Mythras

Developed and Written By
Pete Nash and Lawrence Whitaker
Based on material originally created by Steve Perrin, Ray Turney, Warren James and Steve Henderson

Editing
Lisa Tyler and Brian Pivik

Proof Reading
Ben Monroe and Lisa Tyler

Design and Layout
The Design Mechanism

Artists
David Benzal, Simon Bray, Sarah Evans, Alex Ferreiro, Eric Lofgren, Dan MacKinnon, Pascal Quidault, Sergio Sandoval, Lee Smith, Antonio Vazquez

Cover by Pascal Quidault. Rear Cover illustration by Lee Smith.

Special Thanks
John Hutchinson, Carol Johnson, Brian Pivik, Simon Bray, Bruce Mason, and all the members of, and contributors to, The Design Mechanism forums

Find Us At
www.thedesignmechanism.com and www.MYTHRASrpg.com.
Facebook: https://www.facebook.com/The-Design-Mechanism
G+: https://plus.google.com/communities/113034383032729983266

Revision 3, October 2018
ISBN: 9781911471066

Playtesters
Steven Alban, Nathan Baron, David Paul Bass, Mark Burr, Ben Cable, James Carrington, Chris Donnelly, Colin Driver, Tim Eldred, Tim Evans, Elena Tomàs Ferré, David Finch, Chris Furness, Chris Garland, Chris Gilmore, Tom Griffith, Mark Hare, Kevin Hicks, John Hutchinson, Sebastian Jansson, Donnel Johnson, Joshua Kitz, Marcus Knapp, Dan Lee, Emma Lee, James Lodge, Adam Lundgren, Jordi Mateu Martínez, Bruce Mason, Aiden McAneny, Brad Milburn, John Milward, Daniel J Mooney, Chris Morrell, Alex Morris, Blain Neufeld, Eric Oates, Michael Parkin, Peeter Piegaze, Christopher Pinder, Ben Quant, Warren Ricker, Graham Robinson, Sebastian Sandman, Peter Schofield, Nick Southwick, Howard Tytherleigh, Jordi Romà Vega, Silvia Romà Vega, Ioan Wigmore, Erik Willis, Brian Wombwell, Russ Zabel

About the Cover

In search of the Eight Treasures of Meeros, Anathaym travelled into the ancient forests of Sykei. She knew the risks: Sykei had ever been the home of the slargr, and it was her hope that she would avoid their hunting trails: the map sold to her by that wily merchant seemed reliable, as did the shield and spear he'd supplied.

Never trust a merchant...

Anathaym didn't hear the slargr - a massive, old male - until it was upon her. She barely had time to whisper her Bladesharp spell. The slargr's huge, clawed fists seized her shield as she brought it into position, just as she'd been trained, and the old leather straps, older, perhaps, than the slargr, groaned and snapped. She cursed the merchant but then she was calm. All she needed was to use her spear to place some distance between her and the monster...

The merchant, she decided, would pay later...

Published under licence in the UK by Aeon Games Publishing games.aeonbooks.co.uk

The Design Mechanism

CONTENTS

INTRODUCTION	**4**
Organisation	4
Glossary of Terms	5
CHARACTERS	**6**
Designing A Character	6
Characteristics	6
Calculating Characteristics	8
Attributes	8
Standard Skills	11
CULTURE & COMMUNITY	**13**
Culture	13
Barbarian	14
Civilised	14
Nomadic	15
Primitive	16
Background Events	17
Community	21
Families	21
Allies, Contacts, Rivals and Enemies	22
Passions	22
CAREERS	**26**
Age	31
Bonus Skill Points	32
Starting Equipment	32
Magic	33
Cult Membership	34
SKILLS	**37**
How Skills Work	37
Standard Skills	38
Professional Skills	44
Different Situations	50
Skills Summaries	53
ECONOMICS & EQUIPMENT	**54**
Income, Living Standards and Class	54
Bartering and Haggling	55
Equipment	56
Armour	57
Accommodation	58
Clothing	59
Food	59
Livestock	59
Tools	60
Melee Weapons	61
Ranged Weapons	61
Siege Weapons	62
Vehicles	62
One Handed Weapons	63
Shields	63
Two Handed Weapons	64
Siege Weapons	64
Vehicles	64
Equipment Manufacturing and Quality	65
Ranged Weapons	65
GAME SYSTEM	**68**
Acid	68
Action, Time and Movement	69
Ageing	70
Asphyxiation, Drowning and Suffocation	71
Blood Loss	71
Character Improvement	71
Disease and Poison	74
Encumbrance	77
Falling	78
Fatigue	78
Fires	79
Healing from Injury	80
Inanimate Objects	81
Luck Points	81
Passions	82
Survival	82
Traps	82

Visibility	84
Weather	84
Combat	**86**
Components of Combat	86
Combat Styles	86
Combat Rounds	88
Weapon Size and Reach	94
How Combat Works	94
Special Effects	95
Special Effects Summary	100
Close Combat	101
Ranged Combat	107
Hit Locations	109
Optional Rules: Rabble & Underlings	111
Magic	**112**
Tailoring Magic	112
Magical Disciplines	112
Magical Traditions	113
How Many Abilities?	114
Ritualistic Casting Times	115
Magical Energy	115
Characters & Magic	118
Using Magic	119
Folk Magic	**121**
The Nature of Folk Magic	121
Access to Folk Magic	121
Ubiquitous Folk Magic	122
Using Folk Magic	122
Folk Magic Spells	123
Spells	123
Animism	**130**
Trance and Binding	130
Spirit Societies, Cults & Traditions	131
Defining Spirits	132
Locating and Gaining Spirits	134
Using Spirits	136
Spirit Combat	137
Animism Tricks	140
Spirit Types	142
Mysticism	**154**
Seeking the Truth Within	154
Paths and Talents	155
Starting Mystics	155
Using Mysticism	156
Talent Descriptions	157
Sorcery	**161**
Manipulating the Cosmos	161
Schools and Spells	163
Using Sorcery	164
Spell Descriptions	165
Theism	**178**
Calling on the Gods	178
Cults and Miracles	179
Using Theism	180
Miracle Descriptions	182
Miracles by Cult Rank	190
Cults & Brotherhoods	**192**
Cults	192
Brotherhoods	193
Why Join?	194
Membership	195
Availability by Culture	196
Progression	196
Ranks	197
Benefits	199
Restrictions	201
Sample Gifts	202
Other Aspects	205
Cult and Brotherhood Centres	205
Sample Organisations	206
Example Organisations	210
Creatures	**214**
Intelligence and Instinct	214
Creature Abilities	214
Creatures as Characters	218
The Statistics Block	219
Creature Competence	219
Armed Combat Considerations	222
Designing Your Own Creatures	223
Creatures	224
Chaos Features	275
Non-Human Hit Locations	276
Games Mastery	**278**
This is Your Game	278
The Petersen Rules of Good Gaming	278
Preparation and Game Aids	279
Creating Characters	280
Investigations	282
Using Passions	282
Combat	283
Social Conflict	287
Using Traps	288
Creatures as Player Characters	289
Magic	289
Cults and Brotherhoods in the Campaign	290
Index	**294**
Appendix: Play Aids	**301**

Introduction

Mythras comes from a long tradition of roleplaying game systems based around a common set of principles, and using percentile dice (d100 or d%) to resolve most activities. There are several similar systems available, all of them broadly compatible, but each with their own nuances and unique approaches.

The core rules are straightforward and intuitive; usually, a player rolls d100 and aims to score equal to, or less than, a value (a skill or passion, for instance) on his or her character sheet that represents a certain chance of success. However, the game includes many rules that add greater depth, modify results, or enhance the play experience. While most can be considered necessary for play, none are essential. Indeed, if you do not like a rule, find it confusing, or find it slows things down, feel free to ignore it completely. As with any roleplaying game there will be ambiguities and questions raised: no set of rules will ever cover every eventuality perfectly, and to everyone's satisfaction. However, where something is unaddressed, there should be something in this book that can, with a little tweaking and a little thought, address it. Mythras is a very flexible, intuitive and forgiving game system. Use the game as you want to and need to. Do not be constrained or constrain yourself. Part of Mythras's longevity has been its adaptability, and that adaptability always comes through what its players and referees bring to the table. This is your game: *Your Mythras Will Vary.*

In bringing you Mythras there is a large roster of people to thank: the credits page lists all those involved in helping bring you this game. There are, however, a few people worthy of a very special mention:

- *Dr John Hutchinson* for his valuable contributions that helped get this project underway.
- *The many, many loyal fans* of the game who encouraged us and supported us whilst writing the rules.
- *Our families* for allowing us to have this vision and for sharing it with us.

We very much hope that you enjoy Mythras. We have enjoyed making it for you.

The Design Mechanism, May 2016

Organisation

Mythras is divided into 16 chapters and an appendix.

Chapters 1 to 3: Character Creation

Character creation is covered in these three chapters, with each chapter building on the last. Basic Character Creation starts the process with Culture and Community, and Careers and Development adding further depth. Players should start here to create their first Mythras characters.

Chapter 4: Skills

Each of the skills used in Mythras are explained in depth, with descriptions of the different way skills can be employed.

Chapter 5: Economics and Equipment

This chapter looks at the use of money and social class in Mythras, examining income, its use, and different social levels in Mythras's cultures. All manner of adventuring equipment, from armour and weapons, through to tools and vehicles, are then described. This chapter also includes rules for building and repairing items.

Chapter 6: Game Mechanics

Rules for a myriad of different situations are covered here, including rules for character experience, advancement, and training.

Chapter 7: Combat

Fighting – close combat and ranged – is this chapter's focus. It describes how combats work, need to be run, the use of Special Effects, and other combat techniques.

Chapter 8: Magic

This is the introductory chapter for Mythras's five different magic systems. It explores the fundamentals of magic in its different forms. The chapter offers suggestions and advice on structuring magic in a Mythras campaign, and how to gain, manage, and restore magic points.

Chapters 9, 10, 11, 12 and 13: Magic Systems
Folk Magic, Animism, Mysticism, Sorcery, and Theism are the different magic systems Mythras uses, each with its own chapter. The various differences are explained, and the powers offered by the magic system explored.

Chapter 14: Cults and Brotherhoods
Religious, magical and secular organisations, as well as other kinds of societies are detailed in this chapter. Cults are an important part of Mythras, and they are covered in significant detail along with templates for many different kinds of cult, order, school and so on for Games Masters and Players to build upon for their own campaigns.

Chapter 15: Creatures
Insects, mammals, fish, and monsters from myth and legend are this chapter's focus. As well as providing statistical entries for well over 50 creatures, extensive notes are given on how to use creatures in Mythras games, including using different races as player characters, and designing your own creatures.

Chapter 16: Games Mastery
This chapter offers copious notes, thoughts and guidance on how to Games Master Mythras games. Areas for consideration are summarised, options explored, and different ways of using the rules offered. An invaluable chapter for new and old Mythras Games Masters alike.

Appendix
Character sheet and other play-aids.

Glossary of Terms
Many different terms and phrases are used throughout Mythras to denote certain features, functions and game effects. A glossary of the most frequent, and important, follows:

Attributes: Game abilities derived from one or more Characteristics: Action Points, Hit Points, Magic Points, and so forth.

Characteristic: One of seven identifiers used in character creation: Strength, Constitution, Size, and so on.

Combat Round: A period of five seconds used to measure the detailed activities during combat.

Cycle: The sequence in which all characters act, taking turns, during a Combat Round.

Dice Step: Used to denote a change from one dice type to another. The usual progression is: 1d2, 1d3, 1d4, 1d6, 1d8, 1d10, 1d12.

Differential Roll: Where a degree of success is needed to judge the outcome of a matching of skills.

Grade: Used to indicate the progression in difficulty of skills.

Initiative: A measure of when a character acts during a Cycle.

Intensity: A spell or magical effect's level of power.

Magical Discipline: A type of magic, such as Folk Magic, Animism, or Sorcery.

Magical Tradition: A specific grouping of spells or magical effects within a Magical Discipline. A Mystical Tradition, for example, includes specific magical abilities exclusive to that Tradition.

Magnitude: A spell or magical effect's ability to resist being dispelled.

Opposed Roll: Where two or more dice rolls are made and the results directly compared to determine a winner and loser.

Special Effect: A particular effect generated during combat when one participant secures a better level of dice success than an opponent.

Skill: A capability a character has in a particular field. Skills are rated on a 1 to 100 (and above) scale.

Turn: The point at which a character acts during a Cycle.

XdY: Where this formula is used – 3d6 for example – the first number indicates the number of dice used, and the second indicates the type of dice (four sided, six sided, eight sided, and so on).

XdY+n: This formula signifies rolling the appropriate dice and adding a number. 2d6+6 means roll two six-sided dice and add six to the result.

Dice Used in the Game
Mythras uses the standard range of roleplaying polyhedral dice: d4, d6, d8, d10, d12, and d20. Additionally, the game calls for the use of a d2 and d3:

d2: Roll any die. An odds number equals 1 and evens equals 2. Or flip a coin.

d3: Roll a six-sided die; 1-2 = 1, 3-4 = 2, 5-6 = 3.

For 1d100, take a pair of d10 and decide which one will be the 10s and which the units. The result is a number between 01 and 00 (100). This is sometimes known as 'd%'.

Each die has its own uses. D100 is most frequently used for skill rolls. D20 is used for identifying a location struck during combat. The others are used in different combinations generally for weapon damage and injuries.

All the dice used can be bought from good game stores, and online, in sets or individually.

Rounding of Numbers and Results
On some occasions you will be required to divide numbers - typically the rating in a skill (such as for determining a critical success, which is 1/10th of the skill's value). Whenever a division result creates a fraction, always round up to the whole number. So, for instance, 1/10th of 64% is 6.4; this is rounded up to 7.

Characters

This chapter outlines the initial steps for Character Creation. The following chapters provide additional detail, but the essentials are found here.

Every player in MYTHRAS controls a character. A character is the player's alter-ego, his role in the game, and is usually very different, physically and mentally, to the player. MYTHRAS characters can be from a variety of races – although humans are probably the most common, and certainly the best choice for beginning players – and every race is defined in the same way.

The basic character is defined by a series of different elements that describe the character's capabilities. These elements are:

- Characteristics: such as Strength or Charisma
- Attributes: things like Height or Movement
- Standard Skills: expertise in fundamental abilities which everyone shares

Most of these elements are described in terms of numbers, and some are dependent on or calculated by others. What each element means, and how they are determined, is described in the following sections.

Designing A Character

Characters are usually recorded on a character sheet, which is a handy way of organizing all the information about the character. A blank character sheet is included on pages 302-303, but it is recommended that you first design your character using scratch paper, and then transfer the information to a character sheet once you have gone through each step of the character creation process. Work through each element one step at a time before proceeding to the next. Use a pencil and have an eraser handy; certain numbers such as skill values will change several times during the character creation process.

Character Concept

A good place to start is to have some idea of what sort of character you want to play; a hardened warrior for example, or a cunning thief. Your character concept does not need to be elaborate at this stage; simply an idea that will help guide certain choices such as race and profession. A few character ideas are listed to provoke your imagination.

- *Fierce barbarian hunter*
- *Young, naïve wizard*
- *Bad-tempered gemstone miner*
- *Chivalrous, yet disgraced champion*
- *Suspicious, spirit-worshipping shaman*
- *Overly-curious explorer-scholar*
- *Unscrupulous mercenary*

Non-Human Species

Humans are the easiest characters to play and are probably the most common race found in most MYTHRAS campaigns, but one need not be confined to just humans. It is possible to play just about any sapient species because all creatures, regardless of type, are defined in the same way. The Creatures chapter offers a number of alternatives along with detailed character creation options for non-human species. However, if this is your first MYTHRAS character, stick with the rules for humans given in this chapter before branching out into something more exotic.

Characteristics

Every sapient creature, be it human, elder race, or monster, is defined by seven characteristics. Each characteristic tells you something about your character; how strong or fast he or she is; how clever or healthy. Characteristics are at the core of every MYTHRAS character, and form the basis for most of the other elements such as Attributes and Skills. The seven characteristics are:

- Strength (STR)
- Constitution (CON)
- Size (SIZ)
- Dexterity (DEX)
- Intelligence (INT)
- Power (POW)
- Charisma (CHA)

Before calculating the characteristics, the following section explains what each represents.

Strength (STR)

STR represents physical strength: how much one can lift, how hard one can hit, and so on. Characters with a high STR are likely to be more heavily muscled whilst those with a low STR are somewhat on the scrawny side. STR is a component of the Damage Modifier (see page 9). If a character is reduced to zero STR he lacks the ability to move or lift objects, becoming bedridden until STR improves somehow (through natural healing or magic, for example).

Constitution (CON)

CON is measure of health and hardiness. Those with a high CON are physically tough, and likely to be more resistant to disease or poison. Those with a low CON are less resilient, and may be prone to sickness and tire quickly. CON is a component in determining Hit Points (see page 10), and Healing Rate (see page 9). If CON falls to zero for any reason the character dies.

Size (SIZ)

SIZ measures mass and helps indicate height and weight. The larger the SIZ the heavier or bigger the creature is likely to be. Most creatures' SIZ has a higher minimum value than other characteristics, representing the smallest example of an adult of that race; which in the case of humans is 8. SIZ is used to help figure Hit Points (see page 10), as larger, heavier creatures tend to have greater endurance against damage. SIZ can also be used to determine a character's Damage Modifier, since mass helps to increase the force of a blow. SIZ provides rough limits to Height and Weight, depending on the character's body frame (see page 9). If SIZ drops below the species minimum they are considered to have wasted away to the point they are bedridden.

Anathaym's Saga

The cover of this book shows a female warrior, Anathaym, battling for her life against a creature intent on killing her. Throughout Mythras we'll be using Anathaym as an example of a character and, through her, showing how the Mythras rules work. Her saga begins here, with character creation. Emma, the player, is creating her first Mythras character and has already decided that she will call her Anathaym. Emma's Games Master, Steve, has told all the players that his Mythras campaign will be set in a fantasy world based heavily on ancient Greece, so Emma and her fellow players, Dave, Colin, and Jo, know a little about the world their characters will inhabit, and how to picture it.

Anathaym's world centres on a city-state called Meeros. The rules examples make mention of Meeros frequently, its inhabitants and general culture (which is late Bronze Age). Meeros's enemies are the barbarians known as the Badoshi Warlords.

As well as Anathaym several other example characters are used: Kara - Anathaym's sister and a priestess; Zamothis - Anathaym's combat tutor; Xenos - A Meerish warrior and Anathaym's hated rival; Kratos - A sorcerer bent on destroying Meeros; Mju - a wandering mystic of the plateau desert nomads.

Meeros is used simply as a backdrop for the rules examples; the world is not developed beyond these illustrations, and it does not form a Mythras default setting. Games Masters can, of course, use Meeros in their own games developing it as they need if they so desire.

Dexterity (DEX)

Agility, balance, and reflexes are measured by DEX. Characters with high DEX are fast, nimble, and graceful of movement. Those with a low DEX tend to be lumbering and clumsy. DEX is an important aspect of Action Points (see page 8), and Initiative Bonus (see page 10). If a character is reduced to zero DEX they suffer functional paralysis, unable to move until the situation is rectified.

Intelligence (INT)

INT is measurement of cognitive ability. It indicates the capacity for a character to think both logically and creatively. Those with a lower INT score are not necessarily stupid, but they are likely to be constrained in how creatively they can employ their wits. Creatures with an INT of 7 or below are considered sentient, retaining animal level instinct, and able to react to stimuli. Individuals with an INT of 8 or higher are deemed fully sapient. INT is a factor in calculating Action Points (see page 8), and Initiative Bonus (see page 10). If INT is reduced to zero the character becomes completely mindless.

Power (POW)

Power is a measurement of a character's soul, spirit, inner drive, and capacity for magic. It encompasses a number of different things and is a relatively abstract measurement, but is also one of the most important. POW is the characteristic that marks a character out to the gods or other supernatural powers, and is an indication of divine or magical potential, as well as being an indication of the force of their personal determination. POW governs a character's Magic Points (see page 10), and Luck Points (see page 10). If a character's POW ever drops to zero they lose all independent will.

Charisma (CHA)

Charisma measures personality, and is independent of physical appearance. Someone with a high CHA for example, might be ugly or plain to look at, but blessed with a charm and wit that more than compensates for not being handsome. Likewise a low CHA might indicate someone who is radiantly beautiful but utterly shallow or simply meek. A good CHA is often useful for those who wish to be leaders or centres of their local community. Diehard loners and submissive followers tend towards the other extreme. CHA affects a character's Experience Modifier (see page 9). If CHA is ever falls to zero, the character can no longer socially interact with others, becoming so painfully shy or antisocial they are ignored or even driven away.

Calculating Characteristics

Each characteristic has a numerical value to determine how potent it is. Characteristic values can be calculated in one of several ways; either by random dice rolls or by allocating a predetermined number of points. Which method to be used is governed by the Games Master.

Games Masters are free to modify rolling techniques or values to suit their own campaigns. For instance if the Games Master wished randomly rolled player characters to be more heroic, or at least free from handicap, he could permit the re-roll of an unusually low result; or allow the player to take up to three points from one characteristic, and assign them to another providing the new scores do not exceed the normal characteristic range; or even permit one of the dice used to roll each characteristic to be substituted for its full value. Likewise if using point allocation, a character can simply be assigned a larger pool of characteristic points.

By default, the following options are suggested.

Dice Roll, In Order

Roll the indicated dice for STR, CON, SIZ, DEX, INT, POW and CHA taking each rolled score as it comes. Since the results of these rolls can be somewhat random, it is often better to decide on a character concept after the dice are rolled. Otherwise the final characteristics may preclude a preconceived role.

The dice used depends on the creature or race chosen. For humans roll 3d6 for STR, CON, DEX, POW and CHA; then 2d6+6 for SIZ and INT. Other species use the dice listed against their entry in the Creatures chapter.

Dice Roll, Assign

As above, except that the player may exchange values between characteristics with the same dice range. For example when rolling up a human, the player could swap values between the STR, CON, DEX, POW and CHA characteristics which share a 3d6 range, or between the SIZ and INT characteristics with their 2d6+6 range – but never switch over rolls from one group to the other.

Points Build

Instead of rolling dice to determine characteristics, players build their character from a preset pool of 75 points. Certain rules apply to the points build option:

- 1 point in a characteristic costs 1 Point from the Points Build pool
- Characteristics cannot be *lower* than the minimum value or *greater* than maximum value of that characteristic
- All Characteristic Points must be used in the design process. Points cannot be held over or used for anything else.

Attributes

Each character also has a set of attributes. These are particular capabilities derived from the characteristics, or determined by them that are used to govern certain factors of game play. The attributes are:

- Action Points
- Damage Modifier
- Experience Modifier
- Healing Rate
- Height and Weight
- Hit Points
- Initiative Bonus
- Luck Points
- Magic Points
- Movement Rate

Action Points

How often a character can act in a combat round (see the Combat chapter) is determined by Action Points. How they are used is discussed in more detail on page 91, but to determine a character's base number of Action Points take the sum of INT and DEX, and consult the chart below:

The Reasons Why…

Action Points

INT + DEX	*Action Points*
12 or Less	1
13–24	2
25–36	3
For every additional 12 points	+1

- *INT: Clever characters can more easily exploit openings and opportunities that lend them an edge in combat*
- *DEX: Agile characters react more quickly, and can therefore act more often during combat*

Optional Rule: Fixed Action Points

*Those who have 3 Action Points have a significant advantage over those who only have 2, and this may be frustrating for some players. At the Games Master's discretion, **all** characters can start the game with either 2 or 3 Action Points, regardless of INT and DEX.*

Damage Modifier

The bonus amount of damage a character inflicts when they physically strike or apply force. It is generally used in combat situations, but can also be utilised when attempting to break objects. The damage modifier is an extra die roll which is either added to, or subtracted from, the damage inflicted by the weapon or tool. If a negative damage modifier takes a weapon's damage to zero or below then no damage at all has been inflicted.

Add together STR and SIZ, and consult the Damage Modifier table:

Damage Modifier

STR + SIZ	*Damage Modifier*
5 or Less	−1d8
6–10	−1d6
11–15	−1d4
16–20	−1d2
21–25	+0
26–30	+1d2
31–35	+1d4
36–40	+1d6
41–45	+1d8
46–50	+1d10
51–60	+1d12
61–70	+2d6
71–80	+1d8+1d6
81–90	+2d8
91–100	+1d10+1d8
101-110	+2d10
111-120	+2d10+1d2
121-130	+2d10+1d4
Each 10 points	Continue Progression

The Reasons Why...

- *STR: stronger characters can apply more brute force*
- *SIZ: greater size usually indicates greater mass or leverage*

Experience Modifier

Over the course of play characters improve their skills and capabilities. This is achieved through the use of Experience Rolls which are explained in more detail on page 71.

A character's CHA score may adjust the number of Experience Rolls the character has, reflecting the relationship he has with his peers, and his reputation in his community. If CHA is high people are willing to put themselves out to help train or support the character whilst they undergo tuition. Conversely, if CHA is particularly low, there may be some difficulty improving one's capabilities without the assistance of others; finding someone to spar against for example.

The Reasons Why...

- *CHA: charismatic characters possess greater force of personality and the ability to encourage co-operation from friends, comrades, and peers*

Experience Modifier

CHA	*Experience Modifier*
6 or Less	−1
7–12	0
13–18	+1
Each 6 points	+1

Healing Rate

After receiving injuries, a character needs to recuperate. Healing Rate determines how quickly they naturally recover from wounds. Depending on the severity of the injury (see page 80), the Healing Rate denotes how many Hit Points are recovered per day, week or month.

Healing Rate

CON	*Healing Rate*
6 or Less	1
7–12	2
13–18	3
Each 6 points	+1

Height and Weight

A character's height and weight depend on two things: SIZ, and the character's body frame. Three body frames are provided; lithe (slender, athletic, underweight), medium, and heavy (broad shouldered,

Height and Weight

SIZ	*Height (cm)*	*Lithe (Kg)*	*Medium (Kg)*	*Heavy (Kg)*
1	1-45	1-5	1-7	1-9
2	46-80	6-10	8-14	10-18
3	81-105	11-15	15-21	19-27
4	106-120	16-20	22-28	28-36
5	121-130	21-25	29-35	37-45
6	131-140	26-30	36-42	46-54
7	141-150	31-35	43-49	55-63
8	151-155	36-40	50-56	64-72
9	156-160	41-45	57-63	73-81
10	161-165	46-50	64-70	82-90
11	166-170	51-55	71-77	91-99
12	171-175	56-60	78-84	100-108
13	176-180	61-65	85-91	109-117
14	181-185	66-70	92-98	118-126
15	186-190	71-75	99-105	127-135
16	191-195	76-80	106-112	136-144
17	196-200	81-85	113-119	145-153
18	201-205	86-90	120-126	154-162
19	206-210	91-95	127-133	163-171
20	211-215	96-100	134-140	172-180
21	216-220	101-105	141-147	181-189
Each point	+5 cm	+5 Kg	+7 Kg	+9 Kg

Hit Points Per Location

CON+SIZ

Location	1–5	6–10	11–15	16–20	21–25	26–30	31–35	36–40	+5 pts
Leg	1	2	3	4	5	6	7	8	+1
Abdomen	2	3	4	5	6	7	8	9	+1
Chest	3	4	5	6	7	8	9	10	+1
Each Arm	1	1	2	3	4	5	6	7	+1
Head	1	2	3	4	5	6	7	8	+1

barrel-chested, overweight). Players are free to pick their preferred frame depending on how they envisage the character. If non-humans are being created, race may limit the choice of body frame.

To calculate height and weight, which is measured in centimetres and kilos, cross reference SIZ with the body frame selected. The result is a range of values that your character's height and weight falls into. You should choose the actual value from within this range.

The Height and Weight table can, of course, be used to determine the physical properties of anything, but is primarily designed to reflect humanoids. Other creatures however can have more extreme body frames beyond those given here. See the Creatures chapter, page 224.

Hit Points

Hit Points represent how much injury an area of the body can withstand before it becomes useless, possibly resulting in incapacitation, and ultimately the character's death. The body of every creature is divided into separate locations – humans for example have seven; the head, chest, abdomen, arms, and legs – each location with its own hit points.

Some creatures, such as monsters or different classes of animal, by their very nature often have radically different body structures, yet each location they possess still has Hit Points. When a location's hit points are reduced to a certain level through damage of any kind, then the character suffers certain consequences that reflect the severity of the injury. For further information concerning wounds see page 80.

To calculate the Hit Points of each location, add CON and SIZ together and cross-reference on the Hit Points table.

The Reasons Why...

- *CON: healthy, resilient individuals can withstand more punishment than frailer ones*
- *SIZ: greater bulk helps absorb damage, and reduce the significance of an injury*

Initiative Bonus

The moment at which someone reacts in combat is governed by initiative. Initiative Bonus acts as a modifier to initiative rolls; the higher the bonus, the faster one responds in a combat situation, determining when you can act. Further factors – armour for example – modify it. The Combat chapter goes into more detail on how Initiative works (see page 90).

Initiative Bonus is the average of the DEX and INT characteristics.

The Reasons Why...

- *INT: clever fighters can predict attacks and anticipate their opponent's strategies*
- *DEX: faster characters react and respond more quickly than slower ones*

Luck Points

Luck Points represent that strange force differentiating adventuring heroes from everyday folk. Call it fate, karma or simple good fortune. Luck Points can be used to:

- Re-roll the dice, if they are unfavourable
- Mitigate physical damage or other unfortunate circumstances
- Gain an edge at a vital moment in combat

Exactly how they are used, and when, is described on page 81.

Once a Luck Point is spent, the pool decreases; when one is out of Luck Points, no more are available – unless the Games Master makes an impromptu award – until the next game session when they replenish to their normal value.

Luck Points

POW	Luck Points
6 or Less	1
7–12	2
13–18	3
Each 6 points	+1

The Reasons Why...

- POW: power is a measure of luck and divine favour; a gift of fate, or the ability to cheat it

Magic Points

Mystical abilities and spells cast in Mythras usually rely on Magic Points. Since the availability of magic may be limited by a campaign setting or to specific magical professions, some characters will find this Attribute superfluous.

For those who can utilise such powers, a character's Magic Points are equal to their POW. These points are used to cast spells, the cost of which is dependent on the type of magic used. When the caster runs out of Magic Points he has exhausted his ability to cast any spells until they are replenished.

The Reasons Why...

- *POW: Power is a measure of both willpower – used to command the magical fabric – and the psychic strength the character channels from their environment*

Movement Rate

Movement is not calculated from Characteristics but is a default value which differs between species. The base Movement Rate for humans is 6 metres, although certain skills can improve this. The section on Movement, on page 69 offers more detail.

Standard Skills

By default, every Adventurer has a range of Standard skills allowing him to perform a variety of actions with varying degrees of expertise. These skills are detailed more fully in the Skills chapter, but cover a range of everyday activities and local knowledge which anyone can use without specialised training. At this point of character creation, players will only need to know the base values of each Standard skill.

The basic score of each Standard skill is determined by the sum of two characteristics or a multiple of a single characteristic. The value represents the character's innate competence in a given area, in effect their raw talent before any formative training received as part of his culture and profession.

The Standard Skills Table shows how the basic values are calculated, along with a brief description of what the skill is and does. The score represents the percentage chance of success for a skill; so, an Athletics score of 25 is expressed as 25%. How skill percentages work, and more detailed skill descriptions are provided in the Skills chapter.

Note that the basic percentages for some skills will be modified by both culture and profession, so these starting values will change as character creation progresses.

Standard Skills

Skill	*Basic Percentage*
Athletics	STR+DEX
Boating	STR+CON
Brawn	STR+SIZ
Conceal	DEX+POW
Customs	INTx2
Dance	DEX+CHA
Deceit	INT+CHA
Drive	DEX+POW
Endurance	CON x2
Evade	DEX x2
First Aid	INT+DEX
Influence	CHA x2
Insight	INT+POW
Locale	INT x2
Native Tongue	INT+CHA
Perception	INT+POW
Ride	DEX+POW
Sing	CHA+POW
Stealth	DEX+INT
Swim	STR+CON
Unarmed	STR+DEX
Willpower	POW x2

Anathaym's Saga

Emma prepares to create Anathaym, a human adventuress. The campaign uses the assigned dice roll method, so characteristic rolls are made first, and then allocated to the characteristics as the players wish. Emma rolls the following on 3d6: 11, 7, 13, 9, and 16. Since humans calculate their SIZ and INT using different dice, she then rolls 2d6+6 twice, and gains a 10 and 14. After some thought Emma assigns them thus: STR 11, CON 13, SIZ 10, DEX 16, INT 14, POW 7, CHA 9

For a human, Anathaym is of average strength, and fairly hardy. She is small, reasonably smart, yet is somewhat unlucky. On the other hand she has excellent reflexes. Last but by no means least, her charisma is a little below average, probably indicating she is slightly shy.

Characteristics assigned, Emma now figures Anathaym's attributes.

Action Points: *with INT and DEX totaling 30, Anathaym has 3 Action Points. She can think and act quickly in perilous situations.*

Damage Bonus: *Anathaym's STR 11 and SIZ 10 give a total of 21, which means she has no Damage Bonus. Although Anathaym has a small physique, her strength partially counteracts her stature, preventing any loss of power when attempting to damage something.*

Experience Modifier: *Anathaym's CHA 9 results in no Experience Modifier. Anathaym is somewhat unassuming, finding it a little difficult to make friends and accept others into her trust.*

Healing Rate: *Anathaym's CON 13 results in a Healing Rate of 3. Whilst unexceptional in terms of size and strength, Anathaym heals from her wounds quickly.*

Height & Weight: *Emma has decided that she would like Anathaym to be slender. So she cross references Anathaym's SIZ on the Lithe column for her Weight. At SIZ 10 she is between 161 and 165 centimetres tall – Emma settles on 165 – and she weighs between 46 and 50 kilos. Emma decides that Anathaym is at the lower end of the scale, and opts for 47kg. Emma reasons that Anathaym is willowy to the point of looking ascetically thin – an appearance which leads many to underestimate her.*

Hit Points: *CON 13 and SIZ 10 means Anathaym's Hit Points will be average, her hardiness compensating for her small, slight frame. Adding CON and SIZ gives a result of 23 which denotes that she has 5 Hit Points in her Head and Legs, 7 in her Chest, 6 in her abdomen, and 4 in her Arms. Anathaym is tougher than she looks.*

Initiative Bonus: *With INT 14 and DEX 16, Anathaym has a Initiative Bonus of 15. She often acts first in combat, seizing the initiative.*

Luck Points: *Anathaym has a POW of 7 which grants her 2 Luck Points. Thus, twice a game session, she can call upon these Luck Points to aid her in a variety of different ways.*

POW 7 gives Anathaym only 7 Magic Points. She isn't particularly concerned; she's smart and agile, and those traits are more important to her.

Anathaym's Standard Skills work out as follows:

Athletics 27%, Boating 24%, Brawn 21%, Conceal 23%, Customs 28%, Dance 25%, Deceit 23%, Drive 23%, Endurance 26%, Evade 32%, First Aid 30%, Influence 18%, Insight 21%, Locale 28%, Native Tongue 23%, Perception 21%, Ride 23%, Sing 16%, Stealth 30%, Swim 24%, Unarmed 27%, Willpower 14%.

Clearly at this stage her weakest Standard Skill is Willpower, reflecting her shyness and lack of self-confidence; whereas her best is Evade indicating Anathaym's natural grace and coordination. These raw talents will be further improved by her cultural upbringing and chosen profession as described in the following two chapters.

Combat Styles

A Combat Style is the skill relating to fighting and the use of weapons. It is a diverse skill with many specialisations related to the culture or profession which teaches it. Most fighting traditions encompass training in multiple weapons, along with the techniques required to use them all effectively, whether singly or in combination. In addition they often assume a situational element, such as fighting as close order infantry or whilst mounted. Therefore a Combat Style is an umbrella skill that melds together many related aspects of fighting under a single ability, removing the need to purchase multiple sub skills.

All Combat Styles have a Basic Percentage equal to STR+DEX.

Since most people can pick up a weapon and instinctively either swing, throw or fire it, Combat Styles are considered Standard Skills. Yet due to their potentially diverse nature, they are categorised and defined separately, under names suitable to the genre of the game setting.

For example, a campaign centred on professional gladiators, where set-piece bouts between conflicting weapon techniques is important, a character might learn the Combat Style (Retiarius) or Combat Style (Murmillo); whereas a travelling merchant campaign might feature wandering tribesmen with Combat Style (Horse Nomad) instead. The precise weapons covered by a particular style are normally defined by the Games Master (for further details see Combat page 88).

Characters learn Combat Styles as part of their culture and profession, as described in the following two chapters. Some sample Styles are offered opposite to show the range and versatility of Combat Styles – but these are simply *suggestions*; various Mythras supplements offer many more variations and creative styles, and both players and Games Masters are encouraged to develop their own, unique combinations to fit their campaigns.

Sample Combat Styles

Style Name	*Suggested Weapons*	*Suggested Trait (See Page 89)*
Street Brawler	Fists, Feet, Knife, Club	Batter Aside or Unarmed Prowess
Assassin	Dagger, Shortsword, Bow or Crossbow	Assassination or Ranged Marksman
Barbarian Warrior	Greatsword, Broadsword, Battleaxe, Shield	Do or Die, or Intimidating Scream
Cavalry or Mounted Knight	Sword, Long Spear/ Lance, Shield	Beast-back Lancer or Mounted Combat
City Watch or Hoplite	Spear, Shield, Shortsword	Cautious Fighter or Formation Fighting
Gladiator	Shortsword, Buckler, Net, Trident	Daredevil or Mancatcher
Marine or Pirate	Falchion (or Rapier), Club, Main Gauche	Excellent Footwork or Swashbuckler
Master Archer	Dagger, Shortsword, Long Bow	Ranged Marksman or Skirmishing
Meerish Slinger	Shortsword, Shield, Sling	Knockout Blow or Shield Wall
Noble Warrior	Longsword, Shield, Main Gauche, Bow	Defensive Minded

Culture & Community

Culture and community play an important part in MYTHRAS character creation. Culture determines the kind of society in which the character was raised, and so prescribes certain outlooks and philosophies he or she might have. More practically, culture helps define the values of the various skills that shape your character's overall capabilities. Community details the family, both immediate and extended, which helps to define kinsfolk and relationships with them.

Culture

There are four basic human cultures: Barbarian, Civilised, Nomadic and Primitive.

A description of each cultural background follows and includes a view of the culture from the perspective of one of its members. Incorporated in the description is a list of skill bonuses and new skills appropriate to that culture. Players should apply the skill bonuses immediately to the Standard skills on their Character Sheet, and add the additional new skills, known as Professional Skills (introduced in the next chapter), to the appropriate section of the sheet. In many cases a cultural background lists a range of skills and invites the player to pick one, or more, that will gain a bonus: in this way players from the same cultural background can ensure that their adventurers are different in the areas they have developed.

Also note that each culture comes with several Passions (see page 82). Passions are optional rules for MYTHRAS but they can add a great deal of depth and characterisation to the adventurer you are creating. If Passions are being used, then the Cultural Passions define ingrained preferences and prejudices for that culture. If Passions are not required, then simply ignore the entries.

Cultural Skill Points

Each culture lists a variety of Standard Skills that the character learns as part of his formative development within that society. These are core abilities which all characters from the same specific culture improve to some degree. Characters also learn a number of more specialised or esoteric Professional Skills according to their personal interests, and have the option of learning a cultural Combat Style.

Professional skills are further explained in the Skills chapter on page 44, but in brief they represent those skills which cannot be attempted without years of rigorous study and specialised training. Whereas a character has a basic ability in all Standard Skills, they have zero ability in any Professional Skill unless chosen as part of their cultural upbringing or career.

When applying cultural skills perform the following steps:

- Apply the static bonuses to Customs and Native Tongue: these are +40% to each, irrespective of the culture chosen.
- Select three Professional Skills from the options offered
- If desired, select a single Combat Style
- Distribute 100 points amongst the listed Standard Skills, the chosen Professional Skills, and the Combat Style (if selected), increasing that skill by 1% for every point spent on improving it. Players are free to choose how much each skill is improved by, but each skill must receive a minimum of 5% and cannot receive more than 15%.

Chosen Professional Skills start off at their base characteristic value as per Standard Skills. Some Professional Skills such as Crafts, Languages or Lores offer choice of a specialisation. In these cases the speciality chosen should be one which suits that culture.

Characters need not invest any points into a Combat Style if they are disinclined to do so, as some cultures have non-combatant members whether due to gender, caste or philosophy. Cultural Combat Styles usually reflect the informal training received by the community for hunting, personal protection or civil defence.

Each culture comes with a range of evocative names for Combat Styles. However, no weapons are defined, because Combat Styles are intended to be flexible tools for the Games Master to tailor the weapons to the particular culture or setting. Refer to the Combat Style section in the Combat chapter for further guidance.

Barbarian

Tribal in nature, barbarians tend to shun civilisation, viewing those who live in large towns and cities as weak and corrupt. Although their own settlements are also sedentary, they tend to be far smaller and closer to nature. Barbarian tribes occupy distinct territories, often half tamed wilderness, which they regard as their own for hunting, grazing and farming purposes. Most are adept in the use of weaponry as they must overcome many dangers throughout their lives – facing creatures of the wilds or mustering to defend their lands against rival tribes. Since they live in small communities the ties of kinship and clan are strong elements of their society.

Skills

Standard Skills

Athletics, Brawn, Endurance, First Aid, Locale, Perception; and either Boating or Ride.

Example Combat Styles

Barbarian Fyrdman, Berserker, Horse Eater, Seaborne Reiver, Weapon Thegn, Wolf Hunter.

Professional Skills

Craft (any), Healing, Lore (any), Musicianship, Navigate, Seamanship, Survival, Track.

Cultural Passions

- Loyalty to Clan Chieftain
- Love (friend, sibling or romantic lover)
- Hate (creature, rival or clan)

The Barbarian's Voice

'The people of the towns and cities call us barbarians because our houses are not made of mortared stone, and we choose not to crush ourselves together like too many fish in a shallow pond. They call us barbarians because we choose not to write down what we see, hear and say, but to memorise it as song. They call us barbarians because we fight amongst ourselves sometimes. They call us barbarians because they simply do not understand. Living in brick boxes must do something to the wits.

We choose to be close to the ground that gave rise to all of us. Our homes are made from the things we can readily find and shape, and we do not believe in building high or covering the ground in dressed marble. Life is hard; we appreciate it that way. It is good to feel the rain on our cheeks and the sun on our backs as we go about our business. Why lock ourselves away? The gods created us to experience the world, and you can't do that if you spend all your time imprisoned within walls. We accept the world for what it is and how it is. Town and city folk seek to make it something else. We appreciate comfort and warmth just like they do, but we take life as it comes, not as how we would like it be. A bed of good, fresh straw is as comfortable as any slab stuffed with feathers – and probably cleaner, and certainly better for the back.

Do not believe what you hear from them about our lack of laws. Our laws are embodied in our customs and traditions. When we transgress we expect to be punished. When we transgress badly we expect the punishment to be bad, too. We believe in saying what we mean, meaning what we say and doing what we have promised. Some view this as harsh, such as when we stone liars to death, but this means we do not have liars in our midst. Those tempted to transgress know the consequences and think twice. This helps us to live in harmony.

You question our raids? Well, do the civilised folk not make wars? Of course they do! When they make war thousands die, innocent victims amongst them. For us, we raid to settle scores and to build our strength – not just the strength of the tribe but the strength of character too. We expect to be raided and our neighbours expect us to raid them. Just as the hawk takes the dove on the wing. Life is a cycle and we are part of it; and when we raid, a few might die, but most do not. And when we die we are ready for it and unafraid. Through raiding we understand our place and keep it, just as the wolf knows its territory and keeps that.

So come and break bread with us. We do not care that you live in the stinking, narrow, disease filled streets of Meeros; as a visitor to our hearth you are a guest and will be treated as such. You will be served first, above even the headman, and we will share with you all that we have, keeping nothing back. In return we ask for news and stories, and perhaps a small token of your appreciation for our hospitality in the form of a song or a dance. Come, the elders are waiting.'

Civilised

The Civilised culture is epitomised by a semblance of law and order, underpinned by complex social codes, and supported by a bureaucracy. Civilised people believe themselves superior to all other cultures because their achievements tend towards permanence: sprawling cities, imposing temples, celebratory monuments, and the recording of history and events in books, tomes, and scrolls. Of course, this is a thin veneer. The most civilised of cities can be more lawless than any barbarian frontier settlement; and the social codes may be cruder than the hospitality rituals of nomads. But the Civilised culture prides itself on its achievements, its infrastructure, its professional artisans, and its ability to easily extend its reach to wherever it wishes to go.

Skills

Standard Skills

Conceal, Deceit, Drive, Influence, Insight, Locale, Willpower.

Example Combat Styles

Citizen Legionary, City-state Phalangite, Levied Archer, Light Skirmisher, Street Thug, Town Militia.

Professional Skills

Art (any), Commerce, Craft (any), Courtesy, Language (any), Lore (any), Musicianship, Streetwise.

Cultural Passions

- Loyalty to Town/City
- Love (friend, sibling or romantic lover)
- Hate (rival, gang, district or city)

The Civilised Voice

'Isn't this a fine city? I mean, isn't it the finest you've ever seen? Safe, too. The militia sees to that, and although you might see the odd beggar wandering around the marketplace you're as likely to be attacked as you are to get eaten by monsters. We have rules, you see. Without rules we're no better than animals. Rules help us live together without fighting, and to make things we can sell so that we can move up in the world.

It's about order and a certain degree of comfort. And it's about education. I have listened to the priests and studied with philosophers, which helps me run my business. Because I run my business I can buy education for my children so they can run businesses too, when they're older. I can buy my wife the things we need to bring up the children, and sometimes there's a little left over for a treat. Sometimes. And to pay the taxes. It's very important that we pay the taxes.

But mostly it's about protection. That wall around the city is there for more than show. It keeps the Badoshi out and lets us live in peace. The garrison patrols the borders, and the wall, and alerts us when enemies are near. Not that they'd dare attack us! We have the most important city in the whole region. Attacking us would invite hatred from our allies. So we are safe.

Well, yes, of course there's crime. There's always someone who isn't prepared to work for it and steals instead. Why, only last week my shop was turned over, and the day's takings stolen. And yes, there are muggings, and murders too, but the militia always catch the perpetrators; and when they do! Well, then they'll see our marvellous court in action. The Queen herself presides, you know, and she's a fair woman. She can tell when someone's guilty just by staring at them. And don't bother appealing; if you're guilty, you're off to the quarries. That's unless you've been stealing, in which case you lose fingers.

What I like most about the city is the wider community. It's about meeting new people every day, each with a new story to tell. I like seeing my neighbours, even if they are a bit loud sometimes, and I like the atmosphere of market day or Gods' Day when everyone's excited and out for a good time. I like having a roof over my head, and a warm bed to lie in at night (even if it is damp). I like having a door I can close on the world when I get fed up with it, and knowing that I don't have to go out with a spear to hunt my next meal.

Me? Give up the city? No chance!'

Nomadic

Nomadic people are constantly on the move, with no home and hearth to call their own. They may wander aimlessly about, or might have several camps they move to and from throughout the year. They raise few crops and instead follow the migrations of animals or fish, perhaps even herding their own domesticated beasts. Nomads are adept at subsisting on what they can quickly and easily scavenge from their surroundings, letting nothing go to waste. The skills of the nomad culture should be tailored to their environment. Some journey vast distances on foot, others live in caravans or ride strange creatures, and some drift across the oceans on great floating rafts.

Skills

Standard Skills

Endurance, First Aid, Locale, Perception, Stealth; and two of the following: Athletics, Boating, Swim, Drive or Ride depending on the primary mode of travel.

Example Combat Styles
Camel Cavalry, Feathered Death Flinger, Horse Lord, Whale Hunter, Wheeled Warrior, Wolf Runner.

Professional Skills
Craft (any), Culture (any), Language (any), Lore (any), Musicianship, Navigate, Survival, Track.

Cultural Passions

- Loyalty to Tribal Chieftain/Khan
- Love (friend, sibling or romantic lover)
- Hate (creature, rival or tribe)

The Nomad's Voice

'In the winter we move down to the shelter of the valleys where our people have made camp every year for fifty generations. We wait until the ground thaws, living all the while on the dried meats and fruits laid down in the autumn and protect ourselves from the snow and cold. Last year we arrived in the valley to find it had been occupied by savage, diseased wolves, and we had to drive them out and cleanse the place with fire. A dozen died in that fight. A dozen hands fewer to tend the herd and forage.

In the spring we move to the high plateau, where the hunting is good. The Great Hunt takes place in that time, when the strong go and find antelope, leopard, and yak, and the rest move the herd up out of the valley. Those are good days, and we give thanks to the spirits, and sacrifice a cow or two. We meet the other clans at the Great Sky Cairn, and exchange news, and gifts. There is always a feast, and many sore heads, but we agree the business for the year, and discuss what the game trails are like, and how the pasture holds out. Last year one clan brought with it a monster they had captured and tamed. It was a scaly thing with tusks and hide like tree bark; the shamans said it was unnatural, but the other clan kept it as a watchdog.

And then in the summer we move out across the high plateau where we graze our animals and gather fruits to prepare for the winter. Sometimes we battle, seeking to hold the best grasslands, or raid barbarian settlements lurking in the forest, but mostly we know peace. It is difficult to keep enemies when you're always on the move. Neither do we waste. Waste is an insult to the gods! We eat, or find a use, for everything we hunt. We honour what nature provides, and do not squander it. It brings tears to the eyes and heart to see the waste in the stinking cities.

Why do we follow this life? Because of the animals, because of the seasons! The world moves and so must we. If you stay in one place you sap the earth and it stops giving. Stay in one place and sooner or later enemies or monsters find you, and before you know it you're fighting every day instead of every now and again. By moving we learn the land and take its best. If you set down roots, you become like a plant and we are not plants. We have legs and we walk and run like the deer walk and run. We are free and being free we must move freely. Our hunters and herders are strong because we keep our blood moving and stay in time with the seasons, moving when the earth and the spirits say it is time to move. Never stop moving. Even when death claims us, we go to the Great Hunting where all is spring and the game is good, and the spirits look after us as we have looked after them.

We have a good life.'

Primitive

Of all peoples primitives are those that live closest with the land, in tune with its hidden secrets. Other cultures commonly dismiss them as little more than animals, yet they merely eschew the technology that so many others take for granted; relying instead on flint spears and arrows, and their skill for survival in the wild. Living in extended family groups, primitive cultures gather around very simple dwellings that can range from caves and areas of natural shelter through to lean-tos or very basic huts. Primitives are typically hunter-gatherers with either few, or poorly developed, systems for farming and husbandry. However, certain cultural beliefs, often based on superstitions, can be very well defined. Few primitive cultures have developed anything approaching a written language although paintings and other pictorial symbols serve as a means of communication.

Skills

Standard Skills
Brawn, Endurance, Evade, Locale, Perception, Stealth; and one of either Athletics, Boating or Swim.

Example Combat Styles
Flint Death Dealer, Ghost Warrior, Head Hunter, Jaguar Brother, Jungle Savage, Savannah Hunter.

Professional Skills
Craft (any), Healing, Lore (any), Musicianship, Navigate, Survival, Track.

Cultural Passions

- Loyalty to Chief/Headman
- Love (friend, sibling or romantic lover)
- Hate (something that scares or intimidates you)

The Primitive Voice

'The world is full of fear. It is a wrathful place and we know its wrath. So we hide. We try to keep the gods happy with sacrifices of blood but still they punish us. We asked the wise woman why the gods are so angry, and she told us it is because we are not perfect, like they are, and it is our fault. So now we know. Can we be perfect? I don't think so. I think the gods like it that way. I think they like having something to blame and then punish. So we fear them.

Our home is the great cave that runs deep into that mountain. When the gods send the monsters to eat us we flee deep inside while the warriors hurl their spears and the shaman makes her chants. We paint our victories on the cave wall and tell stories about them so the children will know that even though the gods are angry at us we are a strong people and want to make things good. We eat the monsters we kill and make weapons and tools from the bones.

Our wise woman told us that the people who live in the woodlands two days from us made the gods even angrier because they stole the secret of fire, so we went and killed them. We thought the gods would be pleased with us for killing the thieves but that night they sent a great plague and more monsters, so maybe the wise woman was wrong, but she probably wasn't. I wonder how you get to be a wise woman?

Our chieftain married the young woman who we took as a slave when we killed the enemies, and we know that is wrong because her hair is red. Red is the colour of the trickster god but the chieftain won't listen. He was challenged and killed the hunter who challenged him and ate his heart. He gave the brain to his new wife so she might eat and gain some wisdom. Perhaps that's how you get to be a wise woman? Because she has red hair we fear her, and we fear the chieftain because he's changed. She's put a spell on him, we think. That's probably how her people stole fire from the gods. I think she did it.

I made my first spear yesterday. I knapped the flint myself, and tied it firm with the twine I made from dried pig gut. It is very straight and very sharp. I went looking for an enemy to kill, and found someone lost in the hills not far from our cave. I tested my spear on him and it stuck so deep I nearly broke the haft getting it out. I ate his heart without bothering to make it hot, and now I have his soul. I'm not sure I want two souls, so I will go to the wise woman and give her the skull from the enemy I tested my spear on, and she will take the second soul from me. It will be my slave then, and I will make it worship me like a god, and I will make it fear me.

Because the world is full of fear.'

Anathaym's Saga

Steve, the GM has already decided that the characters are residents of a civilised city-state named Meeros, loosely based upon the myths of ancient Crete. Anathaym is therefore from a Civilised culture.

She begins by adding the default 40% bonus to Customs and Native Tongue, then chooses the three Professional Skills she learned growing up in Meeros; deciding upon Courtesy 23% (INT+CHA), Lore (Geography) 28% (INTx2), and Streetwise 16% (POW+CHA).

Anathaym now has 100 points to assign to the listed Standard Skills and the three Professional Skills she selected. She applies them thusly: Conceal +5, Deceit +5, Drive +5, Influence +10, Insight +10, Locale +5, Willpower +10, Courtesy +15, Lore (Geography) +10, and Streetwise +15. The remaining 10 points she withholds since she wishes to learn a Combat Style.

Steve says that, as a citizen of the city, Anathaym can take the Meerish Slinger style, learning as a child the art of slinging which was augmented with the city's civic training in shortsword and medium shield. The style starts with a base score of 27% (STR+DEX), and she adds her remaining 10 points to it.

Finally, for her Passions, Anathaym takes Loyalty (City), Love (Sibling), and Hate (Rival). These will be determined later.

After applying her cultural modifiers Anathaym's skills are: Athletics 27%, Boating 24%, Brawn 21%, Conceal 28%, Customs 68%, Dance 25%, Deceit 28%, Drive 28%, Endurance 26%, Evade 32%, First Aid 30%, Influence 28%, Insight 31%, Locale 33%, Native Tongue 63%, Perception 21%, Ride 23%, Sing 16%, Stealth 30%, Swim 24%, Unarmed 27%, Willpower 24%; Courtesy 38%, Lore (Geography) 38%, and Streetwise 31%; Combat Style (Meerish Slinger) 37%.

Background Events

Background Events are notable things that have happened in the character's life before he began his career as an adventurer. Some are formative; some are fortunate and some are unfortunate. Background Events are optional, but using them adds to the character's history, and can be used by creative players and Games Masters as hooks for scenarios or even complete campaigns.

If using Background Events you may feel free to choose an event that appeals or roll randomly. Random rolls may produce very interesting, but potentially conflicting results. If a roll is not to your liking or seriously disrupts the idea and concept you have for your character then do re-roll the event. Background Events should enrich the character – not disrupt it.

If your starting character is older than the Mythras standard, then you may gain multiple rolls on this table (see Age, page 31). If you roll a result twice, re-roll one of the results. If two results contradict each other either discard both and roll again, or agree with the Games Master how best to make both results work together.

The Background Events tables begin on the next page.

Background Events

1d100	Event
01	A case of mistaken identity resulted in a period of imprisonment or some other punishment for your character. You have long wanted to find whoever it was who was responsible for the crime you were punished for.
02	A curse has been placed upon your family. For generations all children of the opposite gender to your character have died in tragic circumstances. It falls to each generation to select one who will find a way to lift the curse, and you are the chosen one.
03-04	A girl in your community wants you to carry messages to a boy in another community. She pays you well enough and you believe that the messages are love letters. But can you be sure? Why are these two not allowed to communicate directly? What would happen if they did? What would happen if anyone else found out? And why did she choose you to be her messenger?
05-06	A group of travelling players visited your community and stayed for several weeks. They performed feats of legerdemain, juggling and acrobatics. As a child you were enthralled, and spent as much time as you could with them. Then you were kidnapped, carried far away from your homeland and abandoned. How did you escape? Did you even make it home?
07-08	A priceless object owned or protected by your family was stolen by enemies. On his deathbed the head of the family made you swear to retrieve it from the thieves. You're not sure what the item is or why it is so special, but loyalty to your deceased relative drives you to complete your oath.
09-10	A relative or family member has bequeathed you a secret: the whereabouts of a lost legendary heirloom; the location of an imprisoned deity; or maybe the rituals for a special spell. The information is shrouded in family myth, and you have been oath-sworn to either protect this secret or find and awaken it.
11-12	A sibling has been betrothed to someone from your childhood that you consider an enemy. You are forced to make a sullen peace with this new in-law but your hatred still burns beneath. What is worse is that you fear your sibling is being turned against you. What can you do to set matters to rights?
13	You believe yourself to be suffering a divine or magical curse. Moan, groan and whinge at every opportunity, or remain completely stoic at every misfortune that befalls you in the future.
14-15	An old, warlike relative has died, bequeathing you a useless suit of armour which will fall apart the first time it's used. However the scratches and dents tell of great battles and a life of adventure. Despite the shoddiness of the armour you are very fond of it and, when wearing it, you feel as if the spirit of your relative is watching over you.
16-17	A scholar, priest or mystic visits your community, and demonstrates his almost supernatural wisdom. You are fascinated by what you see but the individual does not remain long enough for you to learn more. You do, however, receive dreams that show you meeting up with this person again and learning from him. When, where, and how will form a future part of the story.
18-19	Distant relatives demanded that you be sent to stay with them. Your father could not refuse – why was that? The relatives treated you well but were always cold and distant with you, despite insisting that you live with them for several years. On returning to your true family, they had also become distant with you. What is at the root of this strangeness? Why have you been caught in the middle?
20	Fate has closely watched over you as you grew to adulthood. Siblings have drowned, friends died from plague, parents disgraced, but you have emerged unscathed from everything. Are you truly blessed by the gods?
21-22	For some reason you have shamed your family and have been cast out. What did you do? Is there hope of reconciliation? Were you to blame or were you just a scapegoat for someone else? At first you lived on your wits, but people in your community grew suspicious and shunned you.
23-24	It transpires that one of your parents is, in fact, a member of a noble family (and possibly even a prince or princess) who has turned their back on their heritage to live a simple life. This does, however, mean you are an heir to a noble estate or title. Will you ever realise your inheritance?
25	On your birthday two years ago it rained frogs. Last birthday it rained lizards. What will it rain this year? More to the point, why does it rain strange things on your birthday?
26-27	Playing one day you discovered a dead man – a warrior – in the cellar or outbuildings. Who was he? And more importantly who killed him? Was it your father, or worse still your mother, who had been looking rather nervous of late...
28-29	Somehow you have picked up a loyal companion or retainer. Maybe a childhood friend; perhaps a hanger-on from some chance encounter. This does not necessarily make your companion a welcome presence, but the relationship has somehow endured over the years.
30-31	You come into possession of a mundane item that a friend or family member claims is magical. So far the item has not exhibited any magical properties, and it could well be that some form of quest is needed to activate its magical abilities. Worse, the item if known about may attract unwelcome attention. What the abilities are remain for the Games Master to determine at an appropriate time.

1d100	Event
32	You have been marked as special by the gods. You carry with you a symbol or marking that is of great reverence to a particular religion or cult. The gods and the cult in question may be very far from where you were born, and may even be an enemy of your culture, but this makes no difference.
33-34	You have a favoured and beloved pet which follows them everywhere. It has no abilities or special powers, but offers comfort and companionship.
35	You have studied with a noted master, scholar or wise man. Whenever you meet up with the teacher, you can request personal tuition for one or more of your related Professional Skills.
36-37	You have suffered some form of horrific attack that has left you psychologically scarred, and extremely wary about the situation or thing which harmed you. This might be nearly dying from drowning, man-eating lions or necromantic magic. Whatever it is, gain a new passion of Fear (thing which harmed you) or roleplay your subsequent trepidation.
38-39	You have sworn a fervent oath with a member of the opposite sex. You are compelled to help this person, and never betray him or her. By some intuition you are always aware of their presence in your dreams, and sense any danger he or she is subject to even when many miles apart.
40-41	You were born into a once rich and powerful family that has somehow fallen on rough times or suffered a severe blow to its reputation. Perhaps the family name is a mockery, or reviled, or even revered still by those who know the truth.
42-43	You were born with an unusual sensitivity to a particular substance, species of creature or type of supernatural power. When the subject in question is nearby, you suffer a mild physiological effect such as tingling fingers, sneezing or headaches. Upon a successful Perception roll you can determine the rough location of the detected thing.
44-45	You were either born with, or somehow received, a mark, blemish or scar that resembles a glyph. The symbol does not exhibit any power yet, but all who see it remark on it – some acting with wonder, and others fear. A quest of some kind is needed to awaken the glyph; but is this wise? Only time will tell.
46	You are magically gifted, attracting the attention of a scrying sorcerer, the priest of a cult or a wandering shaman. If permitted, you may choose to enter a magical profession. If magic-using characters are not permitted, you instead become the focus of that magician, who desires to extract your inherent power via some suitably nefarious, and possibly fatal, means.
47	You awoke one morning to find a valuable object, one with significant religious or ruling importance, lying in bed with you. The question of how precisely it got there aside, do you keep the object with the intent to sell or use it later, or do you return it, thus placing yourself under suspicion of its theft?
48-49	When you were a child you nearly died from a fatal disease, but since then you have never, ever been ill. Are you simply paranoid about any type of infection or do you believe you are immune to any form of contagion?
50	Several years ago you were attacked by an unidentifiable wild beast, which nearly killed you. The creature vanished but since that time you've felt an ominous presence when wandering the edges of your homelands. Thus far the beast has not reappeared, yet perhaps it's merely biding its time. What was the creature, and why is it hunting you?
51-52	You spent your childhood as a slave before either escaping or being freed. The experience had a significant effect upon you. How do you view slavery now? Do you hate and fear it, or did the experience institutionalise you?
53-54	The eldest surviving member of your family harbours a great secret, and many times they have told you that when you are old enough, it will be entrusted to you. What is this secret? When will the time be right? Your Games Master will decide, but until then you must be patient. Can you contain your curiosity?
55-56	As a child you witnessed some ceremony or ritual that had a profound effect on your psyche. The chants and dances haunt your dreams, and you feel compelled to discover what it was you witnessed. The outcome of the ritual is unknown, it might be for good or ill; you do not know. Its true nature must be discovered through adventuring.
57-58	Your family was hunted by powerful foes. Why is this? Why did your family need to keep moving and hiding? What do the pursuers want? Are they still following you? Should you confront them? You are sick and tired of being on the run.
59-60	You are a bastard-born. Your mother swears your father was a man of note and station, but she herself is of low status, and you are considered even lower than she is. Where your father is, no one knows, but you would love to meet him some day and discover the truth about him. Perhaps, if reunited with your father, the stigma of your birth might be erased.
61-62	You are adopted. Your true parents either abandoned you or were killed, and the family that raised you has always accepted you as one of their own – except for certain jealous relatives who see you as an imposter, and would gladly have you cast out of the family so their own offspring might benefit. You have had to fight their resentment for most of your life but now things appear to be coming to a head.
63-64	You came across a tinker or peddler on the road. He offered to read your fortune for a silver piece, but you had no money, and instead offered to share your meal with him, which he accepted. Reading your palm he declared you would become a great hero and travel the world, but not before encountering 'A great sorrow, a great victory, and a great reversal.' You have often wondered what he meant because none of those things have come to pass. Might the tinker have been lying?

1d100	*Event*
65-66	You come from a family that is artistically adept. Their fame has spread far and wide, granting you access to high status patrons if you yourself are an artist, craftsman or performer. Conversely it is a constant source of irritation when casual acquaintances are taken aback at your lack of talent.
67-68	A sibling committed a heinous crime that has brought shame on your family. They fled soon after, vanishing entirely, casting suspicion on you. Were you yourself falsely blamed for the crime? Or did you willingly confess, to preserve the remnants of your family's honour? Is blood truly thicker than water?
69-70	You are a twin. Your brother or sister has similar characteristics and skills to yourself but you are clearly different people. Are you close, as twins usually are, or estranged? You always seem to know where your sibling is, even if relations between you are not good.
71-72	You are the sole survivor of a horrific catastrophe. Your entire family was wiped out by some tragedy leaving you to fend completely for yourself.
73-74	You met a great hero (or villain) at a time when he or she was unknown. You suspected, perhaps, that this person was destined for greatness (or infamy), but you still became friends before you parted. Will they remember you? Will you still be friends?
75-76	Your elder brother or sister is (or was) a great hero for some reason, and you live somewhat in their shadow. You are desperate to prove that you are your sibling's equal, and want to outdo their deeds, proving that your family can produce more than one hero.
77-78	Your family crossed a wealthy or influential family and have suffered because of it. That family is now your Enemy.
79-80	Your family follows a religion or philosophy unaccepted by the rest of your community. Possibly they have kept their beliefs hidden, or perhaps they simply ignore the sneers and cold looks. Whatever, it marks you as different, and the increasing persecution has made your convictions stronger.
81-82	Your family has a reputation for luck. Everything your family does turns-out splendidly; it has wealth it has never seemed to work for; it has a strong reputation; no ill has ever befallen it. You have, however, heard something that makes you suspicious of this charmed life you've led. How did you family come by this luck? Was a much higher price – perhaps a darker price – paid for it?
83-84	Your family performed a great service for a wealthy noble or person of influence. As a reward you were taken into that person's service. You gain this powerful patron as an Ally.
85-86	Your family was ever cruel to you. Why, you do not know, but your siblings always seemed to receive better treatment and more favour. You have always been denied. That is why, at the first opportunity, you left them behind, forgetting them and seeking the life of an adventurer.
87-88	Your hereditary line is slowly becoming extinct, every year one member of the diminishing family dies in a frightful and twisted 'accident'. What is behind this run of misfortune? Are you family cursed or has some evil agency taken to expunging your blood line? Are you next?
89-90	Your family was involved in some community event that has made them either famous or infamous. The legacy of what they did follows you everywhere. What did your family do? Can you shake the reputation? Do you want to?
91-92	Your family was wealthy once, but is now reduced to poverty. How did it lose its fortune? Was it due to circumstance or the actions of others? If others, how did they ruin you – and how will you make them pay?
93-94	Your family, previously poor and beggared, has ever struggled to survive. Yet when you were a lad somehow your father attained great wealth. How did they come by this money? What effect did it have on the family? Will somebody arrive to reclaim or perhaps terminate the mysterious fortune?
95-96	Your family, through financial need, sent you into service with another family of some prestige. As their ward you have learned many things about them including a dire secret that, if revealed, would get you killed. What is this hidden truth? What damage could it do? Decide with your Games Master.
97-98	You accidentally killed a close friend or sibling when playing together. The horror of the situation caused you to flee, remaining silent about the tragedy. When the adults finally went out to search for the missing adolescent no trace could be found, although they searched the area where you left the body. You have lived with the guilt ever since, but whatever became of you compatriot? Did they escape death or did something unspeakable happen to the body?
99-00	You recently experienced a supernatural epiphany which shook you. Whilst out alone a god personally came to speak with you, or perhaps a host of spirits manifested and danced about you. The event, whatever it was, may be seen as a blessing by the local community or conversely deemed blasphemous. In more secular societies the experience, if reported, could be viewed as the onset of insanity.

Community

Having determined the character's culture it is now time to develop his community ties. Community consists of a number of related elements: family, contacts, background events and passions. Passions have been mentioned in the Culture section earlier, but you will find the rules for them here.

Work through each of the Community elements as described below adding the details to your character sheet. This is an opportunity to really bring your character to life – to work out what family he has, what friends and enemies he might have made, what strange or odd things may have happened to him in his past, and what things drive his loyalty, his loves and his hates.

Character Social Class

Social Class measures the prosperity, resources and social position of characters. Their class influences the starting money available to them, and likely Background Resources – things to which the character has access and can return to when not adventuring. It is additionally used to determine income between adventures (see the Economics and Equipment chapter).

Unless it has been predefined as the consequence of a Background Event or specifically decided by the Games Master, a character's Social Class is rolled randomly – although it can be chosen or re-rolled if the Games Master permits. There are four separate tables, one for each culture, which determine the class the character or his family have enjoyed for most of their life.

Class defines broad categories of social strata, but may have more subdivisions as determined by the game setting. In general the more advanced the culture, the more complex its social structure. Players should confer with the Games Master to decide what precise title or rank is appropriate for their character.

The Social Class tables start on page 24.

Starting Money

All characters begin the game with commodities or currency worth:

- Barbarians: 4d6 x50 silver pieces
- Civilised: 4d6 x75 silver pieces
- Nomadic: 4d6 x25 silver pieces
- Primitive: 4d6 x10 silver pieces

Multiply the character's starting money by the Money Modifier to determine the available cash or commodities the character has. At the Games Master's discretion additional money generated by the Money Modifier may be in the form of goods or chattels rather than ready coin.

The Background Resources reflect additional items the character either can start the game with – such as a mount (horse, camel or beast appropriate to culture) – and things he can call upon, such as servants or slaves.

Families

Every character comes from a family. The family might be rambling with dozens of members or small and tightknit with only a handful of kin. The family's reputation might help or hinder the

Anathaym's Saga

To determine her Social Class, Anathaym rolls d100 and gets 97. Fortune has smiled upon the heroine since she is descended from the Aristocracy. The Games Master decides she is closely related to one of the city's ruling oligarchs, granting her a privileged position in society and allowing her to live in her family's well appointed home.

For her starting money Anathaym has 4d6 x75 SP - her roll is 9 which gives her 675 SP in total. As a member of the aristocracy her Money Modifer of 5 increases this to 3,375 SP personal wealth. The Games Master says that Anathaym has 1,000 SP in ready coin, with the remaining 2,375 SP being in the form of jewellrey and clothes.

Next Anathaym checks the status of her parents – her roll of 37 indicates that only her father remains alive, her mother dying whilst she was a little girl. She then rolls 19 on the siblings table and gets a 1 on the 1d4 for how many brothers and sisters she has. Emma decides her character's one sibling is a sister by the name of Kara.

The Games Master thinks it is wise to delay the generation of her extended family until later. However a roll of 51 on the Family Reputation table shows that whilst Anathaym's family is not prominent, it has no black marks against it. A further roll of 77 on the Connections table results in one Rival.

The Games Master decides that Xenos *will be Anathaym's Rival. They come from families of a similar background, and even grew up together. But, as Xenos has matured he has become something of a debauched wastrel who constantly mocks Anathaym's diligence. He also harbours designs for her sister, Kara, and Anathaym is determined to protect Kara from this rat. Xenos has broken many hearts, caring nothing for the wreckage he leaves behind. Anathaym is determined this will* not *happen to her sister...*

character, or its connections might prove useful for all sorts of reasons now or in the future.

If desired, roll 1d100 on each of the Family tables below to determine parental status, the number of siblings the character has, and the extended family's structure. Next determine the family's connections and reputation. Does the family enjoy respect in its community? Do its connections bring it a level of power or prestige? Are there are skeletons in the closet that might threaten stigma or ostracism? Does reputation bring allies or enemies?

It is recommended to leave the details of large families vague. One way of developing a story for Mythras characters is to introduce family members – such as that shrewish aunt or roguish cousin – through roleplaying and scenario development. Keeping details vague at this stage gives the Games Master the flexibility for creating such introductions. Family tables start on page 25.

Allies, Contacts, Rivals and Enemies

Allies, Contacts, Rivals and Enemies are people, or perhaps organisations, that a character has developed a relationship with for either good or ill. At this stage all one needs to do is give these supporting characters a name (Contact: Gundleus the Sage, for example, does just fine; or, Enemy: Cult of Yethis); fleshing out the details can come later.

- Ally: a friend, colleague or relation who shares the same cause as the character and will offer help and guidance when called upon. Depending on their personality the Ally may want a favour in return or might provide aid for free.
- Contacts: people of potential influence the character knows. A Contact is an acquaintance who can help, not one who will.
- Rival: those who oppose the character for the same or similar goals, and will attempt to interfere with or harass him.
- Enemy: someone who wishes the character harm, and will go to lengths to ensure the character suffers in some way. Enemies may take direct or indirect action, possibly trying to influence contacts and allies to bring about the character's misfortune.

Allies, Contacts, Rivals and Enemies are intended to act in the background, providing occasional interactions with the character but not always being prominent in their lives. These can be good sources of background information and, in certain circumstances, drive crucial parts of a scenario, but they are generally intended to be bit-players in the characters' stories rather than fully-fleshed non-player characters. Of course, they may well develop into fully-formed non-player characters as a campaign develops, and so Games Masters should keep careful note of who they are, how they look and act, what they know, and how they have (and will) interact with the character. This will maintain consistency in how they are portrayed.

Personal Connections

Why are the characters adventuring together? What connects them and forms the companionship? It is recommended that each player choose at least one of his fellows and, working with the chosen colleague, devise a reason for the relationship. Some examples:

- *Childhood friends who have continued together into adulthood.*
- *Members of the same community or culture.*
- *Members of the same profession, or, if from different professions, have had chance to meet and do business.*
- *A lucky encounter in a tavern, inn or other social establishment.*
- *A shared acquaintance (such as a third character in the group).*

Starting characters wishing to form a personal connection as part of their background are rewarded with a pool of Luck Points available to the entire party, rather than just a single individual. The number of Luck Points starts at two and increases by 1 per character who has formed a personal connection within the group. This pool of points functions in a very similar way to the individual Luck Points a character has, but are there for the benefit if all those within the group. They can only be drawn upon by a character when he is actively helping, or intends to help, another character (this can be anyone in the group needing help; not just the character with whom a relationship has been established).

For example, the players in Steve's game decide that they will all hail from the same city, Meeros, and belong to families that have known each other for years, the characters growing-up together. There are four players altogether: Emma (playing Anathaym), Kathrine (playing Kara), James (playing Hallax), and Rob (playing Tor-Irdeen, a minotaur character). Clearly Rob's character is unlikely to have grown-up with the humans, so Steve rules that connections will come later, through play. But for the humans of Meeros the Group's Luck Points equal 5: two points to start with, plus one point for each human, and the connections they have formed. Steve tells Rob that in the first session of game play, Tor-Irdeen will be introduced and given a chance to form a connection with the humans. Depending on how successful this plays out, then the Group Luck Points will increase to 6.

Passions

Using Passions in Mythras is optional but their use can greatly assist players and Games Masters in deepening the nature of the character, introducing plot hooks based on a character's desire or prejudices, and helping the player to understand who his character is, what drives him, and so on.

Passions are measured in the same way as skills; they have a starting value based on two characteristics and are rated between 1 and 100 (or higher). Passions represent several things:

- Loyalties and allegiances
- Strongly held beliefs or ideals
- Emotion felt towards someone or something

A Passion can be improved in the same way as a skill or it can be either increased or decreased by the Games Master depending on circumstances. *Aild, for example, may have Loyalty to Achaius, his clan chief, at 70%. However if Aild were to make an alliance with an enemy clan that Achaius disapproves of, then the Games Master could, quite reasonably, have Aild's Loyalty drop to 50%, representing an erosion of his fidelity. Conversely,*

PASSIONS TABLE

Object of Passion	Examples	Starting Percentage
A person, in a romantic or familial context	Lover, Sibling, Wife, Parent, Aloof or Unsuspecting Object of Desire	30% plus Loved one's POW+CHA
A person in a platonic context (a friendship or loyalty, for example)	Leader, Teacher, Ruler, Master, Rescuer, Priest, Enemy	30% plus Character's POW and subject's CHA
A person in an averse context	Enemy leader, Rival worker, Husband of Desired Lover, Murderer of Friend, Thief	30% plus Character's POW and subject's CHA
An organisation or group of people	Family, School, Temple, Religion, Local Community, Military Unit, Guild, Nobles	30% plus Character's POW+INT
A race or species	Foreigners, Non Humans, Tigers, Supernatural Beasts, Ghosts, Primitives	30% plus Character's POW x 2
A place	A Country, Home Town, Holy Place, Capital City, Graveyards, Mountains	30% plus Character's POW+INT
An object or substance	The Iron Throne, Diabolic Relic, Magic, Darkness, Ancient Heirloom, Gemstones	30% plus Character's POW x 2
A concept or ideal	An Ethic, Moral Code, Freedom, Personal Honour, Betrayal, Dishonesty	30% plus Character's POW+INT

Achaius might grant Aild a favour which increases the Loyalty to 80%, demonstrating the strengthening bond.

A Passion can be for anything – a person, an organisation, an ideal, even an object. Passions are typically described by a verb such as: *Comfort, Desire, Despise, Destroy, Espouse, Fear, Flee, Foreswear, Hate, Love, Loyalty to, Protect, Repudiate, Respect, Seek, Subvert, Torment or Uphold.*

The verb describes the nature of the relationship. Loyalty, for instance, does not always indicate respect; Respect does not always indicate love; Despising something is not the same as hating it; Loving someone is not the same as being loyal to them. The verb used should therefore reflect how the character feels either personally or culturally towards the subject.

A Passion can be established at any point in the game – either during this phase of character creation or, and perhaps most interestingly, during game play. All a character needs to do to establish a Passion is stipulate that he intends to form the passion and give it an appropriate adjective: Love (Elissa), for example; or Shun (Sorcery).

The starting value of the Passion varies according to its type - see the Passions Table, opposite.

All the Starting Percentages may be modified by the Games Master to reflect deeper or lesser devotion; thus, Love (Elissa) might begin for a character at 55%, using the above Starting Percentage calculation, but, because the character is so faithful to Elissa (a childhood sweetheart), the Games Master decides to increase the Starting Percentage to 75%, taking into account the lifelong devotion.

Where a person or people are concerned, the Passion does not need to be reciprocated. It is up to the Games Master to decide if it is or not, and the Player must decide if unreciprocated love will strengthen his character's Passion, or weaken it. If the decision is made to strengthen the Passion (unrequited love often drives the heart to deeper fondness or infatuation), then the Passion value can be increased (or decreased, if the depth of feeling is diminished) by 1d10%.

This section only details what Passions represent and their default values. How Passions are used in the game is discussed in Chapter 6.

MARRIAGE

This is purely optional, but is the character married or betrothed to be married? Marriage is the most common way for families to advance their status, position and power, and so making marriage arrangements, even for children who are not yet old enough to be married, is common. To decide Marital Status roll 1d100 for the character and compare it with the character's base value Influence skill. If the result is equal to or less than base value Influence then the character is Betrothed – that is, has been promised into a marriage. If the 1d100 roll is equal to or less than 10% of the character's Influence then the character is already married.

How happy or prosperous this marriage is depends entirely on the player and Games Master. Take a little time to think about the nature of the relationship: is it a political or economic betrothal? Does Social Class play a part? Do the two partners love each other? Perhaps they hate each other. If love or hate are involved then consider establishing a Passion to represent the depth and nature of the relationship.

And, if the character is married, have any children formed from the union? Again this can be an agreed situation between the player and Games Master. Or the player can roll 1d4-1 to determine the number of children present. If there are children, then roll 1d4 to determine the ages of the children. If the age rolls are identical, then the character has produced twins or even triplets. If the character starts play middle aged or older, roll the children's ages on the Age Table (see page 32) as if they were one category younger.

Social Class Tables

Barbarian Social Class

1d100	Class	Example Title	Money Mod	Background Resources
01-05	Outcast	Exile, Outlaw	0.25	Nothing but the clothes on their back, and maybe some personal armament
06-15	Slave	Bondsman, Caxtos, Peon, Serf, Thrall	0.5	Resides on owners property; owns a few keepsakes
16-80	Freeman	Churl, Commoner, Feine, Freedman, Karl, Labourer	1	Rented accommodation or farmland; possesses own tools or livestock, simple weapons
81-95	Gentry	Ealdormen, Flaith, Hauldr, Reeve, Thane	3	Owns a house, and either a farmstead, business or ship; furniture; tools, weapons & armour, mount, several servant or slave retainers; support from locals
96-100	Ruling	Chieftain, Cyning, Eorl, Jarl, King	5	As above but lives in a great hall and possessions are of excellent quality; fealty from a country or smaller region

Civilised Social Class

1d100	Class	Example Title	Money Mod	Background Resources
01-02	Outcast	Beggar, Mendicant, Vagabond, Vagrant	0.25	Nothing but the clothes on their back, and maybe some personal armament
03-20	Slave	Chattel, Captive, Helot, Servant	0.5	Resides on owners property; owns a few keepsakes
21-70	Freeman	Citizen, Peasant, Proletariat, Tenant, Vassal	1	Rented accommodation or farmland; possesses own tools or livestock; simple weapons
71-95	Gentry	Bailiff, Equite, Master, Official, Steward, Warden	3	Owns property, farm or business; furniture, tools, weapons & armour, mount, several servant or slave retainers; support from locals
96-99	Aristocracy	Archon, Baron, Count, Duke, Lord, Nawab, Noble, Oligarch, Patrician, Satrap	5	Owns several properties, extensive farmlands or multiple businesses; expensive furniture, tools, weapons & armour, mounts, many servants or slaves; fealty from regional inhabitants
100	Ruling	Caliph, Czar, Dictator, Emperor, Imperator, Maharajah, Mogul, Pasha, Pharaoh, Potentate, Prince, Rajah, Shah, Sultan, Tyrant	10	As above but of priceless quality; fealty from a dominion or nation

Nomad Social Class

1d100	Class	Example Title	Money Mod	Background Resources
01-05	Outcast	Outlaw, Rebel	0.25	Nothing but the clothes on their back, maybe some personal armament, and mount or small boat if suitable
06-10	Slave	Bool, Convict, Prisoner, Thrall	0.5	Resides on conquered lands, or in owner's yurt or vessel, owns a few keepsakes, plus tools or simple weapon
11-90	Freeman	Arad, Haran, Kinsmen, Subjects	1	Possesses own mounts, cart or small boat; owns yurt or similar, half a dozen livestock, weapons, simple armour, a slave or two
91-100	Ruling	Chieftain, Emir, Khan, Khaqan, Sea Lord, Sheikh	3	Owns many mounts, carts or boats; large yurt or similar, several dozen livestock, good weapons, good armour, some slaves, fealty from tribe and conquered peoples

Primitive Social Class

1d100	Class	Example Title	Money Mod	Background Resources
01-05	Outcast	Outlaw	0.25	A weapon and a few knickknacks
06-80	Freeman	Tribesman	1	Simple home, tools, and primitive weapons
81-100	Ruling	Chieftain, Elder	2	Large hall; valuable skins, totems, trophies, tools, cooking implements, decorated primitive weapons, simple armour; support from tribe

Family & Connections Tables

Parents Table

1d100	Parents
01-20	Both Parents living
21-40	Single Parent – Father
41-60	One birth parent plus step–parent
61-80	Single Parent – Mother
81-00	Both parents dead

Siblings Table

1d100	Siblings
01-10	None
11-30	1d4
31-70	1d6
71-90	1d8
91-00	1d10

Extended Family Table

1d100	Grandparents	Aunts & Uncles	Cousins
01-10	None	None	None
11-30	1d2-1	1d2	1d3
31-70	1d3-1	1d3	1d4
71-90	1d3	1d4	1d6
91-00	1d3+1	1d6	1d8

Reputation Table

1d100	Reputation	Allies, Contacts, Enemies and Rivals
01-15	Family has a poor reputation	1d3 Enemies or Rivals
16-35	Family's reputation is sound, but there may be a few skeletons and secrets better left locked away	1 Enemy or Rival
36-65	A sound family reputation	-
66-85	Family enjoys a good reputation although there may be those either inside or outside the family who could tarnish it	1 Contact or Ally
86-00	Family's reputation is untarnished and of excellent standing	1d3 Contacts or Allies

Connections Table

1d100	Connections	Allies, Contacts, Enemies and Rivals
01-20	No connections of note	None
21-80	Family enjoys reasonable connections within its community	Roll 1d4. On a 1 you gain an Ally; 2 a Contact; 3 an Enemy; 4 a Rival
81-90	Family is well connected in the community and is known to those commanding local power	As above but roll twice
91-95	As above, but the family also enjoys some status with those commanding regional power	As above but roll thrice
96-00	As above but the family also enjoys some status with those commanding national power	As above but roll four times

CAREERS

This chapter develops the character's skills through a profession, possible cult membership, the allocation of Bonus Skill Points, and some starting equipment, and determining what magic the character might (or might not) possess.

CAREERS

Every MYTHRAS character starts the game having been trained in a career. The occupation he chooses may not necessarily be the one he continues to follow as he begins his adventuring life, but it is the career he embarked on as part of the transition to adulthood, and it further defines his skill development.

The careers available to a character are dependent on their cultural background; in some cultures the range of available occupations is quite narrow because the needs of the community are simple; or social traditions will push young adults along a certain path. In others, the list is more diverse, reflecting a more complex community with wider needs that have diversified over the centuries.

Players are nominally free to choose which career they wish their character to learn, provided the Games Master deems it suitable. The following table gives some guidance as to the common types of vocation available to each cultural type. It is not definitive and may differ significantly in more exotic game settings. For example a campaign based in a land where magicians are slain at birth could prohibit the selection of magic using professions.

Similar to cultural backgrounds, each career offers the chance to improve a range of Standard and Professional Skills commonly utilised by that occupation. Some grant access to Magical Skills or extra Combat Styles. Unlike cultural backgrounds, characters need not invest their points in every available skill, but may tailor which ones are taken as those fitting for their specific role or culture.

Characters develop their career skills in the following way:

- *Select up to three skills from the Professional Skills available to that career.*
- *Distribute **100 points** amongst the career's listed Standard Skills and whatever Professional Skills were chosen, increasing each skill by 1% for every point spent on improving it. Not all of the available skills need to be improved, but no individual skill can receive more than 15%.*

Newly chosen Combat Styles and Professional Skills start off at their base characteristic value. Choosing a Style or Professional Skill previously gained via cultural background simply allows the character to further apply some of their career skill points at this stage. Some of these skills such as Craft, Language or Lore offer choice of a specialisation. In these cases the speciality selected should be one which suits the character's culture.

EXAMPLE CAREERS BY CULTURAL BACKGROUND

Civilised	Barbarian	Nomad	Primitive
Agent	Beast Handler	Beast Handler	Beast Handler
Alchemist	Crafter	Crafter	Crafter
Beast Handler	Entertainer	Fisher	Fisher
Courtesan	Farmer	Herder	Hunter
Courtier	Fisher	Hunter	Physician
Crafter	Herder	Merchant	Sailor
Entertainer	Hunter	Official	Scholar
Farmer	Merchant	Physician	Scout
Fisher	Miner	Priest	Shaman
Herder	Mystic	Sailor	Thief
Hunter	Official	Scholar	Warrior
Merchant	Physician	Scout	
Miner	Priest	Shaman	
Mystic	Sailor	Thief	
Official	Scholar	Warrior	
Physician	Scout		
Priest	Shaman		
Sailor	Thief		
Scholar	Warrior		
Scout			
Shaman			
Sorcerer			
Thief			
Warrior			

Agent

Agitator, Assassin, Detective, Informer, Spy…

The work of an agent is to report upon, and operate covertly against those his employer wishes to keep an eye on. They watch, discover, and act secretively. Anyone might be an agent – servants, beggars, noblemen, even children. Likewise those that employ agents might be anybody from a jilted lover or struggling merchant to the ruler of a nation. Agents mostly deal with passing of information or minor acts of sabotage, although a few sometimes perform assassination if the cause, or payment, is right.

Skills

- Standard Skills: Conceal, Deceit, Evade, Insight, Perception, Stealth; Combat Style (Concealable Weapons Style)
- Professional Skills: Culture (any), Disguise, Language (any), Sleight, Streetwise, Survival, Track

Alchemist

Apothecary, Herbalist, Poisoner, Perfumer…

Alchemists concern themselves with creating, or trading in, a wide range of chemical and herbal substances which are used by the local community. These concoctions can vary in purpose – soaps, polishes, dyes, disinfectants, acids, oils, unguents, perfumes, narcotics, medicines, poisons – the list is almost endless. The larger the society they reside in, the more likely that the alchemist will specialise in making or selling one specific type of compound.

Skills

- Standard Skills: Customs, Endurance, First Aid, Insight, Locale, Perception, Willpower
- Professional Skills: Commerce, Craft (Alchemy), Healing, Language (any), Literacy, Lore (Specific Alchemical Speciality[1]), Streetwise

Beast Handler

Animal Breeder, Beast Tamer, Menagerie Keeper…

Beast handlers make their living by capturing, trading, breeding, caring for, or domesticating creatures for a variety of different roles in the community. Examples include horse-whisperers, falconers, hound masters, snake wranglers, and the like. Some raise ostensibly wild animals for domesticated use, whilst others tend the beasts on display in private menageries. A few even take captured beasts and turn them into guardians, battlefield weapons, or competitors for pit fights and gladiatorial events.

Skills

- Standard Skills: Drive, Endurance, First Aid, Influence, Locale, Ride, Willpower
- Professional Skills: Commerce, Craft (Animal Husbandry), Healing (Specific Species), Lore (Specific Species), Survival, Teach (Specific Species), Track

1 *Such as Acids, Narcotics, Poisons, etc.*

Anathaym's Saga

Coming from a civilised city-state Anathaym has a wide selection of careers she could potentially follow. Indulged by her father she requests training as a soldier, the career he himself followed before retiring to a life of politics. Believing his daughter will soon tire of the gruelling discipline, her father tolerantly agrees to apprentice her under the tuition of weapon-master Zamothis, a famous warrior.

To her father's growing alarm, Anathaym flourishes under the guidance of the aging master. From the Warrior career she selects the following three professional skills: Lore – Military History 28% (INT x2), Lore – Strategy and Tactics 28% (INT x2), and Survival 20% (CON+POW).

She then spends her 100 points, dividing it amongst the available career skills thusly: Athletics +10, Endurance +10, Evade +10, Lore – Military History +10, Lore – Strategy and Tactics +10, Survival +10, Unarmed +10, Combat Style (Meerish Slinger) +15, Combat Style (Meerish Infantry) +15

Her new Meerish Infantry combat style covers training in spear, hoplite shield and javelin – something her tutor feels she'll need to be proficient in if she wishes to join the ranks of the Meeros Scarlet Spears, the regiment her father once commanded.

After applying her career modifiers Anathaym's skills are now: Athletics 37%, Boating 24%, Brawn 21%, Conceal 28%, Customs 68%, Dance 25%, Deceit 28%, Drive 28%, Endurance 36%, Evade 42%, First Aid 30%, Influence 28%, Insight 31%, Locale 33%, Native Tongue 63%, Perception 21%, Ride 23%, Sing 16%, Stealth 30%, Swim 24%, Unarmed 27%, Willpower 24%; Courtesy 38%, Lore (Geography) 38%, Lore – Military History 38%, Lore – Strategy and Tactics 38%, Streetwise 31%, and Survival 30%; Combat Style (Meerish Slinger) 52%, Combat Style (Meerish Infantry) 42%.

Courtesan

Concubine, Escort, Harem-girl, Houri, Paramour…

Professional companions, courtesans make their living through providing company, conversation, dance, singing, and sometimes other services to those who can afford it. The attitude towards courtesans can vary dramatically according to their culture, some are little more than tavern girls only there to draw in customers, whilst others are revered by the high ranking wealthy. The most famous and skilled courtesans may literally have princes begging at their feet. Courtesans can be both male and female.

Skills

- Standard Skills: Customs, Dance, Deceit, Influence, Insight, Perception, Sing
- Professional Skills: Art (any), Courtesy, Culture (any), Gambling, Language (any), Musicianship, Seduction

Courtier

Advisor, Conspirator, Delegate, Diplomat, Sycophant…

Traditionally members of the gentility or nobility, courtiers are those summoned into the service of a ruler or government to act as an adviser, a companion, an aide or simply as a lackey. Chosen for their ability to be persuasive, insightful or discreet, they are often the power-brokers behind domestic and foreign policy. Some courtiers are in fact ambassadorial representatives from another, foreign nation. Courtiers see and hear much about the affairs of state, and may

> **CAREERS AND SOCIAL CLASS**
>
> *MYTHRAS does not impose any immediate restrictions on what careers are available to what social class but it is something players and Games Masters may wish to consider. Some social classes will look down on members who practice certain vocations, risking censure or perhaps even expulsion from their rank. One culture might forbid nobles becoming merchants due to the risk of financial corruption, whilst another may restrict the practice to only those who are part of the nobility, creating an enclave of merchant princes.*
>
> *Games Masters should decide if a career is denied to a particular social class, but some interesting roleplaying possibilities can present themselves if a character decides to ignore social norms, and enter a vocation usually treated with disdain. How will that character be viewed: pioneer or social pariah? What are the consequences? How will the profession accept him? These are all golden opportunities for roleplaying and plot development.*

learn a great deal about politics and scandal in high places. Whatever their political standing, the machinations of courtiers can save or undermine a nation.

SKILLS

- Standard Skills: Customs, Dance, Deceit, Influence, Insight, Locale, Perception
- Professional Skills: Art (any), Bureaucracy, Courtesy, Culture (any), Language (any), Lore (any), Oratory

CRAFTER

Artificer, Artisan…

Skilled artisans, professional craftsmen cover a huge range of trades: from basket making through to weaving. Most craftsmen specialise in one particular area, but it is not uncommon to find those skilled in a second field related to their primary craft. Some crafters have associated experience in buying materials and selling their own wares, depending on their scale of their business. Primitive crafters may simply be individuals who produce objects for their family or tribe. Civilised crafters on the other hand might be part of a family enterprise or members of an official guild. Some crafts may be unavailable or illogical for particular cultures, such as a smith for primitives.

SKILLS

- Standard Skills: Brawn, Drive, Influence, Insight, Locale, Perception, Willpower
- Professional Skills: Art (any), Commerce, Craft (Primary), Craft (Secondary), Engineering, Mechanisms, Streetwise

ENTERTAINER

Acrobat, Bard, Dancer, Player, Poet…

Professional entertainers, have a range of skills in which they can specialise. Acrobats perform feats of balance, gymnastics, and hand-eye co-ordination. Actors present plays or ribald pantomimes. Dancers entertain with diverse dances ranging from the erotic to ceremonial. Musicians use their instruments to perform private concerts or provide background music. Poets recite great works of literature, and lyric poetry, whereas singers perform choral works, often as choirs. Story-tellers recount apocryphal tales, and so on. Entertainers sometimes learn several complimentary arts to increase their repertoire and create unique acts. For instance, a bard might combine the arts of music, singing and poetry.

SKILLS

- Standard Skills: Athletics, Brawn, Dance, Deceit, Influence, Insight, Sing
- Professional Skills: Acrobatics, Acting, Oratory, Musicianship, Seduction, Sleight, Streetwise

FARMER

Gardener, Estate Owner, Forager, Harvester, Ploughman…

Farmers cultivate the land, raising or harvesting crops, but they are often generalists in a range of skills necessary for foraging or maintaining their chattels. Usually their produce is food and other useful flora, such as medicinal herbs or plants which produce fibres for clothing. Not all agriculturalists necessarily tend a farm or plantation. Some wander through wild regions harvesting the naturally occurring vegetation, whilst others are employed to supervise formal gardens for rich patrons. Likewise not all farmers are necessarily yokels tied to a small pasture, orchard or vineyard. Many cultures may place high status on owners of large estates who manage the running of their property.

SKILLS

- Standard Skills: Athletics, Brawn, Drive, Endurance, Locale, Perception, Ride
- Professional Skills: Commerce, Craft (any), Lore (Agriculture), Lore (Animal Husbandry), Navigation, Survival, Track

FISHER

Beach Comber, Net Tender, Pearl Diver, Whaler…

Fishermen work the waters, braving the elements and dangers to bring back its bounty. Mostly they trawl for edible food, anything from shellfish to whales. A few seek commodities other than food however, particularly valuable items like rare shells, pearls or even medicinal types of water plants. The social rank of fishermen depends on the value of what they recover; a primitive island based culture for example, might grant high status to those who bring back the greatest amount or most dangerous produce. Fishermen do not necessarily need boats, and neither are they tied to the sea. Many live beside lakes or along rivers, using nets, baskets, and weirs to trap their catch.

SKILLS

- Standard Skills: Athletics, Boating, Endurance, Locale, Perception, Stealth, Swim
- Professional Skills: Commerce, Craft (Any), Lore (Primary Catch[2]), Lore (Secondary Catch[2]), Navigation, Seamanship, Survival

2 These represent different techniques of fishing, such as whaling, lobster potting, trawling, and so on.

Herder

Breeder, Herdsman, Sacred Goose Tender, Wrangler…

Herders are those who raise and tend flocks of creatures, not necessarily domesticated animals; anything from goats to migrating mammoths. Most herdsmen spend days or even weeks out on the plains or hills, ensuring their beasts have sufficient food and water, whilst also watching for predators. A herder does not necessarily raise his own livestock; some hire themselves out to escort herds over large distances to far off markets or use their skills to purchase stock for less discerning customers. It can be a solitary profession, but herdsmen generally know the land, the seasons, and the habits of their animals.

Skills

- Standard Skills: Endurance, First Aid, Insight, Locale, Perception, Ride; Combat Style (Specific Herding or Cultural Style)
- Professional Skills: Commerce, Craft (Animal Husbandry), Healing (Specific Species), Navigation, Musicianship, Survival, Track

Hunter

Forester, Poacher, Scavenger, Stalker, Trapper…

Responsible for finding, tracking, and killing creatures, the hunter, like the herder, is knowledgeable about the land and the behaviour of animals. A hunter may hunt in a variety of ways: simple stalking, trap laying or driving creatures into pens. The purpose of the hunt depends on the culture of the hunter. Most seek out prey for the simple purpose of gathering food, but some hunters specialise in the extermination of deadly predators or the culling of animals for valuable body parts: furs, horns or teeth for instance. Hunters often learn a supplemental craft for preserving or skinning the creatures they kill.

Skills

- Standard Skills: Athletics, Endurance, Locale, Perception, Ride, Stealth; Combat Style (Specific Hunting or Cultural Style)
- Professional Skills: Commerce, Craft (Hunting Related), Lore (Regional or Specific Species), Mechanisms, Navigation, Survival, Track

Merchant

Broker, Hawker, Money Lender, Smuggler, Trader…

Merchants come in many forms: the street vendor, small shopkeeper, wily caravanserai, intrepid merchant-venturer, and many more. Although their methods or merchandise are different, all have one thing in common: to trade commodities (be it goods, food, livestock, people, property or even money) for the highest profit. Merchants know a bargain, and how to drive a good one; and not all trade in legal merchandise. Due to their dealings as middle men, many merchants pick up some knowledge of foreign cultures and languages.

Skills

- Standard Skills: Boating, Drive, Deceit, Insight, Influence, Locale, Ride
- Professional Skills: Commerce, Courtesy, Culture (any), Language (any), Navigation, Seamanship, Streetwise

Miner

Prospector, Quarryman, Sapper, Well Digger…

Miners are those who excavate the ground, for a number of reasons. Some dig for ore and precious metals, a few seek out special types of stone for building or statuary, whilst others dig to create catacombs or sewers, or to penetrate the defences of towns. Whatever the purpose, miners are prepared to go deep into the ground, risking life and limb. As a result, miners tend to be both physically and mentally strong; used to working in hot, cramped conditions for hours on end.

Skills

- Standard Skills: Athletics, Brawn, Endurance, Locale, Perception, Sing, Willpower
- Professional Skills: Commerce, Craft (Mining), Engineering, Lore (Minerals), Mechanisms, Navigation (Underground), Survival

Mystic

Guru, Hermit, Illuminate, Master…

Mystics are those who seek mastery of the world by the attainment of perfection, spiritual insight or by becoming inured to physical discomfort. Depending on the culture from which they originate, mystics may be found as anything from reclusive mountaintop hermits to respected teachers of martial or artistic schools. The path of their development is always via mastery of self, and most are sagacious as an result of their studies.

Skills

- Standard Skills: Athletics, Endurance, Evade, Insight, Perception, Willpower; Combat Style (Cultural Style)
- Professional Skills: Art (any), Folk Magic, Literacy, Lore (any), Meditation, Musicianship, Mysticism

Official

Minister, Overseer, Steward, Tax Collector…

Officials are those appointed or elected to an office, charged with performing certain administrative duties and granted a degree of authority to ensure their commands are followed. Examples include slave managers of large estates, guild masters, bureaucratic scribes, legal advocates or tax collectors. Depending on the size and complexity of the organisation or government, most officials control a body of men to help perform their duties.

Skills

- Standard Skills: Customs, Deceit, Influence, Insight, Locale, Perception, Willpower
- Professional Skills: Bureaucracy, Commerce, Courtesy, Language (any), Literacy, Lore (any), Oratory

Physician

Doctor, Healer, Medicine Man, Torturer, Vivisectionist…

Physicians have detailed knowledge of how the body works, although they do not necessarily use that learning to heal. Some instead offer their skills to extract information by coercion, or further the depth of their education by questionable practices. A physician can take many guises, some examples being the medicine man of a tribe with his totems and fetishes; a local hermit or wise woman with their knowledge of herbs and poultices; or a court physician who can cure fevers and agues with complex chemical remedies. Depending on the sophistication of the culture, many doctors embellish their treatments with ceremonial theatrics, bogus medications, and manipulative psychology.

Skills

- Standard Skills: Dance, First Aid, Influence, Insight, Locale, Sing, Willpower
- Professional Skills: Commerce, Craft (Specific Physiological Speciality[3]), Healing, Language (any), Literacy, Lore (Specific Alchemical Speciality[4]), Streetwise

Priest

Arbiter, Cultist, Druid, Mendicant, Prophet…

Priests can take a variety of different roles in society; an official leading worship of the gods, an illuminated seer leading followers on an exodus to find their god, an administrator in a theocracy, and so on. Priests do not necessarily need to be religious or even believe in the faith they serve, whilst others might be granted miracles from their deity to reward suitable propitiation.

Skills

- Standard Skills: Customs, Dance, Deceit, Influence, Insight, Locale, Willpower
- Professional Skills: Bureaucracy, Devotion (Pantheon, Cult or God), Exhort, Folk Magic, Literacy, Lore (any), Oratory

Sailor

Captain, Galley Slave, Marine, Pirate, Raft man…

Sailors and boatmen have a myriad of roles upon the lakes, rivers, and seas, from the simple crew of a trading ship to hardened convict rowers. Those sailors employed as professional raiders or marines are often given shipboard combat training. Wise to the ways of the waves, but superstitious with it, sailors are used to long dangerous travels, and the hardships that go with it.

3 *Prosthetics, Scrimshaw, Torture, Vivisection, etc.*

4 *Such as Herbs, Medicines, Poisons etc.*

Skills

- Standard Skills: Athletics, Boating, Brawn, Endurance, Locale, Swim; Combat Style (Specific Shipboard or Cultural Style)
- Professional Skills: Craft (Specific Shipboard Speciality[5]), Culture (any), Language (any), Lore (any), Navigate, Seamanship, Survival

Scholar

Annalist, Librarian, Philosopher, Skald, Scribe…

The keepers and seekers of knowledge and learning, scholars and scribes are people who are fascinated by knowledge and the powers contained within it. Scholars are not necessarily confined to dusty libraries or suffocating scriptoriums; they may be active explorers and archivists, intent on advancing their learning or collections of tomes. Neither are they dependent on literacy to learn; some scholars memorise and hand down their knowledge orally. Some scholars are specialists in particular areas of knowledge, such as a lawspeaker who is employed to memorise and quote legal codes during law cases.

Skills

- Standard Skills: Customs, Influence, Insight, Locale, Native Tongue, Perception, Willpower
- Professional Skills: Culture (any), Language (any), Literacy, Lore (Primary), Lore (Secondary), Oratory, Teach

Scout

Bounty Hunter, Explorer, Pioneer, Ranger, Wayfarer…

Scouts are those who thrive beyond the reach of their native civilisation. They may be pioneers seeking out new territory or rangers employed by the military to keep an eye on the borders. Some are employed to seek out natural commodities which they sell to merchants of more settled lands, whilst others are hired to hunt down fugitives. A few are scholarly explorers, high ranked men seeking to document new cultures or simply folks cursed with chronic wanderlust. Hardened by their life, scouts often live from what the land provides, understanding the plants, animals and seasons of the wilderness they inhabit.

Skills

- Standard Skills: Athletics, Endurance, First Aid, Perception, Stealth, Swim; Combat Style (Specific Hunting or Cultural Style)
- Professional Skills: Culture (any), Healing, Language (any), Lore (any), Navigation, Survival, Track

Shaman

Animist, Diabolist, Exorcist, Madman, Witch Doctor…

The medicine-man, the witch-doctor, the wise-woman: all can commune with the spirits and the ancestors; understanding the secrets of the spirit plane which lies over, under, and around the world we

5 *Carpentry, Sail Making, Rope Making, etc.*

live in. The shaman has great insight and power, or so they would have you believe. Not all have magical powers, some merely follow the rituals and traditions handed down to them. Others are outright charlatans using trickery to fool the gullible members of their community. Despite the primitive associations, many civilised cultures also believe in the powers of the spirit world, propitiating dead ancestors for instance.

Skills

- Standard Skills: Customs, Dance, Deceit, Influence, Insight, Locale, Willpower
- Professional Skills: Binding (Cult, Totem or Tradition), Folk Magic, Healing, Lore (any), Oratory, Sleight, Trance

Sorcerer

Enchantress, Magi, Warlock, Witch, Wizard…

The dedicated practitioners of sorcery who seek to control the world around them through spells, incantations and rituals that are not necessarily tied to any gods or spirits, but directly alter the fabric of reality. A sorcerer is often fascinated by all aspects of magic, driven to master its subtleties, and discover lost incantations. Some gain their power from a lifetime of studying dusty tomes, whereas others might offer sacrifices to learn from the diabolic entities of forbidden realms. A few are deceivers with no supernatural powers at all, using legerdemain and prestidigitation to fool others into paying them respect.

Skills

- Standard Skills: Customs, Deceit, Influence, Insight, Locale, Perception, Willpower
- Professional Skills: Folk Magic, Invocation (Cult, School or Grimoire), Language (any), Literacy, Lore (any), Shaping, Sleight

Thief

Burglar, Conman, Fence, Mugger, Tomb Robber…

Thieves are those who delight in stealing, or are forced to steal from others to support themselves. They range from petty criminals who mug or pickpocket folk on the streets, to gang leaders and golden-tongued swindlers. Whilst thieves thrive in urban environments they also exist in less civilised cultures too, operating as outlawed brigands, and raiders of neighbouring tribes. Some thieves specialise in tomb robbing, stealing the grave goods of the dead. A few independently wealthy cutpurses and burglars are simply bored individuals who thieve for adventurous excitement.

Skills

- Standard Skills: Athletics, Deceit, Evade, Insight, Perception, Stealth; Combat Style (Concealable Weapons Style)
- Professional Skills: Acting, Commerce, Disguise, Lockpicking, Mechanisms, Sleight, Streetwise

Creating a Custom Career

Players can create custom careers subject to the following guidelines:

- *Agree the career with your Games Master. Your concept of 'Death Knight Assassin' might not fit with the themes and style of the Mythras game.*
- *Standard Skills: Choose up to seven Standard Skills and seven Professional Skills for the profession, reflecting its nature. Remember that magical abilities are considered Professional Skills.*
- *Also remember that Combat Styles are treated as Standard Skills. Try to avoid granting Combat Styles except to those careers where physical conflict is a regular occurrence or fundamental to survival.*

Warrior

Bodyguard, Champion, Mercenary, Pit Fighter, Soldier…

Professional soldiers are the warrior class of a community; this is the career of the fighting man. Most of their time is spent patrolling, guarding and training – focusing on the use of weapons, close-quarter tactics, and the study of enemy styles to make the most of any future opportunities. The warrior may or may not follow a particular martial code, and similarly he might focus on finesse or simple brute-force.

Skills

- Standard Skills: Athletics, Brawn, Endurance, Evade, Unarmed; Combat Style (Cultural Style[6]), Combat Style (Speciality Style[7])
- Professional Skills: Craft (any), Engineering, Gambling, Lore (Military History), Lore (Strategy and Tactics), Oratory, Survival

Age

How old is your character? An Adventurer may start as young or old as the player desires, subject to the agreement of the Games Master. It is recommended that beginning characters start as youths or young adults, but much depends on the setting, and whether the game will be but a short one-off adventure or a long running campaign.

A table is provided, breaking age into Age Categories. Note that this table can be used for non-human characters by simply substituting the actual number of years for longer or shorter lived races. A character's age has a direct effect on their skill competence; as older characters naturally have more life experience than younger compatriots.

6 *This is the warrior's default starting cultural style.*

7 *Speciality styles are those catering to particular troop types, martial school or career (see Combat Styles on page 86 in the Combat chapter).*

To determine how old a character is, a player may either choose an age within the Age Category permitted, or simply roll the value randomly.

AGE TABLE

Age Category	*Age*	*Bonus Skill Points*	*Maximum Skill Increase*	*Background Event Rolls*
Young	1d6+10	100	+10	0
Adult	2d6+15	150	+15	1
Middle Aged	3d6+25	200	+20	2
Senior*	4d6+40	250	+25	3
Old*	5d6+60	300	+30	4

AGE TABLE NOTES

Bonus Skill Points *determines how many additional skill points the character has to spend on developing his skills – see the following section.*

Maximum Skill Increase *limits how many of the Bonus Points can be applied to any one particular skill.*

Background Event Rolls *are used for characters starting at different ages, requiring the player to potentially roll additional times on the Background Event Table in the Culture and Community chapter.*

****Ageing**: If a character is Senior or older he is subject to Ageing; see the rules for Ageing on page* *70*.

BONUS SKILL POINTS

At this stage every character gains an additional pool of 'free' skill points based on age, which can be distributed amongst his existing skills. These are provided so that the character can be rounded out, and given particular interests or areas of expertise. The default for adult characters is a pool of 150 points, with a limit of assigning no more than 15 points per skill. If characters are younger or older, then the number of Skill Points and restrictions will differ, as previously indicated on the Age Table.

The number of Bonus Skill Points does not necessarily need to be tied to age. If the characters are to be seasoned veterans, cultural heroes or even the sons of gods, the Games Master is free to grant additional points or modify the maximum number which can be applied to a specific skill.

Bonus Skill Points are used in the following way:

- Allow the character the option of choosing one final new Combat Style or Professional Skill, reflecting a personal hobby or interest.
- Distribute points amongst whatever skills the character currently has; increasing each skill by 1% for every point spent on improving it. No individual skill can receive more points than indicated by their Age Category.
- Save for the optional hobby skill, no points may be assigned to those Combat Styles or Professional Skills not learned as part of their Culture or Career.

STARTING EQUIPMENT

Every character begins with some starting money and starting equipment, determined by their culture and social class. In addition they may augment their belongings by buying additional items (or upgrading ones they already have) from the Equipment section of this book.

The table on page 33 gives some examples of personal possessions available to a character of that social class. These are merely guidelines, and are open to change according to the campaign or setting.

ANATHAYM'S SAGA

As a member of the aristocracy Anathaym begins the game with the following:

Four sets of good quality clothing: a court dress, day, and evening wear and a formal gown. Mostly though, she opts for a simple, but well-made, tunic akin to the kind worn by Meerish soldiers.

Four weapons, chosen from her father's armoury: a shortsword, dagger, spear, and shield. Her sling she makes herself from a length of strong leather.

A suit of Meerish Hoplite armour - again chosen from her father's armoury. Although the protective value is determined by 1d3+3 roll, the Games Master declares that Anathaym is given a mixture of leather and bronze with appropriate Armour Point values.

She also has a horse, chosen from the family stables. Anathaym's mount is a chestnut gelding named Arrow, for his speed and sharp temper.

CLOTHING

Finery and decorations are dependent on the culture and its climate. The higher the class the more exclusive the fabric used in its manufacture. An example would be rough spun wool for the poor, followed by linens, brocades, and silks as social class or wealth increases. In a land full of silk worms and no sheep, these relative values may be reversed. Decorations are also culturally dependent. Feathers may be the height of décor for a primitive tribe, whilst embroidery using gold threads may be de riguer for a barbarian king. Example decorations are fabrics of bright or rare colours, the attachment of precious substances, pelts or fur trims, detailed embroidery and pattern woven fabrics.

WEAPONS

Not everyone in a society is expected to be armed; in fact some cultures expressly forbid weapons to those of a particular class or caste. The most common weapons are usually simple and inexpensive; spears and axes for example which can be mass produced or improvised. Only the higher classes tend to have 'prestige' weapons such as swords which require significant amounts of time to manufacture.

ARMOUR

Perhaps even more restricted than weaponry, few members of the lower classes possess armour, and what they own is usually hand crafted from fabrics or leather by their own family. Culture and environment plays a big part in who is expected to own armour, for example it would be rare to see common folk of a city storing armour at home, whereas it might be ubiquitous amongst a tribe of horse nomads. Metallic armours tend to be restricted to the wealthy or those of noble class, and are often passed down as heirlooms.

Background Equipment Table

Class	*Clothing*	*Weapons*	*Armour*	*Transport*
Exile	One set of ragged, probably dirty clothes	One well used weapon of a provenance suitable to the character's origin	Roll 1d6-3. If the result is greater than zero the outworn armour is worth that many AP, and covers 1d3 locations. Otherwise no armour is owned	None
Slave	One or two sets of clothes of a quality suitable for the position and type of work performed by the slave	None	None	None
Freeman	Two sets of common, undecorated clothes suitable to the freeman's occupation	1d2 simple weapons suited to the culture. Axes, clubs, knives, spears, slings, and the like	Roll 1d3. This represents the Armour Points for the armour the character has. Armour is available to cover 1d6 locations	Own back, Raft, Handcart or Beast of Burden
Gentry	1d6+1 sets of clothing, made of good quality fabrics and a modest level of decoration	1d3+1 weapons of higher status, and/or quality. Swords, maces, shields, bows, great weapons, and so on	Full set of protection worth 1d2+2 Armour Points	Hired or Slave Porter, Boat, Wagon or Riding Mount
Aristocracy	1d6+3 sets of clothing, made of expensive fabrics and sporting lots of decoration	1d3+3 weapons of expensive quality, decorated with precious substances	Full set of protection worth 1d2+3 Armour Points	Palanquin, Ship, Chariot or Several Fine Mounts
Ruling	1d6+6 sets of clothing, made of rare, priceless materials and as opulent as good taste allows	1d3+6 weapons of exquisite craftsmanship, each of which are priceless due to heredity or materials	Full set of protection worth 1d2+4 Armour Points	Expensive Palanquin with matched Bearers, Warship, Exquisite Carriage or Several Magnificent Mounts

However, culture and setting might restrict the type of armour available to upper classes; for example the sons of a primitive tribal chieftain might not have access to iron mail hauberks, but could conceivably possess a type of hoplite plate carved from the bones or scales of monsters instead.

Transport

Choose a vessel or mount suited to the culture or environment the character comes from. Examples are given based upon the primary mode of travel: foot, vessel, wheeled or mount. Some interpretation or leeway may be required, for instance a freeman from a nomadic society might be expected to at least own a mount, or perhaps it is something loaned to him by the patron or patriarch of his family.

Magic

Mythras offers several different types of magic. Whether characters begin play with access to these arts depends on their cultural background, starting career, and the accessibility of magic in the setting. More information on the kinds of magic available, how they differ, how they work and the spells or abilities they begin with is given later in the respective magic chapters. For now, it is necessary only to know what sort of magic, if any, a character has learned, rather than a detailed knowledge of how it works.

Folk Magic

Usually only learned by petty magicians or common folk in lands where magic is ubiquitous, folk magic has minor effects upon the world, outshone in comparison to the higher arts, but can be potent for all that. Folk magic originates from, and is connected to, the natural world, and the emotions of those within it. The ability to use folk magic is controlled by the skill of the same name.

Animism

Animists derive their magic from the summoning and control of spirits and other supernatural creatures. These beings of the otherworld are negotiated with or enslaved at the animist's determination, forming agreements with allied spirits or binding the less willing into fetishes for later use. In exchange the animist must follow strict taboos or fulfil binding contracts. Animism relies on the skills of Trance and Binding.

Mysticism

Mystics draw their magic from the knowledge of self mastery and understanding. Their insight into the inner self allows them to achieve incredible acts of mental and physical excellence, making them difficult to defeat in direct confrontation. Whilst their magic does not extend beyond themselves, they themselves become a tool to manipulate the world about them. Mysticism uses the skill of the same name in addition to Meditation.

Sorcery

Sorcerers express their magical abilities by twisting the laws of the world using the invocation of powerful spells. Whilst sorcery is exceptionally flexible, it can often be unbound or dismissed by the strength of other magics. Yet their independence from supernatural beings means sorcerers never need to rely on anyone but themselves. Sorcery uses the skills of Invocation and Shaping.

Theism

Theists are those who are rewarded with power from the gods in exchange for loyalty and service. Their miracles are potent as they merely channel their gods' own divine power, and can be utterly devastating. Yet maintaining the bond requires continual dedication and constant sacrifices to ensure the deity remains appeased, or at least aware of their worshipper. Theism requires the skills of Devotion and Exhort.

Character Creation Complete

Working through the first three chapters should now have left you with a well-rounded, competent character with an established culture, career, community and back-story. You have everything you need to begin play.

Hopefully the character creation process will have also set you thinking about your character's life, history and aspirations. What does he want from life? Why is she adventuring? What are the things driving this character to risk life and limb?

These are not questions that need to be answered immediately. Many answers will suggest themselves through play, and one of the joys of Mythras is discovering more about your character as he or she develops in experience and maturity.

Cult Membership

An optional stage for character development is cult or brotherhood membership. Many cultures of all types initiate their young adults into a cult or other form of social organisation as a rite of passage. If the character joins a cult it is likely one that either reflects the faith and beliefs of their family or their choice of career. Cults and Brotherhoods offer access to training, and perhaps magic as well as providing a social, cultural, and professional network that characters will find useful.

Cults and Brotherhoods are covered at length in their own chapter beginning on page 192. If Games Masters allow cult membership at this stage of character creation it is suggested that no character should have a rank higher than Common Member.

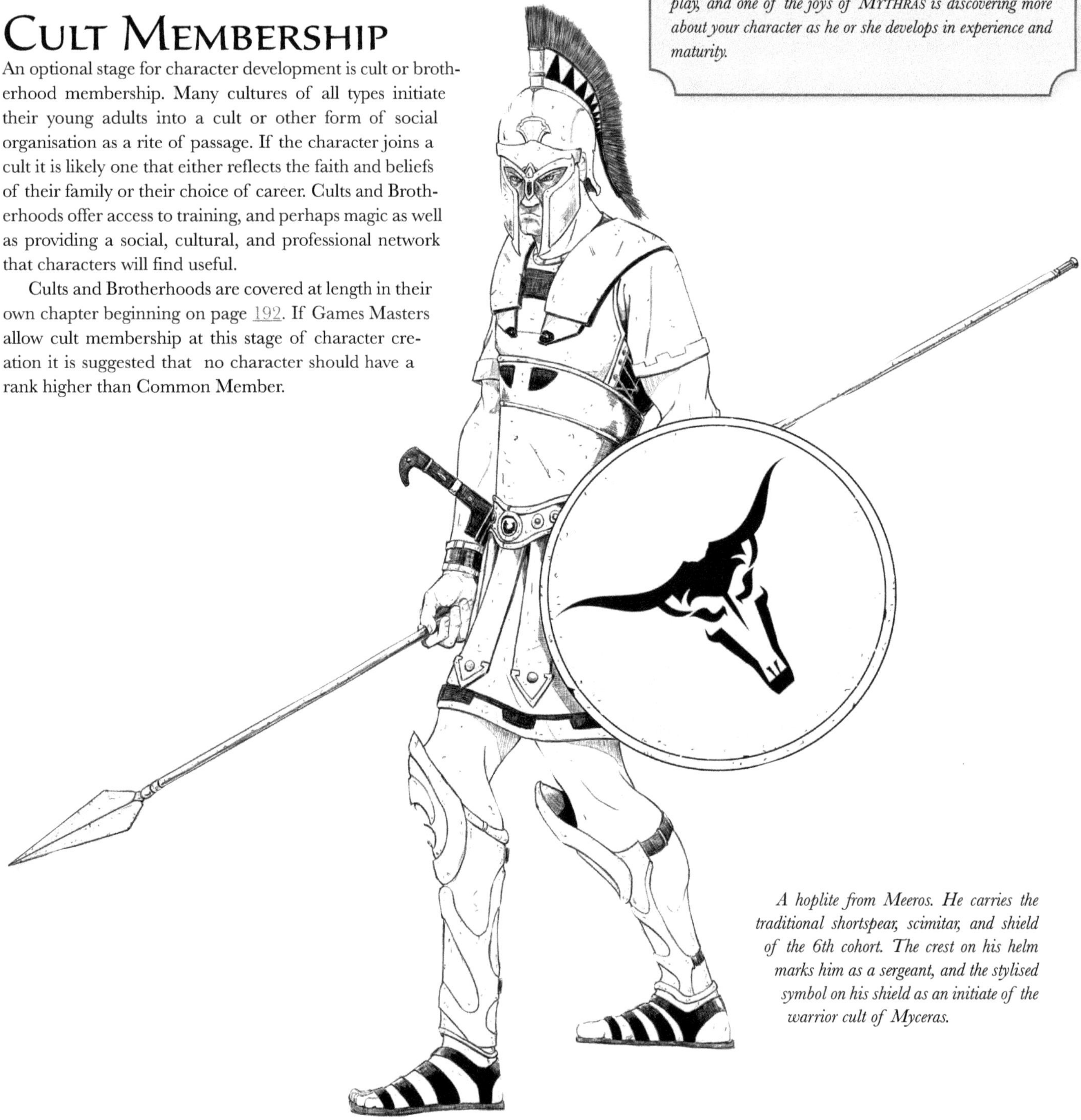

A hoplite from Meeros. He carries the traditional shortspear, scimitar, and shield of the 6th cohort. The crest on his helm marks him as a sergeant, and the stylised symbol on his shield as an initiate of the warrior cult of Myceras.

Basic Character Creation Elements

1

Characteristics

3d6 for STR, CON, DEX, POW and CHA. 2d6+6 for INT and SIZ. Allocate results to fit the concept. Results may be allocated in the order listed, or distributed as the Games Master and players agree.

Alternatively distribute 75 points amongst the characteristics. Minimum 3 (8 for INT and SIZ), maximum 18. Use all the points.

2

Action Points

INT + DEX	Action Points
12 or Less	1
13–24	2
25–36	3
For every additional 12 points	+1

3

Damage Modifier

STR + SIZ	Damage Modifier
5 or Less	−1D8
6–10	−1D6
11–15	−1D4
16–20	−1D2
21–25	+0
26–30	+1D2
31–35	+1D4
36–40	+1D6

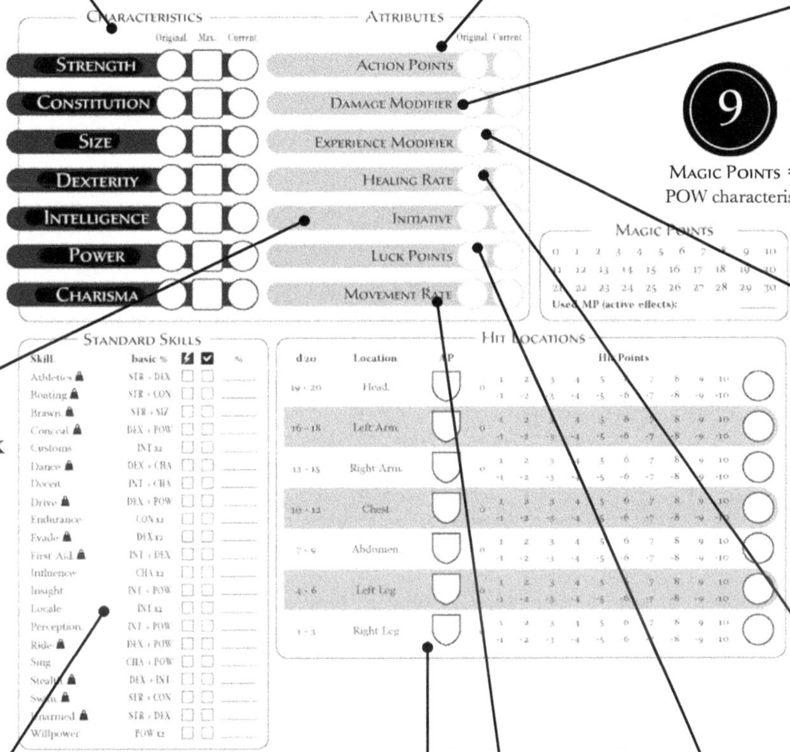

9

Magic Points = POW characteristic

4

Experience Modifier

CHA	Exp. Modifier
6 or Less	−1
7–12	0
13–18	+1
Each 6 points	+1

8

Initiative Bonus = Average of INT & DEX

5

Healing Rate

CON	Healing Rate
6 or Less	1
7–12	2
13–18	3
Each 6 points	+1

11

Skills & Combat Styles

These are calculated using the characteristics listed for each skill. At this stage you generate only the beginning values; skills will increase as you progress through Cultures and Community, and Careers and Development.

6

Movement = 6m for Humans

10

Hit Points Per Location

CON+SIZ

Location	1–5	6–10	11–15	16–20	21–25	26–30	31–35	36–40
Head	1	2	3	4	5	6	7	8
Chest	3	4	5	6	7	8	9	10
Abdomen	2	3	4	5	6	7	8	9
Each Arm	1	1	2	3	4	5	6	7
Each Leg	1	2	3	4	5	6	7	8

Hit Points appear on the second page of the character sheet and are shown here for clarity.

7

Luck Points

POW	Luck Points
6 or Less	1
7–12	2
13–18	3
Each 6 points	+1

Character Creation Summary

1 Character Concept

- Decide on the kind of character to play. Keep it simple for now. More will come.

2 Characteristics

- If playing a human, 3d6 for STR, CON, DEX, POW and CHA. 2d6+6 for INT and SIZ. Allocate results to fit the concept.
- Alternatively distribute 75 points amongst the characteristics. Minimum 3 (6 for INT and SIZ), maximum 18. Use all the points.

3 Calculate Attributes

- Use the characteristics to determine Action Points, Damage Modifier, Experience Modifier, Healing Rate, Hit Points, Luck Points, Movement and Initiative Bonus as described in pages 8 to 10.

4 Standard Skills

- Calculate Standard Skills by adding together the appropriate characteristics.

5 Culture

- Decide on a Cultural Background: Barbarian, Civlised, Nomadic or Primitive. Allocate 100 points amongst the listed Standard Skills, the chosen Professional Skills and the Combat Style for the chosen culture. Skills must have a minimum of 5% and cannot receive more than 15%. Customs and Native Tongue gain +40% each.
- Decide on Cultural Passions: Loyalty, Love and Hate.
- Calculate your character's Starting Money.

6 Background

- Roll or choose a Background Event from pages 18 to 20.
- Roll for Social Class (or choose according to the campaign), for Parents, Family Standing, Connections.

7 Career

- Choose a Career from those available to your character's culture.
- Distribute 100 points amongst the career's listed Standard Skills and whatever Professional Skills were chosen, Not all of the available skills need to be improved, but no individual skill can receive more than 15%.
- Identify if the career uses magic and consult the appropriate Magic chapter for information on spells and so forth.
- Consider Cult or Brotherhood membership as described in the Cults and Brotherhoods chapter starting on page 192.

8 Bonus Skill Points

- Depends on age, but default characters have 150 points, with a limit of assigning no more than 15 points per skill. Choose one additional Professional skill as a hobby speciality.

9 Equipment

- Determine Starting Equipment based on Social Class.
- Buy any additional equipment needed using the Starting Money determined as part of culture and social class. Refer to the Economics and Equipment chapter starting on page 54.

10 Finally...

- Don't forget to give your character a name. Look to establish Connections with other characters.

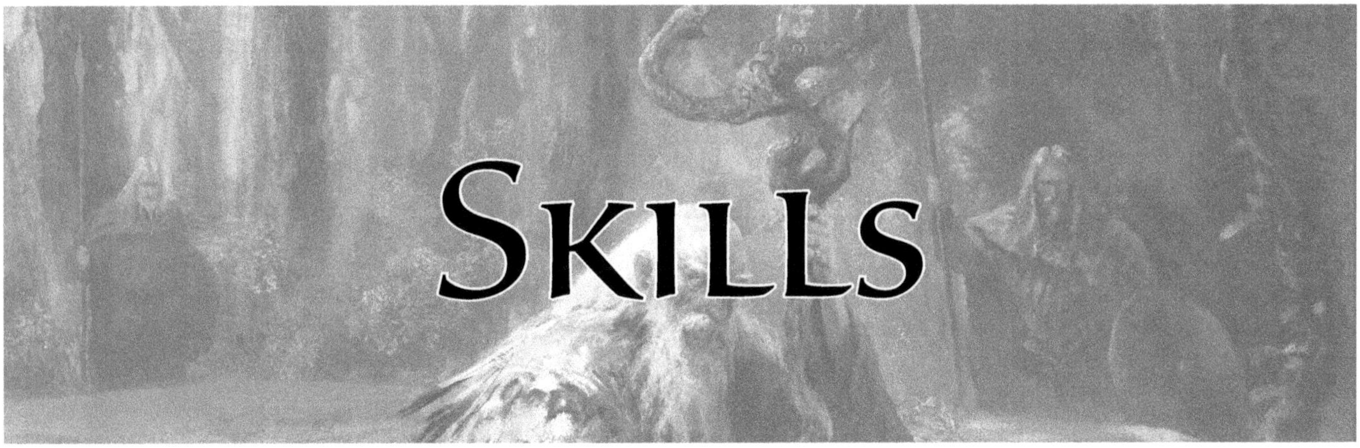

Skills

If characteristics and attributes define what a character is like, skills define what he can do. As explored in the previous chapters, all characters have a diverse set of skills drawn from their vocation and cultural backgrounds. This chapter explains how skills work, and provides greater definition for each skill used in Mythras.

Skills are divided into two categories: Standard and Professional. Every character has the same set of Standard Skills. Professional Skills differ between individual characters and reflect expertise developed within a career and, to a certain extent, their culture. Despite these distinctions, Standard and Professional Skills work in the same way.

This chapter looks, first of all, at the basics of how skills work. Then the skills, Standard and Professional, are described. The chapter then concludes with some additional rules for how to handle skills in different ways, and under different circumstances.

How Skills Work

A skill has a base value based on two characteristics; or one characteristic multiplied by two. There is no upper limit to a skill's value; it can exceed 100 and, in the course of play, characters can expect to see their skills reach such heights.

Whenever a character is called upon to resolve some form of test, challenge or professional ability 1d100 is rolled and compared with the skill's value:

- Equal to, or less than, the skill indicates a success
- Greater than the skill's value indicates a failure

There are certain special cases concerning success and failure that should be noted.

- Any roll of 01-05 is always a success
- Any roll of 96-00 is always a failure, irrespective of how high the skill's value

Criticals and Fumbles

Criticals and Fumbles represent spectacular successes and catastrophic failures; those cases where a character has either excelled in his attempt or failed miserably and utterly.

- A Critical success is equal to one-tenth of the skill's value (and this includes skills that receive a modifier – so modified skills may have a greater or lesser chance of a Critical outcome). Round fractions up when calculating a Critical success's range. For example, if a skill is modified to twice its normal value – from 40% to 80% say, then its critical range would be a roll of 08 or less.
- A Fumble is roll of 99 or 00. Skills with a value of more than 100% fumble only on a roll of 00.

The precise nature of a Critical or Fumble result is left to the Games Master to determine. The consequences could be wondrous or dire, depending on the circumstances. However, some examples of Critical and Fumble outcomes for each skill Mythras uses are given in the skill descriptions later in this chapter.

Automatic Successes

There will be some occasions where a roll against a particular skill just isn't necessary – either because the task at hand is easily accomplished, or because, with enough time and concentration, success is guaranteed. Riding a horse at a gentle canter across an open meadow is an example of an Automatic Success where simply being skilled in the activity means that straightforward actions do not require any skill roll to resolve them. A crafter carving a piece of wood into a chair leg is another example where a skill roll is not necessary; it takes time to accomplish, but the craftsman knows how to do the work and, if he is not rushing, success is assured. A thief, undisturbed, with a set of lockpicks, can successfully pick the simple lock of a treasure chest given enough time to do so.

When to Roll?

Part of the fun and drama of Mythras comes in making a roll against a skill to see if success or failure is the outcome. It can be tempting to call for skill rolls for each and every challenge but, as outlined above, there are some cases where rolls are not needed. A list of likely scenarios where skill rolls are redundant is as follows:

- The activity or task is very routine to the character
- The character has enough time and all the tools necessary
- The circumstances and environment do not impose any stress
- There are no significant consequences to failure

Skill rolls should be used when they have a dramatic purpose. For example, although riding a horse at a gentle canter requires no skill roll, fleeing at a gallop from pursuing bandits does. Carving a chair leg may be a routine task for a carpenter, but carving an exquisite chair leg, with blunt tools, and in only a few hours, for a demanding sultan who executes those who do not please him, would need a skill roll. It is usually obvious when a dramatic purpose arises and a skill roll is necessary, but if in doubt, consider the consequences of failure: are they crucial to the plot? Does the chance of failure heighten tension, and make for an exciting possibility? Will a failure – or even superb success – add fun to the game? If the answer is Yes to any of these, then have the character make a skill roll.

Modifying Skills

There are some occasions where a skill roll is required but the chances of success need to be adjusted to reflect particular conditions. Fleeing bandits, for instance, might require an Athletics roll. But what if the character is fleeing through darkness or through treacherous undergrowth? In such a case the Games Master can insist on modifying the skill of the character to reflect the circumstances.

Mythras uses a series of grades to determine how a skill is modified. These are as follows:

Difficulty Grade Table

Difficulty Grade	*Skill Modifier*
Automatic	No need to roll
Very Easy	Double the skill value
Easy	Add half again to the skill value
Standard	No adjustment.
Hard	Reduce the skill value by one third
Formidable	Reduce the skill value by half
Herculean	Reduce the skill value to one tenth
Hopeless	No attempt can be made

Where a character is already suffering a penalty from other circumstances the hardest difficulty grade takes precedence.

Mythras does not provide a definitive list of situations and challenges which can incur skill modifications. What sort of modification is required for any particular skill or context is ultimately up to the Games Master to decide; according to the capabilities of the characters, his perception of the difficulty of the situation, and the dramatic tension at that particular moment.

Simplified Difficulty Grades

Whilst difficulty grades are designed to scale with character skill, some Games Masters may find applying penalties results in the slowing down of their game. As an alternative the following option is provided:

Simplified Difficulty Grade Table

Difficulty Grade	*Skill Modifier*
Very Easy	+40%
Easy	+20%
Standard	None
Hard	-20%
Formidable	-40%
Herculean	-80%

Standard Skills

Standard skills are common to everyone. They represent innate abilities and skills that most people employ on a regular basis from any walk of life.

Athletics (STR+DEX)

Athletics covers a range of physical activities, including climbing, jumping, and running. If an adventurer is wearing armour, the distances he can climb, run or jump are affected by the Armour Penalty. The Movement section on page 69 describes these effects.

Climbing

With the right surface (hand and footholds), the right equipment (ladders, ropes, pitons), and enough time, characters can climb any surface without the need for a roll. Under normal circumstances, use the following guidelines:

- Climbing a rough or rugged surface (branching trees, scaffolds, piles of rubble, and so on): Half the Armour Penalty (rounded up) is subtracted from the character's base Movement. If the result is zero or less, they are too encumbered by armour to climb.
- Climbing a steep surface (pitched roofs, steep hills, and so on): The Armour Penalty is subtracted directly from the base Movement. If the result is zero or less, they are too burdened by armour to climb.
- Climbing a sheer surface (walls, cliff faces, and so on): Double the Armour Penalty is subtracted from the base Movement. As with previous situations, if the result is zero or less, the character cannot climb.
- Tests should be made for treacherous surfaces (such as sheer cliffs or wet surfaces), and if a character is distracted, or even attacked, during his ascent or descent.

A critical success permits the climber to scale the surface extremely quickly or avoid any hidden danger involved with the attempt.

A failure merely indicates that the climb was aborted.

A fumbled Climbing roll results in a fall; furthermore the character cannot attempt an Acrobatics roll (if he has that skill) to reduce falling damage.

Jumping
A successful Athletics roll allows one to jump up to twice one's own height horizontally or up to half one's own height vertically (if the character has at least a five metres run-up available). If the jumper is jumping from a standing position then these distances are halved. Any jump of over half a character's maximum distance results in him falling prone on landing.

- If wearing armour reduce the jump distance in metres by half the Armour Penalty to a minimum of one normal step.
- For every full 20% a character has in Athletics, he can add an extra metre to a horizontal jump, or 20cm to a vertical one, if he has space to perform a run up.

On a critical success the character adds a further metre to his total distance, and remains upright on landing.

A fumbled roll indicates the character has landed awkwardly. He must immediately make an Endurance roll. If the Endurance roll is a success 1 point of damage is sustained to one leg. If the Endurance test fails, then 1d4 points of damage is inflicted instead.

Running
A higher Athletics skill allows a character to run at a higher speed over short or long distances.

- For every full 25% a character has in Athletics, he can add an extra metre to his base Movement when sprinting, or half that when running over longer distances. In certain situations where space may be limited, such as Charging within a melee, the character can decide not to apply this bonus, and remain at his base racial or species movement.

On a critical success the character adds a further metre to his Movement rate.

A failure causes the runner to increase a level of fatigue.

A fumbled roll indicates the character has pulled a muscle or torn a ligament, and must cease running. He must immediately make an Endurance roll. If the Endurance roll is a success 1 point of damage is sustained to one leg. If the Endurance test fails, then 1d4 points of damage is inflicted instead.

Throwing
Athletics can also be used for hurling large, unwieldy objects over distance or tossing smaller items with accuracy. Throwing is restricted for sports or improvised missile weapons - everything from small stones to bar stools. Weapons which are thrown using a specific technique to ensure it strikes point or blade first (rather than just achieving distance), such as javelins, axes or knives, use their Combat Style instead.

- A thrown object has a maximum range of one metre for every point the character's STR exceeds the object's SIZ.

Boating (STR+CON)
The Boating skill covers the operation of small floating craft on rivers, lakes, and close inshore. Appropriate vessels are generally boats, canoes or rafts which travel short distances, and are unsuited to the rigours of the open sea. Most are propelled using oars, paddles, punts or simple sails; or can even be towed by animals. Ships with large crews or designed for long, overseas journeys are covered under the Seamanship professional skill.

The skill measures a character's competence in propelling a boat in the right direction and dealing with adverse conditions. With no distractions and optimal conditions, a Boating roll is unnecessary, although lesser skilled characters may take longer to get where they need to as they manage the boat's handling.

A critical Boating success increases the vessel's Movement rate by one tenth.

A failed Boating roll implies the boat's movement rate is halved or it failed to reach its intended destination; for instance navigating to an isolated rock positioned above a waterfall.

A fumbled Boating roll indicates losing an oar, taking on water or some other serious inconvenience. If the weather is bad or the water violent, then a fumble causes the boat to capsize.

Brawn (STR+SIZ)
Brawn is the efficient application of technique when applying raw physical force. The skill covers acts of applied might, including lifting, breaking, and contests of strength.

Lifting
A character can lift and carry up to their STR in SIZ up off the ground, or drag double this amount, without needing a Brawn roll. As a mass equivalent, 1 point of SIZ equals, roughly, 5 kilograms. For every full 10% he possesses in the skill the character may add an extra point of SIZ or 5kg to his total.

For SIZ or mass above this the character needs to succeed in a Brawn roll. The maximum weight a character can briefly lift is equal to twice their STR, plus whatever bonus they gain from their skill.

Failing the Brawn roll may result in injury; the character must make a successful Endurance roll or suffer 1d3 points of damage to a random location below the head.

Fumbling the Brawn roll automatically results in injury.

Note that the size and shape of an object might make it impossible to lift, even if it is within the character's weight capacity.

Breaking
A character can use Brawn to break objects with their bare hands – such as shoulder barging a wooden door. Take the character's maximum lifting capacity in SIZ and apply that value to the Damage Modifier table on page 9 to determine how much damage can be inflicted with each Brawn attempt, remembering that failed rolls may result in injury.

Contests of Strength
Brawn rolls can also be used in opposed tests for breaking free from the grip of others, arm wrestling, and tugs of war. Such events are handled as a simple opposed roll. However, there comes a point where technique cannot overcome superior size and strength. In a contest, if a character's Damage Modifier is smaller than his opponents, his Brawn roll suffers a penalty; a difference of one step raises the difficulty to Hard, whilst two steps increases it to Formidable, and so on. Naturally the penalty is suffered by his opponent if the character is the stronger.

Conceal (DEX+POW)
Conceal is the counterpoint to Stealth, being the concealment of large objects rather than the character themselves. For instance conceal could be used to hide a chariot behind some rocks, or sweep away the wheel ruts of the chariot so its path cannot be tracked. The skill is versatile in application, anything from hiding a scroll in a library to disguising the presence of a trap or secret passage.

A critical success using Conceal indicates that the object has been hidden so cunningly that rolls attempting to discover it are one difficulty grade harder.

A failed Conceal roll means that the object will automatically be found if actively searched for.

A fumbled Conceal roll indicates that the attempt backfires spectacularly with the object falling, rolling, blowing out of its hiding place so blatantly (or otherwise revealed in an appropriate manner) that it draws the attention of everyone nearby.

Customs (INT x2)

Customs represents the character's knowledge of his own community; its social codes, rites, rituals, taboos, and so on. The skill is used when it is essential to accurately interpret or perform any socially important custom or to behave in a particular way.

A critical success with Customs indicates that the character has acted in an exemplary fashion or perceived a very subtle social nuance that will be of immediate or later value.

A failed Customs roll results in wry humour or minor irritation. A fumbled Customs roll indicates that the character has badly failed to observe his community's customs, and may have even given offence – whether intentional or not.

The ramifications of a fumbled roll depend very much on the nature of the culture or community, and may thus have very different outcomes, ranging from harsh rebuke, through ostracism, exile or even violent punishment.

Dance (DEX+CHA)

Just about every culture uses dance in some way – either as recreation or as part of important rituals. It might be a court dance, a war dance, or a simple set of movements accompanying a prayer or ceremonial chant. The Dance skill measures a character's ability to move rhythmically and accurately (to a reasonable degree) when called upon to do so.

A critical success results in a dance that is expressive, fluid, and perhaps deeply affecting for those who witness it. The dance is as persuasive as any Influence roll, and can be used as such in situations resting on communication and personal credibility. Alternatively any subsequent Influence test is given a bonus equal to the critical score of the Dance skill. Of course, a critical Dance roll may very well result in tumultuous applause, and tokens of admiration and appreciation.

A failed Dance roll signifies a lacklustre performance.

A fumbled Dance is clumsy to both the dancer and those who watch it. The dancer trips or stumbles. Passion is lost, the execution is weak, and the dance fails to convey what it is meant to. Any skills resting on communication and personal credibility will suffer a penalty at the discretion of the Games Master.

Deceit (INT+CHA)

Deceit covers all instances where a character attempts to mask the truth and offer a deceit of some kind; barefaced lying, misleading a guard or even bluffing (or cheating) during a card game. The skill also covers instances where hiding true emotions or motives is necessary (feigning pleasure when one is bitterly disappointed perhaps, or attempting to seem welcoming and open when the opposite is true). Deceit forms a counterpart to the Insight skill, and can be used to oppose Insight rolls when others are attempting to discern either truth or motive.

On a critical success the character has pulled off the deceit convincingly to the point where the truth will not be questioned in the future by those who are subject to the deception – unless something happens to expose the truth.

A failed Deceit roll indicates that the character lacked conviction or believability, prompting further investigation.

A fumbled Deceit roll represents a miserable failure to deceive – one so transparent that others may have difficulty believing the character at a future time.

Drive (DEX+POW)

Drive covers the control of wheeled or drawn vehicles, whether by one or more beasts of burden or more esoteric means: such as carts, carriages, chariots or sleds. Drive rolls are needed when a character wants to do something out of the ordinary with a vehicle – traverse treacherous terrain, jump obstacles, and so on. A roll is also necessary if the vehicle being driven is drawn by different beasts than the driver is used to (horses instead of oxen, for example) or there are more or fewer beasts teamed together to pull the vehicle (a four-horse wagon when the character is used to a two-horse team). In cases where either the beasts or their number are radically unfamiliar, a tiger drawn chariot for example, then the roll should be made more difficult.

Where two or more vehicles are contesting with each other, perhaps to overtake or force another off the road, the drivers should determine the result with an opposed Drive test.

A critical Drive roll either increases the vehicle's Movement rate by one tenth or permits the driver to perform some feat of skilful or flamboyant driving.

A failed Drive roll halves the vehicle's Movement.

A fumbled Drive roll indicates either that the vehicle has broken down in some manner (wheel comes off or the harness breaks for example), or if the vehicle is engaged in a high speed or dangerous manoeuvre, it becomes unstable and overturns. An overturning vehicle requires all occupants to make a successful Acrobatics or Evade roll to leap clear of the wreckage, or sustain an amount of falling damage commensurate with its speed (see page 78).

Endurance (CON x2)

Endurance is a character's capacity to endure physical stress, pain, and fatigue. It measures the body's ability to deal with potentially damaging or debilitating conditions, and is a general gauge of resilience, stamina, and metabolism. Endurance, like its counterpart Willpower, is used in any number of ways, but most specifically to resist the possible effects of injuries, including harmful poisons and disease.

In most cases Endurance is used in Opposed Tests but there are some circumstances where it is used as a standard skill roll.

A critical Endurance roll usually indicates that the character has managed to shrugoff the worst possible assault on his body. In the case of injury he is often able to act when ordinarily he might be incapacitated.

A failed Endurance roll results in the character succumbing to whatever stress or injury it has been put under. A Fumbled roll means that the character is overwhelmed by the circumstances and becomes incapacitated. In the case of disease or poison he automatically fails any further resistance rolls against it.

Evade (DEX x2)

Evade is used to escape from observed, impending danger, and can be used against ranged weapons (by diving for cover, for example), avoiding traps, changing the engagement distance in combat, and generally getting out of the way of a potential physical hazard. It can also be used as a resistance roll for certain types of magic.

Usually Evade will be opposed by another roll, but it may also be a standard roll in its own right. Trying to negate damage by leaping clear of a crashing vehicle, as mentioned in the Drive skill, is an example of a standard Evade roll. The typical circumstances for opposed rolls are as follows:

Avoiding Missiles

Evade is opposed by the Combat Style of the attacker.

Thwarting a Trap

Evade is opposed either by the trap's Potency or its original designer's skill rating at the time the trap was made or set.

Evading a Harmful Spell

Opposed by the spell caster's score in the casting skill.

Manoeuvering in Combat

Opposed by the attacker's Evade skill.

Again, like Endurance, Evade is most often used in Opposed Tests. When used as a standard test, a critical Evade roll ensures that the evader retains some form of advantage or composure afterwards, such as avoiding all damage or slipping completely clear of further danger.

Anathaym's Saga

Anathaym, investigating a ruined temple, comes across a sarcophagus in the catacombs. She tries to open it, and triggers the centuries-old dart trap set by the sarcophagus's designer. The trap-setter's skill at the time was 65%; Anathaym's Evade is 57% which she must pit against the trap in an opposed roll.

Amathaym scores 45, and the Games Master rolls 31. Both are successful but Anathaym wins the contest with the higher roll. The trap is sprung as Anathaym lifts the sarcophagus lid, shooting a hail of darts towards her face; but Anathaym throws herself desperately to one side and, fortunately for her, the darts strike the wall behind.

Brushing herself down as she stands, Anathaym reflects on the dangers of ancient tombs, unaware of the guardian mummy lurching towards her from behind...

A failed roll usually means the character suffers whatever misfortune they were attempting to avoid.

If the Evade roll is fumbled, then the character has left himself wide open to the hazard, for instance sustaining maximum damage from a trap or ending up prone, and vulnerable to a follow up event.

The effects of Criticals and Fumbles during combat is a special case (see the rules for Evading in the Combat chapter, page 103).

First Aid (DEX+INT)

First Aid measures a character's ability to treat minor injuries and stabilise severe ones. First Aid may be applied only once per specific injury. Thus a character that is slashed twice in the leg may have each wound treated separately. If suffering some form of bodily harm which simultaneously affected several body areas at once, such as being burned by Dragon Breath, then a First Aid attempt is permitted for each individual location.

A character can self-administer First Aid, although depending on the circumstances (such as the location of the wound, its degree of severity and so forth) the roll may be subject to a greater degree of difficulty.

Applying First Aid takes 1d3 minutes. Neither party can do anything else during the treatment. When tending life threatening trauma, the patient is temporarily stabilised until the result of the

First Aid Actions

Injury	*Successful Treatment*
Asphyxiated	The victim begins breathing again.
Bleeding	The blood flow is staunched.
Impaled	The impaling item is removed without causing further damage to the victim.
Unconsciousness	As long as the unconsciousness is not the result of poisons or narcotics then the injured party is restored to awareness.
Minor Wound	Treatment restores 1d3 hit points to the injury.
Serious Wound	Treatment restores the location to partial functionality.
Major Wound	A successful First Aid roll on a location suffering from a Major Wound does not return any Hit Points, nor restore functionality; but it does stabilize the area, and prevent immediate death resulting from the damage. More skilled healing is required to treat Major Wounds.

application is known. An injury that has had a previous form of First Aid applied cannot benefit from First Aid again, whether successful or not, until it has fully healed.

First Aid relies on having appropriate equipment – bandages, at the very least – available for the treatment. These can be improvised (a torn cloak to make a bandage or sling, for example) if necessary.

A critical First Aid improves the result of the treatment. On a Minor Injury it recovers 1d6 Hit Points, on a Serious Injury it recovers 1d3 Hit Points, and on a Major Injury it restores partial functionality (if possible), and permits it to heal naturally.

A fumbled First Aid attempt causes more harm than good: the injured location suffers a further 1 point of damage, potentially increasing the severity of the injury.

Influence (CHA x2)

Influence measures a character's ability to persuade others. It is used in a wide variety of situations; from changing someone's mind, through to bribing an official or guard.

Influence rolls are typically opposed by the Perception, Willpower or another Influence skill, depending on the circumstances, and are modified by how much a character is trying to influence behaviour. Attempting to persuade a close friend to loan you their horse may be relatively easy. Getting a usually incorruptible bureaucrat to accept a bribe is more difficult.

A critical success indicates that the character has been incredibly persuasive, so much so that not only is the character successful in what he is trying to attain but his next Influence test with the same person, no matter when it takes place, is one grade easier than the circumstances would normally dictate (A Standard roll becomes an Easy roll, for example, or a Hard roll becomes a Standard one).

A failure merely means that the persuasion was refused, with no subsequent issues.

On a fumble not only does the Influence roll fail; it also insults or offends the person being influenced. The specific reaction depends on the individual and the situation. It also means that further Influence attempts with this individual become one difficulty grade harder.

Insight (INT+POW)

Insight is the ability to read or intuitively define another's verbal and non-verbal behaviour (such as body language or the manner of speech) to establish their motives and state of mind. Insight is used to determine if someone is telling a lie (and it can be opposed by the other person's Deceit skill), or to predict how someone feels about a particular situation. Insight can equally be applied to particular situations as well as other people: is that tavern a haven for trouble? Could the bandits be planning an ambush in the nearby hills?

On a critical success the Insightful character gains an in-depth understanding of the other person's current motives, thoughts and feelings. Using either Deceit or Influence against that person in a subsequent roll is one grade easier than circumstances would dictate (Easy rather than Standard; Standard rather than Hard, for example).

A failure simply means the character cannot discern anything specific at that time. On a fumble, the character completely misjudges the person's motives and actions. The Games Master should offer the character a series of private, deliberately misleading hints regarding the person's motivations and likely actions. It also makes consequent Deceit and Influence rolls one difficulty grade harder.

Locale (INT x2)

Locale measures a character's understanding of local flora, fauna, terrain, and weather in the area where he has spent the majority of his life, usually within his community. The character knows the common plants, trees and animals, their properties and behaviour: where the best fish can be found; the movements of game creatures; where to find shelter; the likely weather for the season, and the most common regional dangers. In neighbouring, yet unfamiliar locations Locale should be made one or more grades harder.

A critical success guarantees the character finds what he is looking for in abundance or knows precisely what something is. Subsequent skill rolls related to the subject of that Locale roll (Survival, for instance, or Track) become one grade easier.

A failure implies too little evidence to unambiguously identify or predict, or that whatever is being searched for cannot be found.

A fumble means the information needed is not just unobtainable but utterly misunderstood. Subsequent skill rolls dependent on that use of Locale become one grade harder.

Native Tongue (INT+CHA)

Native Tongue is the ability to speak one's own language, the one learned whilst growing up in one's home culture. It measures articulation, eloquence, and the depth of the speaker's vocabulary.

Unlike other skills, Native Tongue is not rolled against directly. Instead it is treated as a static representation of overall fluency, limiting the level of conversational interaction. This is described in more detail under the Language skill on page 47, but starting characters usually begin play fully fluent in their mother tongue.

The skill can be used in two ways. Firstly it can help to understand dialects of neighbouring peoples which share a common linguistic basis or origin. In such cases the skill is treated at least one grade harder, potentially affecting the character's fluency. Secondly, it can be used as a cap on verbal skills which require a good grasp of language. See Capping Skills on page 50.

Perception (INT+POW)

Perception is used for both passive observation and focussed detection; whether hunting for something specific, a general scan of an area or simple awareness of their surroundings. Specific conditions – darkness, for example – may affect the difficulty grade of the skill roll depending on the primary senses being utilised. Strong scents might make an olfactory Perception roll Easy rather than Standard, whereas trying to eavesdrop on a conversation in a crowded and noisy tavern would make the roll Hard.

A critical Perception roll reveals things that otherwise would not have been detected in addition to that which the roll was being used for.

Failure indicates nothing in particular was discerned.

Fumbling a Perception roll means that even the most blatantly obvious things are overlooked or misconstrued, potentially increasing the difficulty of subsequent skill checks. For instance, a fumbled Perception roll when trying to spot a trap might make an Evade roll Hard or even Formidable rather than Standard.

Ride (DEX+POW)

Ride covers the ability to control and remain mounted on those creatures that are trained to be ridden. The skill can be applied to a diverse range of beasts, everything from mules to elephants; even flying or swimming creatures such as giant eagles or dolphins.

Riding an unfamiliar species is always one difficulty grade harder; whilst riding a species of a different medium (a horseman riding a dragon, for example) is two grades harder. Wild, untamed creatures cannot be ridden in a constructive manner until they have been broken and trained to be riding beasts.

A critical Ride result allows the rider to perform a feat of flamboyant riding (such as a jump or wingover) or temporarily increase his mount's Movement by one tenth.

A failure causes the mount to drop a level of fatigue.

A fumbled roll means that an accident occurs; either to the rider (who might fall off) or the mount whom suffers some form of injury, going lame or breaking one of its limbs for example.

Sing (POW+CHA)

Carrying a tune is covered by Sing, anything from monotonous chants through to complex arias. Singing is an inherent part of most cultures, a prime source of entertainment, and perhaps used in its rituals. Important songs might be used for courting, inspiring soldiers before battle, or simply recounting a historical deed. The skill reflects the user's ability to maintain rhythm, keep in key and remember the correct words.

A critical Sing success can have one of several effects. If singing to earn money, increase by half again the amount earned due to the audience's appreciation of the performance. If being used to impress someone, a follow-up Influence or similar skill become one difficulty grade easier to make.

A failed Sing roll signifies a bland performance. If fumbled, then the song was off-key, out of tune, and poorly received. Halve the earnings and any attempts to influence or deceive afterwards become one grade harder.

Stealth (DEX+INT)

Hiding out of plain sight, or moving with minimal sound are covered by the Stealth skill. Cover and conditions, such as darkness or loud background noise, improve the grade of the skill according to specifics of the environment. Similarly adverse conditions, such as a lack of cover or a quiet night will decrease the skill's grade. Circumstances also affect the difficulty of the attempt. For instance, a warrior wearing heavy armour can easily conceal themselves behind a wall providing they stand still or move very slowly, whereas moving quickly might cause their armour to jingle.

A critical roll means that any subsequent attempts to use skills to locate the character; follow him, observe him, and so forth are one grade harder.

A failure indicates that they are blatantly obvious, providing someone is bothering to locate them.

On a fumble the Stealth attempt has backfired and signals the character's presence rather than disguises it, or causes them to suffer some accident or misfortune; such as hiding on a window ledge then being knocked off when someone opens the shutter to investigate the strange noise.

Swim (STR+CON)

Without development the ability to swim is limited to being able to thrash around, and keep one's head above the water for a short time.

Higher Swim percentages indicate being able to negotiate deeper and stronger waters, with less risk of drowning. Making a Swim roll therefore depends entirely on the conditions. Rough seas, strong currents, white water and rip-tides all reduce the grade of the skill no matter what the character's affinity for water might be. Under normal conditions a character's maximum swimming speed per round is equal to their base Movement rate, plus an extra metre for every full 20% they possess in Swim.

A critical Swim roll allows the character to add a further metre to his Movement rate.

Failing a Swim roll has no immediate consequences, save that the character gains a level of Fatigue.

If a Swim roll is fumbled then controlled movement ceases as the swimmer begins suffering cramps or is overwhelmed by turbulent conditions; future Swim rolls become one grade more difficult. From that moment on, all the swimmer can do is try to keep their head above water until help arrives or they become exhausted, at which point they'll likely start to drown. See the rules for Asphyxiation on page 71.

Unarmed (STR+DEX)

Unarmed is a universal Combat Style common to all characters, measuring the ability to defend oneself without the aid of weapons. The Unarmed skill covers the brawling and wrestling techniques known by that culture. However there are, of course, specific styles that enhance the ability to fight without weapons, offering advantages to those who learn them as a separate Combat Style.

As Unarmed is a Combat Style its critical and fumble effects are covered by the rules for combat, as detailed in the Combat chapter.

Willpower (POW x2)

Willpower is a measure of a character's ability to concentrate, channel his force of will in a particular direction, or harden his psyche to possible mental shock. It is also a measure of personal resolve. The skill is used in all manner of situations where mental resilience is required, and this includes resisting magic. Although not a measure of sanity it can be used to endure traumatic events that would shake even the sanest, stable mind. Willpower is the mental counterpart to Endurance.

Again, like Endurance and Evade, Willpower is most often used in Opposed Tests. When used as a standard test, a critical Willpower roll indicates that the character has hardened his mind and spirit to the extent that no further attempts to influence him, or shake his resolve, will work. In the case of resisting magic, a critical success means that no further mentally afflicting spells cast by the opponent have any effect on the character for the remainder of that encounter.

The effects of failing a Willpower roll depend on the situation and circumstances – usually temporary capitulation to whatever is being done to him. A fumbled Willpower roll means that the character is utterly overwhelmed. His will is broken, and he has no means of resisting whatever it is that assails him mentally or spiritually. In the case of resisting shock or spells a fumbled Willpower roll means that the psychological effect of the spell becomes permanent until healed.

Optional Rule – Limits to Endurance and Willpower

There are limits to mental, and physical endurance; barriers beyond which the mind, and body cannot be pushed, and surrender becomes inevitable. Games Masters may wish to rule in their campaign that Endurance cannot exceed CON x5, and Willpower cannot exceed POW x5. The starting values for each skill are both calculated as normal, but have a defined limit.

Professional Skills

Professional Skills differ between characters and represent more specialised forms of training and experience. Some Professional skills are gathered through cultural background and a character's career, as the name suggests. Although they differ between characters they work in the same way as Standard Skills.

Certain magical skills are also classed as Professional Skills: Invocation and Shaping are the two skills associated with Sorcery for example. These are only briefly described here. For more details see the relevant magical chapter.

Acting (CHA x2)

Acting governs the art of being able to impersonate and convey a completely different character, whether in a staged performance or in a social situation. The actor portrays a personality and mannerisms different to his own in a convincing manner. Coupled with the Disguise and Deceit skills, this is a powerful way of becoming someone else entirely. An Acting roll is needed when it is essential to perform convincingly: on stage, for example, or attempting to pass oneself off as another person.

A critical success is thoroughly convincing. In a performance context it guarantees a standing ovation or similar. In a social context then the actor is the character he portrays. It also means that any subsequent skill roll, such as Deceit, Influence or similar, is one difficulty grade easier (Easy rather than Standard, for example).

Failed rolls signify a lacklustre performance.

Fumbling an Acting roll means the performance convinces no-one, and is so bad that even the most unperceptive will see through the act, or perhaps worse, laugh and jeer.

Acrobatics (STR+DEX)

Acrobatics covers acts of balance, gymnastics, juggling and tumbling. The skill can be used in its own right as a way to impress an audience, but also to help mitigate damage from falls. With a successful roll a character can move at full speed and sure-footedly across an unstable or narrow surface. If trying to mitigate damage from an unexpected fall, a successful Acrobatics reduces the distance as explained on page 78, *Falling*.

Acrobatics can be substituted for Evade if the situation warrants it. The benefit of this is that if the roll is a success, the character automatically avoids ending up prone.

A critical success doubles the movement rate when balancing or negotiating an unstable surface.

Failing an Acrobatics roll results in an unimpressed audience, or the premature aborting of whatever trick or tumble was attempted.

A fumbled Acrobatics roll means that balance and agility has been completely lost, causing the character to either fall off whatever he was balancing upon, drop a juggled object in a spectacularly bad way, or injure themselves performing an acrobatic tumble – suffering 1d4 points of damage to a random location.

Art (POW+CHA)

There are many specific art forms. Painting to Poetry; Literature to Sculpture. A character chooses an Art specialisation when taking this skill. Subsequent Art forms are advanced in separately. A roll is made whenever a character must impress or convince through his artistic medium.

A critical success indicates that artist creates something of stunning quality, elegance or beauty – worth half the standard value again of like products. Any subsequent skill rolls made to influence whomever commissioned the work, or those that simply admire it, become temporarily one grade easier.

Failing the roll creates something insipid, which neither impresses or sells for more than the materials used to create it.

A fumbled Art roll renders an artistic disaster. The effects of such a terrible situation need to be determined by the Games Master but, at the very least, represent a complete waste of time, materials, and talent that, if viewed publicly, could influence reputation.

Binding (POW+CHA)

Binding is a magical skill used by animists to exert their will over spirits and creatures of the otherworld. It is used to bind spirits into fetishes, and control their actions once bound. Additionally, it can be used to summon and coerce a known spirit to perform a deed for a mutually acceptable service, forging a contract between them.

Moreover the skill is used when engaging in Spirit Combat, and also measures the authority an animist has within a spirit cult. For further details see page 131 of the Animism chapter.

Binding is not limited to animists. The skill can be learned by other magical practitioners, and used in the binding of supernatural entities such as elementals and demons.

Bureaucracy (INT x2)

Understanding administrative procedures, records, and unspoken conventions are covered by the Bureaucracy skill. It is used to interact with officials or discover pertinent civic information. Depending on the sophistication of their culture, bureaucrats need not necessarily be literate. However their Bureaucracy skill cannot exceed the score of the Language or Literacy skill in which they work. Whenever red-tape or administrative landscapes need to be navigated, a Bureaucracy roll is necessary.

Critically succeeding in Bureaucracy lends a deep insight into the procedures and formalities of whatever it is the character is attempting to accomplish, achieving it in half the usual time. It also means any subsequent skills relying on the Bureaucracy roll are one grade easier (Influence, for example, or Deceit).

A failure results in becoming stonewalled or relevant documents misplaced, the user's inability to follow customary procedure resulting in subsequent skills relevant to the situation becoming one grade harder.

If the roll is fumbled then access is forbidden or the character alienates a key personage – so that their enquiry or request will never be satisfied.

Commerce (INT+CHA)

Commerce is used to evaluate the worth of goods and commodities, and to trade them for the best possible price. It is also used to understand the intricacies of business transactions in addition to securing a profit. A further use is in finding the best way to dispose of stolen and illicit goods – again for the best possible price. Commerce is obviously used when trading, and it can be opposed by either an opponent's Commerce skill or Willpower, reflecting the opposing side's attempts to further the deal in their favour. It is also used to judge the market value of goods, gaining an idea of price and where it will be best traded.

In transactions where rolls are not opposed, a critical success allows the character to secure the commodity or service at half its usual price, or sell it for double.

Failing the roll indicates that the commodity or service is secured at twice the price, or sold for only half the value.

A fumble means the character has insulted the purchaser or seller to such a degree that the transaction is lost. Alternatively it may indicate that they are cheated instead, ending up paying for something worthless or unwittingly selling something of potentially great value at a fraction of its cost.

Also see the section on Haggling, page 56.

Courtesy (INT+CHA)

This skill covers understanding how to act appropriately in a social or formal situation: modes of address, rituals, and conventions of behaviour, and so forth. It includes everything from who to bow to, and when, to how low; from when to use a particular title, to when it is appropriate to act informally.

Critically succeeding in a Courtesy roll makes any subsequent skill roll relevant to that situation one difficulty grade easier.

Failing a Courtesy roll means the user has not impressed the company with his attitude or manners; making any subsequent skill rolls a grade harder.

A fumbled Courtesy roll creates severe embarrassment and humiliation and, at worst, gives insult that, depending on the circumstances, could have a dire outcome. No further social intercourse is possible after a fumble.

Craft (DEX+INT)

Each Craft is a specialised form, and there are as many crafts as there are professions for them. Like Art, Craft is used to create the subject item. How long it takes depends entirely on the nature of the product: weaving a rug takes longer than throwing a pot, for instance, but time is not necessarily the most important factor: it is the skill of the crafter, the quality of the resources, and attention to detail.

A critical success creates an item of superior quality, in terms of durability, utility or beauty.

A failed Craft roll indicates a sub-standard result undermining its robustness, function or aesthetics.

A fumbled roll creates an item that is functionally useless and valueless. Alternatively an accident occurs during the crafting process, causing damage to property, stock or the crafter themselves; a pottery kiln collapsing or a smith striking his hand with a hammer for example.

Culture (INT x2)

Culture is the more specific form of the Standard Skill of Customs, relating instead to societies foreign to the character's own. Each Culture skill must be given a particular nation or society to which it applies. Mechanically it works in the same way as the Customs skill.

Devotion (POW+CHA)

Devotion is a magical skill which reflects the commitment of priests, and their ilk to the service of a deity or pantheon of gods. It not only measures the depth of devotion to a deity, but also governs the magnitude of any theistic miracles called upon by the theist, and the recovery of these blessings at an appropriate holy place.

Additionally the skill can indicate the standing of a theist within a religious cult. For further details see page 178 of the Theism chapter.

In some settings Devotion is not limited to professional priests. It may be adopted by those who simply wish to show respect to the gods even if they do not actively practice Theism, or indeed if the gods exist at all!

Disguise (INT+CHA)

Effecting a convincing disguise, using appropriate materials (costumes, cosmetics, wigs or hairpieces), is covered by the Disguise skill. Creating the disguise requires time and attention to detail, as well as access to the right materials to make it convincing. If some, or all, of these elements are not present then the Disguise roll's difficulty grade is made one or more steps harder.

Disguise can be augmented with Acting to enhance the overall effect of a deception (vice versa when performing), and so the two skills are complementary.

A critical Disguise roll results in a completely convincing masquerade so potent that even their own mother or a lifelong enemy probably wouldn't recognise them.

Failing a disguise roll results in such a meagre attempt it permits passive onlookers the chance to see through it.

A fumbled Disguise roll either produces a disguise so crass that it instantly penetrated; or one which fails at a spectacularly inopportune moment. No amount of great acting can salvage the illusion when a false nose peels away or a poorly fitted costume rips off.

Engineering (INT x2)

The design and building of large-scale structures, from houses to bridges, gates to siege engines, is in the remit of the Engineering skill. Rolls are necessary when planning large scale projects to ensure correct construction, but are also made when an engineer wants to assess a structure's integrity for whatever reason (state of repair or weak spots, for example).

A critical success highlights any unnoticeable major flaws or problems with the item under study. It also makes subsequent rolls dependent on the structure one grade easier. Alternately it may allow a tougher, more resilient construction to be built (a tenth more Hit Points or Armour Points).

Failing an Engineering roll results in a construction which is sub-standard (a tenth fewer Hit Points or Armour Points) or an inability to determine any structural information.

A fumble actively introduces a major flaw into a project or disastrously assesses the condition of an item, providing incorrect and misleading information. Subsequent rolls dependent on the Engineering check are made one grade harder.

Exhort (INT+CHA)

Exhort is the magical skill used to call upon and channel the power of the gods. It includes knowledge of the history, myths, rituals, practices, prayers, and powers of the god or pantheon, and is essential to Theistic magic, being used to manifest divine miracles. For further details see page 178-179 of the Theism chapter.

Folk Magic (POW+CHA)

Minor, petty magics are cast using this skill. It represents the character's knowledge of charms, cantrips or blessings, and how competent the user is when casting them. For further details see page 122 of the Folk Magic chapter.

Gambling (INT+POW)

The Gambling skill measures a character's competence in games of chance, and especially where money is staked on the outcome. It is used to assess the odds of success or failure or spot when someone is cheating. The skill can be used in an opposed or unopposed manner, depending on the situation. Spending the night in a faceless gambling den might only require a straight test, whereas a high stakes dice game involving notable personages may instead require several rounds of opposed rolls.

A critical Gambling success usually permits the character to win a game outright or clean out one of the participants.

Failure simply results in the character losing that hand or stake.

On a fumble, the character has completely misread the odds or has tragic bad luck. He loses everything gambled and is thrown out of the game.

Cheating allows a character to roll twice and take the best result. However each time this is attempted the cheater must roll an opposed test of their Sleight skill against the Perception or Gambling skill of everyone else playing. Failing to beat all the observers means that the cheater has been detected, with suitable results.

Healing (INT+POW)

Healing is the in-depth knowledge of medical procedures, based on cultural practices. In a primitive or barbarian culture, for instance, healing will be based on the knowledge of herbs, and natural cures. In a civilised culture, drugs and more advanced treatments will be more common. In all cultures Healing includes the ability to set bones, suture wounds, and so forth. Obviously applying healing requires appropriate resources, and most practicing healers will have such things to hand (needles, gut or thread for sutures, herbs for poultices, and so forth). There are three main areas of Healing:

Treating Serious Wounds

A successful Healing roll restores 1d3 Hit Points to a Seriously Injured location. On a critical success this is raised to 1d3+1. If fumbled, damage is increased by 1 Hit Point.

Treating Diseases and Poisons

If Healing is performed prior to the onset time, it counteracts the disease or toxin entirely, providing it overcomes the Potency of the malady in an opposed roll. If performed on a character who has already succumbed to the disease or toxin, a successful Healing roll permits the victim a new chance to resist, making it one grade easier. A critical success increases it by two grades. A fumble however, makes the resistance roll one grade harder.

Surgery

Surgery is the only way, other than magical healing, that a character can recover from a Major Wound. A successful First Aid roll is needed to stabilise a Major Wound (see the First Aid skill on page 41), and then a Healing roll can be made to set a shattered bone, stitch together the flesh of a stump or excise foreign objects lodged in tissue, so that the location can begin the road to recovery.

As long as the Healing roll is a success, the injured location begins to heal as normal for a location suffering a Major Wound (see Healing on page 80). On a critical success the location regains 1 Hit Point immediately; whereas on a fumbled Healing roll the patient must succeed in a Endurance roll or die from the procedure. Surgery cannot re-attach a severed limb.

Invocation (INT x2)

Invocation is a magical skill essential to Sorcery. It is the sorcerer's ability to successfully cast spells learned from a particular grimoire or mentor. It is a combination of understanding the formulae of the spell, the correct mental state, accompanying gestures and incantations, and so on. Increasing competence in this skill also improves the final intensity of the spells cast with it.

Each Invocation skill must be tied to a specific source of sorcerous knowledge, whether that be a particular spellbook, school of wizardry or even a demonic patron. For further details see page 161 of the Sorcery chapter.

Language (INT+CHA)

This skill covers the speaking and comprehension of languages other than the character's own. Akin to Native Tongue (see page 42), the Language skill is not rolled against directly, but is treated as a static representation of overall fluency. Its value is used by the Games Master to limit the level of spoken interaction when the players converse with personalities in the game. Use the Linguistic Fluency table as a guideline.

Linguistic Fluency

Language %	*Conversational Fluency*
01-25%	Knows only a few simple words, cannot phrase sentences
26-50%	Can understand and communicate in fragmentary, simple sentences, such as "Where temple?" or "How much food?
51-75%	Fluent enough for general conversation
76% +	Able to express yourself with eloquence

Each Language skill is specific to a particular national or regional language which must be chosen at the time of learning. It can help to understand similar dialects which share a common linguistic basis or origin. Depending on the divergence, the skill roll should be treated at least one grade harder, possibly reducing the character's fluency.

Language is also used as a cap on verbal skills which require a good grasp of language. See Capping Skills on page 50.

Literacy (INT x2)

Speaking a language fluently does not mean one can read and write it. Literacy is a specific skill, and different cultures and societies display different levels and approaches towards it. In some, literacy is reserved for the nobility, bureaucratic or religious classes. In others it is unknown with oral traditions prevailing instead.

Naturally Literacy is specialised according to its associated language, including Native Tongue. Before once can be literate in a Language one must be able to speak it. Literacy cannot exceed the character's related Language skill. The skill works similarly to Language in terms of how much of a document can be comprehended.

Literacy does not necessarily imply writing, as there are an infinite number of ways to record information. Some cultures might carve symbols into trees or lengths of bone, whereas others record history in complex patterns of knots in a tapestry. Neither are all forms of literacy based on phonetic alphabets; hieroglyphs and ideograms also being commonplace.

Lockpicking (DEX x2)

Lockpicking is the ability to open a mechanical locking system without the aid of a key or other device made specifically for the lock. It includes the techniques of levering open bolted or barred doors and windows without causing damage. The difficulty of the lock usually depends on the ability of the locksmith who created it, requiring an opposed test of Lockpicking versus Mechanisms skill of the crafter.

Where no skill value is provided for the lock a Games Master may adjust the difficulty grade of the Lockpicking skill instead, according to the lock's complexity. A thief attempting to pick an expensive and expertly crafted mechanical doorlock of a kind he has never seen before, might have to make his Lockpick roll one or two grades harder, for example. And some locks – invisible, recessed bolts and deadlocks – might be impossible to pick.

On a critical success the Lockpicker not only opens the lock silently and efficiently, but subsequent attempt to pick the same kind of lock becomes, for a short while, one grade easier.

A failure simply means the lock could not be picked.

On a fumble the lock becomes jammed: lockpicks break in the mechanism, or the mechanism is damaged internally. Whatever the cause, the jammed lock will ultimately attract attention.

Lore (INT x2)

Lore covers a specific body of knowledge which must be chosen when the skill is first learned. Astrology, Astronomy, Geography, History, Monsters, Mythology, Politics, Strategy and Tactics: these are all typical examples of Lore skills. Skill in a Lore means the character understands its fundamentals, how it can be applied to immediate challenges and problems, and can use the Lore to recall useful information.

A critical Lore success grants a high degree of insight into what is being studied. It also means that a subsequent skill roll relevant to that Lore becomes one grade easier. For example, a commanding officer who critically succeeds in a Lore (Politics) roll knows that not only is the approaching troupe part of a diplomatic envoy, but they are mercenaries unhappy with their situation. If he later tries to influence the mercenaries to change sides his roll would become one step easier.

Failing a Lore roll results in no useful information being gained.

A fumbled Lore roll indicates a complete misunderstanding of the subject. Facts are wrong, and subsequent skill rolls dependent on the Lore skill's accuracy become one grade more difficult.

Mechanisms (DEX+INT)

Mechanisms represents the knowledge and skill to assemble and disassemble mechanical devices, such as traps. The skill of Mechanisms generally involves the creation of delicate contraptions with small working parts, as opposed to Engineering, which deals with massive constructions. It is a distinct discipline from Lockpicking and cannot be interchanged with that skill.

The time taken to deal with a mechanism depends entirely on its scale and complexity. Repairing a large cartwheel might take half an hour; whilst building a poison-needle trapped lock might take an entire week. When deciding on how long a Mechanism skill attempt should take, Games Masters need to consider the size, intricacy, tools needed, and any specific conditions. As a rule of thumb, Mechanisms rolls take a minimum of 1d3x10 minutes but this is for simplest and most straightforward of mechanical challenges. The timeframe may very well extend to months.

On a critical success the character achieves success in half the usual time, and with flawless results. Any future rolls attempting to disable or circumvent the Mechanisms are one grade harder.

A failure results in a device which is temperamental and prone to breaking down; attempts to bypass or render it inoperative are one grade easier.

On a fumble the mechanism is utterly broken, and has to be thrown away and started again from scratch.

Meditation (INT+CON)

Meditation is the ability to reach a state of deep relaxation and concentration, through emptying the consciousness of all distractions: external and internal. Technically a magical skill, it is a fundamental part of Mysticism controlling the depth of focus needed when augmenting skills to superhuman levels. As competence in Meditation improves, the more potent a mystic's abilities become.

Being a useful skill, Meditation need not be limited to just mystics. Since it helps to shut out distractions and relaxes the body, it allows the user to achieve rest even in the most uncomfortable of locations. A successful roll permits a character to recover Fatigue or Hit Points in situations normally forbidden by the rules.

Musicianship (DEX+CHA)

Musicianship covers the playing of musical instruments; from a simple reed pipe to a complex stringed instrument such as a harp. Each iteration of Musicianship is applied to a group of similar instruments. A musician who can play a reed pipe can also play a flute, panpipes or a recorder because the fundamentals are the same. He could not, however, play a harp or lute.

The chief groups of instruments are:

- Bow Strings (violin, cello, fiddle, and so on)
- Keyboards (piano, organ, clavinet, and so on)
- Percussion (drums, tom-toms, and so on)
- Plucked Strings (harp, lyre)
- Strummed Strings (lute, guitar, banjo etc)
- Wind (pipe, flute, trumpet, and so on)

A critical success indicates the musician creates music of stunning quality, elegance or beauty. Any subsequent skill rolls, such as Influence, become one grade easier.

Failing a Musicianship roll renders in a lacklustre performance. A fumbled Musicianship roll results in a musical disaster. Perhaps the instrument breaks or the piece of music performed is taken as a gross insult. The effects of such a terrible situation need to be determined by the Games Master but, at the very least, represent embarrassment that could influence reputation.

Mysticism (POW+CON)

Mysticism is a magical skill essential to Mystics. It measures their facility to perform superhuman acts through the channelling of inner resources, and either harnessing or suppressing certain passions or concepts. As competence in this skill improves, so does the mystic gradually approach perfection in those skills which are the focus of his training.

Each Mysticism skill must be tied to a specific foundation of mystical knowledge. This can be a religious sect, a book of esoteric teachings or perhaps a mountain-top residing hermit. The skill is more fully described in the Mysticism chapter on page 155.

Navigation (INT+POW)

Whether using prominent landmarks, the stars or the varying taste of seawater, the ability to accurately direct travel is covered by the Navigation skill. Each Navigation skill covers a specific region or environment, such as Open Seas or Underground for example. It should be made during unusual journeys or when in completely unfamiliar territory.

A critical success in Navigation allows the user to locate a shortcut, such as a fast current or hidden pass.

Failing the roll results in delays due to uncertainty or temporarily losing the path.

A fumbled Navigation ends up with the user becoming utterly lost, unable to even backtrack.

Oratory (POW+CHA)

Oratory is the art of delivering a speech to large group of people with the aim of conveying or swaying a point of view. It is a skill frequently used by politicians to drive home a policy, but is also used by commanders to inspire troops, and impose discipline on the battlefield. Wherever mass persuasion is needed, Oratory, rather than Influence, is used.

On a critical Oratory roll the orator sways the group completely to his argument, even winning over the most ardent of detractors. Subsequent rolls related to the Oratory are one difficulty grade easier.

A failed Oratory roll goes nowhere; people are as dispassionate or hostile as before.

On a fumble, the orator has alienated his audience, perhaps made himself look foolish, and may even have managed to compel the audience to believe the opposite of what he wanted to convey. Subsequent rolls dependent on the Oratory become one grade harder.

Seamanship (INT+CON)

This skill is used in exactly the same way as Boating (see page 39) but is instead applied to large waterborne vessels powered by sail or banks of oars. It also covers the maintenance and upkeep of a ship: assessing when repairs are needed, where it is safe to anchor, the dangers of violent weather, and so forth.

Seduction (INT+CHA)

Seduction is the romantic or sexual persuasion of another person, a skill very different to Influence. It uses explicit signals – verbal and non-verbal – to elicit a sexually positive response. It also takes a significant amount of time: successful Seduction may take hours, days or weeks to achieve depending on the morals of the target, who always has the opportunity to resist a Seduction attempt with Willpower.

A critical Seduction roll yields a potent result, entrancing the victim or causing them to fall passionately in love (or lust). Subsequent skill rolls taking advantage of this relationship become one grade easier.

A failed Seduction leads to the seducer being rebuffed to some degree.

A fumble ends up causing emotional hurt or insulting the target. This completely ruins any further chances of seduction for the time being; it also makes subsequent skill rolls one grade harder. A disastrous Seduction attempt can lead to intensely grave consequences.

Shaping (INT+POW)

Shaping is a magical skill that is the counterpart to Invocation. Successfully invoked spells can be manipulated or shaped by the sorcerer to meet specific requirements; extending their range, adding multiple targets, increasing duration, and so on. The Sorcery chapter on page 161-163 defines how Shaping works in detail.

Sleight (DEX+CHA)

Sleight covers attempts to palm or conceal small objects (legerdemain and prestidigitation), and includes attempts to pick pockets, cut purses or cause a visual distraction. Naturally it is an essential thieves' skill.

Characters can attempt to manipulate any item as long as it is no larger than their hand. Sleight can be attempted with living creatures provided that the user has somewhere or something to conceal them with, a hat or baggy sleeve for example, but the skill becomes one grade harder to perform. Some objects, due to their size and mass cannot be manipulated with Sleight at all but require Conceal instead. Observers can pit their Perception skill against Sleight attempts to become aware of the deception.

On a critical Sleight success the character has manipulated the object so successfully that any subsequent attempts to locate it are one grade harder.

Failure means that the object is not concealed, and will be automatically detected if any effort is made to locate it.

If fumbled, not only is the item unconcealed, but it is dropped or otherwise fully exposed at a most inopportune moment.

Streetwise (POW+CHA)

Streetwise represents knowledge of places and social contacts within a settlement. It covers everything from identifying potentially dangerous neighbourhoods, to finding local services – legal or illegal. How long a Streetwise attempt takes depends on what is sought. Finding a good inn will take less time than locating a fence for stolen goods or a fake trading permit.

A critical Streetwise success locates the precise person or place necessary to gain what he is seeking for, without unnecessary bribes or intermediary steps, which can result in the formation of a new contact.

Failing a Streetwise attempt merely results in wasting the time spent looking.

A fumbled Streetwise means the character not only fails to find what is being sought, but also comes under unwanted, potentially dangerous attention: from local thugs or muggers to the resident militia, depending on circumstances.

Survival (CON+POW)

This skill covers surviving in a rural or wilderness environment where the benefits of civilisation are absent: foraging, building a fire, finding shelter or a safe place to sleep. When properly equipped rolls are usually unnecessary since the character may be carrying a tent, food supplies, and so on. Only when separated from their equipment or when environmental conditions turn bad does it become essential to utilise this skill. A roll is usually made once per day in such conditions.

A critical success indicates that the character locates a good source of food or shelter, and does not need to make a further Survival roll for a number of days equal to the critical range of his skill (one-tenth).

Failure results in the character gaining an automatic level of fatigue that does not lift until conditions change or the next Survival roll is made. A fumbled Survival roll ends up with a disastrous accident of some kind; encountering a fierce creature, suffering exposure or consuming poisonous food for example.

Teach (INT+CHA)

Teach allows the user to pass on their knowledge and techniques in an easy to understand and constructive manner. Without this skill even the most capable of masters will suffer problems instructing others. Similarly to certain other skills, Teach is not rolled against directly, but acts as a limit to what actually can be taught to more advanced students. For further details see Training on page 73.

General vs. Specific Teaching

Depending on the amount of complexity Games Masters wish to introduce, teachers may specialise in a particular area or range of subjects.

For example, Kara's philosophy teacher specialises in Teach (Meerish Philosophy). This covers the teachings of the great Meerish philosophers, historians, and cult priests.

If treated in this way Teach can function almost as a Combat Style, encompassing several different skills or areas of study. A thieves' cult might employ teachers who instruct in the related arts of Disguise, Stealth, and Sleight, under the Teach (The Hidden Path) skill.

Cults frequently employ teachers who train their members in specific cult skills (see page 199 of the Cults and Brotherhoods chapter).

Track (INT+CON)

The Track skill is used for tracking any form of game or quarry. It uses both obvious and ambiguous signs of passing to remain on the quarry's trail, including footprints, bruised leaves, scattered pollen, displaced rocks, and so on; small, tell-tale signs that are invisible to the non-skilled. Track rolls need to be made periodically, especially if conditions change abruptly (a rain shower, for example, will disturb certain signs). How often depends on how cunning the quarry has been. Conceal rolls can be used to oppose a Track roll.

With a critical success the tracker remains on the trail of someone or something not attempting to hide their spoor, irrespective of conditions, and does not need to make any subsequent Track rolls to locate the quarry.

Failing causes the tracker to lose the trail, forcing them to backtrack in order to pick it up again.

Fumbling a Track roll loses the trail utterly, forcing the user to abandon the pursuit or hunt. Alternately the tracker may wander blithely into a prepared trap laid by the stalked victim.

Trance (POW+CON)

Trance is a magical skill used by practitioners of Animism to attain the correct psychological state that permits the perception of, and transition into, the Spirit World. Further detail on how Trance works is given in the Animism chapter beginning on page 130.

Different Situations

Although the basic rules for using skills in Mythras are very straightforward, there are a multitude of different circumstances that arise during play that require skills to be handled in a slightly different way. The following sections look at these circumstances and situations, and show how to handle them.

Reattempting Skills

In some situations a character will fail a skill attempt but be left in a situation where he could potentially try again. Example cases might be picking a lock or attempting to climb a sheer wall. Instead of simply denying any further attempts, kindly Games Masters may permit a follow-up, last-ditch attempt. However, the character will suffer some trepidation or lack of confidence which increases the difficulty of the skill roll by one grade.

If this second effort also ends in failure, the character is assumed to have given it his 'best shot', and cannot make any further attempts for the foreseeable future.

Augmenting Skills

It is possible for one skill to aid another. This is called *Augmenting*. Anathaym, for example, may find herself being chased by nomad raiders through countryside she knows well, and they do not. She could, in this case, augment her Drive with her Locale skill, knowledge of the local terrain giving her an advantage.

The Games Master will decide if augmentation is appropriate and possible. Any skill being used to augment another must be appropriate to the circumstances. In Anathaym's example Locale is appropriate because she knows the area. If she was in unfamiliar territory it would not be permissible.

- Characters can only augment the primary skill with a single other skill.
- An augmenting skill increases the value of the primary skill by twice its Critical range (ie, 20% of the skill). So, in Anathaym's case, using Locale 33% she would increase her Ride by 7%, giving her a Ride of 45%. However, the chances for Critical and Fumble are the same as if the primary skill was unaugmented; so Anathaym would still only score a Critical success on a roll of 4% or less.
- Characters can augment other character's skills to assist them. All the above rules apply, so a character being aided cannot augment himself in addition. Likewise a character can only contribute one of his skills to assist another. So, for example, Anathaym, trying to scale a high wall, could have her Athletics skill augmented by a companion's Brawn (representing a hitch-up).

Capping Skills

To 'cap' a skill with another means that for a particular roll, the primary skill is restricted to the value of a secondary skill, providing the latter is lower. This is normally done in situations where a character's full knowledge or ability is limited by unusual circumstances.

Capping is a useful alternative to applying a difficulty modifier, especially in circumstances where the character is limited by their own capability.

Anathaym's Saga

Anathaym has a Lore (Strategy, and Tactics) skill of 48% which she normally rolls without penalty when organising battle plans with her native Meerish compatriots. Travelling across the plains of Korath however she is forced to use the local language with her hired nomadic bodyguards, in which she is far less fluent, knowing only a few basic words – Language (Korathian) 23%. Spotting an approaching enemy patrol of Zingriffi raiders, Anathaym attempts to organise her nomads to lay an ambush. In this circumstance the Games Master rules that her halting command of the local language will prevent Anathaym from being able to clearly explain her plan; capping her Lore (Strategy, and Tactics) skill to the value of her Language (Korathian).

Contested Rolls

Contested Rolls are used whenever a skill is actively resisted by an opponent. This can be anything from a character influencing a reticent guard to a sorcerer casting a spell against a monster. There are two types of contest: *Opposed Rolls* and *Differential Rolls*.

Opposed Rolls

Mythras frequently pits one skill against another – Stealth versus Perception when a thief attempts to cut a nobleman's purse, say; or Deceit versus Insight when the same thief tries to deny the attempt when he is caught – are good examples of times where skills are matched against each other. These are known as Opposed Rolls, and are used where a challenge will result in either win or lose, pass or fail.

An Opposed Roll is determined thus: both participants roll their respective skills. The winner is the one who gains the better level of success. If the participants score the same level of success (a standard success each, or a critical each), then the winner is the one who has the highest dice roll still within the success range of the skill.

For example, Lodz, a thief of Meeros, attempts to cut the purse of Senator Odas. This calls for a Sleight roll by Lodz which, the Games Master says, will be opposed by Odas' Perception. The dice are rolled: Lodz scores 45 on his Sleight skill of 70%, and Odas scores 63 on his Perception of 66%. Both have succeeded in their rolls but, because Odas has rolled higher than Lodz, and is still within his skill range, he is judged the winner. Lodz has successfully cut the purse, but Odas has quite clearly seen him do it.

In a bid to save his skin, Lodz attempts to lie his way out of trouble. 'The cord snapped, sir!' Lodz protests. 'I merely caught your purse as it dropped, and was about to return it to you.' This calls for a Deceit roll for Lodz, opposed by Odas' Insight roll. Lodz has Deceit 78%, and rolls 07 – a critical success. Odas has Insight 64%, and rolls 62. Here, Lodz quite clearly has the better level of success: a critical against Odas' standard success. Lodz manages to sweet-talk his way out of a sticky situation, and he walks away thankful, but ruing his bad luck at so nearly being caught.

If both participants fail in an Opposed Roll then either:

- Describe the situation, leaving both sides hanging in dramatic tension, then re-roll the contest to establish a winner
- The Games Master should produce some explanation or circumstances that suit the nature of the failure

In the Lodz and Odas example, both of them failing in the initial rolls would mean that Lodz failed to cut the purse, and Odas failed

Opposed Roll Examples

Activity	Opposing Skill Examples
Bargaining/Haggling	Commerce vs Commerce, Influence vs Commerce
Chasing/Racing	Athletics vs Athletics, Athletics vs Endurance, Ride vs Ride
Deceiving or Lying	Deceit vs Insight, Sleight vs Perception
Displaying Loyalty	Passion vs Passion, Passion vs Insight, Passion vs Influence
Getting out of the Way	Evade vs Athletics, Evade vs Mechanisms, Evade vs Ride
Hiding or Sneaking	Stealth vs Perception; Stealth vs Track
Pulling Rank	Influence vs Willpower, Deceit vs Willpower
Staying the Course	Endurance vs Endurance, Endurance vs Brawn
Swaying a Crowd	Oratory vs Willpower
Test of Strength	Brawn vs Brawn, Brawn vs Endurance
Test of Wills	Willpower vs Willpower, Seduction vs Willpower

to notice him trying: it is easy to re-roll the contest. In the case of Lodz trying to lie his way out of trouble, if both fail in their rolls then the Games Master informs the players that both of them are suddenly distracted by the sounds of a skirmish across the marketplace as a brawl breaks-out between rival merchants. Lodz can make a swift exit, and Odas has his attention absorbed by the merchants' squabble.

Opposed rolls are frequently used in certain battle situations to overcome the effects of wounds or oppose a combat special effect. They are also used to resist poisons and disease, or shrug off the effects of baleful magic.

Differential Rolls

Differential rolls are similar to Opposed rolls except that instead of a simple win or lose result, the difference in levels of success are calculated. Primarily used for the resolution of combat (see page 94), Differential Rolls can also be used in other situations where the Games Master wishes to increase the detailed results of a contest.

A Differential Roll is determined in the following manner: Both participants roll against their respective skills and suffer the results of their roll as if tested in isolation. There is no outright 'winner' per se, but whoever gained the higher level of success gains an advantage equal to the difference in the success levels between them (assuming one participant gains at least a standard success or better). If both participants score the same level of success (a standard success each, or a critical each), then there is no additional effect.

Differential Roll Results

Result of Rolls	Antagonist Critical	Antagonist Success	Antagonist Failure	Antagonist Fumble
Protagonist Critical	*No Benefit*	*Protagonist Wins 1 level of Success*	*Protagonist Wins 2 levels of Success*	*Protagonist Wins 3 levels of Success*
Protagonist Success	*Antagonist Wins 1 level of Success*	*No Benefit*	*Protagonist Wins 1 level of Success*	*Protagonist Wins 2 levels of Success*
Protagonist Failure	*Antagonist Wins 2 levels of Success*	*Antagonist Wins 1 level of Success*	*No Benefit*	*No Benefit*
Protagonist Fumble	*Antagonist Wins 3 levels of Success*	*Antagonist Wins 2 levels of Success*	*No Benefit*	*No Benefit*

Simplifying Subtraction with Skills over 100%

Games Masters may find ad hoc subtraction for skills over 100% slows down the flow of their game. As an alternative suggestion, penalties should be rounded up to the nearest 10%. Thus in a contest involving a skill of say 113%, instead of subtracting 13% from everybody in the contest, the Games Master can simply round the penalty up to 20% which is a faster calculation.

Opposed Skills Over 100%

If the highest skilled participant in an Opposed or Differential Roll has a skill in excess of 100%, that participant subtracts the difference between 100, and his skill value from the skill of everyone in the contest, including himself. This reduces the skill value of the opponents but leaves him retaining the advantage.

The identification of who has the highest skill must be calculated after any other modifiers for circumstances have been applied.

Group Rolls

Group Rolls are a time-saving way for Games Masters to determine the success of a group of individuals involved in the same task. There are two separate forms of Group Roll: *Team Rolls* and *Sorting Rolls*.

Team Roll

In a team test, success is co-operative; everyone reaps the benefit from a single success. If the group of bandits hunting Anathaym are all trying to search for her hiding place in the forest, then any successful Perception roll will reveal her to all the bandits. The Games Master rolls once for the highest skill in the team (the highest Perception skill among the bandits, for example), and if the roll is a success, everybody in the team succeeds. If the roll is a failure, everybody fails.

A 'reverse' team test can be used in a situation where one failure can spell disaster. For example, if a group of hunters are attempting to stalk a deer, any failed Stealth test will startle the quarry. In this case, the hunter with the lowest Stealth skill rolls a Stealth test. If he succeeds, everyone succeeds. If the roll is a failure, everybody fails.

Sorting Roll

In a sorting test, success is individual. For example, the same group of bandits are being chased by Anathaym, which calls for opposed Ride tests. Some of the bandits have a Ride skill of 40%, some of 50%, and some of 60%. The Games Master makes a group roll for the bandits, which results in a 49. Those with skills of 50% or more succeed, while the slower bandits - those on a skill of 49 or lower - begin to fall behind (unless the remainder of the bandits slow their progress to allow their fellows to keep up).

Games Masters need to judge when to use multiple rolls to a group roll. Multiple rolls – one roll for each individual in a group - is more realistic, but is time consuming. If it is important to keep a game flowing and individual skill successes are not so important, a Group Roll is more effective.

Proportional Skill Success

Occasionally it may be necessary to determine the success of a large group of people performing the same task, in a situation in which there is no margin for error. In this case, simply take the skill being used and apply that as the percentage of success for the whole group.

For example: a group of 100 troops are attempting to wade across a fast-flowing river a short distance from a high and treacherous waterfall. This calls for an Athletics skill test. A failed skill test for an individual would result in their being swept away by the current. Rather than rolling 100 skill tests, or using a Group Roll to determine whether all 100 soldiers make it across, the Games Master can simply rule that the Athletics skill for the group represents what proportion of that group successfully completes the task. If the troops have an Athletics skill of 75, then 75 of them will make it to the other side of the river, and the remaining 25 will be swept away.

Skills Summaries

All Combat Styles are STR+DEX

Standard Skills

Skill	Basic Percentage	Skill	Basic Percentage
Athletics	STR+DEX	Influence	CHA x2
Boating	STR+CON	Insight	INT+POW
Brawn	STR+SIZ	Locale	INT x2
Conceal	DEX+POW	Native Tongue	INT+CHA
Customs	INTx2	Perception	INT+POW
Dance	DEX+CHA	Ride	DEX+POW
Deceit	INT+CHA	Sing	CHA+POW
Drive	DEX+POW	Stealth	DEX+INT
Endurance	CON x2	Swim	STR+CON
Evade	DEX x2	Unarmed	STR+DEX
First Aid	INT+DEX	Willpower	POW x2

Skills in italics are used in Magic.

Animism: Binding, and Trance

Mysticism: Meditation and Mysticism

Theism: Devotion and Exhort

Sorcery: Invocation and Shaping

Professional Skills

Skill	Basic Percentage	Skill	Basic Percentage
Acting	CHA x2	Literacy	INT x2
Acrobatics	STR+DEX	Lockpicking	DEX x2
Art	POW+CHA	Lore	INT x2
Binding	*POW+CHA*	Mechanisms	DEX+INT
Bureaucracy	INT x2	*Meditation*	*INT+CON*
Commerce	INT+CHA	Musicianship	DEX+CHA
Courtesy	INT+CHA	*Mysticism*	*POW+CON*
Craft	DEX+INT	Navigation	INT+POW
Culture	INT x2	Oratory	POW+CHA
Devotion	*POW+CHA*	Seamanship	INT+CON
Disguise	INT+CHA	Seduction	INT+CHA
Engineering	INT x2	*Shaping*	*INT+POW*
Exhort	*INT+CHA*	Sleight	DEX+CHA
Folk Magic	*POW+CHA*	Streetwise	POW+CHA
Gambling	INT+POW	Survival	CON+POW
Healing	INT+POW	Teach	INT+CHA
Invocation	*INT x2*	Track	INT+CON
Language	INT+CHA	*Trance*	*POW+CON*

Passions

Object of Passion	Starting Percentage
A person, in a romantic or familial context	30% plus Loved one's POW+CHA
A person in a platonic context (a friendship or loyalty, for example)	30% plus Character's POW, and subject's CHA
A person in an averse context	30% plus Character's POW, and subject's CHA
An organisation or group of people	30% plus Character's POW+INT
A race or species	30% plus Character's POW x 2
A place	30% plus Character's POW+INT
An object or substance	30% plus Character's POW x 2
A concept or ideal	30% plus Character's POW+INT

Economics & Equipment

This chapter is concerned with money: how much characters have, and what it buys. MYTHRAS uses the Silver Piece (SP) as the standard unit of currency in the game, with the cost of most equipment, goods and services being measured in SP. One Silver Piece is the standard price for one day's food, drink, and accommodation for one person, of stark quality; that is to say, breakfast and an evening meal, with some form of cheap beverage, and a place to sleep for the night.

It therefore costs a character around 7 SP a week personally to live at subsistence level. Depending on where the characters are located, coinage may not even be used (or may be viewed with suspicion). Some cultures value barter and payment in kind more favourably than the chink of silver.

Other coins are available as well. The standard currency for MYTHRAS consists of the Copper Piece, Silver Piece and Gold Piece. The exchange rate is:

- 10 Coppers = 1 Silver
- 100 Silvers = 1 Gold

Thus a single Gold Piece would provide a MYTHRAS character with reasonable food for 100 days. Three or four Gold Pieces would see a character roughly all the way through the year, if he is frugal.

Some cultures, typically farming, nomad and barbarian communities, measure wealth in terms of livestock. A single large herd animal, such as a cow, is worth around 100 SP. A pig or sheep is worth around 25 SP, and a flock of hens around 15 SP.

Anathaym's Saga

As MYTHRAS is not setting-specific the names of coins are very generic, but Games Masters should create something evocative for their coinage.

Silvers could, for example, be shillings, royals, pounds, and so on. Coppers could be pennies, bits or farthings. Gold could be wheels, Imperials or something equally grandiloquent.

In Meeros the copper piece is known as an Obol, the silver as a Drachm, and a gold a Zarig.

Income, Living Standards and Class

A character's income is a reflection of how much he makes in a given period of time. Whilst income equates to wealth, it is most common for average workers to generate income not in terms of coin, but in terms of food and shelter, or access to land which, if tended, annually generates an amount per year equivalent to their yearly income in terms of coinage. Other common forms of recompense include training – magical and mundane – favours, and trade in kind.

Civilised cultures are most likely to use coinage for income and expenditure – although only those social classes with any form of prosperity will use coins on a frequent basis. Lowly classes will rely on barter, favours, and payments-in-kind for most transactions, with coins being a rare and treasured luxury.

An individual's standard of living is determined by their total expenditure each year on essentials: food, drink, lodging, clothes, gifts, and so on. It is natural for most people to spend nearly all their income achieving, or maintaining, the highest possible standard of living that they can. Note that this income may be required to support any additional dependents they may have, such as children, household servants or perhaps even a troop of personal guards. Those who spend more are likely to be at the top of their social class; those who are frugal and pinch pennies can exist on about 25% less than the amounts listed in the Social Class table, and will save some of their income, but may show a lower standard of living for their class.

Anyone seeking to be socially mobile must increase their living expenditures accordingly. Note, though, that social rank often does not rely on comparatively equal incomes. A barbarian chieftain may very well be accorded more respect, and wield more power, than a civilised rich noble, yet have nowhere near the same income in terms of cash and value in property.

The Minimum Maintenance Costs table opposite compares the minimum required expenditures required over time to maintain the standard of living for that social class. It does not necessarily indicate the actual amount a member of that social class earns, which can be higher, but it can be used as a basis for deciding how much money a particular social class may have available in ready coin or other commodities.

Social Class	*SP per Day*	*SP per Week*	*SP per Year**	*Typical Home*
Exile	Lives a hand to mouth existence			None/Lives Rough
Slave	1	7	375	Shared Shack/Hut
Freeman	2	15	750	Hut/Cabin/ Rented Room
Gentry	10	75	3,750	House/Apartment
Aristocracy	50	350	20,000	Large Villa/ Mansion
Ruling	250	1,750	100,000	Palaces/Estates

**Depends on the campaign setting. Assumes a year length of roughly 360 days with totals rounded up for neatness*

Character Income Between Adventuring

Characters are unlikely to spend all their time adventuring and, between adventures, will be engaged in professional and cultural pursuits. Characters can therefore expect some form of income from 'normal' day to day business according to their social class.

For example a noble might earn a regular income from taxing the inhabitants of his lands, or receive a stipend from his father, requiring no direct involvement on his part; whereas a baker might be employed slavishly baking loaves every day.

A character can expect to earn an applicable SP amount for his profession and social class. This assumes all is well in the world and no disasters, natural or otherwise, have affected the ability to generate income. However, if a more accurate reflection of downtime income is needed, roll on the Seasonal Income table adjusting the 1d100 roll as follows:

Seasonal Income Table

1d100	*Profitability*
01-10	Disastrous: Reduce Income by 50%
11-20	Poor: Reduce Income by 25%
21-60	Normal: No adjustment to Income
61-80	Prosperous: Increase Income by 25%
81-00	Very Prosperous: Increase Income by 50%

The table represents the downtime profitability during the length of time the character was working or supervising his holdings, anything from several days to a year. During this period any number of things may have occurred from the failure of a harvest or theft of his property, through to an unexpected demand for particular produce or the expansion of a business.

For example, a self-employed Baker (a freeman) might expect to earn 30 SP in a week under normal circumstances. The 1d100 result is 06. One winter is especially bad, and the price of grain is driven up due to shortages, forcing the baker to absorb the majority of the loss in order to keep his customers. The baker only earns 50% of his usual Seasonal amount, for a total of 15 SP, which fortunately is just enough to keep supporting his family, and business. If his basic income had been less then he might have had to sell his bakery or resort to illicit means in order to prevent himself dropping a social class, perhaps being forced into servitude as a slave to pay off his debts.

Characters can expect to spend the income indicated in the Minimum Maintenance Costs table on general living expenses. Of course, they can squander any windfall or spend less if prepared potentially to drop their living standards, albeit at the risk of their reputation suffering in some form.

Bartering and Haggling

In most societies shopping for services or goods is rarely straightforward. Coinage tends to be confined to civilised cultures, but in primitive, barbarian and nomad cultures, barter is far more common. Even where currency is actually used, traders rarely sell anything for a 'standard' price, as the value of most objects is subjective, and most purchases are haggled over.

As was once wisely said, an item is only as valuable as the amount somebody will pay for it.

Bartering

Bartering successfully depends on tendering something someone else needs in exchange for what is being offered. A civilised character in a barbarian stead might offer coins in exchange for food, but coinage does not necessarily offer any immediate advantage to the barbarian. To barter successfully then, the character must have something the other party finds valuable in their normal environment.

Trading in kind usually works well: offering to chop wood for a morning in exchange for a bowl of stew and a bed for the night, for example. More complex or specialised goods and services are less likely to succeed – unless the character can convince the other party of the need and utility.

Anathaym's Saga

Anathaym decides she wishes to purchase a new sword. Venturing to the bronzesmith's quarter in Meeros, she spots an intriguing blade suited to her tastes, and begins to bargain with the seller. The Games Master decides to use the Haggling rules which require resolution based on a differential roll. Anathaym has an Influence skill of 28% which the merchant opposes with his Commerce skill of 63%.

The dice are rolled. Whilst Anathaym manages to succeed in her Influence roll, the merchant Criticals his, resulting in the seller winning by one level of success. According to the Haggling Outcome Table this means that although Anathaym negotiates well, the merchant's impressive sales pitch convinces her to pay a quarter over the normal price for such a weapon. Anathaym considers herself fortunate however, if she had failed the roll the merchant would have won by two levels of success, which would have been even more expensive!

Bartering works in the following way:

- The character makes an offer of something. If this is a common commodity or an essential service appropriate to the other party that is obviously going to be of benefit, then the barter succeeds.
- If the character is intending to offer something of less obvious value/utility or something esoteric, then he makes a Customs or relevant Culture roll (see Barter Modifier Table below). If successful, he has spotted a way of pointing out benefits not realised by the other party. This changes the difficulty grade of either Influence or Commerce, whichever is being used to effect the transaction.
- Next the character makes an Opposed Influence or Commerce roll. The other party resists with either Willpower or Commerce - whichever is higher.
- If the character wins the Opposed roll, what he offers is accepted. If he fails, it is not. If the Adventurer fumbles the opposed roll, then there is a good chance he has insulted the other party, meaning that offence has been taken, even if not intentionally offered.

Barter Modifier Table

Customs/Culture	Influence Bonus	Commerce Bonus
Critical	Easy	Very Easy
Success	Standard	Easy
Failure	Hard	Standard
Fumble	Formidable	Hard

Haggling

Reducing a price to a reasonable amount is known as Haggling. In some cultures haggling is a major source of social interaction, a prime source of daily entertainment.

A skilled negotiator can achieve substantial discounts through careful haggling, although it is rare for any seller to allow themselves to make a loss on any transaction. To do so on a regular basis would soon place them out of business. Prices listed in the Equipment section assume a 'standard' profit margin for the seller, enough to reasonably support themselves.

The process works in a slightly different way from Bartering, in that participants use Insight rather than Customs to gain an advantage in the negotiation. This is followed by a Differential Roll of Influence or Commerce against Willpower or Commerce. The outcome of the roll is determined by the difference in success levels between buyer and seller:

Haggling Outcome Table

Difference in Levels of Success	Purchaser gains Advantage	Seller gains Advantage
3	25% of the Standard Price	200% of the Standard Price
2	50% of the Standard Price	150% of the Standard Price
1	75% of the Standard Price	125% of the Standard Price
Equal	Standard Price	Standard Price

Equipment

The remainder of this chapter is given over to equipment: armour, weapons, clothing, tools and other sundries characters rely on when adventuring.

Any piece of equipment is described in terms of one or more elements (some apply more than others). These are:

- Cost (in SP or CP)
- Armour Points: the natural resilience of the item to damage
- Hit Points: how much damage the item can sustain before being destroyed or rendered useless
- Encumbrance: how much the item contributes to Encumbrance (see page 77) limits; a combined measure of weight, mass, and restriction

Some items, typically clothing, and very small, light things, have only cost listed: it can be assumed that such things do not contribute towards Encumbrance limits and can be damaged relatively easily. Others, such as weapons, armour, and tools, display all four elements.

Equipment Price

All items listed in this chapter represent standard quality examples. Items of better or worse quality are available at an either an inflated or reduced cost. The section on Equipment Quality, starting on page 65, provides guidance on costs, enhancements/drawbacks or higher and lower quality goods.

The prices quoted assume availability is good. When there is a short supply of something, prices will rise and, depending on the commodity, may be anywhere between 10% and 1000% higher than quoted (1d100x10%). The environment, too, will affect availability and therefore cost. Items, and commodities are generally easier and cheaper to obtain in larger settlements with established markets and traders. In remote or rural areas all but the most basic of locally produced goods and foodstuffs will be more difficult to obtain; and will command a higher price, if available at all.

Culture/Milieu

Depending on the setting for your Mythras game, not all items will be available. One would not expect clockwork mechanisms or wheeled vehicles to be available in a Mythras setting modelled on Ancient Mesoamerica, for example. Equipment is therefore provided with a Culture/Milieu classification to help Games Masters identify what is and isn't available in a particular setting. This is a rough guide only, but one that helps recreate an authentic atmosphere (if one is needed; your Mythras setting may be deliberately anachronistic).

The Culture/Milieu classifications are:

- Prehistoric (P): Items likely to be found in settings and cultures that have not progressed much beyond the Stone Age.
- Ancient (A): Items likely to be available in settings and cultures equating to the Bronze and Iron Ages.
- Medieval (M): Items likely to be available in settings and culture equating to the European Middle Ages.
- Renaissance (R): Items likely to be available to settings and cultures equating to the European Renaissance.
- Enlightenment (E): Items likely to be available in settings and cultures equating to the European Age of Enlightenment (17th and 18th Centuries).
- Industrial (I): Items found in settings and cultures that have embarked on an Industrial Revolution.

Armour

Worn for protection against physical harm, armour reduces the amount of damage a Hit Location sustains by its Armour Point value. Armour of any kind therefore offers a significant advantage in combat, and helps improve the chances of survival. The downside to armour is that it can be heavy and restrictive to movement; fighting for a sustained period in metal armour takes its toll in terms of fatigue, and also slows down the ability to react.

Armour is ranked according to the manner in which it is constructed and overall coverage, not the actual material it was made from. For example it is perfectly permissible to manufacture a scaled helm made from sewing boar tusks to a leather cap, or a suit of half-plate from cuir bouilli dinosaur leather or carved jade. Of course some materials are stronger than others; a bronze breastplate will be thinner and lighter than an equivalent made from rhino hide. Thus the material used to manufacture the armour affects its Encumbrance (ENC).

No matter what material the armour is made of, it cannot be layered with other types – such concepts are already incorporated as part of its construction. Armour is assumed to come with whatever lining or padding would normally be expected as part of the complete panoply.

Each type of armour is defined by the following qualities:

- AP: The number of armour points given to each location covered by this armour. If a character is wearing multiple pieces of armour on a location, only the highest armour point score is used although the ENC incurred is cumulative.
- ENC: The typical weight and bulk of the armour. Use the Material Types table to adjust ENC for more unusual materials.
- Cost: The cost, in Silver Pieces, per location covered. Price assumes the armour is made from common local material, more exotic substances increase this cost.
- Milieu: Typical milieus where this type of armour occurs.

The Armour Table lists each of the characteristics by armour type, and also summarises the encumbrance and cost for a full suit, covering all seven Hit Locations, for the armour in question assuming construction from standard materials. The Armour Penalty for a full suit of the same armour is given in parentheses.

In the Material Types table, no cost adjustments are given for the construction of armour from more unusual materials, only its effect on ENC. The availability and additional cost of such substances is wholly dependent on the campaign setting. For instance, chitin armour would be impossible in a game where giant insects did not exist. Likewise if chitin is only available to primitive or hostile cultures, it might be vastly more expensive for someone in a civilised culture to purchase armour made from the material, assuming somebody in the city could actually craft or import it. On the other hand, it might be the default armour substance for tribesmen lacking metallurgy.

Linothorax

Bezainted

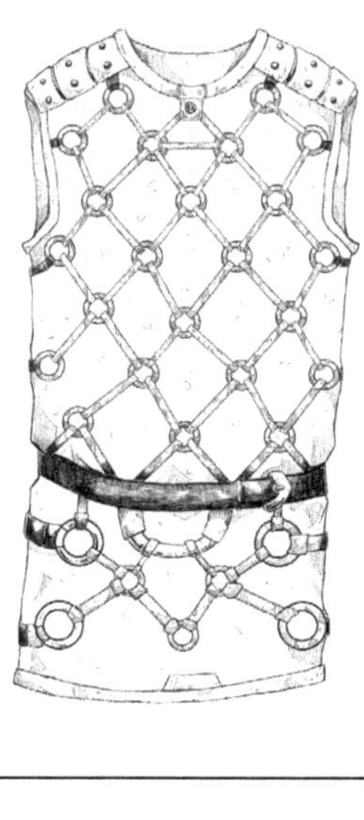

Mail

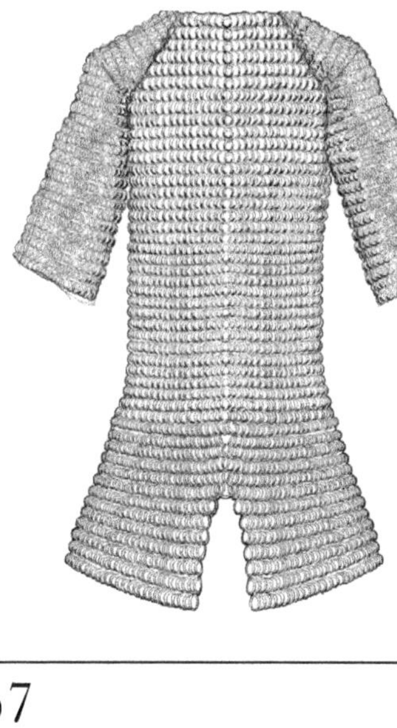

Hoplite Cuirass

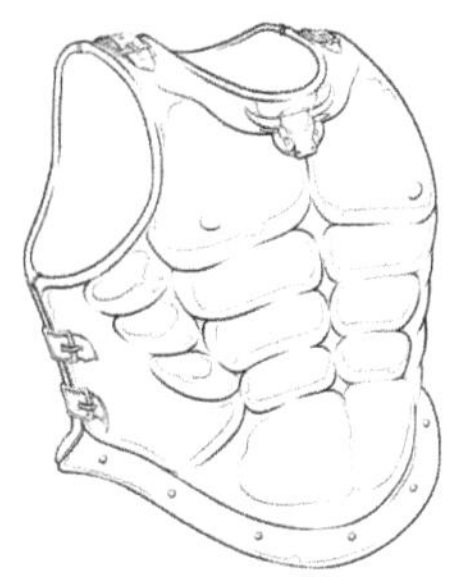

Armour Table

Base Material	Construction	Example	AP	ENC	Cost per Location	Suit ENC/Cost/ Armour Penalty	Milieu
Flexible	Natural/Cured	Furs, Hides	1	2	20	14/140/3	Any
	Padded/Quilted	Aketon, Gambeson	2	1	80	7/560/2	Any
	Laminated	Linothorax, Bezainted	3	2	180	14/1260/3	A-M
	Scaled	Brigandine, Lamellar	4	3	320	21/2240/5	A-R
Rigid	Half Plate	Hoplite Plate	5	4	500	28/3500/6	A-R
	Mail	Mail Hauberk, Laminar	6	5	900	35/6300/7	A-R
	Plated Mail	Splinted Chainmail	7	6	1400	42/9800/9	M-E
	Articulated Plate	Gothic Plate	8	7	2400	49/16800/10	M-E

Material Types Table

Material	ENC Modifier	Notes
Bone	x1.5	Bulky though light, desiccated bone can be used in Laminated, Scaled, and Plate construction
Bronze	x1	Bronze, like iron, is considered the default material for rigid armours
Chitin	x0.75	Lighter than other rigid materials it can be used for Laminated, Scaled, and Plate armours. Chitin can only be carved however, not moulded, so large armour segments must come from insects of suitable size
Iron	x1	Similarly to bronze, iron is considered the default material for rigid armours
Ivory	x1.25	Teeth, and tusks can be fashioned as part of Laminated, Scaled, and Plate
Leather	x2	Leather can be tanned or boiled to make it rigid, and thus used in the construction of any armour save mail, providing it is thick enough; crocodile skin for a suit of half plate for example. Furs, and Hide armour is by default assumed to be made from leather
Linen	x1	Linen or its woollen equivalent is considered the default material used in flexible armours up to Laminated
Shell	x2	Shell armour tends to be thick, and heavy to make up for its fragility, but can be used in Laminated, and Scaled armour; or if the source creature is of sufficient size, single pieces carved down to shape for Plate
Silk	x0.75	Tougher, and lighter than other fabrics, silk can be used to make flexible armours
Steel	x0.75	Superior in strength to iron or bronze, it is can be fashioned into thinner, lighter pieces for rigid material armours
Stone	x3	Not often used due to its weight, stones such as jade or obsidian can be carved, and ground into small pieces suitable for laminated or scaled armours, or large single segments worn as impromptu half-plate cuirasses

Armour and SIZ

Flexible armour will generally fit one point of SIZ more or less than the SIZ it was designed for. Rigid armour is crafted to fit a wearer of specific proportions, so it will only fit the same SIZ and frame for which it has been designed.

Armour Penalty to Initiative

Armour can be heavy and impede movement to some degree. The vast bulk of those who train in weapons also train in armour, and so become accustomed to armour's rigours, but this does not mean they are free from its more restrictive effects.

Mythras simulates this through the Initiative Penalty. The more armour one wears, and the heavier or more encumbering it is, the greater the Initiative Penalty. This penalty is applied to a character's Initiative. Its calculation is simple enough; add together the ENC for all the armour worn, and then divide by 5, rounding up. A full suit of plated mail, having an ENC of 6 per location, and covering seven locations has an Armour Penalty of (6x7)/5 = 8.2, rounded up to 9. Thus a character wearing a full set would reduce his Initiative by 9 points.

Anathaym's Saga

Meerish Warriors wear Hoplite Half Plate armour: helm, greaves, vambraces, breatsplate, and kilt. Anathaym therefore has her seven Hit Locations covered with armour having an ENC value of 4 per piece. The total ENC is therefore 28, and her Initiative Penalty due to the Hoplite Armour 28/5. Her Initiative Penalty is therefore -6.

Accommodation

Accommodation can be permanent or temporary, fixed or transportable. Prices for rented temporary accommodation, such as a room at an inn, are per night. Food is extra.

As always, accommodation costs will vary with seasons and demand. In busy periods – markets, festivals, and so on – prices will climb with demand, and larger towns and cities will charge more, in general, than smaller ones.

Accommodation Table

Accommodation Type	Cheap	Reasonable	Superior
Common room floor/ stables	0.5	-	-
Shared room/ dormitory	1	1.5	-
Private room	2	5	10
Rented hovel or shack (week)	10	-	-
Rented cabin or cottage (week) – sleeps small family	15	25	50
Rented house or apartment (week) – sleeps large family	30	50	75
Rented villa or mansion(week) – sleeps small entourage	100	250	1000
Hovel or shack to buy	100	-	-
Cabin or Cottage to buy (per bedroom)	750	1,250	2,500
House or Apartment to buy (per 2 bedrooms)	3,000	5,000	7,500
Villa or Mansion to buy (per 4 bedrooms)	20,000	50,000	200,000
Tent (per person capacity)	1	3	5

Clothing

All characters begin the game with a set of clothes appropriate to their culture and social class, but through wear and tear it will become necessary to replace existing garments as well as buy new ones appropriate to the local conditions or to celebrate unusual occasions. Those of high Social Class may even be required to continually purchase new sets of clothes simply to keep up with fashion.

The following prices are merely guidelines. There is technically no upper limit as to how much an item of garb can cost once you take into consideration exotic fabrics, embroidery, dyed colours, and decorations of precious furs or jewels.

Assuming more or less continual wear, cheap clothing can be worn for a year before it is rendered to rags. Reasonable clothing lasts for twice that before being reduced to cheap status. Superior clothing lasts for three years of wear, and then is downgraded to reasonable status.

Repairing clothing is a normal part of everyday life. In most cultures it is commonplace to provide garments, footwear or the fabric to make such things as part of an employee's annual wages.

Clothing Table

Garment	Cheap	Reasonable	Superior
Boots	25	50	100
Cap or Hat	3	6	18
Gloves, Socks or Underwear	5	10	20
General Coat or Cloak	20	45	90
Vest or Tabard	10	20	50
Tunic or Dress	15	30	75
Sandals	4	8	20
Shoes	20	45	90
Trousers, Skirt or Kilt	12	25	60
Shirt, Smock or Shift	8	16	35
Winter Coat or Cloak	30	75	150

Food

Food is not specified by any particular type in Mythras as it can vary dramatically according to culture: assume that food bought is a meal which, for a very basic, cheap meal typically includes some kind of broth, pastry or bread, and some brewed or dairy beverage. More expensive meals include larger portions of meat or fish, a wider range of seasonal fruits and vegetables, and a better grade of beverage. A superior meal consists of several varied courses, and luxuries of some sort such as rare meats, spices or imported fruits.

Trail rations consist of food preserved for long life, such as dried and cured meats, cheese, bread (usually unleavened flatbread for ease of transport), and cereals, either nuts or grains.

Characters need to eat and drink at least once per day or begin to suffer penalties, see Survival on page 49.

Food Table

Type	Cheap	Reasonable	Superior
Meal at a tavern or inn	1	3	8
Ale or Beer for an evening	1	1.5	3
Wine or Spirits for an evening	2	4	6
Trail rations (7 days)	7	9	12

Livestock

In many communities livestock represents cash wealth, and may even form the local currency. Livestock needs to be fed and tendered. The cost to maintain livestock in bought food (grazing will usually be free during appropriate seasons, but stockpiled food is essential in inclement seasons) for a week is usually a twentieth of the animal's price.

A creature's inherent worth is not simply dependent on how much food it produces when butchered. Some are valued for their ability to draw vehicles or ploughs, whilst others may be a source of valuable materials such as ivory or chitin. A few creatures might even be kept for their ability to fight or hunt.

The following table only offers general livestock. In more exotic settings one can expect to see a greater range of creatures available, anything from giant insects to flying beasts. Higher quality usually reflects better physical characteristics or training, but can be merely based upon the creature's aesthetic beauty.

Livestock Table

Item	*Poor Quality*	*Reasonable*	*Superior*
Bull	500	1000	3000
Calf	30	60	180
Camel	1100	2200	6000
Cow	100	200	600
Fowl	1	2	4
Goat	25	50	100
Horse (cavalry/ war-trained)	3000	6000	10,000
Horse (heavy draught)	1400	2800	8000
Horse (riding)	1200	2500	7000
Ox	150	300	800
Pig	25	50	150
Sheep	25	50	150

Tools

Tools include all the items any self-respecting adventurer can be expected to own: rope, sacks and bags, candles, lanterns, and so on. All items in this list are deemed to be of reasonable quality.

Tools	*ENC*	*Cost*
Abacus	1	8 SP
Astrolabe (Ancient onwards)	1	200 SP
Backpack/Satchel (holds up to 20 ENC)	1	5 SP
Bedroll	1	1 SP
Bit & Bridle	1	15 SP
Block & tackle	1	15 SP
Bottle, glass/earthenware	—	2 SP
Candle, 6 hour	1	1 SP
Chain, 2m	2	40 SP
Chest, Large (holds up to 100 ENC)	5	80 SP
Chest, Small (holds up to 50 ENC)	3	40 SP
Cooking Pot (for travel)	2	3 SP
Craft tools (basic tools to match a handicraft)	2	75 SP
Crop (riding)	—	15 SP
Crowbar	1	25 SP
Doorjamb	2	5 SP
Driver's whip	—	25 SP
Falconer's Kit	1	30 SP
Feed/mount rations (per day)	1	5 CP
Fine wine goblet (glass – double for silver)	—	8 SP
First aid kit (useful for 10 applications of First Aid skill)	—	25 SP
Fish hooks (20)	—	1 SP
Fishing kit	1	15 SP
Fishing Net	4	10 SP
Flint & tinder	—	1 SP
Game Snares, and Traps	1	1 SP
Goad	1	25 SP
Grappling hook	—	5 SP
Hammer/Saw/Mallet/Chisel	1	1 SP
Healer's kit (useful for 10 applications of Healing skill)	1	150 SP
Hourglass (Ancient onwards)	1	20 SP
Knife (tool, not weapon)	—	5 SP
Ladder, rope 3m	4	2 SP
Lantern, basic	1	10 SP
Lock picks	—	75 SP
Lockbox	1-4 depending on size	75 - 250 SP
Lodestone	—	5 SP
Milling Stone	2	8 SP
Mirror (hand glass)	1	12 SP
Mug/Beaker/Dish/Plate (wood – double price for metal)	—	5 CP each
Musical instrument	2	70 SP
Nails or tacks (50)	—	2 CP
Oil flask	1	1 SP
Papyrus or paper sheet (double the cost for vellum)	—	5 CP

Tools	*ENC*	*Cost*
Oil flask	1	1 SP
Papyrus or paper sheet (double the cost for vellum)	—	5 CP
Pickaxe	1	35 SP
Pole, 3m	1	1 SP
Quills , and ink for writing	1	30 SP
Quiver	—	2 SP
Razor, folding	—	3 SP
Rope (hemp), 10m	2	10 SP
Sack, large (holds up to 60 ENC)	1	5 CP
Sack, small (holds up to 30 ENC)	—	2 CP
Saddle, riding	3	60 SP
Saddle, war	4	90 SP
Saddlebag (holds up to 2x20 ENC)	2	20 SP
Saw, hand	1	1 SP
Scythe/Sickle	2	30 SP
Sextant (Renaissance cultures, and later)	1	25 SP
Ship's Compass (Medieval cultures, and later)	1	70 SP
Shoes, horse	1	10 SP
Spade/Hoe/Pitchfork	1	25 SP
Torch, 1 hour	—	4 CP
Torch, 6 hour	1	8 CP
Waterskin or Canteen (holds 2 litres of liquid)	1	5 CP
Wax, block	1	2 CP

Melee Weapons

The weapons listed here cover a wide gamut of societies and periods. Some weapons, such as swords, axes, and spears, are ubiquitous, whereas others have firm cultural and period groundings. In many societies it is deemed both necessary and desirable to carry some means of defending oneself. Customs always vary though, and the type of weapon carried depends very much on circumstances. Having a sword and dagger anchored to one's belt may not be thought unusual, for instance, whereas carrying a halberd or greatsword would be deemed unthinkable unless one is actively preparing for war.

All weapons are governed by a series of characteristics which are as follows:

- *Damage: The amount of damage the weapon delivers if an attack is successful.*
- *Size: Every weapon is rated for its mass, leverage and stability. The Size is used to determine the weapon's ability to inflict and parry damage (see page 94). The size categories are Small (S), Medium (M), Large (L), Huge (H), and Enormous (E).*
- *Reach: Every weapon is also rated for its Reach – its length and ability to hold a foe at bay due to its length. The longer the weapon the greater its ability to prevent an opponent getting close enough to inflict damage with their own weapon. The Reach categories are Touch (T), Short (S), Medium (M), Long (L), and Very Long (VL).*
- *Combat Effects: The design of the weapon allows it access to weapon specific Special Effects. Swords, for instance, slice and stab, and so are permitted access to the Impale and Bleed effects, whereas a mace is unable to produce those effects but could inflict Stun Location instead (see Special Effects page 95).*
- *ENC: The weapon's combined encumbrance and weight*
- *AP/HP: All weapons are rated for their Armour Points and Hit Points; their ability to withstand direct damage, and how much damage they can tolerate before breaking. Those weapons that rely on metal for their damage capability are assumed to be either bronze or iron.*
- *Traits: Some weapons, due to their specialised nature, have certain qualities, or traits, that differentiate them from weapons of a similar style. The common traits are:*
    - *Barbed – If impaled it will cause full rather than half damage on being yanked free.*
    - *Defensive – If used to parry an attacking weapon, that weapon is considered one size smaller than it actually is. So a Large sword is considered Medium, and a Medium sword is considered Small. Weapons already Small in size are unaffected.*
    - *Double Ended – If broken in combat, the length remaining in the hand can be reversed, and used as a shorter version of the original weapon.*
    - *Entrapping – As per the Defensive trait, but also allows use of the Pin Weapon special effect without needing to roll a Critical.*
    - *Flexible – If the opponent is using a shield to parry, the shield is considered one size smaller than it actually is. So a Huge shield is considered Large, a Large shield is considered Medium, and so on.*
    - *Mount – The weapon must be used from the back of a moving mount.*
    - *Offensive – The weapon cannot be used to parry.*
    - *Passive Block – The weapon can passively block multiple Hit Locations, which must be contiguous to one another.*
    - *Ranged Parry – The weapon can parry ranged weapons.*
    - *Set – The weapon can be set to receive a foot or mounted charge.*
    - *Stealth – The weapon must be used from ambush.*
    - *Thrown – The weapon can be used as a ranged weapon as well as a hand-to-hand weapon.*

- *Cost: The weapon's cost in Silver Pieces.*

The melee weapon tables begin on page 63.

Ranged Weapons

Ranged weapons deal damage at a distance, and do not require physical contact between combatants; such as a thrown rock, a bullet from sling or an arrow from a bow. Being able to harm an opponent from range has clear advantages: one can take advantage of cover and greater protection and, unless the opponent has a ranged weapon himself, the chances of you being injured are lessened.

Since dealing damage at range inevitably means imparting velocity to some form of projectile, ranged weapons are difficult to defend against. Without a shield or other form of solid cover that can disperse the energy of a projectile, ranged weapons cannot be parried; meaning that the best defence, if one is aware of an incoming missile, is evasion. However evasion often puts the defendant into a situation where returning an attack, even a ranged one, is difficult.

Ranged weapons have very similar characteristics to Melee Weapons, although there are some differences as noted below:

- *Damage: The amount of damage the weapon delivers if an attack is successful.*
- *Damage Modifier: Not all ranged weapons can take advantage of a character's damage modifier. A Yes or No entry dictates whether or not the user's damage modifier can be applied.*
- *Force: Each ranged weapon possesses a force rating equivalent to the 'Size' of close combat weapons. In the case of projectiles, this does not relate to the firing weapon itself, but rather to how much 'impact' its ammunition has. The value is used to determine whether the weapon can overcome any shield which may parry it. The size categories are Small (S), Medium (M), Large (L), Huge (H), and Enormous (E).*
- *Range: This is a measure of the weapon's effectiveness at three distances separated by slashes, representing the maximum Close, Effective and Long ranges of the weapon or its ammunition. Ranges are expressed in metres. Note that distance penalties to the user's skill are independent from the weapon, see page 108.*
  - *Close Range – The distance over which Choose Location may be used as a non-critical special effect, provided the target is stationary or unaware of the impending attack.*
  - *Effective Range – The distance over which there are no significant modifiers on the weapon's accuracy or power.*
  - *Long Range – The distance over which the weapon can still inflict harm, but the amount of damage is halved, and its Force is reduced by one step.*
- *Load: This shows how many turns are required to load or reload a weapon which fires ammunition.*
- *Combat Effects: As per Close Combat weapons.*
- *Impaling Size: The effective size of the weapon or its ammunition if it succeeds in an impaling attack.*
- *ENC: The weapon's combined encumbrance and weight.*
- *AP/HP: All weapons are rated for their Armour Points and Hit Points; their ability to withstand direct damage, and how much damage they can tolerate before breaking. Those weapons that rely on metal for their damage capability are assumed to be either bronze or iron.*
- *Cost: The weapon's cost in Silver Pieces.*

[1] ***Thrown javelins may use the Pin Weapon special effect against shields, without needing to roll a Critical.***

RANGED WEAPON AMMUNITION

Weapons such as bows and crossbows use ammunition to deliver damage. Arrows, quarrels, darts and bullets can be made by anyone with the appropriate craft skill, for example Craft (Fletcher) for arrows, as long as the appropriate raw materials, and a suitable work area or workshop are available for the task. If bought from a craftsman then the costs are as follows:

- Arrows (per sheaf of a dozen) 4 SP
- Quarrels (per sheaf of a dozen) 3 SP
- Lead sling bullets (per bag of twenty) 1 SP
- Blowgun darts (per half dozen) 2 SP
- Thrown darts (per sheaf of a dozen) 2 SP

Ranged Weapon tables begin on page 65.

SIEGE WEAPONS

Most siege weapons are used to lob simple bolts or stones at targets. They are so powerful that a direct hit will generally cripple or kill most armoured humanoids with a single shot. However, it is often only siege weapons which can hurt larger creatures such as giants or dragons . If not being used in battle most siege weapons are used to reduce fortifications, breaching holes in walls or destroying defensive towers hosting their own siege weapons.

The following weapons do not use handedness, damage bonuses or ENC being beyond such issues. The Size of their projectiles is rated as Beyond Enormous (BE), meaning that no shield will protect against the force of such impacts. Due to the nature of the weapons, Range only has two values; Effective Range and Long Range.

NOTES ON SIEGE WEAPONS

- Reloading time is measured in Combat Rounds, not Turns.
- Crew: This is the minimum and maximum crew required to operate the weapon. Each extra person above the minimum value reduces the Load time by 1.
- Siege Weapon Combat Effects are included for attacks against large or colossal creatures. They are superfluous against fortifications.

Siege Weapon tables begin on page 64.

VEHICLES

Most vehicles are drawn by one or more animals, and move at the animal's rate. The number of animals required, for the animals to maintain their standard movement rate, is noted in the Draw column of the vehicles table. Reduce the movement proportionately if fewer animals are used. Generally drivers will not exceed the required number of animals because this decreases control, stability, and integrity.

The amount a vehicle can carry in terms of driver(s), and passengers, and cargo (total ENC) is indicated in the Load column. Again, drivers will refuse to exceed these load amounts because control, and stability becomes more difficult.

Vehicle tables begin on page 64.

One Handed Weapons

Weapon	Damage	Size	Reach	Combat Effects	ENC	AP/HP	Traits	Milieu	Cost
Ball & chain	1d6+1	M	M	Bash, Entangle, Stun Location	2	6/8	Flexible	M	250 SP
Battleaxe	1d6+1	M	M	Bleed, Sunder	1	4/8		A-R	100 SP
Broadsword	1d8	M	M	Bleed, Impale	2	6/10		A-E	175 SP
Chain	1d4	M	M	Entangle	1	8/6	Flexible	A-I	10 SP
Club	1d6	M	S	Bash, Stun Location	1	4/4		All	5 SP
Dagger	1d4+1	S	S	Bleed, Impale	—	6/8	Thrown	All	30 SP
Hatchet	1d6	S	S	Bleed	1	4/6	Thrown	All	25 SP
Falchion	1d6+2	M	M	Bleed	1	6/10		A-M	200 SP
Flail	1d6	M	M	Bash	1	3/6	Flexible	A-M	25 SP
Knife	1d3	S	S	Bleed, Impale	—	5/4		All	10 SP
Lance	1d10+2	H	VL	Impale, Sunder	3	4/10	Mount	A-M	150 SP
Longsword	1d8	M	L	Bleed, Impale	2	6/12		M-R	250 SP
Mace	1d8	M	S	Bash, Stun Location	1	6/6		A-R	100 SP
Main Gauche	1d4	S	S	Bleed	—	6/10	Entrapping	M-E	180 SP
Military pick	1d6+1	M	M	Stun Location, Sunder	3	6/10		M-E	180 SP
Net	1d4	S	L	Entangle	3	2/20	Entrapping, Thrown	All	20 SP
Rapier	1d8	M	L	Impale	1	5/8		E	100 SP
Sabre	1d6+1	M	M	Bleed, Impale	1	6/8		E-I	225 SP
Scimitar	1d8	M	M	Bleed	2	6/10		M-E	200 SP
Shortspear	1d8+1	M	L	Impale	2	4/5	Set, Thrown	All	20 SP
Shortsword	1d6	M	S	Bleed, Impale	1	6/8		All	100 SP
Trident	1d8	M	L	Impale	2	4/10	Barbed, Thrown	A-M	155 SP
Whip	1d3	M	VL	Entangle, Stun Location	1	2/8	Entrapping, Flexible, Offensive	A-M	100 SP

Shields

Shield	Damage	Size	Reach	Combat Effects	ENC	AP/HP	Traits	Milieu	Cost
Buckler	1d3	M	S	Bash, Stun Location	1	6/9	Ranged Parry; Passive Blocks 2 locations	M-E	50 SP
Heater	1d4	L	S	Bash, Stun Location	2	6/12	Ranged Parry; Passive Blocks 3 locations	M	150 SP
Hoplite	1d4	H	S	Bash, Stun Location	3	6/15	Ranged Parry; Passive Blocks 4 locations	A-M	300 SP
Kite	1d4	H	S	Bash, Stun Location	3	4/15	Ranged Parry; Passive Blocks 4 locations	M	300 SP
Peltast	1d4	L	S	Bash, Stun Location	2	4/12	Ranged Parry; Passive Blocks 3 locations	A-M	150 SP
Scutum	1d4	H	S	Bash, Stun Location	4	4/18	Ranged Parry; Passive Blocks 5 locations	A-M	450 SP
Target	1d3+1	L	S	Bash, Impale	2	4/9	Ranged Parry; Passive Blocks 3 locations	A-E	150 SP
Viking	1d4	L	S	Bash, Stun Location	3	4/12	Ranged Parry; Passive Blocks 4 locations	M	300 SP

Two Handed Weapons

Weapon	Damage	Size	Reach	Combat Effects	ENC	AP/HP	Traits	Milieu	Cost
Battleaxe	1d8+1	L	M	Bleed, Sunder	1	4/8		A-M	100 SP
Garrotte	1d2	S	T	-	—	1/2	Stealth	A-I	15 SP
Glaive/Rhomphaia	1d10+2	L	L	Bleed, Sunder	2	4/10		A-M	250 SP
Great axe	2d6+2	H	L	Bleed, Sunder	2	4/10		A-M	125 SP
Great club	2d6	H	L	Bash, Stun Location	3	4/10		All	50 SP
Great hammer	1d10+3	H	L	Bash, Stun Location, Sunder	3	4/10		M-E	250 SP
Greatsword	2d8	H	L	Bleed, Impale, Sunder	4	6/12		M-E	300 SP
Halberd/Poleaxe	1d8+2	L	VL	Entangle, Impale, Sunder	4	4/10	Set	A-E	200 SP
Longspear	1d10+1	L	VL	Impale	2	4/10	Set	All	30 SP
Longsword	1d10	L	L	Bleed, Impale, Sunder	2	6/12		M-E	250 SP
Military flail	1d10	L	L	Bash, Stun Location	3	4/10	Flexible	A-M	250 SP
Pike/Sarissa	1d10+2	L	VL	Impale	4	4/12	Set	A-M	90 SP
Quarterstaff	1d8	M	L	Stun Location	2	4/8	Defensive	All	20 SP
Xyston	1d10	L	VL	Impale	3	4/10	Set; Double Ended	A	100 SP

Siege Weapons

Weapon	Damage	Range		Load	Crew	SIZ	Combat Effects	AP/HP	Milieu	Cost
		Effective	Long							
Scorpion	3d6	150m	300m	4	1/1	BE	Impale, Sunder	4/15	A-M	750 SP
Ballista	4d6	200m	400m	5	2/4	BE	Impale, Sunder	4/25	A-M	1,000 SP
Mangonel	5d6	250m	500m	6	2/4	BE	Bash, Stun	4/50	M	1,250 SP
Onager	6d6	300m	600m	7	3/6	BE	Bash, Stun	4/75	A-M	1,500 SP
Couillard	7d6	350m	700m	8	3/6	BE	Bash, Stun	4/100	M	3,000 SP
Trebuchet	8d6	400m	800m	9	4/8	BE	Bash, Stun	4/150	M	5,000 SP

Vehicles

Vehicle	Occupants/Load ENC	Draw	Milieu	Cost
Two wheeled cart (hayrick, ox cart or similar)	6/60	1	A-I	60
Two wheeled wagon (goods cart, carriage or similar)	10/100	1	A-I	175
Four Wheeled Freight wagon	10/200	2	A-I	500
War Chariot	2/20	2	A-I	1200
Sedan Chair (carried by humans)	1/10	2	A-I	400
Palanquin (carried by humans)	4/40	8	A-I	2000
Stage Coach (covered and comfortable)	8/200	4	R, I	8000
Heavy Coach (covered and comfortable)	12/400	8	R, I	15000

Ranged Weapons

Ranged Weapon	Damage	Dam. Mod	Force	Range	Load	Combat Effects	Impale Size	ENC	AP/HP	Milieu	Cost
Atlatl	—	—	+1 Step	+0/+25/+75	1	—	—	1	1/4	P	10 SP
Blowgun	—	N	—	10/20/30	2	—	—	—	1/4	P	30 SP
Bolas	1d4	N	—	10/25/50	—	Entangle	—	—	2/2	P-A	10 SP
Dagger	1d4	Y	S	5/10/20	—	Impale	S	—	6/8	All	30 SP
Dart	1d4	Y	S	5/10/20	—	Impale	S	—	2/1	P-A	10 SP
Discus	1d4+1	Y	L	5/20/40	—	Stun Location	—	—	2/3	A	30 SP
Hatchet	1d6	Y	S	10/20/30	—	Bleed	—	1	4/6	All	25 SP
Heavy crossbow	1d10	N	H	20/150/300	4	Impale, Sunder	S	2	4/8	M-E	350 SP
Javelin	1d8+1	Y	H	10/20/50	—	Impale, Pin Weapon (Shield)	M	1	3/8	A-M	20 SP
Light crossbow	1d8	N	L	20/100/200	3	Impale	S	1	4/5	M-E	150 SP
Long bow	1d8	Y	H	15/125/250	2	Impale	S	1	4/7	M	200 SP
Net	—	N	—	3/5/10	—	Entangle	—	3	2/20	All	20 SP
Recurve bow	1d8	Y	H	15/125/250	2	Impale	S	1	4/8	A-M	225 SP
Short bow	1d6	Y	L	15/100/200	2	Impale	S	1	4/4	P-M	75 SP
Shortspear	1d8	Y	L	10/15/30	-	Impale	M	1	4/5	All	20 SP
Sling	1d8	N	L	10/150/300	3	Stun Location	—	—	1/2	P-M	5 SP
Staff sling	2d6	N	E	5/25/50	4	Stun Location	—	2	3/6	A-M	20 SP
Stone/Rock	1d3	Y	S	5/10/20	—	Stun Location	—			All	
Trident	1d8	Y	L	10/15/30	—	Barbed, Impale	M	2	4/10	A-M	155 SP

Equipment Manufacturing and Quality

With the right resources characters can make, repair, and enhance the quality of items they acquire. The right resources are the skills to do the job (usually a Craft skill, or Engineering/Mechanisms); tools, and other equipment, such as a forge, workbench, and so on; and, finally, time.

Resources

Access to resources is essential to the task. These will differ from one job to another but will, at the very least, involve suitable tools, materials, and a suitable place of work (a forge or workshop for example).

The availability of resources determines a number of things:

- Whether or not the task is possible
- How long it takes to complete
- The quality of the output

It is the Games Master's responsibility to decide if available resources are suitable, and in the right quantities. If they are not then the grade of the skill being used for the task should be reduced appropriately– and if there is a true dearth of materials, the skill might be reduced by several grades. Some repairing, and manufacturing tasks will be simply impossible without the right elements, and Games Masters will need to adjudicate based on local circumstances (does a village have a working forge? Is iron, and wood available?), and on common sense.

Circumstance Modifiers

The following modifiers may be applied, depending on circumstances:

Resource Modifiers Table

Circumstances	Skill Grade
No tools	Hopeless
Improvised tools	Herculean
Poor Quality/Incomplete tools, or lacking crucial resources	Formidable

Task Rounds

Building or repairing something is measured by Task Rounds. This is a variable amount of time dependent on what is being done. Again, Games Masters should decide how long something is going to take, but the suggested Task Round table below offers some suggestions, and inspiration:

Sample Task Rounds

Task	Appropriate Skill	Task Round Unit
Repairing clothing	Craft (Needlework)	5 minutes – 1 hour
Forging metal	Craft (Blacksmith)	5 minutes – 30 minutes
Forging a sword	Craft (Weaponsmith)	1 – 5 days
Erecting a wooden or stone structure	Engineering	6 months – several years
Sharpening a blade	Mechanisms or Craft (Weaponsmith)	3 to 5 minutes

Completing the task requires a roll against the relevant skill. Note the level of success:

- Critical: 50%
- Success: 25%
- Failure : 0%
- Fumble: –25%

Continue making skill rolls, each taking one Task Round, until 100% has been achieved – or until time, resources, and budget are exhausted. Thus, a competent worker will usually be able to accomplish the work in four to five Task Rounds, assuming a reasonable skill level. Reaching 100% means the final result is of an acceptable standard. Anything less is below par, and may be flawed in some way. If time is pressing or constrained then the number of Task Rounds can be reduced: this will constrain the ability to reach 100%. For example, if a blacksmith is ordered to shape, and fit a horseshoe in two Task Rounds (half the usual time needed) then, unless he scores two critical successes with his skill rolls the finished shoes will have no more than 50% of their effectiveness (meaning they are incorrectly shaped, do not fit properly, and may come loose or even injure the horse).

With enough time it is possible to exceed 100%. The percentage achieved at the end of the period available indicates the overall quality of the product or task, as shown in the Item Quality table, opposite. Exceptional quality offers enhancements to the product. The final percentage reflects the quality of the product or completed task.

Enhancements

If a task exceeds 100% in four or fewer Task Rounds it automatically gains Enhancements as indicated in the Item Quality table. If a project only reaches 100% within four Task Rounds, the maker has the option to continue refining it. To do this he works on it for a single further Task Round at one difficulty grade harder and, depending on the result of the skill roll for that Task Round, may enhance it. However, there is a risk that the maker overworks the item, taking away from its quality rather than enhancing it.

- Critical Success: 2 Enhancements
- Success: 1 Enhancement
- Failure: No Enhancements
- Fumble: Reduce Quality by 25%

If the task took greater than four Task Rounds to achieve 100%, then the base object is mediocre and cannot be improved. The Enhancement is determined by the nature of the object.

Item Quality Table

Total Score	*Result*	*Enhancements*
150	Excellent	2
125	Good	1
100	Acceptable	0
75	Flawed	The product will break or wear out 25% faster than normal; or its Hit Points and value are reduced by one quarter reflecting its flawed durability.
50	Poor	The product will break or wear out 50% faster than normal; or its Hit Points and value are reduced by half reflecting its flawed durability.
25	Shoddy	The product will break or wear out 75% faster than normal; or its Hit Points and value are reduced by three quarters reflecting its shoddy durability.
0 or less	Unusable	The product is simply of no use whatsoever.

Enhancements can be stacked: so an item with two Enhancements could benefit from being highly efficient, for example, conferring a 10% bonus to the using skill. However no item can benefit from more than two Enhancements of the same type.

Choose from the following:

Enhancements Table

Enhancement	*Effect*
Desirable	The item's value is doubled.
Durable	The item's Hit Points are increased by one.
Resilient	The item's Armour Points are increased by one.
Efficient	The item of such quality that it confers a 5% bonus to the skill required to use it.
Effective	If a weapon it gains +1 to its Damage rating. Other items reduce ENC value by 1d2 points.

Using the Task Rules in Other Circumstances

The rules presented for making and repairing equipment can be applied to many different situations. Using the same basic mechanics any situation requiring an investment of time, effort and skill, and requiring a quality of outcome, can be simulated. Some examples are given below:

Social conflict - where characters are engaged in argument, debate, negotiation, politics, diplomacy, and so on.

Affairs of the heart – seductions, courtship, proof of love (or even hatred).

Sieges and wars of attrition – use the Task rules to simulate the progress of a siege or extended battle over a long-term period.

Chases and pursuits – use the Task rules where pursuits take place over days or weeks, rather than in detailed time where an immediate result is more desirable.

Games Masters will no doubt find their own uses for these rules.

Game System

Many different things can occur during a Mythras game. Some are resolved through skill use or one of the major game mechanics such as combat or magic; others require their own rules for adjudication. This chapter provides rules and guidance for a variety of different scenarios that Games Masters and players will encounter whilst playing the game.

The list is not exhaustive but should represent most common situations. If Games Masters find there are other situations that require some form of game-system adjudication, and that these situations seem to occur frequently, then they are encouraged to develop their own rules to cover these special circumstances, using those given in this chapter as a basis for replication or development.

Briefly this chapter includes rules for:

- Acid
- Action, Time, and Movement
- Ageing
- Asphyxiation, Drowning, and Suffocation
- Blood Loss
- Character Improvement
- Disease and Poison
- Encumbrance
- Falling
- Fatigue
- Fires
- Healing from Injury
- Inanimate Objects
- Luck Points
- Passions
- Survival
- Traps
- Visibility
- Weather

Acid

Acids come from many different sources and are used extensively in alchemical research. The most important factor with any acid is its concentration, rather than its type. All acids are therefore classified as either Weak, Strong or Concentrated. Mythras assumes that contact with the acid is significant or sustained, rather than just a droplet or two.

A splash or spray of acid lasts only for a few Combat Rounds before it loses potency. Immersion in a considerable volume of acid inflicts the damage every round until the victim or location is removed and treated.

For generic acids it is assumed that armour protects against the effects of acid but does not stop it, its Armour Points being reduced by the acid's damage until it reaches zero hit points, at which point the damage is then transferred to the hit location it protected. Armour reduced to zero Armour Points is considered useless as the acid burns through bindings, straps and joints.

Although the Acid table assumes the action of acid on living flesh, not all acids affect non-organic substances equally. Some can eat rapidly through metal, whilst others barely mark it. If desired it is entirely permissible to have strange acids which affect only metal or other specific materials instead of flesh.

Acid Table

Acid Type	*Damage*	*Duration*
Weak	1d2	1 Combat Round
Strong	1d4	1d2 Combat Rounds
Concentrated	1d6	1d3 Combat Rounds

Action, Time and Movement

How quickly time passes in Mythras depends on circumstances. Activities in roleplaying games rarely elapse in real time unless characters are conversing with each other or with non-player characters. For the most part, timescales for different forms of activity are inflated or condensed depending on what is being done.

The key timescales and what actions and motion can be accomplished within them, are as follows: Combat Rounds, Local Time and Strategic Time.

Combat Rounds

A Combat Round, dealt with more fully in the Combat chapter, represents five seconds of real time. Combat Rounds are used to measure short, frenetic bursts of activity that take seconds to complete. They can be useful for measuring very detailed activities that require a blow-by-blow resolution. For example, a chase between hunter and prey can be measured in Combat Rounds, representing the twists and turns that happen very quickly during any tense pursuit.

Local Time

Local Time represents a few minutes to a few hours, and is used to measure activities that do not require the detailed attention of a Combat Round, but require a specific concentration of effort with a definite end result. Picking a lock might take five minutes, and this is a measure of Local Time. Observing the patrols made by teams of guards around a castle's walls might require several hours, but is still a measure of Local Time. Manage Local Time in the following way:

1. The character states his intention (Local Time starts)
2. The Games Master decides how long this takes to accomplish
3. Any appropriate skill rolls are made and the results noted
4. The Games Master communicates the results, and the time taken in step 2 passes (Local Time ends)

Local Time may then continue, move into Combat Rounds or become Strategic Time

Strategic Time

Strategic Time is measured in days, months or even years. Use Strategic Time for those occasions where it is not necessary to know the detail, simply the outcome – 'You ride for ten days and reach the city by dawn on the eleventh day.' 'After a whole day of watching the guard patrols you now understand their movements and patterns.' 'It takes a week to craft the sword.'

Strategic Time is mostly concerned with how far characters travel depending on the mode of transport used. The Strategic Time Travel Table offers examples for various conditions. The travel times assume a travelling day of around 10 to 12 hours with regular stops for rest, water and food.

If characters need to increase the distances given in the Strategic Time Travel Table, then they can effectively add half again to the distance travelled in the Strategic Time period but gain an enduring level of Fatigue as a result. Naturally an appropriate skill roll (Drive, Ride, Athletics, and so on) also needs to be made to successfully increase the distance covered, along with dealing with any hazards that might need to be resolved in Combat Rounds or Local Time.

Strategic Time Travel Table

Travel Example	*Distance Covered (kilometres) per Day (10-12 hours)*
Walking	30 per Day
Horseback at casual speed	60 per Day
Wagon at casual speed	15 per Day
Open Sea, favourable conditions	150-300 (in a 24 hour period)
Open Sea, unfavourable conditions	0-60 (in a 24 hour period)
Coast or River, favourable conditions	30-60 per Day
Coast or River, unfavourable conditions	0-30 per Day

Movement

Movement is broken down into three 'gaits' which are Walking, Running and Sprinting.

Walking is the average speed a member of a particular species ambles along at when in no particular hurry. This is normally referred to as a creature's base Movement Rate.

Running is a trot or jog, at a speed which can be maintained over long periods. Basically, anything faster than a walk. Maximum running speed is triple Movement Rate, which may vary according to the bonus granted by Athletics skill.

Sprinting is flat out movement at top speed, which can only be maintained for brief periods. Peak sprinting speed is five times Movement Rate, which again may be increased according to whatever bonus is granted from Athletics skill.

The Comparative Movement table summarises the typical walking distances covered by creatures of differing base movement rates, for a variety of time periods. Tactical movement during combat is explained in more detail on page 101 (Engagement).

Scenes

Scenes are an abstract time measurement based on definable events or interactions. They can last for Combat Rounds, Local or Strategic Time, and duration is based on activities being engaged in by one or more characters. Some spells, for instance, last for a Scene, which means that duration is variable but based on that Scene's need. For example, if a Folk Magic spell, such as Bladesharp, is cast successfully, it will last for one active scene. This will be either as short as the duration of an entire combat, or as long as a Local Time event where Bladesharp might be required. Scenes always have active player participation. For instance an evening spent in a tavern gaining information is a Scene, because it requires the characters to participate. However a long-distance trip by sea, where the Games Master stipulates that several days pass without incident, is not a Scene.

The Games Master always determines when a Scene starts and ends. For the most part it will be obvious and important only where magical effects need to be measured.

Comparative Movement Table

Time Period	Movement 4m	Movement 6m	Movement 8m	Movement 10m	Movement 12m	Movement 14m
Combat Round	4m	6m	8m	10m	12m	14m
Minute	48m	72m	96m	120m	144m	168m
Hour	2.9km	4.3km	5.8km	7.2km	8.6km	10.1km

Moving In Armour

Worn armour acts against character Movement Rates, and certain kinds of actions such as swimming or climbing. The armour's Initiative Penalty is applied to Movement of different kinds in the following ways:

- Walking: Armour does not interfere with walking movement, although it can increase the Fatigue level (see page 78)
- Running or Sprinting: Subtract the Armour Penalty from the running and sprinting speed. The result is how fast the character can move during chases or when charging. For example, a character wearing a full panoply of Hoplite Plate armour would reduce both gaits by 6m.
- Swimming: Take the character's swimming speed (see the Swim skill page 43) divide by two (rounding up), and subtract the Armour Penalty. If the result is zero, the character cannot move, and barely keeps himself afloat. If the result is negative, then the character sinks. For example, even if our character was a top class swimmer (84%), wearing full Hoplite Plate with its -6 penalty, would still cause him to sink if he attempts to swim in his armour (Swim speed of 6+4, divided by two, then subtract 6 equals -1).
- Climbing rough surface (branching trees, ladders, scaffolds, and so on): Half the Armour Penalty (rounded up) is subtracted from the base Movement Rate. If the result is zero or less, they are too burdened by their armour to climb. Thus, our hero in his Hoplite Plate armour can still scale easily climbable objects, as his Climbing movement is 6 – 3 = 3.
- Climbing a steep surface (pitched roofs, steep hills, and so on): The Armour Penalty is subtracted from the base Movement Rate. If the result is zero or less, they are too burdened by their armour to climb. Thus, our hero in his Hoplite Plate cannot climb as his Climbing movement is 6 – 6 = 0.
- Climbing a sheer surface (walls, cliff faces, etc): Double the Armour Penalty is subtracted from the base Movement Rate. As with climbing a rough surface, if the result is zero or less, the character cannot climb.
- Jumping: Reduce the distance in metres the character can jump (see the Athletics skill, page 38) by half the Armour Penalty (rounded up). For standing jumps this impairment is halved.

Anathaym's Saga

Anathaym, like all humans, has a base Movement Rate of 6. In addition she is a proficient athlete with an Athletics skill of 52%. From these her maximum movement rates are calculated as:

Walking 6m – base Movement Rate of a human.

Running 21m – Base Movement Rate plus one for her Athletics skill, multiplied by three.

Sprinting 40m – Base Movement Rate plus two for her Athletics skill, multiplied by five.

Ageing

All characters age, and with age come certain consequences. The signs of ageing start at Early Middle Age (40 years for humans – other species might age at greater or lesser rates). As a character passes into a new Ageing Band he must make both an Endurance roll and a Willpower roll at the grades noted. If a roll is failed then he experiences Ageing Effects as shown in the Ageing Effects table.

Each characteristic affected by ageing reduces by 1d3 points. These points can be recovered or at least partially counteracted through characteristic improvement, representing efforts made to keep themselves trim and alert as they grow older. If any characteristic is reduced to zero from ageing, the character dies due to his terminal frailty.

What specific debilitating effects arise as part of the ageing process are up to the Games Master to define. For instance, reducing STR, CON or DEX represents general wear and tear on the body, with creaking joints, and a gradual loss of mobility. Reducing INT indicates that age is starting to play tricks on the mind and memory, whilst reducing CHA indicates the character is getting craggier, and more short-tempered perhaps, as they get older.

Age Bands

Age Band	*Endurance and Willpower Roll Grade*
Early Middle Age (40-49 for humans)	Easy
Middle Age (50-59 for humans)	Standard
Late Middle Age (60-69 for humans)	Hard
Old Age (70-79 for humans)	Formidable
Advanced Old Age (80-89 for humans)	Herculean
Dotage (90+ for humans)	Hopeless

Ageing Effects Table

1d6	*Physical Ageing (Failed Endurance)*	*Mental Ageing (Failed Willpower)*
1–2	STR	INT
3–4	CON	POW
5–6	DEX	CHA

Asphyxiation, Drowning and Suffocation

Characters can hold their breath for a number of seconds equal to their Endurance skill. However the character must be prepared (filling the lungs with as much air as possible); if not, then the period is halved if the character was in a passive situation, or reduced to one fifth if the character was engaged in strenuous activity.

Once the period of held breath is over, characters must make an Endurance roll:

- If the roll is a critical success, no further deterioration occurs.
- If the roll is successful, the character accrues an extra level of Fatigue.
- If the roll fails, the character sustains 1d2 extra levels of Fatigue that round.
- If the roll is fumbled, the character sustains 1d3 extra levels of Fatigue that round.

Without aid, death from asphyxiation is usually swift. If the asphyxiation ends before the character dies, they recover Fatigue levels lost to suffocation relatively quickly; regaining one level per minute.

Depending on the method of asphyxiation, the Games Master may wish to prevent full recovery, imposing an enduring level of Fatigue to represent damage to the lungs caused by smoke or water inhalation.

Blood Loss

Blood loss due to external and internal wounds, usually sustained in combat, can wear a character down very quickly. Its effects are measured by the accumulation of Fatigue levels, in a manner similar to asphyxiation since blood is needed to oxygenate the body's muscles and vital organs. Significant blood loss is suffered in the following circumstances:

- The Bleed Special Effect (see page 96)
- Injury resulting in a Major Wound (see page 110)
- Diseases and Poisons that result in Bleeding (see page 75)

Unrestrained blood loss typically results in death unless some form of medical attention or healing magic can be applied to control the bleeding.

Unlike asphyxiation, the effects of serious blood loss on Fatigue are enduring. A character recovers Fatigue lost to bleeding at a rate of one level per day, starting the day after his exsanguinations cease.

Character Improvement

Every MYTHRAS character has the opportunity to improve with time. Improvement can be undertaken in several areas:

- Increasing existing skills
- Increasing characteristics
- Increasing passions
- Learning new skills
- Learning new magical abilities and spells

Experience Rolls

The mechanism for most character improvement is the Experience Roll. Games Masters dispense Experience Rolls at an appropriate juncture in the campaign: at the end of every successful scenario or storyline; or after perhaps two or three sessions of play if the story is a long one which will take time to complete. The frequency is at the Games Master's discretion. A high frequency of Experience Rolls will lead to the characters developing at a faster rate.

There is no right or wrong time to give Experience Rolls, but natural breaks in the story may suggest suitable times. The Games Master is, however, always the decision maker here. Whilst players cannot demand Experience Rolls, they have a right to expect them at certain times – as their characters will not be able to develop without them.

How Many?

The number of Experience Rolls given in any one sitting should be between two and four, but it can be lower or higher depending on how long it has been since the last set of rolls, and how well the characters performed or have been played.

It is recommended that all characters be given the same number of Experience Rolls, which helps maintain fairness and parity in character progression – although even with the same number of rolls characters may progress at different rates, as the mechanics for Experience Rolls illustrate.

The only exception to this guideline is where a character gains an additional roll (or suffers a reduction in rolls) for their Experience Modifier as described on page 9. This modifier should only be permitted in situations where the character can put their influence to good use or suffer its consequences, such as returning home at the conclusion of a scenario. Thus it is not intended that the bonus should be applied at the end of each and every session, especially when the characters are isolated or exploring off in the wilderness.

Experience Rolls do not need to be used there and then. They can be reserved for future use at the player's discretion. The main reasons for reserving use of a roll are:

- To increase Characteristics
- To buy new Professional Skills
- To put towards developing a new magical Tradition (explained in the Introduction to Magic chapter).

Increasing Existing Skills

Any skill on the character sheet, Standard or Professional, can be increased by spending one Experience Roll.

- The player rolls 1d100 and compares it to the skill being increased. The character's INT is added to the roll.
- If the number rolled is equal to or greater than the skill being improved it increases by 1d4+1%.
- If the number rolled is less than the skill selected, the skill still increases but only by 1%.

If a character fumbled any skill during the course of the preceding session(s) – i.e., between the last set of Experience Rolls and the present one – the fumbled skill gains a free increase of 1%. It is a truism that we learn more from our mistakes than our successes, and this represents the reflection a character undergoes following a disastrous failure. Multiple fumbles of the same skill do not stack.

Freely Improving Skills

Normally players have full discretion over which skills to improve, no matter their location or circumstances. Sometimes, however, it may be unrealistic for a character to practice Lockpicking when he is currently on a ship, and has done nothing but fight sea monsters for the last few game sessions. In such cases it is reasonable for the Games Masters to request that characters only attempt to improve skills which they have recently used, or for which the situation exists to practice them. For example, if the ship-bound character arrives at a civilised port it is quite likely he can find a local thieves' guild or locksmith with whom he can practice.

Some caution is required that the Games Master is not too restrictive, as this can lead to a bias in a subset of those skills which are most often used in his campaign, leading to disproportionate character development. Instead, if a character wishes to improve unusual skills, the Games Master should use this to create a roleplaying opportunity or an eventual subplot for his campaign.

Games Masters can, if they wish, increase the dice step if they want to have skill progression move at a faster rate without giving Experience Rolls on a frequent basis: so, instead of increasing by 1d4+1 skills increase by 1d6+1. If adjusting the default dice roll in this way, Games Masters should set the expectation at the start of the campaign and not veer from it.

Increasing Characteristics

A creature's rolled characteristics are regarded as its peak natural development, a combination of its birth and environment as it was growing. Thus just as some horses are bigger, stronger and tougher than others, humans and other sapient species can grow up to exhibit fairly diverse physical and mental characteristics.

Characteristics can, like skills, be improved through Experience Rolls, which represent training regimes. However, such increases are artificial boosts which normally atrophy after the training exercises cease, characteristics dropping back to their natural levels whether the workouts were daily calisthenics sessions to increase CON or memory tests to enhance INT.

To achieve and maintain characteristic increases requires that a character reduce his regular allotment of Experience Rolls by one or more points. This represents the continual and intensive effort spent to push his body beyond its normal capability.

Each Experience Roll sacrificed in this manner boosts the trained characteristic by one tenth of its rolled species maximum. Thus a human who engaged in regular weightlifting to build up his STR could, at the cost of reducing his normal allotment of Experience Rolls by one, gain +2 points to his Strength. A minotaur on the other hand would gain +3 points to Strength as his species maximum is 24.

When a characteristic increases, all attributes and skills derived from it increase too (if the characteristic increase is enough to create an attribute change). Thus, increasing STR by one point will also increase each skill that uses it as a component by one point too. In addition Damage Modifier may also increase if the new STR value moves the character into the next Damage Modifier band.

No matter how much training is undertaken, no characteristic can exceed its species maximum – which is simply the highest possible result from the characteristic roll. Once the character decides to cease his exercise regime, his trained characteristic drops by one improvement step the next time he receives Experience Rolls, and again the following time, the atrophying continuing until the characteristic has returned to its natural value.

SIZ is the exception to the above rules. It cannot be increased through mundane means.

Increasing Passions

As described under Passions on page 82, the value of a passion may be increased with Experience Rolls in exactly the same way as a skill. If supported by play, the Games Master might even allow a passion to be reduced by the use of an Experience Roll.

For example, constant spurning from an unrequited love might eventually wear down the passion of even the most ardent lover, especially one who wishes to pursue a relationship without the ghosts of the past haunting them.

Permanent Characteristic Improvement

Some players may bemoan the significant and continual costs of characteristic improvement. In these cases the Games Master can ignore a certain level of realism, and instead focus on fun, allowing permanent characteristic boosts for a one-off Experience Roll cost.

This method must be treated with a degree of caution however, since not all Games Masters reward players with the same frequency or number of Experience Rolls; thus the default costs may be too cheap or expensive. Additionally games where characteristic improvement is too prevalent can quickly lead to many characters with identical attributes, each tweaked to take advantage of natural break points within the system.

The following method utilises the current and minimum characteristic values so that it scales for all creatures. Although it sometimes throws up an oddity between characteristics rolled on different dice, this should be considered a feature of that particular species. Since most creatures are generated using no more than three or four dice, this method remains both simple and comparatively fair.

Cost to increase a characteristic by one point = 1+creature's current characteristic value, minus the species minimum for that characteristic

Thus a human with DEX 12 would need to invest 10 Experience Rolls (13 – 3) to raise DEX to 13.

Learning New Skills

Some characters may wish to study new Professional skills which they never had the chance to learn from their culture or career. Before they can start investing Experience Rolls they must first find a source of knowledge from which to learn. This could be as prosaic as a professional tutor such those provided by cults or brotherhoods. Alternately it might be a more exotic source of education, an ancient and crumbling training scroll or an ancestor spirit bound to the community's sacred stone tiki.

Once a source of education is found, the character must spend an entire month of study and practice to garner a basic grounding in that skill. This costs 3 Experience Rolls plus whatever in-game costs are required to pay the teacher (if one exists), and purchase (or rent) whatever equipment and tools may be needed.

Training

Skills can be improved without expending Experience Rolls, through help of a mentor; either a trainer or a teacher.

Characters must spend one full week in training to benefit from a training increase. At the end of the training period the skill being trained improves by the die roll indicated on the Training Chart, with any modifiers due to the Teaching skill.

How much a mentor charges for his services depends very much on the nature of the campaign and the setting. They might accept manual labour or favours in return for training, or insist on hard coin. In the case of abstract promises the Games Master must set the terms and the character should meet them, or else face some form of consequence if they are not met.

In terms of hard coin, a week's training costs 1 Silver Piece for every 5% the mentor has in the skill he is training. If he also knows how to teach, this amount increases by 1 silver piece for each 10% he has in the Teach skill. So, a mentor with 70% in Lore (History) could charge 14 SP; or 19 SP if he also had Teach 50%.

Training Improvement Table

Degree of Difference	Skill Improves By
21-30%	1d2
31-40%	1d3
41-50%	1d4
51-60%	1d6
61-70%	1d6+1
71-80%	1d6+2
81-90%	1d6+3
91-100%	1d6+4
Each 10%	+1

Trainers

A trainer is someone who works with the character, helping them to practice a particular skill hoping, through coaching and mentoring, to improve the character's skill. Characters can act as trainers for other characters but it is usual to seek out someone who, through years of specialised study and greater experience, has more benefits and insight to offer.

A trainer must have at least 20% more than the character in the skill being trained, and the degree of improvement rests on the difference:

Teachers

A teacher is a professional trainer who possesses the Teach skill, using it to improve the quality of his tuition. They utilise the same Training Chart above, but modify the amount increased according to the result of a Teach roll:

- Critical Success: Skill improvement increases by two Training steps
- Success: Skill improvement increases by one Training step
- Failure: No effect on improvement
- Fumble: Skill improvement decreases by one Training step, which may result in the character gaining no improvement through the training

Limits to Training

Training comes with some limitations:

- Only one skill at a time can be trained.
- A trained skill must be next improved using an Experience Roll; it cannot benefit from the training procedure again until it has been increased in this way.
- Trainers can only tutor a single student at a time, whereas teachers may educate multiple students at once. As a guide, divide the trainer's Teaching skill by 10 to determine how many students that teacher is prepared to train at one time.

Cults and Brotherhoods

Cults and guilds may offer training at a reduced cost, or free of charge, to their members. The training costs outlined earlier are therefore considered a standard guide; cult or brotherhood members may be offered a reduced rate, but this may be dependent on rank and standing within the organization. The Games Master may need to set these limits.

Anathaym's Saga

Tired of having sand kicked in her face by Xenos during combat training, Anathaym decides that she needs to be as strong as her hated rival, so that she can properly humiliate him the next time they face off in the sparring circle. With her STR 11, SIZ 10, and no Damage Modifier she is at a significant disadvantage, especially when wrestling.

Thus Anathaym throws herself body and soul into a punishing training schedule, her player deciding that she'll use all three of Anathaym's regularly assigned Experience Rolls to increase her STR. She boosts her characteristic by +6 but at the expense of consuming all her free time (preventing any other skill improvements to be made). The Games Master also rules that it takes six weeks of campaign time for her to achieve this new strength.

When Anathaym next turns up at the combat school, Xenos inevitably makes some foul comment concerning her new 'manliness' which she seizes upon to challenge him. The arrogant noble insultingly looks her muscular physique up and down (STR 17), then offers to arm-wrestle with her. However, although her Damage Modifier is now in parity with Xenos' (+1d2) she still loses the match, her rival being slightly more experienced in applying his Brawn in these tests of machismo.

Anathaym rages at her humiliating defeat, but master Zamothis approaches his student and sardonically suggests that if she spent time actually practicing her combat skills instead of turning herself into an ox, she might actually simply punch out her opponent the next time. Anathaym hears the wisdom in his words and ceases her weightlifting, planning to invest some of her future Experience Rolls in becoming more skilful in unarmed combat.

Following the advice of Zamothis, Anathaym seeks out her mentor to be schooled in the art of unarmed combat. In her single-mindedness to become an expert of the Meerish Infantry combat style, her Unarmed skill has languished at a mere 37%. Master Zamothis on the other hand is an expert with 85%, and a Teach skill of 79%.

After ten days of intensive training Anathaym benefits greatly from her mentor's wisdom. The difference in skill between them is 48% which on the Training Chart table normally results in a 1d4 bonus. However, Zamothis also critically succeeds his Teach roll, increasing the table result by two steps. This boosts the improvement roll to 1d6+1, and from this Anathaym gains 5%, raising her Unarmed skill to 42% - well worth every bruise.

Disease and Poison

Some of the most feared things which can affect characters are the myriad diseases and poisons which infest the dark and grim places of the world. There's nothing quite as unsettling than a plague which strikes the character's home city, especially when they are still within its gates. Likewise finding a venomous serpent in the bed or being attacked by giant scorpions can be moments of high drama.

Diseases and poisons are near infinite in their varieties but, for game purposes, are handled in the same way.

Disease and Poison Traits

All diseases and poisons manifest a number of traits important to their effects.

Application: The method of how the disease or poison is introduced into the victim.

- Ingestion - Effects take place through either eating or drinking.
- Inhaled – Effects take place through breathing or snorting.
- Contact – Effects take place through absorption through the skin.
- Injected – Effects take place when the substance is injected into the body through piercing.

Potency: The virulence of the disease or poison. This value is set against an appropriate resisting skill (usually Endurance or Willpower) in an opposed roll. If character wins the roll they shrug off its effects. If however they lose the roll, then they suffer all of the disease or poison Conditions, each at the appropriate time.

Resistance: How the disease or poison is resisted – either Endurance or Willpower, but may have more exotic resistance requirements. Resistance can be rolled at the time of exposure, or deferred until the Onset Time to conceal the fact the character might have been infected or poisoned.

Onset Time: Many diseases and poisons do not take immediate effect. The delay is called the Onset Time, and this can be a matter of seconds, minutes, hours, or even longer. Poisons or diseases possessing multiple effects may have different onset times for each one as described under Conditions.

Duration: How long a disease or poison's Conditions last.

Conditions: Every toxin has one or more Conditions. These have specific effects as described in the Conditions table, below, and if a victim fails to resist he suffers all the Conditions described.

Antidote/Cure: If the toxin can be treated it will be noted here. Otherwise all non-magical diseases and poisons can be alleviated by specific healing magic, such as the Cure Malady spell. Successful treatment prevents any further conditions from occurring, yet in some circumstances may leave the victim suffering enduring effects that have already been inflicted.

Disease and Poison Conditions

Condition	Effects
Agony	Victim is hindered by intense pain. Whether in a location or the entire body, any skill roll involving use of the affected area must also be less or equal to the character's Willpower, otherwise the attempt fails, and they moan or scream in pain.
Asphyxiation	Victim suffers asphyxiation – he collapses incapacitated, unable to breathe. The rules for Asphyxiation, found on page 71, are used. Asphyxiation may be asthmatic in nature meaning the victim only suffers shortness of breath, or complete respiratory failure resulting in death. In the later case a victim can be kept alive by winning an opposed test of the First Aid skill against the Potency of the diease or poison.
Bleeding	Victim suffers from either internal bleeding or surface haemorrhaging which leads to the effects described in the Blood Loss section on page 71.
Blindness	Victim becomes blind.
Confusion	Victim cannot use any knowledge, communication or magic skill.
Contagious	Victim can transfer the poison or disease by touch.
Deafness	Victim loses his hearing.
Death	Victim collapses incapacitated, and dies after a number of rounds equal to his CON characteristic.
Dumbness	Victim's vocal chords are paralysed, preventing verbal communication.
Exhaustion	Victim gains an extra level of Fatigue, on top of any they are currently suffering from.
Fever	Victim's body temperature fluctuates wildly – from hot to cold – and muscles ache. All skills suffer a difficulty grade of Hard.
Hallucinations	Victim experiences delusions and cannot differentiate between real and imaginary experiences. His skill and abilities are unaffected but his ability to relate to the real world is seriously impaired. Under its effects the sufferer tends to experience visions related to his strongest Passions, and any skeletons kept in the cupboard, often leading to irrational acts.
Maiming	Victim suffers a permanent loss of 1 Hit Point in the location(s) affected, due to necrosis of the injured tissue.
Mania	Victim is driven to follow some compulsion; such as avoiding water, paranoia, self mutilation, and so forth. The mania induced by the disease or poison will be noted in its description.
Nausea	Victim cannot eat, and must roll against his Endurance every time he performs a stressful physical action to avoid being physically sick. Vomiting lasts for 1d3 rounds during which he cannot act. Long durations of Nausea may cause starvation.
Paralysis	Victim is unable physically to move. The affected area, if a location, cannot be used for the duration. If it affects the whole body, the character cannot move at all.
Sapping	Victim has their Magic Points (either the Attribute or current number) reduced. Apply the Potency of the disease or poison on the Spirit Damage table (page 131) to calculate the dice roll used. Lost Magic Points do not recover until the duration ends.
Unconscious	Victim loses consciousness for a period specified in the description. When consciousness is regained the victim suffers a level of Fatigue.

Sample Diseases

These are samples of various diseases encountered during Mythras play, to be used as they stand or as a template for Games Master designed infections.

Pyrohoxia

A rather strange disease, pyrohoxia is carried by feral animals such as rodents, and transferred by a successful bite. The infection gradually spreads to the brain, where it begins to twist the perceptions and aggression of the victim. No obvious signs exist of pyrohoxia infection, although the behaviour of the creature which bit them may offer clues. Within several weeks of the bite the victim starts to suffer increasingly painful headaches, and the eyes turn bloodshot. At this point the hallucinations begin, strengthening over the course of a week into violent waking nightmares.

The victim then passes into the terminal stage of the disease, which induces constant shivering accompanied with a mania to get warm by whatever means possible. Eventually this climaxes with a suicidal desire to jump into fires, lava or even set themselves alight; usually resulting in a paroxysm of violent destruction as they burn to death. Even if restrained from self-immolation, the victim dies from brain swelling.

Application: Injected
Potency: 80
Resistance: Endurance
Onset time: 1d6+6 days
Duration: 1 week + 1d3 days

Conditions: Disease manifests with the start of Hallucinations. After one week they also start to suffer from Mania (Fire). If the victim somehow survives to the conclusion of the disease, they then suffer Death.

Antidote/Cure: Can be cured by the Healing skill up until the onset of Mania, at which point the disease must be treated magically.

Red Pox

Red pox is a nasty disease spread by skin contact with a person already infected, or with something they have touched. The chance of catching the disease from an object remains for 1d3 days after contact, making it quite difficult to contain the disease once an outbreak occurs.

Victims initially suffer a minor rash, but within a day come down with a serious fever which usually renders them bedridden for the entire duration. During this time the rash evolves into gruesomely itchy pustules which burst open at the slightest movement, weeping small trickles of blood – especially from the armpits and groin. This stage can last up to a week or more, potentially proving fatal.

Application: Contact

Potency: 50

Resistance: Endurance

Onset time: 1d6+6 hours

Duration: 1d6+3 days

Conditions: Once the disease manifests the victim becomes Contagious. 1 day later they begin to suffer Fever and Bleeding. Each day the pustules weep blood the victim loses one level of Fatigue, which does not recover until the duration of the disease has completed.

Antidote/Cure: Can be cured by the Healing skill.

Soul Leech

Dreaded by priests, shamans and sorcerers alike, soul leech drains their magical vitality, reducing them to powerless prestidigitators. Although the disease starts with an innocuous enough cough combined with a degree of lassitude, it soon becomes apparent that their paranormal strength is ebbing when spells tire them more easily.

The only extraneous sign of this weakening is that the victim's own web of subcutaneous veins begins to glow a faint purple when examined in pitch darkness, a by-product of the disease consuming their Magic Points. Magicians suffering this malady often try to bluff through their lack of power hoping that the disease will end before a rival can take advantage.

Application: Inhaled

Potency: 65

Resistance: Endurance

Onset time: 1d6 days

Duration: 1d3+3 weeks

Conditions: Sapping. Each week the victim reduces his Magic Points attribute by 1d6 points. Since these do not recover until the disease ends, a magician can eventually be reduced to a level of utter powerlessness. After the disease concludes, the Magic Points attribute recovers at a rate of 1 point per day.

Antidote/Cure: Can be cured by the Healing skill if rare, mystical ingredients (the precise nature of which depends on the setting) are used.

Sample Poisons

Cobra Venom

Perhaps the quintessential venomous snake, a cobra's venom has several effects depending on its application. If injected via bite, the venom will inflict a burning pain shortly followed by respiratory difficulty which can lead to death. Even surviving a cobra bite comes at a horrible cost, the bitten area suffering permanent necrotic damage. If the venom is spat at the eyes instead of respiratory paralysis the venom can often inflict permanent blindness.

Application: Contact (eyes) or Injected

Potency: 75

Resistance: Endurance

Onset time: Instant if spat in eyes, 1d6+4 minutes if bitten

Duration: 1d3+3 days

Conditions: If spat into the eyes both Agony and Blindness are instant, lasting the entire duration. Bitten victims also begin with Agony but can struggle along until 1d6+6 hours after the bite when Asphyxiation strikes, usually resulting in death, unless First Aid is successfully applied to keep the victim breathing. Survivors will then suffer Necrosis, losing 1 Hit Point per day from the location bitten, until the venom is somehow purged or it naturally ends.

Antidote/Cure: Can be ameliorated with the Healing skill. However blindness, if not treated before the end of the venom's duration becomes permanent. Likewise, each day of Necrosis suffered before successful treatment inflicts permanent damage.

Lotus Dust

Lotus dust is the natural pollen produced by the blossom of the rare and deadly ebony lotus flower, which grows in the depths of remote jungles. It takes the form of a fine yellowish powder with a sweet, cloying scent; although to smell it is death since the pollen in its natural state is lethal when inhaled or tasted, causing the heart of the victim to burst. Whether from fear or ecstasy is unknown, for few beings ever survive long enough to tell.

Despite its dangers many sorcerers breathe the fumes of burning lotus dust, which instead of bringing near instant death, infuses the mind of the imbiber with fantastical visions of other worlds. It is said that they learn dark secrets from the euphoric dreams, though few have the strength of will to extract themselves from such visions.

Application: Inhaled

Potency: 90

Resistance: Willpower

Onset time: 1d3 rounds

Duration: Instantaneous in its natural state, 2d6 hours if smoked

Conditions: Death if natural pollen. Paralysis and Hallucinations if smoked. At the end of a narcotic dream, the smoker must make another resistance roll otherwise subside into an endless coma, still trapped within his lucid visions.

Antidote/Cure: Can be treated by an infusion of the rare Golden Lotus which brings complete recovery, otherwise magic must be used.

Sleeping Draught

Sleeping draughts are often used to capture or rob characters, who unwittingly imbibe the tasteless concoction hidden in a mug of ale or glass of wine. By the time the character awakens, they are usually weak and nauseous – if not from the after-effects of the sleeping draught, then due to the alcoholic hangover which accompanied it.

Application: Ingested

Potency: 60

Resistance: Willpower

Onset time: 1d6+4 minutes

Envenomed blades: a favourite of every assassin

Duration: 1d6+3 hours

Conditions: Unconsciousness. Victim falls into a deep sleep, and cannot be woken until the duration ends.

Antidote/Cure: Can be counteracted by the Healing skill, and use of a strong stimulant.

Encumbrance

Encumbrance represents both the mass and bulk of an item. The greater the encumbrance value the more difficult it is to carry it.

Correlating ENC with SIZ can be a challenge: light but bulky items often impose just as much of a burden as small but heavy ones. As a rule of thumb 3 ENC is equivalent to 1 SIZ, but, depending on the item, Games Masters may want to adjust the ratio down to 2:1 or even 1:1. A head-sized lump of lead, for instance, is far heavier than a similar sized lump of rock. Conversely a large sack loosely filled with goose-down might have a ratio of 5:1. As always, common sense should prevail in such circumstances.

Items that have a zero ENC value are, on their own, inconsequential; however consider that 20 zero ENC items equal 1 ENC.

Encumbrance Capacity

Characters can carry a total ENC equal to their STR x2 with relative ease. Everyday clothing does not contribute to this capacity, but armour does – see the notes on Armour ENC below.

If the total ENC borne exceeds STR x2 then the character is considered to be Burdened. This has the following effects:

- Skills using STR or DEX as part of their base (including combat skills) become one grade harder
- Base Movement Rate drops by 2 metres, and the character can no longer sprint
- Carrying the load counts as Medium activity for Fatigue purposes

If the borne ENC exceeds STR x3 then the character is considered to be Overloaded. The effects are thus:

- Skills using STR or DEX as part of their base (including combat skills) become two grades harder
- Base Movement Rate drops to half normal, and the character cannot move faster than a walk
- Carrying the load counts as Strenuous activity for Fatigue purposes

Characters cannot carry a total ENC more than their STR x4, either the mass or unwieldy bulk of the objects proving to be too much to bear for more than a short distance.

Armour ENC

When considering its encumbering nature, armour has a number of different effects: it not only hinders Initiative (see Armour Penalty), and slows gaits faster than a walk (see Moving in Armour page 70), but also burdens its bearer with its bulky weight.

Anathaym's Saga

Anathaym owns a partial suit of bronze Hoplite Plate. This comprises a crested helm, a cuirass and two bracers. The panoply covers five of her body locations, and has an Armour Penalty of -4 which counts both against her Initiative, and her running and sprinting speeds due to the hindrance the strapped pieces have on her body movement.

Additionally the armour has a total ENC of 20 simply due to the weight of the heavy bronze. If she carried the armour on her back, whilst also bearing her spear, shortsword and hoplite shield, Anathaym would have a total Encumbrance of 20+2+1+3=26 which is more than twice her STR of 11, rendering her Burdened.

However, if she wears her armour instead, the ENC of the panoply is halved, reducing her total Encumbrance to 10+2+1+3 =16, leaving her a little extra capacity to carry extra equipment, and not be hindered by her load.

The amount armour counts towards Encumbrance Capacity depends on whether it is worn or carried.

- When worn, only half the total ENC of the armour is counted towards Encumbrance
- When carried, the full ENC value of the armour is counted towards Encumbrance

Non Human Encumbrance

Whilst the encumbrance rules work fine for human scaled characters, they can begin to break down for creatures of larger or smaller dimensions. The best way to avoid scaling issues is to assume that arms and equipment for each species scale in proportion with their user's size. Thus a great axe used by a minotaur would be slightly larger than one used by a (human) royal guard, as would its armour.

To calculate the encumbrance of proportionally sized equipment, add together all the ENC values of everything carried by the creature, then multiply the final result by the ratio of the average SIZ of a member of that race divided by the average SIZ of a human.

Final Encumbrance = Total ENC x (Average SIZ of species/13)

Alternative Encumbrance Rules

Keeping detailed track of encumbrance adds considerable effort to maintaining character sheets, especially when items are picked up or looted, and as a consequence many groups simply hand-wave encumbrance as being an unnecessary hassle in general play. For those who still wish to keep a rough track of encumbrance but want something less maths intensive, consider the following alternative, which does not track items carried in strict terms of their ENC value.

- *All characters can carry a number of Items equal to half their STR without being encumbered. Over STR/2 and up to STR, they are considered Burdened. Over STR to STRx1.5 they are Overloaded.*
- *One Item is equivalent to anything that can be comfortably carried in one hand. Things that are two-handed or are strapped to an arm (a shield, say) count as two Items. Note that the SIZ of the creature will influence what is considered one or two items. For a giant, a greatsword could comfortably be counted as one item, whereas for human-sized creatures it would clearly be two.*
- *Worn armour of any kind does not contribute towards ENC. If carried, then it counts as its equivalent Armour Penalty value.*

Continuing with the minotaur example, we find its proportional size ratio is 1.7 (22/13). Thus a minotaur wearing full Hoplite panoply and wielding its great axe would have a total encumbrance of 27 (28 halved plus 2 for the great axe, and the total multiplied by 1.7) Still well within the unburdened limit of STRx2 which for an average minotaur is 34.

Although this sum may require a few seconds to work out, it simplifies the entire process to a single calculation, and avoids time consuming book keeping.

Falling

The amount of damage suffered in a fall depends on the distance of the drop. Armour points do not reduce falling damage.

Falling Distance Table

Distance Fallen	*Damage Taken*
1m or less	No damage.
2m to 5m	1d6 points of damage to a random location.
6m to 10m	2d6 points of damage to two random locations.
11m to 15m	3d6 points of damage to three random locations.
16m to 20m	4d6 points of damage to four random locations.
Each +5m	+1d6 damage.

- Damage is rolled separately for *each* location; it is not spread among them.
- Creatures of smaller size suffer less from a fall. Those of SIZ 8 to 9 treat the distance fallen as one metre less. A creature of SIZ 6 to 7 treats the distance fallen as three metres less. A creature of SIZ 4 to 5 treats the distance fallen as five metres less. A creature of SIZ 2 to 3 treats the distance fallen as eight metres less. A creature of SIZ 1 or less treats the distance fallen as ten metres less.
- Creatures of larger size suffer more from a fall. For every 10 points above SIZ 20 the creature adds +1d6 to the damage. Thus a SIZ 35 creature which drops from a height of 2m would take 3d6 damage to a random location.
- Acrobatics can be used to mitigate falling damage – a successful roll allows the character to treat the fall as if it were two metres shorter than it actually is. In addition, as long as the roll is successful and the character does not suffer a Serious or Major wound due to the fall, the character lands relatively safely and is not prone.
- Characters falling onto soft surfaces may treat the distance they fall as halved for the purposes of damage. This is always at the Games Master's discretion.
- Characters falling onto damaging surfaces (such as a pit of spikes) will suffer the effects of the surface to all locations that are damaged in the fall.

Falling Objects

A falling object imparts an amount of damage based on its SIZ and the distance of the fall. An object imparts 1d6 damage for every 6 points of SIZ (or fraction thereof), plus an amount of damage equal to the Damage Taken column of the Falling Distance - including any reductions for objects of smaller size.

Falling from a Moving Vehicle

Damage sustained from a fall from a moving vehicle, such as a chariot, depends on the vehicle's speed and the distance fallen. Assume that the speed, in metres per Combat Round, is equal to half the height shown on the Falling Distance table. A chariot moving at 20m per Combat Round would inflict 2d6 damage to two random locations if a character should fall from it.

Fatigue

Fatigue measures tiredness and its incremental effects. It is an important aspect in Mythras as it is used to track many different things from strenuous activity to the debilitating effects of disease or magic.

Physical Effort

The primary way of accruing Fatigue is by engaging in some form of physical activity. The more arduous the exercise or work, the more quickly it tires the character. There are three classes of effort: Light, Medium and Strenuous. The length of time a character can engage in an activity without becoming fatigued is determined by his CON, as detailed under each category. Once this time has elapsed characters must make an appropriate skill roll – either Athletics, Brawn or Endurance – to resist gaining a level of Fatigue.

Unless the recipient of some form of magic that naturally extends wakefulness, all characters need sleep. A character can remain awake for a number of hours equal to twice CON before needing to make an Endurance roll. If successful, the character can continue to function normally for a number of hours equal to half CON before needing to make a further Endurance roll, although this roll will be one grade harder than the last. Each failed roll accrues one level of fatigue.

Effects of Fatigue

Every failed roll accrues a level of Fatigue. Each level of Fatigue carries penalties for skill use, movement, Initiative and Action Points. Asphyxiation, Blood Loss, and some types of magic also contribute to Fatigue accrual.

For most characters, activities of any kind become near impossible when the level of Incapacitated is reached. At this stage the character is still conscious but incapable of anything but the most desperate of activities.

Beyond Incapacitated, characters cannot act at all. The Fatigue levels – Semi-Conscious, Comatose and Dead – are generally reserved for measuring the most extreme effects of suffocation, disease, blood loss, starvation, exposure, and so forth.

It is perfectly possible to accrue Fatigue from several sources, potentially making some situations more dangerous.

For example, a thief climbs the flanks of an extinct volcano to reach a long-forgotten temple, in which fantastically precious jewels are reputed to be hidden. By the time he crests the crater rim his Fatigue level has reached Tired. Spurred on by sighting the ruins upon an island at the centre of the flooded

Fatigue Levels

	Skill Grade	*Movement*	*Initiative*	*Action Points*	*Recovery Period*
Fresh			No Penalties		
Winded	Hard	No Penalty	No Penalty	No Penalty	15 minutes
Tired	Hard	-1 metre	No Penalty	No Penalty	3 hours
Wearied	Formidable	-2 metres	-2	No Penalty	6 hours
Exhausted	Formidable	Halved	-4	-1	12 hours
Debilitated	Herculean	Halved	-6	-2	18 hours
Incapacitated	Herculean	Immobile	-8	-3	24 hours
Semi-Conscious	Hopeless	No Activities Possible	No Activities Possible	No Activities Possible	36 hours
Comatose	No Activities Possible	No Activities Possible	No Activities Possible	No Activities Possible	48 hours
Dead	Dead				Never

Physical Effort Table

Effort	*How Long?*	*Example*	*Skill Roll*
Light	CON in hours	Activity that places no strain on the body. All reasonable activities at a steady pace.	Very Easy grade roll vs either Athletics, Brawn or Endurance according to the task (Athletics for exercise; Brawn for heavy lifting; Endurance for general activities).
Medium	CON in minutes	Manual labour; sustained physical exercise.	As above, but at Easy grade.
Strenuous	CON in seconds (rounded up to the next Combat Round)	Combat; struggling against the elements; physical activity in extremely adverse circumstances.	Standard grade roll vs either Athletics, Brawn or Endurance according to the task (Athletics for exercise; Brawn for heavy lifting; Endurance for Combat).

caldera, the thief foolishly undertakes the swim before resting; in the process losing several more levels of Fatigue from failed Swim rolls. When the scaly guardian of the sacred temple pulls him under the surface, the fatigue accrual from drowning starts from his current level of Exhausted, and he swiftly dies, lacking the energy to put up much of a fight.

Recovering from Fatigue

Characters recover from Fatigue depending on their Healing Rate. The amount of complete rest needed to recover from each level of accrued Fatigue is equal to the Recovery Period divided by the character's Healing Rate.

Note that the table represents fatigue recovery for physical exertion. Fatigue recovery can be much faster when recovering from asphyxiation or slower if recuperating from blood loss.

Managing Fatigue

Managing Fatigue, and its effects makes for additional book-keeping. To simplify things, Games Masters can decide that only certain types of activity contribute towards Fatigue. But common sense should apply. A character dressed in full plate armour, in a tropical jungle, on a hot summer's day, could not spend three hours hacking his way through the foliage without suffering fatigue in some way. Similarly carrying heavy loads, trekking uphill, foot chases, long swims or digging out an ancient necropolis are all going to take their toll on a character, potentially tiring him at a crucial moment.

Fires

Fires are always a source of danger when used as a weapon or rage out of control. They damage both people and objects; how much is dependent on the intensity of the source. The Fire Intensity table below gives five different intensities for heat damage, with some examples.

The damage inflicted per round is given in the Damage column. Being relatively small, Intensity 1 and 2 sources apply their damage to a single Hit Location, usually that touching the source. Intensity 3 and 4 sources are larger, applying damage to nearest 1d4+1 Hit Locations, indicating the degree of radiant heat. Intensity 5 sources affect all Hit Locations simultaneously.

Fire clearly has the ability to ignite flammable materials. If not extinguished immediately such materials combust within a number of rounds as indicated by the fire's Intensity. Once ignited, flammable materials burn until physically extinguished. Damage is applied directly to the Hit Points of the material, ignoring Armour Points and to any flesh beneath. If left uncontrolled it spreads to a number of Hit Locations, per round, equal to its Intensity.

Fire Intensity Table

Intensity	*Examples*	*Time to Ignite*	*Damage*
1	Candle	1d4	1d2
2	Torch	1d3	1d4
3	Campfire	1d2	1d6
4	Room filling conflagration	1d2	2d6
5	Volcanic lava	Instant	3d6

Healing from Injury

Natural healing from wounds and injuries is based on the character's Healing Rate. The Healing Rate dictates how many Hit Points are recovered in a location depending on the injury's nature:

- Minor Wounds: Days
- Serious Wounds: Weeks
- Major Wounds: Months

Thus a character with a Healing Rate of 3 who suffers damage taking him to −3 in a Hit Location, a Serious Wound, will heal naturally at a rate of 3 Hit Points per week until his wound goes above zero, and then heal 3 Hit Points per day until fully recovered.

There are certain restrictions on natural healing:

- The healing character cannot engage in strenuous activity: otherwise the Healing Rate is reduced by 1d3. Thus, a character recovering from even a Minor Wound could find his progress halted if he decides to engage any physical tasks that might exacerbate his injuries.
- Natural healing will not begin to heal a Major Wound until that location has been treated with a successful Healing roll (see page 46). Non-dismembering Major Wounds which are not treated within a number of days equal to one twentieth of the Healing skill become maimed, permanently reducing the Hit Points of the location.

Guidance on how to stage combat to take into account these lengthy healing times is provided in the Games Mastery chapter (see Pacing Combat Encounters page 285).

Magical Healing

Some magic can heal the wounds suffered by a victim. Yet there are specific restrictions as to what level of wound can be treated by each spell. For example the Common Magic spell Heal cures only Minor Wounds, whereas the Sorcery spell of Regeneration can heal both Minor and Serious Wounds. There are few magics which can reverse the traumatic injuries of a Major Wound.

No matter how petty the healing spell or miracle, its application is always enough to stabilise any type of wound, preventing bleeding and immediate death even if it doesn't actually cure the underlying injury. Note that this only applies to gross physical trauma, not to conditions brought about by suffocation, poison, and the like.

Permanent Injuries

Some Major Wounds, and certain poisons or diseases inflict maiming injuries; for example horribly crushed and severed limbs, or the necrotic effects of venoms. The result of this damage permanently reduces the Hit Points on that location, forever weakening it. A location maimed in this way uses the diminished Hit Point value to calculate its new Serious and Major Wound thresholds.

For permanent injuries caused by accident or battle, roll 1d3 and consult the following table to see the extent of the maiming:

In those cases where the maiming involved the loss of a limb, reduce the d20 numbers for that Hit Location by an appropriate amount. For example the Right Arm of a humanoid is normally struck on a roll of 13-15 on a d20. If however the arm was severed at the elbow then locations 13-14 no longer exist, and being struck there means the attack actually misses! Characters vindictive enough to target such a maimed limb using Choose Location must roll a 1d3 to see if they actually hit the remaining parts.

Permanent Injury Table

1d3	*Hit Point Reduction*	*Maiming Result*
1	Character permanently loses one third of the Hit Points in that location	If a limb, this represents the maiming of a hand or foot. If the head, the character loses one of his sensory organs, eye, ear, nose or tongue Anywhere else it denotes a disfiguring scar.
2	Character permanently loses two thirds of the Hit Points in that location	A limb is maimed from the elbow or knee down. The head loses two sensory organs. Torso exhibits a gruesomely horrible scar.
3	Location is reduced to a single Hit Point	Limbs are maimed from the shoulder or hip down. The head either loses three sensory organs, half the face or the entire jaw. Chest or abdomen shows such a horrific scar or deformation nobody seeing the healed wound can comprehend how the victim survived.

Anathaym's Saga

After months of practice Anathaym finally succeeds in defeating Xenos in the practice circle, humiliating the proud noble by tripping him, and forcing his surrender at spear point in front of his friends. She spends that evening foolishly drinking wine in celebration. When she eventually leaves the tavern, the warrioress is too drunk to notice the sinister cloaked figures who follow, and drag her into a dark alleyway.

Whilst two of her assaulters pin her down, the third draws a club which he smashes down onto her spear hand, twice, pulping every bone in the appendage. Then, the men pick her up, laughing cruelly, and Anathaym recognises the supercilious voice of her rival as she passes out. When she finally awakens she discovers herself abandoned in the dry hills many leagues from Meeros.

Suffering from the pain and delirium of the Major Wound, it takes four days to stumble back to Meeros, but she finally reaches the city's modest Shrine of Healing, located in the poor quarter. The serving acolyte explains that the wound is beyond her powers to heal magically, and too much time has already passed to avoid it being maimed. However, she successfully performs her Healing roll, ensuring that the hand does not become infected and can start to recover, albeit with slightly twisted fingers and frozen knuckles.

Anathaym has little choice but to heal naturally. With her right arm at -6 it would normally take a month at her Healing Rate of 3 to recover to the point at which the Major Wound is reduced to just a Serious one. The maiming injury however, has permanently reduced her limb by two Hit Points. This new level means the Serious Wound threshold of that arm is now -1 Hit Point, so it takes two months to recover – at which point another visit to the acolyte magically cures the remaining damage.

Her right hand crippled to the point of near uselessness, Anathaym is driven by her hatred for Xenos, and begins to learn how to use her spear left handed...

Inanimate Objects

All inanimate objects possess Armour Points and Hit Points which are used to determine resistance to damage and destruction. Armour Points reduce damage before Hit Points are affected. Once an object's Hit Points have been reduced to zero, it is useless.

Usually inanimate objects offer no resistance to damage, save for their Armour Points. However in the case of items that can restrict or offer a significant resistance to breakage attempts (such as a barred door, or ropes used to restrain hands and feet), the character must succeed with either a Brawn, Unarmed or weapon attack roll, as appropriate, to inflict damage. A successful roll deals damage to the item as per the weapon type; a failed roll has simply failed to apply enough force or damage to the item to deteriorate its condition. Refer to the description of the Brawn skill to determine what damage it inflicts.

The Inanimate Objects table gives some example objects, along with their Armour Points and Hit Points.

Using Weapons Against Inanimate Objects

Using a weapon against an inanimate object with Armour Points equal to or greater than those of the weapon deals damage to both the object and the weapon. For instance, using an axe on an anvil may damage the anvil, but the axe itself will be destroyed long before the anvil is. The Games Master should exercise discretion on which weapons or tools can affect which objects. A chisel, for example, is explicitly designed to carve wood or stone whilst a sword, although sharp, is not. The chisel would therefore not take damage from something it is attempting to carve whereas a sword most likely would.

Inanimate Objects Armour and Hit Points

Object	Armour Points	Hit Points
Boulder	10	40
Castle gate	8	120
Castle wall (2m section)	10	250
Chain/shackle	8	8
Club	4	4
Dagger	6	4
Hut wall (2m section)	3	15
Iron door	12	75
Rope	6	3
War sword	6	10
Wooden chair	2	6
Wooden door (normal)	4	25
Wooden door (reinforced)	6	30
Wooden fence (2m section)	4	5

Luck Points

Luck Points help differentiate heroes from the rank and file. They represent a character's ability to potentially turn failure into success, and even cheat death,

Every character starts with a number of Luck Points as described in the Attributes section of the Basic Character Creation chapter. Luck Points can be used during play and, at the beginning of the next session, replenish to their usual value.

For example, Emma and her friends meet every Friday for their weekly Mythras game. One Friday night Emma, playing Anathaym, is given cause to use all her character's Luck Points for a variety of reasons. Out of Luck Points, Anathaym manages to survive with no catastrophic consequences till the end of the game session. However, when the players reconvene on the following Friday, Anathaym's Luck Points will have replenished back to their normal value.

Luck Points only increase if the POW characteristic increases, or some form of magic provides a temporary increase in some fashion.

Using Luck Points

Luck points can be used in a variety of ways. Only one Luck Point can be used in support of a particular action. Each of the following options costs a single Luck Point.

Cheat Fate

Characters can use a Luck Point to re-roll any dice roll they make or swap the numbers already rolled, when rolling a d100 for example. This can be a skill roll, damage roll or anything else that has some effect.

Characters can even force an opponent to re-roll an attack or damage roll made against them.

Desperate Effort

If a character has exhausted his Action Points during a fight and needs to find that last burst of desperate energy to perhaps avoid a messy demise, he may spend a Luck Point to gain an additional Action Point.

Mitigate Damage

A character who suffers a Major Wound may spend a Luck Point to downgrade the injury to a Serious Wound. This reduces the damage taken to one Hit Point less than what would be required to inflict a Major Wound.

Group Luck Points

The Personal Connections boxed text on page 22 describes how, when characters form personal connections during character creation, the group as a whole gains a pool of Luck Points distinct from those available personally. This pool of Group Luck Points is available to all members of the team to use in precisely the same way as personal Luck Points but only when the character wanting to draw upon the pool needs to do so to aid one of his fellows.

The Games Master should keep track of the Group Luck Points pool (or the players can do this, nominating one of their number to keep track). Group Luck Points refresh in the same way as personal Luck Points: that is, the pool is fully restored at the beginning of the next game session. However if Games Masters feel that the Group Luck Points pool is offering too much of an advantage, or even being abused, it can be made to replenish at an appropriate point in the story – at the end of an adventure for example, or after a reasonable period of down-time.

PASSIONS

Introduced during the character creation chapters, a Passion is any deeply held commitment that has the capacity to influence events during play. Although they can be used as stand-alone abilities (to call them skills is to do them a disservice), passions are further expanded below to explain in more detail how they work, and how they can influence MYTHRAS characters and campaigns.

In summary, Passions can be used thus:

- To augment another skill, reflecting the depth of one's feeling and how it drives action.

  When used in this regard the Passion adds one fifth of its value to a skill being used, as long as the augmentation is thematically and dramatically important.
- As an ability in its own right to drive choices, desires, and emotional actions and responses.

  When used in this way a standard roll is made against a Passion to determine how strongly the character thinks and feels about something. If a roll is a success then the character acts in-line with what the Passion would dictate. If the roll fails then the character can act freely without feeling constrained by the Passion's drives.
- To oppose other Passions – even those held by the same character. This is typically used where two Passions would conflict. For instance a personal love might dictate a course of action that would be contrary to an oath or loyalty. Here use an opposed roll between the two Passions with the more successful determining how the character acts.
- As a general measure of depth of commitment, belief, and loyalty to a cause. The higher the Passion's value, the more committed the character is. Characters with similar Passions can compare and contrast their ratings to determine who exhibits the deeper commitment.
- To resist some form of psychological manipulation or magical domination. In certain cases where a character is being forced into performing an act contrary to his Passions, he may use substitute his Passion for the usual Willpower in the opposed roll.

During character creation characters establish up to three starting Passions; however new Passions can be developed at any point during a MYTHRAS game session if the circumstances warrant it. One might instantly develop 'Hate X' where someone else does something that would strongly invoke hatred to arise. A lord or chief calling for an oath would immediately establish a Passion of 'Loyalty to X' as soon as that oath is taken or sworn – something explored further in the Cults and Brotherhoods chapter.

Passions developed during play in this way cost no Experience Rolls, and are established there and then. Of course, characters can also choose to establish a Passion during improvement, at the cost of an Experience roll to gain a Passion at its base value: see the chart on page 23 of the Culture and Community chapter.

DEEPENING AND WANING

Passions can increase during a game independently of Experience Rolls, based on the strength of whatever occurred to trigger the increase. Also Passions can, and do, wane. A strongly held belief can be shaken by many things leading to that Passion being either reduced or, in more extreme circumstances, reversed completely.

For instance, a character with 'Trust Chieftain' might, if his chieftain acts treacherously, either reduce his Passion or turn into 'Distrust Chieftain' at the same percentage. The Games Master needs to determine if a Passion reduces or reverses. If it reduces then it does so according to the strength of the source of the change.

The Deepening and Waning table shows by how much the Passion changes.

DEEPENING AND WANING

Change	+/-
Weak	1d10
Moderate	1d10+5
Strong	1d10+10

Further advice for Games Masters on using Passions to drive a scenario or campaign is provided in the Games Mastery Chapter.

SURVIVAL

Characters may find themselves in hostile environments: deserts, arctic landscapes, mountains, rain-lashed moorlands, and so on. In such environments characters may find themselves battling the elements, and the three big killers: exposure, starvation, and thirst.

Each danger has a specific onset time before a critical point is reached, after which debilitation occurs at a steady rate:

- Exposure occurs when the body is insufficiently protected against a hostile environment. Assuming suitable clothing it usually starts to take effect after CON hours. The subsequent Exposure Rate can range from daily to mere minutes depending on the weather conditions. See Temperature, page 84.
- Starvation takes place after an extended period without food. Critical levels of starvation begin after a number of days equal to half CON. After this the Starvation Rate is daily.
- Dehydration begins after CON x4 hours; although in arid or hot environments this might be CON x3 or even CON x2. The ensuing Dehydration Rate depends on the ambient aridity or humidity of the environment. See Precipitation page 84.

Once any of the above conditions take hold characters start to accrue Fatigue levels. An Endurance roll is required at onset, which is then repeated every time the Exposure, Starvation or Dehydration Rate cycles. If the roll is failed then a level of Fatigued is accrued.

Care should be taken to apply any skill penalties suffered for the current level of Fatigue. Eventually their increasing debilitation steadily wears down the character's capabilities until Incapacitation is reached. Thereafter, without help death will swiftly follow.

TRAPS

Traps are ubiquitous devices used by every culture from the digging of pitfalls to capture animals to death-traps guarding tombs for all eternity. These devices are built for a range of purposes, each specifically tailored to raising an alarm, capturing interlopers, or maiming and killing thieves outright.

Constructing traps requires that the builder knows either the Mechanisms or Engineering skill. Small traps such as bear traps or trapped locks require Mechanisms, whereas large scale constructions like spiked pits or rolling boulders need Engineering.

Beyond hiring the constructing craftsman, traps often have very expensive component or manual labour costs. As a general guideline alarms cost the skill of the creator in copper pieces, ensnaring traps the same in silver, and death-traps require payment in gold.

All traps have a Difficulty rating which represents how difficult it is to perceive, disarm or avoid. This value is treated as its skill when resisted in an opposed roll.

Despite the many entertaining tales told by storytellers, traps – especially those intended to kill – rarely have a method of cleverly avoiding or reversing their effects once set in motion. Without magic or good fortune, those caught in a death-trap usually succumb to its highly efficient purpose. In short, they are not intended to be survivable. Unless the trap has some cunning design or is some sort of enduring magical enchantment, once it has been sprung it must be manually reset.

Trap Traits

Traps are described using the following traits.

Purpose

The purpose of the trap.

- Alarm – Trap sends a silent or audible signal that it has been triggered.
- Ensnaring – Trap is designed to capture anyone who triggers or enters it.
- Maiming – Trap is intended to critically injure whoever triggers it.
- Death – Trap is intended to kill those who activate its lethal devices.

Trigger

The way the trap is set off.

Difficulty

The challenge rating of the trap, which is equal to the value of the Mechanisms or Engineering skill which created it. For instance a scything blade trap built into the base of a treasure chest by a craftsman with Mechanisms 70% grants the trap a Difficulty of 70%. The trap would thereafter use this value in opposed rolls to see if the blade can be spotted, evaded or disarmed.

Resistance

How the trap is resisted – typically using Brawn, Evade or parrying with a Combat Style which uses a shield. Resistance is rolled when the trap is triggered.

Effect

What happens when the trap is sprung, and the victim(s) fail to resist. Usually this results in the alerting of antagonists if an alarm or the capture of victims if designed to ensnare. Maiming and death-traps obviously injure the victim, although some death-traps utilise other means than direct damage to inflict harm, such as drowning or poison. To restrict overly deadly traps, the damage inflicted by these devices is limited by the skill of its creator. Force is noted for those traps which fire projectiles which can be parried.

Building Traps

Use the Task rules (page 66 onwards) as the basis for building traps, with the task round measured in hourly increments depending on the sophistication of the device. If Enhancements are achieved, boost the trap's Difficulty by +5% for each Enhancement gained.

Death Trap Damage Limits

Maker's Skill	Damage	Size/Force
1-10%	1d2	Small
11-20%	1d4	Small
21-30%	1d6	Medium
31-40%	1d8	Medium
41-50%	1d10	Large
51-60%	2d6	Large
61-70%	1d8+1d6	Huge
71-80%	2d8	Huge
81-90%	1d10+1d8	Enormous
91-100%	2d10	Enormous

Sample Traps

These are example traps which Games Masters can use as templates to create their own devious devices.

Crushing Roof

This trap often takes the form of a small room or short length of corridor. The trap has a lure of some sort, usually something of an artistic or valuable nature which attracts the victim to enter. Most crushing roof traps are dead ends with only one entry, perhaps with a false door on the other side; although rarely they are utilised as additional security to prevent illicit access to a real doorway.

When triggered the entry portal slams closed with a metal portcullis which locks into place. The roof then gradually lowers, its support pillars sinking into the floor as their supporting sand flows away; or if the ceiling is suspended from some sort of ratchet device, the chains play out.

Due to the difficulty of carving entire roofs from a single piece of rock, most ceilings are actually made of plastered wood, weighted on top with large rocks to provide extra mass. Unless the creator deliberately incorporated a secret trapdoor in the ceiling to provide an emergency escape route, victims typically suffer a long, slow demise as the weight of the roof crushes them to death.

Purpose: Death

Trigger: Moving the lure object

Difficulty: 80%

Resistance: Evade to dive clear of the room before the entry slams shut. If several characters are trapped within the chamber, they may attempt to support the roof with Brawn whilst a companion attempts to open the door or find something with which to wedge or support the roof. In this circumstance add the SIZ and STR of every resisting character to calculate their combined Damage Modifier, and use this value with the highest Brawn skill of the party against the trap's Damage Modifier of 2d8.

Effect: Once the ceiling lowers far enough, victims become pinned to the floor, and receive 2d8 damage per round to a random Hit Location (armour does not protect), eventually crushing every bone in their body.

Pitfall

A pitfall is an archetypal trap used by every culture. It can take the form a simple dug pit, covered by branches and leaves or reach the sophistication of stone walled sumps beneath hinged false floors which are counterbalanced to swing back up into place after a victim drops in.

Pitfalls need not be particularly deep. If designed for capture, a simple amphora or lobster pot shape will prevent escape by climbing, as will walls which are chiselled smooth or made from crumbling material which gives way under a character's weight.

Pits which are instead intended to kill usually line the floor with dozens of stakes, closely packed so that a falling character will inevitably become impaled. Other options could include filling the bottom with a weak acid, water deep enough to drown in, or starving rats.

Purpose: Ensnaring or Death
Trigger: Walking across the false surface covering the pit
Difficulty: 60%
Resistance: Either Evade to jump clear or a Hard Athletics roll to catch the edge as they drop.
Effect: The drop into the pit inflicts 2d6 damage to a random Hit Location, armour does not protect. Secondary effects are left to the Games Master's imagination.

Spear Trap

Spear traps are complex devices requiring hidden niches or a separate chamber in which their mechanical launchers must be set. Their primary mode of operating is to drive a spear through a wall or floor, powered by a counterweighted lever or compressed spring.

The manner of their placement can be quite inventive. Instead of the traditional spear hidden behind plaster or bas-reliefs, some versions have the spear in plain sight, held in the raised hand of an innocuous looking statue for instance, whose arm might pivot down to stab a victim from above.

Purpose: Maiming
Trigger: Stepping on a pressure plate or moving an object
Difficulty: 75%
Resistance: Either Evade to dive aside or a Hard parry roll if wielding a shield.
Effect: The spear inflicts 2d8 damage to a random Hit Location, but can be (partially) parried by a shield if its size is sufficient to counteract the spear's size of Huge. If the trap gains one or more levels of success over the victim it can apply Special Effects, such as Impale.

Visibility

The table opposite gives rough distances in metres for the visibility of man-sized objects, according to the ambient weather and quality of light. Whilst intended to represent human sight other species may have more acute vision; the eyesight of an Iqari for instance (see page 252) might triple these distances.

The SIZ of what someone is trying to observe also affects its visibility, as will other factors such as obscuring undergrowth, background terrain, and possible camouflage. Assume targets with SIZ 10 or below halve the range at which they can be spotted, and that larger objects increase the range by one multiple for every 10 points of SIZ over 20. So a SIZ 22 minotaur can be seen at double the distance, whereas a SIZ 37 cyclops could be spotted at triple the distance.

The same values can also be used for the primary senses of other creatures, such as an acute sense of smell or hearing. However in these cases it an alternate modifier should be applied rather than SIZ.

Visibility Table

Conditions	*Daylight*	*Twilight*	*Moonlight*	*Moonless Night*
Clear	500	300	50	25
Overcast	400	250	50	25
Moderate Fog	150	100	25	15
Dense Fog	50	30	15	10
Wind-driven snow	35	25	10	5
Sand/dust storm	20	15	10	5

Weather

Weather conditions can have a significant effect on the local environment. The main aspects of weather are precipitation, temperature, and wind. These are detailed for the purposes of modelling weather magic, reduction of character skills, and calculating the effects of weather on Survival. No tables are provided to generate random weather conditions, which are very much setting dependent.

Precipitation

Precipitation relates to the amount of moisture which falls out of the sky. Depending on the temperature it can range between rain, sleet and snow, with hail falling during storms. The base chance of it raining is equal to the relative humidity. The amount of rain per hour and duration of the fall can be calculated by looking up the relevant entry on the Precipitation table.

Normally precipitation has little effect on characters save to slow down travel if excessive rain causes flooding, or snow begins to drift, obscuring or blocking paths. Rain also makes characters wet, which may increase their chance of suffering exposure if the ambient conditions are windy or cold.

Temperature

Temperate can vary dramatically due to climate, season, and elevation, depending on the campaign world and where scenarios are set. The following table provides a guideline for the effects of extreme temperature on characters.

Wearing suitable local clothing permits a character a grace period of their CON in hours before exposure sets in. After this point they need to seek shelter or start to suffer Fatigue loss (see Survival page 49). Wet characters shift the Exposure Rate one step cooler. Light or moderate gale force winds also shift Exposure Rate by one step cooler, whilst strong gales and storms shift it two steps.

Wind Table

Wind STR	*Sample*	*Skill Grade*	*Movement Rate*
0-15	Calm Day/Light Breeze	Standard	Normal
16-30	Moderate Breeze	Standard	Normal
31-45	Strong Breeze	Standard	Two Thirds
46-60	Light Gale	Hard	Two Thirds
61-75	Moderate Gale	Hard	Half
76-90	Strong Gale	Formidable	Half
91+	Storm/Hurricane	Formidable	One Third

Temperature Table

Temp oC	*Climate*	*Risk of Exposure*	*Exposure Rate*
Below -20	Glacial	Yes	Minutes
-19 – -10	Freezing	Yes	15 Minutes
-9 – 0	Cold	Yes	Hourly
1– 10	Chill	Yes	Daily
11 – 20	Cool	No	None
21 – 30	Warm	No	None
31 – 40	Hot	Yes	Hourly

Precipitation Table

Relative Humidity	*Typical Cloud Cover*	*Amount per Hour*	*Duration*	*Dehydration Rate*
0-12	None	None	None	Hourly
13-25	Scant cloud	Very light (0-1mm)	1d10 minutes	2 Hours
26-37	Scattered cloud	Light (1-2.5mm)	1d6 x10 minutes	3 Hours
38-50	Heavy cloud	Moderate (2.5-10mm)	1d2 hours	4 Hours
51-62	Slightly Overcast	Heavy (11-25mm)	1d3 hours	4 Hours
63-75	Moderately Overcast	Very Heavy (26-50mm)	1d6 hours	3 Hours
76-87	Completely Overcast	Monsoon (51-80mm)	1d8 hours	2 Hours
88-100	Storm Clouds	Deluge (81+mm)	1d12 hours	Hourly

Wind

Wind, especially very strong winds, can have an adverse effect on activity. A wind's Strength (STR) is expressed in kilometres per hour of velocity. Its effect on physical skills – those involving STR or DEX – is detailed in the Skill Grade column; effects on Movement Rate in the Movement Rate column (for example, a Light Gale of STR 50 reduces human walking speed to two thirds or 4 metres; whilst a STR 95 Storm reduces it to 2 metres).

Combat

Combat is an important feature of Mythras. Violent confrontation has ever been a way of settling problems, from vengeance driven fights between nemeses, to the clash of armies in times of war. Combat need not be a savage battle to the death. Some combat encounters can be swashbuckling duels which end without injury, or perhaps light-hearted bar room brawls.

There are a number of central concepts which are an inherent part of Mythras combat:

- Combat can be a very deadly business: Even the greatest hero can be hacked down if seriously outnumbered, receive grievous wounds if abjuring armour, or suffer 'the slings and arrows of outrageous fortune' if luck turns her back.
- Combat need not end in death: Although commonplace in some genres, battles do not have to conclude with the demise of opponents. It is as easy to end a fight with the submission or capture of a foe without necessarily killing them.
- Combat is both abstract and tactical: Whilst the rules are not specifically designed for tabletop miniatures, tactical manoeuvres and techniques are a vital part of how combat plays. A comprehensive range of options exist to take advantage of the situation if one participant gains the upper hand over another.
- Combat is exciting: Since combat is inherently dangerous, a well orchestrated duel or melee will exhilarate players; the advantage swinging to and fro with innovative use of tactical choices and techniques.

Mythras combat can be either gritty or cinematic: The rules allow for the emulation of any genre, from the grim realism as recounted from Viking Sagas to the highly visceral encounters in works of fantasy – such as written by Howard, Leiber or Gemmell – and mythological epics like the Iliad or Mahabharata. Whatever the setting, Mythras is designed to handle all such confrontations.

Whatever the intent of participants, their armaments or the situation they find themselves in, all forms of physical combat are handled using these rules in this chapter.

Combat Components

Mythras uses a number of terms and concepts to explain the core elements of Combat. These are explained in the following sections, but in overview, these are:

Combat Styles
The skill of wielding a group of weapons learned as part of a culture or profession.

Combat Rounds
Book keeping time segments of five seconds each.

Combat Actions
Possible acts a character can perform during a round by the expenditure of an Action Point.

Weapon Size and Reach
How difficult it is to parry a particular weapon, and the distance it can engage at.

Engagement
Combatants can hit or be hit by a direct opponent, depending on circumstances.

Special Effects
Special combat manoeuvres which can be performed if one combatant gains the upper hand.

Combat Styles

Fighting skills are purchased as styles. Each style is a 'package' of multiple weapons, related by culture, career or even schools of combat, which avoids the necessity of learning each individual weapon separately. Deciding how many weapons should be included into a single style is ultimately a choice determined by the Games Master. However, some guidance is provided here to help tailor Combat Styles to match a particular campaign theme.

Sample Combat Styles

Some basic Combat Style samples cna be found on page 12. Some additional suggestions, found elsewhere in these rules, are:

Meerish Infantry (Spear, Hoplite Shield, Javelin)
Meerish Slinger (Sling, Shortsword, Shield)
Centaur Warrior (Spear, Shield, Short Bow)
Dwarven Legionary (Axe, Hammer, Shield, Crossbow)
Elven Ranger (Sword, Spear, Shield, Bow)
Lizardman Savage (Axe, Shortspear, Target Shield)
Big Hitty Things - Ogres (Club, Hammer, Thrown Rock)
Striped Death - Tiger (Teeth, and Claws)
Crushing Doom - Giant Snake (Constrict, Bite, and Writhe)

The most important aspect of Combat Styles is that the character learns how to use each weapon in the style, both singly and in combination, so that they might be interchanged as necessary. Combat training does not focus merely on using a specific weapon or weapons under best conditions, but also covers what to do when placed at a severe disadvantage. Such cross-training is a primary part of preparing a combatant for the unpredictable events of the battlefield, where weapon breakage or becoming disarmed is always a potential possibility.

Almost all characters begin with the chance to learn a cultural combat style. This is supposed to reflect a basic education in those weapons available for a member of that society and social rank, reflecting the training given for community (or perhaps personal) defence. Thus a barbarian karl may be expected to know how to use a spear, hand axe, and bow – the fundamental weapons and tools of a commoner; whereas a thane from the same community, growing up with access to better weapons, may be trained in swords, spears, and shields instead.

Some careers such as hunter or warrior offer the option to learn further styles. These should reflect more unusual weapons, or weapons normally restricted from someone not of their profession. So continuing the previous example, if the karl decided to become a mercenary he might learn a new style, diversifying his competence to include glaives, great axes, and thrown axes.

Anathaym's Saga

As part of her cultural background, and civic duties, Anathaym learned the Meerish Slinger style, combining the art of slinging with the close combat skill in shortsword, and peltast shield. During the hot summers of her adolescence she trained as part of a skirmishing unit learning how to sling stones at targets, whilst sometimes wielding a shield in her off-hand.

At the same time she was also taught how to use a shortsword, again both with, and without a shield, to prepare her for close combat if ever her unit was ever engaged in melee during a battle. She even knows how to fight with just a shield if she ever loses her shortsword in a fight. This adaptability holds her in good stead, since provided she is using at least one of her cultural weapons, she'll never suffer a situational penalty due to her comprehensive preparation.

Games Masters should avoid, if possible, replicating the same weapon within additional Combat Styles. If unavoidable, common sense should be applied, such as limiting the character to use the relevant Combat Style skill if the weapon is used in combination with a second weapon available only to that specific style, or permitting them to use the style with the highest value when wielding that particular weapon singly. Duplication of weapons simply reflects superfluous, repetitive training.

Choosing how many weapons should be part of a Combat Style depends ultimately on how important combat will be within a campaign. Some suggestions are:

- Combat Styles are very exclusive: Each style pertains to one particular two-handed weapon or a specific paired weapon combination. Best used for combat heavy campaigns such as a game focused on gladiators, where each gladiatorial type has its own precise weapon combination (net and trident for example). Exclusive styles necessitate a greater investment of skill points during character generation, and subsequent investment of Experience Rolls to achieve diversification, which may slow down the development rate of combative characters.
- Combat Styles are cult or school specific: Each style specialises in a few weapons of noted significance to a particular cult or school of combat. An evil brotherhood of assassins may, for example, train in unusual signature weapons like blowpipes and garrottes. Schools of combat might reflect the battlefield armaments of a mercenary company, or an ascetic martial arts school. The suggested number of weapons should range from two to three per style.
- Combat Styles are career specific: Each style is limited to the core weapons used by a professional combatant of that career, for example a legionary soldier should demonstrate competence in

shortsword, dagger, scutum, and javelin. The number and type of weapons should roughly match those of a similar historical context, between three or four per style.

- Combat Styles are weapon class based: Each style incorporates every weapon of a particular design or damage type. An example may be 'All Swords', incorporating everything from shortswords to greatswords; or 'Bludgeoning Weapons' covering clubs, hammers, maces, and anything else which relies on bashing to inflict damage. As can be surmised, these categories can potentially include dozens of weapons.
- Combat Styles are all-encompassing: These styles are inclusive of any, and all melee weapons, ranged weapons or both. This option is only recommended for campaigns where combat is infrequent, secondary to other forms of interaction.

It should be obvious that not all Combat Styles will be equal, or necessarily need to balance with one another. Such considerations are intended to be based on culture, social class and career – not be limited by game mechanics.

Weapon Choices

When deciding on which particular weapons are included within a Combat Style the following should be considered:

- Two handed weapons generally have an advantage in both terms of weapon reach (see page 61), and how much damage they inflict, but leave the wielder vulnerable if the weapon is lost.
- Shields are the best defensive weapons, able to block fairly large weapons in addition to protecting against ranged attacks - which other weapons cannot normally parry.
- Using two offensive weapons simultaneously offers the wielder a greater range of engagement distances and grants some security if one weapon is broken, dropped or disarmed during combat. Secondary off-hand weapons must be at least one size category smaller than the main weapon, unless both are small.
- Ranged weapons grant the ability to strike from beyond the immediate reach of an enemy, typically at the cost of a lower rate of attack unless using anachronistic firearms or sorcerous devices. A Combat Style could potentially include unusual weapons such as siege engines.
- Unarmed combat styles allow the user the opportunity to fight and defend themselves without the need of weapons. They are also useful in situations where an opponent has closed inside the reach of a wielded weapon. An unarmed attack can be made with any part of the body, except for the torso. Thus limbs, wings, tails and even the head can be used.

Combat Style Benefits

Combat styles possess another function beyond simply learning a group of weapon skills. Since each style is taught by a particular culture or career, they are inherently optimised for the environment or military tactics that group normally fights with; for instance a horse nomad learns to fight from the saddle, or an infantryman trains to fight in close order formation. Therefore, as an additional bonus, every Combat Style *may* gain one or more traits which grant it an advantage under certain circumstances. This can be thought of as an inbuilt technical advantage the style offers for those particular situations. However, a trait is only intended to be used with the weapons and situations of that particular style.

There are limitless diverse and potential benefits a Combat Style can enjoy. The adjacent table merely suggests a few possibilities, and is intended to offer flavour rather than overwhelming tactical advantage. Games Masters are encouraged to create further ones to match their campaign setting.

Note that some of these benefits can potentially be applied, by extension, to the Unarmed skill – either learned via culture or added later as part of a profession.

Use of Weapons Not Covered by a Combat Style

Occasionally characters may be forced to pick up an unfamiliar weapon, using it either independently or in conjunction with a trained weapon. A character with a Sword and Shield style might, for example, be forced to use a mace, or mace and shield together.

By rights, using an untrained weapon forces the user to fight at his base Combat Style percentage. However, much depends on the weapon and how similar it is to something the user is experienced with. Some guidelines on using unfamiliar weapons are as follows:

- If a weapon is *substantially* different from a trained weapon – in weight, size, length and method of use – then offensive and defensive actions are made at the base Combat Style skill (ie, STR+DEX).
- If a weapon is *reasonably* different from a trained weapon – say a greatsword when the combatant is trained with a broadsword – then offensive and defensive actions are based on the existing Combat Style but are two grades more difficult.
- If a weapon is *broadly similar* to a trained weapon – say a shortsword when the combatant is trained with a broadsword – then offensive and defensive actions are one grade more difficult.
- If a weapon is *similar* to a trained weapon – a scimitar say, as opposed to a broadsword – then the character uses his existing Combat Style with no penalty.
- If a combatant is using an *unfamiliar* weapon in conjunction with a trained weapon, such as a shield, then the trained Combat Style is used, but is one grade harder. This simulates the compensation in the overall style the combatant must make (adjusting balance, accounting for heft, and so on) necessary to use a combination of trained and untrained weapons.
- The penalty imposed by use of an unfamiliar weapon cannot reduce the user's skill below the default level of STR+DEX.

Combat Rounds

To emphasise its visceral nature, MYTHRAS combat is tracked on a blow by blow basis. In order to ease bookkeeping but still reflect the differences in speed or numbers of attacks, fights are broken down into Combat Rounds of five seconds each. During this period combatants may make hand-to-hand attacks or defend against them, manoeuvre into and out of combat, fire or throw a ranged weapon, and so on.

Combat Style Traits

Trait	Description
Assassination	Allows the user access to the normally restricted 'Kill Silently' special effect.
Batter Aside	If the fighter's Damage Modifier is two or more steps greater than his opponent's, his weapon is considered one size larger for the purposes of bypassing parries.
Beast-back Lancer	Performing a mounted charge with this combat style does not incur the one step difficulty penalty to hit.
Blind Fighting	Allows user to ignore any penalties imposed due to poor lighting or temporary blinding.
Cautious Fighter	Can use the Change Range action to automatically withdraw from engagement with no need to roll
Chariot Fighting	Style allows those riding in a chariot to ignore the skill cap placed upon their combat rolls by the driver's Drive skill.
Daredevil	May use Evade to dodge blows in hand to hand combat without ending up prone.
Defensive Minded	Increases the Size of your weapon when parrying by one step, provided no offensive action is taken that round.
Do or Die	Allows dual weapon combinations to use the Flurry special effect, provided that each subsequent attack utilises the alternating weapon.
Excellent Footwork	When fighting on slippery, wobbling surfaces the user can ignore the skill cap placed on combat rolls by the Acrobatics skill.
Formation Fighting*	Permits a group of three or more warriors to draw into close formation, placing more open or disordered opponents at a disadvantage (provided the 'unit' cannot be outflanked), and thus reducing each foe's Action Points by one if they engage.
Hidden Weapons	Allows the user to utilise seemingly innocuous objects noted as part of the style as deadly weapons, with no chance of accidental breakage despite apparent delicacy (fans or musical instruments for example).
Intimidating Scream	Style encourages frequent yells and bellows in combat to intimidate foes, making any psychological resistance rolls inflicted on an opponent one grade harder.
Knockout Blow	When attacking with surprise treat any Stun Location as lasting minutes instead of turns.
Mancatcher	The style grants its user an advantage when entangling or immobilising opponents, making a foe's opposed rolls to evade or break free one difficulty grade harder.
Mounted Combat	Style allows rider to ignore the skill cap placed upon combat rolls by the Ride skill.
Ranged Marksman	When using a ranged weapon, shift a random Hit Location roll to an adjoining body location.
Shield Splitter	Permits clubs and axes to roll the weapon's damage twice and pick the best result, but only when using the Damage Weapon special effect against shields.
Shield Wall*	Allows a group of three or more shield users to overlap their protection, adding one to the number of locations which can be protected with passive blocking and resisting Knockback, Leaping attacks, and Bash as if using the Brace action.
Siege Warfare	The style permits its user to ignore the skill cap placed upon combat rolls by the Athletics skill when making assaults whilst scaling walls or crawling through tunnels.
Skirmishing	The style permits launching ranged attacks whilst at a run (but not whilst sprinting).
Swashbuckling	Style allows the user to engage in attacks and evades made whilst jumping or swinging into (or disengaging from) combat, ignoring any skill cap placed on it by the Athletics skill.
Throw Weapons	Any nominal melee weapon in the style can also be thrown at no penalty to skill, but when used in this way a weapon's damage roll is halved.
Trained Beast	Intended for styles which emphasise fighting in close coordination with an animal companion (such as trained birds of prey, pet wolves, and so on), the user may utilise any of his Action Points to defend against attacks launched at his beast.
Unarmed Prowess	Permits the user to treat his Unarmed blocks and parries as 'Medium' sized, enabling him to better defend himself from armed opponents.
Water Combat	The style allows its user to ignore the skill cap placed on combat rolls by the Swim skill.

** Requires everyone else in the group to also have this benefit, otherwise the coordinated effort fails to lack of one or more participants being trained in the correct technique.*

Anathaym's Saga

Anathaym is trained in two separate Combat Styles, Meerish Slinger, and Meerish Infantry. After considering the options available, the Games Master decides to grant the Meerish Slinger style the Skirmishing trait, and the Meerish Infantry style the Formation Fighting trait. Thus her cultural and career styles now look like this:

Meerish Slinger: (Skirmishing) sling, shortsword and peltast shield
Meerish Infantry: (Formation Fighting) spear, hoplite shield and javelin

Note that Anathaym is limited to ranged weapon skirmishing with her sling, and formation fighting with spear and large shield. During the hundreds of hours she trained in combat, she only ever practiced slinging at a running gait, since javelin throwing was learned as part of being a close ordered unit. Similarly she learned the tactics of fighting shoulder to shoulder only whilst using a spear and large hoplite shield, and wouldn't feel comfortable trying to fight as a formation with a shorter weapon and smaller shield.

Similarly to real life, most combat engagements – once joined – are concluded in a matter of seconds rather than minutes. In game terms this means several Combat Rounds (usually three or less) unless participants withdraw to perhaps reset initiative, reassess their tactical situation or simply to grab a momentary rest before re-engaging. Only fights between well matched foes or sequences of opponents tend to last longer.

Combat Rounds use several important terms:

- Initiative: The order of who acts when during a Cycle of a Combat Round.
- Cycle: The countdown through initiative values from the highest to the lowest, so that each participant has a chance to take their Turn when their number is reached. There can be several cycles per Combat Round.
- Turn: Upon each turn, participants perform a Combat Action, which comprises of a declaration, any necessary dice rolls (including reactions), and the resolution of the action.

Each term is described in more detail, below.

Initiative

Initiative determines participants' order of actions during the cycles of a Combat Round. It is rolled at the start of a fight. Unless something occurs to change the situation, such as certain Combat Actions or Special Effects, initiative remains in play until it is forced to be re-rolled.

Anathaym's Saga

On the plains outside the city Anathaym is practicing with shortsword and shield against her weapons tutor, Master Zamothis. Both she and her mentor have 3 Action Points each, but Anathaym rolls a better initiative. Going first she decides to attack (Proactive, 1 Action Point) which Zamothis effortlessly deflects (Reactive, 1 Action Point). Thus far they have each used one Action Point – Anathaym to attack and Zamothis to parry. Then it is her mentor's turn, and he returns with an attack (Proactive, 1 Action Point), forcing her to block (Reactive, 1 Action Point). Now they have used two Action Points each.

Both have now taken their respective turns, but each still has a Combat Action remaining; so the Games Master cycles back to the highest initiative again; allowing Anathaym to attack a second time that round. Zamothis again parries the blow and the round ends, since neither has any Action Points remaining. Thus going first allowed Anathaym to use her actions to attack twice and parry once.

Calculating Initiative

Initiative is calculated by each participant rolling 1d10 and adding their Initiative Bonus. Whoever gained the highest result acts first, followed by the second highest, and so on. When two or more participants tie scores they act concurrently.

Initiative Penalty

Characters who wear armour are hindered by the encumbrance of their protection, slowed by its inherent mass and bulk. As described on page 58, a penalty is applied to Initiative equal to the total ENC for all the armour worn, divided by 5, and rounded up. For example, a full suit of Hoplite Plate armour, covering all seven hit locations, with an ENC value of 4 per location, imposes an Initiative penalty of $(7x4)/5 = 6$.

Cycles and Turns

Once initiative has been determined, the participants have the potential to perform several Combat Actions during each Combat Round. The number of times they can act is equal to their Action Points, but when they can act is limited to whether the action is proactive or reactive.

Proactive actions can only be attempted on the character's own Turn; that is to say, when it is his initiative. Proactive actions are those in which the character is the instigator, such as making an

Anathaym's Saga

As Master Zamothis continues his lesson Anathaym notices three belligerent centaurs, armed with bows, gallop out of a nearby gorge towards them. She cries out a warning and interposes herself between her momentarily surprised mentor and the approaching raiders.

All three centaurs roll higher initiatives than Anathaym. Each one, on its turn, spends an Action Point to fire an arrow at the female warrior. In response Anathaym defends herself against the fusillade with her shield, forcing her to block three times, once per arrow. This costs all three of her Action Points, so when her turn arrives she is unable to do anything and indeed cannot act for the rest of the round.

The Games Master cycles back to the highest initiative, but fortunately for Anathaym the centaurs each spend their second (and last) Action Point nocking new arrows to their bows. Thus the end of the second cycle is reached, and since nobody has any Action Points remaining, a new round is begun.

attack with a weapon. Only one proactive action may be attempted per cycle. If no proactive action is selected, the character is assumed to have used Dither by default.

Reactive actions are those taken by a character to counter or resist an act made against them. Only one reaction attempt is permitted for each threat, an example would be trying to parry an attack. However, any number of reactions may be made per cycle, provided that the character has Action Points to spend.

The end of the cycle is reached once every participant has taken their turn. If anyone still has Action Points remaining then a new cycle is begun for those characters with Action Points available. This continues until all available Action Points have been expended, at which point the round is over, and a new one begins.

Combat Actions

Combat Actions are those acts which can be performed during battle. Drawing a weapon, casting a spell, or diving clear from an attack are all examples of Combat Actions. Most are concerned with elements of combat itself, but some relate to activities outside the to and fro of spells and weapons.

As previously mentioned, how often a character can act per round is limited by their available Action Points. These are spent over the course of each Combat Round to perform various Combat Actions. Once a combatant's Action Points are expended, they may no longer act for the remainder of that round, and must wait until their points reset at the beginning of the next.

Unless otherwise specified any Combat Action (save for 'free' actions) costs one Action Point. Thus combatants need to carefully consider how and when they use their points. They may act as aggressively or defensively as they wish, dynamically reacting to the evolving circumstance of the combat.

Proactive Actions

The following are activities a character can attempt on his Turn by spending an Action Point. Note that some actions such as spell casting or reloading may take several turns to complete; each turn costing its own Action Point.

Attack

The character can attempt to strike with a hand-to-hand weapon or use a ranged weapon.

Brace

The character braces himself by taking a firm stance, and leaning into the direction of a forthcoming attack. For the purposes of resisting Knockback or Leaping Attacks the character's SIZ is treated as 50% bigger. Against the Bash special effect SIZ is doubled. The benefits of bracing are lost once the character moves away from the place they planted themselves.

Cast Magic

The character can attempt to cast a spell, call for a miracle, invoke a talent or summon a spirit. Complex magics may require several turns in order to complete the casting. Once concluded, the magic can be released at any moment up until the caster's next turn; at which point it can be held for later effect; but this requires the Hold Magic action (see below) to maintain it in preparation for later release.

Keeping Track of Action Points

It can be tricky to keep track of Action Points during a round, especially if characters make a habit of using Combat Actions such as Delay or casting spells which require more than one turn to complete. As an aide to simplify book keeping, the use of tokens (coins or poker chips are ideal) is recommended.

Give each player a number of tokens equal to their Action Points, then each time they act or react, remove one of the tokens – tossing them into a used pile in the centre of the table. In the case of the Delay action, the token can be moved half way, indicating a held action which can be triggered at a later point. For spell casting a separate pile could be formed which keeps track of how many turns have been invested thus far.

When each round concludes the players can reclaim a requisite number of tokens from the discard pile. Of course other methods can be used, such as using dice as trackers or even tallying Action Points on scrap paper.

Change Range

The character can attempt to close on, or retreat from, an opponent; changing the range at which he is fighting to take best advantage of his weapon's reach or disengage from engagement entirely. See Weapon Reach - Closing and Opening Range on page 106.

Delay

The character conserves his action so that he can instead perform a Reactive Action at a later time, such as an Interrupt or Parry. The Action Point cost of delaying is covered by whatever act is finally performed. If the delayed action is not taken before the character's next turn (on the following cycle), then the character is considered to have Dithered, and the Action Point is lost.

Dither

A character can decide to simply waste his turn doing nothing useful.

Hold Magic

Once casting is complete, the character may hold a spell, miracle or spirit in temporary check, awaiting the best moment to release it. The magic may be held back for as long as the character continues to take this action on his subsequent turns, but allows free use of the Counter Spell reaction if pertinent to his spell.

Mount

The character can mount or dismount a riding beast. Particularly large mounts may require several turns to complete.

Move

Provided he is not engaged with an opponent, the character can move any distance the Games Master deems suitable for the situation. The Move Combat action is not required for every instance of movement during combat.

One does not need to spend an Action Point on Move to engage an opponent. For instance, a character crossing an open field to engage a group of archers would spend 1 Action Point to cover the distance. He would not, though, need to spend a further Action Point to initiate combat with one of the archers when he reaches their vantage point. He may use his next turn solely for his attack roll.

ANATHAYM'S SAGA

Backtracking the centaurs' trail, Anathaym and Zamothis discover the raider's encampment in a small cave-filled canyon far to the west of Meeros. Using the cover of darkness they creep close enough to see a sorcerer by the name of Kratos, whom the herd is serving, about to perform a human sacrifice of a youth tied spread-eagled between frighteningly carved totem poles. Zamothis orders Anathaym to deal with the black wizard, then yells loudly and, bedecked in his bronze hoplite armour, heroically leaps down into the midst of the centaur warriors to cause a distraction.

Anathaym runs to engage the sorcerer and Initiative is rolled, resulting in Kratos gaining the higher Initiative. Spotting her approach the sorcerer immediately begins invoking a diabolical spell, one which the Games Master determines will take two turns to cast. He marks off the first of Kratos' Action Points for the round. Guessing at her imminent doom, Anathaym on her turn tries to stab the sorcerer, forcing Kratos (who has no weapons) to Evade in a desperate attempt to avoid the blow. Rolls are made, and the sorcerer successfully throws himself backwards into the shadows, but is now prone upon the rocky ground. This concludes the cycle, with Anathaym having used one Action Point, and Kratos two.

The next cycle begins with the sorcerer in apparent difficulty. He has one Action Point remaining, and has the choice of either kicking at the warrior in the hope of perhaps tripping her (leaving him at the mercy of Anathaym's sword for the rest of the round) or continuing his half cast spell. Facing little chance of mercy Kratos uses his turn to complete his spell and rolls against his Invocation skill. Despite an imposed difficultly grade of Formidable for lying on his back, he succeeds, and disappears in a puff of greasy, black smoke. Anathaym is left on her turn with nobody to attack, so revises her intentions and starts cutting the youth's bonds...

To summarise, use the Move Combat Action for:

- Moving up towards a combat
- Perform a dramatic action within combat (swing from a handy chandelier, for example)

Move is not necessary to engage an opponent.

OUTMANOEUVRE

The character can engage multiple opponents in a group opposed roll of Evade skills. Those who fail to beat his roll cannot attack him that Combat Round. See the section on Outmanoeuvring on page 104.

READY WEAPON

The character may draw, sheath, withdraw or reload a weapon. Retrieving a nearby dropped weapon requires two turns: one to move and reach down for the weapon, and a second to return to a readied stance. Some missile weapons require several turns to reload.

REGAIN FOOTING

If unengaged with an opponent, the character can regain his footing from being tripped or knocked down. If engaged, the character must win an opposed test of Brawn or Athletics with the opponent before standing.

STRUGGLE

If the character is the victim of a certain types of attack or Special Effect, he may attempt to extract himself from the situation. For example breaking free from a Grapple or Pin Weapon.

TAKE COVER

Take Cover is a proactive action which allows someone to duck behind whatever cover is available in their immediate vicinity, gaining some degree of protection against incoming fire. Unlike Evade it does not leave the user prone, but it does rely on some form of cover being available (for example, ducking back around a corner in a corridor or crouching down behind a table in a bar).

REACTIVE ACTIONS

This list specifies reactions which can be used at any time during the Combat Round as a response to an imminent threat. As in the previous list, a reaction costs an Action Point to perform.

COUNTER SPELL

The character can attempt to dismiss or counter an incoming spell, miracle or spirit. This assumes the countering magic has a casting time of one Turn, otherwise it must be prepared in advance, and temporarily withheld using the Hold Magic action. Successfully intercepting magic in this manner is assumed to negate the entire spell or miracle, even those with multiple targets or areas of effect.

EVADE

The character can attempt to dive or roll clear of threats such as incoming missiles or a charging attack. Using Evade leaves the character prone, unless mitigated by some special consequence. Thus the character's next turn is usually spent taking the Regain Footing action to stand again. See Evading on page 103.

INTERRUPT

(Delaying characters only) Halts an opponent's turn after his declaration in order to take your own delayed turn. Assuming no change in the tactical situation, the opponent continues his turn after yours is completed. If unable to still achieve his original declaration, the opponent's Action Point is wasted. An interrupt can also be used against anyone passing close by the delaying character, within weapon reach.

DELAY AND INTERRUPT

Delay is intended to be a way of allowing a character to conserve all of their Action Points in a Round for reactive actions; for example parrying.

Interrupt, on the other hand, is intended to permit pre-emptive actions which could, but do not necessarily, involve combat, such as slamming a door shut, knocking a siege engine off target, waiting for the clear shot, and so on. It is also worded to allow characters to intercept those that try to dodge or pass close by them.

Neither Delay nor Interrupt are intended to be used as a way of gaining an Action Point advantage over a closing opponent: it is not in the spirit of the rules to permit the withholding of actions until engagement has been initiated.

Parry
The character can attempt to defend against an incoming attack using a combination of parrying, blocking, leaning, ducking or side-stepping footwork to minimise the blow.

Free Actions
Free actions can be performed at any time during the Combat Round, and cost no Action Points to perform.

Assess Situation
If unengaged, a character can make a Perception roll at no Action Point cost. Success in the roll alerts them to any relevant changes in the tactical situation (such a spotting a foe beginning a charge).

Drop Weapon
Dropping a weapon is a Free Action.

Signal
If unengaged, gesturing or signalling to one or more participants (as long as they can perceive the sign) is a Free Action.

Speak
A character can speak at any time during combat, but what is said should be limited to short phrases which can be uttered in five seconds or less; for example 'Time to die!', 'Look out behind you!' or 'Damn you to hell!'

Use Luck Point
Using a Luck Point – to re-roll a particular result for example – is a Free Action.

Ward Location
The character guards a particular Hit Location from being hit by dedicating one of his weapons to statically cover the area. Any blow which lands on that location has its damage automatically downgraded as per normal for a parrying weapon of its Size. The ward continues until the dedicated weapon is used to attack or actively parry. Establishing a ward or changing the Hit Location covered must be performed prior to an opponent rolling to attack the character. Due to their design, shields can cover multiple areas. For further explanation see Passive Blocking, page 105.

WEAPON SIZE & REACH

Every weapon in MYTHRAS possesses a number of different attributes from the damage it deals to how many hands are required to wield it. Two of these ratings, Size and Reach are important due to their mechanical effect. Size is used to determine the weapon's ability to impose and parry damage (see Damage Reduction in this chapter), whilst Reach can affect whether an opponent lies within range of being struck (see Weapon Reach - Closing and Opening Range on page 106).

Size categories are *Small, Medium, Large, Huge,* and *Enormous.* Reach categories are *Touch, Short, Medium, Long,* and *Very Long.* Some monsters and weapons further extend these categories beyond the scope of human characters, as illustrated in the Creatures chapter.

Both of these ratings are largely abstract in nature, simplified to help speed play. Size is a combination of a weapon's mass, leverage and stability. Reach is more a measure of its length and ability to hold a foe at bay due to how far it extends beyond the hilt or grip.

The Equipment chapter provides default Size and Reach values for common weapons, but the following guidelines are provided for those Games Masters wishing to design their own armaments.

The unarmed attacks of creatures are assigned similar categories according to their physical characteristics. See page 222.

WEAPON SIZE CATEGORIES

Size	Description
Small	Human unarmed combat, and light single handed weapons less than a kilo in weight, such as a dagger
Medium	Single handed weapons over a kilo in weight, a mace for instance
Large	Long hafted thrusting weapons, two handed spears being a case in point
Huge	Two handed slashing, chopping or bashing weapons, like greatswords
Enormous	Weapons used by very large creatures, for example a tree trunk used by a giant

WEAPON REACH CATEGORIES

Reach	Description
Touch	Human reach in unarmed combat, knuckledusters, spiked kneepads, and so on
Short	Weapons less than half a metre long; such as a dagger or short sword
Medium	Single handed swung weapons longer than half a metre, like a ball and chain
Long	Single handed thrusting weapons, or two handed swung weapons, a great axe for instance
Very Long	Two handed or mounted thrusting weapons, polearms or lances for example

KEEPING TRACK OF ATTACK ROLLS

As will be further explained in the rules, some Special Effects and certain types of injury require an opposed roll of some sort against the attacker's original attack roll. The same thing applies to offensive magic. For this reason it is a useful habit for players to leave the percentage dice lying untouched on the table until the attack and consequences have been fully resolved. In this way the dice provide a record of what number was actually rolled, thus helping to avoid lapses of memory or unnecessary dispute.

HOW COMBAT WORKS

Fighting in MYTHRAS is resolved in a blow by blow progression, each attack or parry representing a single swing, cast or shot of a weapon. Any offensive action is permitted the chance to be resisted by a reaction. Thus even if a character manages to strike an opponent, the foe is permitted its own roll to see if it can parry the blow before it lands. The same philosophy is used whether the attacks are missile weapons against targets diving for cover, or trying to break free from the iron grasp of a giant octopus.

ATTACKS AND PARRIES

Close combat is handled in the following step by step manner:

1. On his turn the attacker spends an Action Point, rolls against his Combat Style and notes the result.
2. If desired, the defender spends an Action Point, rolls against his Combat Style and notes the result.
3. The success level of the results are compared as per a Differential Roll.
4. Any difference grants the combatant with the superior roll one or more Special Effects (see below).
5. If the attacker achieved a success or critical, he may roll weapon damage and apply their Damage Modifier (if any). If applicable, a Hit Location is determined for the blow.
6. If the defender achieved a success or critical, reduce any damage inflicted according to the comparative sizes of the weapons involved.

It should be noted that any Special Effects generated by the exchange are independent of whether or not damage is inflicted. It is quite possible for a defender to gain the higher success level, yet still suffer injury.

DAMAGE REDUCTION

If a defender succeeds in parrying, then he can reduce an attacker's damage, if any, according to the comparative Size of the weapons used.

- Parrying an attack with a weapon or shield of *equal or greater* Size deflects *all* damage
- Parrying with a weapon or shield of *one Size less* only deflects *half* damage
- Parrying with a weapon or shield *two or more Sizes less* fails to deflect *any* damage

For example, parrying a great axe (Huge) with a hoplite shield (also Huge) would block all damage; parrying it with a pike (Large) would halve the damage, and parrying it with a shortsword (Medium) would stop no damage at all.

Damage Reduction Table

		Attacking Weapon				
		Small	*Medium*	*Large*	*Huge*	*Enormous*
Defending Weapon	**Small**	All	Half	None	None	None
	Medium	All	All	Half	None	None
	Large	All	All	All	Half	None
	Huge	All	All	All	All	Half
	Enormous	All	All	All	All	All

Parrying a Missed Attack

If the attacker misses his initial attack roll, the defender has the option of whether or not to spend an Action Point to parry. Although it may seem disingenuous to parry an attack which will miss anyway, a skilled defender can use this to his advantage to gain one or more Special Effects, potentially weakening or incapacitating a foe, and preserving their next turn for some other action.

Unable or Unwilling to Parry

In a situation where a defender is unable to parry due to having no Action Points remaining, or, confident in his ability to weather the blow, elects not to parry, he is treated as having automatically rolled a failure. This has the consequence of granting a successful attacker one or more Special Effects.

Failed Rolls and Fumbles

If both combatants fail their rolls, or the defender decides not to take advantage of a missed attack, then the attack-parry sequence ends, and combat continues on to the participant with the next highest Initiative.

Fumbling a Combat Style roll has no additional effect other than the chance it provides his opponent to inflict multiple (and more dire) Special Effects against him. If a combatant fails when his opponent fumbles, then he misses the opportunity to take advantage of his foe's clumsiness.

In the rare circumstance that both opponents fumble, Games Masters are encouraged to describe some hilarious or amazingly improbable event occurring which temporarily takes both out of the fight.

Retroactive Parrying With a Skill over 100%

Allowing a character to parry only those attacks which will hit is an essential part of maintaining the unpredictable flow of combat. However it does start to cause problems when the defender has a combat skill exceeding 100%, since what was originally a successful roll by the attacker may become downgraded to a miss if the penalty provided by the defender's superior skill is retroactively applied.

To avoid messy calculations or causality issues, the best way to handle this situation is to only permit the defender to impose his over 100% skill penalty if he pro-actively defends, declaring his parry before the attacker rolls. This has the added benefit of preventing superhumanly skilled opponents from being near-immune to attacks without the need to expend Action Points to defend themselves.

For example; despite his best efforts to outmanoeuvre them, Master Zamothis is surrounded by centaur opponents. The grizzled warrior is worthy of his title, possessing (amongst others) a Combat Style (Meerish Infantry) skill of 120%. However he is surrounded and faces the tough choice of whether or not to use his remaining two Action Points to defend himself. Since his skill is so high that it would provide a penalty to his attackers, the Games Master asks his player if he wishes to declare his parry in advance (thus reducing the centaurs impending attack skill by 20%) or withhold parrying until it is seen whether the centaurs hit or miss at their normal skill.

Special Effects

Fighting is far more than simply injuring or killing an opponent. Combative arts teach many methods of defeating a foe, perhaps rendering them helpless or forcing them into situations where they must capitulate, without necessarily needing to actually cause them harm. Special Effects represent these techniques, and control how they occur in play.

Whenever opponents engage in a Differential Roll of their respective fighting skills (Combat Styles or Evade for example), any resulting difference in success levels indicates an opportunity for Special Effects to occur. This reflects one combatant manoeuvring his opponent into a disadvantageous situation which can be exploited using a cunning trick or tactic.

The number of Special Effects received depends on the difference between the levels of success, as illustrated on the Differential Roll Results Table (see page 51).

If any Special Effects are won during an exchange, they must be selected before Damage and Hit Location, if any, are rolled. In cases where the recipient is badly wounded in addition to receiving a Special Effect, Endurance rolls are resolved after the application of the effect.

Special Effects cover a diverse range of situations and techniques. Some are designed specifically for attacks, whilst others are intended for defence, and a few are adaptable for either circumstance. Certain Special Effects can also be limited to particular weapon types or specific dice rolls, requiring a Critical or Fumble result on their skill check for instance.

When two or more Special Effects are gained, the combatant may freely mix and match which ones are selected, providing he meets the prerequisite conditions for each one. Some effects can be stacked. For example, an attacker who rolls a critical success and wins two Special Effects could choose Maximise Damage twice, rather than choosing two separate offensive manoeuvres.

Special Effect Descriptions

Accidental Injury

The defender deflects or twists an opponent's attack in such a way that he fumbles, injuring himself. The attacker must roll damage against himself in a random hit location using the weapon used to strike. If unarmed he tears or breaks something internal, the damage roll ignoring any armour.

Arise

Allows the defender to use a momentary opening to roll back up to their feet.

Bash

The attacker deliberately bashes the opponent off balance. How far the defender totters back or sideward depends on the weapon being used. Shields knock an opponent back one metre per for every two points of damage rolled (prior to any subtractions due to armour, parries, and so forth), whereas bludgeoning weapons knock back one metre per for every three points. Bashing works only on creatures up to twice the attacker's SIZ. If the recipient is forced backwards into an obstacle, then they must make a Hard Athletics or Acrobatics skill roll to avoid falling or tripping over.

Bleed

The attacker can attempt to cut open a major blood vessel. If the blow overcomes Armour Points and injures the target, the defender must make an opposed roll of Endurance against the original attack roll. If the defender fails, then they begin to bleed profusely. At the start of each Combat Round the recipient loses one level of Fatigue, until they collapse and possibly die. Bleeding wounds can be staunched by passing a First Aid skill roll, but the recipient can no longer perform any strenuous or violent action without re-opening the wound. See Blood Loss page 71.

Blind Opponent

On a critical the defender briefly blinds his opponent by throwing sand, reflecting sunlight off his shield, or some other tactic which briefly interferes with the attacker's vision. The attacker must make an opposed roll of his Evade skill (or Weapon style if using a shield) against the defender's original parry roll. If the attacker fails he suffers the Blindness situational modifier for the next 1d3 turns.

Bypass Armour

On a critical the attacker finds a gap in the defender's natural or worn armour. If the defender is wearing armour above natural protection, then the attacker must decide which of the two is bypassed. This effect can be stacked to bypass both. For the purposes of this effect, physical protection gained from magic is considered as being worn armour.

Choose Location

When using hand-to-hand melee weapons the attacker may freely select the location where the blow lands, as long as that location is normally within reach. If using ranged weapons Choose Location is a Critical Success only, unless the target is within close range, and is either stationary or unaware of the attacker.

The Head? Again?

Some Games Masters may find the Choose Location special effect a rather sour annoyance, especially if their players continue to take down foe after foe with exactly the same blow. What might surprise many people to know is that this behaviour is exactly matched by real life combat. Not only is the head is the closest part of the body to strike, but shields tend to be held beneath the level of the eyes, exposing the head and part of the face so that you can see your opponent.

There are several techniques which can help prevent foes being chopped down with the same blow. First, and most obvious, is to wear a helmet, which after shields was the most prevalent type of protection used throughout history. Secondly is to use the Ward Location action. This is a perfectly natural thing to do, since once an opponent has suffered a wound he will tend to try to keep that weakened area covered so that it cannot be struck again. Third, the Prepare Counter Special Effect (page 98) can be used to anticipate (and neutralise) predictable tactics.

Last but by no means least the Games Master should himself use a range of diverse and interesting Special Effects, showing that Choose Location can be eclipsed by manoeuvres such as Bleed, Stun Location or even Bash in the right circumstances!

Circumvent Cover

Assuming that the shooter is using some high-tech weaponry, they can fire around the target's cover. In most cases this will require something along the lines of self guided ammunition. If used as a trick shot, for example bouncing a laser blast off a mirror or ricocheting a bullet off a wall, then the special effect should be treated as a Critical Success only with a commensurate reduction in damage.

Circumvent Parry
On a critical the attacker may completely bypass an otherwise successful parry.

Close Range
Permits the character to automatically change the engagement range between himself and his opponent, so that they end up at the Range favoured by the shorter weapon (see Weapon Reach - Closing and Opening Range page 106).

Compel Surrender
Allows the character a chance to force the surrender of a helpless or disadvantaged opponent; for example someone who has been disarmed, is lying prone unable to regain his footing, has suffered a serious (or worse) wound, and so on. Damage is not inflicted on the target, they are only threatened. Assuming the target is sapient and able to understand the demand, the target must make an opposed roll of Willpower against the original attack or parry roll. If the target fails, they capitulate. Games Masters may wish to reserve Compel Surrender for use against non-player characters only.

Damage Weapon
Permits the character to damage his opponent's weapon as part of an attack or parry. If attacking, the character aims specifically at the defender's parrying weapon and applies his damage roll to it, rather than the wielder. The targeted weapon uses its own Armour Points for resisting the damage. If reduced to zero Hit Points the weapon breaks.

Disarm Opponent
The character knocks, yanks or twists the opponent's weapon out of his hand. The opponent must make an opposed roll of his Combat Style against the character's original roll. If the recipient of the disarm loses, his weapon is flung a distance equal to the roll of the disarmer's Damage Modifier in metres. If there is no Damage Modifier then the weapon drops at the disarmed person's feet. The comparative size of the weapons affects the roll. Each step that the disarming character's weapon is larger increases the difficulty of the opponent's roll by one grade. Conversely each step the disarming character's weapon is smaller, makes the difficulty one grade easier. Disarming works only on creatures of up to twice the attacker's STR.

Drop Foe
Assuming the target suffers at least a minor wound from a siege weapon, firearms shot or similar, they are forced to make an Opposed Test of their Endurance against the attacker's hit roll. Failure indicates that the target succumbs to shock and pain, becoming incapacitated and unable to continue fighting. Recovery from incapacitation can be performed with a successful First Aid check or using some form of magic or narcotic stimulant if such exists in the campaign. Otherwise the temporary incapacitation lasts for a period equal to one hour divided by the Healing Rate of the target.

Duck Back
This special effect allows the shooter to immediately duck back into cover, without needing to wait for their next Turn to use the Take Cover action. The character must be already standing or crouching adjacent to some form of cover to use Duck Back.

Enhance Parry
On a critical the defender manages to deflect the entire force of an attack, no matter the Size of his weapon.

Entangle
Allows a character wielding an entangling weapon, such as a whip or net, to immobilise the location struck. An entangled arm cannot use whatever it is holding; a snared leg prevents the target from moving; whilst an enmeshed head, chest or abdomen makes all skill rolls one grade harder. On his following turn the wielder may spend an Action Point to make an automatic Trip Opponent attempt. An entangled victim can attempt to free himself on his turn by either attempting an opposed roll using Brawn to yank free, or win a Special Effect and select Damage Weapon, Disarm Opponent or Slip Free.

Flurry
An unarmed creature or attacker can make an immediate follow-up attack using a different limb or body part, without needing to wait for its next turn. A human attacker might follow up a punch to the abdomen with a knee to the face for example. The additional attack still costs an Action Point, but potentially allows several attacks in sequence before the defender can respond offensively.

Force Failure
Used when an opponent fumbles, the character can combine Force Failure with any other Special Effect which requires an opposed roll to work. Force Failure causes the opponent to fail his resistance roll by default – thereby automatically be disarmed, tripped, etc.

Grip
Provided the opponent is within the attacker's Unarmed Combat reach, he may use an empty hand (or similar limb capable of gripping such as claws, tails or tentacles) to hold onto the opponent, preventing them from being able to change weapon range or disengage from combat. The opponent may attempt to break free on his turn, requiring an opposed roll of either Brawn or Unarmed against whichever of the two skills the gripper prefers. If the gripped victim wins, they manage to break free. Note that some attackers using Brawn may be so strong that no amount of brute force or cunning technique can overcome their grip (see Brawn page 39).

Impale
The attacker can attempt to drive an impaling weapon deep into the defender. Roll weapon damage twice, with the attacker choosing which of the two results to use for the attack. If armour is penetrated and causes a wound, then the attacker has the option of leaving the weapon in the wound, or yanking it free on their next turn. Leaving the weapon in the wound inflicts a difficulty grade on the victim's future skill attempts. The severity of the penalty depends on the size of both the creature and the weapon impaling it, as listed on the Impale Effects Table above. For simplicity's sake, further impalements with the same sized weapon inflict no additional penalties. To withdraw an impaled weapon during melee requires use of the Ready Weapon combat action. The wielder must pass an unopposed Brawn roll (or win an opposed Brawn roll if the opponent resists). Success pulls the weapon free, causing further injury to the same location equal to half the normal damage roll for that weapon, but without any damage modifier. Failure implies that the weapon remained stuck in the wound with no further effect, although the

Impale Effects Table

Creature SIZ	Small Weapons	Medium Weapons	Large Weapons	Huge Weapons	Enormous Weapons
1-10	Formidable	Herculean	Incapacitated	Incapacitated	Incapacitated
11-20	Hard	Formidable	Herculean	Incapacitated	Incapacitated
21-30	No Effect	Hard	Formidable	Herculean	Incapacitated
31-40	No Effect	No Effect	Hard	Formidable	Herculean
41-50	No Effect	No Effect	No Effect	Hard	Formidable
Each +10			Follow table progression		

wielder may try again on their next turn. Specifically barbed weapons (such as harpoons) inflict normal damage. Armour does not reduce withdrawal damage. Whilst it remains impaled, the attacker cannot use his impaling weapon for parrying.

Kill Silently

Restricted to those trained in a Combat Style with the Assassination benefit. It allows the attacker to neutralise a victim in complete silence, covering their mouth or grasping them about the neck whilst simultaneously stabbing, cutting or garrotting them. This prevents the victim from crying out or otherwise raising an alarm for the entire round. In addition, if during this time the attacks inflict a Serious or Major Wound, the victim will automatically fail its Endurance roll. Kill Silently can only be used on a surprised opponent, and only on the first attack against them.

Marksman

Permits the shooter to move the Hit Location struck by his shot by one step, to an immediately adjoining body area. Physiology has an effect on what can be re-targeted, and common sense should be applied. Thus using this special effect on a humanoid would permit an attacker who rolled a leg shot, to move it up to the abdomen instead. Conversely shooting a griffin in the chest would permit selection of the forelegs, wings or head.

Maximise Damage

On a critical the character may substitute one of his weapon's damage dice for its full value. For example a Hatchet which normally does 1d6 damage would instead be treated as a 6, whereas a great club with 2d6 damage would instead inflict 1d6+6 damage. This special effect may be stacked. Although it can also be used for natural weapons, Maximise Damage does not affect the Damage Modifier of the attacker, which must be rolled normally.

Open Range

Permits the character to automatically change the engagement range between himself and his opponent, so that they end up at the Range favoured by the longer weapon (see (see Weapon Reach - Closing and Opening Range page 106).

Overextend Opponent

The defender sidesteps or retreats at an inconvenient moment, causing the attacker to overreach himself. Opponent cannot attack on his next turn. This special effect can be stacked.

Overpenetration

If shooting at lineally positioned opponents or into a densely packed group, this special effect allows the shot to travel completely through the first victim to strike a second behind them, assuming that it overcomes the first target's body armour. The second victim however, only suffers half damage due to attenuation or slowing down of the shot. Overpenetration is generally of more use with high powered weapons that inflict large amounts of damage or those which have some sort of armour piercing ability. Any other special effects inflicted on the first target are not applied to the second.

Pin Down

Similar to Press Advantage, this special effect forces the target to make an Opposed Test of their Willpower against the attacker's hit roll. Failure means that the target hunkers down behind whatever cover is available, and cannot return fire on their next Turn. Note that Pin Down works even if no actual damage is inflicted on the target (perhaps due to a successful evasion or shots striking their cover instead), as it relies on the intimidation effect of projectiles passing very close by.

Although a pinned victim is unable to fire back for the requisite time, they can perform other actions provided they don't expose themselves to fire in the process, such as crawling away to new cover, communicating with others, reloading a weapon, and so on.

Pin Weapon

On a critical the character can pin one of his opponent's weapons or shield, using his body or positioning to hold it in place. On his turn the opponent may attempt to wrestle or manoeuvre the pinned item free. This costs an Action Point and works as per the Grip special effect. Failure means that the pinned item remains unusable. In the meantime, an opponent lacking a weapon or shield in the other hand may only avoid an attack by evading, using his Unarmed skill or disengaging completely.

Prepare Counter

The defender reads the patterns of his foe and pre-plans a counter against a specific Special Effect (which should be noted down in secret). If his opponent attempts to inflict the chosen Special Effect upon him during the fight, the defender instantly substitutes the attackers effect with an offensive or defensive one of his own, which succeeds automatically.

Press Advantage

The attacker pressures his opponent, so that his foe is forced to remain on the defensive, and cannot attack on their next turn. This allows the attacker to potentially establish an unbroken sequence of attacks whilst the defender desperately blocks. It is only effective against foes concerned with defending themselves. Foes that find themselves constantly locked under an unceasing sequence of Press Advantage will likely disengage from the combat, call for help, or use Prepare Counter to give attackers a nasty surprise.

Rapid Reload
When using a ranged weapon, the attacker reduces the reload time for the next shot by one. This effect can be stacked.

Remise
The attacker performs a sequential follow-up attack with a weapon of size Small on his opponent's next turn, which forces the foe to change their proactive action into a reactive one.

Scar Foe
The opponent is given a scar that will disfigure them for the rest of their life, for example a slice across the face, or an artfully inscribed letter across the chest.

Select Target
When an attacker fumbles, the defender may manoeuvre or deflect the blow in such a way that it hits an adjacent bystander instead. This requires that the new target is within reach of the attacker's close combat weapon, or in the case of a ranged attack, is standing along the line of fire. The new victim is taken completely by surprise by the unexpected accident, and has no chance to avoid the attack which automatically hits. In compensation however, they suffer no special effect.

Slip Free
On a critical the defender can automatically escape being Entangled, Gripped, or Pinned.

Size Matters...
Some Special Effects may feel unrealistic when fighting against opponents of a significantly larger size. For instance using Bleed or Trip Opponent against an immense wyvern is not as easy as when applying them to a human. In these cases the Games Master should make opposed skill rolls to resist such effects a difficulty grade or two easier for the larger foe according to the verisimilitude of the setting. Conversely using them on smaller opponents may make the opposed skill check harder for the target.

Spoil Spell
The character automatically ruins any spell in the process of being cast, providing the blow overcomes Armour Points and injures the target.

Stand Fast
The defender braces himself against the force of an attack, allowing them to avoid the Knockback effects of any damage received.

Stun Location
The attacker can use a bludgeoning weapon to temporarily stun the body part struck. If the blow overcomes Armour Points and injures the target, the defender must make an opposed roll of Endurance vs. the original attack roll. If the defender fails, then the Hit Location is incapacitated for a number of turns equal to the damage inflicted. A blow to the torso causes the defender to stagger winded, only able to defend. A head shot renders the foe briefly insensible.

Special Effects Summary

Special Effect	*Offensive*	*Defensive*	*Specific Weapon Type*	*Specific Roll*	*Stackable*
Accidental Injury		X		Attacker Fumbles	
Arise		X			
Bash	X		Shields or Bludgeoning		
Bleed	X		Cutting Weapons		
Blind Opponent		X		Defender Criticals	
Bypass Armour	X			Attacker Criticals	X
Choose Location	X			See Description	
Circumvent Cover	X		Ranged Weapons		
Circumvent Parry	X			Attacker Criticals	
Close Range	X	X			
Compel Surrender	X	X			
Damage Weapon	X	X			
Disarm Opponent	X	X			
Drop Foe	X		Siege Weapons, Firearms		
Duck Back	X		Ranged Weapons		
Enhance Parry		X		Defender Criticals	
Entangle	X	X	Entangling Weapons		
Flurry	X		Unarmed		X
Force Failure	X	X		Opponent Fumbles	
Grip	X		Unarmed		
Impale	X		Impaling Weapons		
Kill Silently	X		Small Weapons	See Description	
Marksman	X		Ranged Weapons		
Maximise Damage	X			Attacker Criticals	X
Open Range		X			
Overextend Opponent		X			X
Overpenetration	X		Ranged Weapons	Critical Only	
Pin Down	X		Ranged Weapons		X
Pin Weapon	X	X		Critical Only	
Prepare Counter		X			X
Press Advantage	X				
Rapid Reload	X				X
Remise	X		Small Weapon Only		
Scar Foe	X	X			
Select Target		X		Attacker Fumbles	
Slip Free		X		Defender Criticals	
Spoil Spell	X				
Stand Fast		X			
Stun Location	X		Bludgeoning Weapons		
Sunder	X		Axes, Two Handed Weapons		
Take Weapon	X	X	Unarmed		
Trip Opponent	X	X			
Weapon Malfunction	X		Ranged Weapons	Attacker Fumbles	
Withdraw		X			

Anathaym's Saga

One of the centaurs battling Master Zamothis becomes infuriated at the grizzled warrior's near impenetrable defence. When it finally rolls a critical attack, Zamothis once again parries with his Hoplite shield which would normally be enough to block any damage from the centaur's great club. So rather than attacking the warrior, the enraged beast aims for the shield instead, and selects Damage Weapon as its effect. The blow from the club inflicts 11 points of damage which when applied to the shield, overcomes its 6 Armour Points and reduces it to 10 Hit Points. The resulting cracking noise alerts Master Zamothis, who realises he will soon be in serious trouble..

Meanwhile, Anathaym cuts the youth free, but as he flees to the entrance of the canyon, one of the centaurs spots the escape and closes in for an attack, waving a dangerous looking halberd in wide circles above its head. Anathaym interposes herself and engages the savage warrior in combat. Rolls are made resulting in Anathaym gaining a normal success, and the centaur fumbling!

With two special effects to select, Anathaym decides she doesn't want to be hit by the halberd so chooses Disarm Opponent and Force Failure. Normally this would prove troublesome for the heroine, her shortsword suffering significant penalties to knock the larger weapon out of the centaur's hands. However, because she has also taken Force Failure, the centaur automatically fails the opposed roll and his weapon clatters to the ground, leaving him unarmed.

Sunder

The attacker may use a suitable weapon to damage the armour or natural protection of an opponent. Any weapon damage, after reductions for parrying or magic, is applied against the Armour Point value of the protection. Surplus damage in excess of its Armour Points is then used to reduce the AP value of that armour(ed) location – ripping straps, bursting rings, creasing plates or tearing away the hide, scales or chitin of monsters. If any damage remains after the protection has been reduced to zero AP, it carries over onto the Hit Points of the location struck.

Take Weapon

Allows an unarmed character to yank or twist an opponent's weapon out of his hand. The opponent must make an opposed roll of his Combat Style against the character's original Unarmed roll. If the target loses, his weapon is taken and from that moment on, may be used by the character instead. Take Weapon differs from Disarm Opponent in that the size of the weapon is largely irrelevant. However, the technique only works on creatures of up to twice the attacker's STR

Trip Opponent

The character attempts to overbalance or throw his opponent to the ground. The opponent must make an opposed roll of his Brawn, Evade or Acrobatics against the character's original roll. If the target fails, he falls prone. Quadruped opponents (or creatures with even more legs) may substitute their Athletics skill for Evade, and treat the roll as one difficulty grade easier.

Weapon Malfunction

The attacker's weapon malfunctions in such a way that it is rendered useless until time can be spent repairing it.

Withdraw

The defender may automatically withdraw out of reach, breaking off engagement with that particular opponent.

Close Combat

Close combat is hand to hand fighting in its classic sense, when combatants strike each other with wielded or natural weapons. Although the basic combat rules have been described previously, this section further details a number of tactical and environmental situations which may affect those in close combat.

The following guidelines offer ways to make close combat more interesting and help to further explain some concepts hinted at earlier in this chapter.

Situational Modifiers

The Situational Modifiers table (below) provides some common situational modifiers that may be applied when fighting in particular situations, or as the result of a Special Effect.

Unless stated otherwise, these modifiers are applied to attacking, parrying, and evading equally. The difficulty grade column suggests a suitable skill penalty for that situation. Where two or more situations are pertinent to the character, use the most severe. See Modifying Skills page 38.

Close Combat Situational Modifiers

Situation	*Difficulty Grade*
Attacking a helpless target	Automatic
Attacking in a confined situation	Hard
Defending while on lower ground or against mounted foe	Hard
Fighting while on unstable ground	Hard
Fighting whilst crouching or from one knee	Hard
Fighting in poor visibility (thick fog, snowstorm)	Hard
Defending against an attack from behind	Formidable
Fighting while prone	Formidable
Fighting in partial darkness (dim illumination)	Formidable
Fighting in pitch black conditions (no illumination at all)	Herculean
Blinded or loss of primary perceptive sense	Herculean

Engagement

An important concept of close combat is that of Engagement. A character is considered Engaged if he is within melee weapon range of his opponent. This does not necessarily require that both combatants can reach each other; only that one of them can be potentially struck by the other.

Once a character has engaged with an opponent he can no longer freely depart that fight (Charging is a special exception). It requires some form of deliberate act to break contact with the foe, who might not wish to allow him to depart. This is normally performed via a combat action such as Change Range or Outmanoeuvre, but sometimes an unexpected chance to disengage occurs by use of a Special Effect. Fleeing from a battle requires that engagement is broken first.

Certain circumstances will allow a character to engage with multiple foes simultaneously, provided the enemy are in close proximity with each other. This can occur in many ways, for instance closing with a line of soldiers blocking a bridge, or jumping down into the middle of a tight packed rabble. In such situations not only does the character have the option of which foe he strikes, but the reverse is also true.

Withdrawing from Engagement in this circumstance depends on the distribution of foes. Obviously retreating from the middle of a pack will be near impossible, whilst withdrawing from an organised formation might be automatic, providing the enemy doesn't wish to break ranks.

Close Combat Mechanics

The remainder of this section provides further guidelines concerning combat under different tactical circumstances.

Charging

Charging is the act of moving quickly to increase the force and impact of an attack. There are two main types of charging, depending on whether the attacker wishes to stop in engagement range with the target or continue sweeping past, through or over the target.

The common principles of a charge are as follows:

- A charge requires at least one full Combat Round of movement at running or sprinting speed prior to contact
- A charge imposes a penalty to the attack roll, increasing it by one difficulty grade
- A charge increases a bipedal attacker's Damage Modifier by one step; or the Damage Modifier of four (or more) legged creatures by two steps. In addition, the Size of the attacking weapon is improved by one step

The recipient of a charge has three options; attempt to parry, evade or simultaneously counterattack the charging attacker.

Parrying a charge attack holds some significant risks, depending on the size and strength of the attacker. The primary danger is suffering knockback, which may leave a victim prone even if they suffer no other damage from the impact. Use of the Brace combat action in advance of the charge attack can help mitigate the effects of knockback. The secondary threat comes from the bonus to the charger's weapon size, which may permit a blow to penetrate or overcome the defender's parrying weapon.

Evading a charge attack is more of a gamble, but in some circumstances may be the only option. The defender must make an opposed roll of his Evade skill versus the charging opponent's combat skill. If the defender wins he throws himself completely clear of the charge, otherwise he is hit. Any difference in Level of Success results in Special Effects as normal.

Counterattacking sacrifices the defender's opportunity to actively defend against the charge in exchange for a chance to injure the attacker. In such cases both sides are treated as having failed to parry, although they can still benefit from Passive Blocking. The wielder of the weapon with the longest Reach strikes first, potentially hindering his opponent from launching the subsequent blow. If using long-shafted impaling weapons which can be 'set' against a charge, the defender may substitute his own Damage Modifier for that of the charging opponent (or its mount if the attacker is riding).

Charging into Contact

Some charges are intended as a method to crash into an opponent, then remain in place to take advantage of any chaos caused. An example of this would be a barbarian warrior, armed with a great-axe, throwing himself at a shield wall, hoping that the impetus of his charge will help him smash through the defender's shield or knock him over.

Once the charge strikes home, the attacker is considered engaged with his opponent. From that moment on combat proceeds normally. All benefits gained from the charge are lost after the first attack.

Anathaym's Saga

Although disarmed the centaur is still dangerous. On its next turn it clips Anathaym with a hoof sending her reeling backwards, momentarily stunned. When she gathers her senses she sees that her foe has galloped off to pluck up a lance, and is now galloping back towards her, weapon levelled for a charge!

Cursing that she only brought her peltast shield, Anathaym realises that attempting to parry the lance would result in the weapon passing right through the shield (shield size Large versus a lance size Huge, but boosted to size Enormous during a charge). Not wishing to be impaled she decides to try and dive clear. The centaur makes an opposed roll of his weapon skill against Anathaym's Evade. Both achieve normal successes but Anathaym gets the higher roll and leaps clear, ending up prone. On her next turn she regains her feet, but by this time the centaur has been carried clear by the speed of his attack, and is now slowing in preparation for another charge...

Fearing that she will eventually fail if forced to keep on evading, Anathaym looks around frantically for some other option, and spots the halberd she earlier knocked from the centaur's grasp. She quickly grabs the weapon and, using it like a spear, sets it to receive charge then braces herself; completing her arrangements just before the centaur contacts her again.

Since both weapons are of equal reach, the Games Master declares that the attacks are simultaneous. The centaur's attack is rolled first, and to Anathaym's great relief the mighty beast just misses her with its lance, thanks to the attack difficulty being raised to Hard. Her own attack is a hit however, and since the halberd is set she uses the centaur's own Damage Modifier against itself, in this case 1d8 (1d4 increased by two steps for the charge). This added to the 1d8+2 for the halberd, and the special effect for not defending, Anathaym impales the weapon through the centaur's chest for 14 points of damage, giving it a Major Wound. The centaur collapses in gouts of blood, unable to continue the fight.

Charging through Contact

The second type of charge is one which uses the momentum to carry the attacker through, and clear of an engagement. It is normally limited to mounted combatants or creatures of significant size unlikely to be hindered by an impact with smaller foes. For instance an enraged aurochs could quite easily charge through a group of warriors, tossing or trampling over a victim as it passes, before continuing on out of close combat range.

The speed of such charges prevents the attacker and defender from exchanging more than a single action with each other, namely the charge attack, and the defender's reaction to it (Parry, Evade or Counterattack). Since the charge attack occurs on the attacker's turn, they will have already been carried clear by the time the defender's turn arrives.

Note that charges are not limited to just running, but can be performed by flying or swimming creatures in the relevant environment.

Cover

Cover is used by opponents to obstruct attacks against them, whether from ranged or close combat. This occurs by either physically blocking a blow due to the toughness of the interposing material, or by obscuring where precisely the foe is. For example a guard standing behind a crenellated wall may have his lower body shielded, whereas a thief hiding somewhere behind a curtain may be hidden from direct attack. The precise value of cover depends on the thickness of its protection and the extent of its coverage.

In the case of partial cover, any attack against a target which lands on an obscured Hit Location will be blocked to the extent of the cover's inherent protection. Thus in the case of the guard covered by the crenellated wall, any attack which would normally hit his abdomen or legs would be stopped by the stone fortification.

The effects of cover can be partially negated either by use of the Choose Location special effect to aim at visible parts of the target; or striking through the cover if the weapon is capable of penetrating it. When using ranged weapons however, Choose Location normally requires a critical success, which makes taking cover against missiles extremely worthwhile.

In situations where cover is total but the attacker knows his attack will penetrate, he may strike blindly at the hidden target. In such cases the attack roll is one grade harder, and Choose Location may not be taken if a special effect is won. This assumes the cover is not so extensive as to permit the target to move freely behind it. Thus, someone lurking behind a small bush could still be attacked, even though the attacker might not be able to see his quarry, but if he was behind a lengthy hedge his position could not be accurately predicted.

Evading

Protecting oneself from attacks such as volleys of ranged weapons, headlong charging beasts, and even destructive magical spells can be exceptionally difficult, especially if the consequences will overwhelm or ignore a shield. In these situations often the best thing for a character to do is fling themselves to the side or dive behind cover to escape. This is known as evading.

Evasion attempts require an opposed roll of the attacker's pertinent skill versus the Evade skill of the defender. This could be anything from the Drive roll of a charioteer to the spell casting roll of a magician. If the attacker wins then they inflict damage as per normal. If the defender wins damage is completely avoided. Whatever the result, the evasive gambit leaves the defender prone, usually requiring him to regain his footing on his following turn.

If the winner of the opposed roll achieves one or more levels of success over his opponent, they may select suitable Special Effects as per normal combat.

Evading may be made more difficult or rendered impossible depending on the circumstances:

- The character is helpless or entangled
- There is nowhere to evade to (balancing on a ledge whilst scaling a cliff, for example)
- A mounted character may only evade by flinging themselves clear of the saddle

Evading is not normally performed in close combat due to its inherent disadvantages. However, a character facing a hand-to-hand attack against which he has no applicable defence due to the lack of a weapon (or an inferior sized one which won't block the damage) may have no other choice.

In such cases evading provides only a temporary respite from a determined opponent who decides to follow up, preventing the prone character from regaining their feet. Nothing prevents a prone character from attempting to evade subsequent attacks, with the proviso that they suffer a 'Fighting while prone' situational penalty as they continue to roll aside or scrabble backwards away from their attacker.

Evading Creatures

Creatures that lack thick natural armour to bull through attacks, or the intellect or skill to actively parry them, are often forced to evade in close combat in order to defend themselves.

In these circumstances, most creatures lacking humanoid form, quadrupeds or serpents for example, have an inherent advantage over bipedal characters; in that they rarely go prone when evading, due to their shape or multiple limbs.

As a rule of thumb, whenever such a creature attempts to evade an attack, they only end up prone if they fail their Evade roll (the skill check, not the opposed test).

Flying Combat

Fighting against flying creatures, and full scale aerial battles provide a rather interesting dynamic to close combat, since most airborne creatures require constant movement to remain aloft.

Attacking Ground-Based Targets

It can be difficult for ground-based characters to defeat airborne foes. Of course in some encounters the flying creature will hover or land on the combatant, allowing combat to proceed normally. In others the flying creature may fly back and forth, sweeping down to make attacks before continuing back out of range. In the latter situation it is recommended that each 'strafing' run is treated as Charging through Contact, see Charging page 102. This can make airborne creatures deadly opponents unless ground based defenders have some sort of ranged weaponry or cover.

Aerial Combat Aloft

Combat between aerial creatures or characters mounted on flying beasts should be handled slightly differently. Unlike ground based fighting it often takes a significant period of time to jockey into a position where one airborne opponent can assault the other. Each brief engagement only allows one of them to attack before the flying creatures travel apart, requiring them to manoeuvre again to see which gets the upper hand in the next pass.

Thus at the start of each round combatants must make an opposed roll of their Fly skills (or Ride if a mount). The winner is the one who can attack that round. If facing multiple opponents use a group opposed roll, and all those who beat the lone participant

Aerial Tactics

Airborne combat can be spiced up by introducing terrain and environmental factors. Clouds can be used for ambushes or places to escape battle. Tall buildings and narrow canyons can offer a dramatic setting in which to set chases, with the participants playing a deadly game of chicken if they fail their flying or riding rolls. An aerial battle could even involve support fire from the ground, forcing combatants to hoard their Action Points to evade deadly ballista bolts whilst trying to beat their flying opponents.

may attack it that round. Attacks are resolved in a similar manner to charges, the recipient allowed to parry, evade or counterattack.

In the case of particularly large creatures or those travelling at high speed, the Games Master may wish to increase the manoeuvring time between passes, for example perhaps 1d3 rounds for a griffon or 1d6 rounds for a dragon. In these cases it is wise to limit mounted archers or spell casters to acting on each pass, since most of the intervening time the rider will be thrown about in aerial acrobatics or the enemy target will be out of range.

Knockback

An attack which imparts more damage than the SIZ of the recipient will, by default, result in him being knocked back. The damage in this circumstance is accounted before any reduction due to parrying or armour.

On receiving such a blow, the recipient must pass an easy Acrobatics or standard Athletics roll to avoid falling prone. They are also thrust backwards one metre for each five points of damage (or fraction thereof) in excess of their SIZ. Proactively using the Brace combat action can reduce or even negate the effects of knockback.

Knockback differs from the Bash special effect in that Knockback is the automatic and accidental side effect of tremendously powerful blows, whilst a Bash is a deliberate technique which relies on timing and leverage.

Leaping Attacks

There are some animals, monsters, and even people who leap upon their victims in order to knock them prone. Leaping attacks can be launched from a variety of situations, but most are triggered as part of an ambush or at the conclusion of a charge. A few creatures have the ability to leap atop an opponent without the need for a run-up or superior height.

A leaping attack is resolved with an opposed roll of the leaper's Athletics skill versus the defender's Brawn or Evade skill. If the leaper wins then the defender is automatically knocked prone, with the attacker astride them. If the attack fails, the defender has weathered or sidestepped the impact. If the winner of the opposed roll achieves one or more levels of success over his opponent, they may select suitable Special Effects as per normal combat.

No damage is inflicted as part of the leap (unless they possess the Leaper creature ability page 216); however a subsequently prone victim cannot recover his footing until either his attacker leaves him, or he eventually wins a Special Effect permitting him to Arise.

If the target is a quadruped, then it may substitute Athletics for Evade, and makes the attacker's initial Athletics roll one difficulty grade harder. In addition, leaping attacks only work against opponents of up to twice the attacker's SIZ. A target can make themselves more difficult to knock down by proactive use of the Brace combat action, provided they are aware of the impending leap attack.

Mounted Combat

Unless learned as part of specifically mounted combat styles (see Combat Style Benefits page 88), the combat skills of a rider may not exceed their Ride skill. The advantages of being mounted are considerable however:

- A mounted warrior rolls a 1D10+10 for the Hit Location of bipedal creatures, provided the target is lower than the rider.
- A mounted warrior can withdraw freely from engagement on his turn provided his mount moves faster (i.e. has a higher Movement value) than the opponent, and the mount itself is not engaged in attacking.
- A mounted warrior may, at the cost of an Action Point, substitute either his own Combat Style or Ride skill instead of his mount's, to defend it against attacks.
- A mounted warrior may combine his SIZ with his mount's for the purposes of avoiding Knockback, provided he passes an unopposed Ride roll.
- A mounted warrior may, when charging with a braced weapon, substitute his own Damage Modifier for that of his mount. A weapon braced for a charging attack cannot be used to parry. If the weapon impales it must be left in the body of the target, or else break or dismount the rider as the mount continues past.

Multiple Opponents

Facing multiple opponents in MYTHRAS is often exceptionally dangerous. Whilst a character suffers no specific penalties to his combat skills, he can soon become swamped by his opponents and rapidly run out of Action Points with which to defend himself. Once all his actions have been expended the character is treated as having failed his parry roll against any subsequent attacks, which in addition to any damage inflicted also leaves him vulnerable to Special Effects.

The best tactics to use against being outnumbered are:

- Constrain the avenue of attack so that fewer opponents can engage simultaneously
- Fight as a formation to place disordered opponents at a disadvantage
- Outmanoeuvre around multiple opponents so that they interfere with one another
- Withdraw then flee the combat as quickly as possible

Outmanoeuvring

A character facing multiple opponents can use movement to limit the number which can attack him at any one moment in time. This works by constantly shifting position, forcing some foes to start running around the flanks of their companions to re-establish reach or lines of attack, generally causing them to interfere with one another. Outmanoeuvring requires that the character has room to move about, and is not pinned in a confining area. It also assumes that the character is engaged with the entire group of foes, rather than a specific individual.

An example of outmanoeuvring in action would be a group of guards trying to arrest a drunken barbarian in a tavern. The warrior could manoeuvre around the tables, chairs, and roof supports to block the majority of his foes whilst he whittles them down one by one.

Outmanoeuvring requires that the character engages his opponents in a group opposed roll of Evade skills. Every participant, both the manoeuvring character and those foes who wish to corner him, must spend an Action Point. Then they each roll once, and those who fail to beat the manoeuvring character's roll cannot attack him for the remainder of that Combat Round, being blocked by their allies or terrain features.

If the manoeuvring character beats all of his opponents he has the choice of safely engaging a single foe for the rest of the round or Withdrawing from the fight completely.

Passive Blocking

Passive Blocking is the placement of weapons and shields in such a manner so that they effectively act as cover. Characters armed with a weapon may hold it in such a way that it covers a chosen location (or locations when using a shield), but at the cost of being unable to actively parry with it (see Ward Location page 93). Any attack which hits those locations automatically receives the benefit of the weapon or shield, reducing damage as normal. The technique is commonly used when a warrior wishes to guard a weak spot or wounded location.

It may seem paradoxical to sacrifice the ability to parry, potentially opening up a passively blocking character to an unopposed attack. However there are many situations it is a valid tactic: for example when used by inexperienced troops or those lacking full sets of armour. In addition there is nothing which prevents a two weapons or weapon and shield combatant from using his other weapon to actively parry.

Since passive blocking works in the same way as cover, the Choose Location special effect cannot be used to bypass the block in close combat, though opponents can still use the effect to strike other unblocked areas. Assuming a shield, passive blocking against missiles becomes even better, since for ranged weapons Choose Location is a critical only.

Crouching down behind a shield allows a character to double the number of locations covered whilst passive blocking.

Pulled Blows

Occasionally a character may wish to avoid maiming or killing an opponent. This is achieved by 'pulling' a blow, limiting the force placed behind it or striking with a less lethal part of the weapon. A pulled blow halves the damage inflicted on a successful hit. However, the intent to pull a blow must be stated before the attack is made, since it is near impossible to withhold a fully committed strike once it has been launched.

Surprise

Surprise occurs when an unexpected attack is launched against opponents unaware of the attacker's presence or intention. An ambush would be an example of the former, whilst treacherously turning on an unsuspecting ally during amiable conversation illustrates the latter.

The effects of surprise on a target are potent:

- The target suffers a -10 penalty to initiative
- Until their Initiative arrives they are considered flat footed and cannot defend themselves
- The first attack on the target, if successful, gains a bonus Special Effect
- For the remainder of the round they may not perform any offensive action

For example, an assassin who sneaks up on an oblivious guard, wins the initiative, and successfully strikes from behind would gain two special effects – one for the attack's success against the guard's automatic failure; and a bonus one for surprising him. If the assassin were using a dagger he could then choose Select Location: head, and Kill Silently, quietly stabbing the guard in the throat.

As surprise can be so devastating, targets of such an attack should be permitted a chance to detect the impending conflict. For instance, an ambush might allow an opposed roll of Perception versus Stealth; or Insight versus Deceit for a betrayal. Difficulty modifiers should be applied in situations where the target is hindered, such as being inebriated or dozing lightly. Conversely a bonus should be applied if the target is suspicious or forewarned. If the target wins the opposed roll then the effects of surprise are negated.

Sweep Attacks

Sweep attacks occur when weapons or creatures of unusual size attack a closely clumped group of opponents – the scything tail of a huge dragon for example – striking several foes simultaneously. A sweep attack is made by applying a single attack roll of the weapon or creature to all targets in its path. Each defender must resolve the effects of the attack separately, and any special effects imposed on the attacker are treated as having occurred concurrently.

Sweep attacks can also be used for other 'area affect' assaults, such as the overhead smash of a giant's tree trunk club or the unstoppable charge of a giant triceratops. The games master decides how many foes are caught in the attack based upon the length or trajectory of weapon, and his visualisation of the conflict.

Unarmed Combat

Unarmed combat is the default Combat Style available to any person or creature, which covers the skill of fighting using only the limbs and natural armaments of their own body. Some beasts have a variety of natural weapons, each with a different reach and size, which can make larger creatures particularly dangerous – able to stand off at longer range, and still launch blows capable of smashing through the stoutest shields. The unarmed combat techniques used by animals and monsters are examined in more detail in the Creatures chapter.

Although unarmed combat seems superfluous for warriors who utilise weapons, it still provides a number of advantages:

- Unarmed combat can be used interchangeably with any other weapon style, provided the target is within reach of the attacker's natural weapons.
- Unarmed combat can be used offensively for either striking or grappling an opponent. It is important for the user to declare which he intends in advance, since the resolution of each is handled slightly differently.
- Unarmed combat can be used defensively to parry a weapon attack. Damage is reduced as per normal, according to the comparative Sizes of the natural and wielded weapon. Even if no damage was stopped, the parry attempt might still prevent the defender from suffering one or more Special Effects.

Note that if an unarmed combatant can step within the reach of an armed opponent, he will reduce the effective Size of his opponent's weapon, making it quite possible to parry blows without suffering injury.

Parrying Weapons Whilst Unarmed

As previously described a Parry is actually a combination of parrying, blocking, and footwork to deflect the force of a blow. It is not simply interposing an object into the path of an attack to stop it dead – for example using a forearm to block the sweep of a sword – since such an action would likely result in a mangled arm.

Instead most unarmed and armed combat styles use more subtle techniques to gain maximum deflection for the minimum risk. Examples include, but are not limited to: Pressing against the hand or hilt of a weapon to change its line of attack, stepping very close to cut down angular momentum of swung weapons, deflecting thrusts by knocking aside the point or haft, or even grabbing a weapon on the haft or blade near its grip.

Such methods rely on several points however; firstly that the parrying creature is intelligent enough to understand and use said techniques, and secondly that they are within unarmed range. The latter point is perhaps the most crucial, and demonstrates the dangers of facing an armed opponent with a longer reach.

Striking

Using unarmed combat to throw simple damage-inflicting strikes is resolved in the same way as normal weapon attacks. Some Special Effects are specifically reserved for unarmed combat, namely Flurry, Grip, and Take Weapon.

Calculating the damage, Size and Reach of natural weapons is defined on page 222 of the Creatures chapter. Human unarmed attacks, for instance, have a size of Small, reach of Touch, and inflict 1d3 damage.

Some creature's natural weapons and unarmed combat styles may add other effects or impart inherent Special Effects on a successful strike. For example the gripping jaws of a crocodile or the poisoned stinger of a giant scorpion.

Grappling

Grappling attacks are resolved using an opposed roll of the attacker's Unarmed skill versus the combat skill used by the defender. If the attacker wins then they establish the grapple, but if the defender wins the grapple fails. As with Evade, if one of the combatants achieves one or more levels of success over his opponent, they may select an equal number of Special Effects.

The effects of grappling depend on the location struck. A grappled limb is rendered inoperable whilst grappling the head or torso imposes a difficulty penalty of Hard against any skill the opponent attempts. In addition, on his following turns the grappler may make unarmed attacks to inflict damage (equal to his Damage Modifier) on the body part by crushing, twisting or strangulating it. The defender may oppose with his own Unarmed or Brawn skill in order to reduce or block the damage.

A grapple continues until the victim manages to break free. Escape attempts are performed on the victim's turn using the Struggle combat action. This requires an opposed roll of either Brawn or Unarmed against whichever of the two skills the grappler prefers. If the grappled victim wins, they manage to break free. Note that some attackers using Brawn may be so strong that no amount of brute force or cunning technique can overcome their grip.

Grappling requires that the limb or appendage is empty, and is capable of hooking, sticking or gripping.

Unusual Combat Conditions

There are certain circumstances and environments which may prevent a character from fighting at his full ability. Several are specifically noted below, but other situations may occur which aren't covered by the rules. In such cases the Games Master should apply similar rules as appropriate to the fight. For example, a battle upon a treacherously slippery ice floe may require that combat skills be capped by Acrobatics.

Climbing

A climbing character has all of his combat skills capped by the value of his Athletics skill. Bipedal characters are limited to fighting with a single limb, requiring the other three to remain clinging to the vertiginous surface they are scaling.

Swimming

A swimming character has all of his combat skills capped by the value of his Swim skill. Since water (and other fluids) impose significant drag, only thrusting weapons are effective whilst submerged, and even those are reduced to half damage. Other weapons are slowed to the point of impotence. Unarmed combat attacks which involve biting, strangulation or ramming are unaffected.

Weapon Reach – Closing and Opening Range

Weapon Reach, and its associated mechanics for Closing and Opening Range are optional rules for those desiring more realistic combat.

In general terms when two combatants face one another armed with weapons of greatly disproportionate reach, the wielder of the longer weapon can keep his opponent at bay, preventing him from attacking. If however, the wielder of the shorter weapon can step inside the effective reach of the longer, then the tables turn and the combatant with the longer weapon will find himself unable to parry with that weapon.

The following rules assume a Reach difference of two or more steps between the longer and shorter weapon. Thus a dagger (Short) against a falchion (Medium) would suffer no penalties in combat, whereas the same dagger against a great axe (Long) would.

Fighting at the Longer Reach

If fighting at the Reach of the longer weapon, then the user of the shorter weapon cannot directly attack the wielder of the longer. They are still considered to be engaged since the longer weapon can still reach them.

In this situation the user of the shorter weapon can attack the longer weapon of his opponent, try to close the range between them, or hope to win an applicable Special Effect. If the longer weapon is in fact the natural armament of a creature with superior reach, such as the tentacle of a colossal squid, the user of the shorter weapon can directly attack the limb assaulting them.

The intimidating threat of longer reach is an inherent advantage of two handed weapons, which offsets the disadvantage of not using a shield.

Fighting at the Shorter Reach

In the converse situation where the fighters are engaged at the Reach of the shorter weapon, the user of the longer weapon will find he cannot parry the attacks of the shorter.

The user of the longer weapon can still attack with the haft or hilt of his now encroached weapon, but its efficacy is significantly reduced. In this circumstance the weapon's Size is reduced as many steps as the difference between the two weapons' Reach, and only inflicts 1d3+1 damage due to the necessity of striking with the haft, pommel, guard from an awkwardly cramped position.

At this point the best option for the user of the longer weapon is to reopen the range between them, draw a shorter backup weapon, defend themselves with their Unarmed skill, or hope to win a useful Special Effect. In a last ditch situation the encroached fighter can attempt to Evade instead.

Closing Range

A character that is being held at range by a longer weapon must close on his opponent before being able to attack him. Two methods are available to do this.

- Close Range Special Effect – automatically closes, but cannot be used unless a character has generated an opportunity for a Special Effect.
- Change Range Combat Action – costs an Action Point, and is used on a character's Turn.

In the latter case of attempting to Change Range, the character's opponent has two options, described below. In both cases if the opponent has no Action Points left – or chooses not to spend an Action Point – then the attempt to close is automatically successful.

- The combatants match Evade skills in an opposed test. If the character initiating the Change Range action wins then he can close the range to a desired distance. If the opponent wins then the existing range is maintained.
- However, if the opponent decides to attack the closing character instead, then he must make an opposed roll of his combat skill versus the closing character's Evade skill. If the opponent wins, he strikes the character, and any difference in Level of Success results in Special Effects as per normal combat. Whether or not the blow lands, the closing character bridges the distance, and gains the advantage of having the shorter weapon.

Opening Range

Opening Range works in the same way as Closing Range – but obviously in reverse. The character can use Change Range to completely withdraw from engagement. See Withdrawing below.

Withdrawing

Withdrawing from a fight means that the character extricates himself from close combat weapon range. This can be done in a myriad of ways, from physically pushing an opponent away, side-stepping a committed attack or unexpectedly taking several large steps backward. At this point they have not fled the battle entirely, but have briefly opened up enough space to have disengaged that opponent, and consider new tactical options.

Withdrawing is automatic when using the Withdraw special effect. Otherwise a character must attempt to break free by use of the Change Range or Outmanoeuvre combat actions, in which case the opponent(s) may resist.

Once he has disengaged himself, the withdrawing character may on his next turn (for the cost of an Action Point):

- Reroll initiative
- Flee the battle entirely
- Seek out a new opponent to engage
- Perform some other suitable act not covered here

Ranged Combat

Ranged combat incorporates all forms of weaponry which require to be shot, thrown or slung to strike their target. The ranged weapons a character can use are listed as part of their combat styles - anything from throwing stones to firing a huge trebuchet.

Ranged attacks are resolved in an identical way to close combat. However, ranged weapons can normally only be parried with shields; those without must rely on natural cover or use Evade to dive out of the line of fire. Thus against lightly armoured foes, ranged weapons can be formidable deterrents.

Each ranged weapon has a number of specific attributes which determine its effectiveness. The ones which have a key bearing on combat are as follows:

Force

The ranged weapon equivalent of Size. It measures the penetrative power of that weapon or its ammunition to determine whether the blow overcomes a (shield) parry.

Damage Modifier

This attribute shows whether or not the Damage Modifier of the attacker can be used to boost the ranged weapon's damage roll. In general only bows and thrown weapons allow the user to apply their Damage Bonus.

Range

Three numbers separated by slashes, representing the maximum Close, Effective, and Long ranges of the weapon or its ammunition. Close range is the distance over which the Choose Location special effect may be used, provided the target is stationary or unaware of the impending attack. Effective range has no significant modifiers. At long range the weapon can still inflict harm, but the amount of damage is halved and Force is reduced by one step.

Reload

The time taken to reload a weapon which fires ammunition.

Situational Modifiers

The table on page 108 provides some situational modifiers specific to ranged weapons. Where two or more situations are pertinent to the character, use the most severe.

Ranged Combat Situational Modifiers

Situation	Difficulty Grade
Light Wind*	Hard
Moderate Wind*	Formidable
Strong Wind*	Herculean
Gale, Storm or Worse*	Hopeless
Target is Running	Hard
Target is Sprinting	Formidable
Target obscured by mist or is in partial darkness	Hard
Target obscured by thick smoke, fog or is in darkness	Formidable
Target is completely obscured	Herculean
Blinded or loss of primary perceptive sense	Hopeless
Target prone	Formidable
Attacker is prone**	Herculean
Attacker is on unstable ground	Hard

**Assumes the thrown weapon or ammunition is vulnerable to crosswinds; and supersedes the normal penalty imposed by winds on physical skills .*

***Penalty can be negated if using a crossbow from a prepared position.*

Ranged Combat Considerations

Whilst ranged weapons appear to be extraordinarily potent they do suffer a number of restrictions, and have special rules covering their use. Specific notes concerning ranged attacks are as follows:

Aiming

By spending additional time aiming a ranged weapon, a character can potentially increase his chance to hit. Aiming requires an entire Combat Round steadying the weapon, and waiting for the best opportunity to release, for example withholding a bowshot for a momentary lull in the wind or until a target moves between two obstructions. By aiming, the character may reduce the difficulty of a Situational Modifier by one grade. Additional rounds spend aiming grant no further advantage.

Distance Penalties

The difficulty of hitting a target increases rapidly with the distance which separates it from the marksman. Distance is considered independent of a weapon's Range, the latter being the performance characteristics of the weapon over set distances.

Distance penalties can be offset by the size of the target being aimed at. Hitting a mammoth at fifty metres is far easier than hitting a human at the same range. The table overleaf indicates the difficulty grade adjustment of hitting various sized objects over incremental distances. These stack on top of other ranged combat situational modifiers.

These values assume an active target in the open field. If shooting a static object at a known range, for example a straw butt during a competition, the Games Master may reduce the difficulty by a step or two.

Whilst there are few creatures which achieve such gargantuan scales, there are other objects which can reach sizes in the hundreds; such as buildings, fortifications, and troop formations. On the battlefield the near impossibility of striking a single man is replaced by the use of volley fire, saturating an area densely packed with men; in the hope that a small proportion of projectiles will strike home.

For characters with a more destructive bent, statistics for siege engines are included in the Economics and Equipment chapter.

Firing into a Crowd

Firing into the swirling ebb and flow of a melee can be a risky business, even for the most proficient marksman. The unpredictable movement of crowds and engaged opponents can easily result in an ally straying into the line of fire, during the time it takes for a ranged weapon to travel the intervening distance to its intended target. Thus there is always a risk of accidentally striking someone other than the original target being aimed at.

When firing at a specific target at the edge of a crowd or melee, the attack suffers a difficulty grade of at least Hard. If trying to fire through a group to hit a target in its midst, or on the other side, the penalty should be raised to Formidable.

The result of the dice roll is very important. A marksman who passes his attack roll despite the difficulty penalty has aimed true, and will hit his intended target. If however the marksman fails the roll, but would have succeeded if not for the firing into a crowd penalty, then an adjacent victim is struck instead. If more than one target is in the line of fire, the Games Master should determine the victim randomly.

No matter who eventually becomes the target – intended or not – if they are aware of the impending attack, they are free to Evade or Parry as normal. Any special effects won as part of the attack only apply to the original target, not any accidentally struck bystander.

Firing on the Move

A character is still permitted to use ranged weapons even whilst mounted on an animal or vehicle. However in these circumstances their combat skill is capped by the Ride or Drive skill of the person controlling the conveyance, which may or may not be the attacker

Distance Penalties

		Target SIZ					
		10 or less	11-20	21-40	41-80	81-150	151-300
Distance	1-20m	1 Step Harder	No Effect	1 Step Easier	1 Step Easier	2 Steps Easier	2 Steps Easier
	21-40m	1 Step Harder	1 Step Harder	No Effect	1 Step Easier	1 Step Easier	2 Steps Easier
	41-60m	2 Steps Harder	1 Step Harder	1 Step Harder	No Effect	1 Step Easier	1 Step Easier
	61-80m	2 Steps Harder	2 Steps Harder	1 Step Harder	1 Step Harder	No Effect	1 Step Easier
	81-100m	3 Steps Harder	2 Steps Harder	2 Steps Harder	1 Step Harder	1 Step Harder	No Effect
	101-120m	3 Steps Harder	3 Steps Harder	2 Steps Harder	2 Steps Harder	1 Step Harder	1 Step Harder
	121-140m	4 Steps Harder	3 Steps Harder	3 Steps Harder	2 Steps Harder	2 Steps Harder	1 Step Harder
	Each 20m	Follow table progression					

Realistic Range Penalties

Trying to hit a man-sized target with a human powered missile weapon is actually much harder than most people expect. A shot must take into consideration physical factors such as cross winds, variances between weight, flexibility and air resistance of each piece of (ostensibly identical) ammunition, and the necessity to arch a shot or throw. Even humidity and heat can significantly affect the performance of weapons such as bows.

Further complicating the matter are the difficulty of judging range accurately, and the diminishment in the perceived size of a target as range increases. And this is assuming a stationary object! Complexity is further increased when attacking a moving target, because of the time it takes for the weapon to reach the destination; even more so if that target starts to move erratically.

Taking all these factors into account, it soon becomes evident that there is a huge difference between how ranged weapons are portrayed in fantasy and the realities of the real world. In actual fact most bow and spear hunters rely primarily on stealth to get very close, and are rarely able to hit large prey in the wild at ranges over a few tens of metres. Fortunately MYTHRAS errs on the side of the heroic.

himself. For example an archer riding in a two man chariot would have his attack skill capped by the Drive skill of his driver.

Ranged attacks cannot usually be performed if the attacker himself is moving at a gait faster than a walk, since their aim is constantly thrown off by the physical movement. One exception to this are warriors trained in a Combat Style specialising in Skirmishing, see page 89. However in this case the attacker's attack percentage cannot exceed his Athletics skill.

Anathaym's Saga

Seeing that Master Zamothis is in trouble, Anathaym abandons the impaled halberd, and unwinds her sling from her forehead. At the start of the next round she casts a lead slingshot into the tight melee surrounding her desperately manoeuvring mentor, aiming at a black coated centaur of prodigious musculature.

Her combat skill (Meerish Slinger style) is normally 67%. Since she does not wish to accidentally strike Zamothis the roll is considered Hard, reducing her skill to 45%.

Anathaym passes the attack roll, and selects the Stun Location special effect against the unsuspecting creature. Unluckily she rolls minimum damage, and her shot glances off its hindquarters with no apparent effect.

Her first attack unnoticed, Anathaym reloads, and at the end of the round casts again. This time she does not do so well, rolling 52. This not only fails to strike the black centaur but since it is less than her normal skill (without the firing into a crowd penalty), it means she has struck a bystander. The Games Master states there are two other possible targets in immediate proximity, a second (chestnut coated) centaur, and Master Zamothis himself. A dice is rolled to see which of the two is struck, and to her horror Anathaym inadvertently hits her oblivious mentor. Fortunately this time the slingshot inflicts no special effect, but still manages to draw a glare from the grizzled warrior when the shot clangs off his crested bronze helmet.

Impaling Ranged Attacks

Ranged weapon projectiles which result in an impale, such as an arrow or thrown javelin, clearly cannot be yanked free of the wound on the next turn by the marksman who threw or fired the weapon. However nothing stops a character in close combat with the transfixed victim from subsequently attempting to grab the impaling weapon to tear it free.

Note that the Size of an impaled weapon is different from the Force it struck with. Ranged impaling weapons have a special column denoting their actual size when considering the hindrances caused by the Impale special effect.

Loading Ranged Weapons

Before a ranged weapon can be used it must either be readied or loaded. This can often take significant time, slowing down a ranged combatant's rate of fire.

Throwing weapons, for example javelins, necessitate the weapon be drawn or plucked up in preparation. This normally only requires one turn to complete, as per the Ready Weapon action providing it is within reach. If a second throwing weapon is held in preparation in the off-hand, the caster can swap it over to his throwing hand as a Free Action.

Projectile weapons, such as slings or bows must be loaded. The number of turns it takes to load a ranged weapon is listed in its Load column on the Ranged Weapons table, page 65.

A character can reduce the time spent loading or readying by use of the Rapid Reload special effect.

Hit Locations

Most successful (weapon) attacks land on a specific hit location. This can be determined randomly or in some circumstances be selected by Special Effects such as Choose Location. To randomly calculate which location is been hit, roll 1d20 and compare the number rolled with the relevant humanoid or creature Hit Location table.

Animals and monsters usually have slightly different hit location tables than humanoids to reflect their own unique physiology. These are listed as part of each being's description in the Creature chapter. The humanoid Hit Location table is repeated here for ease of reference.

Humanoid Hit Locations

1d20	Hit Location
1–3	Right Leg
4–6	Left Leg
7–9	Abdomen
10–12	Chest
13–15	Right Arm
16–18	Left Arm
19–20	Head

Note than some attacks, especially magical ones or those produced by particular monsters (a dragon's fiery breath for example) may strike several Hit Locations simultaneously. Individual Hit Locations may be armoured, either from worn protection or the natural toughness of the creature's outer surface. This is important when considering Damage and Wound Levels below.

Damage and Wound Levels

If an attack strikes successfully, it causes damage according to the damage rating for the weapon (see the statistical entries for close combat and ranged weapons in the Economics & Equipment chapter, pages 63 to 65). A shortsword, for instance, inflicts 1d6 damage.

The rolled damage for the weapon or attack is modified by the certain conditions in the specific following order:

- Apply the Damage Modifier for the character making the attack
- Modify the damage from any weapon enhancing (or reducing) magic
- If parried, reduce the damage appropriately as per the comparative weapon sizes
- If the hit location is armoured, reduce damage by the Armour Points value

If the damage inflicted by the attack is above zero, then the hit location sustains that amount of damage, with the damage total being immediately removed from the location's Hit Points. Note how many Hit Points the location has remaining, and the wound category that results.

- Minor Wound: Hit Location still has positive Hit Points
- Serious Wound: Hit Location is reduced to zero Hit Points or below
- Major Wound: Hit Location is reduced to a negative score equal or greater than its starting Hit Points

Use the following rules if a location receives a Serious or Major wound. Note that wounds requiring Endurance checks test them in an opposed roll against the value of the original attack roll. This reflects the ability of highly skilled warriors to make more deadly strikes. Endurance rolls are not repeated unless the location is wounded again.

Wounding Opponents with an Endurance over 100%

When a serious or major wound is inflicted against an opponent that possesses an Endurance over 100%, the opposed test should take into account the penalty applied by the higher skill in the contest. In the rare cases where Endurance is the higher skill, it is recommended that the penalty is imposed retroactively to attacker's skill – potentially downgrading the success level of the original attack roll.

This does not mean that the attacker missed his original attack, merely that the deadliness of the wound is reduced and it becomes easier for the victim to win the opposed test.

Minor Wound

Minor wounds are cuts, scratches, bruises and sprains. They hurt, may bleed, but are not significant enough to slow down or hamper the victim.

Serious Wound

If a location is reduced to zero Hit Points or below, the victim receives a Serious Wound. The location is permanently scarred, and the victim cannot attack or start to cast spells (but can still parry or evade) for the next 1d3 turns due to being stunned or distracted by the pain of the wound.

A character suffering a Serious Wound to a limb must immediately make an opposed test of his Endurance versus the successful attack roll of his enemy. Failure results in the limb being rendered useless, until the location is restored to positive hit points. If a leg, the victim drops prone. If an arm, he drops whatever he is holding unless the object is strapped on (use common sense here).

A character suffering a Serious Wound to the Abdomen, Chest or Head must immediately make an opposed test of his Endurance versus the successful attack roll of his enemy. Failure results in unconsciousness for a number of minutes equal to the amount of damage sustained in the attack causing the Serious Wound. First Aid or Healing skills can be used to help an unconscious victim regain consciousness, but he will not be able to rejoin any combat until he has received further healing to the Seriously Wounded location.

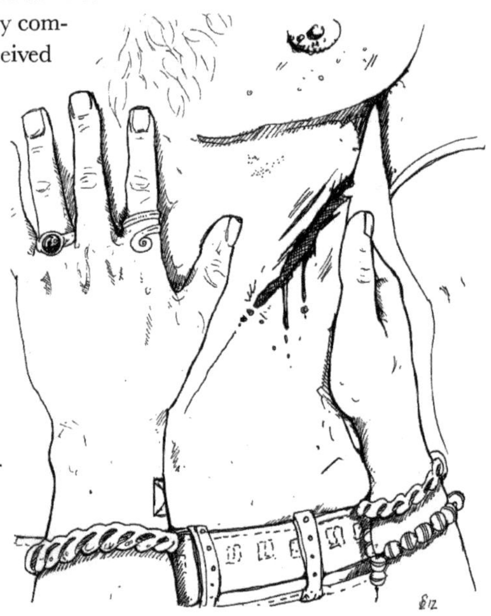

At the Games Master's discression, even if the character remains functional, all tasks requiring use of that body location will suffer an ongoing penalty of one difficulty grade, until the injury is reduced to a Minor Wound.

Major Wound

If a location is reduced to a negative score equal or greater than its starting Hit Points, the character receives a Major Wound. The character is immediately incapacitated, unable to continue fighting.

A limb is considered to be severed, transfixed, shattered or ripped off by a Major Wound. The character drops prone, physically incapacitated, and must immediately make an opposed test of Endurance versus the successful attack roll of his enemy. Failure results in unconsciousness from the agony. If a severed, punctured or ripped-off location is not treated within a number of minutes equal to five times his Healing Rate, the character dies from blood loss and shock.

The victim of a Major Wound to the Abdomen, Chest or Head drops unconscious, totally incapacitated and must immediately make an opposed test of Endurance versus the successful attack roll of his enemy. Failure results in an instant and gratuitous death (decapitated, chopped in half, impaled through the heart, torn apart, and so forth). If he survives, and the location is not treated within a number of Combat Rounds equal to twice his Healing Rate, he still dies from blood loss and shock.

Since most Major Wounds require some form of surgery or major magic to heal, the sufferer will be very unlikely to recover

Anathaym's Saga

Giving up on her sling, Anathaym recovers her shortsword and rushes to aid Master Zamothis, who despite cutting down two of the formidable centaurs is becoming rapidly exhausted. Just as she arrives, the big black centaur smashes through the last of her mentor's shield, and with its return blow catches Zamothis full in the head. Despite the protection of his helmet the aging warrior is knocked down, out of the fight with a Major Wound.

Anathaym screams with fury and leaps astride the centaur's back, taking it completely by surprise. On her next turn she stabs with her shortsword. The gods are with her and she rolls a critical success. Since the centaur was unable to defend with its club, she gains two special effects and chooses Maximise Damage and Impale, driving her blade deep into its back. Although this might have finished off a human, the centaur is somewhat tougher. On its own turn it rears, throwing her off. Anathaym fails her Athletics roll and lands prone – unarmed and helpless before the enraged creature.

As it raises its great club to finish her off, the forgotten Master Zamothis spends a Luck Point to perform a Heroic Last Action and rallies long enough to cast his knife at the centaur. It flies true, striking the beast in the chest, near to where the tip of Anathaym's shortsword emerges. This is enough to give the centaur a Serious Wound, forcing it to make an opposed roll of its Endurance against the attack roll of the thrown knife. Zamothis wins with the higher roll, and the centaur chief collapses with a look of surprise.

The remaining centaurs take this as an omen, and lacking the steadying presence of their sorcerer, turn tail and flee. Anathaym crawls over to the now unconscious body of her beloved mentor and performs First Aid on his cracked skull, saving his life. Then with the help of the rescued youth, they carry the old man back to Meeros.

from a major wound in time to rejoin combat. Depending on the available treatment the wounded location will be potentially maimed (see Healing from Injury page 80).

Heroic Last Actions

In special cases where key characters receive a Major Wound, the Games Master might allow a heroic last action - such as spitting out one last spell, attempting to cut down their slayer, crawling away to hide, or trying to tourniquet their own wound. They must have working limbs applicable to the action, and burn a Luck Point. They get a single opportunity to attempt their action, and then immediately collapse into unconsciousness, and probable death.

Optional Rules: Rabble & Underlings

Only use these optional rules when the characters are facing a ravening horde of inconsequential and expendable adversaries. Competent NPCs and major villains should be treated differently

A mainstay of some fantasy literature is the scene of heroes scything down hordes of faceless opponents, be they enemy soldiers, fanatical cultists or even ravening demi-humans. To portray such battles in MYTHRAS can not only be time consuming enterprises, but are also difficult to pull off satisfactorily considering the ever present risk of becoming outnumbered or rolling a fumble at the wrong time. Luck Points can only help so far.

A better way of modelling these types of encounter is to provide weaker foes or simplify the book keeping required to keep track of injuries. MYTHRAS offers alternate options to dealing with this issue, thus speeding up combat considerably.

Rabble

Rabble are foes who intimidate by their numbers but in actual fact have little prowess or willingness to remain in combat once blood is shed. They can take many forms from vicious beggars who set upon drunken characters when they stumble home from the tavern along dark alleyways; or the mindless adherents of a dark cult – eager yet incompetent. In terms of conflict, members of a rabble use the following guidelines:

- Rabble have little or no armour
- Rabble are too incompetent to be able to use Special Effects
- Rabble have Hit Points equal to one fifth (rounded up) of the CON+SIZ of an average member of that race
- Once they receive any damage, they cease fighting
- If the damage is less than their Hit Points they flee cursing or yelling in fear
- If the damage equals or surpasses their Hit Points, they collapse clutching the wounded location, and weeping or screaming in agony
- If the damage is double their Hit Points, they die in a spectacular and grotesque manner
- Once one third of their number are dead or wounded, the rest of the rabble break and take flight

Underlings

Underlings are competent foes usually sent en-masse to harass Adventurers: thuggish bodyguards irregular troops in the opening stages of a battle, for example. Despite not being tracked as full characters, underlings can prove deadly if they catch their targets unprepared. Similar to rabble, Underlings use the following guidelines:

- Underlings wear moderate amounts of armour
- Underlings are freely able to use Special Effects
- Underlings have Hit Points equal to one fifth of the CON+SIZ of an average member of that race
- Once they receive two injuries, they cease fighting and if possible, withdraw cursing or yelling in fear
- If the damage equals or surpasses their Hit Points, they automatically fail the Endurance roll, suffering the effects of a Serious Wound in the location struck
- If the damage is double their Hit Points, they die in a gruesomely violent manner
- Once half their number are dead or wounded, the rest of the underlings withdraw from the fight

Magic

Magic comes in many forms and derives from numerous sources, but all forms of magic have one thing in common: the ability for the user to overcome or manipulate the natural order of the world to achieve specific, supernatural effects. The theist's magic derives from the relationship with his god; the sorcerer's magic derives from the rituals and formulae he has mastered; the animist's magic comes from his relationship with the spirits; and the mystic's magic comes from within himself. Despite their sources and the relationships that drive them, all these magicians are able to perform remarkable feats that are beyond the capabilities of non-practitioners.

Tailoring Magic

Magic is one of the most variable aspects of any roleplaying game. Whilst elements such as how character generation or combat works are ubiquitous no matter what the setting, almost every historical and fantasy genre has its own idiosyncratic style of magic – how it is prepared, cast, and the scale of effect it can produce.

To ensure flexible adaptability, magic in Mythras has been given a range of options so that it can support a wide array of settings and styles. The following sections describe different alternatives with which magic can be tweaked. These suggestions are intended to inspire Games Masters to create unique magical ecologies, helping to overcome issues where a default system may appear at odds with the setting concept the Games Master wishes to model.

Although at first glance the range of options may seem somewhat overwhelming, there are in fact only a few core considerations required:

- What magical disciplines are available?
- What magical traditions control magic?
- How many magical abilities do traditions provide?
- How long does magic take to cast?
- How is magical energy generated and recovered?
- Can characters start with magic?

Magical Disciplines

Mythras provides rules for five distinct magical types, which for ease of reference are called disciplines. Others exist, and will no doubt be explored in future supplements. Each of the following magical disciplines receives its own chapter describing in detail how that magic works, how characters come by it, and what spells, spirits or other abilities are available.

Although each discipline provides a unique and interesting style of magic, a Mythras campaign does not have to include all five. Games Masters should consider whether each discipline is suitable for his game setting. A campaign based on an archipelago of tropical islands might only include Animism; whereas a more inclusive game world might be based upon opposing cultures, one dominated by sorcerers, and the other theist priests, but both of which also practice mysticism in addition.

Note that every discipline of magic has its own strengths and weaknesses and are not necessarily balanced with one another. The five core disciplines are:

Folk Magic

Folk Magic is the most basic form of magic available, and is usually associated with hedge wizards, witches, wise women, and so forth. These are simple spells and cantrips that offer limited magical effects and can, where permissible, be used by anyone. Folk Magic is frequently taught by communities from an early age with the types of spells reflecting community necessities. This means that the Folk Magic taught by a Barbarian culture will differ to that taught by a Civilised one. Folk Magic is also taught by some professions or cults to aid their members in their jobs and duties. Folk Magic can therefore be accessible and available to all – in theory. In practice, Folk Magic might be heavily restricted depending on the campaign setting.

Animism

A higher magical discipline, Animism is the practice of dealing with the spirit world and spirits that are bound to the mortal realm in some form. Animists are shamans and totemists who deliberately develop relationships with spirits to work magical effects, usually on behalf of a community but also for obtaining personal power. Animists believe that all things, be they animate or inanimate, organic or non-organic, are possessed of a spirit or soul. A relationship with that spirit allows its power to be drawn upon and used by the animist. Animism usually teaches a profound respect for the natural and spirit worlds, inculcating in its practitioners a need for restraint and reciprocation. This does not mean, though, that there are no rogue shamans; even animism has its share of selfish individuals prepared to ignore this respect in favour of gaining greater personal power at the expense of the spirit world.

Mysticism

Mysticism achieves its effects through a combination of deep inner understanding of the fabric of reality, and channelling energy to produce a resulting action. The mystic attains this state of understanding through constant contemplation of the world around him, discerning its truths and meditating on the very nature of existence. This process is quite often linked with the asking of philosophically challenging questions, but it is more common for the mystic simply to understand both his place in the universe, and how the universe itself is placed. This comprehension forms a path to unlock the mystic's inner potential. Mystics, ultimately, seek to transcend the fetters of the natural world, and achieve a higher state of consciousness that places them directly at one with the forces of the cosmos. The reality though is far more complex, because every accomplished mystic knows that an even higher state of existence can be attained, one that transcends even the powers of the gods.

Sorcery

Sorcery is the manipulation of underlying laws that directly control the very fabric of creation. These formulae are complex equations: a mixture of mathematical, psychological, existential, and supernatural principals that allow the sorcerer to grasp a portion of reality and bend it to his will. Sorcerers do not need to rely on gods for their powers; nor do they need to engage with spirits to achieve their effects. Their manipulation of these metaphysical equations makes sorcery very powerful and very flexible. However, it also means sorcerers are viewed with suspicion, and even fear and hatred by those who come by their magic through less direct means. And, because sorcerers have little need for gods or spirits, it is not uncommon for them to develop a certain degree of arrogance and disdain for those who choose to venerate such entities. Although some sorcerers maintain a healthy respect for the gods, and may even practice worship themselves, this does not lessen the fact that the sorcerer is, through his magic, attempting to perform acts that others may consider as the province of greater beings.

Theism

Theists draw their magic from their gods. Through worship and devotion, those that dedicate themselves to a deity channel these powers in the form of miracles, and thus gain the ability to work similar effects in the mundane world – albeit in a much diluted form. A worshipper of the Storm God might be able to summon lightning; a worshipper of the sun god might be able to create brilliant daylight even in the midst of the blackest night. The magic theists can call upon is always based on the nature of the god or pantheon being worshipped. The strength of devotion to a god has a direct impact on the power of the magic worked; assuming that the deity retains some awareness of his worshippers, maintaining a cordial relationship with the god is necessary to receive its power.

The Games Master's Saga

Steve designs his campaign to make use of all the available magical disciplines, assigning them on the basis of culture and species:

- *Folk Magic is known to all cultures and sapient species*
- *Animism is practiced by the wild tribes of bestial centaurs, satyrs and minotaurs*
- *Mysticism is studied by the remote nomad clans of the high plateau desert*
- *Sorcery is ostensibly forbidden in all cultures and is rare beyond isolated individuals*
- *Theism is favoured by both the civilised city states (of which Meeros is central), and the barbarian hordes of the Badoshi Warlords.*

Magical Traditions

Although people may be born with the capacity to work magic to greater or lesser degrees, the actual skill of using it is normally taught and cultivated via some kind of social organisation; such as a cult, order or a mentor. These are known collectively as traditions. For example, the Cult of Myceras and the Cult of the Seven Badoshi Devils are both traditions based upon religious organisations, but worship different gods and teach their priesthoods different miracles.

Some traditions are not limited to providing a single discipline of magic, but can combine two or more. A sorcery order could offer both Folk Magic and Sorcery to its members; the former providing petty cantrips to lower ranking apprentices, whilst adepts and above are taught more potent spells of the higher art.

It should also be noted that membership of a tradition need not necessarily grant access to magic. One could be a faithful worshipper of Myceras, and hold the rank of lay member in his cult, yet still have no ability to cast theistic magic.

As part of setting up the magical traditions in a campaign Games Masters should give some thought to what type of organisation or social groups will provide it. Some examples follow.

Cults

Organised sects who venerate a religion, a philosophy or an individual, cults receive a great deal more attention in their own chapter. By and large cults only teach magic to their members, and are likely to restrict certain types or magic and spells to those who attain higher ranks within the cult. Cults can teach any kind of magic, depending on their nature. Some may mix magical styles (theism and animism, say) whilst others may have only one, and so on.

Guilds

Guilds are professional bodies that represent and guard members of that occupation. Because they are focused on protecting their market, and because they are concerned with more mundane skills, guilds are unlikely to offer higher magic, focusing instead on Folk Magic – and only those spells of direct use and relevance to the profession.

Royalty and Noble Houses

Kings, queens and emperors might attain royal power through their command of magic, or through the support of those who wield it. In some settings a monarch might be truly a divine appointment, the living representative of a deity in the world. Conversely the power to work magic might be dependent on inheriting the correct noble bloodline. Magic can be of any type, although in most works of fantasy, magic-wielding monarchs tend to be either theists or sorcerers. Outside the royal sphere magic use may be outlawed: it could be a threat to the monarchy, and thus needs to be suppressed. More benevolent monarchs might use magic for the greater good, but where magic keeps the monarchy in power, it is usual for all sources of power to be jealously guarded.

Individual Teachers

The wandering hedge magician, hermit-mage, old and wise counsellor… fantasy is awash with examples of learned individuals who find and mentor an apprentice in the magical arts. Such practitioners are usually specialists in one form of magic, and may even be an established part of a community, training the young adults in those magical powers they will need to continue contributing to society, or making their way in the world. Primitive and nomadic cultures often rely on this form of patronage, lacking the population numbers and organisation to support more formalised magical tutoring.

Social Castes

Similar to magic restricted to nobility, social castes can denote what type of magic is available or taught to a person depending on the birth caste they belong to. Settings with magic limited by social caste should probably offer a range of different types according to birth rank, hereditary lineage or something similar. Someone of the priestly caste might automatically join the predominant religion and be indoctrinated into Theism for example; whereas a lower born member of the warrior caste may be restricted to only learning mysticism.

Species Specific

Some races or species are naturally predisposed to magical knowledge. Elves or satyrs, for instance, are associated with considerable magical powers. Within the species magical skills are natural capabilities that only need training and refinement. Depending on what type of magic they were inherently gifted with, the relevant magical skills could be considered Standard for that species. Typically species specific magic tends to be of one type: Folk, Animism or Theism the most common. Magic such as sorcery and mysticism may be learned but is generally not a natural accoutrement.

Totems

Many cultures adopt totems or other symbols that become a focus and provider of magical power. The most prevalent examples are those practicing animism, but there is no reason why totems should be confined solely to spirit magic. Sorcery orders may gain their knowledge through totemic practices; and idolatry in theistic worship is very similar. Rather than an organised cult of teachers, it is the totem itself which is the channel for magical knowledge and skill, granting magical lore to those that establish suitable bonds with it or are born into the correct family, tribe or race to understand its lore.

The Games Master's Saga

Further detailing his campaign world, Steve develops the traditions which will teach and control magic. He constrains the practice of each discipline thusly:

Folk Magic is taught as both an adjunct to religious cults and via individual teachers, such as hedge wizards or witches.

Animism can only be learned by those beast races which still possess an animal affinity to a particular totem spirit. Thus centaurs venerate Great Horse, their species totem, with whom only they can form a bond. Knowledge is tightly held by clan shamans.

Mysticism is only taught to magically eligible nomads of the correct birth caste; their path of mysticism dependent on which astrological conjunction is at the apex of the sky as the child emerges from its mother.

Sorcery, forbidden due to its diabolic overtones, is secretly studied by lone practitioners who stumble upon the art, or under the tutelage of reclusive sorcerers living in remote places.

Theism is jealously guarded by the innumerable cults which propitiate the gods. Each of the city states has its own unique patron deity, the temple to which acts as the cult centre for that god. The Badoshi on the other hand have a pantheon of seven demons which is universally worshipped by all the tribes.

How Many Abilities?

Abilities are the spells, talents, miracles or spirits provided by magical traditions. The number of abilities a tradition offers is completely setting-specific. A world in which cult theocracies rule entire nations may offer more miracles to its priesthood than a setting where grimoires of sorcery are exceptionally rare, each containing but a single spell. Several elements can adjust the amount and proclivity of abilities available to a tradition.

Firstly, traditions normally structure the learning path of the magical abilities they provide. Members only gain access to more potent magics at higher levels of achievement and rank. For example; if a sorcery order knows the particularly deadly spell Wrack, it is highly unlikely that it will be taught to students until they have attained a certain degree of knowledge, maturity and seniority to be entrusted with its power and secrets.

Secondly, traditions may teach more than one type of magic. A cult might combine Folk Magic with Theism for instance, granting a broader range of abilities. In this case the Games Master can grant a similar number of abilities per discipline, or limit the number given to the more powerful one.

A Games Master should consider how versatile he wishes magic to be in his setting and adjust the number and availability of abilities to suit. But, as a rule of thumb, use the Spells by Organisation table as a guide:

Spells by Organisation

	Low Magic	*Medium Magic*	*Magic Rich*
Number of spells, spirits, miracles, talents etc an organisation possesses:	1d3	1d3+3	1d3+6

In selecting what magical abilities are available, balance is key. Just because a spell, miracle, talent or spirit is listed in MYTHRAS does not mean that everyone should have access to it. Create spell lists; choose wisely. Don't feel compelled to use every ability found in these rules. Indeed, some of the magics found in Mythras can be exceptionally powerful. If Games Masters feel these would destabilise his game then they should be either be omitted completely, withheld or reserved for potent non-player characters.

Thus it is probably unwise to allow players to devise their own traditions and spell lists – at least not without Games Master guidance and approval.

The Games Master's Saga

After choosing what sort of traditions to use, Steve must come to a decision on how many abilities each magical tradition should provide. Steve decides that he'd like his setting's cults, schools and paths to grant a wide range of powers. Selecting the Magic Rich category allows each to provide between 7-9 spells, spirits, and so on; tweaking the actual number dependent on the importance and central role of the tradition.

Since Theism is the dominant form of magic in the campaign world, Steve also grants each divine cult an additional 7-9 Folk Magic charms in addition to their full range of 7-9 miracles. This substantially augments the potency of theistic cults in comparison to traditions based on other types of magic, but Steve thinks it will give his setting a uniquely distinct flavour.

Although Steve likes the idea of making all magic long and difficult to cast, he finally chooses to go with the default casting times but keeping the option to boost the casting chance if spending additional time in preparation; since he wants magic to be an active part of the to-and-fro of combat.

Ritualistic Casting Times

By default each type of magic in Mythras has a casting time of mere seconds. Whilst this permits magicians to utilise their powers more freely, especially in combat situations, it can pose some problems when trying to replicate the feeling of extreme effort it often takes for magic to be cast in some genres.

There are several methods of handling this issue:

- Grant casters the ability to roll an Easy skill check if spending one minute in preparation, or Very Easy if spending an hour, but only for the purposes of casting the spell (and any subsequent resistance checks)
- Increase the default base casting time from Turns to Rounds, Minutes, Hours or even Days instead
- As above, but in duress allow a magician to speed up casting at a skill penalty of one difficulty grade per time frame advanced

Of course ritualistic casting times need not be universally applied to all magical disciplines, which can grant one type of magic a significant speed advantage over others. For example Sorcery and Animism could have their base casting time increased to minutes, whilst Mysticism remains unmodified. This will have a significant effect on a campaign setting, but can create some rather unusual, yet entertaining, twists in how magic is utilised.

In general, increasing the length of casting times will turn magic into a more thoughtfully applied tool – rather than a method of applying greater firepower – and encourages careful planning. It can generate a huge amount of atmosphere, especially if the magician must augment this preparation time with the inscription of magical sigils, tossing of powders, use of ritualised objects or even singing and dancing.

Games Masters should take care when applying ritualistic casting times. Although it can add ambience to a setting, players with magic-using characters may feel hampered by increased preparation times, and some magical abilities may lose a degree of applicability if they cannot be cast near instantaneously.

Magical Energy

Although knowledge of magical powers may be prevalent in a setting, it does not automatically follow that the magical energy required to invoke them is as widespread, or even available. Having the skill to transform a man into a leopard is useless if you don't have the energy to cast the spell or request the miracle from the gods.

Whilst every character has an attribute known as Magic Points, derived from their characteristic POW, this merely represents the capacity to hold or store magical energy, not necessarily the ability to generate their own.

Of all the considerations required to tailor Mythras magic to a campaign setting, where magical energy comes from (and how to recover it) is perhaps the most important.

Where Do Magic Points Come From?

Magical energy should come from a particular source as defined by the campaign setting. The following options need not be generic; for example some types of magic might require particular sources different from each other. Also the setting might permit a few sources to be used in combination, so that there are several methods of gathering Magic Points.

- Self: the simplest and most convenient source of Magic Points, characters generate their own magical energy
- Sacrifice: magical energy is 'harvested' from the sacrifice of living creatures
- Magical Locations: magic is naturally produced at foci such as ley-lines, temples, and the like
- Destruction of an inanimate object: magic may come from a ethereal or mineral substance of limited supply, gems for example
- Consumption of a substance: the consumption of particular herbs, narcotics or animal products may provide magical energy
- Veneration: in a similar manner to the worship of gods, magic points might be provided to individuals who tap into, or become the focus of, organised worship

Characters must have access to the source of their magical energy to be able to regain expended Magic Points. If they do not, then points used in the process of casting spells or using magical abilities cannot be regained until the source is obtained.

Self

Here, the character attracts and stores magical energy from the world around him. Recovering Magic Points is simply a matter of resting, and letting his body absorb the natural magical emanations of the world until his points are restored. He need do nothing else. This has been considered the default source of Magic Points in other games, but Games Masters should not feel limited by it.

Sacrifice

Sacrifice is a common trope of both the Sword & Sorcery genre and historical religious practices. It requires the ritualised death of a 'victim' to produce a number of Magic Points, which can then be sent to an otherworld entity such as a god, spirit or demon in order to propitiate them; or the magical energy can be absorbed by the person performing the sacrifice.

The amount of magical energy produced by such an act is an important consideration. Traditionally the most minimal sacrifices are livestock animals, whilst the most potent are sapient beings. With that in mind, Mythras assumes as a default that the amount of Magic Points harvested by a being's death is equal to their POW. This can be raised or lowered as deemed fitting for the setting.

How many Magic Points for Sacrificing a...

Sacrificial Magic Points are a perfect way to represent the transference or generation of magical power in many historical or gritty Sword & Sorcery settings. Using this method however, will prompt the frequently asked question of 'How much magic is this creature worth?'

As a general rule of thumb, Games Masters should treat tiny animals, especially those which can be raised en-mass (such as doves) as capable of only producing a single Magic Point. Small animals (snakes, cats etc) as only generate 1d3 Magic Points, medium sized creatures (goats, pigs, and so on) produce 1d6 Magic Points, and large animals (cows, bulls, horses) 2d6 Magic Points. Only truly huge, magical or sapient creatures should provide 3d6 MPs or more.

Although at face value this may appear to provide a boundless source of Magic Points, there are several important limitations to keep in mind. Firstly very few cultures or societies have 'excess' livestock available for the purposes of ritual offerings.This is why it is called a sacrifice; because it may cost the community dearly to provide an animal from their subsistence level herds or flocks. In places where animals are freely available for purchase, then the requirement becomes a question of finances, as a horse or cow is not a cheap commodity.

Secondly each cult is likely to have a specific type of creature it requires as the preferred sacrificial victim, meaning that killing the wrong beast may net the character no Magic Points at all. Even if the correct species of creature is located, it may be required to be in perfect health, possess an unblemished skin, be of a particular colour, and so on. Once these factors are taken into consideration, it is doubtful that adventuring priests, sorcerers or shamans would travel about with a string of such animals in tow, which will require care, feeding, guarding, and so on.

Note that those magicians seeking sapient victims for sacrifice had better belong to a culture which supports such activities. Needless killing of prisoners or slaves for the purposes of invoking magic has dark connotations, especially when that magic is used for personal gain rather than being intended for the care and protection of the community.

Magical Locations

Here, a geographical place or physical structure acts as a conduit for natural magical energy which individuals can then absorb, replenishing diminished resources. The individual must spend a given period of time at this location, resting, praying, meditating, and so on, for Magic Points to accrue. How much magic depends on the strength of the place, and its environment. Some locations may only provide Magic Points to particular types of magical disciplines – e.g. druid groves might only produce Magic Points for Animists.

Give a location a Magical Strength of either 25%, 50%, 75% or 100%, depending on its size and importance. The Magical Strength is the percentage of a character's Magic Points that can be regained. For example, a character with a normal stock of 16 Magic Points spending time at a shrine with Magical Strength of 25% would only be able to recover back to a level of four Magic Points; whereas attending a major temple with Magical Strength 100% would allow him to restore his full 16 Magic Points.

The amount of time taken to replenish Magic Points should depend on the overall strength of magic in the campaign. See Recovering Magic Points below for guidance.

Destruction and Consumption

These work in similar ways to Magical Locations. The thing destroyed or consumed should be given a Magical Strength of 25%, 50%, 75% or 100%, depending on its quality, purity and other crucial factors. When destroyed or imbibed, Magic Points are recharged back up to the level indicated by the percentage, at the rates suggested in the Recovering Magic Points section..

Veneration

Characters who orchestrate the ceremonial worship of supernatural beings are able to tap into magical energy produced by the worshippers. Others, who attain the status of heroes and demigods, may even use the veneration of themselves as a source of Magic Points. The amount of Magical Strength provided by each ritualised ceremony is dependent on the number of people who offer veneration, as follows:

Less than 100:	25%
100-999:	50%
1000-9,999:	75%
10,000 or more:	100%

Recovering Magic Points

How quickly Magic Points return is vital to the feel of a campaign. Rapid return allows potent powers to be thrown about with impunity, whereas slow recovery makes each act of magic an important decision and rare occurrence.

Only some sources of Magic Points permit natural recovery: Self, Locations and Veneration. These assume complete rest, comfort, and freedom from threat or stress. Camping in an occupied dungeon or resting in the wilderness during the depths of winter would prevent recovery; whereas returning to somewhere safe and sheltered like an inn would permit it.

- 1 Magic Point per hour – Good for Magic Rich campaigns
- 1 Magic Point per day – Good for Medium Magic campaigns
- 1 Magic Point per week – Good for Low Magic campaigns
- Magic Points return at particular conjunctions – This option is perfect for settings with strong celestial or religious overtones, the Magic Points of a source only being available at specific times, such as those tapped from Veneration occurring on holy days sacred to that god, or magic from a megalithic stone circle flowing when the moon is full.

Whilst Medium or Low Magic recovery rates appear to be crippling for player character magicians, they do emphasise the rarity of magic in some genres. On the other hand they offer a balanced game when characters have access to some of the most potent spells.

In fact the slow Magic Point recovery of a Low Magic campaign is perfect for campaigns involving antagonists armed with deadly magic, allowing characters to survive the wrathful persecution of say, a sorcerer, if after casting a couple of powerful spells he has to recover for several months before trying his diabolical magic again.

Magic Points from other sources can be recovered by performing a ritual sacrifice, formal destruction of certain objects or the relaxed imbibing of other substances. Those acts in themselves should require at least an hour of effort, unless the magician wishes to hasten the experience and risk the loss of the magical energy generated.

The Rule of Recovery

As a general guideline, it is suggested that characters cannot recover more Magic Points than what is naturally produced by the local environment or their last 'recharge'. Thus a character who rests in a magical location which can produce 50% of his magical strength, cannot visit several of these places in succession in order to completely regenerate his Magic Points. Neither can a magician sacrifice several goats in sequence and add each offering together to fully top up.

The same principle applies to settings where several different forms of magical power generation exist in parallel. A character who recuperates at a dolman, performs a sacrifice, and is venerated by his army of worshippers may only recover as many Magic Points as provided by the most productive of those three sources.

Of course, games in which magicians recover Magic Points naturally should ignore this rule, at least where it applies to the number of Magic Points generated from self.

Running Out of Magic Points

The consequences of running out of Magic Points are, again, a campaign decision, and should be dependent on the setting. MYTHRAS's default position is that, when Magic Points reach zero, no more spells or magical abilities can be used, but there are no further consequences for the character.

Additional options are offered below:

Fatigue Accrual

Characters can continue to cast magic or use magical abilities, but gain one level of Fatigue for each Magic Point expended in the spell or ability attempted. Note that in certain circumstances this could kill the caster if a fumble is rolled.

Hit Point Attrition

As for Fatigue Accrual but, instead, the caster suffers 1 Hit Point of physical damage to all Hit Locations for each spell or ability attempted, no matter what its potency, magnitude or intensity. The magician can keep on casting spells until he has incurred the equivalent of a Major Wound, but at this point he is risking imminent death. Natural healing processes are needed to restore expended Hit Points; they do not regenerate with Magic Points.

Unconsciousness

On reaching zero Magic Points the character automatically falls comatose and remains that way until at least 1 Magic Point has been regained. Depending on the source of Magic Points, this might mean extended periods in a coma, or even eventual death if not cared for in the interim.

Willpower

On reaching zero Magic Points the magician must make a successful Willpower roll to remain conscious. He is not prevented from trying to cast a new spell, but each subsequent attempt requires a new Willpower roll, at an additional difficultly penalty. Thus the second check is Hard, the third Formidable, and so on. If the magician fails they collapse into unconsciousness for a random number of days up to the number of Willpower checks taken (so failing the third check would be 1d3 days of unconsciousness).

ENDURANCE OR DIE

Reaching zero Magic Points represents the exhaustion of life-force. The magician must make a successful Endurance roll or die, his psychic reserves having being spent completely. If the magician rolls a critical success he regains 1 Magic Point immediately.

These options can, of course, be mixed and matched if Games Masters desire, creating any number of custom variants that lend a unique feel and character to how magic manifests itself in the campaign.

CHARACTERS & MAGIC

MYTHRAS does not automatically assume that everyone can use magic or, even if they can, have access to it. Magic is not a right and nor should it be. Achieving any skill in magic usually requires following a career that teaches it as a specific discipline. This is certainly very true of the higher magical paths such as Animism and Sorcery. It may be possible for characters to have a smattering of Folk Magic spells if this fits with the setting and level of magic within it. Generally magic should be something to be marvelled at, respected and feared.

BECOMING A MAGICIAN

Unless magic is ubiquitous within a campaign, not all characters begin with the knowledge or capability to perform magic. As can be seen in the Careers and Development chapter, the specific skills required to learn magic are by default restricted to certain professions. Of course that need not be the case in all settings, but it works as a general guideline.

There are a number of deliberations a Game Master must work out prior to allowing magic using characters to be created.

Is the ability to use magic restricted to a particular inborn gift? If so:

- Does the gift need to be nurtured during childhood to bring it to fruition, or can it be trained at any time of life?
- How extraordinary is the gift, is it commonplace or ultra rare?
- Does possession of the gift grant instant access to particular cults or brotherhoods?
- Are those that bear the gift persecuted if they do not engage in formal training?
- If formal training is unavailable, can magicians teach themselves?

If magic is available to anyone provided they have the knowledge then:

- Do cults, brotherhoods, and so on restrict access to it to preserve their own power base?
- Is membership of such an organisation restricted to a certain social class, career, culture, and so on?
- How far is magic taught by the culture the character belongs to?

THE GAMES MASTER'S SAGA

Continuing his theme of Sword and Sorcery, Steve decides that magicians are rare and exalted, requiring specialised training from childhood. Access to higher magical powers is restricted to characters that pursue a specific magical profession, specifically those who take the mystic, priest, sorcerer or shaman career. However, he likes the idea of Folk Magic being somewhat more commonplace, but restricted to those who those who devote themselves to a specific cult or possess a mentor willing to teach them.

In his game the three main player characters are Anathaym, Kara and Mju. As part of her back-story during character generation, Kara began her adolescent life as a sacred dancer in the temple of Myceras where her natural affinity with the god was recognised. So she was trained to enter the priesthood permitting her access to Theism.

Mju was born a mountain nomad under the constellation of the Jackal, nominally a lowly caste of hunter-scavengers, but blessed by a lunar eclipse and the falling of seven stars. This auspicious astrological sign destined him to be educated as a mystic of the Path of Shadows.

Of the three only Anathaym starts with no magical skills, having trained since childhood to be as great a warrior as her father. Since she did not begin the campaign as a professional magician she can never adopt any of the higher magical arts, but could still learn some minor Folk Magic charms if she finds the right cult to join.

STARTING MAGIC

Characters permitted to learn magic start with knowing a number of abilities (spells, miracles, spirits or talents) based upon the value of the appropriate magical skill in that tradition (Binding, Devotion, Folk Magic, Invocation or Mysticism). Once the game begins they are restricted in what additional abilities they can learn, and when they can learn them.

At character generation, a magician character knows one relevant spell or ability for each 20% (or part thereof) he has in his magical skill.

LEARNING NEW ABILITIES

Once a character enters the game, learning further abilities must be paid for by the investment of Experience Rolls, and a commensurate amount of study time. As previously mentioned, Games Masters may wish to limit the availability of certain abilities according to cult rank, ensuring that characters learn the secrets of their path in a particular order, and withholding the most potent abilities until the cult deems them responsible enough to be trusted with such knowledge.

The values provided in the table are merely suggestions. These can be changed if necessary, dependent on the flow of Experience Rolls permitted. Since they are important advancements both to personal power and progression within a tradition, their costs should be a significant investment. However, a character can break down the total investment of time and Experience Rolls into instalments over several sessions of play.

At some point magician characters are likely to have learned all the abilities provided by their cult, school or path. Depending upon the game world, this need not be the end of their magical development. A character might be able to join a new cult, find another cache of sequestered knowledge or even seek tuition by a more renowned master. Such efforts require the starting of another skill specific to the philosophy of the new tradition.

Experience Roll and Time Costs

Magic Type	Type	Experience Rolls	Time
Folk Magic	Cantrip/Charm	3	1 Week
Animism	Spirit	5	1 Month
Mysticism	Talent	5	1 Month
Sorcery	Spell	5	1 Month
Theism	Miracle	5	1 Month

Learning New Traditions

Nothing prevents a character from joining a new tradition, provided that:

- The new tradition uses the same magical discipline, for example a theist cult can only join other theistic traditions
- There is no antipathy between the new tradition and any others the character may already be a member of
- The Games Master is willing to permit the character to join a new tradition

This assumes that magic cannot simply be learned by anyone who decides to start studying it. In this case there may be no restriction to joining traditions which teach new styles of magic, save for the usual conflicts of interest. Games Masters should beware of characters learning multiple magical disciplines if this does not suit their campaign setting.

In general it takes six months of dedicated study and the permission of its highest ranking masters, to gain the new tradition at its base percentage, and whatever initial spells or talents the student is capable of learning. This costs the same amount of Experience Rolls as would normally be required to learn whatever new Professional skills are necessary for that tradition, plus the cost of each spell learned.

Creating New Traditions

Some characters may wish to create their own religious or totemic cults, sorcery schools, mystical paths or any other type of tradition they conceive of. Existing traditions are complete philosophies and cannot be added to without tremendous research and effort, which would probably be resisted by the status quo of their masters. However, new traditions can be created with fewer problems, although progressing in this manner is inherently more expensive in time and effort than following an existing one.

Thus it can sometimes take years, if not a lifetime, of dedicated practice to formulate a new tradition in comparison to learning an established one. Yet a practitioner who creates a new tradition would be its grandmaster and founder, ever remembered for his efforts.

Creating New Traditions

Ability Added	Months Required	Experience Rolls Required
1st	3	7
2nd	6	13
3rd	10	19
4th	15	25
5th	21	31
6th	28	37
Each +1	+ (Ability Number+1)	+6

Mju's Saga

Mju starts the game as a student of the art of mysticism. He has a score in Meditation of 52%, and Mysticism (Path of Shadows) 57%. Thus he knows three mystical talents (one for each 20% of his Mysticism skill).

After several sessions and the completion of a major adventure, Mju finds himself with 5 Experience Rolls with which he wishes to learn another of the talents taught by the Path of Shadows. The Games Master however says that Mju has already learned all of the talents available to one of his lowly standing. If he wishes to progress further, he must prove himself worthy to his guru and be formally promoted to the rank of disciple.

Mju sighs patiently, and instead uses the Experience Rolls to improve his other skills, hoping to impress his master by diligently practicing in those areas the old guru is always complaining are lacking.

Later...

Mju is a faithful disciple of the Path of Shadows, but finds it does not teach all of the physical feats he wishes to learn. Encouraged by his master, he decides to go into retreat and meditate upon a new path of mysticism.

Studying on his own, in the remote depths of the desert plateau, Mju notices the plucky little mice that scamper and hop amongst the rocks. Experiencing an epiphany he uses the rodents as the source of his new path, attempting to mimic their abilities. It takes him 3 months of contemplation and practice, and 7 Experience Rolls, to emerge with his newly developed branch of mysticism, which he names the Path of the Jerboa. This starts at the base Mysticism percentage of POW+CON, and he gains (chooses) the first talent.

Seeking to further his path, Mju remains in isolation, spending another 6 months and 13 Experience Rolls to add a second talent. At this point he feels he has done enough and must now see how his new path will serve him in the world.

Using Magic

Mythras uses a number of default assumptions concerning the casting of magic. Since the same fundamental concepts are utilised by each discipline, they have been collated here for easy reference and avoid unnecessary duplication.

The following rules are intended to be globally applied to all of the magical disciplines – namely Folk Magic, Animism, Mysticism, Sorcery and Theism. However, as with all of the guidelines offered in this chapter, the Games Master is free to tinker with these as desired so that they fit with his play style and campaign setting.

Casting Requirements

Whether the passionate entreaties of a theist calling upon his god or the esoteric hand movements of a mystic, all magical disciplines are assumed to use ritual words and gestures to aid in the focussing of concentration required for their proper incantation.

By default the following freedoms are required:

- Clear thought, unclouded by detrimental magic, narcotics or emotional stress
- The ability to gesture or symbolise with at least one free hand
- The ability to make appropriate vocal sounds to invoke the formulae or request
- The ability to accurately perceive or sense a potential target, if the spell has to be targeted

Where one or more of these are denied to a magician, each missing element increases the difficulty grade of the appropriate magic skill. A hedge wizard who is bound and blindfolded could attempt to cast Folk Magic, but does so at a Formidable grade. With enough penalties it may become impossible to perform any form of magic.

Restricted Actions During Casting

Whilst performing magic, no matter what discipline, characters are only able to:

- Move at a maximum of walking pace
- Perform Free or Reactive Actions

Therefore characters cannot attack any foes whilst preparing a spell, or make any attempt to run or indeed perform any other skill. This reflects the deliberation needed to focus on the spell and channel the energy for it to have its desired effect.

At the Games Master's discretion, some reactive actions such as parrying or evading may make completing a spell more difficult due to disruptions incurred to the normally required somatic gestures or mental focus.

Interrupting Casting

All types of magic have casting times measured in Turns. This means a magician performing more complex invocations can be slowed down in their casting by reacting to threats which eat up their available Action Points. However, unless the caster suffers some dramatic shock, all this does is delay the final completion of the magic.

To totally disrupt casting normally requires that the magician be injured or mentally suborned. The chance of this depends on the precise circumstances:

- Minor Wounds force the caster to make a Willpower check, failure makes the casting one difficulty grade harder
- Serious Wounds force the caster to make a Willpower check, passing makes the casting one grade harder, whilst failing makes it two grades harder
- Major Wounds automatically causes the casting roll to fail
- Succumbing to mental domination automatically causes the casting roll to fail

Dismissing One's Own Magic

Characters can dismiss any magic they have personally cast as a Free Action. No roll is needed for dismissing a spell; simply the decision needed to cease its effects.

Stacking Magic

In all circumstances, magic of different disciplines cannot be stacked together to produce greater effects. Thus a Folk Magic spell cannot add its effect to that produced by a theist Miracle for example. In addition, magic of the same discipline which has a similar purpose cannot be stacked. So two weapon enhancement magics such as Fireblade and Bladesharp cannot work together.

In situations where two incompatible spells are in simultaneous existence, the magic with the greater Intensity take precedence, suppressing or subsuming the lesser magic. Where both magics are of equal Intensity, the newer magic replaces the previous one.

Magnitude and Intensity

These two terms are methods of describing the potency of magic. Magnitude is used to see how difficult it is to dispel the magic whereas Intensity reflects its level of effect. More detail concerning these terms is described for each discipline.

Although Intensity (and sometimes Magnitude) are based upon the value of a magical skill, they are not modified by any difficulty grades applied to the casting roll. For example, the Intensity of a sorcery spell is one tenth of the sorcerer's Invocation skill, no matter whether the casting roll is Easy, Hard or even Herculean..

Enduring Magic Costs

As a general rule, the Magic Points attribute (or pool) of a magician is temporarily reduced by the cost of all his ongoing active magic. He is unable to start recovering Magic Points used to cast a spell (or similar ability) until that magic is dismissed or expires.

Folk Magic

Folk Magic is the lowest level of magic available to Mythras characters. Depending on the setting Folk Magic represents:

- Simple cantrips and spells taught within a community to aid daily chores and tasks
- The magic of hedge wizards and witches who have not exposed themselves to the higher forms of magic
- A magical tradition with wide accessibility but a relatively low level of power

Although Folk Magic might appear to be weak in comparison with magical approaches such as animism, theism and sorcery it can, if used wisely, be a very powerful tool. The balance comes in its relative ubiquity: Folk Magic may be more commonplace and easier to learn which leads to a wider range of use whilst not necessarily being confined to specialists.

The Nature of Folk Magic

Folk Magic is an unseen force that permeates the world and is not derived from the gods but is an echo of the very earliest stages of creation. Maybe it comes from life force, geomancy or perhaps the cosmic radiance of constellations, but, whatever its source, its power is ubiquitous to those who know how to tap it.

Folk Magicians have attuned their senses to this faint resonance, tapping into the background energy to work magic on mundane things around them. In worlds where magic is limited, these magicians are valued for the small charms and blessings they can provide to their community. In settings where it is more commonplace, people use petty magics to ease their lives, aiding them in daily chores.

Since the focus of Folk Magic is to reduce effort or augment comfort, few of its spells are overtly specialised in the ways of death and combat. Those arts are left to practitioners of higher magics.

Access to Folk Magic

Given its nature Folk Magic can be accessed in a number of different ways:

- Through a culture reflecting secrets known by a social group.
- Through a career representing knowledge used by a vocation.
- Through a cult or brotherhood that has, over time, mastered these magical forces.
- Through an individual practitioner who may be willing to share their knowledge.
- Through self-realisation from study or inner connection with the world about them.

Games Masters need to decide how Folk Magic is made available. It might be very common, with every cultural group having access to certain spells that aid and support daily life. Or it might be restricted to specific groups or individuals, with the uninitiated aware of its existence but unable to use it. Depending on the campaign setting, not every character can or should have access to magic.

Starting Folk Magic

As an exception to the general rule of thumb, characters from careers which specialise in Folk Magic may start with a number of spells equal to one tenth of their Folk Magic skill.

In campaigns where everyday people are permitted to pick up the skill as a hobby or as part of their cult or culture, non-magical career characters only start with the default number of spells as described in the previous chapter (see Starting Magic on page 118).

These default values may be changed as the Games Master desires.

Learning Folk Magic

Folk Magic is usually taught by someone skilled in its use. If available culturally or professionally then such teachers are likely to have taught Folk Magic during a character's formative years. If being learned during the course of a campaign, it costs three Experience Rolls, and takes one week to learn a new Folk Magic spell.

Learning spells may also come with a monetary cost – depending on the teacher and perhaps the spell. Precise costs will be dependent on circumstances, but as a general rule it costs 100 Silver of goods or services per spell. Games Masters should adjust the base cost according to how common Folk Magic is generally, who is teaching it, and whether or not the student has the benefit of cult or brotherhood membership, special friendships, and so on. Tuition in Folk Magic may also be free in certain circumstances: attaining a particular rank in a cult, say, or in recognition of services rendered.

For example a Healing cult might offer tuition in the Heal spell at a rate of 50 Silvers to its members; whereas a local witch might offer to teach the spell at a base rate of 150 Silvers to the same student. A mother might even offer to teach her child the spell for free when he or she leaves home for the wide world.

If a Games Master wishes, professional folk magicians may develop new spells for a suitable cost in Experience Rolls and time. As a rough guideline, use the incrementing costs as presented on the Creating New Traditions table on page 119.

Ubiquitous Folk Magic

The table below is included for those campaigns where Folk Magic is available to common folk, rather than being restricted to specialist hedge wizards and witches. Each of the standard careers has been presented with a list of generic spells useful to that particular profession.

Some spells are more prevalent than others, and Games Masters are encouraged to tweak the lists to fit their campaign. For example, ostensibly similar careers may differ by one or two spells depending on the background culture and environment. Some of the rarer spells may be available to members of particular cults or brotherhoods.

Career-Specific Folk Magic Spells

Career	*Suggested Folk Magic*
Agent	Alarm, Befuddle, Bladesharp, Bypass, Find, Incognito, Knock, Mimic, Ventriloquism
Alchemist	Any
Beast Handler	Beastcall, Find, Might, Mobility, Pathway, Pet, Slow, Speedart, Vigour
Courtesan	Alarm, Appraise, Befuddle, Calm, Cleanse, Find, Glamour, Sleep, Tune
Courtier	Babel, Calculate, Calm, Fanaticism, Find, Glamour, Mindspeech, Translate, Voice
Crafter	Appraise, Bladesharp, Calculate, Coordination, Find, Ironhand, Pierce, Polish, Repair
Entertainer	Babel, Calm, Find, Glamour, Light, Mimic, Tune, Ventriloquism, Voice
Farmer	Beastcall, Bladesharp, Calculate, Find, Might, Preserve, Repair, Vigour, Warmth
Fisherman	Beastcall, Deflect, Dry, Find, Pierce, Preserve, Repair, Vigour, Warmth
Herder	Alarm, Beastcall, Find, Heat, Pathway, Pet, Slow, Speedart, Warmth
Hunter	Bladesharp, Find, Mobility, Pathway, Preserve, Slow, Speedart, Vigour, Warmth
Merchant	Alarm, Appraise, Calculate, Cleanse, Find, Glamour, Lock, Translate, Voice
Miner	Bludgeon, Breath, Find, Ignite, Light, Might, Pierce, Repair, Vigour
Mystic	Avert, Befuddle, Demoralise, Find, Heal, Mindspeech, Spiritshield, Vigour, Witchsight
Official	Alarm, Calculate, Find, Glamour, Lock, Mindspeech, Translate, Ventriloquism, Voice
Physician	Breath, Calm, Cleanse, Cool, Find, Heal, Preserve, Sleep, Warmth
Priest	Any
Sailor	Bladesharp, Deflect, Dry, Extinguish, Find, Pierce, Repair, Vigour, Warmth
Scholar	Appraise, Calculate, Calm, Extinguish, Find, Mindspeech, Tidy, Translate, Voice
Scout	Bladesharp, Bypass, Find, Incognito, Mobility, Pathway, Speedart, Vigour, Warmth
Shaman	Any
Sorcerer	Any
Thief	Bypass, Coordination, Darkness, Demoralise, Find, Glue, Knock, Mobility, Ventriloquism
Warrior	Bladesharp, Bludgeon, Coordination, Fanaticism, Firearrow, Fireblade, Find, Protection, Vigour

Note: In regions predisposed to great heat rather than winter cold, any career offering Warmth as a spell can substitute it for Cool instead (and vice-versa).

Using Folk Magic

Folk Magic takes only a single Turn to cast.Each spell costs one Magic Point which is deducted from the Magic Point total whenever it is successfully cast. Casting any spell successfully requires a Folk Magic roll. The Folk Magic skill covers every spell a character knows. Thus, a character with Folk Magic 70% would cast all their Folk Magic spells at this level: Folk Magic spells do not have discrete skill ratings.

If the Folk Magic roll is a...

- Critical Success: the spell's Magic Point cost is zero.
- Success: the caster loses 1 Magic Point and the spell works successfully.
- Failure: the caster loses 1 Magic Point, but the spell does not work.
- Fumble: the caster loses 1d3 Magic Points for the spell and the spell fails to work.

Due to their minor or petty nature, all Folk Magic spells have a default Intensity and Magnitude of 1.

Limits to Folk Magic Capacity

Characters have no actual limit to the number of Folk Magic spells they can learn, provided that the Games Master permits them to have access to new ones. Such knowledge might be restricted or unavailable in the game world.

Folk Magic Spells

Folk Magic spells are defined by various traits defining the effects of the spell, and any particular limitations. Every spell is different with some having fewer traits than others.

Duration of Folk Magic Spells

Unless a spell has either the Concentration or Instant traits it has a natural duration which lasts the entire scene or action for which the spell was used. A few spells have custom durations noted in the spell's definition. For example, using Pathway to traverse a section of thorny and overgrown woodland would last until the terrain clears, and the spell is no longer necessary.

Traits

Folk Magic Traits are as follows:

Concentration

The spell's effects remain in place as long as the caster continues to concentrate on maintaining it. Concentration requires the caster to be free of all physical and mental distractions: any such disturbance interrupts the concentration, resulting in the spell's immediate dismissal.

Instant

The spell's effects happen immediately. It has no duration.

Ranged

Spells with the Ranged trait can be cast at a distance of up to the character's Folk Magic score in metres. The caster must know the location of the target, such as 'hiding behind the door': if they are unable to directly see or sense the target of the spell, then the Folk Magic roll becomes one grade harder.

Resist (Endurance, Evade, Willpower)

Any spell that is not readily accepted by a target can be actively resisted using either Endurance, Evade or Willpower, as determined by this trait. To successfully resist a spell, the target must win an opposed roll of the relevant skill against the caster's Folk Magic casting result. If the target fails in the opposed roll then the spell takes effect as normal. Note that resisting is usually a passive action if Endurance or Willpower are the being used. If a spell requires the target to Evade then it costs an Action Point to make the Evade attempt. Targets without Action Points to spend in evading will therefore be powerless against the spell's effect.

Touch

The caster must be in physical contact with the target whilst the spell is cast. If a target is intent on resisting physical contact then the caster will most likely fail to complete his spell unless some specific circumstance prevents the target's withdrawal, such as surprise or the Grip special effect. A touch spell merely needs to contact the target or its carried accoutrements in order to work.

Anathaym's Saga

Anathaym has never learned any Folk Magic as its teaching has traditionally been restricted to Meeros's cults, and the priesthood. However Anathaym's sister, Kara, is an acolyte of Myceras, and has been learning Folk Magic as part of her own training.

While Anathaym recovers from the injuries to her right hand, Kara uses the time to teach her the Bladesharp spell - a useful warrior's cantrip, and one generally learned by Meeros's soldiers.

Trigger

Trigger spells can be cast successfully but have their effects delayed by the caster. If the spell is not triggered during the scene it dissipates naturally.

Spells

Alarm

Special Duration

Casting Alarm on a location such as a room or small clearing creates a temporary psychic bond between the area and the caster. If the area is accessed by a living creature with a SIZ greater than 1, the caster is automatically made aware that something has transgressed no matter how great the distance. The Alarm is usually a distinct tingling sensation or mental twinge which will awaken the caster. Alarm can also be used on an individual object, triggering when touched or moved.

The spell does not determine who or what has crossed the alarmed threshold, and neither does it prevent ingress. It lasts until triggered, but the Magic Point used to cast it does not recover until the spell is dismissed or concludes naturally. Once activated Alarm must be cast again.

Appraise

Instant, Touch

Appraise allows the immediate assessment of the quality of physical goods of combined ENC or SIZ equal to the caster's POW. The spell determines whether or not identical looking items are of the same or similar quality, or if one or more is either flawed or of a higher quality. The spell does not work on organic things, only on inanimate objects. Neither does it determine what flaws or enhancements are present; merely that they exist.

Avert

Instant, Ranged

Avert is used to dismiss another Folk Magic spell within range. Avert can be cast reactively to neutralise offensive spells, by using the Counter Magic Reactive Action.

Babble

Resist (Willpower), Touch

Babble mangles anything spoken by its target. It does not affect what the target is thinking, only what is verbally issued. Thus Babble can seriously disrupt orders being issued by a commanding officer to his troops, but it cannot influence what the commander is thinking or his intentions. Depending on the necessity for verbal components, Babble may be able to adversely influence spell casting.

Beastcall (X)

Instant, Ranged, Resist (Willpower)

Beastcall is used to attract a single, specific animal, the type being specified in the spell, within range. The animal summoned cannot be sapient, and it may also resist the spell using its Willpower. If it fails to resist, it is naturally drawn, in a passive fashion, to the caster, whereupon the spell dissipates, and the creature acts as it normally would, finding itself in proximity to the caster. Physical obstacles or adverse actions (such as a wall, river or line of spears, or a harsh yank on a set of reins or leash) also cause the spell to fail.

Befuddle

Ranged, Resist (Willpower)

Befuddle causes confusion within the mind of a corporeal target. The subject of the spell has difficulty thinking straight, forgetting where it is, what it is doing, and why – often lapsing into disassociated lines of thought. Befuddled targets can still act in self defence, but cannot initiate any constructive activity until the spell ends. Any sort of attack or threatening action instantly breaks the spell, whether or not it was directed specifically at the befuddled target.

Bladesharp

Touch

Bladesharp is cast on edged and piercing melee weapons. It increases the damage of a weapon by one dice step, and incidentally leaves the edge honed after the spell concludes. This spell is often used on tools such as logging axes, ploughs and razors. Thus casting this spell on a dagger increases it to 1d6+1 damage, whereas the same spell on a great axe would increase it to 2d8+2 damage. (1d4>1d6>1d8>1d10>2d6>2d8>2d10)

Bludgeon

Touch

Bludgeon is similar to Bladesharp but used on weapons and tools that deal blunt-force trauma rather than cutting or piercing damage. It is normally used to aid with threshing grain, fulling wool, or similar heavy duty work.

Breath

Touch

Breath permits the recipient to hold their breath for an extended period, so that they can temporarily venture into harmful environments, such as underwater; or atmospheres tainted by rock dust, gases, smoke or poisons. The spell lasts for a maximum of half the caster's POW in minutes, during which time the recipient cannot speak or the breath is lost, and they immediately begin to asphyxiate (or become poisoned).

Bypass

Touch, Trigger

Bypass is used to cross the threshold of an area under the effect of an Alarm spell without triggering the Alarm. When cast the spell is held in preparation, triggering on contact with an Alarm spell. Of course the caster must suspect that an Alarm spell exists in the first place. Bypass does not negate the Alarm, and it must be cast for each crossing of the Alarm spell's threshold.

Calculate

Instant, Ranged

Calculate allows the immediate calculation of numbers, weight or size of a thing, be it soldiers amassed in battle formation, the length of a rope or weight of a sack of rice. The spell always yields a precise quantity, but not value or quality. Only items which are directly observable (seen, lifted, smelled, and so on), and within range can be calculated. The spell will work when cast on a container – assuming, of course, that the container is not empty.

Calm

Ranged, Resist (Willpower)

Calm attempts to dampen down the passions or the target, perhaps ensuring that a lovesick paramour doesn't press his suit, a frightened rival doesn't scream for help or that weapons are not drawn in anger. A calmed person is not otherwise mentally affected, thus any sort of assault or threatening action still permits the target to defend themselves, and even attack, albeit they will do so in a calm and level headed manner.

Chill

Instant, Touch

Chill dramatically reduces the temperature of small objects (with an ENC no larger than a third of the caster's POW) down to the temperature of ice water. Useful for rapidly cooling hot items, chilling drinks, and so forth. The spell does not freeze an object, and neither does it cause any damage to its structure: it merely renders it very cold.

Cleanse

Instant, Touch

Cleanse is used to rid an object, person or small area of dirt, grease, grime, bad smells, and so on. It does not organise or tidy the target or area; merely cleans them to a spick-and-span state. This spell is often used to launder clothes. The caster can cleanse an area equal to POW in square metres.

Cool

Concentration, Touch

Cool protects the recipient from the effects of muggy atmospheres and heat prostration, guarding them from any Fatigue caused by the natural environment. The spell does not stop the effects of heat related magic, but will make any resistance roll one difficulty grade easier. Someone under the effects of this spell wearing full hoplite armour could march through a tropical rain forest during the height of summer without harm. Cool affects a target of SIZ up to the caster's POW x2.

Coordination

Touch, Trigger

Coordination enhances manual dexterity and agility when performing a single task. When cast in preparation it permits the recipient a chance to re-roll a single skill check where coordination is required, such as Acrobatics, Lockpicking and so on. The recipient may choose the better of the two rolls, but the spell is expended in the process.

Curse

Special Duration

Curse must be cast in combination with a second spell of a harmful nature. Its one and only effect is to increase the duration of the accompanying spell so that it is continuous. This comes at a cost however, since the Magic Point used to cast the curse does not return until the caster drops the curse willingly, the curse is dispelled, or the spell to which it is bound breaks naturally. Curse is commonly combined with spells such as Befuddle, Demoralise, Dullblade, Repugnance, and so on.

Darkness

Concentration, Ranged

Darkness creates an area of shadow, equal to POW in square metres, which suppresses all light within it. This is enough volume to fill a modest room, a length of corridor or form a small cloud if cast outside. All non-magical light, including sunlight, passing into or present within the boundary is reduced to the equivalent of a dim glow.

Deflect

Touch

Deflect wards the recipient against tiny impacts of foreign material, such as rain drops, a cloud of midges or even flying grains of sand. The protection is limited to individual objects smaller than a child's fingernail, and thus cannot prevent normal missile weapons from striking a character.

Demoralise

Ranged, Resist (Willpower)

Demoralise temporarily fills the target with a sense of despondency towards a particular person, species, situation or object. When confronted with the subject of this despondency, any proactive skill attempts made by the afflicted character related to the source are one grade harder. However a direct assault from the subject instantly breaks the spell.

Thus a character could be given a demoralising dread of heights, ensuring that any Athletic skill used for climbing or Acrobatics skill for balancing would be one difficulty grade harder.

Dishevel

Instant, Touch

Dishevel is the reverse of the Cleanse spell. Objects affected are immediately covered in grime, dust, cobwebs, and so forth. The spell can be used to make brand new objects look old and weathered or help prevent normally well turned out people from being recognised. The caster can dishevel an area equal to POW in square metres.

Disruption

Instant, Ranged, Resist (Endurance)

Disruption is used for damaging or dissembling physical objects without the need for tools. It is commonly employed to drive off or kill living creatures, such as birds or vermin. When successfully cast, Disruption inflicts 1d3 damage to a single random Hit Location or the overall Hit Points of an object. In both cases the damage ignores any armour or natural protection.

Dry

Instant, Touch

Dry removes all extraneous moisture from an object or person, either slicking off to form a puddle or evaporating in a cloud of vapour. It is normally used to dry off after heavy rain or help protect equipment from rotting, but has a number of other versatile uses. The caster can dry an object up to POW x2 in SIZ.

Dullblade

Ranged

Dullblade is the reverse of Bladesharp reducing the keenness of weapons and tools. It reduces the damage inflicted by the weapon by one step, and can never keep a sharp edge.

Extinguish

Instant, Ranged

Extinguish immediately quenches flames and small fires of modest size and heat. It is useful for dousing candles, lanterns, torches or small cook fires, but it will not work on magical or larger, more ferocious conflagrations such as pyres, burning houses or dragon flames.

Fanaticism

Ranged, Resist (Willpower)

Fanaticism is the reverse of Demoralise. It grants the target a wildly excessive or irrational devotion, dedication, or enthusiasm for a particular person, species, situation or object. Its effect is to grant the recipient a temporary Passion equal to the Folk Magic skill of the caster. Fanaticism can be used to counter Demoralise, and vice versa.

Find (X)

Concentration, Ranged, Resist (Special)

Find has many variations, always specific, and learned as separate spells. Some common examples are given below. It works by attuning to the natural emanations of a creature or thing, alerting the caster to its presence within the spell's range. Find can be blocked by dense or thick materials such as metal, or earth and stone at least one metre thick. The spell cannot discern emotions or thoughts.

Find Arrows: Locates ammunition shot by hunters, which miss their target.

Find Flaw: Identifies any flaws in an object, such as hidden imperfections or physical damage.

Find Livestock: Locates a particular type of animal. Can be resisted with Willpower.

Find Loot: Locates precious metals and gems.

Find Object: Locates a lost personal possession.

Find Sickness: Identifies the existence of disease and illness, whether magical or mundane.

Firearrow

Touch

Firearrow causes all missiles thrown or fired by the recipient to burst into flame when released. Ostensibly created to act as a signal flare, it has since evolved into a combat magic. Missiles under its effect add an additional 1d3 damage, but are extinguished if they impale flesh. Those that strike flammable material have a chance equal to the caster's Folk Magic skill of setting alight whatever they lodge in, such as wooden shields, thatched roofs, and so on. Wooden ammunition is consumed as part of the spell.

Fireblade

Touch

Fireblade is similar to Firearrow but is instead cast on hand tools and melee weapons. The original purpose of the spell is to sterilise surgical equipment, aid in slash and burn agriculture or provide illumination during darkness without the need to carry an additional light source. If cast on a weapon it inflicts an additional 1d3 damage, and has the chance of setting flammable materials alight if held to them for several rounds (see Fire on page 79). Wooden hafted weapons under the effects of Fireblade will be consumed as part of the spell.

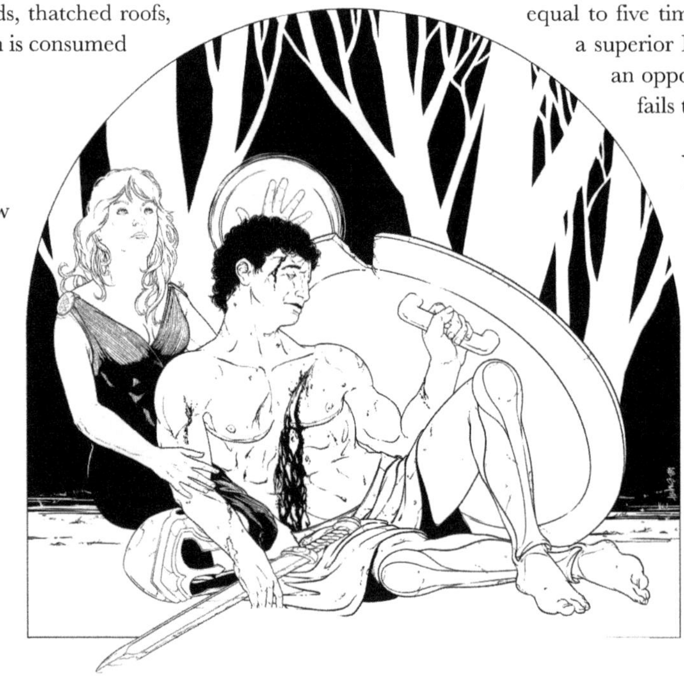

Frostbite

Ranged, Resist (Endurance)

Frostbite works directly on living, organic tissue, inflicting numbness and pain in one of the recipient's extremities, for example fingers, toes, buttocks, nose & ears, and so on. The caster must either touch a specific extremity or roll randomly if cast at range. If the spell is not resisted the area affected suffers sensory numbness followed by lingering pain for the duration, making skill tests utilising that location one difficulty grade harder. Frostbite does not deal direct damage but makes the affected area of limited use for a while. For instance, a victim suffering frostbite to the buttocks cannot sit without extreme discomfort.

Glamour

Concentration, Ranged, Resist (Willpower)

Glamour makes the target alluring so that people are naturally attracted to them. The particular nature of the glamour must be chosen when cast, and can be anything from increased natural beauty, a softer more sultry voice or even a seductively perfumed body scent. Whilst the spell grants no mechanical benefits, it does ensure that the recipient will gain a chance to gather themselves an audience, engage the attention of someone they wish to make contact with, or provide a distraction enabling accomplices an opportunity to perform nefarious deeds.

Glue

Touch

Glue cements together two solid, inanimate objects for the duration of the spell, for example a cart wheel to its axle or a door to its frame. Whilst under the effects of the spell the items, no matter how disparate, cannot be parted unless something actively tries to wrench them apart. In this circumstance the spell has a Brawn skill equal to five times the caster's POW, and fails when a superior Brawn is set against it, defeating it in an opposed roll. Once the spell concludes or fails the items part completely unharmed.

Heal

Instant, Touch

Heal has several different effects depending on the nature of the ailment it is being used on. If the subject is suffering from a minor complaint such as a headache, back pain, hangover, cold, warts, and so on, then the symptoms are immediately lifted. Cast on a location suffering a Minor Wound it restores all lost Hit Points instantly. Against Serious or Major Wounds no Hit Points are recovered. However the spell will stabilise locations, stop all bleeding, and prevent imminent death from inattention.

Heat

Instant, Touch

Heat dramatically increases the temperature of small objects (with an ENC no larger than a third of the caster's POW) up to the temperature of boiling water. This versatile spell is useful for mulling wine, cooking food without a fire, or warming a bed prior to sleep. It does not affect living tissue although it can affect clothing and armour, heating it to uncomfortable levels.

Ignite

Instant, Ranged

Ignite only works on flammable inorganic matter, causing a small object or hand-sized area to burst into flame. Depending on what was set alight, once burning, the flames may then spread unless quenched or countered in some way. This spell is normally used to light candles, torches or lanterns from afar. It can also be used to start a camp or cooking fire in adverse conditions, such as using damp kindling or in strong winds.

Incognito

Resist (Endurance), Touch, Trigger

Incognito alters the facial features of the recipient to a bland, unmemorable countenance. It does not affect the voice, mannerisms or physical size/presence of the recipient, but ensures that visually they do not stand out from the crowd.Anyone under the effects of Incognito is actively ignored by those who might otherwise be searching for him; he is simply overlooked and discounted.

Ironhand

Touch

Ironhand allows the recipient to hold anything that would otherwise cause damage (such as extremely hot or cold items, or those dripping acid) without causing themselves injury. Thus a user could grasp a brand from a fire, lift a bubbling cauldron from a spit or even reach through a steam vent to grab an object on the other side. It does not grant total immunity from damage, merely stops it from conducting through the skin of the recipient's hands. The spell does not protect anything worn on the hand, so rings, gloves, and such like will suffer the effects of the source.

Knock

Instant, Touch

Knock magically unfastens any device that is currently secured with a mechanical bar or lock. It does not work on magically locked objects, only mundane ones. The spell only affects a single fastening, so if there are several locks and bars securing the object, the spell will need to be recast for each one.

Light

Concentration, Ranged

Light must be cast on an inanimate object (this could be a branch, sword blade, spear point, torch, and so on). It produces enough light to illuminate an area as though with a lantern. It can also be cast directly against a Darkness spell to counter it. In this case both spells are consumed, leaving the ambient light to illuminate the area.

Lock

Special Duration, Touch

Lock magically secures any device that already has a mechanical bar or lock present. A Locked device can be opened only by the caster, and cannot be picked by mundane means (such as by a thief using lock-picks) since the magic renders the mechanism immobile; however it could still be forced open by breaking the object the lock is set into. The magic remains in place until opened by the caster, after which the device must be subject to a further casting of Lock to restore the enchantment. The Magic Point used to cast Lock does not recover until the spell is dismissed or concludes naturally.

Magnify

Concentration

Magnify allows the caster to see something twice as close as it really is. Useful for close work as well as out in the field.

Might

Touch

Might permits the recipient to engage in impressive acts of physical brawn. It adds the caster's POW to the recipient's STR, but only for the purposes of lifting, breaking, and contests of strength as defined under the Brawn skill. It does not increase the character's Damage Modifier when inflicting combat damage.

Mimic

Touch, Trigger

Mimic allows the recipient to perfectly mimic the voice and mannerisms of someone the caster has seen and heard personally. It does not affect their physical appearance.

Mindspeech

Concentration, Ranged, Resist (Willpower)

Mindspeech allows telepathy between the caster and a target, enabling verbal intercourse without needing to speak aloud. The caster and target must share the same language, or else the spell will merely transmit unintelligible gobbledegook. Attempting to cast Mindspeech on somebody beyond range automatically fails.

Mobility

Touch

Mobility increases the Movement rate of the recipient by 1d3 metres for the spell's duration. It is often used by hunters, herders, and those seeking to escape pursuit.

Pathway

Touch

Pathway enables the recipient to more easily travel through heavy vegetation, safe from being scratched, snagged or otherwise hindered. Under its enchantment Movement rates are not reduced in woods, jungles, swamps, and similar overgrown terrain.

Perfume

Concentration, Ranged, Resist (Willpower)

Perfume either negates a noxious odour or imbibes an odourless substance with a pleasing fragrance. The spell does not affect the properties of the source of a stench (so a rotting carcass is still rotten) - it merely makes its presence tolerable.

Pet

Concentration, Resist (Willpower), Touch

Pet allows the caster to take mental control of a small creature, sending it off to scout, fetch or perform some other complex task. It can be cast on any creature neither of whose SIZ and INT characteristics may exceed half the caster's CHA. If the targeted creature is the already the loyal pet of the caster it does not need to resist the spell.

Phantasm

Concentration, Ranged

Phantasm allows the caster to weave together insubstantial or near weightless objects so that they take a shape or ghostly form. Thus a spectral figure could be woven from a naturally occurring mist, or a face formed in a pile of dead leaves. Beyond this the spell has little effect, save to frighten, intrigue or disconcert those that view it.

Pierce

Touch

Pierce can be cast on any item with a point, helping it to penetrate thick surfaces. It is normally used to help sew leather, punch holes in metal or hammer pitons into stone. Any weapon or tool enhanced with this spell ignores the first two Armour Points of the person, creature or object struck.

Polish

Instant, Touch

Polish instantly buffs an object of ENC or SIZ of up to the caster's POW to a high sheen making it glossy, shiny, and highly desirable even if the quality of the article is sub-par.

Preserve

Instant, Touch

Preserve prevents organic matter, both vegetable and animal, from bacterial decay and putrefaction for 1d3 months, by sterilising it. If the material is later smoked, pickled or salted it is preserved indefinitely. The spell can halt decay that has begun, but not reverse it. The caster can affect an amount of organic matter with SIZ or ENC equal to their POW.

Protection

Touch

Protection is useful in a wide range of tasks where there is a risk of accidental injury such as working in a foundry or mine. The first time the character would normally take damage that penetrates protective clothing or armour, the Protection spell will trigger, and reduce the damage taken by 1d3 points. The spell then dissipates. The spell only protects against physical damage so won't help against events such as fire, choking, and so on.

Repair

Instant, Touch

Repair fixes physical damage to an inanimate object. Each separate successful casting repairs 1d3 Hit Points of damage.

Repugnance

Concentration, Ranged, Resist (Willpower)

Repugnance twists the appearance of the target so that they cause distaste in all those that see, hear or smell them. The particular effect must be chosen when cast, and can be anything from a great wart on the end of a nose, a high pitched nasal voice or even pungent body odour. Whatever is chosen, it will cause people to turn away from the victim or make excuses so as to leave their presence as quickly as possible.

Shock

Instant, Ranged, Resist (Evade)

Shock produces a mild electrical discharge which may be directed at living things. The caster must either touch a specific extremity or roll randomly if cast at range. If the spell is not resisted, the shocked location is stunned for 1d3 Turns; armour does not protect. The spell makes a loud crack when cast.

Shove

Instant, Ranged, Resist (Special)

Shove allows the caster to telekinetically move an object by giving it a single crude push. The item is not moved with enough force to inflict damage, and is still subject to gravity. The spell affects an amount of ENC or SIZ equal to the caster's POW. Living targets can resist with either Endurance or Evade.

Sleep

Resist (Endurance), Touch

Sleep sends its recipient into a deep, peaceful sleep. It has no effect on creatures with a SIZ greater than the caster's POW. Unless the target resists, it slumbers for a number of hours equal to the half the caster's POW. However the spell takes 1d3 Rounds to take effect before the target falls unconscious. Any attempt to cast this spell in a combat situation automatically fails.

Slow

Ranged, Resist (Endurance)

Slow is the direct opposite of Mobility, slowing Movement Rate by 1d3+3 metres, if the target fails to resist.

Speedart

Instant, Touch, Trigger

Speedart boosts the velocity of thrown or fired missiles so that they travel farther before losing efficacy. The spell increases the effective range by 1.5 times the weapon's normal distance.

Spiritshield

Concentration, Resist (Willpower), Touch

This spell creates a shield around the recipient which deters spirits from entering. Any spirit wishing to attack or possess the recipient must overcome the spell by winning an opposed test of their Willpower against the caster's Folk Magic skill.

Tidy

Instant, Ranged

Tidy immediately restores a number of items (up to the caster's POW) within the spell's range to a neat, tidy, and orderly fashion. Items larger than 3 ENC are shifted to a more orderly position but will require manual intervention to tidy properly.

Tire

Ranged, Resist (Endurance)

Tire inflicts one level of Fatigue on the subject unless resisted.

Translate

Concentration, Resist (Willpower), Touch

Translate permits the caster to understand any language spoken to him, by setting up a psychic link with the target. The translation provided is often imperfect, as complex terms or concepts cannot be comprehended, but it does allow simple communication. The spell works between sapient creatures with a definite, constructed language, and still relies on being able to see, hear or otherwise perceive the target as in normal conversation. If cast upon a creature of animal awareness, communication is restricted to the simple reception of emotional state.

Tune

Instant, Touch

Tune ensures that the musical instrument touched is in perfect pitch no matter the dampness, temperature or its general condition, ensuring that the following performance is unaffected.

Ventriloquism

Concentration, Ranged, Resist (Willpower)

Ventriloquism allows the caster to project their voice anywhere within range. The caster needs only to think the projected words, not actually to speak them physically, which can disconcert those unaware of what is going on. If cast upon a living creature, the caster can take control of their vocal cords, and speak through them instead.

Vigour

Touch

Vigour makes the recipient feel alive and energetic, being used to offset the effects of strenuous physical labour. For the spell's duration, all Fatigue effects gained from laborious activity are ignored (but return on the spell's dismissal). It negates the effects of a Tire spell.

Creating New Folk Magic Spells

There are doubtless many spells Games Masters may want to introduce that are not covered by those provided in this chapter. If inventing new cantrips, some points to bear in mind to keep Folk Magic reasonably balanced are:

- *As noted, Folk Magic spells are limited in their effects. Avoid introducing spells that have multiple or far-reaching effects.*
- *Spells are utility-based; that is, to aid a mundane task in some way. Try to create spells that remain focused on aiding daily life rather than being wholesale forces for destruction.*
- *Note that Folk Magic spells do not, by and large, provide skill bonuses or penalties. Those that affect living things do so in subtle or limited ways.*
- *One does not need to create spells that have a measurable game mechanics effect. Folk Magic spells can provide background colour, flavour, and atmosphere. Clever magicians will find creative uses for them.*

Voice

Concentration, Ranged, Resist (Willpower)

Voice amplifies the recipient's intonation and delivery so that it becomes compelling when issuing verbal commands. All who can hear the speaker are forced to listen. Their vocalisation also carries across and through even the loudest background noise (howling gales, the roar of a waterfall, the clash of arms on a battlefield) up to a range of ten times the recipient's CHA in metres.

Warmth

Concentration, Touch

Warmth protects the recipient from the effects of freezing atmospheres and exposure, and from Fatigue caused by the natural environment. The spell does not stop the effects of cold-related magic cast at them, but will make any resistance roll one difficulty grade easier. Thus a person under the effects of this spell could walk about on a glacier during midwinter in their underclothes without harm. Warmth affects an object of SIZ up to the caster's POW x2.

Witchsight

Ranged, Resist (Willpower)

Witchsight allows the caster to see active magic, enchanted items, and invisible entities (although such things are simply shadowy representations) that lie within range and line of sight. It can also penetrate illusions or discern the true guise of shapeshifted creatures. Beings which wish to remain hidden or disguised must win an opposed test of their Willpower versus the casting roll.

Animism

Animism is magic worked through communion with spirits and the spirit world. It is the magic of shamans and spirit walkers. Such practitioners do not treat with gods or learn their abilities from books or tomes; instead their powers come from the myriad spirits that inhabit the spirit realms, and interact occasionally with the mundane world. Shamans are sensitive to their presence, whether these entities are nature spirits, representatives of particular natural objects, the souls of revered ancestors, or malign things such as disease and curse spirits.

Animism relies on forming multiple relationships with many spirits, that themselves embody magical effects which are made available to the shaman. Gathering spirits requires negotiation, sometimes combat, and frequent expeditions into the Spirit World.

What Are Spirits?

Spirits are a metaphysical manifestation of a particular aspect of the cosmos. Most are intrinsically linked with something existing in the material world that reflects and represents the spirit's nature and influence. A spring in a glade, for instance, may well have a spirit representing its beauty and serenity; a species of animal has a guardian spirit watching over it, an archetype of all that the species is and does; ghosts, and certain restless spirits of the dead, are tied to the place where they died; ancestor spirits are linked to the communities they once inhabited. Spirits are non-corporeal, possess motivations, perceptions and outlooks very different to those of the material world, and have, through their connections with the Spirit World, developed great powers and abilities.

What is the Spirit World?

The Spirit World mirrors the mundane world, and resides close to it, intersecting with it in some places, but is otherwise invisible and quite separate. The Spirit World is unfettered by the laws of physics, meaning that conditions there can be very different to those of the mundane world: time may pass differently or have no meaning; colours may seem more vivid and pronounced. All physical effects in the Spirit World are the results of the spirits themselves. As a plane of existence it is infinite. It has no shape, yet reflects all aspects of the material world so that it seems at once familiar and alien. Spirits fill the Spirit World and whirl constantly through it. Also found here are the faint souls of mortal beings whose spirits are still bound to a material body. These appear as pale shadows, and can sometimes be hard to perceive. Many spirits collect in habitats that mirror mundane world communities and settlements; others congregate in clearly defined regions that are alien or hellish to human perception. Nothing physical can exist there, only the non-corporeal.

States of Being

A soul or spirit that inhabits a physical thing, be it a living body or an inanimate object, is defined as being *corporeal.* A corporeal spirit cannot enter the Spirit World until drawn forth from its material residence.

Conversely a soul pulled from its physical body into the Spirit World is considered *discorporate.* Whilst discorporate, souls are separated from the senses and sensations of their body.

The last state of being applies to spirits that naturally reside in the Spirit World, and lack any tie to a physical body or object. These are defined as *manifested* when they emerge into the mundane world.

Trance and Binding

Animists learn two magical skills, Trance and Binding. Trance enables the animist to perceive spirits and enter the Spirit World. Binding allows animists to summon, dominate, and bind spirits in spirit combat. Every animist learns Trance and Binding as part of his training, which is always conducted by a shaman or high shaman. Would-be animists learn which natural features are linked with a spirit or the Spirit World, and become sensitive to the shifts, and whorls of the Spirit World as it intersects with the mundane world.

Trance (CON+POW)

Trance represents the animist's awareness of the Spirit World, and his ability to move between it and the material world. Anyone with Trance can, on a successful roll, detect, but not observe, the presence

Trance Preparation Time

Cult Rank	Observe Spirits	Converse With Spirits	Project Self or Draw Spirit	Drag Souls
Follower	1 Hour	-	-	-
Spirit Worshipper	1 Minute	1 Hour	-	-
Shaman	1 Round	1 Minute	1 Hour	-
High Shaman	1 Action	1 Round	1 Minute	1 Hour

of spirits within a range equal to their POW in metres. The skill is capable of far more - but such secrets are jealously guarded by tribal shamans, and only revealed to those who progress higher in a spirit cult's hierarchy (see page 196). Each further level of knowledge allows the skill to be used in new ways, permitting observation, communication, and eventually freedom to travel the Spirit Plane.

Interacting directly with the Spirit Plane takes time, normally requiring that a ritual be performed to enter a trance-like state. The amount of time required depends on the ability being used (see Trance Preparation Timetable), and costs a single Magic Point.

If the skill check is successful then the animist can perform the following, dependent on his cult rank:

- Follower - Can observe and identify spirits within range, using their natural senses.
- Spirit Worshipper - Can converse with spirits within range, via empathic communication.
- Shaman - Can project their own soul onto the Spirit Plane. They can also draw a spirit into the material world (or expel a spirit possessing a mortal) for a time equal to their POW in minutes. Spirits unwilling to manifest (or depart) may resist using their Willpower in an opposed roll against the Trance skill of the Shaman[1].
- High Shaman - Can drag the souls of others onto the Spirit Plane with them, at a cost of 1 extra Magic Point per additional person. Unwilling participants can resist using their Willpower in an Opposed roll against the Trance skill of the High Shaman[1].

Shamans and High Shamans may travel the Spirit Plane to observe and locate other spirits. The skill provides an understanding of the abstract geography and nature of the region, and the shaman can travel up to his skill's value in kilometres away from his body. From the Spirit Plane a shaman who succeeds in a Perception test can also distinguish the souls of corporeal creatures in the material world, and thus hunt for particular species or even seek out specific people.

If the roll is a critical success then entering the trance is achieved one step more quickly (with a minimum of one Action). If the roll is fumbled, the shaman is barred from entering the Spirit Plane for a full day.

1 If the unwilling target succeeds in resisting, they cannot be affected by the same Shaman or High Shaman again, until a full day has passed. The range of these abilities is the Shaman's POW in metres.

Binding (POW+CHA)

Binding is the skill used by animists to induce or force a spirit to perform to his will. It has a range of applications:

- It can bind spirits into fetishes, places or creatures, and control their actions once bound.
- It can be used to persuade a spirit to perform a single deed for a mutually acceptable service.
- It can be used to summon a known spirit from across the Spirit Plane, provided its corresponding physical location is within the skill's value in kilometres away.
- It can be used to engage in Spirit Combat.

The POW of the largest spirit which can be coerced, bound or controlled cannot exceed three times the critical range of this skill. Thus a character with a Binding skill of 45% could control spirits of up to 15 POW.

When used to engage in Spirit Combat, the value of the Binding skill is used to calculate the amount of damage inflicted by the animist - see the Spirit Damage Table. The same table is used by spirits for their Spectral Combat skill.

Spirit Damage

Skill Value	Damage Inflicted	Average Roll
01-20	1d2	2
21-40	1d4	3
41-60	1d6	4
61-80	1d8	5
81-100	1d10	6
101-120	2d6	7
121-140	1d8+1d6	8
141-160	2d8	9
161-180	1d10+1d8	10
181-200	2d10	11
201-220	2d10+1d2	13
221-240	2d10+1d4	14
241-260	2d10+1d6	15
261-280	2d10+1d8	16
281-300	3d10	17
Each +20%	Follow above progression	

Spirit Societies, Cults & Traditions

In cultures where animism is the main form of religion, spirits and fetishes are ever present, and a shaman fulfils the same role as a priest. In settings where animism is a core part of belief, spirits are fundamental parts of society, and treated with reverence, respect, and fear – not as magical batteries or buffs. Most people will have a shrine to revered ancestors or several fetishes holding totem spirits, and will take part in ceremonies of remembrance and revitalisation.

Animists who walk the otherworld binding spirits against their will, treating them as accoutrements, will soon gain a poor reputation – not only amongst their peers but also amongst spirits friendly to that culture– and gradually be alienated as a result.

share one simple insight: the world is alive. Each rock, plant, animal, and each cloud, pool and storm has its own spirit.

These spirits, especially the spirits of ancestors, might also be members of a tradition or be friendly towards it. Others simply have no interest in the mundane world. Some may even be actively hostile to members of a particular tradition. Because there are so many ways to approach spirit worship, cults tend to be diverse, but as a rule of thumb each spirit tradition tends to have:

- Direct access to 1d3+3 specific types of spirit which are friendly to the tradition.
- Knowledge of how to locate a further 1d3 types of spirit that are neutral with regards to the tradition.
- At least one enemy or competing cult, its own allied spirits being treated as actively hostile towards the tradition.

Depending on the setting, most will have access to allied medicine, nature and ancestor spirits. These are the core spirits upon which a cult can be based, but it is not necessary for a cult to possess knowledge of all of them. The types of allied spirit can vary with the focus of the tradition.

In settings where animism co-exists with theism or sorcery, guardian spirits become necessary allies or neutral spirits to have access to, whereas they are not really needed in animism-only settings.

Elemental spirits of differing Intensities will be available to cults having particular affiliations to large scale natural phenomena, such as earthquakes or floods. Usually (save for some high fantasy or Sword & Sorcery settings) curse, death and bane spirits are not an active part of any particular tradition, and any shaman attempting to bind them into service is taking a serious risk. The remaining types of spirit are not commonly worshipped, and tend to be propitiated rather than made into allies, unless the campaign requires diabolical spirit cults to act as antagonists for the characters.

Most animists possess enough skill in Trance to see the spirits around them when they meditate. It is highly unlikely that they will ever engage in a life and death battle in the Spirit World, since that is the shaman role. Thus most lay animists are content to master enough skill in Binding to learn the proper means of address and state of mind needed to safely invoke the power of their bound spirits.

The shaman is the bridge between the mortal world and the Spirit World. He lives a life in two realms, and with his help members of the community can pass through to the Spirit World to converse with those who have gone before.

Powerful shamans tend to attract attention in the Spirit World. When viewed there the shaman's soul echo is often the subject of many spirits seeking attention. This can be highly distracting for the shaman, and may attract the attention of predators; but a powerful shaman should have a strong enough web of allies that most hunters would rather stalk less powerful prey. However, player character shamans should expect occasional very unpleasant surprises.

Although most spirit worshippers will be a member of a cult or tradition, the organisation is unlikely to be anywhere near as formal as a theistic cult or mysticism order. Spirit cults tend to be loose affiliations of animists or may simply consist of members of single family, clan or race who venerate particular spirits. These traditions

Defining Spirits

From omnipresent spirits of nature to the restless spirits of the undead, the inhabitants of the Spirit Plane are varied and diverse: but what exactly is a spirit?

Typically a spirit is an intangible entity lacking any physical substance. At their simplest they are magical fragments of life-force cycling between the material world, and the mythic or metaphysical sources of the universe.

Spirits are generally aware of their surroundings and capable of reacting to circumstances. Those with plant and animal sentience use their base empathic drives, such as love, hunger or fear, to communicate. Sapient spirits are fully intelligent, capable of far more subtle communication approaching that of true language.

Souls are spirits that remain tied to a living, physical body in the material world. This isolates them from the Spirit World, denying them the primordial state that they should occupy. The only ways for a soul to transcend to the Spirit World are:

- Through death, sundering the physical and spiritual, liberating the soul to attain its next stage of existence.
- Being made discorporate through the actions of another spirit.
- Using the Trance skill to temporarily free the soul.

The nature of a spirit depends on its source and purpose. An animal spirit roams the Spirit Plane in similar places to its physical counterparts. They are attracted by their kin, and drawn to conceived young within which they incarnate as souls, moving to the material world through the miracle of physical birth. When they eventually die they return to the Spirit World, only to be recycled once again.

Other types of spirit serve different purposes, and their powers have a resonance affecting the mundane world. For example elemental spirits drive the natural phenomenon of the material world via their actions on the Spirit World, having a cosmic emanation that transcends the metaphysical barriers. An angered hurricane spirit tears through the Spirit World, and its anger is felt as monstrous winds on the material world. A restless earth spirit causes the ground to shake through earthquakes and rock slides.

Certain malevolent spirits bring sickness or death. A plague spirit's contagion spreads to the physical world where disease affects many. A curse spirit's malignance lingers across the mundane world, bringing misfortune to those touched by it.

Ancestor spirits are the souls of particularly powerful and revered individuals that retain their identity after death to guard their communities and faithful. Communing with the ancestors can yield advice, guidance, and secrets that provide aid in the mundane world.

Then there are the restless dead: spirits that remain tied to the physical world, unable or unwilling to pass fully into the spirit realm to be reincarnated in the great circle of being. Natural, peaceful death results in the soul passing between the worlds easily, and with grace. Violent, unwarranted death can inhibit the transition, causing the soul to linger in a limbo state between the corporeal and discorporate. Ghosts and other restless spirits yearn for the transition to the Spirit World but have been denied it: in this state they become obsessive, aggressive, selfish entities that can bring pain and torment to the living – even though all they seek is the peace that the natural order of the cosmos dictates should be theirs.

Spirit Intensity

All spirits have an Intensity. Intensity is based on a spirit's POW, and measures three things:

- The benefit it can give to the spirit's controller.
- How difficult the spirit is to bind and control.
- The spirit's ability to influence the material world.

The greater a spirit's POW, the greater its Intensity. The Spirit Intensity table can be used in a number of ways to determine this relationship.

To determine the Intensity of, say, a recently deceased creature, cross reference its POW range from life with its Intensity; most player characters, when they die, will produce Intensity 1 or 2 spirits, for example.

To create a spirit that originates in the Spirit World, decide on its Intensity then roll POW as defined by the Spirit Intensity table (1d6+18, for instance, for an Intensity 3 spirit).

The lowest Intensity spirits are by far the most prevalent, but offer the least amount of benefit. A spirit with an Intensity of zero cannot affect the material world in any noticeable manner. Intensity 6 (and greater) spirits are stretching beyond the control of a lone animist, but may still be summoned, bargained with or even bound by several practitioners working together.

Spirit Intensity

Intensity	*POW*	*POW Range*
0	1d6	1-6
1	1d6+6	7-12
2	1d6+12	13-18
3	1d6+18	19-24
4	1d6+24	25-30
5	1d6+30	31-36
+1	+6	+6

Characteristics

Spirits also possess two other characteristics: either INT or INS (Instinct – see the Creatures chapter), and CHA.

INT/INS This reflects their level of intellect when alive or the corresponding physical creature if one exists.

CHA reflects the force of the spirit's personality in very much the same way as for player characters. CHA varies widely according to the nature and type of the spirit; more detail is provided in the descriptions of specific spirits starting on page 145.

Attributes

Lacking a physical body, the attributes of a spirit or discorporated soul are calculated using different Characteristics to corporeal creatures. Spirit Attributes are reckoned in the following way:

Action Points

Calculate using the sum of INT and POW (see Action Points table page 8).

Initiative Bonus

Figure using the average of INT and CHA.

Magic Points

Calculated as normal, but are used by spirits and souls as their Hit Points. A spirit's Magic Points do not recover whilst bound to a fetish or location, nor when summoned to the physical world; they only begin to heal on return to the Spirit Plane. (Also see the alternative concept of Tenacity on page 139)

Spirit Damage

Based upon the value of a spirit's Spectral Combat skill or a soul's Binding skill: see the Spirit Damage Table on page 131. If a discorporated character lacks Binding, they use half the value of their Willpower on the table instead.

Attitude

Each spirit has an attitude towards animists who approach it: friendly, neutral or hostile. A spirit's attitude affects how it will react to being contacted, to being bound, and what it might do if it ever escapes a binding.

Spirits that belong to the animist's tradition will most likely be friendly to the practitioner, and willing to ally with them. A bear spirit, for example, if being bound by a shaman of the Great Bear Clan, would be friendly towards an approaching shaman; neutral at worst.

Neutral spirits consist of both those that belong to traditions which are not hostile towards the shaman, and those not considered part of any tradition.

Hostile spirits belong to enemy traditions or are inherently antagonistic due to their nature. For example a tradition with wolf spirits will find that most prey animal spirits are distinctly hostile to it. Whilst water spirits and fire spirits are immediately hostile towards each other.

Locating and Gaining Spirits

In the Spirit World spirits can be found inhabiting objects or locations relevant to their originating power; subterranean caves for darkness spirits, forests for plant spirits, and so on. Remote places are generally favoured because there is diminished interference from other, more disturbing sources of magic. In the case of more transient spirits the locale can shift. Lesser herd beast spirits are found following the great migrations for example, with more powerful ones found instead at mythic Death Grounds where the greatest beasts go to die. Frequently the location is a place of striking or beautiful appearance.

Ancestor spirits typically live in communities mirroring their corporeal homes, or may have made for themselves a new home, such as a Feasting Hall, Medicine Lodge or Spirit Manse. Indeed all ancestor spirits may be found in one location but with clear delineations between old culture and origins.

As the mundane and Spirit worlds intersect, animists who want swiftly to access the Spirit World location for a particular kind of spirit, travel to the real-world equivalents of the spirit abode. A shaman wanting to contact the Great Bear spirit would travel deep into the woods and find the hunting trails and territories of mundane bears. A High Shaman seeking to locate and bind a death spirit would travel to a burial or execution ground, knowing that here the links to the Spirit World where such spirits lurk are strongest.

Of course not all animists need to travel blindly through remote wilderness locations to find a specific type of spirit. A guardian of a necropolis might, for example, have immediate access to many ancestor spirits whilst the Spirit Tradition of a nomadic clan may maintain cult knowledge of a dozen secret locations where certain spirits gather (See Spirit Cults page 193).

Locating a spirit normally requires an animist to either:

- Scour the mundane world, using Trance to view the Spirit Plane, on the off chance of noticing a suitable specimen.
- Shift fully into the Spirit World to search for a specific spirit.
- Journey to a location known to his tradition, where particular spirits are reputed to reside.
- Have someone of greater skill, rank or knowledge summon a known spirit for the animist.

Spirits might be relatively easy to locate: knowing how to control one is an entirely different matter. Each spirit has its own idiosyncrasies regarding how it can be found, propitiated or bound. Shamanic cults and spirit traditions possess fragments of this lore, which can influence their skill regarding particular spirit types. For example, the shamans of the Great Bear Clan know that the spirit of the Great Bear should never be approached during the winter when all bear spirits hibernate. They also know that the best place to encounter Grandfather Bear, when he is at his least aggressive, is after making a sacrifice of favoured prey – such as a large salmon caught fresh from the water.

Once located, animists may approach spirits in two ways:

- Negotiation: looking to strike a bargain, in return for a singular service.
- Binding: seeking to bind the spirit into continued service.

Spirit Relationships

Over the course of a campaign, some spirit allies may be willing to undertake tasks for the animist or even fight for him by attacking an enemy in spirit combat. This kind of independent behaviour should be the result of mutual respect or perhaps a debt of gratitude, but must be something that unfolds over time in play. The possibility exists that a friendship may grow between a animist, and an allied spirit, in which case the Games Master should feel free to use the spirit as the animist's future fetch (if suitable for the setting) or as a fully fledged non-player character to continue the relationship.

Spirit Negotiation

Animists will make contact with many spirits over time, some of their own tradition, others not. Rather than binding them all to service as fetishes, most animists attempt to strike bargains – providing something the spirit wants in return for a singular service for the animist.

In negotiation, the spirit must be willing to bargain, and be either friendly or neutral towards the animist. If remaining in the material world this requires the animist to successfully enter a detached reverie using his Trance skill, and possess the ability to communicate with the spirit, in line with a cult rank of Spirit Worshipper or higher. Alternatively the animist can ask a shaman or High Shaman to manifest the spirit in question.

Once communication has been established, the animist may then request the spirit's aid to perform a single task in return for performing a like service for the spirit. Some spirits are willing to enter into a more formal arrangement by providing the animist with their name, becoming an ally. In response the animist agrees to undertake some sort of repeating task or accept some form of geas or compulsion in line with the spirit's nature. On the most abstract level it can assumed that the task will cost the animist a number of Experience Rolls equal to the spirit's Intensity per year to complete the service or suffer the inconvenience.

Such bargains can be settled by decision of the Games Master, or resolved with an Opposed Test of suitable skills, such as the supplicant's Influence skill versus the spirit's Willpower. Failure to reach an accord has no further effect. Fumbling the roll however, may cause the spirit to react with anger.

Spirit Binding

Binding a spirit always requires the animist to engage the spirit directly in Spirit Combat. If he is able to compel a bargain (see page 138) or lower the spirit to zero Magic Points, and its POW does not exceed the limit set by his Binding skill, the animist may then bind it into a fetish, a location, or a creature; each type of binding necessitating its own requirements in terms of use and vulnerability, often in the form of taboos.

Fetish Bindings

A fetish is a ceremonial object that embodies magical power. Any item can become a fetish for a spirit, but amongst primitive cultures, fetishes tend to be items made from an item associated with that spirit (a bear's claw or tooth, for example, or its hide).

Whilst confined within its fetish a spirit cannot be harmed by hostile magic or other spirits; it remains in stasis, unaware of its surroundings. For an animist to use its magical ability a bound spirit must first be called from the fetish, to serve the holder. The binding still exists, but the spirit is now able to exert its power and travel up to its POW in metres away from the fetish.

Over time any animist possessing a fetish takes on some of the spirit's essence. So the owner of a bear tooth holding a bear spirit may feel dozy in winter or take on bearish odour. Fetishes holding curse or sickness spirits may emit a miasma that induces minor symptoms in the holder, making the fetish extremely unpleasant. Conversely a stone holding a Fire spirit would be warm to the touch - which may occasionally be useful.

Since the spirit of a fetish only submits to the control of whoever is holding the object, animists closely, and jealously guard their fetishes. It is usually taboo to touch an animist's fetish without his permission, and those who try risk the animist's ire.

In certain circumstances two or more animists might end up struggling for physical control over a fetish, and by inference the spirit bound to it. In these cases both should roll their Binding skill as an Opposed test, the winner gaining command over the spirit until challenged again.

Location Bindings

A spirit can also be bound to a specific location. This is usually done to protect an area. Unlike a fetish the spirit is able to roam the area specified by the anamist when it was bound, but no further than ten times the spirit's POW in metres from the exact spot the binding occurred.

Within this region the spirit is both visible and vulnerable to direct magical assault, unless it has the Manifestation ability to travel back and forth from the Spirit Plane (although it will still be trapped in the binding area). In return the spirit may use its powers, and freely interact with anyone within the location.

Often hostile spirits are bound to locations instead of fetishes, imprisoning them so they cannot cause harm. In such cases the binding taboo is usually linked to oaths of not trespassing into the area, non-aggravation from otherwise harmless activities like dancing, or the establishment of regular propitiatory sacrifice to placate it.

Only the binder, or the cult he belongs to may exert command over a location-bound spirit. If two or more animists of that cult vie for control over the spirit, it is resolved similarly to struggles over a fetish.

Creature Bindings

Spirits can also be bound into the body of a living creature. In principle the creature is loyal to whoever bound it, or the person they have assigned it to.

Advantages are that the spirit may recover Magic Points naturally, can move freely as allowed by its body and gains immunity from direct magical assault (as per a fetish).

Drawbacks are that it is now vulnerable to physical damage; the spirit's abilities only affect the body it is bound to; the creature must be tattooed or branded with the spirit's binding; and most dubitable of all – unlike Possession – the creature's original soul must be permanently sundered from its body, in effect killing it to make space for the new spirit.

Totemists are avid practitioners of creating such living fetishes, placing spirits into the bodies of their totem animals who then act as animal companions.

Some spirits with the Animate ability can be bound into corpses. In such cases the bound spirit cannot regain Magic Points.

Settings without Spirits

In some fantasy settings magicians are able to travel the ethereal planes in spirit form, yet encounter no ecology of spirits other than the souls of other Animism practitioners. This need not be a hindrance, since spirits are not strictly necessary for an accomplished spiritualist who has mastered the necessary skills.

For example, a practitioner can still use the Trance skill to pass messages over great distances, provide warnings to dreaming mortals, and act as a very effective spy or scout. Similarly the Binding skill can be used to combat opposing psychics, possess the physical bodies of others, and perhaps even kill from afar.

Thus a magician or psychic should never be underestimated just because they lack a comprehensive collection of bound spirits. The utility of their skills is limited only by the imagination of the player.

Fetish Proliferation

In most cultures a Shaman is a combination of priest, doctor, teacher, lawyer, undertaker, and spiritual border guard for their community. Most of their efforts are taken up with mundane affairs, and they have very little time for the exertion required for creating extraneous fetishes. Community members might gain a fetish as an adulthood ritual, and maybe others after significant rites-of-passage.

The number of fetishes prevalent in a community depends on many factors such as whether lower ranked members of the cult are permitted to own fetishes, if fetishes are reserved for those of a particular sex or profession, and whether the tradition has existed so long that previously created fetishes are handed down as heirlooms within families. In general, shamans have more important things to do than provide magic items for wandering characters.

Creating a Binding

The creation of a binding costs one Experience Roll per point of Intensity of the spirit. This represents the time and development needed to prepare the item, location or creature in which the spirit will be held. The ritual usually takes one week, at the end of which the animist should roll the spirit's Characteristics randomly, based on its Intensity. It is always possible that the spirit gained may be too powerful for the animist to control.

An animist can attempt to improve the binding's potency to contain a more powerful spirit of the same type by paying the difference in Experience Rolls. Thus an animist with a fetish capable of containing an Intensity 2 Animal Spirit could upgrade it to hold an Intensity 3 Animal Spirit by paying one Experience Roll. The animist can also replace the spirit of a binding with one of the same type, at no additional cost in Experience Rolls, provided the spirit can be found or a shaman persuaded to do the finding.

The recipient of a fetish or creature binding does not need to have bound the spirit himself. Lower ranking worshippers of a spirit cult often gain spirits through undertaking a ritual in collaboration with a shaman who binds it for them. While the shaman searches, the supplicant fasts and meditates, or sings and dances, purifying himself in preparation for the gift of the spirit. The bound spirit counts against the supplicant's limit, not the shaman's.

Animists of less than Shaman rank are not prevented from undertaking the search and binding a spirit personally, save that such tasks are sometimes dangerous, and would be frowned on by peers of the community if, for instance, the attempt ended with a malicious spirit possessing the would-be fetish maker.

Shamans usually only provide spirits to members of the same tradition or in recompense for great favours. Even then shamans will usually only bind friendly spirits associated with their cult in this manner. Seeking out spirits of a disparate or contrary nature is dangerous for both the shaman and the supplicant.

Physically destroying a binding, by killing the host creature or shattering its fetish for instance, immediately unbinds the spirit it contains. Upon gaining its freedom a spirit can either return to the Spirit World or, if hostile, possibly attempt to attack the animist who imprisoned it. Malicious shamans sometimes booby-trap places with easily broken fetishes containing dangerous spirits.

A spirit can be voluntarily unbound from its binding by its owner. Many reasons exist to do this, such as wishing to replace the spirit with a less damaged version. Owners can only manumit a spirit from its bondage if their Binding skill is capable of handling the POW of the shackled spirit.

Limits to Bound Spirits

The maximum number of spirits an animist can hold in bondage depends on cult rank:

- Follower: ¼ of CHA
- Spirit Worshipper: half of CHA
- Shaman: ¾ of CHA
- High Shaman: All CHA

If this number is ever exceeded, then the strongest spirit or spirits break free, possibly extracting revenge if they were hostile to the binding. Neutral spirits may be simply mischievous.

Using Spirits

A spirit's magical effects are persistent, lasting until it is sent away, countermanded or recalled to a fetish. This can make animists formidable foes. However, manifested spirits are vulnerable to magic that specifically targets spiritual entities. If so dismissed or destroyed, the spirit is gone for good until a replacement can be summoned.

Animists generally use their spirits in one of two ways: call upon a materially bound spirit, or summon a spirit from afar to perform an agreed task. These two different uses have different methods of resolution.

Calling Upon a Binding

Depending on its attitude a bound spirit will see its binding as either a prison or a positive relationship with its owner. Hostile spirits are always seeking to hinder or undermine whoever dared to command it; friendly spirits are sanguine and obeisant. Neutral spirits have little care either way. How the spirit behaves when called upon is thus dependent on its attitude.

Commanding a bound spirit takes an Action, costs 1 Magic Point, and requires a Binding skill roll. Depending on the result of the roll the following occurs:

- Critical Success: The command is not only successful, but costs the animist no Magic Points.
- Success: The spirit is commanded successfully, and performs the deed requested of it.
- Failure: The spirit ignores the command. The animist must wait until his next Turn to try again.
- Fumble: The command is so badly botched the binding is broken, allowing the spirit to return to the Spirit Plane or to turn on the animist if hostile.

A spirit that escapes the authority of the animist, can act freely until it is compelled to obey.

While under control a spirit performs its instruction to the best of its abilities, yet if the animist wishes it to perform a different task, he must issue a new command with the requisite Magic Point cost and Binding skill roll. There is always the possibility of losing control of a spirit and, the more powerful a spirit is, the more dangerous it is likely to be.

If the spirit's POW is greater than the limit set by the user's Binding skill, any attempt to command it fails.

In the specific case of a fetish, the bound spirit emerges from its binding-object as a Free Action to perform the first command given it. Returning the spirit to the fetish costs the animist an Action Point on their Turn, but no further Magic Points. Only if the spirit is neutral or hostile to the animist is a Binding skill check required to succeed.

Summoning a Spirit

Animists can summon spirits they have successfully negotiated with previously or know the true name of - the latter something which is normally held secret by members of the animist's cult or tradition.

To conjure the spirit the animist uses his Trance skill to make contact with the Spirit World (though he need not enter it). Assuming the spirit is within range, the animist may then issue a summons.

Attitude of a Summoned Spirit

Binding Test	*Allied Spirit*	*Neutral Spirit*	*Hostile Spirit*
Animist wins	Spirit repeatedly serves the animist for the remainder of the scenario	Spirit serves once	Spirit serves grudgingly, and attempts to pervert the command
Spirit wins	Spirit serves once then departs in friendship	Spirit departs	Spirit turns on the animist

The summoning attempt costs the animist a number of Magic Points equal to the spirit's Intensity, and requires a Binding test:

- Critical Success: The spirit anticipates its summons, arriving in 1d3 rounds.
- Success: The spirit hears the summons, and arrives in 1d6 minutes.
- Failure: The spirit fails to notice the call. The animist may try again the following day.
- Fumble: The spirit is mortally offended by the manner of the summons. The bond between the summoner, and the spirit is suspended until the animist can offer amends for his affront.

What happens then depends on the spirit's attitude towards its summoner, and whether it owes the animist a service. To determine how helpful or malicious it is, the spirit makes an opposed test of its Willpower against the animist's summoning roll. Refer the result on the Attitude of a Summoned Spirit table.

Note that if the POW of the spirit is beyond the capability of the animist to control, it may act independently or place its own interpretation on a service demanded of it.

Observing Manifested Spirits

In the Spirit World spirits are imperceptible to any corporeal creature, save for those with the Trance skill or some other such ability such as a mystic's Spirit Sense trait. However, spirits brought into the material world are manifested, potentially allowing them to become detectable by natural means.

Spirits can manifest in a number of ways. Normally spirits which augment the animist form a ghostly shape, whirling intangibly as an aura about the summoner. Embodied spirits infest, and actually modify the animist's physique, whereas a possessing spirit lurks ethereally within the mortal shell of the animist. How perceivable the spirit is depends greatly upon the setting.

Spirit Combat

Since most spirits are intangible, conflict must be resolved by other means than the clash of weapons.

Spirit Combat in the mortal realm usually takes the appearance of ghostly shapes swarming the body of their transfixed victim. Nothing stops the mortal from physically responding if they desire, save for futility if they lack magic to affect the spirit assaulting them.

Within the Spirit World however, such combats can be completely abstract in both the challenge presented, and in the appearance of the participants and their surroundings: it does not need to resemble a conventional fight. Instead an attack could be the replaying of a painful memory from the opponent's past life, or forcing them to confront and overcome a hidden phobia. A combat might even be a light-hearted contest: riddling perhaps, or boastful attempts at one-upmanship and humiliation. The outcome though, is usually serious.

Generally only spirits and animists initiate Spirit Combat, as characters without the Binding skill lack knowledge of how to fight in this way.

Engaging in Spirit Combat

Spirit Combat works almost identically to normal combat save that mortal combatants (if present in the Spirit World) use their Spirit Attributes, rather than physical attributes, as described earlier in this chapter.

Rather than wielding weapons, spirits have a Spectral Combat skill to make psychic attacks and parries. Animists use their Binding skill, whereas those uninitiated in Animism must rely on their Willpower skill instead.

As with physical combat, each attack and parry exchange in Spirit Combat is treated as a Differential Roll. If one or more levels of success are achieved then Spirit Combat Special Effects may be selected (see table overleaf).

In addition, a successful attack which is not parried, inflicts an amount of damage equal to the attacker's Spirit Damage roll to the defender's Magic Points. (For settings with no natural Magic Points see Tenacity, page 139).

If the defender runs out of Action Points with which to defend themselves, then they are left wide open, and the attacker may attempt to make an unopposed attack roll. Corporal characters engaged in Spirit Combat in the physical world may forgo their attack in order to cast magic or perform a physical act instead.

Fleeing Spirit Combat is not always possible. If the fight occurs in the material world, characters obviously cannot escape unless they physically depart the area the spirit occupies. On the Spirit Plane however, a discorporated animist can, instead of trying to damage their opponent, declare that they are using a Combat Action to try and escape back to their body. An Opposed test of the animist's Trance skill against the spirit's Spectral Combat is required. If the animist wins they break free, and the combat ends; but if the spirit wins, then the animist fails to get away. It is impossible for souls who do not have the Trance skill to consciously escape from the Spirit World as they have no knowledge or understanding of how to move within it. Only if they defeat or drive off their attacker will they be freed from its discorporation. Otherwise they must be rescued by an animist.

Combat continues until the fight is concluded by use of a Special Effect, or one of the combatants is reduced to zero Magic Points, at which point they are defeated.

Making Spirit Combat Harder

Whilst a successful parry normally blocks all damage in Spirit Combat, Games Masters may wish to restrict the amount of Spirit Damage blocked, if the Intensity of the spirits or souls involved is disproportionate. Thus a spirit one step smaller in Intensity than their foe will only block half the Spirit Damage on a successful parry. Two or more steps smaller means that they cannot block any damage at all, although parrying might still prevent a Special Effect; making bigger spirits very dangerous.

Spirit Combat Special Effects

Special Effect	Offensive	Defensive	Specific Roll	Description
Bleed Essence	X	X	Critical Only	Inflict a psychic wound which leaks 1 Magic Point per cycle, until Spirit Combat ends
Compel Bargain	X			Attacker makes an opposed roll of their Influence against the Defender's Willpower. If successful combat ends, and they force the defender to perform a deed
Drive Off	X		Mortals Only	Spirit must resist attack roll with Willpower or depart the combat
Leech Strength	X		Critical Only	Attacker absorbs the Magic Points inflicted by the attack
Obscure		X	Critical Only	Attacker can no longer perceive the defender, unless attacked again
Possess	X		Spirits Only	Assuming spirit is capable of possession, the defender must resist its attack roll with their Willpower or become possessed
Psychic Stun	X	X		Opponent loses next Turn
Restrain	X	X	Mortals Only	Prevents the spirit from fleeing or engaging others in Spirit Combat
Spirit Lance	X			Roll Spirit Damage twice, and take the best result
Sunder Binding	X	X	Spirit Fumbles	Breaks the fetish or binding the spirit came from
Suppress Ability	X	X	Mortals Only	Shuts down one of the spirit's abilities currently in use
Turn Back		X		Attacker suffers its own Spirit Damage roll instead of the defender
Withdraw		X		The defender may automatically disengage from Spirit Combat, returning to their body (if mortal), fetish or the Spirit Plane (if a summoned spirit)

Consequences of Defeat

If a participant in Spirit Combat reaches zero Magic Points they are reduced to a helpless state. Several things may then happen:

- Possessed: Certain spirits may possess the loser's body, to inflict their malignance. (see Possession and Exorcism page 140).
- Bound: If the loser is a spirit it may be bound into a fetish, location or creature binding.
- Exorcised: If the loser is a spirit currently possessing a mortal, then it can be exorcised from the body of the victim, and forced to return to the Spirit World.
- Dissipated: Spirits with the Deadly ability (page 143) may destroy the loser by tearing their essence apart. If the dissipated spirit was a discorporated mortal, then the physical body dies with the destruction of its soul. Some spirits can recover from being dissipated if they have the Recurring trait.
- Obligation: In exchange for its freedom, the loser must grant one service to the victor. This is one of the more common outcomes of a combat, and forms the basis for animists compelling spirits to do their bidding.
- Expelled: If the loser is a discorporated soul, he may be ejected from the Spirit World.
- Ignored: If the loser poses no threat or interest to the victor, he may simply be ignored. Quite often a victorious spirit has no ability to do anything else to a defeated opponent.
- Sundered: Limited to spirits with the Deadly ability (page 143) such as death spirits. If the loser is a discorporated soul, he may be torn completely free of his material form, normally causing the death of the body but transfiguring the soul into a spirit. What then happens to the sundered soul depends on the victorious spirit, and it may become one of its thralls – perhaps exiled to the mundane world to bring fear to other mortals, or retained as a slave in the Spirit World.

Note that some of the above consequences can only be chosen by spirits capable of that action. Animists, however, are taught the necessary skills to be able to freely choose any of the consequences known to their cult.

Defeat does not inevitably need to result in something bad. Many Spirit Combats are not antagonistic at all, but rather a test of an animist's strength or the abstract representation of a negotiation where the spirit and animist are debating with empathic images and memory. Winning such a challenge sways the loser to regard the victor with respect, perhaps even capitulating a passionately debated issue.

Even if the Spirit Combat was violent the winner may not want to inflict any additional revenge: much depends on the type of spirit to begin with. A peaceful mountain spirit may simply cast a foolish animist back to the material world; a predator spirit may inflict a ritual scar that manifests on the loser's material body, showing that he was bested; a curse spirit will likely be driven to possessing those it defeats; and a disease spirit is likely to infect the victim. Games Masters must adjudicate the circumstances and repercussions according to the spirit's inherent nature.

The Recurring Trait

Normally spirits dissipated as a consequence of losing Spirit Combat are forever destroyed, their essence recycling into the fabric of the Spirit Plane. Spirits possessing the Recurring trait are not eradicated. Although ripped asunder their individual elements gradually reform, eventually restoring the original spirit no matter what is done to it.

Such an involved process takes time. A dissipated spirit requires a number of days equal to its Intensity to reform, plus whatever time is required to recuperate its Magic Points. although in some settings the period can often be longer.

Restored spirits retain their former knowledge, skills, and memory. This often leads to them seeking revenge for their previous destruction – a dangerous situation for any animist. The only ways to deal with such a spirit are to either imprison it in a fetish where it can no longer cause harm, or discover why it keeps recurring. This is normally due to some enchantment or an unfinished task that must be completed before the spirit will rest.

Multiple Opponents versus a Single Spirit

In certain circumstances a Spirit Combat might ensue where one side has a numerical advantage over the other. This may be a group of discorporated mortals facing a single spirit of high Intensity. Conversely it could be an animist ambushed by multiple spirits of minor power.

Whilst single combats between disproportionate foes may pose little threat to the more skilful practitioner, the situation can change if several lesser opponents gang up on a more powerful individual. The normal result of such a one-sided engagement is that the more numerous side is able to launch a number of unopposed attacks, which will begin to whittle down the overwhelmed defender.

Attempting to flee multiple opponents requires that an animist's Opposed disengagement roll beats all of his foes, otherwise he remains trapped by their numbers. Conversely, if a member of the attacking pack decides to flee, then they get away automatically, provided at least one associate remains behind to cover their retreat.

Spirit Combat Options

Using Magic Points as spiritual Hit Points is the default method of measuring damage during Spirit Combat: it poses considerable problems if attacked victims have no magical reserves to prevent Spirit Combat, lessen its effects, or preserve/recover Magic Points quickly. In such situations any spirit or shaman could become unstoppable.

To overcome these circumstances, two alternate methods of running Spirit Combat are provided below.

Tenacity

As well as storing or producing Magic Points, which are used in the mundane world to fuel magic, POW also creates Tenacity Points, which measure a character's resilience when in the Spirit World. Tenacity Points are the focus of Spirit Damage, preserving Magic Points solely for the use of magic, and ensuring that magicians defeated in Spirit Combat are still capable of maintaining their earthly magical powers afterwards.

Tenacity Points cannot be used to cast magic. They are only tracked to judge the psychological endurance of those engaging in Spirit Combat. When reduced to zero the will to resist is broken, leaving the loser unable to avoid the consequences of the defeat.

Adding Tenacity Points has the advantage that all magicians, be they theists, mystics or sorcerers, do not become spiritually weakened by casting magic. Tenacity is independent of magical effort, providing them with a level playing field when placed beside iron willed warrior types.

Modifying Spirit Combat to use Tenacity is a simple case of adding this as a new attribute to complement Magic Points. Tenacity Points lost in Spirit Combat recover every 24 hours, provided the character is sufficiently well rested on their native plane of existence.

> **Mental Resilience**
>
> *Tenacity has the additional benefit of becoming a flexible measure of other mental states. If the campaign is of a kind where supernatural, and alien horrors are capable of shredding the frail sanity of humanity, Tenacity can be used to track deteriorating mental states, with zero Tenacity points reflecting serious psychological damage, and the decline into insanity.*
>
> *Similarly Tenacity could be used for resisting corruption, experiencing battle fatigue, suffering addictions, facing supernatural forces in historical settings, and so forth.*

Physical Damage

Appropriate for nearly all Sword & Sorcery genres, this option is the perfect replacement for personal Magic Points in worlds where magic and violent sacrifice is rife. Nonetheless, it is best suited for campaigns where Spirit Combat is only used to harm and destroy, rather than for abstract challenges.

To avoid the difficulties that corporeal beings face in settings where they have no normal access to Magic Points, any damage they take in Spirit Combat is applied to their physical Hit Points instead of their soul. This approach has several distinctions.

- Spirits can keep Magic Points as Hit Points since they lack a corporeal form.
- All corporeal beings can take about the same amount of damage, regardless whether they are magic users or not.
- Injuries suffered during Spirit Combat become more visceral since damage is applied to locations. Although animists gain an increase in effective 'spiritual' Hit Points, in fact characters become increasingly vulnerable to spiritual beings with large Spirit Damage.
- To offset location vulnerability, Animists and sapient spirits possessing knowledge of armour can manifest psychic protection with a value of one Armour Point per 20% of the Trance skill.

Since spirit damage is applied directly to locational Hit Points, Serious and Major Wounds have duplicate physiological effects on an animist. On the Spirit Plane however, a serious wound prevents the victim from attacking for his next 1d3 Turns, whilst a major wound incapacitates, so that he immediately loses the Spirit Combat.

Note that an animist can physically be killed by this type of combat even though something else might be happening to his soul.

Possession and Exorcism

Possession occurs when a spirit dominates the soul of a corporeal being, usually through a Spirit Combat defeat or the Possess Special Effect. The possessing entity inhabits the loser's body, perhaps seizing control of it. Possession comes in three forms: Dominant, Passive and Covert.

A possessing spirit weaves itself into the victim, so that even if it is drawn forth to engage in spirit combat, part of it remains anchored to the host. No creature can ever purge itself of a possessing entity. Others must first defeat it in Spirit Combat, and then exorcise the spirit, or banish it by successfully casting a specific type of expulsion magic. If the original body of a mortal possessor has been killed in its absence, then its soul usually dies when it is exorcised. Spirits merely return to the Spirit World..

Needless to say, a possessing spirit or soul can willingly abandon a possession at any time.

Dominant Possession

Dominant Possession occurs when the possessing spirit takes complete control of the body. The victim is fully aware that its body has been taken over but is absolutely powerless, unable to take any action at all. The possessor does not have access to any of the memories, skills or magic of the possessed, but substitutes its own instead.

To actively detect a dominant possession requires a successful, unopposed test of either Insight if viewed magically, or Trance.

Passive Possession

Passive Possession occurs when the spirit lodges itself within the victim, but is unable to seize control, allowing the host to remain in full command of its faculties. Instead the spirit 'merely' inflicts its powers on the host's body.

Covert Possession

As per Passive Possession, but the spirit remains hidden. The victim remains unaware of his possession, unless the spirit chooses to inform him of its presence. Some spirits take over the victim's body at night when they are sleeping, thus keeping their existence secret, save for inevitable physical exhaustion, and odd fleeting nightmares.

Detecting a covert possession requires a successful Opposed roll of the investigator's Insight (if viewed magically) or Trance skill versus the spirit's Stealth skill.

Diabolic Spirits

In many cultures spirits have long been thought of as demons or devils, otherworldly beings who take control of the living to wreak havoc in the real world. With the wide range of abilities, and spirit types available, it would be easy for a Games Master to use animism to design fully fledged demonologists, perhaps even using Wraiths as a template for more material demons. The stereotypical hierarchy of the underworld could easily be replicated by assigning increasing Intensity to higher ranked fiends, with Demon Lords possessing Intensity 6 or higher.

Animism Tricks

Animism provides a great deal of flexibility in mimicking most historical or fantasy forms of animism, shamanism and totemism. Yet there are a number of cunning tricks used in novels or recorded in cultural mythology that Games Masters can use, or grant to specific cults as part of their secret teachings.

Rejuvenating Spirits

As described in the Spiritual Attributes section, the Magic Points of a spirit only recover when it is in the Spirit World, since it is the source which provides their magical life-force. Those spirits present in the material world, whether bound to a fetish or manifested via summoning, have no way of recovering their energy, and may eventually wither away depending on how badly they are treated.

In a similar way the souls of corporeal creatures cannot recover their Magic Points whilst present in the Spirit World, since their magical strength comes from the physical world.

Animists whose spirits have been damaged by magical attacks or Spirit Combat may therefore have a difficult choice to make. Manumitting a spirit from a fetish so it can return to the Spirit World will allow it to recover its strength, but there is no guarantee it will permit itself to be re-bound. Conversely failing to liberate a greatly weakened spirit is effectively condemning it to impotence, or even death: something the cult, tradition or donator of the spirit may frown upon.

To overcome this, animists can ceremonially sacrifice their own Magic Points directly to the damaged spirit, restoring its essence. This helps prevent a spirit from withering away, and has no detrimental effect on the animist, who may regain donated Magic Points normally through whichever methods are used in the campaign.

Spirit Traps

A whole array of cunning traps can be prepared using spirits, to guard a particular item or area. The classic method is to construct a fetish from fragile material (or one that will be inadvertently destroyed as part of everyday use) thereby unbinding the spirit held within; such as a log hidden in a wood pile which will be burned for heat, or a carefully inscribed mandala drawn into the sandy floor of a cave. Breaking the fetish allows the spirit to escape; and woe betide those who are in the vicinity. Hostile entities like wraiths, curse or sickness spirits are preferred for such traps because, on release they can engage tresspassers in Spirit Combat to take their revenge.

Binding a Soul into a Living Creature

Binding a soul of a sapient person into another living creature is a nefarious act reserved for those cults that revel in chaos and evil. The host beast is usually something considered insulting or taboo, and usually of little threat to the animist who performs the binding. Whether the original body of the victim is left to die from neglect or is utilised in some other way depends on the objective of the animist. Some Bindings are simply temporary punishments designed to humiliate; the creator permitting the victim to return to his body after the lesson is learned.

Body Snatching

Body snatching takes the concept of soul binding one step further, using it for subversive purposes. A demon ruling a kingdom using the body of its monarch is a familiar trope of Sword & Sorcery fantasy.

To body snatch the animist chooses a victim and, after defeating them in Spirit Combat, binds their soul into another creature. The empty body that remains is then inhabited by the animist, who need not worry about a potentially hostile soul co-habiting the physical shell; nor about triggering the suspicion of anyone in search of possession regarding the snatched body via Trance or other magical means..

Body snatches are nearly impossible to detect, save for the changed personality of the occupant. Physically the disguise is perfect. The animist's own body may be in some danger whilst he takes command of another. In settings where fetches are unknown, the usual stereotype is that the spiritualist literally exchanges bodies with the victim; so that a tenant remains who will, at the very least, feed his temporarily abandoned shell.

Of course if the animist's original body dies he no longer has any place to escape back to, causing his own death if somehow exorcised.

Surviving after Death

A technique passed down amongst a few highly skilled shamans is the ability to survive after death. Since highly skilled animists have rigid control over their own soul, they can hold themselves on the Spirit Plane for some specific purpose, effectively postponing their transcendence to the source of all things or whatever afterlife is destined for them.

In the Spirit World they cannot regain Magic Points, and it is only a matter of time before natural attrition from aggressive spirits finally dissipates their soul. To avoid this, most animists try to locate the nearest living creature they feel capable of discorporating, defeating in Spirit Combat, and possess it. This could be anything from a small animal to their own murderer.

Spirits in Different Settings

In pseudo-historical settings the presence of a spirit, and its effects are normally invisible to the naked eye. Clues can be given to their attendance using other perceptions, skin breaking out in goosebumps or a faint moaning for example – but without some form of magical detection, bound or summoned spirits cannot be targeted.

In low fantasy settings the existence of a spirit can be more obvious. The immediate area around the spirit might take on certain visual cues, for instance hallucinatory morphing of objects seen out of the corner of the eye or an inexplicable deepening of shadows. To target such manifestations without magical aid requires a successful Perception check in each round.

In epic fantasy settings the presence of manifested spirits is clearly seen, and can be directly targeted. The source, and nature of the spirits directly affects their appearance. A totemic shaman for instance may appear to be guarded by a ghostly black wolf which eats any spell cast at its master; whilst a victim of a dominantly possessing sickness spirit may appear to have his skin constantly erupting in weeping sores, and pustules.

The visibility of spirits in a campaign should be considered carefully, as it can set the tone of animist magic. Zero or low visibility makes tackling animists dangerous, but adds greatly to a feeling of suspicion, and fear. Highly visible spirits are far easier to defeat with magic, but provide a very dramatic impact.

Once returned to a living body the shaman can recover Magic Points normally. However the maximum number of Magic Points the shaman can muster is limited by the Characteristic POW of the creature they now occupy.

Of course a shaman who persists in this semi-vampiric manner is vulnerable to being exorcised. If this occurs it may result in the shaman's true death or force them to restart the cycle, depending on how they achieved their first self-aware reincarnation.

Several options are:

- Knowledge of how to survive after death is inherent with gaining the rank of High Shaman. Such animists must succeed in an Opposed test of their Trance skill against the Attack roll which killed them, or else be overwhelmed by the shock of the blow, and unable to prevent their soul from transcending.
- The shaman must succeed in an unopposed Willpower test, but also needs to define what his objective for continued living will be. Once he has achieved this aim the shaman's soul continues to the afterlife.

Binding Huge Spirits

As Spirit Combat suggests, larger spirits can be challenged by a group of animists acting in concert. Whilst fundamentally dangerous (since individual animists could easily be slain with a single backlash) such efforts can be rewarded by overthrowing spirits of impressively large Intensity. The defeat of such spirits permits the animists to bind, dissipate or extract a single service from the entity.

Binding the spirit can be a liability. Choosing to bind the spirit within a fetish effectively imprisons it - a good thing if the spirit in question is malicious or destructive. On the other hand, the spirit's POW may make it impossible to control by anyone calling it out of the fetish.

Requesting a service from the spirit is also risky. Usually the boon is deferred to a later time, granting the spirit a chance to recover. Such requests are normally granted to the cult or tradition of those that managed to defeat it, rather to a specific individual. However this does permit any member of that cult who knows of the bargain and the name of the entity to call upon the owed debt.

Spirit Types

Spirits come in many forms, ranging from minor nature spirits through to powerful kami of major environmental forces, beyond mortal control; mischievous ghosts through to dreadful undead manifestations.

Although spirits are living entities rather than mechanistic spells, they still have specific sources or powers to which they are associated.

- A spirit can be an incarnation of an abstract magical or natural effect
- A spirit can be the individual or collective essence of a species of plant or animal
- A spirit can be the venerated soul of a dead ancestor
- A spirit can be the vengeful remnant of a dead creature

All spirits are sentient, although the degree of sentience varies according to the spirit's representation and type. Ancestor spirits, for example, are fully sapient, and display all the intelligence and coherence of their mortal form; but nature spirits are likely to behave, perceive, and articulate themselves in ways that reflect their origin. Skilled animists are capable of interpreting their (sometimes incoherent) ways of communicating, through their training and exposure to the Spirit World.

Applying Spirit Powers

Animists can use a spirit's powers in three ways; Augmentation, Embodiment, and Abdication.

Augmentation: *The simplest, and safest spirits are Nature, and Guardian spirits who augment the animist. The spirit gives the practitioner a benefit by flowing through or around his body, and is easily returned to a fetish. An animist who walks through some form of magical anti-spirit barrier will strip his augmenting spirits away if it powerful enough to affect them.*

Embodiment: *This is the active task of assimilating a spirit's powers, and advantages into the animist's physical being, directly channelling, and becoming one with the spirit. Elemental or Shape-shifting spirits work in this way. Embodiment can be risky, and demanding: a weak animist who incautiously embodies such a spirit risks being consumed or entrapped by it. Whilst embodying a spirit, the animist is unable to physically cross anti-spirit barriers that are strong enough to stop a spirit of that Intensity.*

Abdication: *This is where an animist surrenders control of his body by willingly letting himself be possessed. This normally applies to ancestor spirits that possess the animist, taking complete command. However other spirits, especially those of great power or authority, might demand use of the animist's body in exchange for performing a service. Should an ancestor or great spirit not wish to depart, there is little the unfortunate practitioner can do. As with embodiment, Animism-suppressing or -countering magics will pose a physical barrier to a possessed animist.*

Designing Spirits

Most of the spirits listed in this chapter are starting examples of a vast range of possibilities. To create new and unique spirits, use the following guidelines:

- Each type of spirit possesses one or more abilities which encompas their powers. Not all spirits are designed to grant an advantage to an animist, some are intended only as challenges for characters to defeat.
- Any advantage a spirit might offer when bound should be capable of being sustained as a permanent effect. The advantage should also be roughly balanced according to other comparable spirits, and the other forms of higher magic (mysticism, theism and sorcery).
- An advantage is always proportional to a spirit's Intensity. Since spirits usually have no defined limit to their POW, spirits often come in weaker and stronger forms.
- All spirits possess certain default skills. Spirits start with a Spectral Combat skill equal to 50%+POW+CHA, and a Willpower of 50%+(POWx2).

Spirit Abilities

Several of the following abilities rely on the spirit first infesting the target, in the form of either dominant, passive or covert possession. This requires that the victim is beaten in Spirit Combat as per Consequences of Defeat (page 138) or it gains the Possess Special Effect.

Animate (Specific Substance)

The spirit can embody itself into non-living matter, allowing it to shape or move the substance as if an actual body. If the material is a pure element such as earth or fire, the spirit may manifest itself physically as per an Elemental with a size in cubic metres equal to twice its Intensity (page 242). If, on the other hand, the material is flesh of a dead creature, it instead provides the powers of an Undeath spirit granting bonuses to physical Characteristics (page 153).

Autonomy

Spirit has the ability to venture beyond the normal distance limits of a binding or its summoner's aura of influence. This allows the spirit to act as an independent scout or messenger.

Bless

The spirit can boost one Attribute or Skill of whomever controls it. The amount increased depends on the Intensity of the spirit, and the specific type of blessing (see Curse Spirit Effects table for associated costs), but no Attribute or Skill may be boosted beyond double its original value.

Cannibalistic

The spirit gains the ability to regenerate its own Magic Points by absorbing the essence of spirits it battles in Spirit Combat. Every successful attack the spirit makes transfers that many Magic Points to its own total. If this exceeds the spirit's own POW, any surplus energy is wasted.

Comprehension
Grants the ability to understand and speak with creatures associated with that spirit or its animal totem. For example, a wolf spirit would allow its user to speak with wolves.

Conjugate
Spirit can maintain a permanent mental link with an animist who summons or binds it, no matter the distance between the two or seperation if one or other is within the Spirit World.

Covert
The spirit has a Stealth skill at 50%+INT+CHA, with which it can hide from active magical or spiritual observation by opposing the Perception skill of the observer.

Curse
The spirit can lower one Attribute or Skill of a victim it passively or covertly possesses. The amount reduced depends on the Intensity of the spirit and the specific type of curse. For example, a victim could be cursed with weakness if possessed by a spirit which reduces their Damage Modifier, or alternately cursed with clumsiness in war by using a spirit which reduces one of the victim's combat styles.

Curse Spirit Effects

Curse Type	*Effect*	*Notes*
Action Points	1 per three full points of Intensity	A possessed victim can be rendered helpless if reduced to zero Action Points
Armour Points	1 per point of Intensity	Only reduces natural armour, not worn armour
Damage Modifier	1 step per point of Intensity	This can reduce a Damage Modifier to negative values
Experience Modifier	1 per two full points of Intensity	If this results in Experience Rolls being lowered to zero, the victim can no longer improve their skills
Healing Rate	1 per two full points of Intensity	A possessed character reduced to zero can no longer heal naturally, and must rely on magic instead
Hit Points	1 per point of Intensity	If a Hit Location is reduced to zero, it is treated as if suffering a Serious Wound
Initiative Bonus	2 per point of Intensity	Initiative Bonus can be reduced to negative values
Luck Points	1 per two full points of Intensity	Bad luck!
Movement Rate	1 per point of Intensity	If reduced to zero the possessed character can barely crawl
Skill	1 Difficulty Grade per two full points of Intensity	The affected skill can be rendered unusable if the Difficulty Grade reaches Hopeless

Deadly
Gains the ability to either Dissipate or Sunder a spirit it has beaten in Spirit Combat (page 137). A spirit may only have the ability to inflict one or the other, not both.

Demesne
A potent ability, the spirit gains dominion over aspects of its environment within a range of one hundred times its POW in metres. Normally the limits of its influence are specified in the spirit's description. For example, a plant spirit could control the growth, flowering and fruiting of vegetation within its area of effect, whilst a truth spirit might prevent falsehoods being uttered. If the demesne of the spirit is challenged by a character, they may attempt to overcome its power by winning an opposed roll of relevant skills. For example, to lie within the demesne of the truth spirit would require opposing the spirit's Willpower with the character's Deceit skill.

Discorporate
Assuming the spirit is not bound, it may drag the soul of a mortal from their body into the Spirit World. The spirit has a base Discorporate skill of 50%+POW+INT. An unwilling target may resist the attempt in an opposed roll of their Willpower versus the spirit's Discorporate skill. If they succeed, they cannot be affected by the discorporation ability of that spirit again, until a full day has passed.

Disease
The spirit carries one or more diseases. Instead of possessing a victim, it instead infects them via Spirit Combat, providing it succeeds in an attack, and gains one or more levels of success over the foe. Once infected, the victim must roll against their Endurance skill to determine the severity of the disease, suffering a reduction if the spirit's Willpower skill is higher, and over 100%.

Depending on the result of the Endurance roll, the severity is as follows:

- Critical: severity is Chronic, effect occurs each week.
- Success: severity is Acute, effect occurs each day.
- Failure: severity is Terminal, effect occurs each hour.
- Fumble: victim is possessed by the spirit, and becomes an asymptomatic carrier of the disease, inadvertently infecting others with whom they come into physical contact.

An imparted disease endures until the sickness is cured magically. The type of condition (page 75) is limited by the Intensity of the carrying spirit. Nothing prevents a spirit carrying a combination of disease conditions, save that the total Intensity cost cannot exceed that of the spirit. For instance an Intensity 3 sickness spirit could carry Bleeding disease, or a combination of Blindness and Fever instead.

- Intensity 1: Confusion, Contagious, Exhaustion, Fever, Hallucination, Nausea, Sapping
- Intensity 2: Blindness, Deafness, Dumbness, Maiming, Mania
- Intensity 3: Agony, Bleeding, Paralysis, Unconsciousness
- Intensity 4: Asphyxiation, Death

If the spirit has more than one condition, they trigger in cascading sequence in assending order of required Intensity. Thus a victim of the previously described Intensity 3 spirit would suffer fever the first time the disease takes effect, then fever and blindness the second, after which (since the blindness might be permanent) the victim will suffer fever each occurance thereafter.

Domination (Specific Species)

Allows totemic spirits to command all living animals related to it within a distance equal to its POW in metres. A serpent spirit for example could dominate all snakes within range.

Endowment (Specific Capability)

The spirit grants the magician a special capability, sense, movement or resistance as owned by the spirit's totem. Usually these take the form of a Creature Ability (page 214), or combat Special Effect. The minimum required spirit Intensity varies, depending on the capability endowed, and nature of the spirit cult.

Eternal

The spirit has Recurring trait (page 138), which enables it to return after being dissipated.

Glamour

Enables the spirit to create illusions within a range equal to its POW in metres. This glamour is a mental illusion that works in a similar way to the sorcery spell Phantom (Sense) (page 171). The spirit can affect one sense per level of its Intensity, with a Magnitude of twice that.

Healing

The spirit is able to cure the effects of disease, if its Intensity is sufficient to counter the condition (see Disease Ability, page 143). It also permits recovery of Minor, Serious and Major Wounds (although they are unable to replace lost limbs), by sacrificing 1 Magic Point per Hit Point healed.

Mana

Permits the spirit to donate its Magic Points to the summoner or holder of its fetish, for use in casting magic or aiding in Spirit Combat.

Manifestation

Spirit may move between the mundane and Spirit World at will. It takes one Action to shift from one to the other. Whilst in the Spirit World the spirit is immune from all attacks (magical or physical) from corporal opponents.

Miasma

Enables the spirit to induce feelings of despair, dread and horror within a radius of its POW in metres. The Magnitude of the effect is equal to twice the spirit's Intensity. Anyone unable to block the magic must succeed in an opposed test of Willpower skills, or else flee the area in abject terror.

Passion (Specific Emotion or Disorder)

The spirit can invoke an overwhelmingly strong passion or state of mind in those it possesses. Although in a few cases they can be used beneficently, most are used in a hostile manner. The following passions and mental disorders provide mechanical effects of how they should be used in play. As with the Disease Ability (page 143), each has an associated number in parentheses, showing the minimum Intensity of spirit required to inflict that state of mind, assuming it manages to possess the target.

Amnesia (1): An amnesia spirit makes the victim chronically forgetful. Although it has no effect on skills, it does prevent them from remembering anything that happens during the period of their possession. This doesn't stop the host from behaving normally (assuming they do not act on knowledge revealed since the amnesia started), only that they have no recollection of it, even after the spirit is expelled.

Confusion (2): Causes confusion during times of stress, or at the malicious whim of the possessing spirit. During a confusion attack, any skill attempt made by the host is resisted by spirit's Willpower in an opposed test. If the victim loses, they do the incorrect thing, possibly striking the wrong target in combat, casting a different spell to what was intended, answering a question which wasn't asked, and so on.

Deceit (1): Induces the possessed victim to lie, cheat and steal, no matter the consequences. They simply cannot help themselves, although they can attempt to disguise their subterfuge through use of the Deceit and Conceal skills.

Fear (2): The possessed host suffers foreboding and timidity, as if they were under the effect of the Demoralise spell (page 125). The subject of the fear must be related to the cult or tradition, thus a sea based spirit could inflict a fear of drowning, and so on.

Greed (1): Also known as Gluttony Spirits, possession causes the host to become enamoured of a specific item, substance or stimulus. Whenever the victim comes into contact with the object of their greed, they will attempt to horde, secrete, covert, consume or immerse themselves to their detriment for the next 1d3 hours. Examples might be alcohol, gold, or even sexual liaison.

Grief (3): Instils a sense of loss so great that the host becomes passively suicidal. They do not actively seek dangerous situations, but will only half-heartedly protect themselves if one occurs. Whenever asked to parry, evade or make an opposed test, to resist hostile magic for instance, the victim must reverse the number rolled on the dice if it would generate a worse result.

Hate (2): These spirits exaggerate the possessed host's natural inclinations towards a particular individual, race, cult or culture, making them irritable and surly. Whenever the opportunity presents itself, usually when unobserved, the victim will succumb to overwhelming hatred; leading them to quarrel with, brutalise, torture, or rarely to even murder the object of their hate.

Love (1): The newly possessed host falls in love with the first compatible partner he or she sees. Once a love object is found, the host is utterly infatuated, gaining a Love (Individual) Passion equal to the Willpower value of the spirit. This is thereafter used as an opposing motivation whenever the host is called to leave their beloved, or work against his or her interests.

Madness (2): Akin to having a demon whispering into your ear, madness spirits force the host – at times of stress – into acts of irrational or gibbering behaviour. Depending on the spirit's inclination, this is done by changing the perceptions of the victim, sadistically torturing them, or instilling a degree of increasing paranoia. Madness attacks last 1d3x10 minutes, occurring whenever a skill check is made by the host, and the spirit overcomes that roll in an opposed test using its Willpower.

Violence (3): Removes all ethical and moral restraints towards using combat to solve problems. Any hint of dissent or outright threat will trigger a violent outburst. Worse still, the host glories in violence so much that they will joyously brutalise all living things within reach, be they friend, foe or even innocents. Violent outbursts can be resisted if the host can overcome the spirit in an opposed test of Willpower, but once triggered, the violence only stops when the host is incapacitated by exhaustion or a lack of responding victims. Note that violence does not necessarily equate to death – most hosts utilising their natural weapons over drawing a weapon, unless directly threatened by one first.

Perceptive

Spirit has the ability to see possessing spirits, bound spirits inside creatures and fetishes, shapeshifted beings, and penetrate illusions in its immediate vicinity. The spirit has a base Perceive Unseen skill of 50%+POW+INT which can be countered by the target of its scrutiny with an opposed test against Conceal, Disguise, Stealth, or a pertinent magical skill.

Persistent

The spirit gains immunity to magical dismissal of any form. This does not mean it is immune to magical damage or Spirit Combat, only that spells such as Banish or Exorcism do not affect it.

Puppeteer

The possessing spirit can control the physical body of others. It can be used benevolently to take control of a totem animal or protect a spirit magician's body whilst he is discorporate. Hostile spirits on the other hand, use this ability to steal the body of a foe to achieve the spirit's strongest desires.

Sagacity

Possesses a skill at a value equal to the spirit's 100% + (INTx2). There is no limit to the type of skill imparted, provided it is relevant to the spirit concerned. So a spirit devoted to war might know weapon skills, whereas one linked to a particular family may provide genealogical knowledge instead.

Shapechange (Specific Species)

Grants the ability to shape change the spirit magician into his cult's totem animal, as described under Shape-shifting spirits (page 152).

Spellcasting

Allows the spirit to either cast magic on behalf of its summoner with a skill of 50%+POW+CHA, or share knowledge of the spells it knows with the holder of its fetish.

Subjugate

Allows the spirit the ability to bind one or more other spirits of lesser Intensity, holding them as vassals without the necessity of a fetish. For spirits of the same tradition, this is usually a willing servitude – a mountain spirit holding several lesser earth elemental spirits, for instance. If the spirits are not associated, the subjugation is more one of forced enslavement. Each lesser spirit held in subjugation reduces the holding spirit's Magic Points by a value equal to its Intensity as an enduring cost. Subjugation ends if the holding spirit is ever reduced to zero Magic Points.

Telekinesis

This ability grants the spirit the ability to move objects in the physical world despite its nominally intangible form. It gains a STR equal to its Intensity, and can shift items up to its POW in metres distant.

Warding

Gains the ability to ward off hostile magic from something the spirit guards, automatically blocking spells with a Magnitude less than or equal to twice the spirit's Intensity. Although magic is blocked, it is not dismissed by contact with the spirit. For instance, weapon enhancement spells do not vanish when the magician is hit, nor is the enchanted weapon prevented from striking them; only that any magical boosting to damage does not occur.

Wither

The spirit is able to physically damage corporeal beings, using its Spectral Combat skill or some other Combat Style it possessed before death. The blows inflicts damage equal to its usual Spirit Damage that ignores all non-magical parries and physical armour; requiring opponents to Evade or flee its attacks.

Example Spirits

The following spirits are presented with base Characteristic ranges and skills. However since the POW of the spirit depends on the Intensity chosen for it (see Defining Spirits page 132), no average Attributes are provided as they fluctuate according to the POW of the spirit.

Nothing prevents a Games Master from adding or removing abilities from the following spirits to create unique entities more suited to their campaign settings.

Spirits That Initiate Combat

Although all spirits have a Spectral Combat skill, it does not mean that an animist can send any old spirit off to engage a mortal in Spirit Combat. Spirits are not ubiquitous fire-and-forget weapons to destroy an enemy's Magic Points. Rather they have a specific purpose, and alternate abilities to back it up.

The important term here is ***initiate****. Whilst a spirit can always fight back when attacked, most cannot start a Spirit Combat except against particular foes.*

Each of the common spirit types mentioned in this chapter has a defined limit clarifying if, and what types of target, that spirit can initiate Spirit Combat with.

Save for a handful of cases (Ancestor, Curse, Death or Sickness spirits for example) none of the described spirits can be used to aggressively instigate an attack against mortals in Spirit Combat.

Ancestor Spirits

Eternal, plus one or more of Discorporate, Sagacity, Spellcasting, and Subjugate

Ancestor spirits are the souls of family members who, after death, reside either in the Spirit World, in the underworld or whatever afterlife is provided by the local pantheon; all depending on the setting. An animist who quests in the Spirit World can always find a way to reach these places, although he will normally only ever encounter ancestors with whom he has a relationship, finding both venerated predecessors and despised enemies. Such spirits can be found continuing their existence in houses, halls, tribes or communities resembling those they occupied before death; or despondently wandering in the gloom of limbo.

Animists may ask questions or request aid from their honoured ancestors; or conversely attempt to bind and imprison an enemy ancestor, preventing it from being called upon by their foes.

Ancestor spirits are a natural source of knowledge and information. In their mortal life they achieved greatness through skills, talents, and deeds that have secured their continued veneration in the afterlife. The spirits of those who died without noteworthy deeds tend to fade and dissipate, once their immediate descendants pass on. Thus most ancestor spirits are noted heroes, remembered many generations after their death, and continually honoured in ceremonies personal and grand, small and large.

A specific ancestor spirit is summoned to the material world by an animist of direct descent. If there is no blood-lineage, a shaman must travel to the home of the ancestor in its afterlife. Once summoned or located, the spirit can be asked questions concerning the family line, or events which happened during its lifetime. Such requests only require a successful Influence roll, the offering of 1 Magic Point – representing a donation of blood or life-force– and cost nothing further.

Animists can also request an ancestor's aid in performing a specific and important service. This comes at a greater cost, involving an immediate sacrifice of at least 1 Magic Point per Intensity of the ancestor, and continued votive gifts to that particular spirit (if necessary this can be abstracted to either spending an Experience Roll each year or one Magic Point each month, if Games Masters prefer). Continued veneration in this way keeps the memory of the ancestor alive, promoting his continued existence. In return the ancestor grants its help to overcome the problem facing the petitioner.

Ancestor spirits are very versatile, and may either agree to perform a single service as a spirit there and then, or offer to incarnate in the body of the descendent if this is a more appropriate act.

Questioning Ancestors

Some animist traditions require the ancestor to inhabit the body of its summoner in the material world, so that it can communicate directly with those who question it; rather than indirectly via a go-between. In settings where this is the norm, an animist must always voluntarily permit the ancestor to possess them unless the animist has travelled into the Spirit Plane to question the spirit in its home in the afterlife. Where an animist has abdicated control of his body, the ancestor will usually respect the trust of the summoner, and leave of its own free will once it has satisfied all enquiries.

Ancestral Demigods

When a soul first departs for the afterlife, it becomes a spirit of equal POW to its living self. However, over time those ancestral spirits which receive regular worship, and propitiation slowly grow in strength. It may take centuries, but ultimately the spirit will transcend their normal species limit to characteristic POW. In this way the spirits of tribal founders, national heroes or even assuaged enemies can eventually become demigods in their own right.

Certain ancestors might be prepared to temporarily inhabit an heirloom or item (such as a tribal treasure) of great personal significance in order to be manifested later. The item can be anything held in esteem by the community, and the ancestor will bind itself to the item as if it were a fetish, and wait within until the appropriate time for it to emerge. Such confinement is extremely unpleasant for the ancestor spirit, and so the expectation is that it last for a very short time – days rather than weeks or months. Any longer, and the ancestor may turn hostile and immediately return to the Spirit Plane upon release, after extracting suitable penance from the summoner.

Physically incarnating requires the descendent to voluntarily permit the ancestor spirit to possess his body. This bargain places the animist at a dangerous disadvantage since he cannot prevent his body from being abused by the ancestor spirit. Unsympathetic ancestors often succumb to long forgotten passions, or attempt extreme acts to further their renown – being in little danger of personal harm if their host dies.

Whilst possessed, the animist may gain access to new abilities, spells, and spirits pertaining to the ancestor. Warrior ancestors have combat skills, shaman ancestors have spirit skills, hunter ancestors have stealth and tracking skills, medicine ancestors have healing skills, and so on.

Residing in another body or object means that an ancestor spirit cannot be called upon by other members of that cult or tradition; for this reason an ancestor spirit usually only remains until it has achieved the summoning objective. Regardless of how the ancestor is incarnated or lodged, it counts against the animist's number of spirits that can be controlled.

Repeated summonings or being summoned for minor or trivial tasks may irritate the spirit, forcing the animist to defeat his ancestor in mock Spirit Combat. If the animist loses, then the ancestor considers the request below its dignity and refuses to help. If the animist wins instead, the ancestor is roused into providing aid, but the ancestor may be considered as either neutral or hostile.

Ancestor Spirit

Characteristics
INT: As per mortal of the species
POW: As per its Intensity
CHA: As per mortal of the species
Culture and Lore skills of their people and region = 100%+(INTx2), Spectral Combat = 50%+POW+CHA, Willpower = 50%+(POWx2)

In addition, the ancestor may take a number of selections, equal to 1d3+Intensity, from the following list of Spirit Abilities:

- Discorporate: allows the ancestor to summon the soul of a nearby mortal descendent into the Spirit World.
- Sagacity: spirit knows a skill relevant to the profession of the ancestor at 100%+(INTx2).
- Spellcasting: holds knowledge of 1d3 Folk Magic spells (which it can cast assuming the ancestor has the Folk Magic skill).
- Subjugate: ancestor has a spirit ally of one less Intensity than itself, which appears within 1d3 Combat Rounds of being summoned (assuming the ancestor has the Trance and Binding skills).

Bane Spirits

Cannibalistic, Deadly

Fragments of pure Chaos or some other source of evil, bane spirits strive to absorb the essence of other spirits. Due to their relationship with entropy, once the Magic Points of the targeted spirit have been reduced to zero, the bane spirit consumes it utterly and irrevocably, so that it is forever destroyed, even those with the Recurring trait.

Bane spirits are abhorred to the point that they are often bound and imprisoned in remote or accursed locations, preventing them from causing irreparable harm. Only the insane, or those driven to suicidal revenge, tend to use them. If imbued into a fetish, bane spirits can be used as a weapon nominally sent against other spirits to engage in Spirit Combat. Bane spirits can destroy other bane spirits.

The majority of bane spirits are oblivious to the physical world, and lack the ability to manifest into the material realm to attack mortals. Instead they fester upon the Spirit World causing untold damage to other spirits which mistakenly stray into their vicinity.

Bane Spirit

Characteristics
INS: 1d6
POW: As per Intensity
CHA: 1d6
Spectral Combat = 50%+POW+CHA,
Willpower = 50%+(POWx2)

Curse Spirits

Curse, Covert, Manifestation

Overtly malicious, curse spirits are sent by animists to possess mortals bringing them misfortune. They can be found in places that have suffered terrible natural disasters.

Curse spirits impose detrimental effects such as reduce Action Points, slow Healing Rate, and so on. The conditions they inflict directly affect the possessed victim, and can only be stopped by exorcising the spirit, assuming the victim is even aware that he is possessed in the first place.

Curse Spirit

Characteristics
INS: 2d6
POW: As per Intensity
CHA: 2d6
Spectral Combat = 50%+POW+CHA,
Stealth = 50%+INS+CHA,
Willpower = 50%+(POWx2)

Death Spirits

Deadly, Manifestation

These spirits are viewed in different ways by different cultures. Some see dying as a natural part of the cycle of existence, and therefore nothing to be feared. Others are horrified by death spirits, seeing them as the tools of depraved animists to spread terror. The spirit's appearance reflects the attitude of the cult or tradition; peaceful bringers of death taking the form of serene angels to guide the victim to the afterlife, whereas murderous slayers might appear as such things like burning skulls, giant poisonous animals or hooded, scythe wielding vultures.

Death spirits are sometimes bound to protect places and objects, or more often summoned to attack specific targets, attacking the transgressor in Spirit Combat either way. If the spirit wins the battle it Sunders the soul of the victim, ripping it free of its corporeal body, and sending it to whatever fate lies in store. This is invariably fatal for mortal creatures but preserves their essence and identity as a spirit.

Death Spirit

Characteristics
INS: 3d6
POW: As per Intensity
CHA: 3d6
Spectral Combat = 50%+POW+CHA,
Willpower = 50%+(POWx2)

Elemental Spirits

Animate, Demesne

Elemental spirits are direct incarnations of the elements (earth, air, fire, water and darkness) or manifestations of natural forces and phenomenon: mountains, volcanoes, tsunami, and so on.

Animists can bind elemental spirits in the normal manner but the object or location must be chosen carefully because, even within the binding, some of the elemental spirit's power is always manifested. A Salamander spirit must be bound into a fetish capable of withstanding heat while an Undine fetish will become damp and clammy.

When summoned or released from a fetish an elemental spirit, if left uncontrolled, will gravitate to the nearest source of its element within range. By itself it is just a spirit, and has no significant effect on the mundane plane. The spirit's power does not truly manifest until commanded to embody itself. As with any control attempt, the animist must spend 1 Magic Point. If the roll is successful, the animist has two choices: Permitting the spirit to animate a suitable volume of its native material, as per a normal elemental, or, embodying the elemental so that it manifests within his own body.

The later choice grants the animist the physical and magical benefits of an elemental. Thus an animist embodying a sylph would be surrounded by a vortex of buffeting winds, but could fly and send out jets of wind to pummel opponents. If a gnome was embodied instead, the animist would take on a gravelly appearance, and be able to sink into the ground as if some sort of amorphous creature of flowing sand.

Whilst embodying an elemental spirit, the Animist is physically immune to the elemental's incidental effects himself, but cannot control their affect on his belongings or companions. So an embodied Salamander will burn away the animist's clothes, consume his equipment, and potentially injure any nearby friends from radiated heat. Furthermore, expelling the elemental spirit is more difficult than for other spirits, as the animist must make a successful Trance roll to successfully force it back into the fetish, each attempt costing an additional Magic Point. Finally, while in his elemental form, the animist is vulnerable to additional damage from an opposing element. For all these reasons, embodying a powerful elemental spirit is a step that is never undertaken lightly.

Animists embodying an elemental spirit gain the abilities of an elemental of a size based on the spirit's Intensity as outlined below.

Elemental Intensity/Size Relationship

Spirit Intensity	*Elemental Size*
1	2 cubic metres
2	4 cubic metres
3	6 cubic metres
4	8 cubic metres
5	10 cubic metres
+1	+2 cubic metres, and so on

The animist's STR, DEX and Hit Points are replaced by the spirit's values (which are rolled as normal for an elemental of its SIZ when first encountered). This normally calls for an adjustment of derived Attributes such as Combat Actions, Damage Modifier and Initiative Bonus. Any special attack the elemental possesses is retained but uses the animist's Unarmed skill value instead.

When the elemental spirit is expelled, any damage it sustained whilst embodied is divided evenly between all the animist's Hit Locations (rounding up as usual). For example if a human shaman took 23 points of damage while in elemental form then he would take 4 points of damage to each of his 7 locations once he returned to his normal form. If the damage is enough to cause a Serious Wound the animist must resist the injury effects by succeeding in a Hard Endurance roll, or a Formidable Endurance roll if a Major Wound. The result of the roll is applied to all the critically injured locations simultaneously.

Although embodying an elemental spirit can be extremely impressive, it also opens the practitioner up to new problems. An animist embodying an elemental spirit will take double damage from attacks using the opposing element, and can be instantly dispersed by contact with an opposing elemental of the same size or bigger in cubic metres. Reducing the elemental form to 0 Hit Points instantly breaks the binding and frees the spirit, possibly also critically injuring or killing the magician in the process. Spells which can dismiss elementals will free the elemental, and destroy the binding if the Magnitude of the magic is equal or greater than twice the spirit's Intensity.

Elemental spirits do not initiate Spirit Combat except against other elemental spirits of an opposite element.

Fetches

Special

A fetch is a shaman's spiritual ally, representing the opening of his consciousness in the Spirit World. Not every Shamanic tradition features fetches, and those that do vary in the nature of the fetch. In some traditions the fetch is the awakened "other half" of the shaman. In this case the fetch and shaman are two sides of the same soul with the fetch perceiving and travelling the Spirit World whilst the shaman exists on the mundane plane.

In other traditions the fetch is a totemic spirit who is drawn to the shaman to become his spiritual guide. In both cases the shaman must undertake a successful quest in order to gain his fetch.

A fetch's abilities vary widely between traditions. In cases where the fetch is the shaman's counterpart, it represents the opening of spiritual abilities to the shaman rather than being an independent being in its own right. The fetch might provide the shaman with exotic powers, such as the ability to shapechange. If the fetch is an animal or ancestor guide then the shaman may gain the ability to communicate with the animals of the fetch's species, control them or gain the traits of that creature; or become party to certain secrets if the fetch is an ancestor.

There are two main choices when designing a fetch, an Awakened Fetch, where the shaman simply unlocks or expands a hitherto hidden part of his soul; or an Allied Fetch which is a separate spirit that forms a lifelong pact with the shaman. Unless otherwise stated, a fetch cannot roam any further from the shaman's soul to which it is bound than his POW in metres. Fetches can grow in experience just as the shaman does. If desired, a shaman can transfer any or all of his Experience rolls to his fetch instead.

Fetch Types

	Awakened Fetch	Allied Fetch
INT:	As the shaman	2d6+6
POW:	As the shaman	1d6+12
CHA:	As the shaman	2d6+6

Spectral Combat = 50%+POW+CHA,
Lore (specific Cult or Tradition) = 100%+(INTx2),
Willpower = 50%+(POWx2)

- Intensity: A fetch's intensity is calculated by cross-referencing the POW of the fetch on the Spirit Intensity Table on page 133.
- Spirit Abilities: A fetch also possesses 1d3+Intensity abilities, selected or rolled randomly from the Fetch Abilities table.

Fetch Abilities

1d20	Ability	1d20	Ability
1	Animate	11	Eternal
2	Autonomy	12	Mana
3	Cannibalistic	13	Manifestation
4	Comprehension	14	Perceptive
5	Conjugate	15	Persistent
6	Covert	16	Sagacity
7	Deadly	17	Shapechange
8	Discorporate	18	Spellcasting
9	Domination	19	Subjugate
10	Healing	20	Warding

Gaining a fetch always brings certain side-effects:

- The fetch may influence the personality of the shaman depending on its totemic nature, for example a bear spirit fetch may cause the shaman to become soporific during the winter.
- The fetch may draw upon the Magic Points of the shaman in times of dire need.
- The fetch will abandon the shaman if he betrays the teachings of his shamanic tradition.

Questing for a Fetch

Questing for a fetch is a dangerous ritual, and if it fails it may cripple or kill the shaman. No mechanics are suggested to abstract this process since such an epic undertaking should be played out in the form of a highly challenging scenario.

Quests usually involve the re-enactment of a cult's mythic foundation to locate or awaken the shaman's fetch, and culminate in a dangerous battle against the traditional enemy of his tradition. The quest includes moral ordeals involving both the shaman's community, and his treatment of spirits, the correct solutions being those endorsed, and taught by his cult. Trials of skill, cunning, and magical strength are also common, the opponents the shaman faces being the friendly, and neutral spirits of his own tradition. The quest helps the shaman reinforce his relationships with the spirit world, and he can use these bonds to aid in the climactic confrontation.

Failing in the final battle usually results in dissipation of the shaman's soul. Few tears are shed at such an occurrence as it generally indicates that the candidate was not in sympathy with the ideas of the spirit tradition, or that they were dangerously overconfident of their own abilities. Either way, it is better for the cult that they failed rather than ending up as a flawed shaman.

Guardian Spirits

Warding

Guardian spirits protect the animist from hostile magic or indeed other spirits. They are found in places where vast magics have been unleashed, such as huge ceremonies or battlefields for example.

Within the mundane plane a guardian spirit protects the holder of its fetish by interposing itself before offensive spells. The spirit can neutralize spells with a Magnitude of up to twice its own Intensity. If the spell's Magnitude is greater, the spirit is unable to affect it. If a guardian spirit encounters an anti-spirit spell, such as Spirit Block or Banish, it may attempt to resist the spell before it is affected.

A guardian spirit offers additional protection by intercepting enemy spirits and engaging them in combat before they can attack the animist. They do not initiate Spirit Combat otherwise.

Guardian Spirit

Characteristics
INS: 1d6+6
POW: As per Intensity
CHA: 1d6+6
Spectral Combat = 50%+POW+CHA,
Willpower = 50%+(POWx2)

Haunts

Eternal, Manifestation, plus one or more of Glamour, Miasma, Spellcasting, Telekinesis and Wither

Haunts are the spirits of the dead who did not receive the proper funeral rites or who have died violently, and are incapable of leaving the material world, denying them progress to the afterlife, and leaving the soul to suffer for all eternity.

Mortals may end up becoming haunts in several ways:

- Cursed by a shaman. By enchanting the soul to be permanently bound to the material world, and forbidding it access to the Spirit World the shaman creates an unliving hell for the deceased.
- Unfulfilled Desires. Dying before an important vow was completed or expiring full of hatred and rage, desiring revenge. In these cases a desperate character can tie themselves to the material world by an act of will (roll POW or less on a d100). This enables them to persist as a spirit until they can complete their last wishes.
- Driven by Passion: A soul can become a haunt by dying whilst overwhelmed by a great passion - unrequited love or despair for instance. In these cases the chance of returning as a haunt is simply Games Master fiat, according to how fitting it would be to the campaign.

Haunts are bound to the material world, an unseen presence fully aware of what is occurring around it but unable to leave the immediate area of the location or item to which they are tied. The object they are linked to can be their unburied remains, their place of death, some object associated with them in life, or something else entirely. Ghost stories of many cultures are filled with varied examples of ties that prevent haunts from passing on.

Although frightening, most of these spirits can do little but appear as ghostly apparitions to hapless observers, and bewail their fate. Nonetheless, some acquire certain powers during their transition to a haunt, each ability costing the haunt dearly in Magic Points to invoke.

Like most spirits a Haunt is usually invisible, it may spend 1 Magic Point to manifest itself visually for up to its POW in minutes. Most haunts must manifest in order to use any of their abilities.

A manifested haunt remains intangible to physical objects, able to pass through solid objects at will. On the other hand it becomes vulnerable to magic, although destroying it with magical damage simply disperses its essence but does not prevent its eventual return. By default all haunts possess the Recurring trait.

Permanently dealing with a haunt is not easy. Trance or magical senses may reveal the location of whatever ties it to the world. If this is an object, destroying it may be enough to release the spirit, but depending on its motivation the haunt may fight against such actions. If on the other hand it is a location or more abstractly, an event, undoing the binding may require determining why the spirit became tied in the first place, and trying to resolve the issue. If tied to its mortal remains, conducting the ceremonies appropriate to the haunt's own culture, and traditions may very well break the bonds, releasing the restless spirit to the afterlife it yearns.

Like bound spirits, haunts cannot regenerate Magic Points normally – but they are able to slowly drain vitality from the natural world around them, a process that creates an unsettling area shunned by animals, and where the plants are stunted and withered. A haunt can tap the Magic Points of any animal or plant that has lower POW than the Haunt's Intensity.

When creating a haunt its skills and Characteristics can be generated randomly or directly taken from the dead person in question. Restless spirits which have persisted for centuries often grow stronger over time, permitting some haunts to achieve higher levels of Intensity.

Haunt

Characteristics
INT: As per Mortal of the species
POW: As per Intensity
CHA: As per Mortal of the species
Spectral Combat = 50%+POW+CHA,
Willpower = 50%+(POWx2)
Add other skills as necessary to give the haunt poignancy or purpose, Sing or Lore (Vital Campaign Secret) for example.

Spirit Abilities: A haunt gains a number of abilities equal to its Intensity, selected from the following list:

- *Glamour: The spirit can create illusions which are experienced by all within a range of the spirit's POW in metres. Each glamour costs 1 Magic Point to create, and affects one sense per level of its Intensity. The ability is often used to replay the events that caused the haunt to be created.*
- *Miasma: The spirit can magically induce feelings of dread and horror to anyone within range of its aura. Each wave of miasma costs the spirit 1 Magic Point.*
- *Spellcasting: Becoming a haunt usually severs the spirit from any form of higher magic, but some may retain the ability to cast Folk Magic. The haunt either uses those spells known whilst alive, or gains 1d3+1 spells such as Befuddle, Curse, Disruption, and so on.*
- *Telekinesis: The spirit has a STR equal to its Intensity which it can use to move items around. This costs 1 Magic Point, and lasts for its POW in minutes.*
- *Wither: The spirit is able to physically damage corporeal beings. For the cost of 1 Magic Point, the spirit can make a single attack with a skill equal to whatever Combat Style or Unarmed skill it possessed before death. The blow inflicts damage equal to its usual Spirit Damage that ignores all non-magical parries and physical armour. Magical Armour Points reduce damage as normal.*

With all the other powers at their command, haunts do not initiate Spirit Combat against mortals.

Medicine Spirits

Healing

Medicine spirits are used to heal wounds or cure disease effects imparted by sickness spirits. They are rarely bound to a fetish save by shamans who can rejuvinate them, since as all spirits, they cannot recover Magic Points naturally in the mundane world. Medicine spirits are therefore usually summoned directly from the Spirit World to perform healing tasks.

Peaceable by nature, a medicine spirit may only initiate Spirit Combat against sickness spirits, their innate foes.

Medicine Spirit

Characteristics
INS: 1d6+6
POW: As per Intensity
CHA: 1d6+6
Spectral Combat = 50%+POW+CHA,
Willpower = 50%+(POWx2)

Nature Spirits

One or more of Bless, Demesne, Domination and Endowment

Nature spirits gather at ordinary occurring concentrations of animals and vegetation, and are entities of the world's natural flora and fauna.

Nature spirits are frequently the subject of totemic veneration where an animal, particular plant or even an area of land, becomes representative of a community – the spiritual guardian and strength of a tribe. Animists who devote themselves to a totem in this way are always on friendly terms with spirits related to their totem, but suffer neutral or hostile reactions from other predating or preyed upon animal nature spirits. Likewise those that venerate a particular region of deciduous forest for instance, will find that the plant spirits within are friendly, but the nature spirits of neighbouring coniferous woodlands are at best neutral, if not actively hostile.

Nature spirits embody a myriad of different abilities depending on the region or creature of origin. In general such spirits should not possess more Spirit Abilities than its Intensity. It can of course select the same ability twice, but only when affecting a different attribute, skill, effect (and so on), and are restricted to things that represent a quality expressed by the corporeal form(s) of the species or plant-life. If two or more nature spirits with the same specific ability are used at the same time by the same animist, only the stronger spirit will take effect.

- Bless: The spirit can boost an Attribute or skill relevant to that totem. A leopard spirit might boost Action Points for example.
- Demesne: The spirit controls the plant life of a particular region. The spirit can control the growth, flowering, fruiting, and defoliation of vegetation within range. These effects are necessarily slow, but thanks to the vitality of the spirit, can be forced to occur out of season.
- Domination: The spirit controls behaviour of members of its own species. Thus a a spider spirit could exert command over every arachnid within range of its aura.
- Endowment: Use a trait possessed by the totemic species, such as a special sense or movement. For instance shark spirits could grant the creature ability of Blood Sense or Swimmer, whilst a Lotus flower spirit might grant Venomous.

Nature spirits do not initiate Spirit Combat except against enemy nature spirits.

Other than its POW, which is based upon its Intensity, the other Characteristics of a nature spirit match those of its corporeal cousins. See the Creatures chapter for further details of a variety of creatures.

Nature Spirits

Animal Nature Spirit	Regional Nature Spirit
INS : As the species	1d6
POW: As per Intensity	As per Intensity
CHA: Equal to INS	3d6
Spectral Combat = 50%+POW+CHA, Willpower = 50%+(POWx2)	
Abilities: See Above.	

Predator Spirits

Bless, Persistent, Puppeteer

These are the more aggressive variants of animal or monster spirits, prowling the Spirit World looking for suitable prey. Useful to animists of less ethical traditions, predator spirits are able to track down a particular soul, no matter the distance, and then rip the victim to shreds. Unlike other spirits, Predator spirits are capable of hunting their prey in the physical world making them perfect to attack targets well protected from spiritual interference.

Two conditions need to be filled to summon a predator spirit into the mundane world.

First, predator spirits require some personal effects (hair, nail clippings, clothing, and so on) to track their prey; the effects must be burned or destroyed during the ritual to summon the spirit.

Second the animist offers the spirit a creature of some kind as part of the summoning ritual. The creature's soul must be defeated in spirit combat by the predator; which then dominantly possesses the host's physical body, creating a warped creature (whether physically or psychologically) that unerringly hunts its victim, not ceasing to sleep or eat until the prey is caught. In fact the creature will reject all food save the flesh, and blood of the victim they are hunting.

Predator spirits often rely on their cunning or stealth to launch attacks, since the creature it possesses is not invulnerable to physical damage. As the victim usually has no warning of his fate the first he will know of his pursuit is the first ambush. If the predator spirit fails to make a clean kill on its initial attack, it retreats to reassess the situation; withholding its next attempt to ensure it has a tactical advantage. If the victim takes flight the spirit pursues; and, because it will never stop, this can cause grave distress to the prey.

The hunt continues until the host is killed or starves to death. At this stage the predator spirit can, assuming it has any Magic Points remaining, attempt to possess a new creature. If defeated, or no new host is nearby, it returns to the Spirit World freed of its obligation.

Animists must consider the host creature carefully. Large animals are obviously more dangerous in combat, but find it difficult to enter civilised places without attracting attention. Smaller creatures can pass unseen more easily, but may find it difficult to keep up if the target flees, or to kill them when caught. Nothing prevents a human (or humanoid) from acting as the host and, if this case, they take-on the wild, animalistic characteristics of a predator. This may be enough of a signal to alert a target to a very big problem.

A number of low Intensity predators can be summoned to hunt as a pack – although each spirit summoning must be treated separately.

Predator Spirit

Characteristics
STR: As per Host
CON: As per Host
SIZ: As per Host
DEX: As per Host
INS: 2d6+6
POW: As per Intensity
CHA: 1d6+6
Spectral Combat = 50%+POW+CHA, Stealth = 50%+INS+CHA, Willpower = 50%+(POWx2)
Spirit Abilities: In addition to Persistent, and Puppeteer, the spirit gains a number of Bless bonuses to its Attributes equal to its Intensity. Popular augmentations are to the creature's Armour Points, Damage Modifier, and Movement Rate.

Shape-Shifting Spirits

Shapechange

Shape-shifting spirits allow animists to change their physical form into that of another creature or being – most frequently a creature or beast associated with their totem or tradition. An animist of the Great Bear Clan could, for example, use a shape-shifting spirit to become a grizzly bear or similar ursine.

Shape-shifting spirits must be embodied by the animist, a risky practice because, like elemental spirits, shape-shifters cannot be automatically recalled or dismissed.

The type of animal form a shape-shifter can adopt depends on the spirit's Intensity. The greater the Intensity the bigger the creature. The Characteristics of creatures assumed are always those of an average member of that species.

Spirit Intensity for SIZ of Creature

Intensity	*Creature SIZ*
1	7-12
2	13-21
3	22-33
4	34-48
5	49-66
6	67-87
7	88-111

Summoning a shape-shifting spirit or calling it from a fetish works as normal. Once embodied the animist must spend a Magic Point, and succeed in a Binding roll to force it back into its fetish or return it to the Spirit Plane. This can be potentially dangerous: if the animist has few Magic Points remaining, he may run out of power before he can return to his own shape – trapping him in his animal form.

In his shifted form the animist gains the average physical Characteristics, Armour Points, Hit Points, Creature Abilities, and natural locomotion of the animal, but keeps his own skills. Physical damage sustained in the animal form is carried over between transformations (and vice-versa), although what might have been a Serious Wound when shifted as a small animal may become a mere scratch when human. Whereas a Serious Wound suffered in the form of a very large creature may translate into a Major Wound, and possibly even death when the animist returns to his original shape.

In the latter case, if the severity of a wound increases after the spirit has been dismissed, the animist must make an unopposed Endurance roll at a penalty of one skill grade per injured location, or suffer the detrimental effects of the injury, based on its severity.

Shape-shifting spirits are usually peaceable, and do not initiate Spirit Combat.

Shape Shifting Spirit

Characteristics
INS: As per Host
POW: As per Intensity
CHA: Equal to INS
Spectral Combat = 50%+POW+CHA, Willpower = 50%+(POWx2)

Sickness Spirits

Covert, Disease, Manifestation

Malevolent beings, sickness spirits inflict misery through infecting victims with the disease they carry. They are attracted by the departure of souls to the Spirit World, gathering close to the bodies of the recently dead; but can also be drawn by congregations of other sickness spirits. Widespread plague can result from a small, localised sickness as more, and more sickness spirits are drawn to the area.

Lone sickness spirits lie in wait in the Spirit World waiting for unsuspecting mortals to approach. They then follow them until they sleep or pass into an unconscious state. At this point the sickness spirit manifests, and engages the target in spirit combat. If it gains a level of success the spirit infects the victim, and wanders off to find another host. Only rarely do they covertly possess a victim in order to come into contact with other mortals.

Animists can bind sickness spirits into a fetish– and some evil shamans revel in such bindings – using them to sicken foes in direct combat.

Unlike mundane diseases, those caused by spirits do not recover naturally even with application of the Healing skill. If the spirit has gone further, and maliciously possessed the victim, then not even the curative spells of Higher Magic will work – since unless the spirit is first driven out, the effects will return after the usual onset period has run its course.

High Intensity sickness spirits are not, thankfully, ubiquitous, and animists very rarely have access to them. Knowledge of lethal sickness spirits is usually reserved to cults devoted to spreading disease. Even then, a tradition will know only a handful of specific diseases, each one an explicit spirit counting towards the tradition's limit. Such dreadful cults are rare, and most likely the subject of sustained attempts to eradicate them, for the good of the world.

Sickness Spirit

Characteristics
INS: 2d6
POW: As per Intensity
CHA: 2d6
Spectral Combat = 50%+POW+CHA,
Stealth = 50%+INS+CHA,
Willpower = 50%+(POWx2)

Undeath Spirits

Animate (Dead Flesh)

Undeath spirits are the souls of dead mortals who thirst to return to the mortal world, usually by reinhabiting their own long dead body. They can often be found clustering near ancient necropolises or battlefields, relatively harmless unless summoned by an animist or provoked by some act of desecration.

The only ability these spirits command is the ability to possess dead corpses, not necessarily their own – raising them as undead. The potency of the spirit empowers the dead remains it occupies, granting a bonus of triple its Intensity to the undead creature's STR, and CON. It also gains the Undead creature ability.

An undeath spirit may only animate a corpse of up to their POW in SIZ. Once in control of a body they are loathe to return to the Spirit World. They are incapable of initiating Spirit Combat.

Undeath Spirit

Characteristics
INT: 2d6+6
POW: As per Intensity
CHA: 3d6
Spectral Combat = 50%+POW+CHA,
Athletics STR+DEX+40%,
Brawn STR+SIZ+20%,
Endurance (CONx2)+20%,
Evade (DEX x2)+40%,
Perception INT+POW+30%,
Unarmed STR+DEX+40%,
Willpower (POWx2)+40%,
Combat Style STR+DEX+40%

Wraiths

Eternal, Manifestation, Wither

Wraiths are angry, malevolent spirits that, whilst anchored to a specific location, can shift between the material, and Spirit Worlds at will. Their anger stems from their partial confinement to the mundane world, and partial denial of the Spirit World; products of a vengeful desire to protect their own tombs or as the by-product of necromantic battlefield sorceries, wraiths are wrathful, malicious spirits intent on venting their grievances.

A wraith is similar to a haunt but far more potent. A wraith that manifests is capable of physically harming mortal foes but remains intangible to physical attacks, and is vulnerable only to magic. A wraith has only one hit location. Reducing its Magic Points to zero temporarily drives the creature back to the Spirit World for 24 hours, after which its Magic Points fully regenerate. The only way to permanently destroy a wraith is to pursue it into the Spirit World, and destroy it there. Cunning wraiths sometimes recognise animists, and withdraw from combat early in order to preserve their Magic Points for potential Spirit Combat.

It is typical for a wraith to manifest as it appeared in life, displaying its arms, and armour. They fight using their Spectral Combat skill inflicting their Spirit Damage on a successful attack. The armour a wraith manifests has an Armour Point value equal to its Intensity, but since wraiths are intangible to physical objects, these Armour Points only block magical damage.

Wraith attacks are as intangible as the wraith itself, so unless parrying with a magically enhanced weapon any blow the wraith inflicts passes through the defending weapon, and armour. Magical Armour Points reduce the wraith's Spirit Damage by the magic's intensity. Wraith weapons inflict a chilling, insidious form of damage which makes the wounds they inflict turn black with necrosis. Such wounds never recover naturally, but require magic to heal.

Should a wraith's opponents not possess magically enhanced weapons, the spirit treats any parry as being an automatic failure, allowing the spirit the opportunity to generate Special Effects: being impaled by a wraith dagger is every bit as nasty as being impaled by a real one. Otherwise combat proceeds as normal save that cunning wraiths will sometimes attack through an ostensibly solid object to catch an opponent by surprise.

A wraith never initiates Spirit Combat, and is unable to pursue enemies beyond its tomb or place of death. Thus outmatched foes always have the option of fleeing these deadly spirits.

Wraith Spirits

Characteristic
INT: 2d6+6
POW: As per Intensity
CHA: 2d6+6
Spectral Combat = 50%+POW+CHA,
Willpower 50%+(POWx2)

Mysticism

Mysticism is the implementation of phenomenal abilities by the force of one's willpower, either via contemplative concentration, or by summoning or suppressing strong passions. The effects of mysticism can be great if used wisely, but despite being modest in comparison to other disciplines in terms of flexibility and raw power, it drains the psychic strength of the user quickly. However, the path of mysticism encourages a philosophy of self improvement, as it augments the natural skills and capabilities of the user.

Mystics do not study spells; instead they learn to channel their energies into enhancing their personal capabilities, sometimes far outstripping those of their fellows. Through a combination of meditative technique and applied knowledge, mystics can increase their likelihood of success with skills, invoke seemingly supernatural powers, and develop incredible reactions to direct threats and other hostile situations.

None of this is achieved through overt magic, but by understanding the true nature of his capabilities, focusing on the energies needed, and channelling them in the right way and at the right time to achieve what is needed. By necessity, a mystic's powers are self-centred: they cannot be conferred on others. Mysticism is a very personal journey that only the individual can experience. What he learns on that journey elevates him far above the norm.

Seeking the Truth Within

The two key skills of mystics are Meditation and Mysticism. Meditation is used to train the mind of a mystic, enabling it to achieve a state of relaxation and perfect self-belief. It also enables them to be able to concentrate on several activities at once. Mysticism represents the depth of knowledge concerning a particular mystical path, granting knowledge of the esoteric abilities - disciplines known as talents - available to that philosophy.

Meditation (INT+CON)

Meditation is the ability to reach a state of concentration by removing all extraneous distractions. Once achieved, this higher mind state permits the mystic to tap their inner powers, and perform feats of parallel thought impossible to non-mystics. Increasing competence in Meditation improves the mystic's ability to concentrate on several mystical abilities simultaneously.

A mystic may maintain a cumulative level of Intensity of active talents equal to their Meditation skill divided by 10. Thus, a mystic with Meditation 66% can manifest a maximum Intensity of 7. This intensity could be applied to a single active talent – in which case no other talents could be used – or split between several talents: Augment X to Intensity 2, Invoke Y at Intensity 1, and Enhance Z to Intensity 4 for example. When a talent becomes inactive, its intensity is immediately released, and can be used for something else.

Mysticism (POW+CON)

Mysticism is the knowledge concerning the secret techniques and abilities taught to a particular Path of Mystic enlightenment. It not only controls the maximum Intensity at which any particular talent can be implemented, but may also govern how quickly the mystic masters each of the talents available to that path.

Mysticism is used to achieve the following effects:

- Augment specific skills by shifting their difficulty grade
- Enhance the mystic's attributes (Damage Modifier, Healing Rate, and so on)
- Invoke particular traits or abilities

A mystic is limited to using each individual talent at a maximum Intensity of one twentieth of the Mysticism skill from which it originates. Thus a mystic with 34% in the Path of the Awakening Dragon would be limited to implementing any of its talents at an Intensity of 2 at most. However, using Meditation he may be able to maintain several of these talents at the same time.

Meditations on Power

Of all the magic disciplines available in Mythras, mysticism is perhaps the least magical. To an external observer, much of what a mystic is capable of achieving seems the result of incredible skill or training, rather than some supernatural force. The source of a mystic's power, at least the Magic Points with which he performs his acts of excellence, lends itself primarily to self generation (see Where Do Magic Points Come From, page 115). This may contradict or undermine the principles behind the magical ecology of the setting if the Games Master does not wish a more exotic form of mysticism.

As an alternative, mystics may provide their own Magic Points by performing long hours of meditation, dance, creating art or even choral singing, thus keeping the restoration of their power both in check, and also in keeping with the philosophy of mysticism.

Paths and Talents

Each incidence of the Mysticism skill must be tied to a specific foundation of mystical knowledge, known as a path. These paths are often based on ancient hermetic teachings, passed down in sacred books or by esoteric gurus or secret mountain-top schools.

A path contains knowledge of multiple mental disciplines called talents – namely skill augmentations, trait invocations, and attribute enhancements – which are defined later on in this chapter. There is no preset limit to the number of talents a path can contain, although the mystical school that has developed the path will have imposed its own limitations based on its particular doctrine. Furthermore the talents contained within a path tend to be linked, and these natural relationships will impose their own limitations.

For example, the Path of Abjuration might include: Augment Endurance, Augment Survival, Invoke Denial (Food), Invoke Denial (Water), Invoke Denial (Sleep), Enhance Fatigue and Enhance Hit Points. Conversely the Path of Shadows might offer Augment Perception, Augment Stealth, Augment Ranged Combat Style, Invoke Adhesion, Invoke Astral Projection, Invoke Dark Sight and Enhance Fatigue.

Paths are therefore the mystical equivalent of Combat Styles: diverse talents and abilities folded into the umbrella skill of Mysticism. A path is usually tied to a profession or philosophy, and depending on the setting it might be rare for an adept to learn more than one.

These different combinations of talents can lend a character some quite remarkable capabilities in a very wide variety of unusual situations that differ from theism and animism.

Starting Mystics

If a character begins the game as a mystic he must choose one path to follow that is built from talents either designed by the Games Master, agreed between the player and Games Master, or chosen from the examples given in the Cults and Brotherhoods chapter. Only one path can be chosen at this stage but others can potentially be learned and developed during the course of play.

It should be noted that some talents are potentially very powerful, and should be considered carefully before being made accessible to characters. Games Masters may wish to limit the availability of certain talents according to cult rank, ensuring that characters learn the secrets of their path in a particular order, and withholding the most potent abilities until the cult deems them responsible enough to be trusted with such knowledge.

Mystic characters begin play with knowledge of a number of talents equal to one twentieth of their Mysticism skill. These will generally be the least potent of the talents available to that path, as suited to a low ranking or novice student.

Learning Talents

Learning new talents is not just a case of handing over cash as if a financial transaction. Rather it necessitates an investment of time and Experience Rolls as described in the Magic chapter on page 118. Even if a character has a sufficient number of Experience Rolls available, consent to learn a new talent must be sought first since knowledge of these arts is carefully restricted by the masters of a path.

Gaining permission to learn new talents usually requires the mystic to demonstrate a certain base competence in skill, loyalty to the master who teaches them, and possibly proof of their readiness by undertaking a difficult or dangerous test. There are countless ways for a mystical order to winnow out those unworthy of learning their most powerful secrets. Roleplaying the interaction between the mystic and his teachers builds the depth of their relationship to that path, and can form the basis for adventures.

Mju's Saga

A faithful student of the Path of Shadows, Mju is already in possession of the talents Augment Perception, Augment Stealth and Invoke Dark Sight. Yet he has been forbidden from learning more of the path's secret talents until he rises to the rank of disciple. To prove himself worthy, Mju is tasked to climb Cloud-reach Mountain a week before the sacred festival of Sun Return, and remain upon its summit for seven days in deep contemplation of the inner meaning of his path.

Mju accepts the challenge, and begins the long trek across the desert of the high plateau to its northern peaks. He has many adventures along the way, at one point aiding a pair of sisters who are seeking an ancient temple of Yethis to clear the ruins of their evil. Eventually he reaches the white tipped mountain, carefully scaling its dangerously sheer slopes. The broken off summit is cold, windswept, and ice covered, but Mju takes this as part of the test, settling himself for days of meditation to ignore the hardships.

During the following days he starts to notice certain oddities about the peak. A slightly rank smell in the brief periods the wind stops blowing. Odd scratches, and perhaps carvings on the rocks which form a natural amphitheatre. Even some ragged scraps of what could be brown crusted desert robes frozen into the ice. Something about all these hints at an unforeseen danger, so Mju augments his Perception skill to keep alert during the remaining days of meditation.

On the night of Sun Return his sharpened hearing picks up the sounds of flapping wings. Mju invokes his second talent of Dark Sight, and spots a vast number of winged beasts all heading for the summit. In desperation he utilises his last talent to augment his Stealth skill, squeezing himself into a narrow crevasse on the downwind side of the peak. All that night the assorted griffons, iqari, and giant eagles dance atop the mountain in a great ritual celebration, and at day break, they fly off in different directions.

When Mju finally returns to the travelling caravan of his master and explains in respectful tones the sights he saw, the old guru knows that unlike many before him, his student passed the test. Promoted to a disciple of the Path of Shadows, Mju is now free to learn the next two talents of his path...

Using Mysticism

Mysticism permits some extraordinary powers which can produce dramatic results. Although less inherently flexible than sorcery, and less crushing than theism, in their own niche mystics can be formidable foes. Their talents can boost their skills to phenomenal levels, grant them unusual physical or mental abilities, and increase their attributes to those of legendary heroes.

To gain access to these inner mysteries requires constant and regular practice. Although expensive in terms of magical strength, being dependent only upon themselves, mystics have no need to enslave spirits or return to temples to regain their effectiveness. Indeed the potent nature of their talents can pose a serious challenge to magicians who follow other disciplines of magic.

Implementing a Talent

Summoning the strength to implement a talent requires a mystic to utter a short mantra or exhale breath in a focussed shout, whilst making some sort of mystical gesture – normally a sweeping or striking motion – which aids concentration. In addition the mystic must satisfy the following conditions.

Firstly the mystic may only implement a talent which he has specifically been taught. Knowing a path does not automatically grant understanding (or awareness) of all the talents which belong to it.

Secondly the mystic must have enough Magic Points remaining to attempt the talent. If too few remain either the talent doesn't work or they may suffer some detrimental effect (see Running out of Magic Points page 117).

Last but by no means least; the mystic must pass the requisite Mysticism skill check. Failure to implement the talent normally results in nothing more than the loss of a few Magic Points.

Consequences of Mysticism

Although mysticism can be used in a number of exotic, imaginative ways from creating mysterious desert hermits to ascetic philosopher monks, it is inevitable that players will eventually want to create warrior mystics; attracted by the thought of augmenting their Combat Style skills or number of Action Points to unbeatable levels.

Games Masters should carefully consider the consequences of allowing mystics access to these types of talents. If permitted, then practitioners of these Paths of Mysticism will be near unstoppable by mortal opponents – which is not necessarily a bad thing provided it is embraced by the campaign setting.

This can be done in a number of ways. A devotee of a mystic warrior tradition may be treated with fear or fawning respect so that the character rarely has to fight. Ordinary soldiers may develop specific tactics to take on such formidable mystics, saturating their defences with volleys of ranged weapon fire or sacrificially attacking en masse, fully expecting half their number to fall. Perhaps mystic warriors are so fearsome that it is forbidden by law for them to kill save in times of war or on specific command of their master.

So unless warrior mystics are commonplace in the setting, the Games Master should expect to have foes scythed down; the only challenges being other mystics, maybe those of an opposing path. To get the better of such a character may instead require political intrigue, use of narcotics or poisons, alternate forms of magic, cunning traps or maybe just playing on the mystic's passions.

Mju's Saga

As a disciple of the Path of Shadows Mju has learned the talents Augment Perception, Augment Stealth, Invoke Adhesion, Invoke Dark Sight and Enhance Fatigue. In addition, after spending nearly a year meditating in the deep desert, he has also created his own Path of the Jerboa, via which he mastered the talents of Augment Athletics and Enhance Movement Rate.

This gives him a total of seven talents. However Mju only possesses a POW of 12 which means he may only maintain the concurrent practice of six talents at any time. After much thought he decides to drop Enhance Movement Rate from his daily mental exercises and keep the others. If needed he can resume the practice of enhancing his Movement Rate, restoring the ability after a week of meditation; but at the cost of dropping another talent from his repertoire.

Costs of Implementing Talents

Talents cost a variable amount of Magic Points to activate depending on their type – see Magnitude and Intensity below– and the success level of the implementation roll.

Once the base cost is known, the Mysticism roll is made:

- Critical Success: the talent works, and only half the Magic Point cost is expended.
- Success: the talent works, and the full Magic Point cost is expended.
- Failure: the talent fails, and a single Magic Point is expended.
- Fumble: the talent fails, and the full Magic Point cost is expended.

Implementation Time

All mystical talents require one turn of preparation per point of their Intensity, and no other action may be performed whilst the talent is prepared. On the last turn of preparation the mystic makes a Mysticism roll and, if successful, the talent is initiated immediately.

Magnitude and Intensity

Magnitude is the Magic Point cost required to call upon a talent. Intensity is the level of effect achieved. These are as follows:

- Augment Skill: 1 Magic Point per level of Intensity. A level of Intensity improves the success chance of the skill by one grade. For example, increasing a skill from Standard to Easy costs 1 Magic Point; increasing it to Very Easy costs 2, and so on.
- Invoke Trait: 2 Magic Points. All traits have a default Intensity of 1.
- Enhance Attribute: 3 Magic Points per step of increase. Each step is a level of Intensity (for example, enhancing Damage Modifier by one step, from 1d2 to 1d4 costs 3 Magic Points; enhancing from 1d2 to 1d6 costs 6 Magic Points, and so forth).

The upshot for mystics is that use of Mysticism can be Magic Point intensive when compared with other types of magic. However, when used creatively, Mysticism can be incredibly potent. A character's natural abilities can be enhanced to a level that is not necessarily available to other magical disciplines.

Duration of Talents

Unless specifically stated in its description, a talent only remains in place for the period of time required to action it. Once the immediate task for which the talent was called upon has been concluded, its effect lapses.

For example, enhancing Movement Rate to run a race should last only for that race, augmenting a Combat Style would be for the length of that melee, whereas inducing Featherlight would remain until the mystic finishes walking over a river.

As a rule of thumb, once a mystic focuses his attention on another, different task, the currently maintained talents drop. However, until a talent is dropped the Magic Points used to implement it cannot start to recover.

Common sense should be applied as to when the talent naturally ends. It is unreasonable to suggest that an augmented Combat Style continues once the mystic's foes have been defeated, or that an invoked perception lasts beyond the investigation of a person or area if the mystic becomes distracted by other events.

Dispelling Talents

Since mysticism is based upon inner focus and strength of will, it is not normally susceptible to magical dismissal via spells such as Avert, Dismiss, Neutralise, and the like. The best way of dealing with mystics is to induce some form of mental or psychological disturbance which may cause their concentration to break; or render them unconscious, whereupon any active talents immediately drop.

When subjected to such a disturbance the mystic is permitted to resist using their Willpower in an opposed roll against the skill actively used against them, in order to maintain concentration. For instance, if injured by a thrown object, the mystic would oppose the Athletics roll of the thrower. Some discretion is required to ensure that the distraction is valid to the situation. A separate Willpower roll is needed for each active talent.

Conversely mystics have no ubiquitous way of defending themselves against direct magical assault, save by augmenting skills such as Endurance, Evade or Willpower.

Limitations to Talents

The maximum level of Intensity at which an individual talent can be implemented is equal to one twentieth of the relevant Mysticism skill.

The maximum combined levels of Intensity of all active talents cannot exceed the Mystic's Meditation skill divided by 10.

No matter how many paths and talents a mystic knows, he may only actively practice a limited number of them. A mystic can concurrently maintain the training of a number of talents up to half the value of his POW. If the mystic wants to change one of the talents regularly practiced, he may discard it from his training regime, and spend a week recalling the talent he wishes to replace it with. A Meditation roll is required to see if the mystic succeeds. If the roll fails, he not only loses access to the dropped talent but must spend another week in meditative practice to re-master the new one.

Talent Descriptions

Talents come in three varieties based upon the boost or ability they grant. These are either skill augmentations, invoking traits or enhancing attributes, as described in the following sections. Each has its own Magic Point costs and scaling limitations.

Augmenting Skills

The mystic augments his skills by concentrating on the nature of the task at hand, and channelling his own positive energies into attaining a desired result. A mystic literally envisages his own success, and then prepares himself to attain it.

Each level of Intensity improves the mystic's chance of success by one difficulty grade (see Modifying Skills page 38). This can be used to counteract situational penalties the mystic is already suffering, or augment them to superhuman levels of skill.

A mystic cannot boost his skill chance beyond the grade of Very Easy. Any levels of Intensity beyond this are ostensibly wasted, but will come into play if the mystic is subsequently penalised by detrimental circumstances.

Invoking Traits

Traits are specialised physical, mental and emotional endeavours akin to the those found for many creatures. All traits by default have an Intensity of 1, making them very useful abilities with which to compliment the mystic's other path talents. A trait confers a specific power for the duration it is implemented.

The available traits are as follows:

Adhesion

The mystic can move freely on vertical surfaces, and even move upside down on a ceiling with no special equipment. Such Movement is always at half the mystic's normal Movement Rate.

Arrowcut

The mystic is able to parry and deflect projectiles (arrows, darts, spears, and so forth) using his bare hands; or weapons not normally permitted to perform such feats, such as swords or whips.

Astral Projection

The mystic can project a visible, albeit ethereal image of himself to a distance in kilometres equal to his Meditation skill. The Astral Protection acts a conduit for the mystic to communicate with and observe a distant location, but he cannot physically interact with it.

Aura (X)

The mystic projects a particular kind of aura (Fear, Intimidation, Serenity, Mastery, and so on) that can be used to present a particular aspect to those who behold him. Overcoming the mystic's aura requires an opposed roll of Willpower versus the mystic's Mysticism roll for invoking the trait. The aura affects all things within a radius of the mystic's POW in metres.

Awareness

The mystic is aware of a particular kind of emanation (threat, love, danger, magic, and so on) within a radius equal to his POW in metres. He cannot gauge specifics; only that the emanation exists and is close by.

Mju's Saga

Mju is travelling the dark streets of Meeros one night hoping to meet an old friend, when he spots a suspicious figure flitting along an alleyway, curved knife in hand. He covertly follows the suspected assassin into the sacred grove, located next to the senate house. Unfortunately for the mystic it is autumn, and the ground is littered with dry leaves which crunch underfoot. The Games Master rules that crossing the leaves unheard is a Formidable task. So Mju takes a few moments to focus on his Augment Stealth talent, implementing it at an Intensity of 3 to ensure success. This costs him three Magic Points and modifies the difficulty grade from Formidable to Easy.

Mju follows the suspicious man into the senate house. Inside the peristyle building it is almost pitch black, little light from the starry night sky penetrating through the roof opening. Momentarily stumped Mju eventually discerns a faint illumination on the far side of the audience chamber, where the knife wielder, holding a softly glowing orb, is conversing with a shadowy cloaked figure.

Despite his augmented Stealth skill, Mju somehow gives away his presence as he creeps closer to the clandestine meeting. In a heartbeat the globe is extinguished. Mju hears the refined accent of a Meerish noble whisper 'kill him' before the sound of departing sandals leave the marbled hall. Hearing no other footsteps Mju realises his life is in extreme danger.

He decides he needs to invoke his Dark Sight talent, taking a voluntary penalty to his Mysticism skill (see Casting Requirements page 119) for not whispering the mantra aloud. Despite this Mju succeeds, and for the cost of 2 Magic Points, reveals the darkened chamber to his mystical senses. The hunting knife wielder has no such advantage, and Mju breaks his neck from behind. A quick investigation reveals the ritual scarring of the Brotherhood of Dust, branded upon the assassin's tongue; the favoured tools of the Badoshi Warlords...

Dark Sight

Allows the mystic to 'see' normally in any level of limited light, even its complete absence.

Denial (X)

The mystic can deny the effects of one specific environmental condition. Denial (Rain), for example, would keep the mystic dry in even the most intense monsoon; Denial (Air) allows the mystic to forgo breathing for an extended period; Denial (Falling) would allow the mystic to briefly levitate above the ground; Denial (Sunlight) would prevent the burning, dehydrating effects of the most intense sun.

Earth Sense

The mystic has a perfect sense of direction, depth and orientation beneath ground, and suffers no penalties to Perception rolls for underground environments.

Echolocation

The mystic senses his environment through reflections of sonic waves. This means that he can perceive others that may be either motionless or hidden. In such circumstances, using a Stealth roll to attempt to remain unperceived by the mystic is one grade more difficult.

Featherlight

The mystic's physical weight becomes negligible, allowing him to balance on impossibly thin or slender surfaces, including those that should not be able to support the his mass (twigs, saplings, and so on).

Formidable Natural Weapons

The hands and feet of the mystic are treated as size Large for the purposes of attacking and parrying in combat.

Heart Slow

The mystic is able to finely control his heart and metabolic rates, reducing them almost to a standstill. Using this trait a mystic must remain completely inactive for its duration but, to all intents and purposes, has no pulse, no heart rhythm, and organic functions have ceased. He becomes immune to other Life Sense attempts and appears to be dead. Once the trait finishes the mystic's faculties are fully restored.

Immunity (X)

The mystic is completely immune to one specific type of damage caused by a particular source. This source can be magical, physical, or energy based, but should be quite narrow in scope. Examples include, but are not limited to: cold, fire, electricity, iron, poison, disease, cutting, crushing, falling, impaling, and so on.

Indomitable

The Mystic is utterly immune to attempts at mind control or domination, including spells and spirit possession.

Life Sense

In tune with the rhythms of nature, the mystic can determine the vitality of any living thing by touch alone. If the mystic touches another he learns of the target's current injuries, Fatigue level, and whether it is currently afflicted by any poison or disease. The mystic is also aware of any form of life within a number of metres equal to his Willpower skill, which may make Stealth difficult to accomplish.

Magic Sense

Similar to Life Sense but instead permits the mystic to detect magical emanations over distance. If the mystic touches another he learns of the target's current magic points, carried enchantments, and active spells.

Night Sight

Allows the mystic to treat partial darkness as illuminated, and darkness as partial darkness.

Pain Control

The mystic is inured to pain and able to work through its effects. Endurance rolls when experiencing any kind of injury are considered to be automatic successes.

Spirit Sense

Similar to Life and Magic Sense, but the mystic's senses are attenuated specifically to the activity of spirits and the spirit plane. The mystic can sense what spirits are active within a radius equal to his Willpower in metres and, if he succeeds in an Insight roll, can gauge the general intensity of the spirit entities. Spirit Sense confers no other powers or protection when dealing with spirits.

Squeeze
The mystic is able to manipulate his body, allowing him to squeeze into recesses and through gaps that would otherwise be impossible. The smallest opening, hollow or volume the mystic may utilise is one third of his SIZ.

Enhancing Attributes
Mystics can enhance an Attribute, temporarily increasing its effectiveness. The following attributes can be enhanced in the ways described below. Luck Points and Experience Modifier cannot be enhanced.

Action Points
Each level of intensity increases available Action Points by 1. The additional Action Points can only be used for defensive actions in combat. Thus, a mystic who spends 6 Magic Points to enhance his Action Points from 3 to 5 may only use these additional Action Points to Parry or Evade. He cannot use the additional points to make additional attacks or cast additional magic.

Damage Modifier
Each point of Intensity increases the Damage Modifier by one step. Thus, at Intensity 3 (for a cost of 9 Magic Points, if available) a mystic's Damage Modifier of +1d2 would increase to +1d8.

Fatigue
Each point of Intensity negates a level of Fatigue. This attribute can be enhanced pre-emptively in anticipation of becoming fatigued. Thus a 'fresh' mystic who spends 6 Magic Points could grant himself two buffer levels of Fatigue which could be lost before he started feeling the effects of his strenuous activity.

Mju's Saga
Sent to spy on the nefarious Badoshi Warlords to assess their plans for war against Meeros, Mju is attempting to sneak into their compound – a lofty valley fortress high in the Grey Peaks. Moving cautiously, he is traversing a long, high corridor which leads to the pleasure gardens of the inner courtyard, and needs to bypass the six alert guards waiting at the end of the passageway. Knowing that if he is seen he will be attacked, Mju considers his options.

First he invokes Adhesion which gives him the ability to traverse sheer surfaces and ceilings. Mju immediately scuttles up the closest wall, and crouches, spider-like, on the ceiling, where none of the guards will think to look. Next he decides to boost his Stealth by Intensity 2. This increases his circumstantial modifier from Standard to Very Good, doubling his base Stealth skill to 160%.

He carefully manoeuvres along the ceiling and the Games Master calls for a Stealth roll to gauge Mju's progress. Luck is against him, and he rolls a 96 which is an automatic failure. Even with their Perception skills suffering a 60% penalty (from Mju's augmented Stealth skill exceeding 100%), one of the guards notices some falling grit dislodged from the ceiling, looks up, and spots the skulking mystic.

Mju immediately leaps down behind the sentries, diving into the luxuriant growth of the flowering gardens. Then in the few moments it takes for the stunned guards to react, he slips into a water lily covered pool. Knowing that the grounds will be thoroughly searched, Mju drops his Adhesion talent, freeing up as much of his meditative capacity as possible to enhance his Fatigue by four levels, whilst still maintaining his augmented stealth.

Three of the Badoshi arrive to check the pool, remaining there for over two minutes to ensure nobody is hiding beneath the surface. Although Mju took a deep breath before immersing himself, he eventually runs out of air, and soon burns through the extra Fatigue levels, almost drowning before the guards leave to search the rest of the garden. Now out of Magic Points, and in serious jeopardy of capture or death, Mju stealthily flees the fortress, cursing its bad stonemasonry...

At the conclusion of the task any negated levels of fatigue return, potentially causing the mystic to collapse into unconsciousness.

Healing Rate
Enhanced Healing Rate works slightly differently to the standard Attribute Enhancement rules. The amount of Hit Points healed is not increased, but the speed at which Healing Rate works is. Each level of intensity improves the speed of recovery by one step as follows

- Combat Rounds
- Minutes
- Hours
- Days
- Weeks
- Months

Usually Minor Wounds heal at a rate of 1 Day, Serious Wounds at a rate of 1 Week, and Major Wounds at a rate of 1 Month. Each level of Intensity changes the speed of healing. Thus, at Intensity 2, hit points are recovered at the following speeds: Minor Wounds 1 Minute, Serious Wounds 1 hour, and Major Wounds 1 day. Enhanced Healing Rate rapidly speeds-up recovery but it will not reattach severed limbs or restore the use of maimed ones.

A mystic may remain in a healing trance for as long as it takes to fully recover. However he may perform no other tasks during this time.

Hit Points

Each level of Intensity boosts Hit Points in every location by 1. So an Intensity 4 Hit Point enhancement would raise all Hit Locations by 4 points. These additional Hit Points absorb damage first, before the natural Hit Points are affected.

However these temporary Hit Points do not change the Serious and Major Wound boundaries, which remain tied to the mystic's natural Hit Points. Enhancing Hit Points after a Serious or Major Wound is suffered does not permit damaged locations to return to functionality.

Movement Rate

Each level of Intensity increases Movement by 2 metres.

Initiative

Each level of Intensity adds 2 to the Initiative roll.

Above: The fabled Floating Citadels of the Azure Mystics. These sages specialise in the Adjuration of the Physical Earth, focusing on the Denial of Gravity. Through their advanced state of enlightenment the Azure Mystics have been able to raise their monastery citadels into the skies. They drift amongst the clouds covering many leagues a day in unguided flight, going wherever the air currents dictate.

Sorcery

Sorcery is the technique of invoking magical effects through the understanding and application of transcendent knowledge. Once a sorcerer comprehends the objective rules of reality, they can employ them in a repeatable and methodical manner. Of course this does not mean a sorcerer can figure out these fundamental laws for themselves, only that once a technique or formula is learned, they can manipulate it in a variety of ingenious ways.

The path of sorcery is often a hard one, requiring much time spent in study and research. Even its reputation can be viewed with an element of suspicion when compared to the worship of communal gods or the veneration of tribal spirits; as those not privy to its secrets tend to regard it with jealousy or perhaps fear, especially when the sorcerer is an aloof recluse without need for or responsibility towards his community.

Not all practitioners are loners. Some take apprentices to pass on the art to those of the next generation, whilst others form schools or guilds in which they share their knowledge in return for mutual protection or a degree of respectability. More sophisticated societies often evolve specialised orders, utilising their unions to practice particular types of sorcery as a profession, from itinerant weather-workers to mercenary spell-swords. At its pinnacle, sorcery can even be used to shield nations from more 'primitive' forms of magic, or provide an increase to the standard of living by the maintenance of innovative enchantments.

Whilst the ability to cast sorcery, depending on the campaign setting, may be limited to those born to it or trained in the art from childhood, each sorcery spell is merely an invocation which can be mastered by those sorcerers willing to spend the time to grasp its philosophical meanings, or at least to memorise the methodology. As such, most orders of sorcery keep the secrets of their most potent magics well hidden, even to their own students, for fear of the spell's power being abused, or corrupting its wielder.

Although sorcery is often viewed as a dark or evil in Sword & Sorcery literature, it need not necessarily be so. Sorcery can be used beneficently or play a key role in societies lacking other forms of magic, depending on the manner in which the Games Master wishes to present it.

Manipulating the Cosmos

The practice of sorcery requires two core skills, Invocation and Shaping. Invocation reflects the depth of knowledge concerning a particular philosophy or school of sorcery; whilst Shaping is the skill of the sorcerer to manipulate the parameters of a spell, so that can be cast in a flexible and innovative manner.

Invocation (INT x2)

Invocation represents a sorcerer's ability to successfully cast spells learned from a particular source, be that a grimoire, mentor, school, extra-planar demon or even an ancient artefact. The precise scope of what the skill covers depends upon the campaign setting, but each incidence of Invocation must be assigned to a specific type or well-spring of sorcery.

The skill encompasses a plethora of magical principles from comprehending the philosophy underlying how that type of sorcery works; to being able to achieve the necessary mental state to manipulate reality. As the value of this skill increases, so does the capability of the sorcerer to create greater changes.

The Intensity of a sorcery spell is equal to one tenth of the Invocation skill used to cast it.

Shaping (INT+POW)

In their default form, sorcery spells are relatively feeble in scope. Shaping is the method used to change the parameters of a sorcery spell so that it can be wrought to meet certain requirements, such as increasing its range or duration.

Once the base concepts of Shaping are known, they can be applied to any spell known by the sorcerer, no matter its school or tradition. Thus sorcerers normally need only learn a single Shaping skill (see Restricting Components of Sorcery Spells page 165).

Shaping is never rolled against when casting sorcery, rather it acts like a governor to limit the degree of modification which can be applied to a spell. The maximum level of alteration is equal to one tenth of the value of the Shaping skill. Thus a sorcerer with Shaping 47% would be able to apply 5 points to shape the parameters of any sorcery spell he cast.

These points may be divided up amongst any of the following components to optimise the spell as desired:

- Combine: Used to fuse together several spells into a single casting
- Duration: Used to extend the period of time the spell's effects last
- Magnitude: Used to penetrate magical defences or resist magical attacks
- Range: Used to increase the distance a spell can be cast over
- Targets: Used to increase the number of targets affected by the spell

Combine

This component permits the sorcerer to combine the effects of several sorcery spells into a single casting, so that they all affect the target simultaneously. This not only saves time on casting, but also preserves Magic Points, as all the conjoined spells share the same shaping components (see Invocation Costs page 165). Use the following guidelines when combining spells:

- A spell may not be combined with another instance of itself; only different spells may be combined
- If the conjoined spells come from different sources, then the lowest Invocation skill is used as the base casting chance
- The conjoined spells must all share the same target or targets
- Any shaping applied to a combined casting is assigned to each, and every one of the spells involved at no extra Magic Point cost
- Each additional spell added using combine, costs one extra Magic Point and increases the difficulty grade of the Invocation roll by one step (see Focus page 165)

Although combined spells might require several different resistance checks, the target only makes a single resistance roll – the result matched against each requisite opposed skill. Thus it is perfectly possible, for example, to save against all the combined spells requiring Resist Endurance whilst simultaneously failing to throw off the Resist Willpower spells.

Duration

Sorcery spells have a default duration equal to the POW of the caster in minutes.

Applying one or more points of Shaping to the Duration component will extend the length of a sorcery spell as noted in the table. The spell remains running for the entire duration, although in some cases part of its effect may require active concentration to function (see Concentration page 166).

Some spells may end up with an extended duration which can last hours, or even longer. In these cases the Magic Point Attribute of the sorcerer is temporarily reduced by the number of Magic Points used to cast that spell until the magic is dropped or expires.

Further Extending Duration

Some Games Masters may find the duration of sorcery to be too limited for how magic works in their campaign setting. The following alternative progression is offered to those that like to greatly extend the active effects of spells. Bear in mind however that until a sorcery spell has finally completed, the Magic Points used to cast it do not recover.

Points of Shaping	*Duration*
None	Caster's POW in Turns
1	Caster's POW in Rounds
2	Caster's POW in Minutes
3	Caster's POW x 5 Minutes
4	Caster's POW x 15 Minutes
5	Caster's POW x Hours
6	Caster's POW x 6 Hours
7	Caster's POW x Days
8	Caster's POW x Weeks
9	Caster's POW x Months
10	Caster's POW x Years
Each point...	Continue progression: Decades, Centuries, Millennia, and so on...

Shaping Table

Points of Shaping	*Combine*	*Duration (Mins)*	*Magnitude*	*Range*	*Targets*
None	None	POW	1	Touch	1
1	2 Spells	2xPOW	2	1m x POW	2
2	3 Spells	3xPOW	3	5m x POW	3
3	4 Spells	4xPOW	4	10m x POW	4
4	5 Spells	5xPOW	5	50m x POW	5
5	6 Spells	6xPOW	6	100m x POW	6
6	7 Spells	7xPOW	7	500m x POW	7
7	8 Spells	8xPOW	8	1km x POW	8
8	9 Spells	9xPOW	9	5km x POW	9
9	10 Spells	10xPOW	10	10km x POW	10
10	11 Spells	11 x POW	11	15km xPOW	11
Each point...	+1 Spell	+1 x POW	+1 Magnitude	+5km x POW	+1

Magnitude

Sorcery spells have a default Magnitude of 1, making them weak and vulnerable.

Applying one or more points of Shaping to the Magnitude component will improve its ability to overwhelm magical defences or resist magical attacks. It has no effect on the Intensity of a sorcery spell which is solely based upon the caster's Invocation skill.

Range

Sorcery spells have a default Range of Touch, requiring that the recipient be within physical reach of the caster.

Applying one or more points of Shaping to the Range component will allow the spell to be cast over greater distances, potentially achieving ranges beyond the immediate perception of the caster. In such cases the sorcerer will need alternate methods of observing the target.

Sorcery spells limited to Touch range may only be cast on others if physical contact can be maintained for the entirety of the Invocation.

Once someone or something is affected by a sorcery spell, it continues even if they travel beyond the spell's Range. Spells which require Concentration (see page 166) lapse into passive mode once the target exceeds this distance, but only for the period it remains beyond the Range limit.

Targets

Sorcery spells have a default Target of one object, creature or person, which may be the caster himself.

Applying one or more points of Shaping to the Targets component will allow the spell to affect an increasing number of multiple targets, each one receiving the full consequence of the magic. That is to say, each target receives an identical copy of the original spell.

Unless specifically permitted by its description, the targets of a spell may not be changed once it is cast.

Sources of Knowledge

The fundamentals of sorcery are as varied as the sources from which its knowledge can be learned. All depends entirely on who, or what, has preserved such arcane knowledge. Although sorcery is often tied to the archetype of reading cryptic old spellbooks, it need not have any relationship with that particular stereotype.

Sorcery might instead be recorded in the form of towering prehistoric pictograms carved into the sides of mountains or be accessible only to those that drink the waters of a legendary well. Perhaps only those that journey beyond the boundaries of reality can master its esoteric secrets.

Of course the theory and practice of sorcery can be passed on by living beings too, without need for books or artefacts. Lone masters might hand down their sagacity as ancient aural traditions to their students. Maybe such wisdom is held only by demons or spirits of the otherworld, which must be summoned and appeased before they teach those who dare to call them up. Sorcery could even be learned by listening to the hidden meanings of mournful hyena howls around campfires at night.

Infinite are the sources of sorcerous knowledge. The only limit is your imagination.

Schools and Spells

A sorcerer's power and spells are restricted to the particular philosophy or tradition of sorcery he studies. Named schools of sorcery, the term represents a collated body of knowledge rather than a formal organisation.

Access to a specific school of sorcery can be held by particular groups, individuals, objects or even locations. Thus a sorcery tradition need not necessarily be taught by a formal cult, rather it can potentially be self-learned if the sorcerer can comprehend the source for himself.

For instance a sorcery cult could be nothing more than a group of loosely affiliated wizards who are all aware, and make use of a particular source; an infamous tome such as the Scroll of Khronus or the psychic powers gained by inhaling the deadly narcotic smoke of the ebony lotus; some discovering the secrets by themselves, others guided by a mentor already privy to the knowledge.

In a similar vein, there are no preset limitations as to how many spells are available to a particular school of sorcery. Yet the spells accessible to that philosophical path will generally be related in terms of metaphysical mechanics as to how they work, or will possess similar supernatural effects.

For example the Stygian Path is a school of sorcery which specialises in manipulating darkness, granting access to the spells: Animate Darkness, Dominate (Reptiles), Palsy, Sculpt Darkness, Smother, Teleport (via Shadows), and Wrack (Darkness). Whereas the Masters of Metamorphosis may learn a school of sorcery that controls the changing of things using the spells: Abjure, Diminish, Enhance, Haste, Regenerate, Shapechange and Transmogrify.

With this in mind, schools of sorcery should be crafted to fulfil a particular concept. They need not be balanced with one another; corrupt diabolic cults might indeed offer more spells than their benevolent counterparts. A grimoire might only grant a single, albeit potent, spell; whereas a respected guild of sorcery could provide a dozen. The precise balance or lack thereof is for the Games Master to decide when designing his campaign.

Further consideration should be made towards whether a sorcerer can join several guilds or discover additional sources of arcane knowledge. Mythras is not predisposed towards the limitless accumulation of innumerable spells, but rather the clever and innovative use of a few. However, this should not preclude such occurrences if that is what is desired.

Starting Sorcerers

A character starting the game as a sorcerer should choose a single school of sorcery to study; one designed by the Games Master, agreed to between the player and Games Master, or chosen from the examples given in these rules or the relevant setting. Only one school of sorcery can be chosen at this stage but others can potentially be discovered during the course of play.

In addition, the source of this sorcery should be decided also; whether it is an object, a mentor or a cult. There is no penalty to being self-taught, a common conceit of the Sword & Sorcery genre.

Sorcerer characters begin with a number of spells from that school equal to one twentieth of their Invocation skill. Once the campaign starts they are restricted in what additional spells they can study, and when they can learn them.

Kratos' Saga

Kratos started out as a modest scribe in the famed city of Meeros. Unfortunately, his increasing interest in the arcane arts soon brought him into conflict with the cult priests of Myceras, who exiled him on suspicion of stealing forbidden texts. The scholar swore vengeance towards the city of his birth and journeyed far into unknown lands in search of true power.

Ultimately Kratos found an old hag who taught him the fundamentals of sorcery in exchange for certain... favours. After a year of subservience, suffering her horrible embraces, Kratos learnt the skills of Invocation (Stygian Path) 32% and Shaping 33%. Then, in a dastardly act of betrayal, he strangled his mentor, stealing the strange crystal which seemed to be the source of her sorcerous knowledge.

Alone in the wilderness, the sorcerer is discovered by a troop of man-eating centaurs. Faced with becoming their next meal, Kratos attempts to invoke a spell to frighten the monsters away. Lacking the skill to affect the centaurs directly, he tries to Animate the shadows dancing about his camp fire.

With his Shaping skill he has four points he can use to manipulate the magic. He uses 1 point to extend the Range of the spell to 16 metres, so that it can reach the centaurs. The remaining 3 points he places into the Targets component, so that he can simultaneously control four separate shadows. His invocation is successful so he sends the amorphous figures of flickering darkness towards the slavering man-horse chimeras. To his great surprise, the centaurs yell in superstitious terror, and prostrate themselves at his feet begging for mercy...

Learning Spells

Learning new spells requires an investment of Experience Rolls as described in the Magic chapter on page 118. Whether or not new spells are available is a different matter. For example, an adept member of a powerful guild may be withheld from freely acquiring the more dangerous spells of the order; only being taught once they demonstrate the correct level of understanding or responsibility. A mage who learns his art from a demon might instead need to provide the entity with a suitable offering (a diabolical deed or rare sacrifice) before he is shown a new spell.

Likewise a self-taught sorcerer who picks up a grimoire cannot learn every spell inscribed within its pages as soon as they have the Experience Rolls to invest. There are limits to how much, and how quickly a sorcerer can understand and absorb knowledge from the complex metaphysical implications of such a work.

As a rough guideline, spells accessible to a school of sorcery are usually linked or entwined in such a way that they must be learned:

- In a particular order; acquisition of lesser incantations being needed to comprehend the underlying techniques to invoke higher ones.
- When a specific degree of mastery is reached, each spell limited to a particular cult rank or value of the Invocation skill may be learned as the sorcerer has demonstrated the necessary level of comprehension.
- Only after the student has shown the correct attitude, behaviour or dedication to be permitted deeper knowledge.

Thus the learning of new spells is not an automatic ability or right. Access to them must be earned through roleplaying and over a period of time in the campaign. A new spell should be regarded as a reward for completing a particularly difficult task, as a consequence of advancing cult rank or even as the result of many months research and study. When knowledge is quite literally power, a sorcerer should not be able simply to purchase spells by handing over a cartload of silver. Although a gift might influence the mind of a sorcerer's mentor, the spell itself is almost always priceless.

Using Sorcery

Although sorcery is not necessarily the most potent type of supernatural power available to mortals, the ability of a sorcerer to shape his magic makes it extremely versatile. Sorcerers can weave a handful of awesome spells into a single, magic-efficient casting; blast small units of warriors with the same spell; or even control the mind of a victim from hundreds of kilometres away. This ability, which greatly augments one or more spell components, enables their magic to far exceed the more rigid parameters of other types.

The inherent flexibility of sorcery extends beyond its ability to be shaped. Unlike animism there is no dependency upon third party spirits which might slip from control. Similarly they need not return to specific holy places to recover their magical strength unlike theists. In effect, sorcery grants its practitioner freedom from needing things or places. All that is required is knowledge of the spell, and enough Magic Points to invoke it.

Invoking a Spell

Casting a sorcery spell requires that the sorcerer performs a short invocation, allowing him to mentally impose the spell's transcendental formula upon the cosmos, changing reality. It may be an envisioning of a complex glyph or articulate utterance of a harmonic mantra. Whatever the procedure, for the spell to work the sorcerer must meet the following prerequisites.

Firstly they must actually know the spell being cast. Simply reading or repeating a spell parrot fashion from something like a scroll will not work if the sorcerer has no understanding of its underlying metaphysics.

Secondly they must have the requisite number of Magic Points remaining. Attempting to cast a spell with insufficient Magic Points

Kratos' Saga

Now in command of a troop of loyal centaurs, Kratos sends them forth to gather tribute and sacrificial victims whilst he spends his time studying the strange artefact he stole. He knows the fist-sized black diamond was the source of the hag's sorcery, from the cold tingling the crystal elicits when he touches it. Some dim memory suggests that this may be the Tear of Yethis, an infamous relic said to be the only remaining fragment of a mighty Serpent Demon who once ruled the world.

After much experimentation Kratos discovers that pouring fresh human blood over the stone causes its holder to experience vivid dreams in which the demon lord appears, passing on forbidden arcane knowledge to he who would learn to master such power. As his skill and arrogance increase, Kratos begins to demand new spells from his diabolical mentor. The demon slyly agrees, providing the sorcerer is willing to pay the hellish price.

In exchange for the ritual slaughter of nine pure virgins from the highest ranked families of Meeros, the demon promises to teach the increasingly corrupt Kratos the magical ability to shift between pools of shadow. The sorcerer readily agrees, little comprehending that the next spell will cost him far, far more.

means that either the spell doesn't work, or something bad occurs to the sorcerer to find the last fragments of power (see Running out of Magic Points page 117).

Thirdly on the last turn of casting, the sorcerer must pass an Invocation skill check. Failing to cast the spell correctly usually results in nothing bad save that the magic doesn't work, or at worst the squandering of a few Magic Points.

Invocation Costs

The cost of casting a sorcery spell depends on how much it is shaped, and the success level of the Invocation skill roll.

Base cost is 1 Magic Point plus an additional one point per spell component modified. For instance a spell which has its Range and Duration components increased will have a base cost of 3 Magic Points. If several spells are woven together using Combine, then an additional Magic Point is added to the cost for each extra spell.

Once the base cost is known, the Invocation roll is made:

- Critical Success: the spell works but only half the Magic Point cost is expended.
- Success: the spell works, and the full Magic Point cost is expended.
- Failure: the spell fails, but no Magic Points are expended.
- Fumble: the spell fails, and the full Magic Point cost is expended.

Invocation Time

The time taken to cast a sorcery spell is equivalent to 1 Turn plus an additional Turn for each spell component modified. This is usually the same as its Magic Point cost except in cases where Combine (or the optional Swiftness component) is utilised.

The Invocation skill check is made on the final turn of casting; the result of the roll occurring immediately.

Magnitude and Intensity

Sorcery spells have a default Intensity equal to one tenth of the caster's Invocation skill. Their Magnitude depends on how many shaping points were devoted to that spell component.

Sorcerers need not apply the entirety of their available Intensity if they desire to limit the spell's effect.

Restricting Components of Sorcery Spells

Not all schools of sorcery need have access to the same component parameters, not even the default ones. A campaign could be created where certain paths of sorcery lack knowledge of a particular shaping technique, perhaps being compensated for by the addition of a different, more exotic component. If used in this way, sorcerers should require a separate and specific Shaping skill for each type of Invocation they know.

The Zemgarian School of Unseen Sorcery for example could teach Shaping but using only the components of Magnitude, Range, Targets and Focus. Whereas the Inebriated Sorcerers of Tzushan may teach their apprentices the components of Combine, Duration, Magnitude and Fortune.

Alternate Components for Sorcery Spells

Other parameters can be added to Shaping, granting sorcery spells additional strange and exotic abilities. Some of these components are not strictly balanced with one another, so care should be taken if introducing them to a campaign.

Ablation – Used with spells which have the Resist trait, each point of shaping applied to Ablation grinds down any protective magic on the target which tries to block the incoming spell; reducing its Magnitude by the level of ablation. This is still the case even if the protective magic successfully blocked the sorcery spell.

Focus – Used to ensure that a spell works, no matter what the mental and physical distractions, each point of shaping applied to Focus permits the sorcerer to ignore one level of difficulty applied against them. This covers the loss of verbal or somatic components, mental state due to narcotics, combining multiple spells, and even penalties applied for suffering wounds. This component cannot raise the casting chance above its base value.

Fortune – Used with spells which have the Resist trait, each point of shaping applied to Fortune allows an additional casting roll from which the sorcerer selects the most favourable result. A spell cast with 3 points of shaping applied to Fortune would permit the sorcerer to roll four times and choose the best roll.

Precision – Used with spells that randomly target Hit Locations, each point of shaping applied to Precision allows the caster to adjust the dice roll by 1 to select the most advantageous location.

Swiftness – Used to hasten the casting of complex or heavily manipulated spells, each point of shaping applied to Swiftness reduces the casting time by 1 Turn, to a minimum of one.

Dispelling a Sorcery Spell

Sorcery spells resist dispelling using their Magnitude. Thus if this component is left unaugmented sorcery can be fairly easy to dismiss.

Limitations of Sorcery

There are no restrictions to the number of concurrent spells a sorcerer can maintain, save that only a single Concentration spell can be focused on at any moment in time.

Due to the boggling complexity of sorcerous invocations, there is a limit to how many spells a sorcerer can keep in his mind. Thus a sorcerer may only memorise a number of spells up to the value of his INT characteristic. In the rare situation that the sorcerer has access to more spells than he has the space to memorise them, spells may be swapped by spending a week of intense deliberation in reclusive isolation to exchange them.

Spell Descriptions

All sorcery spells are defined by several traits which control how each spell functions. By design sorcery spells lack a degree of physical and temporal description since these parameters can be modified by Shaping as it is cast.

This flexibility can make certain spells appear to be remarkably potent, especially those which have their duration or range greatly extended. Such possibilities are intentional, providing an interesting opportunity for those who wish to cunningly manipulate their magic.

Most potential game abuses are handled in the spell descriptions. However, Games Masters who find that certain spell combinations are causing problems should feel free to impose extra restrictions – such as reducing spell functionality, preventing the same spells being available to a single school of sorcery, or using the same tactics against the player characters.

The following two traits are available to sorcery spells:

Concentrationn

The spell's active effects only function so long as the character specifically concentrates on it. During this time the sorcerer is usually restricted to moving at a maximum of walking pace, and performing Free or Reactive Actions (when necessary; use common sense). Any passive elements of the spell continue running without the need to concentrate; for example a Fly spell requires concentration to actually move, but it will simply keep the sorcerer floating in place if his concentration lapses. By default a sorcerer may only concentrate on a single Concentration spell at any one time.

Resist (Endurance/Willpower/Evade)

Offensive spells allow the target to make an opposed test of their Endurance, Willpower or Evade skill (as specified by the spell) against the casting roll of the sorcerer, to avoid the effect of the spell entirely. To resist using Evade, the character must expend a Combat Action.

Be warned that some of the following spells are extraordinarily powerful, included only for the use of major antagonists or as long lost arcane secrets. They are extremely rare and not intended for starting player characters.

Abjure (Substance/Process)

Resist (Special)

Abjure allows the recipient of the spell to abstain from something usually required for life, utterly removing its need (or effect) until the spell ends. Each variant of the spell affects a specific substance or process, which could be anything, including Food, Water, Breath, Sleep, Dreams, Narcotics, and so on. Due to its flexibility, the Games Master should use common sense when more unusual versions of the spell are used, for example Abjure (Narcotics) will not only remove any desire to take narcotics in the first place, but also ensure any already taken will no longer affect the target.

The sorcerer can affect targets with a maximum SIZ of three times the spell's Intensity. If the recipient is unwilling they are permitted to resist using Willpower. Exceedingly rare and exotic versions of this spell exist such as Abjure Pain, Abjure Sensory Perception, and even Abjure Ageing.

Animate (Substance)

Concentration, Resist (Special)

Animate quite literally invests an inanimate object with a semblance of life, permitting it to move under its own power. Each variant of the spell affects a specific type of substance, which can be fairly broad in scope. For example wood, stone, fire, darkness, rope, fabric, and so on. The sorcerer can animate an object with a maximum SIZ of three times the spell's Intensity. Insubstantial substances such as air, fire, darkness or clouds are instead measured in terms of volume, with the sorcerer able to affect a number of cubic metres equal to the spell's Intensity. The animated object gains a default Movement Rate of 1m, which may be incremented by assigning points of Intensity (on a one for one basis) to movement rather than to the amount of SIZ or Volume affected.

Providing they have some degree of flexibility or the ability to extrude portions of themselves, animated objects may perform complex physical manipulations. These are performed by using the sorcerer's own skills, reduced by one difficulty grade. If combined with the appropriate Sculpt spell (see Shaping), the sorcerer can achieve much finer control and ignore this penalty. Where necessary, treat the object as having a Damage Bonus based on twice its SIZ, or as an elemental of equal volume.

To Rock and Roll

The material and shape of an object has important implications on how the Animate spell is used.

For instance, a sorcerer who knows Animate (Stone) 78% could use it to move a boulder of up to SIZ 24 (a little over 200kg), but he couldn't affect a solid cliff face with a much larger size, nor could he break a lump from it unless the fault lines and cracks already existed. However, a more insubstantial material like water is easier to divide up, so there would be no problem splitting off a small pool of water from a lake.

Shape is also vital. Animating a boulder would allow it to ponderously roll about, but it obviously could not pick up an object, open a door (although it might be able to smash through it) or anything else which required limbs or digits to achieve. An animated statue on the other hand would possess the requisite appendages.

Some objects may appear innocuous but can be potentially formidable in the right circumstances. An animated bunch of ropes or a carpet could be an excellent way of entangling opponents, or an animated fire sent dancing through a tent encampment a deadly distraction.

Sorcerers must actively concentrate to cause animated objects to move or perform complex manipulation. If their concentration lapses the object becomes quiescent until the sorcerer can focus his will through it again. Objects which are already under magical control are only affected if the Magnitude of the Animate is equal or greater than the previous effect.

If the animated object is carried or worn by a living creature, then it may resist the spell with Endurance. Whilst the spell can be used to discommode/break such objects, their manipulation cannot be used to directly inflict harm on the creature (see Shrink page 174).

Attract (Threat)

Resist (Willpower)

Attract makes the recipient of the spell a scapegoat for certain, and usually harmful, occurrences. Each variant of the spell affects a specific type of threat, for instance spells, creatures, spirits or even missiles. Often used as a punitive curse or self-sacrificial gesture rather than an offensive weapon, Attract draws all incidences of its particular threat which pass within a radius equal to the spell's Intensity in metres, redirecting them so that they target the recipient instead.

The mechanical effects of the spell depend entirely upon the type of threat:

- Creatures: Attracts aggressive beasts with a SIZ of up to three times the spell's Intensity.
- Magic: Attracts offensive ranged magic with a Magnitude equal or less than the spell's Intensity.
- Missiles: Attracts ranged weapons with a maximum damage (including magical augments) equal or less than the spell's Intensity.
- Spirits: Attracts aggressive spirits with a maximum Intensity of half the spell's Intensity.

Banish

Resist (Willpower)

Banish enables a sorcerer to dismiss a spiritual or demonic entity with a maximum POW of three times the spell's Intensity, back to the Plane from whence it was summoned (or from which it travelled). If the target is unwilling it is permitted to resist using Willpower.

This spell does not work on spirits which are residing within a fetish to which they are bound. If brought forth from the object to perform a service, however, the spirit becomes vulnerable to the banishment; which if successful, sunders the binding. Likewise Banish does not work on spirits currently possessing a victim, but only those which are tricked into abandoning the host first.

Bypass Armour

Bypass Armour affects objects, armaments or the natural weapons of creatures so that they pass through armour. The spell allows the weapon or trap to ignore a number of Armour Points equal to the spell's Intensity. This spell also works against magical protection, such as Damage Resistance or Shield.

Castback

Castback shields the recipient from magic in a somewhat haphazard manner, with the chance that any spell cast at them may potentially be reflected back at its caster. The sorcery can only affect spells possessing the Resist trait which have a Magnitude equal to or less than the Magnitude of the Castback.

In such cases if the recipient of the Castback fails to resist the incoming spell, then it affects him normally. If on the other hand he succeeds in resisting, the reflected spell is sent back to its caster who in turn must roll to see if he himself suffers its effects!

Castback has no way of discerning the difference between hostile or beneficent magic, and affects all spells save those the target casts on himself.

The recipient cannot exceed a maximum SIZ of three times the spell's Intensity.

Damage Enhancement

Damage Enhancement augments the physical damage inflicted by an object or creature. This can be anything from natural weapons, a two handed axe or even the spikes of a pit trap. The magic increases the minimum amount of damage that is inflicted during a successful attack, raising it to the value of the spell's Intensity if the dice roll is lower. The spell cannot inflict more damage than the weapon is normally capable of.

Damage Resistance

Damage Resistance protects an (entire) object or person against physical damage. It provides the recipient with a number of Armour Points equal to the spell's Intensity. These do not stack with existing protection (whether worn or natural) so that only the highest value protection works.

This magic does not necessarily need only to be cast on living creatures. It can just as easily be used to toughen a sword, make a door more difficult to hack through, or render a delicate glass bottle near unbreakable. The target cannot exceed a maximum SIZ of three times the spell's Intensity.

Diminish (Characteristic)

Resist (Willpower/Endurance)

Diminish allows a sorcerer to reduce a physical or mental trait of a living target. Each variant of the spell affects a specific characteristic, diminishing it by 2 points per Intensity of the spell – to a minimum of 1. The target must possess the characteristic in question to be effective.

If the target is unwilling it is permitted to resist the spell, using Endurance if the spell is affecting a physical characteristic (STR, CON, SIZ or DEX) or Willpower if affecting a mental one (INT, POW or CHA). Note that creatures affected by Diminish (SIZ) actually shrink, rather than becoming wasted and skeletal as with the Tap spell.

Dominate (Creatures)

Concentration, Resist (Willpower)

Dominate grants the sorcerer psychic control over a creature of the specific species the spell affects. The spell is limited by the intellect of the target, the caster only able to subjugate creatures with an INT or INS up to twice the spell's Intensity. Those that fall within this range may resist with Willpower.

Whilst the sorcerer concentrates, he may mentally issue commands to the victim, who (in most circumstances) cannot refuse. If the sorcerer allows his concentration to lapse, the victim temporarily regains volition; at least until the next time the sorcerer re-establishes concentration. Dominate does not grant any awareness of what the target is doing when beyond the perception of the sorcerer. In

Kratos wields his Dominate (Reptiles) spell to command a lizardman raiding party of the Zo Swamps to serve him. With this subservient force, the sorcerer plans his revenge against Meeros.

addition, if the target escapes the Range of the spell they are freed from control, although it can established again if they return.

Certain circumstances permit a new resistance roll to break the spell, such as acts which run contrary to the target's strongest beliefs or instincts, for example being forced to murder a loved one. In these cases the subjugated victim may resist using a Passion, Oath or some similarly relevant skill. Suicidal commands instantly break the spell.

Draw (Creatures)

Resist (Willpower)

Draw summons creatures of a specific type within range towards a target. Each variant of the spell affects a family of species, such as fish, felines or birds. It affects creatures up to a maximum SIZ of three times the spell's Intensity, which may resist the summons using Willpower. Those that fail are drawn towards the target, moving at a natural speed suitable to that type of creature.

Physical obstructions may prevent the creatures from reaching the desired location. Upon their arrival, some other magic must be used to control the creatures since Draw provides no protection or domination against them. Aggressive species may potentially rampage or mindlessly attack depending on their natural instincts.

The target of the spell may be an object, location or person – although the latter, if unwilling, may also attempt to resist. If successful the target throws off the curse, and the spell fails.

Although the magic may seem extremely potent, it is balanced by the amount of time required to gather together creatures from overly long distances. In addition, interfering with nature on a wide scale often results in unforeseen (and dire) consequences. Thus Draw is most often used for things like: pestering an individual with insects, clandestinely stealing an entire herd of cattle, or blighting a city with a plague of rats.

Enchant (Object)

Resist (Special)

Enchant enables a caster to make one of their sorcery spells everlasting, but at the cost of seriously reducing their magical strength. Normally enchantments are bound into inanimate objects, something which will last beyond the life of the sorcerer, perhaps even becoming a legendary object. On the other hand a living target can be enchanted, although the spell is often one of a deleterious nature.

A spell which is to be made perpetual must be Combined with the casting of Enchant. In addition, it is limited to possessing only as many points of shaping as the Intensity of the Enchant. The strain of creating the enchantment permanently reduces the sorcerer's Magic Points attribute by the magic point cost of the combined spell. These can be recovered later if the enchantment is unwoven by the original caster or the object (or person) is destroyed. Dismissing or Neutralising an enchantment only suppresses its powers temporarily.

Why Enchant?

Few player character sorcerers are likely to create enchantments since the ultimate cost always comes from their own Magic Points attribute. Although it may seem foolish to enchant objects or people with permanent spells due to this crippling reduction in power, there are some circumstances where it can actually be a reasonable act.

In magically poor settings, recovery of Magic Points may be slow and difficult. An enchanted object in this case, will actually save the sorcerer from expending power, especially if it is a spell which he uses regularly – a carpet enchanted with Fly for instance.

Progression in a magical guild or cult might require the creation of an enchantment, a wizard's staff being a common concept. Combining this with the right spell could create a dangerous weapon of sorcery (Wrack), grant a supplementary pool of Magic Points (Store Manna), or some other imaginative use.

Last but by no means least, a sorcerer can use an enchantment to bless or curse a victim with a persistent effect. A rather infamous example would be changing a prince into a baboon with a permanent Shapechange spell, although with the right shaping entire cities could be damned with some nefarious sorcery.

It is recommended that only objects be permitted to be enchanted with spells requiring the Concentration trait. Enchantments should be recorded with the Invocation skill of the enchanted spell at the time of its creation, along with whatever shaping was performed.

Enhance (Characteristic)

Resist (Willpower/Endurance)

Enhance allows a sorcerer to increase a physical or mental trait of a target. It works in precisely the same way as Diminish, save that it improves a specific characteristic, enhancing it by 2 points per Intensity of the spell – to a maximum of twice the original characteristic value. Malevolent use of the spell may be resisted.

Careful consideration should be taken before permitting characters access to certain versions of this spell, such as Enhance (DEX, INT or POW), due to the potentially unbalancing nature of these spells.

Enlarge

Resist (Special)

Enlarge is the opposite of the Shrink spell. It is used to expand non-living or inanimate objects, the initial SIZ of which cannot exceed a maximum of three times the spell's Intensity. Under its effect, the dimensions and weight of the object are multiplied by a factor equal to the Intensity. For instance a plank of wood subject to an Intensity 7 Enlarge spell it would grow to seven times its length and mass, possibly allowing it to form a bridge.

Normally objects cannot resist the magic, but if it is carried or worn by a living creature, then the victim may resist the spell with Endurance. Used offensively in this way, the creature has the chance to brace itself or simply drop the object as it expands. Thus whilst having a suit of mail grow to five times bigger and heavier may be a hindering inconvenience, it will not cause direct harm. Additionally, an object will stop growing when it meets too much resistance.

Enslave (Creatures)

Resist (Willpower)

Enslave grants the sorcerer power to manipulate large numbers of targets, all of whom must be of the same species as specified by the spell. Instead of crushing the will of its victims, turning them into helpless automatons (as per the Dominate spell), the magic instils a powerful yet wholly artificial zeal or desire within those which it affects – giving them a temporary Passion at a value equal to the caster's Invocation skill. This can be anything from devoted adoration towards the sorcerer to an unremitting hatred for a hitherto friendly nation.

The potential number of victims a sorcerer can Enslave is equal to ten times the Intensity of the spell, multiplied by its Targets component; thus if cast at Intensity 7 with four Targets, the spell will actually attempt to affect 280 victims. These are normally gathered in a crowd or restricted area so that both the sorcerer can see them, and they can hear him. The sorcerer can only enslave creatures with an INT or INS up to twice the spell's Intensity. Those that fail to resist will listen to the words of the sorcerer and be influenced by them.

Whilst under the influence of this spell, victims cannot directly harm the caster, thinking him sacrosanct or a fount of wisdom. However they can baulk at a command if the order brings them into conflict with another Passion of equal or higher value. Enslave is normally used by powerful sorcerers to raise armies, subjugate tribes or corrupt ruling bodies, enabling them to subtly seize power or ensure their own safety in an otherwise hostile society.

Evoke

Resist (Willpower)

Evoke brings an extra-planar being to the presence of the caster; which can be anything from a demon or genie, to an intangible spirit. The only requirements are that it cannot be native to the plane of existence to which it is summoned, that it does not possess a POW greater than three times the spell's Intensity, and that the sorcerer knows its true name. For some settings, each incidence of this spell might be specific to a unique individual.

Although Evoke may summon the entity, it does not grant him any power over the extra-planar being. Unless some sort of magical protection or compulsion is used, the sorcerer is completely at the mercy of the entity, relying on ritual tradition or good nature. Of

Summoning Otherworld Entities

Using Evoke to summon entities from other worlds or dimensions is one of those spells which, according to the genre, commonly requires a great deal of preparation as described in the Introduction to Magic chapter (see Ritualistic Casting Times page 115).

In this particular case, the Games Master could require that the initial summoning of the entity requires roleplaying a long drawn out ritual, with full descriptions of the laying down of protective wards, and any required sacrifices. Then, assuming the summoned creature doesn't just destroy the sorcerer or drag him back to its own realm, some form of negotiation should take place for future services.

Once this deal is struck the entity could be allowed to return home, ready to respond the next time it is called by the Evoke spell. However, these future summonings merely require the sorcerer to call out the being's name whilst casting the spell, allowing it to respond near instantaneously.

course the being may not necessarily attack or punish its summoner, but few are happy about being yanked from their native plane without some sort of suitable raison d'être or a gift to smooth ruffled feelings.

Summoned entities only remain in the world for as long as the Duration of the spell. In addition they cannot travel further from the place of their summoning than the spell's Range.

Fly

Concentration

Fly enables the recipient to move freely through the air at their own behest. The spell can affect a person, creature or object of a SIZ up to three times its Intensity, granting them a base Movement Rate of 6. Further levels of Intensity not allocated to SIZ can instead be used to augment the speed of flight, each point granting an additional 6 metres per round. For instance an Intensity 7 Fly spell could grant a SIZ 14 creature a Movement Rate whilst flying of 18.

Fly requires concentration only when actively moving. If concentration lapses the magic continues, keeping the recipient hovering aloft; although if travelling at high speed it might take a round or two to coast to a stop.

If the spell is used on a beast of burden or an object used to support others (such as a carpet) it must be capable of lifting the combined SIZ of both the creature or object, and those mounted upon it. Otherwise it either fails to take off, or sinks towards the ground at a rate deemed fitting by the Games Master.

Haste

Haste augments the Movement Rate of whatever it is cast on, whether a person, creature or object. The spell can affect targets up to a maximum SIZ of three times the Intensity of the spell. Under its effect, the recipient's Movement Rate is increased by an amount equal to the Intensity. If the target is an inanimate object, it increases the top speed of the vehicle or vessel, but does not provide motive power.

Hide Life

Hide Life conceals the recipient's soul in a specially prepared object called a soul jar, which can take any form the caster desires. It works only on targets with a maximum POW of up to twice the Intensity of the spell. Under its effects the recipient loses a single Hit Point from every location, but in exchange cannot be killed. Each time they suffer an injury, affliction or spell which would normally slay them, at the moment of death their body discorporates and reforms next to the object in which the life force is stored.

It takes the body a period of one month divided by the Intensity of the spell to fully reform and heal. Conversely, if the recipient ventures further away from its soul jar than the Range of the spell, it begins to degenerate, suffering damage in reverse. Dying beyond the reach of the spell is permanent.

Hide Life can be dismissed or neutralised, but requires the counter-magic to be cast directly onto the soul jar, which is normally well hidden or protected. The only other way of ending the spell is to smash the object itself, which may prove hard if it is carved or fashioned out of exceptionally durable material. Although Hide Life prevents death, it does not cease ageing, as many sorcerers who later become withered liches have discovered to their cost.

Hinder

Resist (Endurance)

Hinder reduces the Movement Rate of whatever it is cast on, in a similar manner to Haste. The spell can affect targets of up to a maximum SIZ of three times the spell's Intensity. Those that fail to resist are slowed by a number of metres equal to the Intensity. However, a target's Movement Rate cannot be lowered to less than 1 metre per round with this spell.

Holdfast

Resist (Endurance)

Holdfast magically adheres an object (of a SIZ up to three times the spell's Intensity) to another surface. The bonding is unbreakable by normal means, save for the destruction of the target or the surface it is bonded to. It can only be dispelled by magic if the counter spell can overcome the Magnitude of the Holdfast.

The materials of the two surfaces make no difference to the spell. However, if the target is a living being, it is permitted to resist using its Endurance. This magic is often used to seal doors into their frames, stick weapons into scabbards, or even fasten thieves to objects they were trying to steal!

Imprison

Resist (Willpower)

Imprison creates an invisible barrier around a person or creature, blocking it from leaving the area. The magic only affects corporeal beings with a maximum POW or SIZ of up to three times the spell's Intensity. If either characteristic exceeds the limit the spell fails. The imprisoned creature is permitted a single chance to resist. If they successfully overcome the magic, they can escape.

Depending on the setting, Imprison may require the area of the imprisonment to be pre-prepared with use of powders, glyphs or geometric designs. It is often combined with the Evoke spell to provide some degree of protection when summoning hostile entities.

Intuition

Concentration, Resist (Willpower)

Intuition permits the sorcerer to discern the true emotions and motives of the target, as if he had made a successful Insight roll. The spell can only affect targets with an INT up to twice its Intensity. Although the magic allows a deeper awareness of psychological state, it does not enable the sorcerer to read memories or guarded thoughts. Targets who are aware of the spell may try to veil their feelings, gaining another resistance roll against the caster's Invocation skill, each time they try to deflect the sorcerer's probing.

Mark

Resist (Willpower)

Mark is used to magically tag an object with a mystical sigil, so that it may be located, summoned or even targeted by another spell without being in range of the caster's perception. The magic can mark an object of a SIZ up to three times the spell's Intensity. Whilst the caster is within the Range of the spell, he is aware of the object's distance and direction. Whether or not the magical mark is visible depends on the setting, but once placed it cannot be removed until the spell ends. If cast upon a living creature, it may attempt to resist the effects of the spell.

Mystic (Sense)

Concentration

Mystic (Sense) enables the caster to perceive magic using the sense of perception as specified by the spell. This could take the form of seeing auras, hearing faint tinkling, smelling peculiar scents or even feeling his skin crawl.

Due to the diversity of senses, the magical object need not be in direct perception, but less precise sensory methods may make it difficult exactly to locate the source. The power of Mystic (Sense) permits it to extend into alternate planes, for example the Spirit World, if such exist in the setting.

The sorcerer will be able roughly to judge the Magic Points of objects and people to within 1d3 points. If observing a spell or enchantment with an Intensity equal or less than that of the sorcerer's Mystic (Sense), he may discern what the type of magic (Theistic, Mystic, etc), what it does, and the unique signature of whichever cult, guild or tradition cast it – or if already a member of that group, the individual.

Neutralise Magic

Neutralise Magic suppresses a single spell or miracle on a target, with a Magnitude equal or less than its own. The magic is negated only as long as the Duration of Neutralise Magic, which in most cases is more than enough time for the targeted spell to expire. Magic with a longer duration reinstates itself when Neutralise ends, thus it cannot be used to permanently negate long-running curses or break enchantments for example, but could be used to briefly bring relief or bypass them.

If used against spells or miracles which specifically protect against magic (such as Spell Protection or Reflect), Neutralise Magic takes precedence in those situations when the Magnitude of both is equal.

Neutralise Magic can be used defensively to negate incoming spells using the Counter Spell reactive action. It affects targets with a SIZ up to three times the Intensity of the spell.

Palsy

Resist (Endurance)

Palsy renders a single random Hit Location on the target completely useless, the affected area twitching and unresponsive. The precise effect depends on the location struck. Being hit in the head causes the victim to become completely incapacitated, the chest results in paralysis from the neck down, the abdomen paralysis from the waist down, and a limb simply ceases functioning.

The spell cannot affect Hit Locations which normally possess Hit Points greater than the Palsy's Intensity. Nor can a single casting of the spell be used to target multiple locations on the same victim.

Perceive (Sense)

Resist (Endurance)

Perceive grants the recipient a new and unusual sensory perception. This could be anything from Echolocation to X-Ray Vision. The recipient cannot exceed a SIZ more than three times the spell's Intensity and if unwilling, may resist. Each version of the spell relates to a single unique sense, which can be made up by the Games Master or chosen from the Creature Traits table.

Depending on the setting, the spell may strangely mutate existing sensory organs, or grow exotic new ones, such as giant bat-like ears, delicate antennae or even glowing slit eyes – potentially causing distrust, fear or nausea to observers.

Phantom (Sense)

Concentration, Resist (Special)

Phantom produces an illusory effect on a target, tailored to fool a specific sense. There are many versions of this spell, each one affecting a different type of perception. The most common are used to subvert sight, sound, smell, taste and touch; but others exist to fool more exotic senses such as temperature, magic or emotion. Several phantasm spells can be woven together to form a single illusion, using the Combine component.

Illusions produced by the Phantom spell confuse the senses of those who interact with them, but do not change the underlying reality hidden beneath. As such, phantasms cannot inflict direct harm, but can be indirectly dangerous. For example a visual illusion of a paved floor could hide the existence of a spiked pit beneath it, or the smell and taste of a deadly acid could be hidden under the illusory bouquet of fine wine.

Of course, illusions need not be used to hide danger but could intimidate or bluff instead. The same visual illusion could make a pony appear to be a deadly sabre-toothed tiger, or turn the rags of a beggar into princely robes.

Detecting an illusion is not normally permitted unless the observer has good reason to question its validity. The audible and visual phantasm of a tiger cast on a pony will fool almost anyone, yet a dog witnessing the same illusion would notice that the tiger smelled very strongly of horse, and would have a strong suspicion that it was not all it seemed. In such cases the observer may attempt to resist using their Willpower against the Invocation skill of the caster. Resistance rolls are also permitted if the phantasm attempts to aggressively overwhelm those subject to its illusory effects (see below).

Phantasms can react to their surroundings provided the sorcerer concentrates on the spell. If the caster's attention lapses the illusion enters a relatively static standby mode, still operant but not longer dynamically responding to the environment; so background noises, scents and such like rarely need to be concentrated on.

For instance casting the phantasm of a tiger out of thin air would require the caster to concentrate to make it move or respond to attacks; whereas casting the same phantasm on the pony would need no concentration, since all he has done is changed its external appearance, and the animal will move by itself – although cropping grass and fleeing at the first sign of danger might be giveaways.

Phantom can only be used to replicate senses and memories previously experienced by the caster, or things he can mentally imagine. Thus a sorcerer could create some horrific looking monster with a hundred eyes, but correctly mimicking the taste of Fireberry Juice may be beyond his ability if he hasn't already sampled it. Such minor oversights are often a good way of recognising phantasms.

The following guidelines are provided to help judge the effects of particular sensory illusions:

Sight

Creates a visible yet non-corporeal illusion which cannot exceed a length, height or width of more than the Intensity of the spell in metres. This can range from simply changing the colour of a door to creating a carpet of aggressive, multicoloured snakes which continually wriggle over each other. If used subtly, a visual illusion can help disguise the true appearance of an object or creature, changing skin tones or the pattern of clothing. Creating a fabrication completely out of context with the setting allows the viewer a chance to resist, as does physically interacting with it. Animate illusionary creatures use the relevant skills of the sorcerer to perform physical actions; for example, an illusionary giant spider attempting to avoid a thrown javelin would use the sorcerer's own Evade skill to scuttle clear.

Smell

Reproduces any single scent of something, from a pleasant perfume to the stench of vomit or the smell of cut grass to freshly cooked food. The illusory scent has a detectable radius in metres (to humans at least) equal to the Intensity of the spell. When used creatively, the smell can drive off those who find the odour unpleasant, or cause them to involuntarily gag or choke. Conversely the scent might draw the attention of persons or creatures who find it attractive.

Sound

Generates an audible illusion, anything from a faint, distracting whisper to an overwhelming clap of thunder. The sorcerer can influence the nature and volume of the sound so long as he continues to concentrate upon it. Although very loud sounds can be produced, the illusion cannot cause permanent deafness or damage. On the other hand the volume can be high enough to interfere with verbal communication, or hide the sounds of other things happening. Treat the volume to be equal to ten times the Intensity on the Decibel scale. Any task which requires hearing one's own voice or maintaining concentration (such as spell casting), can attempt to resist, or suffer the usual consequences.

Taste

Produces any taste the sorcerer has previously encountered, from the most subtle of flavourings to mouth fouling tangs. The target of this spell need not just be food or drink, although that it is primary focus. It can be used to make the skin of a lover taste like lemon zest or be applied to a knife so that whatever it cuts is tainted with the flavour of rotted fish sauce. Using this spell offensively is somewhat difficult, but it might be utilised to cause a faux pas; forcing someone to spit something out unexpectedly, or perhaps make somebody abandon a complete meal, allowing the caster to claim it for himself.

Touch

Creates an illusion of tactility, which when combined with other types of phantasm can grant them a greater degree of reality. The sense imposed can range from feathery tickles to resilient impact, although in truth there is nothing actually there. So a target could be goosed from afar or the bite of a phantasmal tiger given crushing force. Indeed the spell is so versatile it can be used to replace the painful lash of a whip with the sense of being gently caressed. Such sensations simply fool those that interact with target, thus the spell cannot inflict, and is itself immune to, damage. Victims may still believe they have been wounded (or not as the case may be), and must resist the spell to avoid psychosomatic effects of receiving wounds, even though they have not suffered any actual harm.

Portal

Concentration

Portal creates a magical gateway connecting two places, which when stepped through, allows instantaneous transportation between the caster's side to the terminus, which may be located anywhere within Range. The portal is large enough for objects or creatures with a SIZ up to three times the spell's Intensity to pass through. However, the portal only remains open for as long as the sorcerer concentrates. If his attention lapses, the portal remains in place, but is impassable.

The appearance of the portal usually depends on the setting. Games Masters should decide whether a portal terminus can be placed blindly, whether it relies on close personal familiarity with the chosen location, or requires use of other magic such as Project (Sense) or Mark.

Conversely portals may require a specially enchanted spot or object to function, such as a set of standing stones. Another consideration is whether sensory information can pass through the portal as if it were a window to another place, or if the surface remains mysteriously opaque.

Project (Sense)

Concentration

Project allows the recipient to send one of his senses beyond his body in the form of an astral projection. This discorporated 'receptor' is both invisible and intangible, permitting it to travel anywhere with no chance of observation save for those with magical perception. Each individual Project spell relates to a specific sense, which is not necessarily limited to just human perceptions. A sorcerer who knows several of these spells can Combine them together, clairvoyance and clairaudience for example.

Wherever the projected sense travels, it relays back its particular sensory information, allowing the recipient to see, listen, touch or so on via the receptor. Whilst one of his senses is projected in this way, the recipient can no longer use it with his physical body. So a sorcerer who projects his hearing off to a distant location becomes deaf until the spell ends or he brings the projected sense back.

Concentration is required for two aspects of the spell: moving the astral receptor, and attempting a Perception check with the projected sense. Relatively speaking the sense moves quite slowly, with a maximum speed of ten times the spell's Intensity in kilometres per hour. When focus lapses, the receptor remains static but it keeps on relaying ambient information. If for any reason the projected sense is detected, it can be dispelled or even attacked with a magically

Death from Afar

Although Project (Sense) is often used to search or spy from remote yet secure locations, its main advantage is that it enables a sorcerer to cast spells at extreme Range, ostensibly safe from reprisal. Whilst this may seem the perfect way to curse or assassinate a victim (and indeed is a staple of the Sword & Sorcery genre), there are certain difficulties with using it in this manner.

Firstly there is no guarantee the sorcerer will actually know the precise location of his intended victim. Of course the location of a public figure such as a king may be guessed at, but it still might take some time to find his exact position, especially if he lacks a regular schedule. Once a victim discovers he is being magically hunted it would be easy to hide or move somewhere unforeseen by his hunter, making it nigh impossible to locate by scrying.

Secondly, after extending the Range of a sorcery spell to reach tens or hundreds of kilometres, few Shaping points remain to augment its Magnitude; meaning that even modest magical protection will block the attack. This is especially true for places such as temple sanctuaries or wizard's towers which tend to be warded against such magical assaults.

augmented weapon or spell – which if successful, transfers the magical effect or damage back to the head of the recipient.

A sorcerer can use Project (Sense) to be able to aim a second spell at a target who is out of direct observation – whether because of distance or blocking obstacles. The piggy-backed spell must also have sufficient Range to reach the target, and cannot possess a greater Intensity than that of the Project spell.

Protective Ward

Protective Ward is an augmenting spell which must be cast in association with one or more other sorcery spells, using the Combine component to meld them together. Its purpose is to form an extended wall to which spells such as Damage Resistance, Spell Resistance or Spirit Resistance can be bound, so that the magic defends an area or volume, rather than individual targets.

The ward can cover an area (or encompass a volume) of up to 1 metre per point of Intensity in width, height and depth. Thus an Intensity 6 Protective Ward could be used to create a simple wall 6 metres wide, a trapezoid pyramid measuring 6m along each vertices, or even a hemisphere 6m in diameter. As preparation before it is cast, the ward must be inscribed upon a solid surface, its sigils or lines either drawn, scratched or etched along the perimeter of the area so protected.

When cast, the sorcerer decides in which direction the ward is permeable, if any. Thus a warding could be set up to affect anything entering the warded area, or conversely anything leaving it. In certain circumstances the caster may wish that the magics woven into the perimeter work in both directions.

Regenerate

Concentration

Regenerate allows the sorcerer to slowly heal injuries by accelerating the natural healing processes of the target. The magic will counteract bleeding and stabilise a dying target, but cannot repair Major Wounds. Targets regenerate a number of Hit Points per hour equal to the Intensity of the spell. These points may be divided across several locations or all applied to one location at the will of the caster. However, the sorcerer must actively concentrate on the spell for healing to occur. If concentration lapses or the spell is terminated early, the amount of Hit Points recovered is proportional to the time spent regenerating.

Repulse (Creatures)

Resist (Willpower)

Repulse is the exact opposite of the Draw spell (see page 168), driving off creatures of a specific type within range of the target. It has a range of useful applications, such as a personal insect repellent or purging homes of vermin. On a larger scale Repulse can keep villages clear of especially dangerous creatures, which might pose a threat to the inhabitants. As a curse it works well too, from driving prey away from a hunter up to the damning of entire cities by repelling people from entering their forbidding gates!

The precise nature of the repulsion is left to the caster to decide. It takes the form of some emotive response, for example disgust, nervousness or outright terror.

Revivify

Concentration

Revivify is used to animate a dead body, creating a mindless undead automaton such as a skeleton or zombie. The spell requires the relatively whole corpse of a dead creature in order to work, although bodies can be assembled piecemeal from dismembered parts of several less intact carcasses, provided time is spent stitching flesh or wiring bone together first.

The sorcerer can revivify corpses with a maximum SIZ of three times the spell's Intensity. The characteristics of the skeleton or zombie are as described in the Creatures chapter, but gain a bonus to STR and CON equal to the Intensity of the spell. All other attributes are based on the original creature.

Being mindless, revivified undead rely on their creator to guide them. Thus they act with physical skills equivalent to those of the sorcerer (capped by the value of the caster's Invocation skill), but if he allows his concentration to relax, they lapse into quiescence until actively guided again. Nothing prevents the sorcerer from further augmenting the undead servitor with other magic or arming it, provided it has the physiology to wear or wield such items.

Sculpt (Substance)

Concentration, Resist (Special)

Sculpt enables a sorcerer to mould the form of a particular substance, shaping it to his will. Each variant of the spell affects a specific type of substance, which can be fairly inclusive, for instance sand, stone, water, metal, and so on. The sorcerer can sculpt a volume or object with a maximum SIZ of three times the spell's Intensity. Insubstantial substances such as smoke, shadows or mist are instead measured in terms of cubic metres equal to the spell's Intensity.

Concentration is only required to actively shape the substance, the spell maintaining the new form until the next change the sorcerer wishes to make. At the conclusion of the spell the substance will retain its final form, provided the material is rigid. For instance a hole opened in a wall would remain, but a statue moulded out of water would collapse.

Although sculpt can create any form imaginable, the actual artistic value or architectural strength of the new shape is limited by the appropriate Craft or Engineering skill; thus a sorcerer who tried to repair the hull of a ship with this spell would only be as effective as his Craft (Carpentry), albeit he'd need no tools, and could perform the task in mere moments.

If the targeted object is carried or worn by a living creature, then they may resist the spell with Endurance. Whilst the spell can be used to discommode/break such objects, their manipulation cannot be used to directly inflict harm on the creature (see Shrink, opposite).

Exotic versions of this spell can be used on living substances, provided the spell can affect the entire plant or creature. Unwilling targets may attempt to resist. No damage is inflicted on those that fail, but their physique and appearance may be warped as the sorcerer desires.

Sense (Object, State or Substance)

Concentration

Sense is utilised as a means to detect valuables, lost possessions or hidden objects from afar. Each incidence of this spell senses a specific type of object, physiological status or unique substance. Such categories are usually quite broad, to ensure some degree of versatility. Examples include precious metals, fresh water, weapons, flesh and bone, edible food, or even undeath.

The caster must concentrate to detect his spell's objective, which reveals its presence by tweaking one of the sorcerer's primary senses. Thus the location of water might be indicated by a gurgling, tinkling noise which strengthens as the caster draws closer to its source.

Sufficient thickness of interposing material will block the spell, which can penetrate a number of metres of solid wood, earth or water equal to the spell's Intensity. Denser materials such as metal or stone reduce this to a number of centimetres equal to the Intensity. Penetrating magical protections require that the Intensity of Sense exceeds that of the protective spell.

Sense cannot discern more insubstantial things like emotions or intents.

Shapechange (to Creature)

Resist (Endurance)

Shapechange morphs the physical body of the target into that of another species. The sorcerer can affect any living creature of a SIZ up to three times the Intensity of the spell. The SIZ of the original form, added to the difference in SIZ between the original and modified form, must be within this range.

The magic transforms the target into an average example of the new species. He adopts the physical Characteristics (STR, CON, SIZ and DEX) of the creature assumed, plus whatever inherent attacks and modes of locomotion it possesses. The recipient may use the creature's base skills or his own, if they are better. Magical or supernatural abilities are not granted, and nor are any of the mental characteristics.

For example, a sorcerer of SIZ 10 who wishes to change into a lion (average SIZ 22), requires a Shapechange of Intensity 8; whereas if the same sorcerer wished to turn into a rat (average SIZ 1), he would only need an Intensity of 7.

There are many variants of Shapechange, each one specific to a species of creature. The categories are quite broad in scope, however, covering an entire family: for example: rodents, canines, snakes, etc. To change into a Wyvern, for example, one would need Shapechange (Draconic); assuming the sorcerer had sufficient Intensity to achieve the new form. The spell only works on living things, which may resist if they are unwilling.

Shrink

Resist (Special)

Shrink is used to miniaturise non-living or inanimate objects, the SIZ of which cannot exceed a maximum of three times the spell's Intensity. The manner in which objects decrease their proportions is different to the Diminish spell, since objects targeted with this magic may be quite small and light. Instead Shrink reduces their dimensions and weight by a factor equal to the Intensity. For example a broad sword has a default SIZ of 1, but if subject to an Intensity 8 Shrink spell it would be reduced to an eighth of its length and mass, making it much easier to conceal.

If the targeted object is carried or worn by a living creature, then they may resist the spell with Endurance. Otherwise the object gets no save against the magic. When used offensively upon worn objects, the targeted item either tears open, squeezes off, or if it is too resilient to break, simply stops shrinking when it meets too much resistance. So using Shrink on a soldier's full helmet might miniaturise it to the point where it is painfully tight and impossible to remove, but it will not inflict any significant harm on its wearer.

Smother

Resist (Endurance)

Smother slowly asphyxiates a target, starving it of air so that it collapses choking and gasping. The magic affects targets with a SIZ up to three times the Intensity of the spell. Those that fail to resist begin to suffocate immediately, suffering damage at the start of the next Round (see Asphyxiation page 71). The spell can also be used on flames to extinguish candles, lamps, and even fires of up to 1 cubic metre per Intensity.

Normally this spell ceases to inflict damage once the victim passes out. Rarer versions possess more dire effects, actually filling the victim's lungs with water, blood, flies or even sand so that they actually die.

Spell Resistance

Spell Resistance provides the recipient protection against magic cast at them. It blocks incoming spells with a Magnitude equal to, or less than, its own. If a spell or miracle manages to overcome this protection, the Spell Resistance suffers no harm, unless of course it itself was the target of magical dismissal.

The negative side of Spell Resistance is that it cannot discern between friendly or hostile magic. Thus someone seriously wounded under its protection may need to terminate the spell or be prevented from receiving magical healing. Spell Resistance affects targets with a SIZ up to three times the Intensity of the spell.

Spirit Resistance

Spirit Resistance blocks spirits and intangible entities of other planes from coming into contact with the recipient. The magic blocks spirits of an Intensity up to half the Intensity of the spell. For example, an Intensity 3 disease spirit would be blocked by an Intensity 5 or 6 Spirit Resistance.

A blocked spirit is unable to touch, discorporate, possess or otherwise engage the recipient in Spirit Combat. Likewise any magic cast by a spirit at the recipient is also blocked unless the Magnitude of the spell exceeds the Intensity of the Spirit Resistance.

Store Manna

Store Manna creates a temporary storage vessel for Magic Points, a reservoir which can charged, then later be called on to power the sorcerer's own spells. It requires an object to be the target of the spell in which the Magic Points are physically stored. This can be anything from an eggshell to an iron idol, but more delicate objects can be prone to breakage. The object can store a maximum number of Magic Points equal to the Intensity of the spell. Travelling further from this object than the Range of the spell cuts the sorcerer off from his Magic Points.

When initially cast, Store Manna has no Magic Points of its own. These must be transferred from other sources; such as voluntary donations from other sorcerers. Depending on the setting, Magic Points might also be gathered from ritual sacrifices, tapping of magical locations, and other more unusual methods (see Where Do Magic Points Come From? Page 115).

If the spell expires, naturally coming to the end of its duration or from being dispelled (or the object is broken), any remaining Magic Points stored within the object are lost.

The sorcerer can only benefit from a single casting of Store Manna at a time, additional castings either not working or replacing the previous incidence of the spell. In addition, the application of the Targets component does not permit multiplication of the Magic Point storage, but simply allows the default number to be split between multiple objects.

Summon

Resist (Evade)

Summon brings a non-living, inanimate object to the sorcerer, teleporting it from wherever it previously rested to his hand or body as desired. The magic can summon an object of a SIZ up to three times the spell's Intensity. Usually this is something he can directly perceive with his own senses, although objects residing at greater distances can be summoned via magical observation, or previously prepared with the Mark spell.

If the object is something in the possession of a living creature, it may attempt to resist the magical theft by snatching it back or diving away. This spell is often used to call forth prepared equipment the sorcerer does not wish to carry, or to arm himself in a moment's notice. Clothing and armour must be prior mounted on a mannequin for it to be instantly settled about the sorcerer's body. When the spell ends the object returns to the precise location it was summoned from.

Switch Body

Resist (Willpower)

Switch Body enables a sorcerer to switch his consciousness with that of another, so that they exchange bodies. The caster can affect targets with a POW up to twice the Intensity of the spell. Unwilling targets who fail to resist become host to the caster's mind, and their own psyche finds itself in the sorcerer's body.

Both the sorcerer and the target retain their own skills and mental Characteristics, but gain the STR, CON, SIZ and DEX of the other's body, which may require recalculation of some attributes.

Since this spell can be used upon creatures as well as sapient beings, the sorcerer takes provisions to ensure his own body cannot suffer harm from the temporary occupant; for instance by leaving it under the supervision of servants or magically binding himself into immobility.

If the sorcerer's body is killed whilst switched with a victim, his consciousness will also die when the spell ends. Using this spell a sorcerer could briefly escape the death of their own body in order to wreak revenge. Casting Switch Body as an Enchantment (see Enchant, page 168) can technically allow a sorcerer permanently to inhabit the body of a target and assume its status or influence, if he can carry off the exchange.

Tap (Characteristic)

Resist (Special)

Tap is used to drain Characteristic points from victims in order to boost sorcerer's own, potentially achieving superhuman levels. Each version of the Tap spell affects a different characteristic. Targets may willingly submit to the spell or attempt to resist its effects, using Endurance if the spell is affecting a physical characteristic (STR, CON, SIZ or DEX) or Willpower if affecting a mental one (INT, POW or CHA).

The number of points drained from each target is equal to the spell's Intensity (down to a minimum of 1 point). The sorcerer however only gains one fifth of these points – up to a maximum of double his original characteristic value. For instance if a sorcerer cast Tap (STR) at Intensity 7 on four targets, each of the victims would lose seven points of STR whilst the sorcerer's own strength would be augmented by +6 points.

Once the spell concludes, the characteristic points of all involved revert to normal. Certain versions of this spell such as Tap (INT) or Tap (DEX) can be very potent, especially if combined with Enchant. When using Tap to steal a creature's SIZ, the magic causes the victim to become wasted and skeletal, rather than shrinking them.

Telepathy

Resist (Willpower)

Telepathy allows a sorcerer to establish mental two way communication with a target, without the need for shared language or even species. The caster can form the telepathic link with beings of an INT up to twice the Intensity of the spell. Non-sapient creatures use their INT equivalent and not their INS. In this case, communication is limited to the exchange of mental pictures or emotions.

The spell also grants the ability to experience memory, if the target is willing to share it. If cast on multiple targets, the sorcerer can decide if everyone connected via the Telepathy can communicate freely, or whether he acts as a hub for numerous private links.

TELEPORT

Concentration, Resist (Evade)

Teleport enables a sorcerer to instantaneously move the recipient anywhere within the Range of the spell. Several limiting factors apply to this transportation, these being that the destination is in direct observation (or tagged by the Mark spell), there is solid footing and no object bars their arrival; otherwise the spell automatically fails. A sorcerer is limited to teleporting creatures with a SIZ up to three times the Intensity of the spell.

Although the spell permits contiguous jumping until its Duration expires, the recipient is forced to teleport back to its origin before selecting a new destination to travel to. Each jump is treated as a Reactive Action requiring the expenditure of an Action Point, and can be used to avoid attacks in an opposed roll in a similar fashion to Evade. When the spell ends or is dismissed, the recipient returns to his starting point. This occurs even if he is dead.

Teleport can be further limited by requiring the presence of a certain material or substance at either end of the jump, through which to pass. For example a sorcerer may only be able to pass from one shadow to another. Likewise this could be pools of water, burning fires or even living trees!

TRANSFER WOUND

Concentration, Resist (Endurance)

Transfer Wound allows a sorcerer to transfer physical damage from himself to the target or vice versa. By spending an Action Point and concentrating on his Turn he may move a single wound of damage equal or less than the spell's Intensity between the target and himself.

Wounds must be shifted between identical or at least roughly similar locations, which cause the spell to fail if cast on a target with alien physiology. When the spell ends, transferred wounds remain where they were last shifted. If multiple targets are incorporated, then damage transferred from the sorcerer is divided equally between each recipient.

TRANSMOGRIFY (TO SUBSTANCE)

Resist (Endurance)

Transmogrify converts the base substance of a creature or object to some other material. Each variant of the spell converts targets to a specific type of substance, which can be as broad or narrow as is suitable for the setting, for example salt, mud or even gold! The sorcerer can transmogrify a target with a maximum SIZ of three times the spell's Intensity. Living creatures and magical constructs are permitted to resist.

The effect of the spell depends on the substance it was converted to. A solid material such as gold will place a living victim into a state of suspended animation which lasts until the sorcery terminates. Unless defaced, the temporary golden statue reverts back to its original form unharmed. If the substance was ice or salt on the other hand, some wearing might occur due to abrasive winds or melting.

Being transformed into a fluid substance usually spells doom for the original target. Objects converted to sand or water collapse under their own weight and may disperse entirely. Those transmogrified into more viscous substances often deform, and living creatures which emerge alive from such an experience are often horribly warped or mutated by the experience.

Whilst it can be used as a horrible curse, transmogrify is normally used in more productive (or at least inventive) ways, anything from tricking merchants to undermining fortifications. Games Masters should restrict this spell to only the most foul sorcerers if it is likely to be abused for the purpose of killing.

TRAP SOUL

Resist (Willpower)

Trap Soul snares the spirit of a corporeal creature so that at the moment of its death, it can be trapped within a specially prepared object or location. The magic can affect targets with a POW up to twice the Intensity of the spell. Unwilling targets may attempt to resist nefarious use of this spell.

Only those beings that die before the Trap Soul spell ends, and whilst still within its Range have their souls imprisoned, unable to depart for the spirit world or afterlife until the object containing them is destroyed, or the spell concludes.

Whilst held within their prison, the soul is unable to communicate, unless contacted by magic with a Intensity greater than the Trap Soul's Magnitude. Sorcerers specialising in necromancy often combine this spell with Enchant to create immortal oracles, to eternally imprison deadly enemies, or to bind the soul of a slain victim to its own place of death or body, where it endures as a Haunt (see page 150).

Kratos's Wrack (Darkness) spell easily overwhelms a Meerish champion. His pain is caused by ethereal serpents that bite and tear, their venom inflicting freezing agony upon his tortured body.

Undeath

Resist (Endurance)

Undeath enables the sorcerer to turn the recipient into an undead monster, gaining the ability to forgo air, food, water, warmth or rest; to experience immunity to disease and poison; and no longer to suffer the adverse effects of Serious Wounds, fatigue or ageing. In effect they gain the Undead creature trait. All this comes at a cost however; whilst under the effect of the magic, the recipient is infertile, no longer heals, and is incapable of generating Magic Points naturally.

The sorcerer can affect living targets with a CON up to three times the Intensity of the spell. Unwilling targets may attempt to resist. Sorcerers who fear death often resort to this spell, and combine it with Enchant to make it permanent, turning themselves into an immortal lich or mummy. Occasionally it is used to impart a terrible curse on those that transgress cult taboos or some equally heinous crime.

Wrack (Substance or Harm)

Concentration, Resist (Evade)

Wrack enables a sorcerer to harm opponents with deadly bolts or waves of sorcerous energy. On his Turn as a Combat Action, he may launch a magical attack against the target or targets, using his Invocation skill as the attack roll, which may be resisted with Evade. Successful attacks strike a random location, the Intensity of the spell denoting the damage it inflicts. Worn armour does not protect, but natural or magical Armour Points reduce damage as normal.

Wrack Damage

Intensity	*Damage*
1-2	1d2
3-4	1d4
5-6	1d6
7-8	1d8
9-10	1d10
11-12	2d6

The caster must concentrate to launch a Wrack attack, but can let the spell drop into dormancy to perform other actions in-between each magical assault.

Each variant of this spell inflicts damage in a different manner, according to the school from which it was learned. For example Wrack (Darkness) taught by the Stygian Path would strike the target with serpent-like tendrils of freezing shadow, whereas Wrack (Death) learned from the Guardians of the Grave, may cause a victim's limbs to rot with necrotic lesions.

Theism

Theism is the belief in, and worship of, godlike beings; it calls upon them to create supernatural effects on behalf of their faithful adherents. The precise manner in which this magic is provided, and how it manifests can vary dramatically according to the setting, but at its heart is the concept that worshippers appease deities with gifts and devotion, in exchange for which the entity lends certain mortals, who have been initiated into its cult, the right to call upon a part of its power.

Worshippers do not study the art of manipulating magic; rather they learn the myths and secrets of those they venerate, gaining insight into their nature, personalities and desires. With this knowledge a devoted worshipper knows how to phrase or frame a request to his gods, so that they feel compelled, or indeed inspired, to help him.

Additionally a worshipper must show his dedication to his divine patrons by offering sacrifice, service, and perhaps even selfless adoration in order to prove himself worthy of their attention. The depth of this piety influences the amount of effort to which deities will move themselves in order to aid a loyal devotee.

Since the divine status of a worshipped entity is often based upon the worship it receives, deities are motivated to watch over their supplicants. This is done in a myriad of ways, from commanding its most devoted priests to establish cults or temples – which in turn provide materialistic support to its worshippers within a community – to elevating zealots as figureheads of high political or military status, by providing them with potent powers.

Worship is the fundamental keystone of this divine (or perhaps infernal) magical ecology. The more worship, or propitiation, a deity receives, the more magical might it garners; which in turn must be given back or used to aid its supplicants or else risk losing their faithful attendance.

Not every being who receives worship is necessarily a god *per se*. One man's deity may be another man's demon. In fact nothing prevents the creation of a theistic culture which venerates monstrous, alien beings from other dimensions. Providing these beings - no matter their origin – are fed, entertained or placated in the correct manner they will channel their power through those who please them.

Calling on the Gods

Calling upon the gods for their power relies upon two core skills, Devotion and Exhort. Devotion reflects the strength and depth of the bond between the theist and his deity, or deities; whilst Exhort is the ability of the worshipper to correctly intonate or phrase his requests, so that his divine patron will respond.

Devotion (POW+CHA)

The nature and strength of any miraculous powers a theist draws upon is based upon his Devotion. The 'skill' is more accurately a relationship the theist has with an individual god, a small faction or family of divine beings, or indeed an entire pantheon. The precise scope of the skill depends upon the campaign setting, but each incidence of Devotion must be assigned to a specific deity or group of deities.

It is the depth of the worshipper's Devotion to his gods which grants potency to any theistic miracles he calls for. Whenever a theist requests aid from a deity, the Magnitude and Intensity of the miracle is equal to one tenth of his Devotion score.

Devotion is often utilised to measure the progression of a worshipper within a cult, the upper echelons being restricted to those who demonstrate the proper dedication. This in turn can limit what miracles are available to a worshipper of particular cult rank; as few religions are likely to grant their most potent powers to mere initiates.

Last but by no means least, in the right circumstances Devotion can potentially be used to resist various psychological attacks, tests of faith or contests of competing passions.

Exhort (INT+CHA)

Exhort is the skill used to coerce the gods to send a worshipper the magical aid he requires. It can be portrayed in several ways, but combines a number of different aspects such as strength of passion, egocentric will, ritualistic knowledge and understanding of divine psychology, to put forth a request which the deity cannot ignore.

Mechanistically the skill works as a simple base chance to successfully channel power from the god. A theist with Exhort (Lord Dark Maggot) 70% has a 70% chance of performing the relevant miracle.

Exactly how a miracle manifests can vary dramatically according to the setting. A successful exhortation can impel the deity to either:

- Channel his knowledge and power through the theist
- Cast the miracle on the theist's behalf
- Manifest before the theist (and all observers) to perform the deed personally

Taking the case of the Demon Lord Ningilin as an illustration, a worshipper who successfully called upon him to destroy a group of sacrilegious enemies with his power of wormy transformation, might find that the god grants the worshipper the words of invocation and magical strength to cast the magic himself; or that the miracle simply occurs without further effort on the worshipper's part; or most worryingly of all, that Ningilin himself steps down from the sky, and personally transforms the interlopers with his own putrescent hands.

Cults and Miracles

A theist's skills are indelibly linked to a specific religion, normally organised and known as a cult. Most cults are ancient faiths and usually accepted – or at least tolerated – by the local culture. Some are limited to a single city or tribe, whereas others can span nations. Even the number of deities incorporated within a cult can vary, with some cults tied to a single divine being, whereas others can consolidate an entire pantheon. In fact a single deity could have a dozen different, independent cults devoted to various aspects of its celestial magnificence!

It is a cult's deities which provide the miracles available to dedicated worshippers. Correspondingly there are no preset restrictions to the number of miracles each cult has, nor even that they should be balanced to one another. In general, the powers offered by the cult reflect the nature of that deity or deities venerated. The only thing which is fairly certain is that the cult's own priesthood will limit the availability of what miracles to which it has access, to those of proven faith and trustworthiness.

For example the Cult of Myceras, war god of Meeros, may grant access to the miracles Beast Form, Berserk, Clear Skies, Consecrate, Fortify, Sacred Band, Shield and Sunspear. Whilst the Cult of the Seven Badoshi Devils might instead provide Bind Ghost, Chameleon, Consecrate, Earthquake, Madness, Perseverance and True Scimitar, each of the seven demigods providing one of the miracles.

Thus cults, like other magical organisations, are similar to Combat Styles: diverse combinations of deities and miracles amalgamated into a single faith. Since cults are often viewed as the patrons of particular careers or irrevocably bound to specific philosophies, it may be unusual for a worshipper to pay more than lip service to more than one faith.

Professional theists who serve the shrines and temples of a cult are often well regarded, if not feared, for their zealous beliefs; and take the trouble to dress, act and behave appropriately to properly revere their patron gods.

Acting Like Your God

In some settings, as his Devotion increases, so does the propensity of the worshipper to act in the ways the focus of that veneration acts. This may not be due to any supernatural link, merely the pressures of cult membership, voluntary geases or even social expectation. Whatever the source of the influence, a worshipper's behaviour or judgment can begin to reflect those of his god, potentially leading to gradual personality changes.

It is believed by many cults that their gods are more able, or at least more willing, to aid those who espouse their divine patron's virtues. Acting in a manner contrary to a god's desires can land that worshipper in deep trouble. Much depends on the nature of the bond between theist and deity; whether it can be an informal relationship, or if the strength of the tie demands a worshipper behave precisely like the god in order to maintain the flow of magical power between them.

Starting Theists

A character that begins the game as a theist must choose a single cult to follow; either designed by the Games Master, agreed between the player and Games Master, or chosen from the examples given in the Cults and Brotherhoods chapter. Only one cult can be chosen at this stage but others can potentially be joined during the course of play.

Theist characters start with knowing those miracles available to someone of their cult rank, but not exceeding a number equal to one twentieth of their Devotion skill. Once the game begins they are restricted in what additional powers they can learn, and when they can learn them.

Kara's Saga

Kara begins the campaign by joining the priesthood of Myceras, specially selected from the virginal dancing girls who entertain the god on holy days with their passionate war dances. Whether her exclusive invitation was due to the political machinations of her father to save her from the lechery of Xenos, or whether the god himself expressed an interest due to her beauty and dedication, Kara does not know.

In exchange for an oath of abstinence and faithful service, she is inducted into the Cult of Myceras as an initiate. Much of her time is spent clearing up the mess produced by the incessant sacrificial offerings requested by the city's warriors, yet during the evenings she is taught the ways of worship. By the time the game starts she has a Devotion of 63% and has learned all four of those cult miracles which Myceras provides to Initiates (1 miracle for each 20% or thereof of her skill).

Learning Miracles

The costs of learning new miracles are based upon an investment of Experience Rolls as described in the Magic chapter on page 118. However, most priesthoods restrict the availability of certain miracles according to cult rank, ensuring that worshippers prove their devotion and loyalty before trusting them with such knowledge. Even the achievement of promotion within the cult does not necessarily grant a character automatic access to any new powers.

Learning miracles may require the theist to prove himself worthy in a number of different ways, depending on the nature of the cult. Some require the completion of a heroic quest to attest their faith or a pilgrimage to seek out a holy spot where their god mythically gained that particular power; whilst others might necessitate the slaying of a worthy sacrifice, or a superior to demonstrate their right to this secret knowledge, or going into seclusion for many weeks inhaling mind-expanding narcotics to seek oneness with their deity.

Thus learning how to call upon new miracles is rarely just a prosaic case of paying enough silver to convince the priesthood – as that is how lay members engage the services of priests to cast miracles on their behalf. To gain these potent powers for themselves, characters must undergo great challenges and moral dilemmas, binding themselves closer to the cult and the deities they revere.

Using Theism

A theist may call upon some of the most potent magical effects available to mortal magicians. However, their exhortations require much preparation, primarily in the form of worshipping and making dedications to the gods. These religious acts are normally restricted to places deemed sacrosanct, so the reach of a cult is often limited to the locales close by shrines, temples or particular holy sites dedicated to the deity or deities in question.

Devotional Pools

Cult members who advance beyond the cult rank of Lay Member may begin to draw upon the gods by use of the Exhort skill. Every miracle they call for must be paid for in advance of the request, by sacrifice or donation of Magic Points into something called a devotional pool. This pool represents the strength of the bond between worshipper and god, and must be regularly topped up.

While Magic Points remain in the pool, the theist can use them to request miracles, but once the pool is expended no more requests may be made. The source of these points need not necessarily be the theist himself (see Donating Magic Points below) but the maximum size of the pool is limited by the theist's cult rank.

- Lay Member – None
- Initiate – 1/4 of the Theist's POW
- Acolyte – 1/2 of the Theist's POW
- Priest – 3/4 of the Theist's POW
- High Priest – All of the Theist's POW

The size of the devotional pool has no bearing on the theist's normal POW capacity for storing personal Magic Points. Assuming the theist is donating Magic Points from his own POW, after the transference is made he can regenerate or recoup Magic Points as normal.

The implication of this method of paying for their miracles is that a worshipper, with enough preparation time, can fully load up both his devotional pool, and his own personal Magic Points in advance of performing some quest. On the downside, refilling his devotional pool requires him not only to return to a place of cult significance, but also personally to donate or transfer the points from his own resources.

Joining More Than One Cult

If the campaign setting permits, nothing prevents membership of multiple cults, providing they are not the antithesis of each other. For instance it may be reasonable for characters to be members of a state religion and a professional cult, and still worship a family deity. In such cases a separate devotional pool must be maintained for each individual cult.

However, there is a limit to how much magical energy can be amassed. No matter how many cults they are members of, the combined amount of Magic Points stored in the pools cannot exceed the POW of the character. Attempting to do so results in Magic Points dissipating from the other pools until the stored total once again equals the theist's POW.

Donating Magic Points

Dedicating Magic Points to their devotional pool requires that the theist be present at a shrine, temple or holy place with connection to the cult's god or pantheon. The ritual takes the form of ceremony, meditation or prayer, and often incorporates some type of offering above and beyond the pure Magic Points – perhaps an animal sacrifice, financial tribute to the priesthood or a gift pleasing to the deity.

The actual source of the Magic Points can be somewhat abstract (see Where do Magic Points Come From? page 115). For example, if Magic Points come from sacrificial offerings, then the theist himself must orchestrate, or at least participate in, the offering. The important concept here is that a worshipper must be physically present at the donation, else the Magic Points generated do not transfer to his devotional pool.

It is recommended that the current number of Magic Points in the pool cannot exceed the size of the most recent donation. Thus a theist with three Magic Points in his pool who sacrifices a white bull (worth seven Magic Points) would raise his pool to seven points, not ten. In this way a deity cannot be appeased with a series of petty offerings which slowly accumulate excessive devotional strength.

Sacrosanct Locations

The concept of only being allowed to recharge their devotional pool at specific holy places may initially seem rather restrictive, but this need not be an overly prohibitive aspect of theism. A worshipper can call upon his god or gods for miracles at any time; they only need to return to a temple to reaffirm the bond with the deity.

This fundamental element of theism should instead been seen as an opportunity by Games Masters to provide challenges and plot hooks with which to entwine his characters, granting them reasons to return to the source of their power, search out lost places of divine significance or build new temples to spread the worship of their cult.

Whilst this works well in settings where cults are localised, it can pose a problem in campaigns where the characters are expected to travel extensively. Assuming the cult or gods are not omnipresent across the game world, Games Masters can aid theists on long or far-reaching quests in various ways. Some suggestions are:

- The deity presenting the theist with a holy relic which acts as a portable shrine or temple
- The ability to build temporary shrines which work a single time if sanctified with a suitable offering
- Allowing theists to worship at foreign temples which enshrine a similar divine being as their own deity
- Making certain natural locations by default, sacrosanct to their deity (all caves, mephitic hot springs or the sea for instance)

Kara's Saga

Kara, now an acolyte of Myceras, is sent to one of the outlying watch towers which guard the city-state's fertile valley territory, garrisoned by a unit of heavy Meerish infantry. Although she left the city well prepared, several attacks by a strange creature have required Kara to cast many miracles, draining her devotional pool to a single Magic Point.

Fortunately her visit coincides with a cult holy day sacred to Myceras and the watch tower incorporates a sanctified shrine to the god. As the attending representative of the cult, Kara leads the soldiers in formal worship of their patron deity. The Games Master declares that the ceremony will generate a number of Magic Points, which Kara may tap in order to restore part of her devotional pool.

Since the squad numbers less than 100 worshippers, the amount of Magic Points she may harvest from the ceremony is equal to one quarter of Kara's POW or 4 MPs. These she transfers into her devotional pool, replenishing it to 4 MP. This is only half of her potential maximum, but even if she held a second ceremony on the next holy day she cannot increase the current number of pool Magic Points beyond four, limited as she is by the size of her congregation. Kara will need to return to the main temple to gather a greater number of Magic Points, or use an alternative source of power.

Requesting a Miracle

Calling for a miracle is simply a matter of performing the correct exhortation to convince the god to channel its power through or on behalf of its worshipper. Such a request depends on a number of prerequisites.

First the theist must have mastered understanding of miracle being requested, as described earlier under Learning Miracles. Without knowing the correct prayer or exhortation, the worshipper cannot convince his deity to perform the miracle.

Secondly the theist must have the requisite number of Magic Points remaining in the devotional pool he maintains with that deity. If too few remain, or the pool has run dry, the god will no longer listen to any requests made to it. Thus a worshipper should, when possible, take care to perform regular donations to their god.

Thirdly, on the last turn of the exhortation the theist must pass an Exhort skill check. This reveals whether or not the worshipper has performed the ritual request in the correct manner. Failure to perform this correctly can result in the god turning a deaf ear to the supplicant, or worse still, punishing them in some manner.

Cost of Requesting a Miracle

The cost of requesting a miracle depends on both its cult level and the success level of the Exhort skill roll:

- Critical Success: the miracle occurs yet there is no Magic Point cost.
- Success: the caster's devotional pool loses the full Magic Point cost, and the miracle occurs successfully.
- Failure: the miracle does not occur, but no Magic Point is taken from the devotional pool.
- Fumble: the miracle does not occur, and 1 Magic Point is taken from the devotional pool.

Initiate level miracles cost one Magic Point, Acolyte level miracles cost two, and Priest level miracles cost three.

Exhortation Time

Requesting a miracle takes an increasing amount of time depending on the cult level the miracle becomes available at:

- Initiate level miracles take 1 Turn
- Acolyte level miracles take 2 Turns
- Priest level miracles take 3 Turns

If the theist wishes to cast multiple instances of the same miracle with a single exhortation roll, then each additional instance adds an extra turn to the time, and adds its full Magic Point requirement to the final cost.

The Exhort skill check is made on the final turn of the exhortation; the result of the skill check occurring immediately.

Magnitude and Intensity

The potency of miracles is based upon the strength of the relationship between a theist and his god. The more devoted the worshipper, the more power the deity can funnel through them. This not only increases the effect of the miracle, but also makes it more difficult for others to dispel.

Miracles have a default Magnitude and Intensity equal to one tenth of the worshipper's Devotion skill value.

A theist need not apply the entirety of a miracle's Intensity if they wish to limit the effect of the god's magic.

Dispelling a Miracle

Miracles may be dismissed by spells or spirits capable of negating magic. Due to the inherent strength of theist miracles, it usually requires a counterspell of great potency to affect them.

Limitations to Miracles

There are no overt limitations to the concurrent number or potency of miracles a theist can maintain, since in effect their god is doing all of the work for them. The only restrictions occur in the need to return to a cult sanctuary to recharge their devotional pool of Magic Points.

Some miracles may possess an extended duration which can last hours, days or even months. In these cases the size of the theist's devotional pool should be temporarily reduced by the number of Magic Points for each miracle which is still active.

Miracle Descriptions

Every divine miracle is defined by a series of traits explaining how it is used in the game, followed by a description of the spell's precise effects. In most cases the physical and temporal parameters of miracles can be hand waved unless the Games Master wishes to keep detailed track during tactical situations.

Theists need not call forth miracles at their maximum effects if they wish to be more selective.

Area (X)

The miracle affects all targets within a specified radius, described as Metres, Tens of Metres or Kilometres. The defined units are multiplied by the Intensity of the miracle to determine the actual radius. If the miracle lacks the Ranged trait, the effect is centred upon the casting theist or whatever he touches.

Duration (X)

The miracle's effects stay in place for an amount of time defined as either Instant, Minutes, Hours, Days or Months. The defined period is multiplied by the Intensity of the miracle to calculate the actual duration, except of course if the miracle is instantaneous. At the end of this period the miracle vanishes.

Ranged (X)

Ranged miracles may be cast upon targets within a range defined as either Metres or Tens of Metres. The defined units are multiplied by the Intensity of the miracle to determine the actual distance. Miracles which lack the Ranged trait may only be cast on others if they can be touched for the entirety of the exhortation.

Rank

The minimum cult rank the spell is available to. This is a guideline only. Cults of gods which specialise or control a particular sphere of power may offer certain miracles to lower ranking cult members.

Resist (Evade/Endurance/Willpower)

Offensive miracles do not necessarily take effect automatically. Resisting targets may make an Opposed Evade, Endurance or Willpower test (as specified) in order to avoid the effect of the miracle entirely. Note that Resist (Evade) spells require the target to have a Combat Action available in order to throw themselves clear.

Note that some of the following spells can be extremely potent. This is deliberate, and Games Masters who fear abuse should limit the availability of these miracles to antagonistic cults, for which they are primarily designed. No specific guidance is provided for whether certain miracles are restricted to the exhorting theist or can be cast on others; nor whether the recipient must be a member of that cult. Such things must be decided when the cult is designed.

Absorption

Duration (Minutes), Rank Initiate

This miracle absorbs incoming magic aimed at the recipient or his equipment, converting its energy into Magic Points which then replenish his personal Magic Points attribute, assuming there is space for the additional points. Excess Magic Points garnered through Absorption simply vanish. Absorption does not affect spells already in existence, prior to the miracle's manifestation. The effects of Absorption depend on the relative Magnitude of both itself and the incoming spell. Any spell absorbed by this miracle is cancelled, and has no effect.

Absorption Results

Incoming Spell's Magnitude is. . .	*Effect*
Equal to or weaker than Absorption's Magnitude	The incoming spell is absorbed, and Absorption remains.
1 or more points stronger than Absorption's Magnitude	Absorption eliminated, and incoming spell takes effect.

Aegis

Duration (Minutes), Rank Initiate

Creates or augments a shield which glows with the cult symbols of the deity. The magical shield takes the attributes of a Hoplite shield, although its parrying Size depends on the Intensity of the miracle. Intensity 1-2 is a Small shield, 3-4 Medium, 5-6 Large, 7-8 Huge, 9-10 Enormous and 11+ Colossal.

The Aegis is immune to all damage. If cast upon an existent shield, it is protected until the miracle ends.

Awaken

Duration (Minutes), Ranged (Tens of Metres), Rank Priest

Awaken brings part of the god's awareness into its consecrated shrine or temple, enabling the deity to animate its sanctified idol or take control of its sacred animal(s), depending on the nature of the cult. It is normally reserved for cult holy days, except in times of emergency. The embodied god cannot leave the consecrated area, but during that time it can awe its worshippers, express its displeasure or defend its own shrine.

The limits of the miracle depend on what is used for the embodiment. An awakened statue or cult idol can have a combined STR+SIZ of up to ten times the Intensity. This value is used to calculate both the idol's Damage Modifier and its Hit Points per location. Its Armour Points depend upon the material it is constructed from, usually 6 for wooden idols, 8 for hollow metal and 10 for stone. The idol performs all actions at the same value as the caster's Devotion skill, has a Initiative Bonus equal to the Intensity, and one Action Point per four levels of Intensity (or fraction thereof). Other physical attributes should be created based upon the shape and size of the idol (see Default Natural Weapons for Unusually Sized Creatures page 222).

Awakened creatures are handled slightly differently. Like idols the deity may awaken a creature of up to a maximum STR+SIZ of ten times the Intensity of the miracle. However, if the shrine or temple lacks a giant example of the sacred animal, the deity can instead awaken multiple beasts provided their combined total does not exceed the limit set by the Intensity. Other than that the creature or creatures possess their normal Action Points, Damage Modifier, Hit Points, Initiative Bonus and Armour Points. They perform skills at either their base (or trained) value or at the value of the caster's Devotion skill, whichever is higher.

Backlash

Duration (Minutes), Ranged (Metres), Rank Initiate

Backlash makes physical assault upon the recipient extremely dangerous, redirecting an inflicted injury back upon the attacker. The magic only affects wounds that inflict equal or less Hit Points than the Intensity of the miracle – translocating the damage so that it affects the attacker in precisely the same location they struck, ignoring any armour.

This miracle affects both hand to hand and ranged attacks, providing the assailant is within range. Even though the recipient may be near immune to injury, it does not provide immunity to any Special Effect they may have suffered as part of the attack.

Beast Form

Duration (Hours), Ranged (Metres), Rank Acolyte, Resist (Endurance)

This miracle transforms the target and all his personal belongings into an animal that is sacred to the cult. The target retains his INT, CHA and POW scores, but exchanges his STR, DEX, CON and SIZ scores for average values for that of the animal type, and gains a bonus to each physical Characteristic of +1 per point of Intensity. He also gains the natural abilities of the creature. The animal cannot be mystical or magical in any way, and the Games Master should have final say as to what manner of creature would fit a specific cult if it is not obvious.

Behold

Area (Metres), Duration (Minutes), Rank Initiate, Resist (Willpower)

Behold summons a vision of what a fellow cult member of lesser rank is currently experiencing. The image requires some sort of cult related paraphernalia in which to manifest, such as a sacred mirror, pool of pure water or even narcotic smoke rising from a brazier.

The view provided is limited to the defined area, centred upon the target of the miracle, which may permit identification of their location if enough clues are visible. Behold conveys only a single primary sense, which for most cults is a visual image. Some however, depending on the deity in question, use sound or even scent instead; in which case the medium through which the information is transmitted is different.

If the target is either magically protected against scrying by a spell of greater Magnitude, held (or hiding) within the consecrated ground of a different cult, or dead, then the miracle fails. The target of Behold may attempt to resist the miracle if desired.

Berserk

Duration (Minutes), Rank Initiate, Resist (Willpower)

The recipient of Berserk is overcome with bloodlust, causing him to disregard his own safety in exchange for being imbued with tremendous stamina and toughness. For the duration of the miracle the Damage Modifier of the recipient is increased by two steps, the Size of his weapon counts as one step larger for the purpose of penetrating parries, and he is immune to all the detrimental effects of Serious Wounds and Fatigue. A Major wound will still incapacitate him.

In return the subject may not Parry, Evade or cast any magic while under the influence of Berserk. However the berserker automatically succeeds in resisting any Special Effect used against him.

Unwilling recipients receive a chance to resist. Normally, the recipient remains in the Berserk state for the entire duration of the spell, but Games Masters may allow a Berserk character to shake off the effects with an unopposed Willpower test. At the end of the spell, the recipient immediately suffers twice the deferred Fatigue levels they would have lost during the entire combat.

Bind Ghost

Duration (Days), Rank Acolyte, Resist (Willpower)

Bind Ghost takes the soul of a creature or person just slain, and temporarily turns it into a Haunt (see page 150) bound to the place of its death. The miracle is usually performed on animal sacrifices or willing volunteers, but in cases where the victim does not wish to be so bound they are permitted the opportunity to resist.

For the duration of the miracle the ghost must obey commands given to it by the theist. However, the way it performs its duties is guided by the nature or personality of the victim. Once the miracle ends, the soul is freed from all obligations, and permitted to depart to its intended afterlife. The theist is limited to binding souls whose POW is no more than twice the Intensity of the miracle.

Bless Crops

Area (Tens of Metres), Duration (Months), Rank Acolyte

When cast on cultivated farmland this miracle protects the crops within its area against naturally occurring bad weather, blight, and insect infestation, guaranteeing a nominal harvest if the magic is maintained from sowing to harvest. Bless Crops can also provide protection against magical disasters, provided the Magnitude of the adverse magic does not exceed that of the blessing.

Breathe Water

Duration (Hours), Rank Initiate

Breath Water permits the recipient to breathe water (the subject will still be able to breathe air as well) for the duration of the miracle. It also protects against pressure if diving deep below the surface of a lake or the sea. Under the influence of this miracle the recipient can speak and cast magic as normal.

Call Winds

Area (Kilometres), Duration (Hours), Rank Acolyte

This miracle permits the theist to bend the winds to his will. The maximum strength of winds they can unleash depends on their cult rank. Acolytes can control or summon up to Strong Breezes, Priests up to Moderate Gales, and High Priests up to Storms (see Weather page 84). If the caster can control the wind he may reduce it to a complete Calm or change its direction if desired. If two or more weather magics are in contest over control of the winds, the spell or miracle with the greatest Magnitude takes precedence.

Chameleon

Duration (Minutes), Rank Acolyte

This miracle permits the recipient to fade into the background, becoming near invisible to normal observation. However Chameleon is only effective when present in an environment specific to the nature of the cult. The Chameleon miracle provided by a sylvan cult, for example, would only be effective in woods and forests; whereas a thief cult might instead provide Chameleon which works in darkness and shadow.

Whilst the recipient remains motionless, crouched or flattened against the terrain, they cannot be spotted by normal Perception rolls relying on vision. If they move however, the constantly shifting patterns across their body will reveal them to sharp sighted individuals. In these circumstances any attempt to interact with the recipient – whether observing where they go, attacking, parrying, and so on – inflicts a penalty against the observer of one difficulty grade per four points of Intensity. Creatures with other primary senses or observers with magical perceptions are immune to this miracle.

Clear Skies

Area (Kilometres), Duration (Hours), Rank Acolyte

This miracle grants a reprieve from cloudy or overcast weather. Rain dwindles, sweltering humidity is reduced, and dark clouds separate to reveal the sky. The scale of the effect depends on the cult rank of the theist. Acolytes can disperse up to Heavy Cloud cover and Moderate rains, Priests up to Moderately Overcast cloud cover and Very Heavy rains, and High Priests up to Storm Clouds and Deluges (see Weather page 84). Clear Skies cannot alter magically-created weather effects of a greater Magnitude.

Cloud Call

Area (Kilometres), Duration (Hours), Rank Acolyte

This miracle gathers together shreds and wisps of cloud, weaving them together to bring rain, block out the sun or even form concealing fogs. Like Clear Skies the extent of the effect depends on cult rank. Acolytes can create Heavy Cloud cover, Moderate rains or mist, Priests can gather up to Moderately Overcast cloud cover, Very Heavy rains or thick fog, and High Priests up to Storm Clouds, Deluges and Pea-soup fogs (see Weather page 84). Cloud Call cannot alter magically-created weather effects of a greater Magnitude.

Consecrate

Area (Tens of Metres), Duration (Months), Rank Acolyte

Consecrate is vital to the creation of sanctified ground, upon which theists may communicate with their gods. It is usually as fundamental a part of a shrine or temple foundation as its cornerstone, but may actually be cast almost anywhere providing some form of temporary altar or image of the deity is erected prior to the casting. The minimum labour required to create a temporary sanctuary depends on the setting, but it should be significant enough to be considered a major effort; for example an entire day of collecting stones and rocks to form a crude altar. In exceptional circumstances it can be cast on cult artefacts.

The effects of the miracle are many fold. Not only does the consecrated area permit cult worshippers to recharge their Devotional Pool (see page 180), but it also allows for a number of additional cult miracles (up to the consecration's Intensity) to be embedded or bound to the area, extending their duration (or held readiness) to that of the Consecrate.

Kara's Saga

After years of faithful service Kara is promoted to the rank of priest, and granted the opportunity to found a new shrine to Myceras in the newly annexed city of Kopash, a known den of thieves and iniquity. Kara finds a suitable plot of ground in the Mercenaries' Quarter, and has constructed a modest roofed portico, within the walls of which is the cult sanctuary where Myceras's bejewelled golden statue stands, beneath the open sky.

When it is finished Kara holds a dedication ceremony, inviting the worshippers of Myceras to attend. During these rituals she casts Consecrate to sanctify the area. At the same time she decides to bind several other miracles into the consecration in order to protect the shrine. She has the choice of only two spells suitable for the task, Beast Form or Sunspear.

Not wishing to bind up too much of her devotional pool in maintaining the shrine defences, she settles on placing a primed Beast Form (Bull) on the statue, and a Sunspear on the altar; requesting that Myceras cast these miracles if anyone attempts to desecrate the cult objects. This reduces the size of her pool by four points, but Kara predicts the investment will be necessary. Sure enough, the following morning Kara discovers a rather distressed thief transformed into a bull and caught within the shrine precinct; sacrificing this bull to the god sends word that this particular shrine is off limits...

These extra miracles need not come from whoever performs the consecration, but the cult rank of the magic cannot exceed that of the consecrating acolyte or priest. Furthermore, each embedded miracle counts against the devotional pool of whichever theist cast it, until the Consecrate itself expires or, if of Instant duration, the miracle is triggered.

Such is the strength of the divine presence within the sanctified area, that requesting miracles from unaligned gods whilst inside the perimeter of the consecration becomes more difficult. Exhorting the deities of neutral cults suffer one grade of difficulty, whereas those of hostile cults are two grades harder.

Corruption

Duration (Hours), Ranged, Rank Acolyte, Resist (Endurance)

This dire miracle is used as a curse against enemies or those that transgress cult tenets. If the target of the spell fails to resist, they begin to deteriorate physically in a manner suitable to the god. This could be anything from pestilent boils, vegetative outgrowths or even a slow transformation of flesh to sand.

At the end of each hour, the victim must make an unopposed Endurance roll and depending on the success level, suffer the following:

- If the roll is a critical success, the victim takes no damage
- If the roll is successful, the victim sustains 1d3 points of damage to every location
- If the roll fails, the victim sustains 1d6 points of damage to every location
- If the roll is fumbled, the victim dies in a horrific transformation of their body

Those who realise what they have contracted either seek out someone capable of dispelling the curse, or return to the cult temple, begging for forgiveness and premature cessation of the punishment.

Cure Malady

Duration (Instant), Rank Initiate

This miracle cures the effects of any mundane disease or poison afflicting the target; or magical ones whose potency is less than the value of the Devotion skill of the caster. If the recipient is suffering from the possession of a Disease Spirit, the spell exorcises the hostile spirit provided its Intensity does not exceed half the Intensity of the miracle (rounded up). For example, an Intensity 5 Cure Malady can exorcise any Disease Spirit of Intensity 3 or less.

Cure Sense

Duration (Instant), Rank Acolyte

Cure Sense enables the theist to cure a specific type of sensory injury such as deafness, blindness, and so on. The effects of the miracle are permanent.

Dismiss Elemental

Duration (Instant), Ranged (Tens of Metres), Rank Initiate, Resist (Willpower)

Dismiss Elemental may be cast against Gnomes, Salamanders, Shades, Sylphs or Undines. The spell affects an elemental of up to 1 cubic metre in size per point of Intensity. Failure to resist the spell causes the elemental to be dismissed, leaving the material substance of its body in place.

Dismiss Magic

Duration (Instant), Ranged (Tens of Metres), Rank Initiate

Dismiss Magic may be cast against either a general target, or a specific miracle or spell. Dismiss Magic will eliminate a combined Magnitude of spells equal to its own Magnitude. A spell cannot be partially eliminated. When used against a spell of equal or lower Magnitude which normally counters magic (such as Absorption, Spell Resistance or Reflection) then Dismiss Magic takes precedence.

If not aimed at a specific spell, Dismiss Magic starts with the most powerful magic affecting the target. If it fails to eliminate any spell (because the spell's Magnitude is too high), then the miracle ends, and no more spells will be eliminated. Dismiss Magic may be fired defensively to neutralise incoming offensive spells, by using the Counter Spell reactive action.

Earthquake

Area (Tens of Metres), Duration (Instant), Rank Priest, Resist (Evade)

Earthquake causes a ground tremor capable of knocking people from their feet and collapsing rigid buildings. At the very minimum, failing to resist the miracle causes the victim to fall prone. If located within a building, built up area or some vulnerable location (such as a forest or beneath a cliff), failing to evade also indicates that the person is struck, and trapped by falling debris. Use the size of the damage dice in a Contest of Strength (see Brawn) to determine the difficulty of being extracted from the wreckage.

Earthquake Table

Intensity	*Secondary Effects*	*Potential Damage*
1	Suspended objects swing.	None
2	Delicately balanced objects topple.	None
3	Walls and buildings creak.	None
4	Plaster and glass windows crack, trees and other tall objects quiver dramatically.	None
5	Heavy furniture moved, wall mounted objects fall, cracks open in walls.	None
6	Modest buildings of earth, wattle and daub or mud brick partially collapse. Minor branches fall.	1d2 damage to a single location
7	Heavy furniture overturned. Buildings of earth, wattle and daub or mud brick destroyed. Buildings of solid timber or masonry partially collapse. Fall of columns, statuary and boundary walls. Major tree limbs fall.	1d4 damage to a single location
8	Modest buildings collapse. Ground cracks conspicuously, rockfalls from steep slopes. Underground pipes and sewers broken. Wooden bridges collapse. Small trees topple.	1d6 damage to a single location
9	Well constructed buildings collapse. Large scale fortifications, city walls and stone bridges damaged. Ground badly cracked. Landslides and avalanches considerable. Big trees topple.	1d8 damage to two locations
10	Few, if any, structures remain standing. Tunnels and caves collapse. Broad fissures in ground. Huge trees topple.	1d10 damage to three locations
11+	Total destruction, even colossal stone monuments suffer partial collapse. Cliffs and mountain flanks shatter.	1d12 damage to four locations

Elemental Summoning

Duration (Hours), Ranged (Metres), Rank Initiate

This miracle calls up an elemental associated with the cult to assist as a personal guard or servant. For example cults associated with the God of Storms would summon sylphs. The miracle summons an elemental of one cubic metre per point of Intensity in 1d3 Combat Rounds, which remains under the command of the theist for the entire duration but cannot stray further than the range. For obvious reasons, the caster must have access to the same volume of the elemental's material to cast this spell successfully. If less material is available, then the caster can summon a smaller elemental if desired.

Entangle

Duration (Minutes), Ranged (Tens of Metres), Rank Acolyte, Resist (Evade)

Entangle animates natural vegetation so that it lashes about, snagging and gripping the target. The victim must resist the miracle or be held immobile for its entire duration.

Enthrall

Duration (Hours), Rank Initiate

Enthrall increases the recipient's sexual attraction, making all those naturally interested in the recipient friendlier and more focussed upon them – which could be a very good or very bad thing depending on the circumstances. Members of the opposite sex (or those of the same sex that would find the target sexually attractive) who attempt to resist any Influence or Streetwise rolls from the recipient suffer one grade of difficulty. Resisting Seduction attempts are treated as two grades harder.

Excommunicate

Duration (Instant), Ranged (Metres), Rank Priest, Resist (Willpower)

Excommunicate can only be called down upon a worshipper of the caster's cult. It severs the mystical link the worshipper shares with their god, causing the target's devotional pool to be drained of all Magic Points, and permanently removing access to miracles from that cult. Unless the target can make amends for whatever transgression caused the excommunication to be cast in the first place, their cult specific skills of Devotion and Exhort become mere academic knowledge with no power.

Exorcism

Duration (Instant), Rank Acolyte, Resist (Willpower)

By means of this miracle, the theist calls upon their god to drive out a spirit currently possessing a corporeal being. Whether the possession is dominant or covert is immaterial. The magic exorcises spirits with an Intensity of up to half the Intensity of the miracle. What occurs next depends on the attitude and type of spirit, but belligerent ones with the power may be tempted to engage other nearby targets in Spirit Combat. Thus this spell can be potentially dangerous for the caster or his fellows.

Extension

Duration (Special), Rank Priest

Extension lengthens the duration of any miracle with a non-instantaneous duration, for as long as the caster wishes to maintain it. Extension can be cast any time, provided the miracle being extended is still functioning. Other than reducing the theist's devotional pool by several Magic Points (three for Extension, and one or more for the extended miracle) the miracle has no other maintenance requirements; unless the Games Master wishes to add any to match his setting.

Fear

Duration (Minutes), Ranged (Metres), Rank Initiate, Resist (Willpower)

This miracle causes the target to be gripped with overwhelming fear. Targets which fail to resist will flee in terror away from the theist, and avoid engaging in combat unless brought to bay. It has no effect on unconscious targets, targets without an INT or INS Characteristic, or targets that are currently under the effect of another emotion-controlling spell of higher Intensity.

Fecundity

Duration (Months), Rank Acolyte

When cast on a person or creature, Fecundity will – depending on its sex - ensure it will bear or sire offspring the next time it performs a reproductive act. Provided the miracle is maintained for the full term of gestation or pregnancy, the progeny will be born healthy. Fecundity also provides the antenatal young protection against magical curses, provided the Magnitude of the adverse magic does not exceed that of the miracle.

Fortify

Area (Tens of Metres), Duration (Instant), Rank Initiate, Resist (Evade)

Fortify strengthens large scale constructions, making them more resilient to damage from natural disasters, siege weapons, and magical attack. The miracle adds its Intensity to the natural Armour Points of all buildings and walls within its area of effect. Offensive magic which seeks to damage or modify a construction under the protection of Fortify has its Intensity reduced by that of the Fortify miracle.

Growth

Area (Tens of Metres), Duration (Hours), Rank Priest

Growth accelerates the growing speed of vegetation, ageing it by one year for each hour until the miracle concludes. Under its effects, trees and bushes can increase in size and verdure dramatically, although at the cost of wildly sprawling, tangled proliferation of every plant within the area of effect. Repeated use of this miracle can potentially grow a thick forest over what had been open fields a few days previously.

Harmonise

Duration (Minutes), Ranged (Tens of Metres), Rank Initiate, Resist (Willpower)

Harmonise causes the target to do exactly what the theist does. If not resisted the victim must mimic every physical move, albeit in a jerky, almost puppet-like manner. It only works on beings with roughly the same physiology as the caster; with limbs or locations not shared by both participants remaining unaffected by the magic. The miracle only controls gross motor skills, and does not permit control of the victim's speech. Use of this magic can humiliate someone from afar, or perhaps even force them into performing a murderous or suicidal act.

If Harmonise is used to force the subject to attack or defend, the combat style rolls are automatically one grade harder to accomplish owing to the jerky movement of the victim.

Heal Body

Duration (Instant), Rank Acolyte

This powerful miracle instantly heals all Minor and Serious Wounds suffered by the target. Like Heal Wound, this miracle has no effect on Major Wounds save to stabilise the injury, preventing death. To repair maimed or dismembered body locations requires the Rejuvenate miracle.

Heal Mind

Duration (Instant), Rank Acolyte

This miracle removes all madness and mental derangements from a single target. In the case of magically-induced madness, the spell works if its Magnitude is equal to or greater than that of the magical disorder.

Heal Wound

Duration (Instant), Rank Initiate

Heals a single body location back to its full Hit Points, provided the injury is no more severe than a Serious Wound. It has no effect on Major Wounds save for stabilising the injury, preventing death.

Heart Seizure

Duration (Instant), Ranged (Metres), Rank Priest, Resist (Endurance)

Another dreadful miracle known to the darkest gods, whoever suffers this dire magic feels the veritable hand of the deity reach within his chest, squeezing his heart or perhaps tearing it out completely. Those that fail to resist the miracle suffer a fatal heart attack and die instantly. If the resistance roll succeeds, the target still suffers a number of Hit Points damage equal to Intensity of the spell, directly to the location where their heart is contained, normally the chest for humanoids. Creatures without hearts are immune to this miracle.

Different forms of this miracle exist, affecting different organs according to the nature of the deity offering it (Brain Seizure, for example).

Illusion

Area (Metres), Duration (Hours), Rank Initiate, Resist (Special)

Illusion is used to change the sensory projections of an area or single target, making it seem to be something completely different. For example a tiger can be made to look like a harmless cat, sound like it meows when it roars, and feel silky soft instead of coarse wiry fur. The theist can adjust one sensory projection per two points of Intensity. Once set, the illusion can no longer be modified.

The largest target which can be affected must be able to fit within the perimeter of the miracle. Unwilling living targets may resist with Endurance. Observers who interact with the illusion are permitted an opposed Willpower roll against the miracle, in order to resist any debilitating psychosomatic effects it creates, e.g. deafness, pain, nausea. Whilst the illusion itself is incapable of causing harm, the underlying target or area remains as dangerous as it was before the miracle.

Lay to Rest

Duration (Instant), Rank Initiate

This miracle is used to ensure that the soul of a recently killed person or creature reaches a deserving afterlife. Its primary purpose is to prevent angry, possibly coerced victims returning from death as vengeful spirits or reinhabiting their bodies as corporal undead.

Leeching

Area (Tens of Metres), Duration (Minutes), Rank Acolyte

Using the blood of sacrifices scattered over an area, this miracle disrupts the flow of magic which enters the zone, dissipating its power. Within the area all magic, even that of the caster, is suppressed by the Magnitude of the miracle. Any encroaching spell whose Magnitude is reduced to zero is rendered inactive until the target of its effect leaves the area. Spells cast within the region with equal or less Magnitude automatically fail.

Lightning

Duration (Instant), Ranged (Tens of Metres), Rank Initiate, Resist (Evade)

This miracle causes a sizzling bolt of lightning to either streak down from the sky, or be projected from the hand or weapon of the theist, towards the target. If the bolt is not evaded, it will inflict 1d6 damage per two points of Intensity to a random hit location. Natural and worn armour offers no protection against this damage, but magical protection does.

Madness

Duration (Days), Ranged (Metres), Rank Initiate, Resist (Willpower)

This miracle infuses the target with gibbering madness. Targets which fail to resist will rant and rave uncontrollably, performing acts of utter insanity in a manner fitting to their personality, plot line and dramatic circumstances. In general, mad characters should be more harmless distractions than ticking time bombs.

In the case of player characters, until the Madness subsides or is somehow cured, the insane victim should be placed under control of the Games Master unless he deems the player is capable of acting out the insanity.

Mindblast

Duration (Days), Ranged (Metres), Rank Initiate, Resist (Willpower)

This spell blasts the intellect of the victim, obliterating their sapience. If not resisted, the victim's INT is temporarily converted to animalistic INS, removing from them the power of speech, writing or any other form of communication. It also prevents them from utilising equipment and devices. If forced to fight in this condition, the victim will by default use their Unarmed skill. Although prevented from utilising complex thought, it does not limit instinct and base cunning.

Mindlink

Duration (Minutes), Ranged (Tens of Metres), Rank Initiate

This miracle allows mind-to-mind communication, theistic knowledge and devotional pool Magic Points to be shared between participants. Its use is normally restricted to those of the same or closely allied cults, since once the magical link is established; there are no safeguards as to what can be tapped from the participants – all of whom must join the Mindlink willingly.

Mindlink has two main purposes. Either it allows an entire cult hierarchy to support a handful of its priests so that they may cast many miracles, powered by the devotional pools of associates and underlings; or it grants lesser ranked cult members the ability (albeit temporarily) to call forth miracles normally beyond their capability.

Each instance of Mindlink connects a pair of individuals in a two way link. Several castings using the same individual but with different partners will make them the hub of a Mindlink network, able to draw on the resources of each of the partners.

If a mental or emotion-affecting spell is cast at someone participating in a Mindlink, then everyone else directly linked to them must also resist the spell or suffer its consequences. Although participants in a Mindlink share deliberately transmitted thoughts, they remain their own entity, and may sever their connection to the Mindlink by willing it so on their turn, or by leaving the spell's range.

Mirage

Area (Metres), Duration (Minutes), Rank Initiate

Mirage obscures a region, covering it with strange optical illusions, usually via the cult associations of the deity. An earth god might cause clouds of swirling sand which form unsettling faces; whereas a sun deity might infuse the area with blinding, shimmering curtain of light. The effect of this disconcerting obscurement is to conceal precisely what stands within the area, and make ranged attacks extremely difficult. Firing at anyone within the Mirage suffers one difficulty grade per four points of Intensity.

Obliterate

Area (Kilometres), Duration (Instant), Rank Priest, Resist (Willpower)

A dire spell to those who seek fame or remembrance after death, Obliterate removes every record of their existence – scouring it from scrolls, clay tablets, carved hieroglyphs, and every other method of inscribing knowledge. In addition the name of that person is wiped from the mind of everyone within range, save for the casting priest, unless they resist the miracle.

Although this miracle is normally used to expunge the glory of those whose crimes are so unforgivable that they must be forgotten for all time, some darker gods offer this as a means for their worshippers to maintain secretive anonymity.

Pacify

Area (Tens of Meters), Duration (Minutes), Rank Acolyte, Resist (Willpower)

Pacify suppresses aggressive and violent behaviour within its area of effect. Those that fail to resist the miracle are unable to cause harm to another, although they may defend themselves using non-harmful techniques. If unthreatened, those subject to the magic will sheathe or drop weapons, stop belligerent demonstration and cease all arguments. The miracle does not change personal opinion, merely makes it difficult to act in a hostile manner.

Perseverance

Duration (Hours), Rank Initiate

Through this miracle the recipient can channel the strength of his god, becoming inured to the effects of hard labour. Whilst the miracle remains active, the target of this spell will not receive another level of Fatigue, no matter the hardship faced. Perseverance does not grant any additional capability to lift, march or work; it just ensures the recipient will keep on going. This miracle has no effect upon Fatigue lost from asphyxiation or blood loss.

Propitiate

Area (Kilometres), Duration (Weeks), Rank Acolyte

Used by cults who try to appease darker, more hostile deities, Propitiate exchanges regular worship for the agreement to leave a region alone. The precise effect depends on the god being propitiated, but the area affected is centred upon the shrine or temple of that cult. Propitiating a lightning deity for example would not necessarily prevent storms happening within the radius of the miracle, but no serious fires or injuries would occur from lightning strikes. Similarly the tremors of an earthquake god would still be felt in a city, but no buildings would collapse – assuming the propitiations were maintained of course.

Rain of (Substance)

Area (Kilometres), Duration (Minutes), Rank Priest

This miracle summons dark brooding clouds which then begin to rain a particular, and most likely horrible substance with specific relevance to the cult deity, anything from blood to frogs. The miracle is intended to inspire awe or terror rather than inflict direct harm, so the actual things raining down are relatively harmless. A rain of spiders for instance would only produce non-venomous types; a rain of fire would look scary, but as each glowing ember reached the ground it would extinguish. During the event, members of the cult should be treated as having the Intimidate ability (see page 216).

Raise Undead

Duration (Hours), Ranged (Tens of Metres), Rank Acolyte

Raise Undead uses the physical remains of a corpse to create either a skeleton or zombie. The miracle infuses the corpse with part of the deity's own consciousness, so that it can obey commands, and act with a degree of independent intelligence. However, the skill capabilities of the undead automaton are limited to those of the theist who creates them.

The number of corpses which can be raised is equal to the Intensity of the miracle. Each skeleton or zombie also gains a bonus to its STR and CON characteristics, again equal to the Intensity. Thus a theist who exhorted his god to grant him an Intensity 9 Raise Dead, could animate 9 skeletons each with +9 to STR and CON. Only creatures of a SIZ equal or less than the caster's POW can be raised.

For further details on skeletons and zombies, refer to the Creature Chapter.

Reflection

Duration (Minutes), Rank Initiate

This miracle reflects incoming magic aimed at the target or his equipment, redirecting it back at the original caster, depending on their relative Magnitudes. It does not have any effect on spells that are already affecting the target, or spells the theist casts upon himself.

Reflection Results

Incoming Spell's Magnitude is...	Effect
Equal to or weaker than Reflection's Magnitude.	Incoming spell reflected, and Reflection remains.
1 or more points stronger than Reflection's Magnitude.	Reflection eliminated, and incoming spell takes effect.

Rejuvenate

Duration (Special), Rank Priest

This miracle heals a single body location suffering from a Major Wound, no matter whether it has been crushed, mutilated or dismembered. The freshness of the injury affects the time taken for the miracle to complete. Provided the recipient is still alive, and the location was wounded within a number of hours equal to the Intensity of the miracle, then Rejuvenate will heal all the damage instantly.

Beyond this threshold the body part must undergo a more traumatic repair, which takes a number of days equal to the Hit Points lost on the location. If the miracle is allowed to lapse before the regrowth has completed, the location remains maimed and unusable, potentially left at a negative Hit Point level which cannot be cured.

Resurrect

Duration (Instant), Rank Priest, Resist (Special)

This miracle can bring the dead back to life by summoning the spirit of the deceased and persuading it to re-enter its body. For obvious reasons the theist must cast Resurrect upon the corpse, which must possess at a minimum, those body locations vital for life. If the target died due to some lingering disease, poison or magical curse, the ailment must be eliminated first or the miracle will fail.

Resurrection is not guaranteed. The deceased spirit will often have desires which preclude their return to life. The spirit may fear the hardship of their life, the lingering pain of wounds, persistent illnesses, the feebleness of old age or may even piously wish to reach their loved ones in the afterlife. On the other hand a spirit might wish to return from the dead to protect their family, seek vengeance against their killer or complete a holy quest.

To judge the primary motivation of the spirit, work out which of their passions or devotion skills has the highest value. If this indicates that the spirit will be unwilling to return to life, it may attempt to resist the miracle using that particular passion or Devotion skill.

Resurrect must be cast within a number of days equal to the Magnitude of the spell after death, otherwise the miracle automatically fails. A resurrected character returns to life with 1 Hit Point on all extant locations.

Ripen

Area (Metres), Duration (Instant), Rank Initiate

Ripen brings forth a single crop of fruits, tubers, roots, nuts, or seeds from the vegetation within the area of effect. The miracle does not guarantee they are edible since that depends on the plants, but does ensure the crop is at the peak of its ripeness, no matter when during the year the miracle is cast. Ripen cannot cause a plant or tree to give forth more than a single crop annually, so if it is used early during the growing season, the vegetation will spend the remainder of the year recovering.

Sacred Band

Duration (Minutes), Ranged (Tens of Metres), Rank Initiate

When cast upon a group of worshippers the miracle binds the recipients together as a sacred brotherhood, sharing their life force between them. This has little effect until one of their number is wounded, whereupon the surviving brothers spread the effects of the injury between them.

Damage is divided evenly amongst remaining recipients, applied to the same location which was injured. Any Special Effects which occur remain only with the originally wounded band member. Thus in a band of six temple guardians linked by this miracle, if one is wounded in the arm for 8 points of damage – normally a Serious Wound – the damage is instead split so that the original target and one other suffers 2 points in that arm, whilst everyone else in the band suffers 1 point.

The maximum number of brothers who can be bound together in the band cannot exceed the Intensity of the miracle. They must also share the same basic physiology, or the miracle will fail.

The obvious application of the miracle is to augment the physical resilience of a unit of cult warriors in battle. However, it can also be used to strengthen a cult champion whilst the remainder of the pious participants remain safely hidden or out of reach of combat.

Sever Spirit

Duration (Instant), Ranged (Tens of Metres), Rank Priest, Resist (Endurance)

This miracle severs the bond between body and soul, with dire effect. If not resisted, the victim is slain instantly. If however, the victim does throw off the miracle, they still receive 1 point of damage for every 2 levels of Intensity to each Hit Location simultaneously – which may, in some cases, still seriously injure or even kill the victim.

Shield

Duration (Minutes), Rank Initiate

This miracle protects the caster from physical attacks. Each point of Intensity grants the recipient one Armour Point on all hit locations. This protection does not stack on top of worn armour, rather it supplants it in those areas less protected than what the miracle itself provides. In some circumstances, even if the protective value of the Shield is less than the worn armour, it may still ward against certain types of magical damage.

Soul Sight

Duration (Minutes), Rank Initiate

This miracle enables the recipient to see the magical aura of anyone he looks at, enabling him to discern that creature or spirit's current Magic Points, as well as the nature of any active spells, the source of their magic, and any enchanted items the creature is carrying. It also permits the recipient to see into the spirit world, and see beyond any visual illusions which may be concealing a creature's true form – although this may not necessarily be a good thing in certain circumstances.

Spirit Block

Duration (Minutes), Rank Initiate

Spirit Block is a powerful way of preventing the malign influences of spirits. The recipient receives complete protection from spirits with an Intensity of up to half the Intensity of the miracle (rounded up). So an acolyte invoking the spell at an Intensity of 7 could protect themselves from Intensity 4 spirits.

This miracle protects against spiritual assault only. Thus it prevents discorporation, spirit combat, possession, and the like. On the other hand, it provides no warding against the spells of a Haunt or physical attacks of an incorporated Predator Spirit for example.

Spirit Block Effectiveness

Intensity	*Recipient is Safe from Spirits of...*
1-2	Intensity 1
3-4	Intensity 2 or lower
5-6	Intensity 3 or lower
7-8	Intensity 4 or lower
9-10	Intensity 5 or lower
Each +2	+1 Intensity

Steadfast

Area (Metres), Duration (Minutes), Rank Initiate, Resist (Willpower)

Used when facing overwhelming odds or terrifying challenges, this miracle renders those within its area immune to any natural mental or emotional manipulation. Magical attacks which generate a similar effect, such as Fear, Fanaticism, Domination, and the like, must exceed the Magnitude of the miracle to stand a chance of affecting the target.

Sunspear

Duration (Instant), Ranged (Tens of Metres), Rank Acolyte, Resist (Evade)

Sunspear summons a shaft of blazing light down from the sky to blast a single target. If not evaded, the scorching light will burn the victim for 1d6 damage per two points of Intensity in every hit location. Natural and worn armour counts against this damage. This miracle will only function in direct sunlight.

Sureshot

Duration (Minutes), Ranged (Tens of Metres), Rank Initiate

Sureshot magically guides the trajectory of missiles thrown or fired by the recipient so that they almost always hit, no matter the situational modifiers or cover; provided at least some part of the target is visible, and they are within range of both the miracle and the weapon itself. Any failed ranged weapon attack roll is treated as a success instead. Fumbles, normal successes and critical successes remain unaffected. The target of the missile attack can still attempt to Parry or Evade as normal.

Thunderclap

Area (Tens of Metres), Duration (Minutes), Rank Acolyte, Resist (Endurance)

This miracle summons a powerful blast of thunder from the open sky, to smite down foes. All non-cult members must resist the magic. Those who fail are knocked prone by the expanding wall of sound, and struck deaf for the remainder of the miracle. Should anyone fumble the resistance roll against the spell, they are struck permanently deaf. Also, any items of glass or pottery will shatter automatically within the area of the spell.

True (Weapon)

Duration (Minutes), Rank Initiate

True (Weapon) augments the harm the recipient inflicts when wielding a cult-specified close combat weapon. The miracle doubles that type of weapon's damage up to the maximum that the weapon can inflict, and increases its Size by one step for the purpose of overcoming parries. Thus under the effects of a True (Sword) miracle the wielder would roll 1d8 twice for a broadsword, but would not receive more than 8 points. Other bonuses, such as Damage Modifier, are not affected.

Miracles by Cult Rank

Initiate Spells Summary	
Absorption	Lay to Rest
Aegis	Lightning
Backlash	Madness
Behold	Mindblast
Berserk	Mindlink
Breathe Water	Mirage
Cure Malady	Perserverance
Dismiss Elemental	Reflection
Dismiss Magic	Ripen
Elemental Summoning	Sacred Band
Enthrall	Shield
Fear	Soul Sight
Fortify	Spirit Block
Harmonise	Steadfast
Heal Wound	Sureshot
Illusion	True Weapon

Acolyte Spells Summary	
Beast Form	Exorcism
Bind Ghost	Fecundity
Bless Crops	Heal Body
Call Winds	Heal Mind
Chameleon	Leaching
Clear Skies	Pacify
Cloud Call	Propitiate
Consecrate	Raise Undead
Corruption	Sunspear
Cure Sense	Thunderclap
Entangle	

Priest Spells Summary
Awaken
Earthquake
Excommuncation
Extension
Growth
Heart Seizure
Obliterate
Rain of (Substance)
Rejuvenate
Resurrect
Sever Spirit

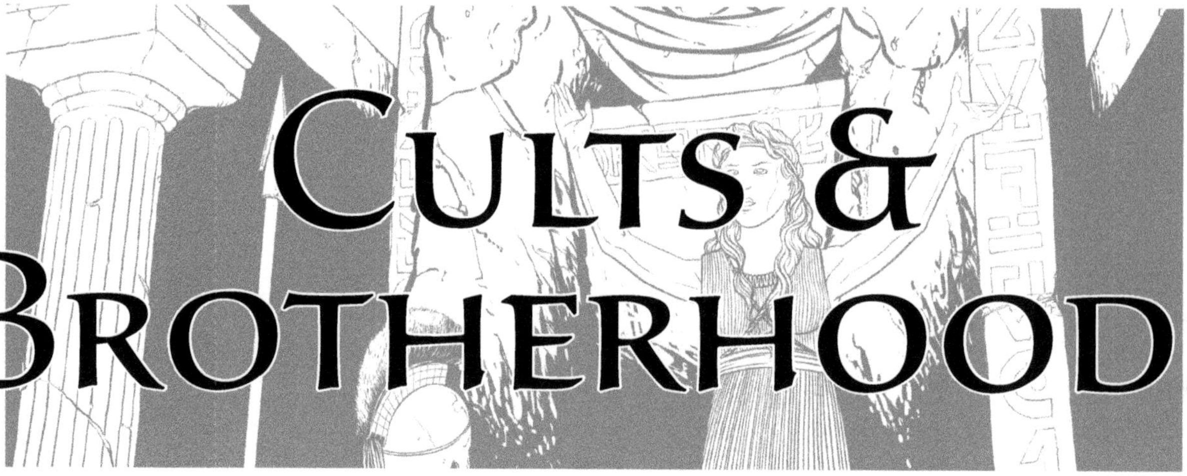

Cults & Brotherhoods

A defining feature of Mythras is its emphasis on membership of a cult – an organisation channelling belief, behaviour and worship – to facilitate community and character progression. As an evolution to this tradition, Brotherhoods have been included, being akin to cults but with an emphasis on professional, rather than religious or magically esoteric, fellowships

Joining a cult or brotherhood depends entirely upon the campaign setting. The Games Master need not include such organisations at all, but to leave them out overlooks their potential as a tool to guide character development, and create bonds of social responsibility, camaraderie and even passions – all of which can be used to craft plots and adventures within the campaign.

If they are to be included Games Masters should weave Cults and Brotherhoods deeply into the cultures of his world. They should be a fundamental aspect of everyday life just as religion, social clubs, and professional guilds still are today. Membership of such organisations mould the opportunities and contacts provided to a character, or conversely block advancement, and colour social opinion of them if they are not members. Thus they can be a powerful tool to hinder or reward characters, and naturally provide a welter of plot twists to a Games Master with little or no effort on his part.

Although the terms are somewhat interchangeable, Cults are organisations which pursue active religious veneration or magical powers as one of their key features; whereas Brotherhoods do not offer magical abilities (unless, of course, one creates a magical brotherhood) but compensate with other facilities and resources focused more on career development.

Nothing prevents membership of several Cults and Brotherhoods, unless they have been specifically denoted as being mutually exclusive in that setting. Both types of organisation add depth and considerable opportunities for roleplaying:, and as we know from the real world, cults, brotherhoods and secret societies abound – a key part of human social development and belonging.

Cults

Cults are organisations which provide a formalised method of worship or the teaching of magic. The nature of a cult is dependent on its focus of veneration. In Mythras this reflects one of the higher magical disciplines: animism, mysticism, sorcery or theism. Animists venerate the spirits and the spirit world; mystics venerate a particular form of teaching which leads to greater understanding and enlightenment; sorcerers venerate the sorcerous principles they practice; theists worship a god or gods hoping to achieve a deeper and more meaningful relationship with their deity.

In most respects all cults work in a similar way. A series of ranks within the cult mark depth of progression, knowledge and achievement. The highest ranks lead and guide the lower ranks, and are party to the cult's most formidable powers and deepest secrets. The lowest ranks generally provide support for the cult in return for mutual support, protection, and sometimes magical aid. Most never bother to advance up the cult ranks, and are happy to stay there, having no aspirations towards personal greatness, but simply seeking a sense of religious or philosophical fulfilment.

- Cults emphasise faith, spiritualism and philosophical practices. They are focused upon the metaphysical.
- Cults offer access to magic, but usually restrict its teaching to more dedicated or professional members of higher rank. However, those of the lowest ranks are normally permitted to petition senior members to cast magic on their behalf.
- Cult membership is very often open to all members of society, but the higher ranks are vocational in their own right. Thus everyone in a tribe might be a member of the common totemic cult, but only those who dedicate themselves to the path of the shaman can progress up the cult ranks.
- Cults often have strictures on how their members demonstrate their veneration, with regular services, rituals, festivals, and the like.
- Cults sometimes have restrictions about how and when they may be joined, and limitations upon later advancement. Membership may be limited to those of a certain age, passing

a particular a rite of passage, being born to a certain caste, and so on.
- Cults are usually an inherent part of communities and cultures, subject to their social restrictions.

Depending on the setting, characters could enrol in more than one cult, assuming the cults are not antipathetic, and that more than a single cult is available to one of their culture, status and profession.

Mystical Orders

Mystical cults seek mystical harmony based on self-discipline, meditation and deep contemplation. They orientate their teachings on philosophical concepts instead of supernatural beings, although they often revere the original source of their learning, be that a god or deified mortal. Thus a mystical cult can be as much of a religion as a theistic cult, albeit the focus being on self-enlightenment or transcendence, rather than direct veneration of any particular entity.

Sorcery Orders

Sorcery cults actively seek to understand, manipulate and control the nature of the universe through research and study. Akin to mystical cults, the order might associate itself with a deity, demon or founder but the personage is not the primary focus of the cult, at least not for the purposes of pursuing magical knowledge. Somewhat more esoteric than other types of cult, sorcery orders are generally modest organisations except in cultures which embrace sorcery in every aspect of life.

Spirit Cults

Spirit cults venerate spirits and natural forces, such as ancestors, nature spirits and elementals. Such spiritualistic worship can take many forms from simple shamanism to exotic types of totemic worship. In many ways spirit cults can be thought of as forerunners of pantheism, but with spirits instead of gods. Spirit traditions can focus on an entire family of similar or related spirit types, or on a powerful patron spirit which provides lesser spirits to its people.

Theist Cults

Theist cults are those which worship a specific god or gods. The number of cults and scope of each depends on the theist culture. Some societies venerate only a single god (monotheism) whilst others venerate a group of deities known as a pantheon (pantheism). Individual gods might be worshipped across many different societies but in different ways. The same Hunter God might be worshipped by barbarian, civilised and nomadic cultures whereas the Trade Goddess is worshipped only by the civilised communities. Cult structures can therefore become quite sophisticated and even complex.

Brotherhoods

Despite the importance of cults to Mythras they will not fit all campaign settings. And even when they do, not all characters want to become cultists. Yet history is scattered with examples of associations and societies, some secret, some not so secret, that fulfil a similar role to cults but offer a different emphasis whilst giving access to very similar resources – primarily support, training, and so on. These organisations are known as 'Brotherhoods' (and, equally, 'Sisterhoods').

Anathaym's Saga

Myceras is the patron god of Meeros. He is the guardian of its defenders, and the strength of its walls, and all citizens of free birth are inducted to his worship when they serve in the city's civic army. Only those who fulfil their military service are permitted to vote, thus the Cult of Myceras holds a position of pre-eminent importance.

As a child Anathaym, watched her father depart to attend the secretive rites and ceremonies of the god. Frustrated, she has been forbidden to accompany him until she receives her first shield, and proves her knowledge of the arts of war on the sands outside the city walls. She longs to serve Myceras as a loyal warrior.

Kara, her sister, on the other hand, was chosen to follow a different path. Called by the god personally to serve as one of the priesthood, she has been invested as an initiate to act as the conduit for Myceras' miraculous powers.

The Scarlet Spears are an elite brotherhood of proven warriors serving the Queen and Temple directly. Meeros's Champion is always drawn from the Scarlet Spears, and to wear their blood-red cloak is to attract the highest respect and honour.

Anathaym, naturally, wants, more than anything, to join the Scarlet Spears as her father once did. She will need to prove herself in battle, and succeed in some great deed in service to the city if she is to have any hope of joining.

Examples of brotherhoods can range from the clandestine support and mutual protection of an organised thieves' guild to the militaristic camaraderie of an elite unit of soldiers. Entry to these brotherhoods often requires some test of worthiness, and demonstration of suitable prowess within the field that the group specialises in. Despite being less metaphysically orientated, many brotherhoods still engage in ritual and follow strict rules of conduct, always alert to those members who'd transgress the rules set up to ensure mutual support, or the respect of the local community.

- Brotherhoods de-emphasise faith and religion. They may figure in the Brotherhood's beliefs but other, more pragmatic values are central.
- Brotherhoods do not offer formalised access to magic. Individual members who are skilled magicians may teach magic to other members, but this is very much an ad hoc affair.
- Brotherhoods are very often vocationally orientated with the aim of supporting members of similar careers, protecting professional interests, and governing prices for services.
- Brotherhoods tend to be less constrained in their ways. Members are not required to attend festivals or rituals for example, and most members go about their daily lives calling on the brotherhood when needed – but duties, save for the direct officers of the Brotherhood – are far less formal than in cults.
- Brotherhoods can generally be joined at any time. Membership is based upon competence or dedication towards an ideal – not a rite of passage.
- Brotherhoods are separate from communities and cultures. Although they operate within them, they transcend community boundaries in ways cults cannot.

Just as cults can have different magical or religious foci, brotherhoods may also come in a variety of organisational structures with very different purposes.

Companies

Companies are groups of people who band together to pursue a particular purpose. By implication companies tend to be small, close knit associations which travel about, or perhaps gather together on a seasonal basis. Examples are exclusive clubs of gentlemen explorers, wandering bands of entertainers, specialist mercenary units or even merchant venturers.

Colleges

Colleges are associations formed by those bound by academic achievement, or by seeking particular avenues of knowledge. Due to their dependence on records, whether memorised, inscribed or written, more formal colleges are often bound to a particular location where the brethren can congregate. Colleges can take the form of monastic scholars serving a great library, travelling bards gathering and passing on news, a secret order of seekers after a lost artefact, and so on.

Gangs

Gangs are localised organisations of small scale, led by the most dominant member and usually self-serving. Most are formed to alleviate boredom, garner a little money or as a means of protection against rival gang persecution. This is not always the case, however. Some gangs form for the purpose of instilling order in societies which lack formal law enforcement, or to ensure respect is paid to local people, businesses or even gods. Examples often take the form of street gangs of adolescent youths, self-elected neighbourhood watches, bands of criminal cutthroats or even informal unions of labourers.

Guilds

Guilds are bodies who regulate the teaching and practice of a particular profession. Fundamentally economic in nature, guilds often establish a stranglehold over all those who would carry on that craft or trade – taking a tithe of each member's earnings in return for protection, market stability, and a formalised recognition of the quality of their products. Guilds often have great reach, spreading across entire nations rather than being limited to a single urban settlement. As such they can have very diverse objectives depending on the craft, for instance a Sea Traders' Guild may have an outpost in every civilised city with a port, whilst a thieves' guild may be limited to operating in a particular ward of a single town.

Regiments

Regiments are military bodies who form an identity based on their prowess, style of fighting, arms and equipment, or even their duty. Their primary purpose is mutual support, ensuring that individual members work together as a team, and providing camaraderie when not on campaign. Regiments are often passionate about their élan or reputation. They can be anything from elite royal bodyguards to mercenary legions feared for their brutality.

Why Join?

Most people are members of a cult or brotherhood, often joining several during their life. The choice of which ones a character should join is dependent upon several things: race, culture and profession. Unless the campaign world is a melting pot of different species rubbing shoulders with one another, humans, for example, will tend to join those Cults and Brotherhoods formed by other humans. Likewise inhabitants of a particular culture will normally only join organisations supported by that culture; and similarly with those who practice specific careers.

The natural choice will be a cult or brotherhood that is related to the biggest part of his upbringing, but it need not be the limited to that. Adventurers are rarely sedentary, and they gain greater exposure to different cultures and viewpoints than most who never leave their home communities. The choice of cult, whether done at character creation or later, through play, raises a few questions that it is worth taking the time to consider:

- How will your character be viewed by your community and peers? Joining an antagonistic or enemy organisation could have profound repercussions for personal safety.
- What Cults and Brotherhoods do your fellow characters belong to? Again, striking a pose that is at odds with those you adventure with could introduce difficulties and tensions that might otherwise be avoided.
- What is your character's goal regarding membership? What sort of relationship and personal power is being sought? All Cults and Brotherhoods offer power of some kind, but there is always a personal cost attached to it: a commitment. Committing to a particular path that one might later come to regret or become disillusioned with could again make life very difficult.
- How far do you intend your character to progress within the organisation? Many characters remain as lay members or novices, but higher standing brings greater power and prestige – always at some cost. To embrace the benefits of higher rank, what are you prepared to sacrifice?

Choosing a cult should not be a knee-jerk choice or one that is seen to offer rapid power with no commitment in the short term. A character ought not to join a war cult simply because he is good with a weapon and likes killing: he should join it if his father was a great warrior, because he wishes to follow a martial profession, and because he wants to ensure that the enemies of his community are defeated.

Players should look carefully at the cult and brotherhoods as they relate to their character's culture, community, background and personal desires. Make the choice based on certain informed decisions. Cults and Brotherhoods, once joined, are more than simply a magical or religious club; they are faiths, and faiths are often vengeful if their principles are ignored or betrayed.

The Games Master is also the ultimate arbiter when it comes to cult and brotherhood choices. He may, quite reasonably, restrict membership only to those who appear both suitable and sincere. If so, then the character must either accept the restrictions or simply choose not to initiate into a cult or brotherhood until later, when more options, determined through actual play, are open to him.

Membership

Characters can join Cults and Brotherhoods in one of two ways:

1. As part of character creation.
2. During game-play, as they learn more about their game world, and the organisations working within it.

Membership is not mandatory – but characters who join a group are likely to have access to certain benefits and resources that non-members will either be denied or find difficult to obtain. Some thought should also be given to the roles these faiths and fraternities play in most societies:

- Individuals usually inherit their parents' and community's beliefs, and are exposed to these attitudes and rituals day-in, day-out throughout their childhood and adolescence. Initiating into a family or community cult is a natural progression, and even desired by many young people.
- Individuals likewise inherit the same profession as their parents, usually working as children to help their father or mother perform their tasks. Thus parents often expect their offspring to follow them into the same career, and thereby brotherhood.
- Cults are very often the basis for community. Not joining or initiating results in social stigma, or even exile or ostracism. Social pressure may be too difficult for some individuals to avoid. Brotherhoods may similarly have a major influence at the family level, perhaps forming a stranglehold on a particular craft or employment, and forbidding non-members from performing that type of work.

As Mythras by default creates characters who are either just entering adulthood or who are young adults, cult membership may therefore be a highly desirable, or an unavoidable, part of character creation.

Membership as Part of Character Creation

During the Careers and Development stages of character creation (see chapter 2) players may opt to initiate into a cult or brotherhood. Joining at the character creation stage offers certain benefits:

- Membership provides immediate context for the character, helping define and identify who he is, what he believes, and where he belongs in the world.
- Having several characters be members of the same or similar organisations, even if they are from different backgrounds and professions, provides a ready-made reason for them to be associating and working together at the start of the game.

Joining a cult or brotherhood during character creation requires no rolls for entry. It is assumed that the initiation forms a natural part of the character's progression from childhood to adulthood.

Mythras divides membership into several levels that reflect dedication or devotion to the organisation. The levels are explained in more detail later in this chapter, but any character who joins a cult or brotherhood during character creation is considered a Common Member with the actual title being based on its nature.

The character has undergone some form of formal initiation, usually as part of the rite of passage from youth to adult, which has created a relationship with the organisation. They follow its principles and general beliefs, but gain no special advantages beyond the support it provides its members.

Characters who start off as professional magicians of a cult are permitted to begin one rank higher, being assumed to have successfully undergone the Initiation Ceremony or ritual associated with the cult. Following the initiation ritual the character undergoes a period of training where he studies with the cult's teachers and elders so that he becomes an active and productive member of the cult. This training is considered part of the overall character creation process. At the end of it the character emerges with the magic skills associated with the cult's nature.

Membership during the Game

Many characters will join a cult or brotherhood during the course of play. They may come across a cult that matches their ideals at that time or find a calling that requires a particular religious or behavioural approach that only a particular kind of organisation can serve.

Joining a cult or brotherhood during play requires a number of things:

1. A demonstration that one is worthy of joining the group.
2. Impressing the organisation's leaders to gain membership.
3. A donation of some kind.

Demonstrations of Worthiness

Such things will vary, but usually the character will need to show that he embodies the same ideals, has similar religious or philosophical beliefs, and understands what the organisation is striving to do. A character may have performed a service for the prospective organisation, or simply acted as a common member for a time (usually a year, but sometimes less), thereby impressing the local leadership. The cult or brotherhood may require a service to be performed – such as a quest or task that confirms the candidate's suitability. Certain background checks may be performed, and a character's reputation assessed.

A character might be asked to renounce a particular mode of behaviour, previous belief or way of life. For example someone who has spent his career as a mercenary and now wants to join a healing cult might be required to foreswear his violent past. Sometimes the choices can be tough, but worthwhile.

This demonstration of worthiness must be quantifiable within the game. That is to say, the character must have done, or will do something, during play, to aptly demonstrate his worthiness. It is usually not enough to have a player say that something has or will be done: one must show, not tell.

Impressing the Examiners

Demonstrations of worthiness must be substantiated. Characters need to convince the cult or brotherhood's leaders of their suitability. Assuming worthiness has been demonstrated, impressing the examiners can be abstracted with a roll against a suitable skill.

For instance, entry into a criminal street gang may require a demonstration of a skill like Stealth, Sleight or Streetwise. If the roll is successful then the examiners have been sufficiently impressed to extend membership. Characters can augment their required roll in the following ways:

- Use of an appropriate Passion.
- Use of an appropriate Communication skill such as Influence, Deceit or Oratory.
- Membership of an allied cult or brotherhood.
- A suitably impressive donation.

Impressing the examiners leads to the character becoming a Common Member of the new cult, irrespective of his station in society or rank in another organisation. From there he can rise in the new group as any other member.

Donations

Usually monetary, but sometimes the presentation of services, goods or property seals the bargain. It shows final commitment to the cult or brotherhood's community, just as the previous demonstrations have proved suitability. It is difficult to quantify how high or substantial a donation should be, and Games Masters will need to weigh up the offering based on other factors. However if the donation is substantial in nature, no matter what form it takes, then Games Masters should make the demonstration of worthiness skill a step easier for the character.

Availability by Culture

The general availability of these cults is suggested in the list of Cultural Background and Cult Types below. However Games Masters should not necessarily feel restricted by this distribution. If, in your campaign, the barbarian culture has a mystical tradition, then allow that type of cult.

Barbarian

Spirit Cult, Theist Cult.

Civilised

Mystical Order, Sorcery Order, Theist Cult.

Nomadic

Spirit Cult, Theist Cult.

Primitive

Spirit Cult.

Progression

Once a character has joined a cult or brotherhood they often seek to rise in the organisation's ranks, in the pursuit of greater respect, reputation or responsibility or simply out of a thirst for knowledge and power. Progression is sometimes limited by the nature of the organisation; cults might only grant access to the higher ranks to those who are professional magicians. Others might slow advancement according to the skills of the character, his completion of a suitably heroic task or even block promotion until a space in the ranks opens up.

Such considerations are, as always, dependent on the campaign setting, and how quickly the Games Master wishes to allow characters to advance. The following guidelines are simply suggestions from which a Games Master can develop his own novel cult or brotherhood structures. For instance the skill requirements of rank can be adjusted to ease progression.

It should always be remembered that just because a character might meet the mechanistic requirements of a particular rank that doesn't automatically grant them the right to achieve it. Promotion within a cult or brotherhood is a very major reward, and should be something strived for by roleplaying. In fact it is encouraged that each advancement is somehow played out as a separate adventure or test to grant further depth to the organisation.

Anathaym's Saga

The preeminent faith in Meeros, those belonging to the Cult of Myceras are granted rights of full citizenship in exchange for being called upon to fill the armoured files of the army in times of war. Since such rights are not hereditary, membership in its exclusive ranks is the most sort after in the city.

Despite this, and other significant benefits, the inability for warriors to progress beyond lay membership rankles with Anathaym as she wants to serve Myceras as fully as she can, and learn the cult's secrets. Kara, who understands these things better than her sister, explains that the priesthood is a Calling. Those who want to progress fully within the cult must give-up their previous lives and careers, dedicating themselves wholly to Myceras.

'You would be forbidden from lifting a spear, drawing a sword or holding a shield,' Kara says, patiently. 'Myceras has chosen you to be one of his warriors; he gave you those talents. Be content with them, and you will find other ways to prosper.'

Reluctantly Anathaym accepts that she would rather be a warrior than a priest, and so sets her sights firmly on joining the Scarlet Spears as soon as she can.

Comparative Rank Titles

Rank	*Theist Cult*	*Animist Cult*	*Sorcery Order*	*Mystical Order*	*Brotherhood*
Common	Lay Member	Follower	Novice	Aspirant	Associate
Dedicated	Initiate	Spirit Worshipper	Apprentice	Student	Apprentice
Proven	Acolyte	Shaman	Adept	Disciple	Journeyman
Overseer	Priest	High Shaman	Mage	Master	Master
Leader	High Priest	Spirit Lord	Arch Mage	Sage	Grand Master

Ranks

Most Cults and Brotherhoods are arranged in a pyramidal hierarchy. Common members form the base of the pyramid, and are the most numerous members of the organisation. These are regarded as part time supporters, affiliate members or retired comrades who may associate in any number of cults or brotherhoods, provided it is done as part of their spare time.

Higher ranks represent professional members of the organisation, working or being educated full time under its edicts. Numbers diminish as one advances up through the ranks until a handful of individuals, or even only one, occupy the upper echelons. Promotion brings greater privilege, prestige, learning, and sometimes magic or other benefits. The heroes, movers and shakers generally fill the highest ranks with the devoted, yet relatively inactive, faithful forming the lower tiers.

Different Cults and Brotherhoods have different names for their ranks. The Comparative Rank table shows the default rank names arranged by each organisation's type and the membership level. Rank names can vary according to setting, but the above suggestions are included for ease of reference to the magic chapters.

A description of each rank follows, outlining their place in the hierarchy, requirements, duties, benefits and magic.

Common

The first step in joining a cult or brotherhood is to become a common member. A character can belong to several organisations as a common member, provided they do not have conflicting purposes or are diametrically opposed. The vast majority of members of any organisation are common members; casual practitioners or worshippers who follow doctrine, and attend regular meetings and ceremonies, depending on its nature.

Common rank reflects the type of folks who are faithful worshippers of a religion, rarely called up levies of a city guard, subscribing members of the beggars' guild, and so on. In effect they are those who have a level of part time commitment to a cult or brotherhood whilst engaged in a different career.

Requirements

Common members must have at least a basic understanding of the beliefs of the organisation, and make a small donation (of time or money) each time they visit the cult's shrine or temple or to pay brotherhood dues.

Duties

Common members have few duties. They are expected to attend important celebrations, festivals or meetings specific to the organisation, but need not attend every one provided they maintain some minimal commitment.

For example Lay Members of a theistic cult would partake in special high Holy Day celebrations, but unless they are aiming to rise in the ranks of the cult, they will not be expected to attend regular ceremonies.

Privileges

Common members will be able to find tutors for any skills the cult teaches. However they must still pay the normal training or tuition rates for a tutor's services. They may seek the aid of the organisation for protection, support, sanctuary, and consultation for personal problems.

Magic

Common members of cults are rarely taught magic, although much depends on the setting. Instead common members have the right to request magic be performed on their behalf, for a suitable donation.

Most cults will be reticent to perform such magics for non-members, as the cult's resources will often be stretched just to satisfy their own brethren, although the purpose or the cult may influence this.

Dedicated

This is the start of the inner membership of the cult or brotherhood, requiring the member to commit themselves fully to serve the organisation. Much of this time is spent performing the drudge work required to keep the organisation running, or at least that which cannot be given over to common members. In addition the dedicated member is expected to learn and practice those skills which the cult or brotherhood deems important.

Since this rank represents the lowest level of professional commitment to a cult or brotherhood, it is difficult for a character to be a dedicated member of more than one organisation at a time, except for closely related or mutually supporting organisations. It should denote those studying for proficiency in a career, such as a neophyte sorcerer enrolled at a university, a low ranking legionary training his martial skills or a young cutpurse learning the arts of thievery at his guild.

Requirements

Dedicated members will have their knowledge and abilities tested to determine their sincerity and eligibility. To be adopted by the cult or brotherhood the character must know at least five of the cult's skills at 50% or more.

Duties

Characters are expected to work or study full time unless specifically sent off to perform tasks or adventures. If possible they must also attend all ceremonies, festivals or meetings.

Anathaym's Saga

As a Lay Member of the cult, Anathaym is expected to attend a few key religious celebrations each year. The praising of Myceras defeating Yethis the demon-snake, which coincides with the founding of the city; and the annual purification of weapons at the beginning and end of the campaign season. Additionally she is required to answer any summons to muster the army whether to attack an enemy or defend the city.

In exchange for her oaths, Anathaym is granted access to tuition in any of the city's civic combat styles, free repair of her arms and armour if broken in the service of Myceras, and the right to sleep on the floor of any shrine or temple of the god.

Last, but by no means least, lay members are permitted to request cult miracles to be cast on their behalf – for as many silvers as foes they cut down under its blessing. A few folk magic spells are also available to any warrior who wishes to learn the skill, but the costs and efforts are significant enough that few partake in the opportunity provided by the priesthood.

Privileges

Dedicated members receive communal bed and board at temples, guild halls, garrisons or wherever their organisation is located. Some also offer a small income depending on whether they provide goods or services as part of their membership. In addition they are provided access to trainers, but do not have to pay full rates for such tuition.

Magic

Dedicated members are eligible to learn the magic taught by that cult.

Proven

Few members of a cult or brotherhood will rise to the position of Proven, a rank that requires dedication and service but where the inner secrets of the organisation begin to be revealed. With the rank comes a degree of independence and responsibility; proven members are given some authority over lower ranks, be that organising the daily duties, command of troops or the education of novices. On the other hand a proven member regains a degree of liberty and can utilise whatever free time they have to engage their own pursuits.

Proven members are often sent off to new locales or encouraged to travel to finish off their schooling. Examples of characters of this rank would be journeyman craftsmen, mercenary sergeants or shrine attendants.

Requirements

Proven members must have been a dedicated member of the cult or brotherhood for a minimum of three years, and must know at least four cult skills at 70% or better. A valuable gift or service must be rendered to the cult, to demonstrate devotion and loyalty.

Duties

Proven members are expected to take charge of the management and education of lower ranking members. They must also attend all ceremonies, services, and meetings essential to the organisation; and to be active in expanding the cult's membership and influence.

Privileges

Proven members may requisition equipment and materials necessary for cult or brotherhood business. They can also commandeer lower ranks to provide any necessary support.

In addition they are paid a stipend suitable to their status, and provided with their own personal chambers in whatever settlement or building they are stationed.

Magic

As for dedicated members, but with access to certain rank restricted abilities.

Overseer

The most senior members of each cult congregation or brotherhood order, overseers are those schooled in its deepest secrets and procedures. Their primary responsibilities are to arrange the bureaucratic or metaphysical running of the local organisation, giving orders to lower ranking members. Whilst most of their time is taken up with these duties, overseers are provided with a greater degree of autonomy, and may formulate their own plans, providing they do not contradict the requirements or objectives of the organisation.

Overseers are often the superiors of their assigned branch or temple, subdividing responsibilities between themselves if the organisation is particularly large. Members of this rank are akin to military captains, guild masters or the head shaman of a tribe. A temple priest for example, would look after an entire congregation and place of worship.

Requirements

Overseers must have been proven members of the cult or brotherhood for a minimum of five years, and must know at least three cult skills at 90% or better.

Kratos' Saga

Kratos has reached the pinnacle of his power, quite literally the right hand claw of Yethis the demon lord. His efforts have recreated the Order of the Stygian Path, a sorcerous cult which spreads the potent, yet foul black magic taught by the diabolical serpent. Most of the cult members are his centaurs, augmented by numbers of ophidians, and even a gorgon. Few of them have minds capable of comprehending the arts of sorcery, so they remain common members who partake in the ritual sacrifices to the demon lord.

A handful of the ophidians however take to the teachings of the Stygian Path, and these he mercilessly corrupts with the dark knowledge of their progenitor. After many years Kratos achieves the title and rank of Arch Mage by the grace of his demonic mentor. As a reward the demon promises to teach the arch mage a secret ritual which will invest the sorcerer with part of Yethis's own power, making him both Immortal and Invulnerable to weapons.

To prepare himself for the ritual of gift giving, Kratos takes ever increasing amounts of mind expanding lotus dust to create the necessary conduit through which he must receive the diabolical gift. When the time comes, Kratos gathers together the entire cult, and begins a three day ritual to open a portal to Yethis in the underworld. The ceremony involves much debauchery and sacrifice, but at its climax something goes dreadfully wrong.

As the wards imprisoning the demon lord sunder, Kratos belatedly realises he has been tricked, and is a mere tool which Yethis has used to gain his own freedom. The sorcerer screams as he is possessed by the demon, his skin turning scaly, and eyes to burning slits, whilst a thick tail slowly grows from under his robes. All prostrate themselves before the demon lord, who bellows in triumph, and slaps the ground with his serpent tail with the sound of a thunderclap. Far away in Meeros the earth trembles...

Duties
Overseers are expected to lead all of the important ceremonies, services and meetings of the organisation. They act as administrators, being responsible for both finances and any political manoeuvrings required to maintain the status (and authority) of the organisation.

Privileges
Overseers may demand any of the resources available to their branch of the organisation. They can also commandeer any or all of the lower ranked members or congregation to provide support for their plans. However unless these are used to further the organisation as a whole, abuse of this power can lead to an alienation from the brethren. If desired overseers can draw on the cult or brotherhood's funds to pay themselves a high wage, and are provided with the best living quarters available.

Magic
Overseers gain full access to all magic available to that organisation.

Leader
The autocrats, spiritual heads and heroes of cults or brotherhoods, leaders are masters of everything the cult stands for, and guide its future. When trouble threatens the organisation, it is they who will fight for its survival and prosperity; not necessarily by arming themselves with weapons, and calling upon the greatest magic, but more often by Machiavellian manipulation – laying down long term strategies and sending out prominent, or perhaps expendable, members to enact their plans.

Reaching the lofty pinnacles of this rank places the entire cult or brotherhood into their hands to do with as they will. Leaders are often charismatic commanders of legions, holy patriarchs of a national religion or skulking arch sorcerers working to overthrow kingdoms from the shadows. Although the rank implies singular authority, many organisations may possess more than one who form a council, such as a secret conclave of master thieves whom control a thieves' guild from behind the scenes.

Requirements
Leaders must have been overseers for a minimum of least ten years, and must have at least two cult skills at 110% or better. They must also have performed an invaluable service for the cult or brotherhood, worthy of recognition as a future guide or custodian; or they must remove the previous leader by whatever means necessary to seize his power.

Duties
Leaders are effectively free to pursue any course of action they desire, provided that the overseers beneath them are suitably schooled and able to function independently of direct management. Most attempt to advance the standing, reach and power of the organisation, but others become drawn to seeking out further magical secrets, deeper enlightenment or even transcendence to divinity.

Privileges
Leaders may utilise the entire resources and personnel of the cult or brotherhood in any way they desire. They may even attempt to change the very precepts of the organisation, corrupting or evolving its nature.

Magic
Cult leaders may try to master new powers or abilities of surpassing potency, beyond the nominal scope of the cult; at a significant risk of bringing doom or disaster if their attempt fails.

Benefits
The following section further emphasises the benefits of joining a cult or brotherhood. These are only suggestions and guidelines which should be used to encourage imaginative design.

Training
Common members of an organisation are offered training but must pay for the pleasure. Although this may not sound like a benefit, it may be the case that the cult or brotherhood are the only ones who offer tuition in that particular field, especially when it comes to professional skills.

Higher ranks are offered training as a matter of course, since it is partly their purpose to ensure their members are well skilled in the areas the cult or brotherhood holds dear. This training may or may not be 'free' but is likely to have been paid for by the member's parents or guardian if enrolled as a youth, or maintenance costs covered by duties the member performs under the auspices of the organisation.

The level and competence of trainers and teachers depend entirely on the size and presence of the organisation, but since training is one of the major advantages of being a cult or brotherhood member, Games Masters should not be too restrictive about providing access to such aid.

As a rule of thumb, use the following to determine training discounts based on rank:

Rank	*Training Discount*
Common	0%
Dedicated	25%
Proven	50%
Overseer	75%
Leader	100%

Protection
Members of a cult or brotherhood can expect to be protected by that organisation, provided of course the character has not transgressed any rules of membership (see Taboos and Geasa below). The type of protection offered depends entirely on what the character is threatened with.

Physical protection or protection against arrest may be as simple as seeking sanctuary at the nearest shrine or holy place, provided of course that those pursuing him are forbidden to enter such sanctums. On the other hand a member may request somebody be assigned to act as a personal guardian. For instance a retired member of a Military Brotherhood whose standing may have lapsed to that of a common member, could reasonably request protection from his old regiment which – out of esprit de corps – assigns a couple of soldiers to go and deal with the problem.

Shelter can also take the form of legal or political protection, the organisation using its standing to discourage active persecution of its members.

Material Aid

Members may also benefit from material aid provided by their cult or brotherhood. Food and lodging has previously been mentioned as a privilege, but this is not the only assistance which can be given. An organisation may provide those who join them full time with the tools of their trade, a newly admitted warrior into a mercenary company might be provided with a set of basic armour and weapons, for example, or someone joining the carpenters guild as an apprentice be given woodworking tools.

Some organisations endow their members with a small wage in addition to bed and board. Such stipends are usually modest at the lower ranks, but can provide a great deal of wealth at upper levels. Much depends on donations provided by common members, payments the organisation collects from undertaking commissions and any supplementary tithes it receives from land ownership or taxation powers granted it.

Material aid need not be limited to only full time members. A lay member of a theistic religion might request support from his cult in times of personal misfortune. Such assistance could take the shape of a simple charitable gift to help them over a brief period of financial difficulty, up to something as significant as calling his religious brethren together to rebuild the member's home if it were destroyed in an earthquake.

Other financial and materialistic benefits are limitless in scope. Trade deals, political support during elections, physical attendance during sickness, funeral services, and so on. In historical and fantasy settings where the concept of communal welfare is completely alien, Cults and Brotherhoods are the only source of this vital support.

Social Status

A more abstract reward of membership is that of social status. Any benefit this provides is purely dependent on the standing or the cult or brotherhood in the local community. A member of a mercenary company, for example, may gain little status, being regarded as barely more than scum by the inhabitants of a city, although he might still be treated with wary respect; whereas a member of the masons' guild could expect deferential treatment, and invitations to exclusive society functions.

Much depends on how important the organisation is in that culture. Wealth, religious standing, political influence, popular opinion and dangerousness all play an important role in its determination.

Magic

Although specifically restricted to cults, the provision of magic is already documented in the previous rank descriptions and examples given in each magical discipline chapter. Yet the fundamental concept of magic availability should be considered further.

By default Mythras assumes that only those who progress above the rank of Common Member are permitted access to the skills of magic casting. This has been adopted to enable the creation of faiths which don't automatically provide magical powers to all of their brethren. Yet there is nothing to stop a Games Master from doing exactly this, if he desires to create a particularly magical setting.

In such cases joining cults should be confined to particular professions, or that type of magic may lose its exclusivity. In those cases where a cult offers more than a single type of magic, Games Masters could grant training in the 'lesser' magic to common members whilst reserving the 'higher' magics to those of more advanced rank.

Conversely Games Masters may restrict access to magic to higher ranks, and indeed it is recommended that more potent spells, miracles, spirits and talents be withheld to specific membership levels, so that a character must prove himself for years before gaining knowledge of those powerful abilities.

Gifts

Gifts are secret teachings provided to those who advance far enough in a cult or brotherhood to be trusted with their knowledge. The nature of a gift can be either magical or mundane according to the wishes of the Games Master and the setting. They are often, although not exclusively, restricted to those of highest rank.

These Gifts vary hugely from organisation to organisation. Some offer them and some do not. Gifts can take the form of treasures, relics, unique spells, lost knowledge, and even special powers granted by extra dimensional entities. Those blessed with their possession are expected to use these Gifts to further the cult or brotherhood's aims: abusing them can lead to their removal, and possibly other sanctions against the miscreant.

Whilst Gifts depend very much on the type of organisation, some examples, with their game effects, are provided below. These are not exhaustive nor prescriptive: Games Masters may invent others to suit the nature of the campaign.

A Gift is reward for loyalty, service and commitment: it is not a power gained simply for attaining a certain level. It is up to the Games Master to decide whether a character has proven his worth to the higher echelons – granting the Gift as an unforeseen reward – or to provide the opportunity to gain such powers in game, dependent on the successful completion of a challenging quest or service. A selection of sample Gifts are given on page 202.

Gifts can work in one of several ways:

1. The Gift works simply when called upon.
2. The Gift costs 1 Magic Point to invoke. It may cost more, depending on the nature of the Gift.
3. The Gift requires a successful roll to invoke. The roll used depends on the nature of the cult. For Theists the roll would be against Devotion. For Sorcerers, against Shaping. For Animists, against Trance. For Mystics, against Meditation.
4. The Gift requires a roll, *and* an expenditure of Magic Points.

The method of managing Gifts depends very much on campaign style. Heroic campaigns might have Gifts working simply when called to do so. More gritty, realistic play would call for either Magic Points or a roll. A low-magic campaign might require a roll, and Magic Point expenditure. Choose in advance how Gifts will be managed to so that characters' expectations when pursuing and receiving a Gift are also managed.

Divine Intervention

Theist cults may benefit from Divine Intervention – that is, the god intervening directly in mortal affairs, usually in response to a prayer from a beloved worshipper. No god is ever compelled to intervene, and intervention may only be staged if the god has some stake in the outcome. Neither can the form of intervention be dictated or controlled by the plaintiff: a god cannot be *compelled* to smite a priest's foes with hails of fire or to pummel a coastal town with a tidal wave. The god (and therefore the Games Master) always decides how it will intervene and to what extent. The intervention may be obvious and crude, or inconspicuous and subtle. Much depends on the god, its nature, its motives, and what it is intervening for.

To invoke Divine Intervention involves the following:

- The plaintiff must be an active member of a theist cult and be of Priest or High Priest rank.
- The plaintiff must not have made a call for intervention within the last month.
- The plaintiff must have an active Devotional Pool (i.e., there must be Magic Points within it).
- The plaintiff makes a Hard Devotion roll, if a High Priest, or a Formidable Devotion roll, if a priest. Success indicates that the god has heard the plea, and will respond in a way decided by the Games Master but in keeping with the god's nature and power.
- The help provided by the god results in the plaintiff's Devotion skill being *reduced* by 1d4+1%.

The availability of Divine Intervention is dependent on the setting. In traditional Swords and Sorcery stories the gods are distant, often uncaring and unwilling to intervene on behalf of their supplicants; in High Fantasy settings intervention may be more common.

Restrictions

Joining a cult or brotherhood is more than simply passing a test and then carrying-on as before, reaping the rewards of membership. There are restrictions involved in maintaining the necessary faith, dedication or bonds of loyalty to the principles held by the cult or brotherhood. Some organisations deliberately embrace these restrictions in order to make membership challenging or exclusive.

The usual methods used to ensure that only the most dedicated and faithful join the ranks of an organisation are those of oaths, superstitions, taboos and geasa. Games Masters are encouraged to use a variety of these, not only establishing each cult and brotherhood with its own unique feel, but also granting some interesting aspects to roleplaying one of their membership.

Some organisations may only have one or two restrictions to become, and remain, a member. Others might possess more draconian constraints, forcing new restrictions with each increase of rank. In history there are examples of priests tied up with so many highly proscriptive edicts that they could barely leave their own homes or temples for fear of transgressing some rule!

Oaths

Belonging to a cult or brotherhood requires loyalty. Failing in that loyalty results in repercussions ranging from rebuke to death, depending on the nature of the group and the degree of infraction. Loyalty is pledged in the form of an Oath.

An oath is more than just a promise to abide by the organisation's rules. It is a pledge of allegiance and commitment on a par with making a lifelong devotion to a god, which in some cases is exactly what is occurring. The oath itself does not accord any special powers or provide access to magic. What it does is bind the swearer to the brethren, and is viewed as a deep and sacrosanct commitment. Throughout history and across all types of societies, oaths are taken very seriously: breaking such an oath is an extremely serious matter.

Sample Gifts

Gift	Effect
Abstinence	Exist without one requirement for life, for example air, food, water, sleep.
Alacrity	The character rolls 1d6+6, rather than 1d10, for Initiative.
Animal Familiar	The recipient receives the companionship of a natural animal. The familiar obeys simple commands but will not go against its nature. The animal's Average SIZ cannot exceed the character's POW.
Change Gender	The character changes from male to female or vice-versa. All characteristics and skills remain the same but the voice and physical functions of the new sex are gained.
Chaotic Blessing	Roll once on the Chaos features table on pages 275 to 276.
Cult Evolution	The character can add a new spell, miracle, spirit or talent to the cult's magical tradition.
Elemental	Gain an elemental helper which may be called once per adventure.
Eternal Life	The recipient will not die of natural causes during the lifetime of the gift, although they are still vulnerable to death through violence.
Healthy	The character's Healing Rate is doubled.
Insightful	The character is immediately aware of the enemies of the cult and those who would directly harm him.
Invulnerability	Character is invulnerable to damage from one specified source: weapons, falling, poison, fire or something similar.
Lucky	When rolling for any skill test, the character can choose which way to read the d100 result. For example, a roll of 90 could be read as 09. Note: if double digits, such as 00, 11, 22, and so forth, are rolled, the result cannot be reinterpreted.
Mighty	The character's Damage Modifier is recalculated, based on the sum of STR, SIZ and POW.
Oracle	The recipient is capable of appraising, with reasonable accuracy, the likely fate of someone he meets. He does not gain a detailed view of the future, but gains a general impression as to whether the individual will be prosperous, lead a full life, die peacefully, and so on.
Polyglot	The character can understand any language spoken to him – but not read or write it.
Perfection	Raise a characteristic by 1d6 up to the species maximum.
Resilience	The character can endure any pain. He never needs to check Endurance to prevent unconsciousness when wounded, and is immune to torture.
Resurrect Loved One	A loved one or favoured companion is brought back from death. This Gift can only be applied to each individual once.
Sanctuary	The character is gifted a special residence that is always safe from the cult's enemies. This residence is usually no larger than a villa, and can take many forms (a tower, a small cave complex, and so on). Enemies of the cult – but not necessarily of the character – cannot pass the sanctuary's threshold.
Reincarnation	If killed then the character's soul is reborn in the body of a suitable creature 1d6 days after death.
Resurrection	If killed then the character rises from the dead 1d6 days after death, their body completely healed of any and all damage done to it.
Robust	The character's Hit Points are recalculated, based on the sum of CON, SIZ and POW.
Sagacity	Raise one cult skill to 100%.
Sense Parallels	Aware of weaknesses in the fabric of reality. Can spot gates and portals to other planes of existence on a successful Perception roll.
Summon	Some cults have a specific creature from the Creatures chapter that can be summoned, acting much like a familiar. This gift allows one creature of the particular type mentioned to be summoned once per adventure. The creature performs one specific action, as directed by the character, and then departs.
Swiftness	The character gains one additional Combat Action.
Weapon	The character is gifted a weapon of the cult. The weapon is always of a special nature, be it magical (having enhanced damage, or enhancing a Combat Style), unbreakable, or having a particular effect against certain cult enemies. Games Masters will need to define the details.
Wellspring	Magic Points are regenerated at twice the usual rate.
Youth	Return to a young body, reversing all ageing effects.

New members swear their oath when joining the cult or brotherhood. Details vary, but at the very least an oath encompasses:

- Loyalty to the organisation
- Loyalty to its membership
- A promise to abide by its rules
- A promise to uphold it values
- A promise to protect its ideals
- A promise to act in the group's best interests – putting them before personal ones
- A promise to keep the cult or brotherhood's secrets safe

Failing in any one of these commitments results in a breaking of the oath. Obviously some situations occur where there is no option and, if the oath-breaker can prove to his peers that not breaking the oath would have resulted in much greater misfortune or detriment for the group, then his position may be viewed with leniency.

Oaths are a type of Passion, and calculated as described on page 22 of the Culture and Community chapter: 30% plus the character's POW+INT.

The oath is used in the following circumstances:

Tough Choices

If a character is forced into a choice that would mean breaking his Oath, he must make two rolls: one for his Oath, and one for his Willpower. If his Oath roll wins the contest then the character abides by his oath – taking whatever consequences come with it. If his Willpower prevails then he has summoned the reserves necessary to break his Oath, and must similarly deal with whatever repercussions that might have – if the organisation discovers the transgression.

If Willpower beats Oath in this way, the value of the Oath is reduced by 1d4+1%: if a character finds he can ignore his Oath once, ignoring it in the future is likely to become easier.

Proving Integrity

If a character finds himself in a situation where he needs to prove his integrity, he can use his Oath in one of the following ways:

- To augment his Influence (or skill appropriate to the circumstances) thereby gaining a bonus.
- To use his Oath directly to prove his integrity beyond doubt: 'As a sworn member of the Guild of Merchant Sailors, you have my word that we shall carry your cargo safely…'

The Oath can be opposed by Willpower, Insight or another, appropriate skill depending on the circumstances. Much depends of course on how that particular organisation is viewed by those the character is interacting with.

Group Standing

The value of the Oath is unconsciously reflected in a character's conduct and carriage when dealing with his peers. In this way the value of the Oath can be used comparatively to distinguish between members of the same cult or brotherhood. Two mercenaries, for example, equally skilled and loyal but vying for a position of trust with their Captain, can compare Oath values. The higher Oath value is more likely to gain favour or sway opinion than the lower. People who take their oaths seriously, and are committed to them have a natural way of reflecting their commitment through body language, emotional signals, and so forth.

Anathaym's Saga

The Cult of Myceras has several oaths, taboos and superstitions which unite its members. To join the cult Anathaym must swear an oath to protect the city of Meeros with her life, and never betray the temple, its priests or her brother worshippers.

In addition cult members are forbidden the following: to leave the battlefield with their backs to an enemy; to go to war or fight whilst rain falls from the sky; and to eat the flesh of a bull without casting its heart and loins on a fire in offering to the god first.

As a lay member she also learns of the superstitions which her brethren stridently believe in, these being: never pass a bull without praising the strength of Myceras, else suffer ill fortune; warriors should wear a helm crested with bull tail bristles, which grants the wearer tenacity; and, just as a bull urinates before charging, a warrior should do the same before battle.

It is not necessary for a character to have an Oath score of a particular value to advance in rank. Oaths are held personally, and it is perfectly possible for someone with a shallow belief in their Oath to advance much further in the organisation than someone who is deeply committed. Indeed, those traitors and potential Oath-breakers driven by ambition might reasonably gain positions of high trust in their cult or brotherhood.

Oaths beyond Membership

Oaths need not– and indeed should not – be confined to joining Cults and Brotherhoods. Oaths can be sworn to lords, masters, and even other characters. The rules work in exactly the same way, and represent the same thing. Remember though that Oaths are a very big, very serious undertaking. Being Oath-Bound represents an obligation to the holder of the Oath. It comes with responsibilities and consequences. It binds two people together. An Oath can over-ride casual responsibilities, friendships and relationships. A character may loathe her queen, for example: but she is Oath-Bound to serve and protect her.

A character can only be absolved from an Oath if the Oath-Holder decides to relieve the obligation. This is dependent on many circumstances but absolving an Oath tends to happen when:

- *A particular obligation or debt has been fulfilled.*
- *Circumstances are such that absolving the Oath is the best way forward.*
- *The Oath-Holder's trust in the Oath or the Oath-Bound has diminished to such a point that the Oath is now meaningless.*
- *The Oath-Holder dies (although remember that some Oaths are sworn to a position rather than an individual: the hated queen's passing does not absolve her servants' oaths to the crown).*

Generally the Oath-Bound cannot force the absolution of an Oath. They might suggest it if the conditions are appropriate, but the accepted convention is that an Oath remains in force until its holder decides to absolve it.

Superstitions

Just about every culture is superstitious, but religions and professions usually have their own peculiar beliefs. Superstitions take many forms, and are usually associated with avoiding bad luck (rather than encouraging good luck). These simple acts prevent one from becoming prematurely noticed by fate, or the supernatural being which overlooks or haunts that particular organisation. A few examples of typical cult superstitions are as follows:

- *Never bid farewell on a bridge (if you want to see the other person alive again).*
- *Seeing a single crow is very unlucky; seeing a single hooded crow signals war is close by.*
- *Placing on a corselet before attaching your greaves will bring death very close.*
- *Burning beef bones when making broth brings a bad harvest and poor hunting.*
- *Malice and envy are to be feared when sparks jump out of the fire.*
- *If thirteen people sit down to dine, the last to rise will meet with ill fortune.*
- *If a bad omen is observed, spit to avoid bad luck, and touch a piece of iron.*

In developing a cult or brotherhood, consider what superstitions will be associated with it. Some might be hidden wisdom whilst others can be odd quirks. Bear in mind the nature of the cult, and the nature of the society or culture of its members. Primitive cults are likely to be more superstitious than civilised ones, but that is by no means a hard and fast rule. All cults maintain distinct peculiarities that most, if not all, members will observe.

It is up to the Games Master to decide whether bad luck will actually occur if the character ignores a superstition. This can take effect by the application of unexplained skill penalties at odd moments, or strange twists of fate causing events to backfire against the blasé character.

Taboos

Taboos are things that are *not* done, both as a matter of cult tradition and as a way of avoiding bad fortune. Usually breaking a taboo is considered as bringing bad fortune on the whole cult or community, and not just oneself. Some typical taboos are:

- Arson
- Cowardice
- Defiling an artefact of the cult
- Eating human flesh
- Heterosexuality
- Homosexuality
- Killing animals sacred to the cult
- Killing innocents
- Looting
- Lying
- Making independent peace with a blood feud enemy
- Marrying
- Murdering outside of a blood feud
- Necrophilia
- Paedophilia
- Rape
- Speaking to a member of a different species or opposite sex
- Theft within the cult
- Torture
- Treachery to the cult
- Worshipping false/foreign gods (indeed, worshipping any gods)

Breaking a taboo usually involves a punishment – a trial or quest, for instance but also by the accepting of a Geas (see below). Punishments can run the full gamut: ostracism to torture to execution. The severity of the punishment reflects the depth of the taboo, and how it reflects on the cult, the society and its members.

Geasa

A geas is an obligation which is often used as a curse or a method of imparting heroic power. If a cult or brotherhood member under a geas violates their taboo, the infractor will suffer dishonour or even death. On the other hand, observing of one's geas is believed to bring power and good luck. In traditional mythology, a hero's doom comes about due to violation of the geas, either by accident, or by having multiple geasa, and then being placed in a position where they have no option but to violate one in order to maintain another.

Generally a cult or brotherhood only possesses geasa which reflect the nature and purpose of the organisation. These are an inherent part of the group's myth and history, explaining its reason for being. A character who breaks his geas, whether consciously or unwittingly, is deprived of all Luck Points from that moment on. Some Games Masters may wish to allow each geas to provide a counterbalancing power (see Gifts page 201). This too is lost if the geas is ever broken.

A geas can be used to reinforce a social condition, such as a vow of chastity or being forbidden to eat meat on festival days. It may also be more perilous, compelling the cultist to act in a way contrary to clan or individual norms in order to atone for some previous crime. It is up to the Games Master to decide how geasa are used in his setting, if at all. Sample geasa include:

- Never use a sword in battle
- Take a vow of permanent silence
- Accept no healing from wounds inflicted in battle
- Wear no armour
- Drink no alcohol
- Take a permanent vow of chastity
- Become a direct slave of the chief or an elder
- Accept exile from the clan, and make no attempt to join another
- Quest into enemy lands and kill X enemies
- Live outdoors permanently, never accepting shelter
- Eat no meat – offer all meat given to the ancestors or clan chief
- Eat no vegetables - offer all vegetables given to the ancestors or clan chief
- Never utter a single lie
- Seek-out and start a blood feud
- Journey to holy place, and remain there in the god's sight for nine days and nights

Anathaym's Saga

In a rash moment of anger Anathaym strikes her rival, Xenos, when he makes an inappropriate remark about her sister. She breaks Xenos' nose, but unfortunately does so in view of several cult Elders. As Xenos is also a lay member of Myceras the Elders deem Anathaym's infraction serious enough to earn her a geas (Xenos, of course, has embellished his side of the story shamelessly, casting himself as the victim of an unprovoked assault). She is ordered to venture into the baleful Forests of Sykei, in search of the lost Crown of Meera, the first Queen of Meeros. The crown is said to be magical, and is one of the Lost Treasures of Meeros. If she survives the task and succeeds then her geas will be lifted, and she may even be feted by her cult. If she fails, she is unlikely to survive. As she leaves the Temple of Myceras she sees the smirking Xenos, and decides that she will succeed in her geas at any cost, and extract a far more subtle revenge on the arrogant nobleman.

Other Aspects

The Cults and Brotherhoods described in this chapter are very rudimentary. Games Masters will need to develop their own details depending on their Mythras campaign setting. Mythras supplements will no doubt offer fully detailed cults for use in games. Often the fine detail of a cult is not necessary – to begin with characters simply need to know the bare bones, so below are some general tips on providing a little more cult development.

- Organisations usually reflect a real-world need: a profession, a way of life, a philosophy. Look to fill these gaps.
- Not all organisations are large. Many are local cults or brotherhoods revering a local nature spirit, a small, forgotten god or a hero known in a particular region.
- Organisations provide meaning. Meaning is usually conveyed through myths, codes, rituals and taboos. Spend some time thinking about these facets as part of developing a cult. Remember that each one explains things in its own ways. There is no single truth.
- Organisations celebrate ceremonial and holy days. At least one day will mark the founding of the cult or brotherhood, and one will mark another major point of importance, reflecting a key myth or deed (such as the martyrdom of a prophet or the greatest victory of a hero). Decide where in your game calendar these official celebrations will appear and their importance to members of different ranks.
- What are the ceremonies for the organisation? Are they formal and highly ritualised such as a ritual offering at a temple or are they loosely structured and simple in approach, like a street party hosted by a guild? Do different celebrations require different ceremonies? Be as vague or as detailed as you wish, but assemble some notes on what ceremonies usually require, using myths, history, and other elements to determine what they consist of.
- Where is the organisation's home? This might be obvious, if the group is local to a small community, but large organisations generally have a base of focus, where the major temple, guild house or secretive retreat is located.
- What happens to those who stray from the cult or brotherhood's path, betray its ideals or attempt to leave? Are magical or secular punishments enforced? What is the greatest consequence which can occur – exile, death or killing of the transgressor's entire family? Is there no sanction at all? Consider the organisation's nature, and outline the punishments, if any, for going against its ideals.
- What gifts, if any, are offered to the highest members of the organisation? Look at the nature and role of the organisation, and select gifts accordingly. Will members of brotherhoods gain supernatural gifts in the form of items? Will the organisation have access to more than one type of gift? Look at the list on page 202 to help you decide what should be specific to the group you're developing.

For further guidance on rounding out organisations, see Cults and Brotherhoods in the Campaign on page 290.

Cult and Brotherhood Centres

Most organisations have a base of some form. This might be as simple as a sacred clearing in an ancient forest where the spirits are most accessible, a remote mountain fortress where a military regiment retires after the campaign season, or something far more elaborate such as a grand temple built at the heart of a city. Depending on their size and spread of their membership, Cults and Brotherhoods may have many properties or holy sites distributed across the world; although only one of these is considered the heart of the organisation.

The nature of these cult centres is related to the organisation to which it belongs, taking almost any form and appearance the Games Master can imagine. Temples, shrines, groves, monasteries, guild houses, palaces, labyrinths, sanctuaries, fortresses, libraries, bastions,

Anathaym's Saga

The cult of Myceras focuses on the rushing flow of the battlefield, inner strength and the purifying light of the sun. Anathaym must choose which of these aspects of Myceras she will follow. She decides on motion since her focus up till now has been her athletic fitness, prowess with weapons, and knowledge of tactics and strategy. As a Lay Member she is permitted to display Myceras's holy symbol of movement openly, and so has it inscribed on the breastplate of her armour. She wants to have the glyph painted on her shield, but this tradition is reserved only for those who have performed certain services on behalf of the god, and so she must wait.

necropolises, schools... the list is endless, as are the locations they can be found in. Not all such centres are buildings or static locations. Some can be wandering or mobile places such as floating sky-cities, drifting raft temples or even the insides of gargantuan, living creatures.

Since there are so many permutations some rough guidelines are provided to describing the staffing and membership of these places. Games Masters are encouraged to add further detail about the organisational structure and additional facilities.

Temples

Temples are sacred places dedicated to one or more demons, gods or even spirits. A temple might have several smaller shrines within its confines, dedicated to other entities of the same pantheon or different aspects of the same being. Temples vary in size but usually have a retinue of staff responsible for the temple's upkeep, and attending to the needs of the faithful – as well as presiding over the ceremonies conducted there.

Every temple is considered sacrosanct, and is protected by spells of the appropriate magical discipline which are maintained by the higher ranked members. Theist temples, for instance, are protected with Consecrate spells since they are important for the regaining of Theist miracles, and this holy ground helps establish the relationship with the god necessary for magical energy to be channelled and replenished. They can also be places of healing, training, and sanctuary. The table below can be used to quickly determine the status, composition and facilities of a temple if one is needed in hurry.

If needing a temple dedicated to the worship of spirits, perhaps venerating dead ancestors or infamous heroes, then simply exchange rank titles and magical skills with those of practicing animists.

Shrines

Shrines are not nearly as organised as temples. They tend to be found near to places closely associated with the object of veneration, and so can be found for both Theist and Animist traditions. Most shrines have somewhere suited to either meditation or contemplation but are unsuited to large ceremonies that must be held outdoors (if the shrine is, indeed, large enough to be considered a building). Shrines, if Theist, are protected by Consecrate spells, and Animist shrines are likely to be protected by a patron spirit. Only larger shrines have a permanent custodian. Most lack anything but the most basic facilities.

Monasteries and Schools

Sorcery and Mystical Orders tend to have monasteries or schools instead of temples (although the faculty might also provide a shrine as part of their facilities). The emphasis is more on study and contemplation than on worship. Protection, at least in the case of sorcery orders, is provided by their diverse range of enchanted spells.

Otherwise monasteries and schools have quite similar compositions to temples: use the Temple table provided earlier to determine the composition of the educational facility, but use triple the number of staff. All monasteries and schools offer training facilities, libraries, extensive dormitories and even infirmaries. Stabling will depend on the building's location.

Rather than drawing large numbers of worshippers on particular holy days, monasteries and schools will have a number of Common Members, equal to five times the number of officers in residence, who act as servants, pilgrims, students, and so on.

Sample Organisations

The following are more fully detailed examples of some cults. Games Masters can use them as they are, changing names as needed, or more appropriately, use them as a guide for purpose-developed organisations in their own games. Each follows the same structure which can be used as a template for developing bespoke cults or brotherhoods.

Name

The name and, sometimes, names, by which the organisation is known.

Mythos and History

How the organisation came to be.

Nature

What the organisation represents; its place in society, and what it seeks to achieve. Also listed here is how the organisation views, and treats apostate members.

Organisation

The organisation's administration, distribution, celebrations or holy days, important sites, and so on.

Membership

The membership requirements for the organisation. If listed as Standard, then the default rank Requirements, Duties and Privileges as detailed on page 195 onwards of this chapter are used.

Restrictions

The oaths, superstitions, and taboos of the organisation, where applicable, are detailed here.

Skills

Skills held important by the organisation, which it both teaches, and form part of its rank requirements. The skills essential for cult membership are listed in italics. Any skills that are taught as an extra benefit are listed in normal type.

Magic

Specific to cults, this lists the magical disciplines and those spells, miracles, spirits and talents available to the organisation.

Gifts

Gifts offered to the organisation's members (usually only those of high rank).

Allies and Enemies

If an organisation has any specific alliances (or antipathies) with another cult or brotherhood, they will be listed here, along with any specific benefits and hindrances these bring.

Temple Facilities

	Minor Temple	*Modest Temple*	*Major Temple*
Usual Staff	1d3+3	1d6+9	2d6+12
Cult Rank and Cult Skill Levels	1d3 x Initiates: Devotion (Deity), Exhort (Deity), and three other cult skills at 50+1d10% 1d2 x Acolytes: As Initiates but with Devotion (Deity), Exhort (Deity), and two other cult skills at 70+1d10% 1 x Priest: As Acolytes but with Devotion (Deity), Exhort (Deity), and one other cult skill at 90+1d10%	1d4+4 x Initiates: Devotion (Deity), Exhort (Deity), and three other cult skills at 50+1d10% 1d3+2 x Acolytes: As Initiates but with Devotion (Deity), Exhort (Deity), and two other cult skills at 70+1d10% 1d2 x Priests: As Acolytes but with Devotion (Deity), Exhort (Deity), and one other cult skill at 90+1d10%	1d6+6 x Initiates: Devotion (Deity), Exhort (Deity), and three other cult skills at 50+1d10% 1d4+3 x Acolytes: As Initiates but with Devotion (Deity), Exhort (Deity), and two other cult skills at 70+1d10% 1d3+1 x Priests: As Acolytes but with Devotion (Deity), Exhort (Deity), and one other cult skill at 90+1d10% 1 x High Priest: As Priests but with Devotion (Deity), Exhort (Deity) at 110+1d10%
Shrines	1d3	1d3+1	1d6+2
Training Facilities?	Yes	Yes	Yes
Library	50% chance, but small (10+1d20 scrolls or books)	Yes, medium (50+2d20 scrolls or books)	Yes, large (100+2d100 scrolls or books)
Lodgings	No	Yes – 2d3 beds	Yes – 1d6+15 beds
Stables	Yes – 1d4 mounts or livestock	Yes – 1d6+6 mounts or livestock	Yes – 2d6+12 mounts or livestock

Shrine Facilities

	Minor Shrine	*Modest Shrine*	*Major Shrine*
Usual Staff	0	0 or 1	1d3+1
Cult Rank and Cult Skill Levels	None	Acolyte: Devotion (Deity), Exhort (Deity), and two other cult skills at 70+1d10% OR Shaman: Binding, Trance, and two other cult skills at 70+1d10%	1d3 x Acolytes: As Initiates but with Devotion (Deity), Exhort (Deity), and two other cult skills at 70+1d10% 1 x Priest: As Acolytes but with Devotion (Deity), Exhort (Deity), and one other cult skill at 90+1d10% OR 1d3 x Shamans: Binding, Trance, and two other cult skills at 70+1d10%, 1 x High Shaman: As Shamans but with Binding, Trance, and one other cult skill at 90+1d10%
Shrines	Simple marker or sacred object	Small building or medium sized sacred area (glade, stone circle, etc)	Medium sized building, or large sacred area (including a medicine lodge, stone circle temple, death house, etc
Training Facilities?	No	No	Yes
Library	No	No	1d3 sheltered areas for sleeping
Lodgings	No	Yes – 1d3 beds	Yes – 1d3+3 beds
Stables	No	No	Yes – 1d3 mounts or livestock

Ancestor Worship (Animist Cult)

Mythos and History

When those dear to the tribe leave this world they go to the Great Spirit Caves where all the ancestors live and have lived, right back to the time of the first men who made the tribe. Here the ancestors hunt, weave, and feast, never go hungry, defeat all their enemies, and watch over the Land of the Living and the great tribe, offering their wisdom and protection. To enter the Great Spirit Caves is an honour, and those who venerate the ancestors and heed their omens are guaranteed a place at the fire, a spear in the Great Hunt, and fine cuts of meat from the kill.

Nature

The Ancestors are spirits of wisdom, hunting, weaving, and survival. They continue in death as they did in life but are free from suffering, injury and disease. Through the ancestors the animal spirits can also be called and summoned by the shamans because the Ancestors are the masters of all animal spirits. The Ancestors provide guidance through omens, signs and portents. Their wisdom is in the trees, the streams, the animals, the birds and the heavens. When the moon blocks the sun, that is the Ancestor's sign for impending war. When the locusts come that is the Ancestors' sign for famine. The Ancestors speak through nature and greatest of all the Ancestors are Grandfather and Grandmother who gave life to the tribe, and taught it its ways: how to hunt; how to make fire; how to birth children, and how to weave.

Organisation

The shamans of the tribe speak directly with the Ancestors, and call upon the animal spirits through them. Grandfather's Day is the shortest day of the year, and Grandmother's the longest. There are many holy places, such as the lightning tree on the lonely hill, and the plunge-pool at the base of the waterfall. Here the Ancestors can be heard most clearly by the shaman, although they can also be heard when the shaman make their great circle of ashes, and perform the Parents' Dance or the Hunting Dance. As the shamans speak with the Ancestors, so they are held holy: without them, the Ancestors will speak only through the signs and omens, and the animal spirits will not come.

Membership

Standard. All males and females reaching the age of twelve initiate into the cult. Males must spend three days and three nights in the wilds, and survive, whilst the hunters hunt them. If caught, they must spend the next year living as a female before they can attempt the Hunt again, and so become men.

Restrictions

- When the moon obscures the sun, war is coming.
- Killing an enemy when one becomes a Man shows greatness and purpose to the Ancestors.
- Never kill a shaman; to do so is to be denied a place in the Great Spirit Caves and to bring doom to the tribe.

Skills

Binding, Dance, Insight, Lore (Ancestors), Perception, Sing, Trance.

Magic

Animism: can summon Ancestor spirits, Guardian spirits, and when necessary create Haunts. Shaman of the cult are allowed to take a fetch.

Gifts

High Shamans gain the Gift of Abstinence. They can do without one of the necessities all others need for survival.

Allies and Enemies

None.

Dervishes of the Open Sands (Mysticism Cult)

Mythos and History

According to oral tradition, the Dervishes of the Open Sands have always haunted the deserts. Nobody remembers who the first mystic was, nor does it matter to them. The sands are always open to those who wish to locate the truths behind reality, by suffering their heat, blindness, and scouring winds.

Why the cult exists is unknown. Its purpose is is equally obscure. Those that cannot endure their loss, despair or self disgust, and who wander into the deserts will always find a path to their acceptant salvation from the Dervishes.

Nature

The dervishes embrace the concepts of freedom, masochism, and physical self mastery. They exist only in the dry hot places of the world, unconsciously drawn to the punishing environment which acts as a path to burn away their mortal sorrows and guilt, purifying the soul so that higher truths can be comprehended.

Find a lone dervish, and he will be a paragon of kindliness and hospitality, sharing what few possessions he has. But gather them together, and they become a force for destructive chastisement. Their numbers never congregate save when they storm out of their desert sanctuaries to perform an act of historical significance; obliterating those who stray from the path of virtue and right-thinking.

Organisation

The Dervishes of the Open Sands have no formal organisation. They simply wander the deserts, alone, leading a life of extreme asceticism. Most of their time is spent gazing at the sun in deep meditation, purifying their soul with its burning light. Soon they become blind which releases them from distraction so that they can truly perceive the world about them. Much of their time is spent in dance, which aids them to think at a higher level. Those who achieve enlightenment often dance their way across the sands when they travel.

Since their fundamental philosophy is based on freedom of movement, the dervishes build no shrines or temples. The entire desert is their sanctuary, whose tribulations are the scourge that frees their mind from their body. When someone enters their realm (mistakenly or not), they are often found by a dervish a short while before death. The dervish will adopt the dying man as an aspirant if they feel that person is ready to undertake the journey of self discovery. However, since all dervishes adopt the penance of silence it requires some effort on the supplicant's part to comprehend what the dervish is offering them.

Often a dervish will pass on their adopted aspirant to a mystic of higher insight, so that he may learn a few more steps on the dervish path to wisdom. Although no formal hierarchy is acknowledged, cult rank is used to demonstrate a level of enlightenment, and more respect is given by cult members to a mystic of higher achievement.

The cult celebrates no particular holy days as such trivialities are beneath consideration.

Membership

Standard. Only those who deliberately seek their death in the desert, or lone travellers who accidentally stray into its wilder regions, are approached by a dervish and given the chance to live. This is as prosaic as following the dervish to the nearest source of food or water, which the dervish himself may not need. There are no age or race limits to those adopted into the cult, only the will to learn the obscure habits and practices of their guardian. To achieve the rank of Student and above, the mystic must render themselves blind by staring at the sun.

Restrictions

There are few formalised restrictions save that cult members are forbidden to harm one another, personal possessions should be given to others more in need of them, and that speaking is forbidden.

Skills

Dance, Endurance, Evade, Meditation, Mysticism (Dervish of the Open Sands), Perception, Survival.

Magic

Mysticism: Augment Endurance, Invoke Dark Sight, Invoke Denial (Food), Invoke Denial (Water), Invoke Indomitable, Invoke Life Sense, Enhance Fatigue.

Gifts

Gifts are gained according to cult rank. Dervishes who achieve the rank of Disciple receive the gift of Robust, those ranked Master receive Invulnerability to Fire/Heat, whilst the few who reach Sage receive Oracle.

Allies and Enemies

Dervishes are both disliked and feared by all who live on the borders of the deserts. Since the mystics restrict their travels to the deepest, most remote areas it is rare that they encounter civilisation. When they do, dervishes are accorded no civility or service: in fact if the mystic appears vulnerable they will be actively persecuted.

The Lich Way (Sorcery Cult)

Mythos and History

Arunis-Sul discovered the spells that master death, and created the tome called, in the common tongue, Ways of the Lich. As his own time in the world came to an end his followers performed the Lich Rite just as Arunis-Sul had formulated it, and so Arunis-Sul did not die but became Arunis-Mort, the Lich Lord. The skin withered on his bones, and his innards fell through his bowels, but he continued in un-life, and continues still, high in the towers of the Black Fortress, served by his unloving army, and commanding all the creatures of the night.

Nature

Those sorcerers who would also command the undead and become un-living, like Arunis-Mort, join the order of the Lich Way, and study the Invocations penned by Arunis-Sul. This is a cult of necromancers and death-cheaters; those who seek to prolong their existence beyond its physical limits, and to control the very nature of death itself. The cult is hated because it takes the recently dead and makes slaves of them: zombies and skeletal servants. Its adherents commune with vampires and demons, practice foul rites including human sacrifice, and prey upon the innocent and unwitting. The cult's nature is corruption, and Arunis-Mort continues to rule over his own creation as the Lich Lord supreme.

Organisation

Arunis-Mort controls the cult from the Black Fortress. This immense edifice of basalt and bone contains his army of the un-living, and many vile fiends from the depths of hell. The Lich Lord is the ultimate arch mage but the other high ranking members of the cult, the Mages and Champions, serve him directly and go forth to do his bidding, and train the adepts of the cult. In time Arunis-Mort intends to create a kingdom of the un-living, and then an empire, corrupting all life as it goes. For this reason the order's members are secretive and solitary, never speaking of their true beliefs. However all initiates of the order are required to seek out the Black Fortress and prostrate themselves before Arunis-Mort. Only then will they be shown the secrets of the Ways of the Lich and, upon achieving Mage status, be taught the Lich Rite so they too will cheat death.

Membership

Standard. Sorcerers who join the order must pledge secrecy and discretion. Failure to maintain either results in the miscreant being hunted by one of the six vampire lords Arunis-Mort commands, and being made a slave in the Black Fortress for eternity.

Restrictions

See Gifts below.

Skills

Deceit, Invocation (Way of the Lich), Lore (Arunis-Mort), Shaping, Willpower.

Magic

Sorcery: Abjure (Decay), Animate (Bone), Dominate (Undead), Enchant, Sculpt (Corpse), Revivify, Sense (Death), Undeath.

Gifts

Upon reaching the rank of Adept, sorcerers of the cult are brought to the Black Fortress and permitted to take one of the following gifts: Eternal Life, Invulnerability, and Mighty, but only in exchange for being cursed with a dire Geas worded to support Arunis-Mort or complete one of his myriad plans. With each increase in rank the sorcerer may take one of the remaining gifts, eventually turning the sorcerer into an immortal, un-living monstrosity.

Allies and Enemies

All are enemies of this diabolical cult. None are allies.

Myceras (Theist Cult)

Mythos and History

In the ancient days when men were but children, a great serpent came to the land and consumed everything. The children were hungry and scared. Darkness came with the serpent and plunged all into night. Then, one day, as Araxis the First Tender watched his herd of cows and bulls, one of the bulls spoke to him. 'Make a sacrifice to the sun, and all shall be restored.' So Araxis led his finest heifer to the foot of the Great Plateau, and made it an offering. Then the stars began to fall as spears, their bright tails dismissing the darkness. From the heavens was a thunderous bellow, and as Araxis watched a vast, bull headed giant came down from the sky, its body wreathed in flame. The serpent rose up to challenge the bull god, but as they wrestled the bright countenance of Myceras burned the serpent and thus defeated, he bound the beast within a tomb imprisoned in shackles of eternal fire. With this, the sun returned to the world.

Myceras taught the people of the hills how to use the sling, and spear. He taught them the arts of war, and how to raise their herds so none would ever be hungry again. He taught them the ways of the beasts, and how to farm them and care for them. Finally he showed them how to make the Army so that the serpent and its followers could be challenged. So was Myceras born and returned to the world.

Nature

Myceras is a diverse cult. He is both the God of War, the God of Farmers and Herders, and the protector God of the city of Meeros. He teaches his followers never to be still and never to be compliant. He teaches bravery and fearlessness in the face of the enemy, and brings the truth that the herd is the centre of all community.

His different aspects are represented as a minotaur as the God of War, as a pure bull as the God of the Herd, and as a flame-wreathed man as the Lord of Light and Fire.

Organisation

The Cult of Myceras is based on a formal priesthood that leads all ceremonies and rituals. The Great Temple of Myceras is the central place of worship although many smaller temples and shrines are found throughout the land, each dedicated to one or two of his aspects. The sacrifice of cows is common: any pure-white heifer born in a herd is marked as a bride of Myceras, and sacrificed on the mid-summer eve in the Fesitival of Light which marks Myceras' return to the world.

Membership

Standard. Only warriors are permitted to become lay members although this is not compulsory. Initiates and above must abandon the pursuit of arms, and be dedicated wholly to Myceras's service as one of his priesthood, a path sometimes taken by retiring soldiers.

Restrictions

- Never leave the battlefield with your back to an enemy
- Never go to war or fight whilst rain falls from the sky
- Never eat the flesh of a bull without casting its heart and loins on a fire as an offering to Myceras

Skills

Brawn, Devotion, Endurance, Exhort, Lore (Herding), Unarmed, Meerish Infantry Combat Style.

Magic

Lay Members with an aptitude for Folk Magic may learn up to three appropriate Folk Magic spells. The cult teaches Bladesharp, Coordination and Might. Initiates gain access to the skills of Theism, and can pray for miracles.

Miracles offered are Beast Form, Berserk, Clear Skies, Consecrate, Fortify, Sacred Band, Shield and Sunspear.

Gifts

Those who show true and selfless dedication to the cult, whatever their rank, are gifted with Robust. High Priests are gifted with either Oracle for those who wish to retire to a life of ascetic contemplation, or Summon for more active cult leaders. This latter gift calls forth a divine bull which acts as a bodyguard and mount for the fortunate recipient. Treat as an Aurochs.

Allies and Enemies

The Serpent God Yethis is the traditional enemy of Myceras. The cult considers all ophidians as enemies, as well as those who learn sorcery.

In addition, cults which fail to show proper subservience to Myceras are also considered enemies, and by association those cities which dare to host them.

Example Organisations

The following tables provide a rough selection of many different types of cult or brotherhood which can be easily modified to fit into a campaign setting. They have not been designed with any sense of game balance, only to illustrate particular themes which should be fleshed out as with the previous examples.

These cults are useful as off-the-cuff references if an organisation is needed in a hurry (to identify likely skills offered for training, and a subset of likely magic to select from).

Brotherhoods

Brotherhood Type	Standard Skills	Professional Skills
Alchemical Society	Insight, Perception, Willpower	Lore (Alchemy), Lore (Minerals)
Astrological/Astronomical Fellowship	Insight, Perception	Lore (Astrology), Lore (Astronomy), Lore (Mathematics)
College/University Alumni	Customs, Influence, Willpower	Lore (Any Two)
Criminal Fraternity	Conceal, Deceit, Endurance	Disguise, Sleight
Masons	Endurance, Insight, Locale	Craft (Masonry), Engineering
Mercenary Company	Athletics, Evade, Two Combat Styles	Lore (Strategy and Tactics)
Merchant Venturers	Influence, Perception	Commerce, Navigate, Seamanship
Midwives	First Aid, Influence, Locale	Healing, Lore (Midwifery)
Physicians	First Aid, Insight, Locale	Healing, Lore (Herbs)
Political Party or Movements	Customs or Deceit, Influence, Insight	Orate, Lore (Politics)
Ship's Company	Athletics, Boating, Endurance	Navigate, Seamanship
Thieves'/Assassins' Guild	Conceal, Deceit, Evade, One Combat Style	Sleight
Trade and Craft Guild	Customs, Perception	Commerce, Craft (Appropriate to the Guild)
Warband	Athletics, Brawn, Evade, Endurance, One Combat Style Appropriate to the Band	Lore (Strategy and Tactics)

Animistic Cults

Cult Name	Standard Skills	Professional Skills	Spirits
Ancestor Cult	Customs, Insight, Perception	Binding, Lore (Ancestors), Trance	Ancestors
Animal Spirit	Athletics, Evade, Ride	Binding, Lore (Animal Spirit), Trance	Animal Spirits, Predator Spirits
Nature Spirit	Insight, Locale, Willpower	Binding, Lore (Nature Spirit), Trance	Nature Spirits, associated Animal Spirits
Healing Spirit	Endurance, First Aid	Binding, Lore (Healing Spirit), Healing, Trance	Healing Spirit, Guardian Spirits
Disease Spirit	Influence, Willpower, Endurance	Lore (Disease Spirit), Trance	Disease Spirits, perhaps Curse Spirits

Mysticism Cults

Cult Name	Standard Skills	Professional Skills	Paths
Monastic Order of Epistemology	None	Language (any), Literacy, Lore (any), Meditation, Mysticism	The Way of All Knowledge: Augment Insight, Augment Language, Augment Lore, Invoke Aura (Wisdom), Invoke Awareness, Invoke Denial (Ignorance), Invoke Magic Sense
Brotherhood of the Healing Hands	First Aid, Locale	Healing, Meditation, Mysticism	Path of Healing: Augment Endurance, Augment First Aid, Augment Healing, Invoke Disease Immunity, Invoke Poison Immunity, Enhance Healing Rate, Enhance Fatigue
School of Impenetrable Silence	Perception, Stealth	Sleight, Meditation, Mysticism	Path of Shadows: Augment Perception, Augment Stealth, Augment Unarmed, Augment Ranged Combat Style, Invoke Adhesion, Invoke Dark Sight, Enhance Movement
Fellowship of the Snake	Deceit, Influence	Oratory, Meditation, Mysticism	Path of Deceit: Augment Conceal, Augment Deceit, Augment Influence, Augment Sleight, Augment Willpower, Invoke Night Sight, Enhance Movement
School of the Leaping Tiger	Athletics, Unarmed	Survival, Meditation, Mysticism	Way of the Tiger: Augment Athletics, Augment Brawn, Augment Endurance, Augment Unarmed, Invoke Formidable Natural Weapons, Enhance Action Points, Enhance Damage Modifier
Order of Asceticism	Endurance, Willpower	Survival, Meditation, Mysticism	Way of Abjuration: Augment Endurance, Augment Survival, Invoke Denial (Food), Invoke Denial (Water), Invoke Denial (Sleep), Enhance Fatigue, Enhance Hit Points
Academy of Enlightened Being	Customs, Influence	Lore (any), Meditation, Mysticism	Way of Reason: Augment Customs, Augment Influence, Augment Insight, Augment Willpower, Invoke Aura (Authority), Invoke Aura (Wisdom), Enhance Initiative

Sorcery Cults

Cult Name	*Standard Skills*	*Professional Skills*	*Spells*
Military Order	Combat Style, Unarmed	Lore (Strategy and Tactics), Invocation, Shaping	Attract Missile, Bypass Armour, Damage Enhancement, Damage Resistance, Haste, Protective Ward, Transfer Wound
Necromantic Order	Endurance, Willpower	Lore (Undead), Invocation, Shaping	Abjure (Decay), Dominate (Undead), Revivify, Spirit Resistance, Transfer Wound, Trap Soul, Undeath
Alchemical Order	Locale	Commerce, Lore (Alchemy), Invocation, Shaping	Diminish (Characteristic), Enlarge, Holdfast, Neutralise Magic, Sculpt (Substance), Shrink, Transmogrify (to Substance)
Scholastic Order	Insight, Perception	Lore (any), Invocation, Shaping	Abjure (Process), Intuition, Mystic (Sense), Neutralise Magic, Perceive (Sense), Project (Sense), Sense (Knowledge)
Hermetic Order	Perception, Willpower	Lore (any), Invocation, Shaping	Abjure (Substance), Banish, Damage Resistance, Mystic (Sense), Protective Ward, Spirit Resistance, Spell Resistance
Dark Forces Order	Insight, Stealth	Disguise, Invocation, Shaping	Castback, Enslave (Creatures), Evoke (Entity), Imprison, Smother, Tap (Characteristic), Wrack
Communication Order	Customs, Influence	Language (any), Invocation, Shaping	Fly, Haste, Intuition, Phantom (Sense), Project (Sense), Telepathy, Teleport
Medical Order	First Aid, Locale	Healing, Invocation, Shaping	Abjure, Damage Resistance, Neutralise Magic, Palsy, Regenerate, Repulse (Vermin), Transfer Wound
Transmutation Order	Endurance, Unarmed	Lore (Creatures), Invocation, Shaping	Dominate (Creatures), Draw (Creatures), Enhance (Characteristic), Haste, Perceive (Sense), Shapechange (to Creature), Switch Body

Theist Miracles

The miracles listed for each of the generic Theist Cults are merely a broad range of suggestions from which a cult can select its own unique subset of specialist magics (see How Many Abilities?, page 114). The miracles Awaken, Behold, Consecrate, Excommunicate and Extension tend to be ubiquitous across most cults - although this is not always the case. When choosing miracles offered by a particular type of cult Games Masters should consider including one or more of these five miracles as part of those offered in its portfolio; but must take into account the cult's nature when making a decision on which of them would be relevant or useful to it. For instance, a War God cult might offer Awaken and Consecrate as part of its miracles, whilst a Trickster cult might instead offer Behold, Excommunicate and Extension.

Theist Cults

Cult Name	*Standard Skills*	*Professional Skills*	*Miracles*
Air/Storm God	Air God: Athletics, Evade Storm God: Athletics, Brawn	Devotion, Exhort, Survival	Berserk, Call Winds, Clear Skies, Cloud Call, Dismiss Elemental, Elemental Summoning (Sylph), Lightning, Rain of Hail, Sacred Band, Shield, Thunderclap
Crafter God	Brawn, Endurance	Craft (Any), Devotion, Exhort	Backlash, Dismiss Magic, Fortify, Harmonise, Leeching, Mindlink, Pacify, Perseverance, Steadfast, True (Weapon)
Death God	Influence, Willpower, Combat Style	Devotion, Exhort	Aegis, Backlash, Bind Ghost, Corruption, Dismiss Magic, Fear, Heart Seizure, Lay to Rest, Raise Undead, Sever Spirit, Soul Sight, Spirit Block, True (Weapon)
Earth God	Brawn, Locale	Devotion, Exhort, and either Engineering or Lore (Mining or Smithing)	Absorption, Backlash, Dismiss Elemental, Earthquake, Elemental Summoning (Gnome), Fortify, Lay to Rest, Propitiate, Rain of Stones, Sacred Band, Shield, Steadfast
Fertility Goddess	Endurance, Locale	Craft (Farming or Husbandry), Devotion, Exhort	Beast Form, Bless Crops, Clear Skies, Cloud Call, Dismiss Magic, Entangle, Enthrall, Fecundity, Growth, Heal Wound, Pacify, Ripen
Healing God	First Aid, Endurance	Devotion, Exhort, Healing	Cure Malady, Cure Sense, Dismiss Magic, Exorcism, Fecundity, Heal Body, Heal Mind, Heal Wound, Lay to Rest, Pacify, Rejuvenate, Resurrect
Hunter God	Athletics, Stealth	Devotion, Exhort, Track	Beast Form, Chameleon, Cloud Call, Dismiss Magic, Entangle, Harmonise, Illusion, Lay to Rest, Pacify, Shield, Sureshot, True (Weapon)
Knowledge God	Customs, Perception	Devotion, Exhort, Lore (Character's Choice)	Dismiss Magic, Heal Mind, Mindblast, Mindlink, Obliterate, Propitiate, Reflection, Soul Sight, Spirit Block, Steadfast

Theist Cults (Continued)

Cult Name	*Standard Skills*	*Professional Skills*	*Miracles*
Sea/Water God	Boating, Swim	Devotion, Exhort, and either Craft (Fishing) or Seamanship	Beast Form, Breathe Water, Call Winds, Dismiss Elemental, Elemental Summoning (Undine), Perseverance, Propitiate, Sacred Band, Steadfast, Thunderclap
Sun God/Fire God	Influence, Insight	Devotion, Exhort, Oratory	Aegis, Clear Skies, Dismiss Elemental, Elemental Summoning (Salamander), Fear, Illusion, Leeching, Mirage, Rain of Fire, Sacred Band, Shield, Sunspear
Trading God	Customs, Insight	Commerce, Devotion, Exhort	Dismiss Magic, Enthrall, Illusion, Mindlink, Pacify, Perseverance, Propitiate, Reflection, Soul Sight
Trickster God	Conceal, Deceit	Devotion, Disguise, Exhort	Absorption, Backlash, Beast Form, Chameleon, Corruption, Dismiss Magic, Enthrall, Fear, Harmonise, Illusion, Madness, Mirage, Soul Sight
War God	Combat Style, Evade, Endurance	Devotion, Exhort	Aegis, Berserk, Dismiss Magic, Fortify, Perseverance, Reflection, Sacred Band, Shield, Steadfast, Sureshot, True (Weapon)

Creatures

Animals, monsters, and creatures of myth, legend and folklore are the focus of this chapter. The primary use of creatures is as adversaries, but they should never be thought of strictly in these terms. Every creature has its own motivations, instincts and drives, just as characters do, and they can be much more than simply sword or arrow fodder. Intelligent, sapient creatures in particular may act with similar degrees of intelligence, guile and cunning as any character and, with the right approach, can be developed into characters in their own right – to interact with as well as to be treated as opponents or obstacles. This chapter therefore offers guidance for Games Masters on how to make creatures, sapient and otherwise, as effective as possible, be this the tactics of pack hunters or how to represent creatures operating on instinct or other motivations.

Most creatures in Mythras are defined by the same characteristics, attributes and skills as player characters. This means that some species, sapient or otherwise, can be used as player characters if Games Masters allow this in their campaign. There are, however, certain differences that help mark creatures and different species, from standard humans, notably Intelligence and Instinct, and Creature Abilities.

Intelligence and Instinct

Some creatures do not exhibit intelligence on the same scale or in the same way as humans. It is usual, for instance, to judge dogs and cats (and most mammals) as being less intelligent than humans because they appear to have limited reasoning and problem-solving capabilities, and are driven far more by base instinct than a reasoned approach to their environment. Where such creatures are concerned, INT is a fixed value determined by the creature's general type (see the Creature INT table below), and a new characteristic, Instinct (INS), is used to figure all attributes and skills that would otherwise rely on the INT score. Creatures calculate INS on 2d6+fixed INT. Thus a wolf, being a mammalian carnivore, has a fixed INT of 6, and an INS of 2d6+6, giving an INS range of 8 to 18 with an average of 13. Its INT though, as measured in sapient terms, is only 6.

INS, then, represents instinctive behaviour but also innate cunning, and other behaviours essential to its nature and survival that would otherwise be penalized or poorly represented by a straight INT score.

When calculating a creature's Initiative Bonus they use their INS instead of INT.

Creature INT Table

INT Value	*Creature Types*
1	Invertebrates (worms, snails, and such)
2	Insects and Crustaceans
3	Amphibians and Fish
4	Reptilian, Avian, and Mammalian herbivores (such as elk or triceratops)
5	Reptilian and Avian carnivores (for example allosaurs or terror birds)
6	Mammalian carnivores (bears, big cats, and the like)
7	Almost sapient Mammals and Monsters (apes, chimera etc)

Creature Abilities

A creature ability is something it can do naturally as a result of its physiology, biology, innate magic, and so forth. Birds, for example, can flap through the air, and so Flying is an ability.
Each of the following abilities is described in terms of its game effects, and how it may affect interactions with others:

Adhering

The creature can move freely on vertical surfaces, and even move upside down on a ceiling with no special equipment. Such Movement is always at half the creature's normal Movement rate.

Allergy
The creature has a powerful allergy or other negative reaction to a specific substance that normally does not inflict damage; such as wine, salt, water, and so on. If the creature is exposed to the substance it suffers 1d6 damage per Combat Round to those locations in contact. Worn armour blocks its normal amount of Armour Points against this damage, assuming the creature is not fully drenched or immersed in the substance. Natural protection, however, does not count.

Aquatic
The creature breathes water rather than air, generally possessing gills or a skin capable of absorbing dissolved air directly. If taken out of water and their breathing organs allowed to dry out, they begin to suffocate after their CON in minutes if remaining passive or half that time if moving or fighting.

Blood Sense
Allows the creature to detect blood over great distances, either carried by wind or water. Traces of blood can be sensed at a distance of half its INS in kilometres.

Breathe Flame
The creature breathes flame over an area as a Combat Action. The flame covers a cone in front of the creature, which stretches for its CON in metres. At the furthest extent, the width of the cone is one quarter of the creature's CON. Any creature caught in the flame suffers fire-based damage to all hit locations, though a character can attempt to Evade to halve this damage. Armour Points count as normal unless otherwise noted.

A creature can only breathe flame once in a specified time period (usually once per hour or once per day). Further attempts to breathe flame within this time require the creature to pass Endurance rolls with each roll becoming one grade harder, or suffer a level of Fatigue.

Burrower
The creature is adept at tunnelling through the ground at its normal Movement rate. Some creatures are limited in the kind of ground they can move through, which is noted in the creature's description.

Camouflaged
The creature is adept at hiding due to its colouration or unusual surface texture. Those attempting to spot the creature suffer a penalty to Perception of two difficulty grades.

Chaos Aura
This creature is tainted by Chaos, and other chaotic creatures can sometimes recognise this. When encountering a creature of Chaos, it can attempt a Willpower roll. If successful, the creature will not be attacked by its enemy, so long as it does not take any hostile action.

Chaos Feature
Creatures tainted with Chaos do not always obey the normal laws of physical growth, and many are hideously malformed. Each Chaos Feature Trait forces the creature to roll once on the Chaos Feature table on pages 275 to 276, applying the effects immediately.

Characteristic Drain
The creature has the innate ability to drain temporary Characteristic points from the target of their attacks. The type of attack, the Characteristic affected, and how to resist the draining effect is detailed in the creature's description.

Cold-Blooded
The creature does not need to eat frequently. One meal a week is sufficient to keep it healthy and well fed, and gorging itself on a large amount of meat will remove the need to eat for a month. Conversely, when exposed to temperatures below 15 degrees Celsius, its reflexes become muted, suffering a penalty of -6 to Initiative, and the loss of one Combat Action per round. Below 5 degrees Celsius cold blooded creatures become completely torpid, entering a helpless catatonic state.

Communal Mind
Though a single creature of this type has only a low INT, a large group of them together possess a vastly improved intellect, potentially achieving sapience.

Dark Sight
Allows the creature to see normally in the complete absence of light.

Death Sense
In tune with the powers of death, the creature can sense the death of living things, and dead flesh at a range of up to half its INT or INS in kilometres.

Disease Immunity
The creature is immune to all diseases. All creatures without SIZ automatically have this ability, although it is not specifically listed in their descriptions.

Diving Strike
Some creatures can plummet from the sky or surge through the waters to attack their prey, striking with incredible force. This is effectively charging for creatures which are not land based. Diving Strike increases both the Size of the attack, and the creature's Damage Modifier by one step, for this attack only. A diving strike may only be used once per round. The creature must be at least one full round of Movement above its target (or possibly below if submerged) in order to use the diving strike.

Earth Sense
Some creatures are so in tune with the underground world that they can work perfectly well in the total darkness of the deep. By sensing vibration and air pressure, a creature with Earth Sense can fight, and make Perception rolls with no penalty as long as their target is no more than their INS in metres away. If using Earth Sense above ground the range is halved.

Echolocation
The creature senses its environment through reflections of sonic waves. This means that it can perceive others that may be either motionless or hidden. In such circumstances, using a Stealth roll to attempt to remain unperceived by the creature is two grades more difficult.

Engulfing
The creature has an orifice which can swallow targets whole. The maximum size of an engulfed victim is figured as half the creature's own SIZ, but may be less than this depending on the creature's

physiology. When engulfed the victim suffers at least one damage roll based on the creature's bite attack before being swallowed – the time spent chewing depends on the creature, and how sensitive its innards are. If still alive a swallowed victim will begin to suffocate, likely dying by asphyxiation before suffering any noticeable damage from stomach acid. Realistically, an engulfed victim lacks the mobility to move inside the digestive tract or the creature is so large that he will die long before he can cut its way out.

Flying

The creature automatically succeeds in everyday moving and manoeuvring whilst flying, and need not roll their Fly skill unless attempting an unusually difficult task, such as flying against a powerful wind, evading a ranged attack in the air, or out-manoeuvring an aerial foe. A flyer may substitute the Fly skill (base STR+DEX) for Evade whilst fighting whilst aloft.

Formidable Natural Weapons

This creature is able to actively parry or deflect attacks using its natural weapons. This is due to a combination of fighting style and possessing natural armament being formed from resilient substances such as horn, chitin or bone which are able to shrug off damage from manufactured weapons. Note that creatures lacking this trait either rely on their natural armour to turn blows or use Evade.

Frenzy

When wounded or exposed to a particular substance - blood for instance - the creature must succeed in a Willpower roll or enter a frenzy. The frenzy lasts a number of rounds equal to the creature's CON. During the frenzy they must only spend Combat Actions on attacking or moving towards combat. Spellcasting, parrying, evading, and anything else is forbidden; all thoughts of self preservation washed away in a red haze. In return, the creature no longer suffers pain or fatigue, and is impervious to mental control. During this time it is immune to all the detrimental effects of Serious Wounds, although a Major Wound will still incapacitate. If still alive, once the frenzy finishes the creature automatically gains a fatigue level of Exhausted.

Gaze Attack

The creature has a gaze attack. This attack may be active (the creature must consciously spend an Action Point on its turn to use it on a foe) or passive (anyone looking at the creature is affected), as listed in the creature's description.

Grappler

If the creature successfully strikes in combat, it can immediately Grapple in addition to inflicting damage. If the creature's attack was parried (or the creature itself is parrying), then the creature is granted the Grip effect against the opponent's limb or the Pin Weapon effect against his weapon instead. The creature always uses its Brawn skill to resist a victim from breaking free.

Hold Breath

The creature can hold its breath for extended periods of time. If prepared and remaining fairly static, the creature can hold its breath for a number of minutes equal to its CON. This period is halved if the creature is active, such as when swimming or fighting.

Immunity

The creature is completely immune to damage caused by one type of source. This source (cold, fire, iron, etc.) will be noted in the creature's listing, but a narrative description may be necessary for some of the more specific immunities.

Intimidate

The creature may intimidate opponents as a prelude to combat or to avoid it altogether: growls, snarls, lowering of horns, and so forth. Opponents must make an unopposed Willpower roll to hold their ground; a success allows a character to stand his ground, whereas a failure indicates that they must spend the next round instinctively placing distance between themselves and the creature. If he fumbles the Willpower roll, then the character flees at maximum speed. A critical success allows the character to ignore any further intimidation attempts by the creature or its brethren during that encounter. The effect continues for as long as the creature continues to act in a threatening manner, which includes it making an attack.

Leaper

The creature uses Leaping attacks as described on page 104 of the Combat chapter, but can combine the leap with a physical attack such as a claw or bite. If the leaping creature wins the opposed leap attack roll, it automatically inflicts damage for one of its natural weapons on the target. This damage cannot be parried except by Passive Blocking.

Life Sense

In tune with the rhythms of nature, this creature can determine the vitality of any living creature by touch alone. If the creature makes a successful Perception roll, it learns of the target's current injuries, Fatigue level, and whether it is currently afflicted by any poison or disease. The creature is also aware of any form of life within a number of metres equal to its Willpower skill, which may make Stealth difficult to accomplish.

Magic Sense

Similar to Life Sense but permits the creature to detect magical emanations over the same distances. If the creature touches another and makes a successful Perception roll, it learns of the target's current magic points, carried enchantments, and active spells.

Multi-Headed

The creature gains an additional Combat Action per extra head possessed beyond the first. These are lost as each individual head is incapacitated or severed. Provided one head remains active, the creature can still control its shared body. When a multi-headed creature resists spells which affect emotions or intellect, it rolls individual saves for each still intact head.

Multi-Limbed

Similar to Multi-headed, the creature gains an additional Combat Action per extra pair of limbs (beyond the first) it can bring to bear during combat – those normally used to hold up or move the creature do not count. These extra Combat Actions can only be used to perform actions with those specific limbs, and are lost as each pair are immobilised or incapacitated.

Night Sight
Allows the creature to treat partial darkness as illuminated and darkness as partial darkness.

Poison Immunity
The creature is immune to all poisons. All creatures without SIZ automatically have this Trait, although it is not specifically listed in their descriptions.

Possession, Covert
A more insidious means of possession, covert possession means, essentially, that the creature's mind or spirit is a hitchhiker in the body of the possessed victim. It exhibits no control over the body whist the victim is conscious, leaving the host completely in charge. In many cases, the possessed host may not even know he is possessed.

Possession, Dominant
More blatant than its covert cohort, dominant possession occurs when the creature's mind or spirit takes full control of a possessed body. The identity (INT, POW and CHA) of the body's owner is subsumed beneath the identity of the possessing spirit. The possessed victim is absolutely helpless, unable to take any action at all, unable even to regain Magic Points, a prisoner in his own body. The possessor is in complete control, though it does not have access to any of the memories, skills or magic of the possessed.

Regeneration
The creature is able to regenerate Hit Points lost to damage. The speed of regeneration varies depending upon the creature. Unless specifically noted, regeneration does not replace lost limbs, and the severing of a vital location (head, chest or abdomen) will still result in death

Swimmer
The creature automatically succeeds in everyday moving and manoeuvring whilst swimming, and need not roll their Swim skill unless attempting an unusually difficult task, such as swimming against a powerful tide or leaping up a waterfall. A swimmer may substitute the Swim skill for Athletics and Evade rolls whilst in water.

Terrifying
The creature's appearance, form or aura is so terrifying it forces viewers to make an unopposed Willpower roll. Success indicates the viewer is shaken for one round and cannot act offensively. Failure causes them to flee in terror. A fumble causes the viewer to collapse unconscious from the shock. Only a critical success allows the viewer to act unhindered. The viewer need not make any further checks for the remainder of the combat, even if more of the same creatures are present. Repeated exposure to a specific type of Terrifying monster may eventually permit the skill check to become one or more grades easier.

Trample

The creature is able to trample beings with a SIZ of half or less than its own, using its Athletics skill to attack. This inflicts damage equal to twice the creature's base Damage Modifier, and increases the Size of the attack by one step. How, and when trample is used depends on the circumstances. If immobile the creature may trample a prone opponent on its turn, but this costs an Action Point. If the trample is performed whist the creature is moving or charging over an opponent, then the trample is a Free Action.

Undead

Being already dead, the creature is immune to the consequences of both fatigue and severe injuries. Undead are thus immune to all the detrimental effects of Serious Wounds. Even Major Wounds do not incapacitate them, although they can still have locations severed or shattered as per normal. Treat the head or chest location of the undead creature as the area where the spirit or magic has been bound. Any location (and those contiguous to it) which is smashed or severed from the bound area ceases to function, but the remainder of the body can continue if it still has limbs with which to act. A Major Wound to the magic-infused location destroys the undead outright. Only fully corporeal dead creatures may possess the Undead trait.

Vampiric

The creature drains its victim's blood, causing an increase in Fatigue levels. The creature must use a bite attack, and cause damage with the bite to be able to drain blood at the rate described in the creature's description.

Venomous

The creature has a venomous bite, sting or other means of attack. The creature's description provides the game mechanic effects for the particular poison used. A venomous creature may, if desired, apply its poison by use of the Inject Venom special effect.

Inject Venom

Whilst the stinger of a scorpion's tail or the fangs of a cobra are extremely threatening, a strike from the natural weapons of a venomous creature does not necessarily indicate that venom was injected. Fangs might not pass a blocking shield or stingers fail to penetrate armour. Using the Inject Venom manoeuvre indicates a specific desire for the creature to poison its foe. In exchange for forfeiting any chance to inflict damage, the creature finds a weak point in the defence/armour, bypassing it only for the purposes of applying its venom – for example a large venomous snake might attack a warrior wearing mail armour and instead of inflicting damage from the bite, ducks past the victim's parry to merely scratch the back of the his sword hand, poisoning him. This combat manoeuvre can be used both offensively and defensively by venomous creatures.

Vulnerable

The creature's natural and magical protection cannot mitigate damage caused by a specific type of source. This source (cold, fire, iron, etc.) will be noted as part of the trait, but a narrative description may be included for some specific vulnerabilities. For example, silver weapons might pass through the skin of a werewolf.

Creatures as Characters

Any sapient creature (with an INT of 8+) can be used as a player character if the Games Master is prepared to allow such exotic characters in their MYTHRAS campaign. Some species, such as elves, dwarves, and trolls are, indeed, fantasy staples, and their general similarities to humans lend themselves readily to play. Others are less suited as player characters, usually due to being creatures of such diverse psychology and physiology that they might not mesh well with the other characters in the players' group. A giant amongst a group of humans or dwarves, for instance, can be an entertaining addition but will pose problems in certain conditions.

Games Masters must carefully consider whether or not to allow a particular species as a player character, and to weigh-up the potential drawbacks before play begins. However a great deal of fun can be had from allowing exotic species into a campaign, as long as both players and Games Masters are aware, and accepting of, the potential complications that might arise. Players, too, must also take into consideration the challenges of playing an exotic creature as a character. Playing an Iqari, for example means the character can fly, but has difficulties communicating verbally owing to its physiology. This may prove to be a barrier to roleplaying – or it may be a terrific opportunity, depending on how the player approaches the role.

It must always be remembered that different races and species have different psychologies and drives. Playing an Iqari in the same way one would run a human character is to do a disservice to that species.

A final consideration is that there is no concept of balance between creatures of different races or species. Whilst their cultural and professional skills may start out at similar levels, their physical or mental capabilities may be far, far superior. Thus permitting someone to play an Iqari character in a party of humans might cause resentment amongst the rest of the players, or pose a difficulty for the Games Master to provide suitable challenges without placing the other characters at risk.

Creature Character Creation

Non-human characters are created in almost exactly the same way as humans. Characteristics are determined using the characteristic dice for that species, which will result in different characteristic values and ranges, but otherwise all the other elements: attributes, culture, profession, and so on, are factored as normal. Of course, creatures may have very different cultural bases resulting in different skills and professions, but nothing stops a Games Master from simply adapting the nominally human tables if it is fitting for his setting.

Space does not permit individual treatments of culture and career for all possible playable species; however some staple fantasy races have been given expanded details for cultural and career options. Some of these can be readily applied to species without such detail, or serve as examples or inspiration for developing appropriate cultural and career packages. For those races that have been given greater depth, notes regarding psychology are also provided, to assist with roleplaying.

Non-Human Points Build

Players who wish to play non-human characters may assign characteristics using the Points Build method (see page 8). The exact same rules apply to building non-humans, except that the starting pool of points will be based upon the totalled average characteristics of the selected species or race.

For example an Iqari being created using the Points Build method would start with a rather staggering 108 points (rounded up) for its seven characteristics. However, an Iqari must have a minimum STR of 15, SIZ and DEX of 14, CON and INT of 8, and a POW and CHA of 3. So there are some limitations on how points can be assigned.

Games Masters should consider carefully whether to allow players to use the Points Build method when creating creature characters. If the natural Characteristics and Attributes of an average member of this species are likely to cause umbrage amongst other players, then a creature which can be tweaked to garner even more extreme Attribute bonuses will likely disrupt the game.

The Statistics Block

Creature statistics are arranged in a table format called the Statistics Block (or Stat Block for short). The block is arranged as follows:

- Creature Name – The creature's name, and any alternatives.
- Description – A description of the creature's appearance, demeanour, temperament, and so on, along with any additional useful notes.
- Characteristics – The characteristic dice for the creature; used when creating a bespoke version of the creature. In parenthesis after each are the average values of the characteristic dice. This is useful when a quick sample of the creature is needed. The averages are also used to calculate the creature's attributes given in its description. Remember that a creature with INS uses this to replace INT when calculating Action Points and Initiative.
- Hit Locations – Every creature has Hit Locations and Hit Points. Humanoid creatures use the same Hit Locations range as humans although there may be some variations depending on precise physiology. Creatures with physiologies differing from humans have a different range of Hit Locations. A summary of the different physiology Hit Locations (quadruped, winged, and so on) are provided on pages 276-277.
- Attributes – The creature's Action Points, Movement, Initiative Bonus, and so forth, are figured using the Average characteristic values but otherwise according to the same rules as for humans, as found in the Basic Character Creation chapter.
- Armour – What armour, natural or fabricated, the creature has. Creatures with natural armour, such as scales or a thick hide, do not incur any Armour Penalty to their Initiative.
- Abilities – Specific abilities possessed by the creature (such as Flying).
- Magic – If a creature uses magic then the type of magic it uses, and the necessary skills (Folk Magic, for instance) are also listed here along with typical spells its uses.
- Skills – Every creature has the skills Athletics, Brawn, Endurance, Evade and Willpower listed. Other skills pertinent to the creature, such as Swim, are listed where needed. The values presented are for a typical young adult of the species, and should be increased for older, more experienced individuals.
- Combat Styles – The Combat Style(s) the creature uses, the percentage, and then the weapons included in the style.
- Weapons – The statistics for the creature's available weapons, as listed in the Combat Style.
- Special Notes – Any game mechanics peculiar to the creature: poisons for example, or breath weapon details.
- Player Character Options – Culture, career, and other information necessary for playing the creature as a player character.

Creature Competence

Just like humans, creatures – especially sapient ones – display different levels of competence in their skills and abilities. Survival of the fittest ensures that the most competent prevail, but even so there will always be differing levels of competence between individuals of a species.

How Skilled Creatures Should Be

The creatures detailed in this chapter all have skill values listed, and these reflect those for a typical young adult member of the species. The values are derived by calculating the base for the skill, just as for human characters, and then modifying the base to reflect experience and knowledge (or developed instincts). Generally a creature will have skill base plus between 20 and 40 percentage points, representing its parental training or self learning during adolescence.

There are, however, those individuals that represent either the fittest, strongest, cleverest cream of the species or the older, wiser, more experienced survivors. When designing creatures as adversaries or points of interaction, Games Masters should take into account these possible exceptions, and adjust skills according to the creature's age, degree of maturity, life lessons, wisdom, and so forth. It is reasonable to increase appropriate skills by a further 20 to 40 percentiles to reflect these elements.

Therefore it is perfectly valid for characters to encounter seasoned creatures which far exceed the average in terms of skill, thus remaining a challenge even for the toughest of adventurers.

How to Balance Creatures Against Characters

The common reason for introducing a creature is combat. In this case the skills the creature has – especially in terms of Combat Styles and skills frequently used in combat, such as Endurance and Evade – should be considered in comparison with the skills of the characters likely to battle it. There is no hard and fast need to balance creatures against character skills: one of the challenges is in seeing how well characters fare against opponents that have a degree of edge; but if characters frequently find themselves facing creatures that have substantially better skills and, perhaps even more importantly, numbers, the likelihood of character injury and death rises dramatically, which can be frustrating for the players.

Here, then, are some guidelines for helping to balance encounters whilst still retaining tension and challenge.

1. Look at the abilities a creature has. Certain abilities give creatures an innate advantage over opponents. Decide how these abilities will be used by the creature, and consider whether the potency of an ability means that the number of creatures of the same type the characters face should be equal to, or less than, the size of the character's party.
2. Consider the example skills of the creature, especially those involved in combat, and compare them with either the average skills of the party or the character with the highest similar skill. If the creature's skills, and certainly its Combat Style, are equal to the characters', or in a range of 10 to 20 points higher, then the challenge posed should still be manageable.
3. Also consider the Armour, Hit Points and Weapons of the creature. Tougher creatures take longer to subdue or kill. Creatures with fearsome weapons will inflict a lot of damage, and could potentially carve a swathe through the characters, especially if encountered in large numbers.
4. Think about the creature's tactics, habits and nature. Some perform hit and run tactics, slowly whittling down their foes whereas others only attack from ambush. Choosing different tactics can radically change how an encounter plays out. See How Creatures Fight below.
5. Understand the effect of numbers. Multiple numbers of smaller, weaker or less skilled creatures can be set against a party, outnumbering them two or three to one if well handled. Creatures which approach equivalence with characters should rarely outnumber the party save for climactic situations. Those that are more potent should themselves be outnumbered by the characters, or else the party be obliterated.
6. Does a creature use magic? If so, will it have had the chance to prepare any spells prior to engagement? Magic using creatures tend be sapient, and so they should use magic with a similar degree of tactical thought as the player characters. The type of magic and spells available will also be helpful in deciding numbers present. Similarly, competency in magic and the spells available may need to be balanced with the characters' own magical skills and spells.
7. Finally, *never* assume that all creatures fight to the bitter end. A cornered animal may have no choice, but whenever circumstances permit it the law of survival takes over, and creatures will flee or surrender, depending on their nature. The fittest only prevail if they survive and learn from their experience and this equally true for all creatures. Only the most desperate and insane will fight to the absolute death. If a pack leader flees, then its followers are likely to follow on its heels. Similarly, unless the creatures view the characters as food, they are unlikely to kill those that submit, flee or withdraw. This simple fact alone can be used to balance an encounter and ensure that complete bloodbaths are a rarity.

Other than this advice Mythras does not provide any *hard* rules to balance creature encounters, since the variables of any conflict are too diverse to model. However, Games Masters should find they develop an instinct for what their group can handle according to the player's roleplaying style and aggressiveness.

How Creatures Fight

Sapient creatures apply their intelligence and reasoning to their environment, opponents and the impending combat It is relatively easy for Games Masters to direct the actions of sapient species because humans, being sapient, naturally relate to reasoning, and reasoned assessments.

Creatures that operate primarily on instinct – animals, naturally, but any creature with the INS characteristic – tend to act differently; which will mean combat situations need to be handled according to how animals and instinct-driven creatures usually act if the combat is to be portrayed with any degree of verisimilitude.

The following notes are designed to help Games Masters prepare and run such encounters in a realistic and challenging manner.

Reasons for Attack

Animals rarely attack without purpose. Random, unprovoked attacks are relatively uncommon, and even the smartest animal usually has a reason for initiating combat. Food is a primary motivator, but it is rare for animals to attack something bigger than themselves unless they operate in numbers large enough to overwhelm the prey. Lone animals, especially those of roughly human size and mass, are likely to steer clear of humans unless absolutely driven by starvation to contemplate an attack. The second motivator is the protection of herd or offspring. If an animal has young, then the young are a target for predators: the parents will therefore instinctively attack a potential predator with the aim of driving it away, and making sure it understands that the young are not an easy feast. Thirdly there are creatures who seek to defend their territory, seeking to conserve its resources for their own use. In all these situations a fight to the death is not necessarily on the agenda.

Judging the Odds

Most dangerous animals prefer to have little to do with humans, and don't take on superior numbers. They normally only fight when the advantage is in their favour; such as one on one or when their victim is sleeping.

Intimidation

Many animals rarely get round to initiating combat. Large herbivores for example will tend to intimidate first. This can be used to scare a party or give them fair warning that something bad might happen if they force the issue. Backing off might 'win' them the encounter, as the animal is likely to also depart peacefully if the threat is removed. After all it doesn't want to be injured either. Predators, too, use intimidation to warn off threats, although the chances of intimidation turning into aggression are likely to be higher, especially if the characters represent an easy meal. Intimidation takes the form of physical and verbal gestures: growling, snarling, lowered horns, raking of the ground and slow, deliberate movements towards the foe which allow energy to be prepared for a blistering assault if necessary. Intimidatory tactics are designed to get the foe to increase its distance, and flee. Only if intimidation fails will most animals launch an attack.

Killing is not always the objective

In some circumstances creatures are not really interested in killing humans, even when deliberately provoked or attacked. In such situations if a creature manages to injure its attackers, it will not necessarily attempt to kill its foe or even inflict a lethal Special Effect. All it really wants is to be left alone, and will cease fighting once resistance ceases, leaving the wounded behind it.

Fleeing rather than death

Many, indeed *most* creatures will flee when wounded. This can turn a simple combat encounter into a tracking challenge or game of cat and mouse, since most animals have superior movement rates and abilities to humans in their natural environment. Superior numbers may influence fight-or-flee decisions, and be instigated by a pack or herd leader, but usually a creature will attempt to flee rather than face certain extinction.

Being Outnumbered

Understand the limits of a lone creature. Placing a large bear against a party using spears will simply see the bear being slaughtered. Do not think that it means the combat system is broken: it is precisely what would happen in real life. The bear might get to wound or maim one or two opponents but ultimately, being outnumbered, it will lose (assuming it cannot flee).

Unusual Tactics

Predators use tactical tricks to catch prey. Games Masters should replicate this. A hunting creature will not willingly attack multiple opponents head-on but it will use stealth and camouflage to creep up on a victim and attack with surprise. If stalking a dangerous foe it will ambush a lone target, not one surrounded by compatriots. A man-eating tiger for instance will leap on someone going into the bushes to relieve himself, or sneak into the outermost tent of a camp. If it incapacitates the victim, it will drag him off into concealment before any cries can summon aid. In these sorts of situations a creature might use Grip and Entangle or have their own special Combat Effects such as Silent Attack or Paralyse. Big creatures with long tails might be able to do sweep attacks to take down multiple foes; those with tentacles might grapple multiple opponents; sabre tooth cats might always begin with knocking a victim prone, and so on.

Using Terrain

Animals adapted to particular environments have an additional advantage. Imagine a giant trapdoor spider which not only grabs the last person in a line (so that the other characters cannot see what happens) but also drags the body into a narrow underground burrow where it can crunch on its victim's body whilst none of his friends can reach him. Other examples might be apes which swing down from high tree limbs to strike or grab opponents, where the dense foliage may block vision and missile weapons. Consider the environment and the creature's place within it, using the nature of the environment against the opponents.

Hit and Run

Very frustrating, but true to the genre of fantastical game hunters is the smart carnivore which injures members of the safari one by one. The animal does not remain around for an extended combat. Instead it lays ambushes, leaping out to make a single bite or claw attack before diving back into cover, and escaping reprisal. It beats its victims by slow attrition until they realise the challenge faced, and adapt their tactics accordingly.

Poison and Leave Them

Similar in concept to the Hit and Run except the venomous creature remains just long enough to give a victim an incapacitating or fatal dose of venom then retreats before it can be hurt. The creature then follows its poisoned victim until it is unable to defend itself and can be eaten, used as an egg incubator, and so on.

Attack by Pack

A classic tactic of wolves, lions, and similar creatures which tend not to face their prey one on one. Most of the pack simply circles the victim whilst one member jumps forward to make a single attack, then immediately evades back out of reach, whilst a new pack member subsequently attacks from another direction. Packs will not attack simultaneously unless the fighting area is too small for them to spread out (as they instinctively prefer). Likewise a herd of herbivores can be a serious threat if they gang up to protect their young (as elephants do) or stampede towards a party.

Fighting at Extreme Close Range

The safest defence for most animals is to close down into extreme close range. This can be done automatically if the creature has leapt on its victim, ambushed it, or charges into contact. The creature could even use the Change Range special effect if the tactical situation starts differently. Once closed upon, the victim will be unable to defend themselves with most weapons, and will probably have to resort to Unarmed Combat. In this situation, provided the animal isn't outnumbered, it should gain the upper hand; especially if it is sitting on top of a prone victim.

Charging

Being repeatedly charged (or dive bombed) by a fast moving animal is especially disconcerting. Using a charge means the victim has a single choice of whether to Evade, Defend or Attack the charging beast as it thunders by. The creature may also have the Trample ability which is really bad for the victim if knocked over during the charge. Between each attack the creature can gallop past, and be out of range or back into cover, then spend an indeterminate period of time preparing for the next attack. A rhino or aurochs would be a good example of a creature using this tactic.

Unarmed Combat Considerations

The Unarmed skill has been subsumed into some creatures' Combat Style, providing a general sense of how they fight with natural weapons. INS-based creatures can normally only attack once with each limb or location per round; thus a giant scorpion with three Combat Actions could attack once with its left claw, once with the right, and attempt one sting per round.

Some animals however, especially herbivores, only possess a single method of attack, which appears to place them at a disadvantage in close combat. In these cases the creature is more likely to evade or simply flee from attack, and should be roleplayed doing so. Other animals might attack using other tactics already explored in the previous section.

Due to their SIZ or morphology, most creatures have natural weapons with a Reach longer than Touch. Opponents gain no advantage closing within this reach (see Fighting at the Shorter Reach page 106) as natural weapons are able to engage at any reach up to their listed maximum.

Unarmed Combat against Weapons

As described in the Combat chapter, unarmed combat can be used defensively to parry a weapon attack. Damage is reduced as per normal, according to the comparative Sizes of the natural and wielded weapon. Whilst this often plays into the favour of bigger creatures, especially when bashing through the defence of an armed opponent, it does not necessarily cut both ways.

It is actually quite rare for non-sapient beasts to actively parry weapon blows, since they lack the intellect and knowledge of how to do so in relative safety. Instead most INS based creatures in fact rely upon their natural armour or use evasion to avoid an attack.

In a few cases however, a creature with an instinctive blocking or grappling combat style might actually be able to parry an attack. Likewise animals possessing resilient armaments of chitin, horn or similar substances may simply flail about, accidentally interposing their natural weapons in the path of a blow. These creatures are given the Formidable Natural Weapons trait, permitting them to parry in combat.

This does not mean that an unarmed creature lacking the Formidable Natural Weapons trait cannot attempt to parry the blow anyway. Doing so can potentially prevent their foe from gaining an automatic combat Special Effect against them; but if the attack is successful the creature must suffer any damage directly to the limb used to successfully parry. Armour Points on that location still count towards protection.

Natural Weapon Combat Effects

Similar to weapons such as swords or spears, natural weapons are able to inflict certain special effects in combat due to their shape and flexibility. The table opposute lists what weapon-specific effects are available to each type of natural weapon.

Default Natural Weapons for Unusually Sized Creatures

The damage capability of a creature's natural weapons is usually a function of its basic size. Some beings however may have unusually big or small examples depending on its physiology and proportions. Humans for example have ineffectual natural weapons, thus the size and damage of their limbs is one step less than default, dropping to 1d3 damage, Size Small and Reach Touch.

Games Masters should treat the following tables as average values. If a creature has more than one type of natural weapon, the Size or Reach of one may be increased, possibly at the expense of reducing the value of another. The values in the following tables have been applied to most of the creatures within this book, with some variation for those with body frames and limbs disproportionate to their mass.

Natural Weapons Special Effects

Type	*Combat Effects*
Beak, Pointed	Impale
Beak, Tearing	Bleed, Grip
Claws/Talons	Bleed, Grip
Hand/Fist	Grip, Stun Location, Take Weapon
Hoof	Bash, Stun
Horns	Impale
Paw	Stun Location
Pincer	Grip, Sunder
Proboscis	Impale
Stinger	Impale
Tail	Bash, Entangle, Grip
Teeth, Crushing	Grip
Teeth, Grasping	Grip, Impale
Teeth, Incising	Bleed
Tentacle	Grip, Take Weapon
Tusk	Impale
Wing	Bash, Entangle

Natural Weapon Damage

Creature SIZ	*Bash/Crush/Claw Damage*	*Bite/Stab Damage*
1-10	1d3	1d4
11-20	1d4	1d6
21-30	1d6	1d8
31-40	1d8	1d10
41-50	1d10	1d12
51-60	1d12	2d6

Natural Weapon Size and Reach

Creature SIZ	*Size*	*Bite Reach*	*Horn Reach*	*Limb Reach*	*Tongue/Tail Reach*
1-10	S	T	T	S	M
11-20	M	T	S	M	M
21-30	L	S	M	M	L
31-40	H	M	M	L	L
41-50	E	M	L	L	VL
51-60	C	L	L	VL	VL

Armed Combat Considerations

Most situations involving armed combat are covered in the Combat chapter. However, due to the scaling imposed by creatures which are either bigger or smaller than average humans, several important modifications are clarified here.

Weapon Modifications for Unusually Sized Creatures

When a creature wields a weapon rather than fighting unarmed, it gains certain bonuses or penalties which reflect the consequence of its size. Thus a mace used by a man, and a mace used by a troll are ostensibly the same style of weapon, proportionately in scale with their wielders; but the troll mace will be somewhat larger, and more massive. This bonus also counts for ranged weapons, providing they are built to scale.

For each 10 points of SIZ over 20 the wielder gains a bonus of +1 step to both weapon Size and Reach. The same general principles are used when modelling proportionally sized weapons for creatures smaller than humans. However, in some cases a degree of interpretation may be required.

For example, whereas the previously mentioned troll sized mace increases Damage, Size and Reach, a halfling sized mace should be one step smaller than normal, so that it had a Damage of 1d6 and a Size of Small. Reach would remain at Short since it is still longer than the halfling's unarmed fist.

If the increased weapon characteristics place the creature beyond the nominal human sized maximums of Enormous and Very Long, blows effectively become unstoppable, and the body of the creature unreachable by most player characters, and thus further steps need not be considered.

If a fight is staged between two colossal creatures, Games Masters can note the number of bonus steps, and base a ruling on the comparative vales to see if a defending creature is capable of deflecting such blows, or can enter range.

Weapon Size and Reach Bonus

Armed Creature SIZ	*Weapon Size Bonus*	*Weapon Reach Bonus*
1-10	-1 Step	-1 Step
11-20	-	-
21-30	+1 Step	+1 Step
31-40	+2 Steps	+2 Steps
41-50	+3 Steps	+3 Steps

Weapon Category Progression

Size	*Reach*
Small	Touch
Medium	Short
Large	Medium
Huge	Long
Enormous	Very Long
Colossal	Unreachable

Wielding Disproportionately Sized Weapons

Sometimes a character might wish to loot a monstrous foe of his weapon, and attempt to use it in combat. This may pose problems however; whilst a human-scaled shortsword may be the equivalent of a mere dagger to a troll, conversely the troll's two handed maul would be too massive to wield for a normal man.

Use the table opposite to discern the largest single handed and double handed 'Size' of weapon a creature can use. This is only a rough guideline since some oversized weapons are used in unusual ways, (couched lances, for example).

Maximum Weapon Size

Character SIZ	*Largest Single Handed*	*Largest Double Handed**
1-10	Small	Large
11-20	Medium	Huge
21-30	Large	Enormous
31-40	Huge	Colossal
41-50	Enormous	Don't even think about it!

* *Use this column for single-handed shields*

Designing Your Own Creatures

Games Masters are encouraged to design their own Mythras creatures – be they creatures from myth and legend, those inspired by popular fantasy fiction, or even unique creations of the Games Master's own imagination. There are two approaches one can take.

Find a creature from this chapter that approximates the new creature, and then modify its characteristics, abilities, skills, and so forth to reflect the new beast. This is usually the easiest method as much of the work is done for you, and the key task is in tailoring the new creature to make it distinct.

The second approach is to build the creature from scratch. Here are some guidelines to assist.

1. Creature characteristics are figured using d3 or d6 multiples in a very similar way to humans. No creature should have more than 4d6 in any characteristic, but bigger, more powerful/faster creatures incorporate a generous addition to this roll. A mammoth, for example, has STR 2d6+40 giving it a range of 42 to 52 and an average of 47.
2. How big is the creature? If roughly human-sized then it is reasonable to use 2d6+6 as the base for its SIZ characteristic. If it is larger then consider by how much, and either adjust the dice used for SIZ or the bonus to the dice roll if a minimum SIZ increase is needed. Note that the creatures presented here use a SIZ value based on mass, and that the Creature Size Equivalency table does not scale linearly. So the bigger the base SIZ the fewer dice should be used – otherwise the dice spread could allow creatures of two to three times the mass of an average specimen.
3. A creature's STR does not necessarily need to be the same as its SIZ, since as creatures grow bigger their strength to mass ratio tends to drop. A lower STR value also helps keep a creature's Damage Bonus within the bounds of survivability for armoured humans – a necessary consideration if your creature is intended to fight against characters.
4. How intelligent is the creature? Sapient creatures – those with the ability to reason, problem-solve and be driven by choice rather than instinct – should have a base of 2d6+6 to place them on a par with humans, if their INT is likely to be in the human range. Of course some creatures may have more refined intellects, or indeed, be rather slow witted, and barely better thinkers than animals. Calculate INS

as described in Intelligence and Instinct at the start of this chapter.

5. The creature's DEX should be assessed and figured in a similar way to STR, SIZ and INT/INS. Fast, agile creatures or those with many limbs will naturally have a higher DEX than humans so adjust the dice and/or dice addition to reflect its DEX relative to a human. Slow sluggish beasts will naturally have a lower DEX rating.
6. POW for most sapient creatures is in the human range of 3d6. However some supernatural monsters or mythical creatures may have a higher propensity for magic in some form, or be products of it. In this case raise the dice or dice addition to reflect any innate magical tendencies or propensities. Mundane animals tend to have less POW, rarely exceeding 2d6, with smaller animals or more primitive insectoid life possessing even less.
7. Charisma is only of importance when designing sapient creatures that interact socially on a meaningful scale and with other species. CHA is a measure of personality and its communication rather than looks and appearance, so use the human range of 3d6 as the base, and adjust upwards or downwards only if the creature's personality is especially extrovert, introvert or alien. In games where the characters are all members of a non humano-centric species, the Games Master can adjust CHA scores so that it is the characters' race who get 3d6, and the weird humans who have less, since they cannot understand or comprehend the culture.
8. Skills should be chosen according to the creature's primary needs and its environment. Sapient, social creatures obviously may have access to the full range of human skills whilst others will have only those skills related to their immediate needs and capabilities. Skill base values are figured as per humans, but should then be subject to further adjustment - say +30% - to reflect the creature's nature.

Abilities follow from the creature's nature. Aerial creatures obviously need the Flying ability; aquatic creatures need the Swimmer ability, and so on. Consider the creature's overall nature, physiology, faculties, environment, and any specific, exotic talents it might display and apply the relevant abilities. It is recommended though that, except in rare cases, few creatures receive more than three abilities from those listed earlier in this chapter.

Comparative Weights

Creatures do not follow the same height and weight progression as for humanoids. Increasing SIZ relates to a different scaling of mass, muscle and bone density. Generally Mythras keeps specific weights abstracted, but should it be necessary to know the rough weight of a creature, use the following SIZ Equivalency Table. The table can also be used for determining the weight of inanimate objects.

Note that since SIZ is abstracted to a degree, the reach and size of natural weapons should be adjusted to cater for differently dimensioned and proportioned creatures.

Creature SIZ Equivalency Table

SIZ	Kilos	SIZ	Kilos	SIZ	Kilos	SIZ	Kilos
1	up to 5	26	238-258	51	2069-2259	76	18001-19600
2	6-11	27	259-282	52	2260-2468	77	19601-21500
3	12-16	28	238-307	53	2469-2690	78	21501-23400
4	17-23	29	308-335	54	2691-2931	79	23401-25800
5	24-35	30	336-366	55	2932-3199	80	25801-27800
6	36-41	31	367-399	56	3200-3490	81	27801-30300
7	42-49	32	400-436	57	3491-3809	82	30301-33100
8	50-55	33	437-476	58	3810-4149	83	33101-36100
9	56-58	34	477-518	59	4150-4531	84	36101-39400
10	59-64	35	519-567	60	4532-4954	85	39401-43000
11	65-70	36	568-617	61	4955-5363	86	43001-46700
12	71-76	37	618-672	62	5364-5863	87	46701-51200
13	77-83	38	673-754	63	5864-6409	88	51201-55800
14	84-91	39	755-799	64	6410-7000	89	55801-59400
15	92-99	40	800-872	65	7001-7600	90	59401-66300
16	100-109	41	873-950	66	7601-8300	91	66301-67500
17	110-118	42	951-1040	67	8301-9000	92	67501-71900
18	119-130	43	1041-1131	68	9001-9800	93	71901-76700
19	131-140	44	1132-1231	69	9801-10800	94	76701-81700
20	141-154	45	1232-1349	70	10801-11700	95	81701-87100
21	155-167	46	1350-1468	71	11701-12800	96	87101-87900
22	168-182	47	1469-1599	72	12801-14000	97	87901-88800
23	183-199	48	1600-1741	73	14001-15100	98	88801-89700
24	200-218	49	1742-1899	74	15101-16600	99	89701-90600
25	219-237	50	1900-2068	75	16601-18000	100	90601-91500

Creatures

The creatures that follow are derived from myth, legend, the natural world and, in a few cases, popular fantasy media. A broad selection is given, and is by no means exhaustive. In some cases similar species with slightly different appearances have been conflated. In the main these are corporeal creatures; the more intangible threats such as ghostly phantoms or wraiths have their own section subtitled Spirits.

There is also a focus on creatures that offer a legitimate challenge to Mythras characters – for this reason we have not included some examples, mainly animals, which would offer little in the way of danger or will typically run and hide when adventurers stray into their territories.

Fighting Quadrupeds

As a rule when four legged animals fight, the creature places its head towards its opponent. Given the size of most quadrupeds, it is difficult for a lone human opponent to strike any location other than the forequarters, front legs or head of the beast. For this reason, it is suggested that when a character attacks such an animal, they roll a d10+10 for the Hit Location. Of course, if the animal is surrounded by multiple foes, then the full range of its target locations should be available.

Acephali

A strange race of humanoids that completely lack any form of head or neck. The acephali's facial features are located instead across its chest and abdomen meaning that these creatures cannot wear any form of clothing or armour across these areas.

Acephali are primitive herders and shepherds occupying hilly terrain. They make crude stone huts and cabins, but prefer natural caves when they can be found. They are a surly, but not necessarily aggressive race, which prefers to keep its own company. Most sapients find the lack of a head extremely disturbing making communication with acephali tense at the best of times.

Given the vulnerability of their chest and abdominal regions acephali prefer ranged weapons and try to avoid melee combat. They are excellent slingers and archers. Some acephali carry a specially crafted heater with an eye-slit carved above the boss allowing for the chest and abdomen to be protected with passive blocking whilst the free arm is used to wield the sling.

Acephali	Attributes	
STR: 2d6+6 (13)	Action Points	3
CON: 3d6 (11)	Damage Modifier	+1d2
SIZ: 2d6+6 (13)	Magic Points	11
DEX: 2d6+6 (13)	Movement	8m
INT: 2d6+6 (13)	Initiative Bonus	11
POW: 3d6 (11)	Armour	Typically Leather
CHA: 2d6 (7)	Abilities	None
	Magic	Folk Magic 56% (Befuddle, Coordination, Firearrow)

1d20	Location	AP/HP
1–3	Right Leg	1/5
4–6	Left Leg	1/5
7–10	Abdomen	0/6
11-14	Chest/Face	0/7
15–17	Right Arm	1/4
18–20	Left Arm	1/4

Skills
Athletics 56%, Brawn 46%, Endurance 52%, Evade 46%, Perception 44%, Survival 52%, Track 54%, Willpower 52%

Passions
Love Solitude 88%, Suspicious of Strangers 80%

Combat Style & Weapons
Acephali Hunter (Sling, Bolas, Bow) 66%, Defensive Stance (Spear, Shield) 56%

Weapon	Size/Force	Reach	Damage	AP/HP
Sling	L	-	1d8	1/2
Bolas	-	-	1d4	2/2 Entangle
Short Bow	L	-	1d6+1d2	4/4
Shortspear	M	L	1d8+1+1d2	4/5
Heater	L	S	1d4+1+1d2	6/12

Ant, Giant

Giant ants are hive-dwellers, and operate under the direction of a queen with individuals taking on very specific roles (typically warrior or worker) necessary for the survival of the hive. Individual ants have highly developed instincts but working together in groups their intelligence shows remarkable degrees of problem-solving. Giant ants are also formidable predators, herding and farming smaller species of mammals and insects for food and, sometimes, incubation of eggs.

Giant ants use their powerful mandibles to seize, squeeze, and crush foes. Once seized the ant uses the Grip Combat Effect to hold onto its prey and, if it continues to resist, moves its thorax around to deliver a powerful sting. If poisoned the victim is allowed an Endurance roll, opposed by the ant's Endurance, to resist the poison. If the roll is failed then the location suffers agonising pain, and cannot be used for 30–CON minutes.

Individual ants are unlikely to engage foes larger than themselves, although packs of ants, working together, will have no hesitation in attacking. Single ants prefer to evade, wait, and send pheromone signals to nearby (or even distant) colleagues, summoning a larger party.

The statistics overleaf are for a worker or soldier ant. Queens are twice as large and twice as strong: 4d6+14 STR and SIZ but have a DEX of only 2d6, reflecting their largely stationery existence in the hive.

Ant, Giant		Attributes
STR: 4d6 (14)	Action Points	2
CON: 3d6+6 (17)	Damage Modifier	+1d2
SIZ: 4d6 (14)	Magic Points	4
DEX: 2d6+6 (13)	Movement	12m
INS: 2d6+2 (9)	Initiative Bonus	11
POW: 1d6 (4)	Armour	Chitin
	Abilities	Formidable Natural Weapons, Venomous
	Magic	None

1d20	Location	AP/HP
1	Right Rear Leg	4/6
2	Left Rear Leg	4/6
3	Right Middle Leg	4/6
4	Left Middle Leg	4/6
5-9	Abdomen	4/8
10-13	Thorax	4/9
14	Right Front Leg	4/6
15	Left Front Leg	4/6
16-20	Head	4/7

Skills
Athletics 67%, Brawn 68%, Endurance 74%, Evade 56%, Perception 53%, Track 66%, Willpower 48%

Combat Style & Weapons
Ant Attack (Mandibles and Sting) 67%

Weapon	Size/Force	Reach	Damage	AP/HP
Bite	M	T	1d6+1d2	1/2
Sting	M	M	1d4+1d2	As for Head

Asipatra

A large bird of Hindu myth, asipatra means 'sword wing', and these creatures are the tormentors of souls in the underworld, carving them with their blade-like wings, and dagger-length claws.

In Mythras these monsters are either summoned from the underworld or have found their way to the mundane world through obscure gateways, portals or tunnels. They aim solely to torment and frustrate, diving and strafing those marked for persecution, inflicting painful slices and cuts. Being made of metal they are exceedingly well-armoured but can still be felled by mundane weapons: note though that they are utterly immune to bladed weapons – swords, spears, axes, and so forth. Arrows and blunt weapons inflict normal damage.

Usually encountered singly, asipatra are summoned for a specific purpose, be it to punish someone or act as guardians. Others that migrate from the underworld come searching for those who have committed some form of sin in the eyes of a particular god, and so can be encountered in numbers; sent as divine punishment for some kind of wrong-doing.

Asipatra confined to the mortal world for any length of time collect spears, swords, and other sharp objects, forming nests from them.

Asipatra		Attributes
STR: 1d6+9 (13)	Action Points	3
CON: 3d6 (11)	Damage Modifier	None
SIZ: 1d6+6 (10)	Magic Points	7
DEX: 4d6+6 (20)	Movement	12m (Flying)
INS: 2d6+5 (12)	Initiative Bonus	16
POW: 2d6 (7)	Armour	Metal Feathers
	Abilities	Diving Attack, Flying, Immunity (Blades)
	Magic	None

1d20	Location	AP/HP
1–3	Right Claw	6/5
4–6	Left Claw	6/5
7–9	Abdomen	6/6
10-12	Chest	6/7
13–15	Right Wing	6/5
16–18	Left Wing	6/5
19–20	Head	6/5

Skills
Athletics 32%, Brawn 23%, Endurance 62%, Evade 60%, Fly 72%, Perception 59%, Willpower 54%

Combat Style & Weapons
Slice and Dice (Claws and Wings) 72%

Weapon	Size/Force	Reach	Damage	AP/HP
Claw	S	S	1d4	As for Claw
Wing Slice	M	M	1d6	As for Wing

Aurochs

Standing nearly 2m at the shoulder, aurochs are a giant Pleistocene cattle species found across much of northern Europe. They are famed for their strength and belligerence. Hunting aurochs is a near suicidal pastime but very rewarding in terms of the quantity of meat provided.

Aurochs prefer to fight by charging threats with their gore attack. If the target is knocked prone and continues to move, the aurochs tramples until the victim stops responding. A successful charge increases the Damage Bonus to 2d8. If lamed an aurochs continues to fight in place until it collapses from exhaustion.

Aurochs horns can span greater than a man's reach, and curve forwards from the head in a perfect charging/goring configuration. Naturally the horns can impale, and this is a standard Special Effect if a charging aurochs manages to gore an enemy. Aurochs horns are capable of both Sundering and Impaling and, if a foe is impaled, the bull on its next turn will attempt to throw its victim with a toss of its head. If the impaled victim is conscious, he may pit either his Athletics or Acrobatics against the Brawn of the bull. If successful, he may land safely on his feet or all fours. If unsuccessful, or if unconscious, the victim suffers the equivalent to a 1d6 metre fall and lands prone.

Aurochs		Attributes
STR: 2d6+24 (31)	Action Points	2
CON: 3d6+10 (21)	Damage Modifier	+2d6
SIZ: 4d6+24 (38)	Magic Points	7
DEX: 2d6 (7)	Movement	12m
INS: 2d6+4 (11)	Initiative Bonus	9
POW: 2d6 (7)	Armour	Tough Hide
	Abilities	Intimidate, Trample
	Magic	None

1d20	Location	AP/HP
1–2	Right Hind Leg	4/12
3–4	Left Hind Leg	4/12
5–7	Hindquarters	4/13
8–10	Forequarters	4/14
11–13	Right Front Leg	4/11
14–16	Left Front Leg	4/11
17–20	Head	4/12

Skills
Athletics 58%, Brawn 89%, Endurance 82%, Evade 34%, Perception 38%, Willpower 38%

Combat Style & Weapons
Gore and Toss (Horns) 68%

Weapon	Size/Force	Reach	Damage	AP/HP
Gore	H	M	1d10+2d6	As for Head
Trample	E	T	4d6	As for Legs

Baboon		Attributes
STR: 1d6+6 (10)	Action Points	3
CON: 3d6 (11)	Damage Modifier	-1d2
SIZ: 1d6+6 (10)	Magic Points	7
DEX: 3d6+6 (17)	Movement	8m
INS: 2d6+7 (14)	Initiative Bonus	16
POW: 2d6 (7)	Armour	Fur
	Abilities	Nightsight
	Magic	None

1d20	Location	AP/HP
1–3	Right Leg	1/5
4–6	Left Leg	1/5
7–9	Abdomen	1/6
10-12	Chest	1/7
13–15	Right Arm	1/4
16–18	Left Arm	1/4
19–20	Head	1/5

Skills
Acrobatics 57%, Athletics 47%, Brawn 40%, Endurance 42%, Evade 74%, Perception 61%, Stealth 61%, Survival 58%, Willpower 54%

Combat Style & Weapons
Ferocious Fracas (Bite, Fist, Thrown Object) 67%

Weapon	Size/Force	Reach	Damage	AP/HP
Bite	S	T	1d4-1d2	As for Head
Punch	S	T	1d3-1d2	As for Arm
Missile	S	-	1d3-1d2	As for Object

Baboon

Baboons are ground dwelling, and typically found in open savannah, open woodland, and hill areas in warm and sub-tropical climates. Ostensibly omnivores, they eat insects and occasionally prey on fish, shellfish, small mammals, birds, smaller primates, and small antelopes. Baboons are foragers and have been known to raid human dwellings, preying on sheep and goats

Troops of baboons usually feature around 30 animals but larger troops are not uncommon. A troop leader can be either male or female, and becomes the dominant figure of the group, choosing mates, and ensuring the choicest foods. Baboons are highly vocal and use their whoops, shrieks and calls to signal to each other and indicate their positioning in the social hierarchy.

The baboon template can be used for larger primates but adding additional bonuses: such as gorillas (+9 STR, +12 SIZ, 2d6+3 DEX) or man-eating carnivorous apes (+12 STR, +15 SIZ, 2d6 DEX).

Bagini

Bagini are vampiric, lustful monsters that are half woman, and half animal – usually a dingo, dog, wolf or hyena. They possess the head and breasts of a human with the rest of the creature being canine in form. In the daylight they appear quite normal, and may even form a friendship with a group of travellers. At night though, the bagini mutates into its true form where it feasts on the males present.

The bagini have two appetites that must be served: the first is their lust, and the monsters seek to be impregnated by males they have befriended so they can give birth to more bagini bitches. The initial seduction is performed as a human but the impregnation itself takes place as the she-demon's true body changes. The second appetite is blood. The bagini bites whilst it ruts, and drinks the blood it draws.

In their true form bagini are incredibly strong, and capable of pinning down a grown man while they satisfy their urges. Their tactic is therefore to drink blood whilst mating and, if possible, continue to drink blood once the mating has finished. A bagini will drain a number of Fatigue levels of blood equal to half its CON before it considers itself satiated, which can often lead to the death of the victim. If disturbed it will fight unless outnumbered. If females are present, bagini will either not approach or attempt to separate the men from the women so their business can be completed with as little suspicion as possible.

A bagini only uses its bite attack during intercourse, and the attack usually comes as a surprise if victim doesn't notice the preceding transformation. The actual bite causes minimal damage but the bagini will consequently drain one Fatigue level of blood per minute thereafter, whilst simultaneously sustaining her coupling. A bagini prefers the throat for its bite so that it can apply pressure to the windpipe of the victim, preventing them from calling out.

If the bite latches on, the victim must win in an opposed Brawn roll to prise the creature off. Failure means they are pinned under the creature's weight, and subject to the Grip special effect. Further efforts can be made to break free, but each subsequent attempt incurs an additional grade of difficulty. Bagini only use their claws in self defence to drive off interlopers which disturb their feeding.

This version of the bagini is based on Australian aboriginal myth. Yet many cultures describe similar creatures, and there is no reason why bagini cannot have more exotic animal types: cat, lizard, or even aquatic species such as dolphin or shark. The latter creates a rather memorable variation on the mermaid legend.

Bagini		Attributes
STR: 2d6+12 (19)	Action Points	3
CON: 2d6+6 (13)	Damage Modifier	+1d4
SIZ: 2d6+6 (13)	Magic Points	11
DEX: 3d6+6 (17)	Movement	8m
INT: 2d6+6 (13)	Initiative Bonus	15
POW: 3d6 (11)	Armour	Fur
CHA: 3d6 (11)	Abilities	Life Sense, Night Sight, Vampiric
	Magic	Folk Magic 62% (Glamour, Sleep)

1d20	Location	AP/HP
1–3	Right Leg	1/5
4–6	Left Leg	1/5
7–9	Abdomen	1/6
10-12	Chest	1/7
13–15	Right Arm	1/4
16–18	Left Arm	1/4
19–20	Head	1/5

Skills
Athletics 56%, Brawn 72%, Endurance 56%, Evade 64%, Influence 62%, Perception 54%, Seduction 64%, Stealth 50%, Willpower 62%

Passions
Insatiable Hunger 80%, Love Sex 80%, Hate Mortals 75%

Combat Style & Weapons
Ferocious Fracas (Bite, Fist, Thrown Object) 67%

Weapon	Size/Force	Reach	Damage	AP/HP
Bite	M	T	1d2+1d4	As for Head
Claw	M	M	1d3+1d4	As for Arm

Bakru

These strange creatures are magical creations: either accidentally, through the misadventure of sorcery, or by the gods out of some obscure whim. Tiny, mischievous creatures that resemble a human child with an oversized head, the bakru's body is made of wood or plant fibres, lending it a strange, gnarled appearance. Their small stature means they can easily hide and in woodland or undergrowth are very difficult to spot. It is possible that bakru have some relationship with elves, and some species may even originate from Faerie.

Bakru are intensely magical and use their magic to cause mischief and havoc for mortals. Any bakru has a number of Folk Magic spells equal to its POW, and a number of Theism spells equal to half its CHA. Games Masters will need to decide precisely what spells are possessed but generally anything that can be used to play pranks, cause annoyance or interfere are appropriate.

These imps cannot be harmed by mundane weapons. However, magical weapons of any kind inflict normal damage. Killing them is said to bring extremely bad luck in the form of a curse. To simulate this, Games Masters may wish to inflict some form of poor luck on any character who kills a bakru, whether accidentally or deliberately. Roll on the accompanying tables to determine the effect and duration of the curse.

Alleviating the curse requires some form of propitiation to the god who created the bakru, if at all possible. Otherwise, some other form of magical healing or alleviation may be necessary, but in such circumstances the Magnitude of the curse is equal to the POW of the dead Bakru.

In those campaigns based on high fantasy, or using the realm of Faerie, bakru are a naturally occurring species. Mischevious, sometimes malevolent, and always a nuisance when they decide to target some hapless human (such as cobblers, peddlers, and the like) who have caused them some slight...

Bakru Curse Type

1d6	*Curse Type*
1	The character's chance to fumble becomes a roll of 90-00 instead of 99-00 for the duration of the curse.
2	All skills become one grade more difficult for the duration of the curse.
3	The character completely forgets one Professional skill for the duration of the curse.
4	The character is subject to at least one level of fatigue for the curse's duration.
5	The character develops a powerfully repellent odour resulting in banishment from public places for the curse's duration.
6	All harmful or manipulative spells directed by the character at an opponent affect himself instead, for the curse's duration.

Bakru Curse Type

1d6	*Duration*
1	1d6 Combat Rounds
2	1d6 Minutes
3	1d6 Hours
4	1d6 Days
5	1d6 Months
6	1d6 Years

Bakru		Attributes
STR: 1d3 (2)	Action Points	3
CON: 1d6+1 (5)	Damage Modifier	-1d8
SIZ: 1d3 (2)	Magic Points	17
DEX: 3d6+6 (17)	Movement	6m
INT: 2d6+6 (13)	Initiative Bonus	15
POW: 3d6+6 (17)	Armour	Wooden Skin
CHA: 2d6+6 (13)	Abilities	Immunity (Mundane Weapons)
	Magic	Folk Magic 70%, Devotion 60%, Exhort 66%

1d20	Location	AP/HP
1–3	Right Leg	1/2
4–6	Left Leg	1/2
7–9	Abdomen	1/3
10-12	Chest	1/4
13–15	Right Arm	1/1
16–18	Left Arm	1/1
19–20	Head	1/2

Skills
Acrobatics 59%, Athletics 49%, Brawn 24%, Deceit 66%, Endurance 30%, Evade 74%, Locale 66%, Perception 70%, Sleight 70%, Stealth 70%, Willpower 74%

Passions
Make Mischief 88%, Take Offence 75%

Combat Style & Weapons
None

Basilisk/Cockatrice

A curious– and deadly – combination of rooster and serpent, basilisks and cockatrice (the former is hatched from the egg of a cockerel by a serpent, and the latter from the egg of a serpent by a cockerel) are small but dreadful magical creatures. Being innately evil they detest all life, and deal with it by the glare which is enough to kill anyone who meets the baleful gaze.

Either creature is about the size of a large rooster with a serpentine body, sometimes with small, useless dragon-like wings, a rooster's head and wattle, and usually two or occasionally four, rooster-like feet. They are highly, highly reclusive, and often prized by sorcerers for many bodily components that are useful ingredients in rituals and spells. The blood of the basilisk is a concentrated acid but its real power lies in its Death Stare. The basilisk must expend both a Magic Point and an Action Point on its turn to activate this dreadful power. This forces an opposed roll of the basilisk's Willpower against the victim's Evade (to avert their eyes in time). If the victim loses he suffers an immediate Major Wound to the Head, haemorrhaging blood from the eyes, ears, nostrils and mouth. A further standard Endurance roll is needed on the next round to avoid death. The Death Gaze is also effective against plant-life, causing all but the hardiest plants to wither and die against the monster's evil glare.

Curiously, these beasts are not immune to their own gaze; if forced to glimpse its own reflection, it must succeed in a Willpower roll or die on the spot.

Basilisks and cockatrices have little need to enter into physical combat, relying on their gaze and Evade for defence. If injured the monster's acidic blood immediately inflicts 1d6 damage to the weapon used (armour points do not protect), with the acid continuing to inflict damage each round for the next two rounds.

Curiously, weasels and similar mammals, such as ferrets and the mongoose, are immune the gaze of the basilisk; their blood, spit and urine contains a venom wholly poisonous to the monster meaning that such animals are safe from any of the basilisk's attacks. Similarly, if a basilisk hears a cock crowing at dawn, it must make an immediate Willpower roll or die immediately, meaning that most basilisks and cockatrice are found far from human habitation.

Certain sorcerers believe that a basilisk can be tamed if raised from the egg by a human parent and will not turn their dreadful gaze against their owner. It takes a brave sorcerer to attempt such husbandry, and braver adventurers to go hunting basilisk eggs, but given the highly magical and lethal nature of the monster, the risks may well be thought to be worthwhile.

Basilisk/Cockatrice		Attributes
STR: 1d6+1 (5)	Action Points	2
CON: 3d6 (11)	Damage Modifier	-1d6
SIZ: 1d6+1 (5)	Magic Points	19
DEX: 2d6+6 (13)	Movement	6m
INS: 2d6+4 (11)	Initiative Bonus	12
POW: 2d6+12 (19)	Armour	Scales
	Abilities	Gaze Attack, Life Sense, Terrifying
	Magic	None

1d20	Location	AP/HP
1-3	Tail	1/4
4-5	Right Hind Leg	1/4
6-7	Left Hind Leg	1/4
8-10	Hindquarters	1/5
11-14	Forequarters	1/6
15-16	Right Winglet	1/3
17-18	Left Winglet	1/3
19-20	Head	1/4

Skills
Athletics 48%, Brawn 30%, Endurance 52%, Evade 66%, Perception 69%, Willpower 78%

Combat Style & Weapons
Gaze Attack (see description)

1d20	Location	AP/HP
1–3	Right Rear Leg	3/10
4–6	Left Rear Leg	3/10
7–9	Hindquarters	3/11
10-12	Forequarters	3/12
13–15	Right Front Leg	3/10
16–18	Left Front Leg	3/10
19–20	Head	3/10

Skills
Athletics 68%, Brawn 79%, Endurance 66%, Evade 46%, Perception 60%, Stealth 66%, Survival 60%, Swim 68%, Track 66%, Willpower 44%

Combat Style & Weapons
Ursine Fury (Bite and Claws) 78%

Weapon	Size/Force	Reach	Damage	AP/HP
Bite	L	S	1d8+1d12	As for Head
Claw	H	L	1d8+1d12	As for Arm

Bear

Bears typically inhabit forested and hilly regions in temperate to arctic zones. They are generally solitary animals although mothers and cubs travel together in packs. The following characteristics represent Grizzly, Kodiak and Polar bears. These are the largest, fiercest, and most unpredictable of the bear species although their need to attack is generally driven by hunger, curiosity and fear. They will roam far and wide in search of food, even entering settlements to scavenge, and prey on smaller creatures. They will pursue and track injured creatures, or those that flee, and leave a discernible trail. Like many predators, playing dead does confuse the bear, and cause it to lose interest which may prove to be a life-saver if attacked. Despite their size and bulk they are swift and remarkable swimmers and climbers.

Bears typically attempt to grip with both claws, and then deliver a bite, although swiping with a claw is also an effective means of disabling an enemy. Playing dead is a tactic oft-cited for dealing with bear attacks. This is fine if the bear is acting defensively. If hungry, and actively chasing prey, playing dead may well be quite the wrong way to act. A hungry bear does not care if its meal is static. Prehistoric ursoids, such as the short-faced bear, tend to be larger and stronger (additional +6 STR, +10 SIZ).

Bear		Attributes
STR: 2d6+18 (25)	Action Points	3
CON: 2d6+6 (13)	Damage Modifier	+1d12
SIZ: 4d6+20 (34)	Magic Points	7
DEX: 2d6+6 (13)	Movement	8m
INS: 2d6+6 (13)	Initiative Bonus	13
POW: 2d6 (7)	Armour	Thick Pelt
	Abilities	Intimidate, Nightsight
	Magic	None

Beetle, Giant

Giant beetles come in many different species. All species are six-legged, and some have wings that fold into the carapace. All giant beetles are naturally armoured with chitin across all surfaces save the underbelly – natural protection against predators although, in their giant forms, only the very largest carnivores are a match for them.

Beetles are not necessarily aggressive. Many beetles are omnivorous, feeding on mouldering plant detritus and vegetation, and other invertebrates (and also small mammals). They prefer warm, dark conditions, and so are often found underground in their vast burrows – a few types are ground-dwellers rather than burrowers.

All giant beetles rely on their armour for defence rather than evading. Grasping, and then attempting to dash their foes (or simply continue biting) is a common enough tactic.

Some creatures, such as goblins, orcs, and even dwarves, actively breed and farm giant beetles for use as beasts of burden and steeds. Species that fly are prized amongst those that put these massive insects to work.

Beetle, Giant		Attributes
STR: 2d6+12 (19)	Action Points	2
CON: 3d6+6 (17)	Damage Modifier	+1d6
SIZ: 2d6+12 (19)	Magic Points	4
DEX: 2d6+6 (13)	Movement	12m
INS: 2d6+2 (9)	Initiative Bonus	11
POW: 1d6 (4)	Armour	Chitin
	Abilities	Burrowing, Formidable Natural Weapons
	Magic	None

1d20	Location	AP/HP
1	Right Rear Leg	5/7
2	Left Rear Leg	5/7
3	Right Middle Leg	5/7
4	Left Middle Leg	5/7
5-9	Abdomen	5/9
10-13	Thorax	5/10
14	Right Front Leg	5/7
15	Left Front Leg	5/7
16-20	Head	5/8

Skills
Athletics 62%, Brawn 68%, Endurance 74%, Evade 26%, Perception 53%, Willpower 38%

Combat Style & Weapons
Beetle Bite (Mandibles) 72%

Weapon	Size/Force	Reach	Damage	AP/HP
Mandibles	M	T	1d6+1d6	As for Head

Boar

Wild boars inhabit woods and forests in most temperate climates. The body of the wild boar is compact; the head is large, whilst the legs relatively short. A boar's coat consists of stiff bristles and finer fur. The colour varies from dark grey to black or brown, are there can be great regional differences in colour.

Adult boars measure around 2m in length, and stand around 1m at the shoulder. Larger specimens are not uncommon. Males are equipped with large, sharp tusks used for foraging and fighting, and these tusks lend the boar its fearsome reputation.

Boars are usually solitary animals outside of the breeding season. All boars are aggressive when threatened, usually attempting to intimidate first, and then launch a powerful charge using the tusks to carve at their enemies. Sows with young will almost certainly attempt to defend their progeny from potential attack, and males can be highly territorial – especially if sows are nearby during the breeding season.

The animals are prized for their rich meat, strong, warm hide, and their tusks which make excellent trophies. Boar hunting, using hounds to track and flush the animals, is a widespread sport throughout most cultures, but a hazardous one. Large, powerful specimens can easily eviscerate unwary opponents, and whilst much of the challenge comes in facing these creatures with a longspear to receive a charge, hunter injuries and deaths are not uncommon.

Some species, such as goblins and orcs, raise boar as mounts, riding them into battle just as any other steed. A boar cavalry, tusks tipped with iron or even spikes or spines, is a terrifying sight.

Boar		Attributes
STR: 2d6+9 (16)	Action Points	2
CON: 2d6+9 (16)	Damage Modifier	+1d4
SIZ: 3d6+6 (17)	Magic Points	7
DEX: 3d6 (11)	Movement	8m
INS: 2d6+4 (11)	Initiative Bonus	11
POW: 2d6 (7)	Armour	Bristled Hide
	Abilities	Burrower, Frenzy
	Magic	None

1d20	Location	AP/HP
1–3	Right Rear Leg	2/7
4–6	Left Rear Leg	2/7
7–9	Hindquarters	2/8
10-12	Forequarters	2/9
13–15	Right Front Leg	2/7
16–18	Left Front Leg	2/7
19–20	Head	2/7

Skills
Athletics 57%, Brawn 63%, Endurance 62%, Evade 42%, Perception 48%, Willpower 32%

Combat Style & Weapons
Goring Grunter (Tusks) 67%

Weapon	Size/Force	Reach	Damage	AP/HP
Tusks	M	S	1d6+1d4	As for Head

BOAR-KIN

Boar-headed humans akin to minotaurs, boar-kin are a product of the gods of chaos. Powerful, aggressive, forest-dwelling individuals, they are as attuned to their environment as are their four-legged relatives, and may even lead packs of wild boar acting as their leaders. Boar-Kin are equipped with the ferocious tusks of their animal cousins, and find socialization with humankind difficult. They have simple psychologies: defend their territory and their lives, and procreate their species. For this latter goal, humans may be actively stalked, seized, and kept prisoner deep in the boar-kin's forest lair.

Boar-Kin, like their four-legged brethren, are largely nocturnal. They are burrow dwellers (like their kin), and may have a large underground lair consisting of a tunnels and chambers beneath the forest floor.

Boar-Kin, if needing a mate, will always try to incapacitate rather than kill so that a potential victim can be captured. Typically boar-kin use their spears, relying only on tusks when in close proximity to their targets. If a boar-kin successfully gouges with its tusks roll 1d10+10 for the Hit Location to reflect the upper parts of the body likely to be targeted by the attack.

Boar-Kin	Attributes	
STR: 2d6+9 (16)	Action Points	3
CON: 2d6+9 (16)	Damage Modifier	+1d4
SIZ: 2d6+9 (16)	Magic Points	11
DEX: 2d6+6 (13)	Movement	6m
INT: 2d6+6 (13)	Initiative Bonus	13
POW: 3d6 (11)	Armour	Bristled Hide
CHA: 2d6 (7)	Abilities	Burrower, Chaos Feature (if a product of Chaos), Frenzy, Intimidate
	Magic	Folk Magic 56% (Befuddle, Coordination, Firearrow)

1d20	Location	AP/HP
1–3	Right Leg	1/7
4–6	Left Leg	1/7
7–9	Abdomen	1/8
10-12	Chest	1/9
13–15	Right Arm	1/6
16–18	Left Arm	1/6
19–20	Head	1/7

Skills
Athletics 59%, Brawn 62%, Endurance 62%, Evade 56%, Locale 66%, Perception 64%, Survival 67%, Unarmed 59%, Willpower 62%

Combat Style & Weapons
Boar-Kin Warrior (Spear, Tusk, Shield) 69%

Passions
Love Chaos 88%, Hate Intruders 80%

Weapon	Size/Force	Reach	Damage	AP/HP
Shortspear	M	L	1d8+1+1d4	4/5
Tusks	M	T	1d4+1d4	As for Head
Peltast Shield	L	S	1d4+1d4	4/12

BONACON

This herbivorous four legged beast has the body of a bull and the head of a horse, the head equipped with oversized sharp, curling horns. Bonacon can be tamed and used as mounts, but capturing these beasts in the wild is hazardous as bonacon are naturally fierce and antagonistic, taking exception to most intruders. If forced to back down, the bonacon flees, expelling a trail of excrement behind it which is spread by its revolving hairy tail.

This strange behaviour has a second peculiarity. Its faeces are poisonous, a result of complex digestive processes that create a pungent, agony and asphyxia-inducing residue inherent in its pellets. Contact between bonacon faeces and exposed flesh results in, first, itching and then an intense burning sensation. Shortness of breath follows as the lungs begin to fail, and then the possibility of death as airways close. One pellet – about the size of a fist – can be used to coat the blade of a Medium sized weapon to create a natural blade venom.

The faeces of a bonacon have a Potency of 70 with itching beginning after 1d4 Combat Rounds. A further Endurance roll against the potency is required after one hour as the affected area is subject to the Agony condition (see page 75). After another 1d3 hours a further Endurance roll, this time at one grade lower, must be made to avoid incurring 1d3 levels of Fatigue owing to shortness of breath. 1d3 hours later the airways start to fail resulting in death in CON minutes if some form of poison cure cannot be found. If at any stage the victim succeeds in resisting the poison then all further effects are ignored.

Bonacon	Attributes	
STR: 2d6+12 (19)	Action Points	2
CON: 2d6+9 (16)	Damage Modifier	+1d8
SIZ: 4d6+12 (26)	Magic Points	7
DEX: 2d6+6 (13)	Movement	10m
INS: 2d6+4 (11)	Initiative Bonus	12
POW: 2d6 (7)	Armour	Tough Hide
	Abilities	Trample, Venomous (faeces)
	Magic	None

1d20	Location	AP/HP
1–3	Right Rear Leg	2/9
4–6	Left Rear Leg	2/9
7–9	Hindquarters	2/10
10-12	Forequarters	2/11
13–15	Right Front Leg	2/9
16–18	Left Front Leg	2/9
19–20	Head	2/9

Skills
Athletics 62%, Brawn 65%, Endurance 62%, Evade 46%, Perception 38%, Willpower 34%

Combat Style & Weapons
Gore and Gouge (Horns) 72%

Weapon	Size/Force	Reach	Damage	AP/HP
Horns	M	S	1d10+1d8	As for Head
Trample	H	S	2d8	As for Leg

Centaur

The classical centaur is a magical cross between human and equine forms: the upper body of a human replacing the horse's head and neck. However other centaur forms are possible: elf, goblin or orc centaurs, for instance.

Centaurs are noted for their intelligence, and often act as teachers, and tutors. They are social and herds of centaurs form their own societies based on either a barbarian or nomadic culture rather than a civilised one – although centaurs display many cultural qualities equating to civilised societies, they can also become wild and bestial, especially when drunk.

It is common for centaurs to form friendship bonds with an individual or a group of individuals, but their loyalties will always be, first and foremost, to their own herd. Centaurs mate with their own kind and cannot mate with humans, but they have human emotions, and so romantic liaisons are not unknown.

Centaurs can study and practice magic just as humans can. Any magical style is open to them, and the style favoured depends entirely on the social, cultural and religious practices of the centaur herd.

Note: The centaur's anatomy means that the Damage Modifier and Hit Points for its upper half are figured using STR x2 and CON x2.

Centaur Characters

Centaurs can certainly be used as player characters although their physiology and general nature may prove to be a challenge in some situations.

Culture

The Centaur culture is roughly equivalent to Barbarian, even though they do not build fixed settlements, and study many cerebral arts. The herd is a cohesive social group with strong traditions and principles. Naturally herds display the same range of characteristics as any society and, although centaurs are, by and large, passive there are herds that enjoy war, raiding and challenging those around them. Indeed, some of the examples found in the Combat chapter show the more aggressive side to the centaur culture.

- Customs+40%, Native Tongue+40%
- Standard Skills: Athletics, Brawn, Endurance, First Aid, Insight, Locale, Perception
- Example Combat Styles: Centaur Warrior, Centaur Berserker
- Professional Skills: Courtesy, Craft (any), Healing, Language (any), Lore (any), Musicianship, Teach, Track

Cultural Passions

- Loyalty to Herd
- Love (Person, Alcohol, Learning, Women)
- Hate (Ignorance, Predators, and so on).

Professions

Craftsman, Herder, Hunter, Physician, Priest, Scholar, Scout, Shaman, Warrior

Starting Money

Centaur characters begin the game with goods and currency worth 4d6 x60 silver pieces.

The Centaur Voice

'Our herd rules these pastures but you are free to pass through as long as you do not approach our mares and foals, and remember that honour should prevail. Indeed, we know many from your city, and I had the privilege of acting as tutor to one of your noblemen: perhaps you have heard of him? No? Ah, well… not all are destined for great things.

We are cautious because there have been raids by the two-legged beastmen of Chaos recently. Only last season our warriors had to drive-away a raiding party intent on spreading disease. One of our mares was captured a year ago and foaled a terrible monstrosity so it is our duty to wipe out their pestilence. We will keep them from reaching your city if we can – even if that costs centaur lives. We fear chaos but will stand against it because purity requires a fight if it is to be preserved.

You look weary. My cave is not far, and our herd is gathering to feast this eve. If you wish you may join us, rest, and eat. There will be many stories told, and competitions held. Why, if you can use that bow you carry you might even beat some of our archers! If not, we can show you some techniques that will improve your skill with it. The choice is yours. If you join us you will be most welcome, and on the morrow I will have two of our warriors provide a guide through the western hills, which is where the chaos nest lurks.

Pass in peace, two-legged brother.'

Centaur		Attributes
STR: 3d6+6 (17)	Action Points	2
CON: 3d6 (11)	Damage Modifier	+1d4 (+1d10 when Trampling)
SIZ: 3d6+18 (29)	Magic Points	16
DEX: 3d6 (11)	Movement	12m
INT: 2d6+6 (13)	Initiative Bonus	12
POW: 2d6+9 (16)	Armour	Hide on equine parts. Any armour for their human locations and barding for the equine locations.
CHA: 3d6 (11)	Abilities	Trample
	Magic	Specialists may follow any magical tradition.

1d20	Location	AP/HP
1-3	Right Rear Leg	1/8
4-6	Left Rear Leg	1/8
7-8	Hindquarters	1/9
9-10	Forequarters	1/10
11-12	Right Front Leg	1/8
13-14	Left Front Leg	1/8
15-16	Chest	0/7
17	Right Arm	0/4
18	Left Arm	0/4
19-20	Head	0/5

Skills
Athletics 58%, Brawn 70%, Endurance 52%, Evade 62%, Insight 59%, Locale 66%, Lore (Various) 66%, Musicianship 62%, Perception 49%, Teach 64%, Unarmed 58%, Willpower 62%

Combat Style & Weapons
Centaur Warrior (Spear, Shield, Short Bow) 68%

Weapon	Size/Force	Reach	Damage	AP/HP
Shortspear	M	L	1d8+1+1d4	4/5
Peltast Shield	L	S	1d4+1d4	4/12
Short Bow	L	-	1d6+1d4	4/4
Hooves	L	M	1d6+1d4	As for Leg
Trample	H	M	2d10	As for Leg

Chaos Hybrid

These foul beings go by many regional and cultural names but are essentially the same thing: a chaos-warped combination of human and animal (goat, sheep, and antelope) that frequently carries disease, and lives only to reproduce, spread its diseases, and bring havoc and suffering to the untainted.

Chaos Hybrids have their own, loosely-knit, primitive cultures based on strength and cruelty. A leader of a pack (known as a Murder) is always the strongest, fiercest, and most ruthless of the bunch, having secured his place through slaughtering any challengers. Given this mind-set and philosophy it is therefore unsurprising to find that Chaos Hybrids have utter contempt for all other sapient races seeing them as prey, a means to spread their contagion and to breed with.

The creatures worship the gods associated with their atrocities: those of murder, chaos, disease and blight. Most other sapient cultures shun them at best, and hunt them down with a view to extermination at worst.

Chaos Hybrids have a chance equal to their Willpower of being cursed (or blessed) with 1d3 Chaotic Features. They are also adept magicians, and most Hybrids can be expected to have a number of Folk Magic spells equal to their CHA. Each pack has at least one priest or shaman with access to the relevant magic.

Note that some hybrids are born with sub-sapient intellects which may cause them to act as little more than mentally impaired beasts.

A Chaos Hybrid carries a disease (see the disease table below) which can be caught through close proximity to the creature (i.e., close combat engagement distances). Chaos Hybrid corpses remain contagious unless burned. The potency of the disease is always equal to the Chaos Hybrid's Endurance.

The diseases in the tableare the most common, but Chaos Hybrids have many dreadful contagions, especially those who worship the spirits and gods of disease. Hybrid shamans go out of their way to locate virulent disease spirits in the Spirit World, bringing them back to deliberately infect an entire tribe.

How Chaos Hybrids are actually created depends entirely on the campaign setting. Such knowledge is often secret, often unknown to the hybrids themselves. Other than the necessity of a human and an animal, the methods can be infinite. Examples include a diabolical sorcery spell that requires ritualised vivisection to exchange body parts. Forcing victims to drink vile potions before invoking the powers of a chaos divinity. An evil spirit which warps its victim after it possesses them. Or literal pools or seas of primeval chaos into which human and animal sacrifices are cast, and only hybrids emerge.

Chaos Hybrid	Attributes	
STR: 2d6+6 (13)	Action Points	2
CON: 1d6+12 (16)	Damage Modifier	+1d2
SIZ: 2d6+6 (13)	Magic Points	11
DEX: 3d6 (11)	Movement	8m
INT: 3d6 (11)	Initiative Bonus	11
POW: 3d6 (11)	Armour	Tough Hide
CHA: 2d6 (7)	Abilities	Chaos Tainted, Disease Immunity
	Magic	Folk Magic 48%; Specialists have either Devotion 58% & Exhort 58%, or Binding 58% & Trance 57%

1d20	Location	AP/HP
1–3	Right Leg	1/7
4–6	Left Leg	1/7
7–9	Abdomen	1/8
10-12	Chest	1/9
13–15	Right Arm	1/6
16–18	Left Arm	1/6
19–20	Head	1/7

Skills
Athletics 44%, Brawn 46%, Endurance 62%, Evade 42%, Locale 52%, Perception 62%, Survival 67%, Unarmed 54%, Willpower 52%

Passions
Love Chaos 88%, Hate Everyone 80%

Combat Style & Weapons
Hybrid Ravager (Spear, Club, Shield) 64%

Weapon	Size/Force	Reach	Damage	AP/HP
Club	M	S	1d6+1d2	4/4
Shortspear	M	L	1d8+1+1d2	4/5
Horns	M	S	1d4+1d2	As for Head
Target Shield	M	S	1d4+1d2	4/9

The Chaos of Chaotic Features

The list of Chaos Features on page 275 provide a way to make creatures disturbing and unpredictable, making even non-descript encounters potentially life threatening. A simple snake or wolf can suddenly become a deadly surprise when it explodes in a spray of acid, or passes through a solid wall to attack a character. Even better is the fact that many Chaotic Features are often undetectable before their horrific effects are felt.

With chaos hybrids in particular, the danger rapidly mounts with numbers. A small troop of half a dozen hybrids can potentially possess up to 18 Chaotic Features between them, rapidly overwhelming adventurers who are not sufficiently prepared, or lack tactical experience to handle the warping effects of Chaos.

It is recommended that Games Masters provide clues or hints to such weirdness prior to any encounter with creatures possessing Chaos Features, so that characters both suffer increased apprehension and are more prepared to flee such a challenge if things get out of hand...

Chaos Hybrid Diseases

1d6	Disease	Symptoms and Effects
1	Mind Rot	1 point of INT is lost every week until the disease is cured. The victim feels sleepy and indolent, the condition worsening with each point of INT lost.
2	Seeping Pox	Suppurating boils begin in a random location and spread to an adjacent location each week until cured. The boils hiss and burst easily leaving horrible welts in their wake. The affected location cannot be covered whilst afflicted and sustains 1 Hit Point of damage after infection. 1d3 points of CHA is lost when the disease reaches the Head.
3	Creeping Chills	The victim is wracked by shivers that no degree of heat can alleviate. He automatically gains 1d3 levels of Fatigue which remains until the disease is cured.
4	Gagging Cough	Whenever strenuous activity is entered the victim must make an Endurance roll. If failed he is subjected to a fit of dreadful, painful coughing that continues for 1d6 minutes. During this time he is unable to do anything save cough and wretch.
5	Red Plague	The victim breaks out in a scarlet rash that covers the entire body. 1 point of CON is lost every day through vomiting, diarrhoea and dehydration. When CON reaches zero the victim dies.
6	Madness Blight	The victim is subject to violent headaches and suffers mild hallucinations whenever they make a skill check which results in a roll of 96+. However, he also descends into insanity becoming paranoid, schizophrenic, subject to violent rages and, after a number of days equal to his POW, irreparably insane.

Chimera

The Chimera of mythology has the head and body of a lion (or lioness) with a serpent for a tail, and the head of a goat emerging from the mid-part of the beast's spine. The serpent is poisonous (treat as cobra venom on page 76), and the goat can breathe fire, whilst the lion's head snarls and rages. Clearly a product of magic and perhaps Chaos, the chimera is a fearsome monster able to handle multiple foes simultaneously. The breath weapon of the goat's head makes it difficult to get close to the creature, its horns defend against attacks from above, and only magical or enchanted weapons inflict normal damage.

Chimera are generally encountered singly, and as guardians of some kind – although some individuals may wander, bringing fear and destruction to those areas they decide to stalk. They are possessed of a ravenous hunger, devouring any fresh meat that happens across their path. In some myth variants the chimera is depicted as having the head of a fire-breathing lion with the horns of a goat. If using such a variation, then remember that the horns can be used as a highly effective impaling weapon.

Killing a chimera can be achieved through decapitating the lion head; killing the serpent or goat heads only serves to deprive the monster of those attacks. The creature can split its attacks easily against separate enemies, assuming they are within range.

Chimera	Attributes	
STR: 2d6+12 (19)	Action Points	5 (multiheaded)
CON: 2d6+6 (13)	Damage Modifier	+1d8
SIZ: 2d6+18 (25)	Magic Points	13
DEX: 2d6+9 (16)	Movement	10m
INS: 2d6+6 (13)	Initiative Bonus	15
POW: 2d6+6 (13)	Armour	Mane and Hide
	Abilities	Breathe Flame, Immunity (Mundane weapons), Multi-headed, Venomous
	Magic	None

1d20	Location	AP/HP
1-2	Serpent Tail	1/7
3-4	Right Rear Leg	1/8
5-6	Left Rear Leg	1/8
7-8	Hindquarters	1/9
9-10	Goat Head	1/8
11-14	Forequarters	1/10
15-16	Right Front Leg	1/8
17-18	Left Front Leg	1/8
19-20	Lion Head	2/8

Skills
Athletics 55%, Brawn 68%, Endurance 66%, Evade 62%, Perception 56%, Willpower 66%

Combat Style & Weapons
Chimeric Chaos (Serpent Head, Goat Head, Lion Head, Claws) 75%

Weapon	Size/Force	Reach	Damage	AP/HP
Serpent Tail	M	L	1d4+Poison	As for Tail
Goat Horns	L	L	1d10	As for Goat Head
Goat Breath	Special		Fire	-
Lion Head	L	T	1d6+1d8	As for Lion Head
Claws	L	M	1d6+1d8	As for Leg

Crab, Giant

Gigantic versions of the familiar marine crustaceans, these crabs can be found in both oceanic and land-based variants although, in the latter case, large bodies of nearby water are favoured.

Giant crabs are capable of burrowing although they tend to remain close to the surface rather than creating deep and lengthy excavations.

All crabs benefit from the natural armour of their carapace, but the giant species of the familiar crustacean takes exceptional advantage. They possess one oversized claw which grants them a distinctive appearance. The giant crab behaves in very much the same way as its smaller cousins, with its sideways scuttle, and its aquatic life style (although land crabs can also be encountered in jungle environments).

Giant crabs are able to parry with either claw making them formidable opponents in combat. Both claws are able to Grip and Sunder. The secondary claw is usually used for parrying blows whilst the main claw is used to deliver them.

Crab, Giant	Attributes	
STR: 2d6+12 (19)	Action Points	3
CON: 3d6+6 (17)	Damage Modifier	+1d8
SIZ: 4d6+12 (26)	Magic Points	4
DEX: 3d6+6 (17)	Movement	6m
INS: 2d6+2 (9)	Initiative Bonus	13
POW: 1d6 (4)	Armour	Carapace
	Abilities	Burrowing, Formidable Natural Weapons
	Magic	None

1d20	Location	AP/HP
1	Right Fourth Leg	8/8
2	Left Fourth Leg	8/8
3	Right Third Leg	8/8
4	Left Third Leg	8/8
5	Right Second Leg	8/8
6	Left Second Leg	8/8
7	Right First Leg	8/8
8	Left First Leg	8/8
9-10	Abdomen	8/10
11-16	Cephalothorax	8/11
17-18	Right Pincer	8/11
19-20	Left Pincer	8/9

Skills
Athletics 56%, Brawn 75%, Endurance 64%, Evade 54%, Perception 43%, Willpower 38%

Combat Style & Weapons
Crushing Crustacean (Pincers) 76%

Weapon	Size/Force	Reach	Damage	AP/HP
Primary Pincer	H	L	1d8+1d8	As for Right Pincer
Secondary Pincer	L	M	1d8+1d8	As for Left Pincer

Crocodile/Alligator

Crocodiles and alligators infest tropical and sub-tropical seas, swamps and rivers where they feed on any form of live prey. Their camouflage is perfect for their environment, and by remaining perfectly still under the surface of murky water the creature can easily go unnoticed. They have little problem tackling prey much larger than themselves using ambush tactics to lunge out from cover, seize the prey, drag it into the water, then drown it. Despite their size and bulk, crocodiles are surprisingly fast and agile, albeit only maintaining this for short periods.

Crocodiles always choose Grip when a Special Effect has been generated, and hold on for as long as possible, using Brawn and Athletics to take the prey into the water where it is submerged and held there, with the creature spinning around and around to facilitate drowning. Spinning does not inflict any additional damage, but it makes attempts to break free from the grip one grade more difficult. Whilst submerged victims are subject to the Drowning rules (see page 71).

Alligators only live in fresh water and tend to be smaller than crocodiles, suffering a penalty of -8 to STR and -8 to SIZ. Prehistoric crocodiles on the other hand can grow far, far larger. To represent something like a Deinosuchus add +12 to STR, +24 to SIZ and double its Armour Points.

Crocodile/Alligator	Attributes	
STR: 2d6+18 (25)	Action Points	3
CON: 2d6+12 (19)	Damage Modifier	+2d6
SIZ: 2d6+30 (37)	Magic Points	7
DEX: 2d6+9 (16)	Movement	6m
INS: 2d6+5 (12)	Initiative Bonus	13
POW: 2d6 (7)	Armour	Thick Scales
	Abilities	Camouflaged, Cold Blooded
	Magic	None

1d20	Location	AP/HP
1-3	Tail	5/12
4-5	Right Hind Leg	5/12
6-7	Left Hind Leg	5/12
8-10	Hindquarters	5/13
11-14	Forequarters	5/14
15-16	Right Front Leg	5/12
17-18	Left Front Leg	5/12
19-20	Head	5/13

Skills
Athletics 41%, Brawn 92%, Endurance 78%, Evade 32%, Perception 49%, Swim 74% Willpower 44%

Combat Style & Weapons
Lurking Death (Jaws, Tail Sweep) 71%

Weapon	Size/Force	Reach	Damage	AP/HP
Jaws	H	M	1d10+2d6	As for Head
Tail	H	L	1d8+2d6	As for Tail

Cyclops

Greek legend refers to two quite distinct races bearing the same name. For Mythras, Cyclopes are a race of single-eyed giants with a taste for flesh of any kind, and a natural skill for metallurgy and constructing fortifications.

The single eye of the Cyclops is found in the centre of the creature's forehead, above the hooked nose. Above the eye is a horn which is the source of magical power for the Cyclops. A typical Cyclops stands around three times the height of a man. Its lower body is goat-like, and covered in rough, shaggy wool terminating in cloven hoofs.

Cyclopes live in isolated areas where they herd livestock (which are eaten raw), and manufacture metal goods in their subterranean forges often located in volcanoes or in caves near the sea. These goods are sold to those who manage to establish a relationship with the creatures, and Cyclopes are capable of forging exquisite weapons, armour, tools and jewellery.

A surly and bad tempered race, Cyclopes are quick to anger, and even those who have formed something approaching a friendship have been attacked with huge rocks, tree-trunk clubs or the forging hammers the Cyclopes occasionally carry. The most unfortunate– and this includes anyone who steal their livestock – are eaten. They are prone to throwing

boulders at tresspassers or even passing ships using their Athletics to aim the huge rocks.

Cyclopes are capable of using Folk Magic, and the horn above their single eye acts as a Folk Magic focus. If taken from a freshly killed Cyclops it contains the remaining Magic Points of the living creature, which can be used to power Folk Magic spells cast by the owner. The capacity of the horn deteriorates over time – one Magic Point is lost every year until the horn becomes useless – but until then, the Magic Points contained in the horn replenish at the same rate as its owner.

If a Cyclops is hit in the head, no matter how much damage is sustained, it must make an Endurance roll opposed by the attacker's combat roll. If the Cyclops fails in the roll it has been struck in the eye, and all physical skills immediately become one grade harder. If it loses with a Fumble, it is rendered completely blind with all skills becoming three grades harder.

Cyclops	Attributes	
STR: 2d6+24 (31)	Action Points	2
CON: 2d6+18 (25)	Damage Modifier	+2d6
SIZ: 4d6+24 (38)	Magic Points	13
DEX: 3d6 (11)	Movement	10m
INT: 2d6+6 (13)	Initiative Bonus	12
POW: 2d6+6 (13)	Armour	Skin & Fur (lower body)
CHA: 1d6 (4)	Abilities	Immunity (Fire)
	Magic	Folk Magic 65% (Bludgeon, Iron Hand)

1d20	*Location*	*AP/HP*
1-3	Right Leg	4/13
4-6	Left Leg	4/13
7-9	Abdomen	4/14
10-12	Chest	2/15
13-15	Right Arm	2/12
16-18	Left Arm	2/12
19-20	Head	2/13

Skills
Athletics 62%, Brawn 109%, Craft (Smithing) 64%, Endurance 80%, Evade 42%, Locale 56%, Lore (Husbandry) 66%, Perception 56%, Unarmed 72%, Willpower 66%

Passions
Resent Intruders 80%, Love Treasure and Metalwork 85%

Combat Style & Weapons
Huge Blunt Object (Hammer, Club) 82%

Weapon	Size/Force	Reach	Damage	AP/HP
Forge Hammer	H	L	1d10+3+2d6	6/325
Cyclopean Club	C	U	2d10+2d6	4/270
Thrown Boulder	E	-	4d6	4/-
Stomp	H	L	1d8+2d6	As for Leg

Dragon

The most iconic, dreaded, and revered of legendary creatures, dragons are immense, winged, fire-breathing reptiles of great intelligence – and, sometimes, wisdom – which are found represented in most cultures and mythologies. Sometimes they are brute killers, preying on the helpless; sometimes they are solitary hoarders guarding huge stashes of treasure; and at other times are wise mystics that seem capable of guiding others as well as preying upon them. Dragons are fully sapient although their intelligence is fundamentally alien to human psychology meaning that their actions, whilst appearing bestial, are driven by their own, peculiar, motivations and desires.

Dragons can talk. They have their own language (Draconic), and may be capable of either speaking other languages or converse mentally, bypassing the need for individual languages. However they communicate their dominating personality constantly seeks to ensnare or trick those that listen to its seductive words. They are also capable of using magic: Folk Magic certainly, and possibly higher forms such as sorcery. The choice of magic any dragon uses is dependent on the campaign, and the way the dragon is used.

Essentially solitary beings, dragons do mate and produce eggs, which are closely and severely guarded. Reproducing is likely a long and difficult business given the relative rarity of these beasts. Usually though, dragons are encountered as individuals, and extremely potent, dangerous at ones at that. A mature or old dragon is capable of handling scores of foes single-handedly although, as with any creature, they do have their weaknesses, and may be prone to a lucky strike that brings them crashing down.

The dragon characteristics provided here are for a young beast, and one that uses Folk Magic to augment its natural capabilities. Older specimens should have their skills, physical characteristics, and natural protection augmented to reflect increasing age and experience. Also note that this is a classic western dragon. Dragons found in eastern mythologies often lack wings (yet still fly), are more serpentine in appearance, and frequently have leonine features rather than reptilian. The same statistics can be used, but different Hit Locations may be required.

A dragon's tail sweep can hit multiple foes, its Attack roll being simultaneously applied to everyone within reach on its rear or flank.

The fire breathed by a dragon stretches in a cone for a number of metres in length equal to the dragon's CON, and a number of metres wide equal to a quarter of CON. Anything caught in the blast ignites if flammable, and the heat is powerful enough to melt unenchanted metals. Repeatedly using the breath weapon within a short period is exhausting though. If breathing fire more than once an hour, the dragon must make an Endurance roll with each roll after the first becoming one grade harder. Failing the Endurance roll gives the dragon one level of fatigue. Dragons therefore reserve their fire for only those occasions where it is absolutely necessary.

The classic dragon covets wealth, collecting and hoarding it in underground lairs and caverns. Not all dragons are so avaricious, but there is no doubting their love for gold, jewels, and finely made things. They can be arrogant and vain, too, displaying obvious contempt for anything smaller, less long-lived, and less intelligent. As with any intelligent creature though, dragons exhibit ahuge range of personality types and, despite their great power, many are friendly - or, at least not prone to violence - towards humans and other such species.

Dragon		Attributes
STR: 2d6+24 (31)	Action Points	4
CON: 2d6+24 (31)	Damage Modifier	+2d8
SIZ: 4d6+36 (50)	Magic Points	19
DEX: 2d6+12 (19)	Movement	12m, 18m (Flying)
INT: 2d6+12 (19)	Initiative Bonus	19
POW: 2d6+12 (19)	Armour	Thick Scales
CHA: 2d6+12 (19)	Abilities	Breathe Flame, Cold Blooded, Dark Sight, Diving Strike, Engulfing, Flying, Formidable Natural Weapons, Immunity (Fire), Terrifying, Trample

Magic: Folk Magic 78% (Avert, Befuddle, Cleanse, Coordination, Curse, Fangsharp, Find Treasure, Glamour, Heal, Mindspeech, Spiritshield, Vigour, Witchsight)

1d20	Location	AP/HP
1-2	Tail	8/17
3-4	Right Hind Leg	8/17
5-6	Left Hind Leg	8/17
7-8	Hindquarters	8/18
9-10	Right Wing	8/16
11-12	Left Wing	8/16
13-14	Forequarters	8/19
15-16	Right Front Leg	8/17
17-18	Left Front Leg	8/17
19-20	Head	8/17

Skills

Athletics 80%, Brawn 120%, Deceit 78%, Endurance 92%, Evade 68%, Fly 90%, Insight 78%, Locale 68%, Lore (Dragon) 68%, Perception 78%, Teach 58%, Willpower 78%

Passions

Covet Treasure 99%, Disdain Lesser Creatures 90%, Abhor Weakness 80%, Love Intrigues 84%

Combat Style & Weapons

Death and Destruction (Bite, Claws, Tail Sweep) 90%, Flame Breath 80%

Weapon	Size/Force	Reach	Damage	AP/HP
Bite	E	L	1d12+2d8	As for Head
Claws	E	L	1d10+2d8	As for Leg
Tail	E	VL	1d10+2d8	As for Tail
Flame Breath	Special		4d6	-
Trample	C	T	4d8	-

Dwarf

Diminutive, subterranean humanoids that often have a propensity for mining and metallurgy, with an accompanying love for treasure, and all things material. The classic view of dwarves is that of a stocky, bearded, gruff species that have no love for elves, and are often portrayed as greedy, calculating and mischievous. That dwarves are short is a given, but most cultures and mythologies have a diminutive species of some kind, and the more materialistic side of their nature is not ubiquitous.

Some dwarves are attuned with nature and earth in similar ways that elves are with the forests. It is probably fair to say that, just like humans, there are numerous dwarven races, all related, with a myriad of different cultures. The things they have in common are a squat, heavily-set stature, a preference for an underground existence, and certain natural enemies (subterranean predators such as trolls, for example). Beyond that, cultural dynamics are as diverse as human societies, although clearly adapted to a life in the tunnels and caverns, and where the natural hazards are very different to those above ground.

Dwarves are naturally suspicious of anyone espousing a different way of life to their own, but not necessarily antagonistic towards them. Living underground means learning to deal with rocks and minerals which results in a capability for mining and metallurgy, but this is by no means a ubiquitous practice. However, given such an insular environment most dwarves are wary, reticent, and probably suspicious where outsiders are concerned.

Strong sunlight is not something they are used to, and many dwarves find that bright, natural light makes them feel sluggish and fatigued. They are, though, generally resilient to cold temperatures, and can function with greater ease in the dark, winter months than in the warm, summer ones.

The characteristics given here are for a typical dwarf from western (and more specifically, Norse) myth. They are base characteristics, and standard for all dwarf species but cultures and, therefore, skills and magic availability will vary. Whether or not dwarves have beards, even females, is entirely up to you.

Dwarven Characters

Dwarves make for good player characters. Their psychology is, though, shaped by their environment and their physical capabilities. As indicated there are myriad species. The notes here are to help design a typical dwarf from northern European mythology.

Dwarven SIZ represents mass, not height. When creating a dwarf, always calculate weight based on the Heavy frame and treat the height as being two SIZ points lower (and always at the lower end of the scale. For instance, a dwarf with SIZ 10 would be 82-90 kg, but its height would be around 151-155cm.

Culture

Dwarves are social creatures bonded into clans and tribes that share the great underground halls and cities. In this respect they most closely resemble the Barbarian culture although there are certain key differences. First of all, gender does not matter in dwarven society: males and females share duties and responsibilities equally. This includes child-rearing, manual labour, hunting, and war. Secondly dwarves tend to downplay the individual in favour of the society. Dwarves know that strength comes from numbers, and that the wants and needs of the individual are always outweighed by the many. They are, however, collectively, an acquisitive, materialistic society, jealously guarding their discoveries and achievements. Dwarves like things and, when removed from the clan, a lone dwarf can become selfish and individualistic very quickly, because the overall dwarvish culture is absent to guide and control his baser instincts.

- Customs+40%, Native Tongue+40%
- Standard Skills: Athletics, Brawn, Deceit, Endurance, First Aid, Locale, Perception
- Example Combat Styles: Dwarven Thane, Dwarf Berserker, Mine Warrior
- Professional Skills: Commerce, Craft (any), Engineering, Lore (any), Mechanisms, Musicianship, Oratory, Survival

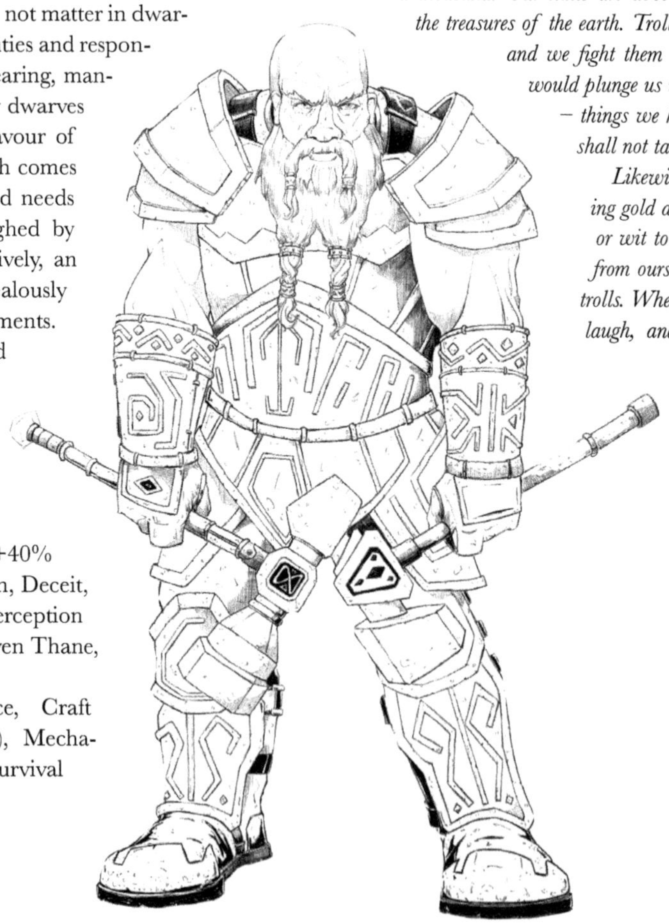

Cultural Passions

- Loyalty to Clan
- Love (Something Materialistic)
- Hate (Either Trolls, Elves or some other race that bears your clan enmity)

Professions

Alchemist, Crafter, Entertainer, Herder, Merchant, Miner, Official, Physician, Priest, Scholar, Scout, Sorcerer, Thief, Warrior

Starting Money

Dwarven characters begin the game with commodities or currency worth 4d6 x100 silver pieces.

The Dwarven Voice

'Of rock and stone we shape the world. Of metal and gem we bend our tools. Above us the world turns, and moves from dark to light but here in the Halls all things stay the same, and that is how they should be. Change is unwanted because it brings uncertainty. Uncertainty breeds indecision, and indecision breeds weakness. We dwarves are not weak. We know what to do, when to do it, how to do it, and the tools to do it with. If something needs doing we do it now. Can you plough a field at night? Can you plant crops in rain? No. The Upper World limits what you can do, and that is why we shun it. In our Halls, we dictate the pace, and the pace is for the good of the Hall. That is the only way.

Our hall is the grandest. The grandfathers of our clan carved it from the living stone a thousand years ago, and each generation has continued the carving. What was once a small settlement of fifty caverns is now a large city of almost a thousand. Our halls are above the silver mines, and so we guard the treasures of the earth. Trolls try to break through now and then, and we fight them with hammer, axe, and spear. They would plunge us into their darkness, and eat our things – things we have strived to mine and build. They shall not take us!

Likewise men come down our passages seeking gold and jewels. They have not the strength or wit to dig their own chambers, and so take from ours. We fight them just like we fight the trolls. When the trolls and men fight, we dwarves laugh, and feast because through killing each other they save us the trouble.

We dwarves are as one. We are like the stone. We are the stone.'

Dwarf		Attributes
STR: 2d6+9 (16)	Action Points	2
CON: 2d6+9 (16)	Damage Modifier	+1d2
SIZ: 1d3+9 (11)	Magic Points	11
DEX: 3d6 (11)	Movement	4m
INT: 2d6+6 (13)	Initiative Bonus	12
POW: 3d6 (11)	Armour	No Natural. Warriors favour heavy armour
CHA: 3d6 (11)	Abilities	Earth Sense, Night Sight
	Magic	Folk Magic 42% (Bludgeon, Light, Lock, Might, Polish, Repair). Specialists favour sorcery, but any magical path is open to them.

1d20	Location	AP/HP
1–3	Right Leg	0/6
4–6	Left Leg	0/6
7–9	Abdomen	0/7
10-12	Chest	0/8
13–15	Right Arm	0/5
16–18	Left Arm	0/5
19–20	Head	0/6

Skills
Athletics 47%, Brawn 66%, Craft (Metallurgy) 64%, Craft (Masonry) 64%, Customs 76%, Deceit 54%, Endurance 72%, Evade 42%, Insight 44%, Locale 56%, Lore (Underground) 66%, Perception 54%, Survival 47%, Unarmed 57%, Willpower 42%

Combat Style & Weapons
Dwarven Warrior (Axe, Hammer, Shield, Crossbow) 67%

Weapon	Size/Force	Reach	Damage	AP/HP
Battleaxe	M	M	1d6+1+1d2	4/8
Great Hammer	H	L	1d10+3+1d2	4/10
Viking Shield	L	S	1d4+1d2	4/18
Crossbow	H	-	1d10	4/8

Elementals

Elementals are physical manifestations of semi-sapient supernatural entities, related to a particular classical element, which usually inhabit the spirit realm. With the right magic they are capable of passing into the mundane world, and assuming a physical form consisting of the substance they represent. The following descriptions relate to the physical manifestations. For information about Elemental Spirits see page 148.

The five elemental types are: Gnomes (earth), , Sylphs (air), Salamanders (fire), Undines (water), and Shades (darkness).

The physical nature, and therefore the characteristics, of each type, differ by the element it is comprised of. Gnomes are corporeal beings of gravel, mud or sand that can, nevertheless, merge with, and pass through the ground seamlessly. Sylphs are formed from blowing winds, shades from stygian darkness and shadows, salamanders from large hot fires, and undines from water or any other liquid capable of supporting its fluid form.

Elemental Characteristics and Attributes

Cubic Metres	STR	DEX	INS	POW	HP	Protection
1	2d6+4	1d6+2	2d6+1	1d6+3	1d6+6	1
2	2d6+8	1d6+4	2d6+2	1d6+6	1d6+12	1
3	2d6+12	1d6+6	2d6+3	1d6+9	1d6+18	2
4	2d6+16	1d6+8	2d6+4	1d6+12	1d6+24	2
5	2d6+20	1d6+10	2d6+5	1d6+15	1d6+30	3
6	2d6+24	1d6+12	2d6+6	1d6+18	1d6+36	3
7	2d6+28	1d6+14	2d6+7	1d6+21	1d6+42	4
8	2d6+32	1d6+16	2d6+8	1d6+24	1d6+48	4
9	2d6+36	1d6+18	2d6+9	1d6+27	1d6+54	5
10	2d6+40	1d6+20	2d6+10	1d6+30	1d6+60	5
Each additional metre	+4	+2	+1	+3	+6	+1 per two steps

Elementals are most commonly encountered when summoned by a particular magician (whether animist, sorcerer or priest), and put into specific service. The magician must have a sufficient volume of its base material in which to manifest it. For ease of reference, this is measured in terms of cubic metres. As a rule of thumb, the larger the elemental the more potent it is. The elementals here are moderate examples. Far more powerful elemental entities exist: sylphs that create hurricanes; vast undines that are incarnate tidal waves; salmanders that, when enraged, and in concert with the Earth God, create the pyroclastic flows of an erupting volcano.

Elementals are naturally immune to magic that is based on their particular element. Salamanders cannot be harmed by fire spells; sylphs are unaffected by magical winds, and so forth. Neither can they be injured by mundane weapons, as their physical forms merely replenish material from the immediate environment, but are disrupted by magical damage providing it is of another type than their own.

Since elementals are amorphous they lack discrete locations. Therefore all damage it suffers is taken from its pool of general Hit Points, and they are immune to serious or major wounds. However, once Hit Points are reduced to zero the spirit animating the elemental can no longer animate its body and dissipates. One does not 'kill' an elemental though; one merely disrupts its manifestation enough to cause it to return to wherever it was summoned from.

The one weakness of an elemental is its vulnerability to the element which opposes or dominates its own. These precise relationships depend on the campaign world, but the upshot is that the elemental takes double damage from magical attacks using the element which is its antithesis.

All elementals possess the traits of Engulfing, Immunity (Own Element), and Vulnerable (Counter-Element). Furthermore they share the same fundamental characteristics and attributes:

Hit Points are rolled rather than calculated. Only damage inflicted by magical spells or weapons affects the elemental, so a sword enhanced with a Bladesharp spell would harm the elemental, but not the damage bonus of its wielder.

Protection represents the natural resilience of an elemental to magical damage. It acts just like Armour Points against any injury the elemental suffers.

Average Elementals

Cubic Metre	Natural Weapon Size and Damage	Action Points	Initiative Bonus	AP/HP	Skills
1	None	2	+7	1/10	Brawn 42%, Evade 52%, Perception 45%, Willpower 64%, Combat 57%
2	M/1d2	2	+9	1/16	Brawn 50%, Evade 56%, Perception 49%, Willpower 70%, Combat 63%
3	L/1d6	2	+10	2/22	Brawn 58%, Evade 60%, Perception 53%, Willpower 76%, Combat 69%
4	L/1d10	2	+12	2/28	Brawn 66%, Evade 64%, Perception 57%, Willpower 82%, Combat 75%
5	H/1d12	3	+13	3/34	Brawn 74%, Evade 68%, Perception 61%, Willpower 88%, Combat 81%
6	H/2d6	3	+15	3/40	Brawn 82%, Evade 72%, Perception 65%, Willpower 94%, Combat 87%
7	E/2d6	3	+16	4/46	Brawn 90%, Evade 76%, Perception 69%, Willpower 100%, Combat 93%
8	C/1d8+1d6	3	+18	4/52	Brawn 98%, Evade 80%, Perception 73%, Willpower 106%, Combat 99%
9	C/2d8	4	+19	5/58	Brawn 106%, Evade 84%, Perception 77%, Willpower 112%, Combat 105%
10	C/1d10+1d8	4	+21	5/64	Brawn 114%, Evade 88%, Perception 81%, Willpower 118%, Combat 111%

An elemental's Action Points and Initiative Bonus are calculated normally. Its Damage Modifier however is based upon STR x2, rather than STR + SIZ. To calculate its natural weapon size substitute its STR for SIZ on the table on page 9. In addition, elementals gain the following skills: Brawn (STR x2)+20, Evade (DEX x2)+40, Perception (INS+POW)+30, Willpower (POW x2)+50, and Elemental Combat Style (STR+DEX)+40.

Elementals injure or damage targets by either striking (pounding, throwing or blasting from afar) or by engulfing the victim entirely. Both methods require a successful attack roll and inflict the elementals' Damage Bonus. Strikes may be parried if the target is using a shield of sufficient size with which to block the substance directed at it, and damage is applied to only a single location.

Engulfing attacks however must be evaded, else the victim suffer the rolled damage to every location simultaneously. Furthermore, unless the engulfed victim can escape they automatically suffer a repeat of this damage at the start of every round. Escaping requires the victim to win an opposed test of either Acrobatics, Brawn or Evade against the Brawn skill of the elemental.

Each elemental has a number of specific abilities corresponding with its type:

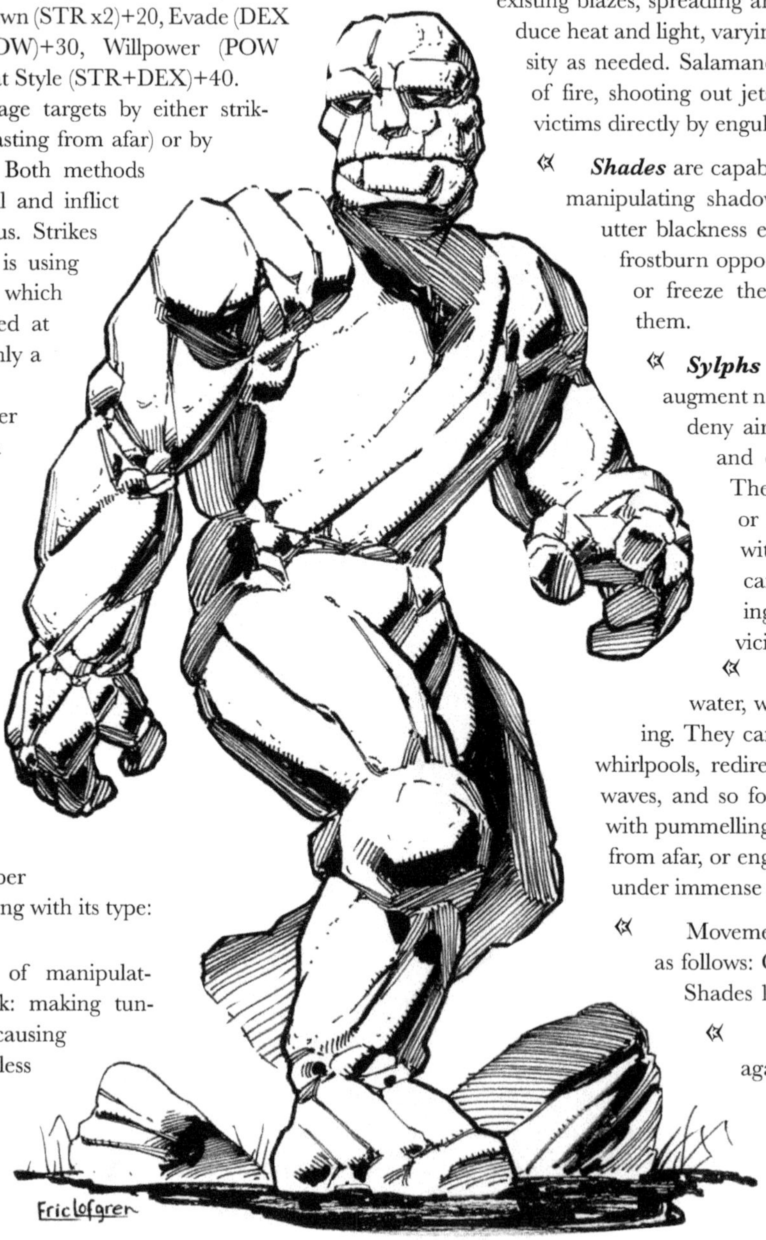

- ***Gnomes*** are capable of manipulating the earth and rock: making tunnels, opening pits, or causing rockslides are effortless activities for a gnome. They inflict damage by bashing foes, throwing rocks or grinding them into mince if they can engulf the victim within their gravelly mass.
- ***Salamanders*** manipulate fire, augmenting existing blazes, spreading and directing them. They produce heat and light, varying the temperature and intensity as needed. Salamanders fight with lashing whips of fire, shooting out jets of flame or by immolating victims directly by engulfing them.
- ***Shades*** are capable of concentrating darkness, manipulating shadows, and creating pockets of utter blackness even in broad daylight. They frostburn opponents with their glacial touch or freeze them solid if they can engulf them.
- ***Sylphs*** create breezes and winds, augment naturally occurring air motion, deny air if necessary (or redirect it), and can lift objects into the air. They inflict damage by tossing or tumbling foes, blasting them with airborne debris or if they can engulf the victim, tearing them limb from limb in a vicious cyclone.
- ***Undines*** manipulate water, whether free-flowing or standing. They can create currents, eddies and whirlpools, redirect tides, lessen (or heighten) waves, and so forth. Undines smash enemies with pummelling waves, shoot high speed jets from afar, or engulf a victim, and crush them under immense pressure.
- Movement rates for elementals are as follows: Gnome 6m, Salamander 8m, Shades 10m, Sylph 10m, Undine 8m.
- Worn armour counts against damage from elemental strikes, but not against Engulfing attacks.

Elf

Elves are natives of the realm known as faerie, a plane co-existent with the mundane world yet distinct from it. Faerie is accessible through the glades, woodlands and forests that form the barriers between them. Elves can come and go between the two at will, although other races may struggle to do so without an elf guide. Elves may even have permanent settlements that belong to neither one realm nor the other but exist in both simultaneously.

The elves have a psychology quite different to that of other species. Otherworldly, wise in natural lore and magic, but often curiously naïve where mundane matters or emotions are concerned. Elves view things through an almost childlike innocence that belies their long lifespan and knowledge of the magical world. Complicated things are both fascinating and difficult to comprehend. Elves favour simplicity over complexity but are, nevertheless, a sophisticated race with their own complex society.

Elves are not necessarily all-wise and benevolent. They can be as cruel, vindictive, malevolent and mischievous as humans; indeed if angered their vengeance can be subtle and painful. When in love their passion consumes all else. They occupy rural and forest idylls but also build great and splendid cities. They lead peaceful lives but are ready to go to war when threatened– and can make tenacious and brutal warriors.

The race tends to be taller than humankind, more slender and graceful (all elves have the Light body frame), and are distinctive with their fine bone structure, narrow, tapering skulls, and narrow, pointed ears. Eye colours vary through the spectrum, from the human tones through to the colour of brilliant gems. Elven society is frequently monarchical, and usually governed by a king, queen or both. The elves presented here are of the western, specifically Celtic folklore. Depending on the campaign setting, the magic available to elves will vary as will their beliefs.

In Anathaym's world the elves have retreated to their shadowy realm, jealous and belligerent at mankind's ascent. The Elf-Kings have long known the practices of sorcery but always shunned its power. Now, they see it is a unique weapon to bring about mankind's fall. Seducing those who covet power, like Kratos, the elves have brought sorcery into the hands of men, and now need only sit back and watch as they begin to abuse its power.

Elven Characters

Elves are otherworldly. They seem remote from mundane events yet exhibit a comprehension of them that proves baffling for humans to understand. Nature is of great importance to them, and so they take great care to preserve their environments although the greatest care is reserved for those areas where faerie is most accessible. As a long-lived species (elves live for many centuries) they do not accept or appreciate time in the same way as humankind, and are often unconscious of the passing of small time increments.

Culture

Elven culture is akin to civilised. Great store is placed on learning and understanding. Deeds, conduct and integrity are important, and desired qualities amongst elves and in others. Dignified manners are expected, and loutish, uncouth behaviour viewed with disdain and suspicion. Most elven societies have a king or queen, and so loyalty to the monarch is paramount. Elves have trouble understanding societies that lack such structures, wondering how people can be properly ordered without a clear, royal leader to guide and represent them.

Cultural Passions

- Loyalty to King/Queen
- Love (Something emotional)
- Hate (any enemy of grace and beauty)

Professions

Agent, Craftsman, Official, Physician, Priest, Shaman, Scholar, Scout, Thief, Warrior

Starting Money

Elven characters begin the game with wondrous goods and strange currency worth 4d6 x100 silver pieces.

The Elven Voice

'We live in the two realms. Both become one world although Faerie is always our ancestral home. All round is beauty, for the world is a beautiful place, and even in its ugliest recesses there is something of wonder to behold. We are happiest though, amongst the glades and woodlands where the animals roam free, and the mighty oaks remind us of the forests of Faerie, whose trees reach far into the sky.

The spirits surround us, and we understand their presence even when we do not communicate with them directly. We know they are always there, watching, and so it behoves us to keep the sanctity of nature, preserving its ways, and taking nothing that is not freely offered.

Above all we value freedom. Freedom in all things: life, expression, meaning. To make a slave of something is to kill its spirit, and so we abhor those who enslave or shackle things to servitude. Yet we are all willing servants of our king and queen because they bring us guidance and dignity, and do not compel us to their whims. Such compulsions are, we observe, human traits. And we have seen over the millennia how humans have tried to impose their will on the world, and have, time and again, failed. Perhaps it is the curse of a short life to have to leave a mark. Look around you: do you see signs of our passing? It is rare for any elf to leave more than a footprint yet you younger races have scarred the earth, and will not live long enough to see these scars.

Yet the younger races intrigue us. Their ways are fascinating and contradictory. Humans can be brutal and artful – sometimes together – and they are driven to such extremes that one wonders why no higher purpose has yet developed amongst them. Dwarves hide away beneath the ground, fearful of the sun, of nature, or beauty even though the things they craft from metal and precious gems are without compare.

Such curious breeds, such curious peoples. Let us show you faerie and true beauty. Come, walk with me.'

Elf	Attributes	
STR: 3d6 (11)	Action Points	3
CON: 3d6 (11)	Damage Modifier	+1d2
SIZ: 2d6+9 (16)	Magic Points	16
DEX: 3d6 (11)	Movement	6m
INT: 2d6+9 (16)	Initiative Bonus	14
POW: 2d6+6 (13)	Armour	No Natural. Warriors wear any armour
CHA: 3d6 (11)	Abilities	Life Sense, Night Sight
	Magic	Folk Magic 64% (Dullblade, Glamour, Light, Mobility, Sleep, Vigour). Specialists favour theism, but any magical path is open to them.

1d20	*Location*	*AP/HP*
1–3	Right Leg	0/6
4–6	Left Leg	0/6
7–9	Abdomen	0/7
10-12	Chest	0/8
13–15	Right Arm	0/5
16–18	Left Arm	0/5
19–20	Head	0/6

Skills
Athletics 52%, Brawn 47%, Customs 72%, Deceit 67%, Endurance 42%, Evade 52%, Insight 69%, Locale 72%, Lore (Faerie) 62%, Perception 69%, Unarmed 42%, Willpower 56%

Combat Style & Weapons
Elven Warrior (Sword, Spear, Shield, Bow) 62%

Weapon	Size/Force	Reach	Damage	AP/HP
Longsword	M	L	1d8+1d2	6/12
Longspear	L	VL	1d10+1+1d2	4/10
Heater Shield	L	S	1d4+1d2	6/12
Long Bow	H	-	1d8+1d2	4/7

Ghoul

Ghouls are undead creatures that feast on recently deceased corpses and carrion. They are only created from sapient races, and no intelligent species is immune to the vile curse that creates a ghoul. Emaciated, blank-eyed, and equipped with sharp teeth and nails, ghouls are driven by an insatiable hunger for necrotic flesh that causes them to frequent burial sites, battlefields and charnel pits where there is a ready source of decomposing meat.

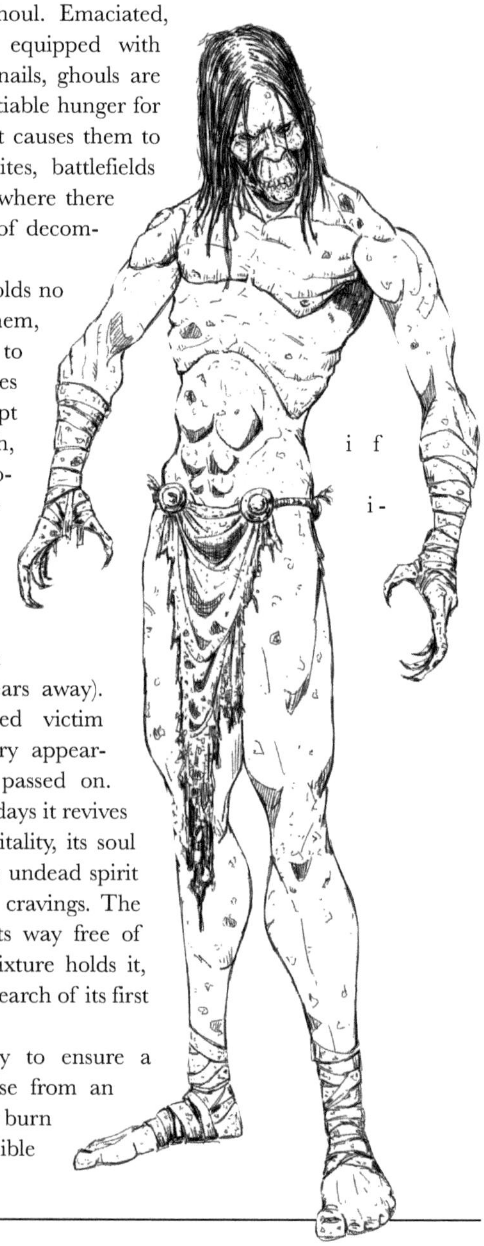

Living flesh holds no attraction for them, but if forced to defend themselves ghouls will attempt to bite which, if successful, introduces the magical curse that creates a new ghoul upon the victim's eventual death (which may be many years away). Once an infected victim dies, it gives every appearance of having passed on. But, after 1d6+3 days it revives with an unholy vitality, its soul corrupted into an undead spirit driven by its foul cravings. The ghoul scratches its way free of whatever burial fixture holds it, and then goes in search of its first meal.

The only way to ensure a ghoul will not rise from an infected body is to burn it as soon as possible

Ghoul	Attributes	
STR: 3d6+6 (17)	Action Points	3
CON: 3d6+3 (14)	Damage Modifier	+1d2
SIZ: 2d6+6 (13)	Magic Points	4
DEX: 3d6+3 (14)	Movement	6m
INS: 2d6+6 (13)	Initiative Bonus	14
POW: 1d6 (4)	Armour	Hardened skin. If buried in it, some ghouls will be wearing armour.
	Abilities	Death Sense, Regeneration, Undead
	Magic	None.

1d20	Location	AP/HP
1–3	Right Leg	1/6
4–6	Left Leg	1/6
7–9	Abdomen	1/7
10-12	Chest	1/8
13–15	Right Arm	1/5
16–18	Left Arm	1/5
19–20	Head	1/6

Skills
Athletics 51%, Brawn 50%, Endurance 58%, Evade 48%, Perception 47%, Unarmed 71%, Willpower 38%

Combat Style & Weapons
Deathless Horror (Claws, Teeth) 71%

Weapon	Size/Force	Reach	Damage	AP/HP
Claws	S	T	1d4+1d2	As for Arm
Teeth	S	T	1d3+1d2	As for Head

– which is one of the reasons why certain cultures cremate, rather than bury, their dead.

Lifting a ghoul's curse can only be done through a Cure Malady spell of a Magnitude greater than the POW of the ghoul which bit them. An infected victim may not even be aware of their fate; those that are, are doomed without magical intervention. Even hacking off a bitten limb will not lift the curse that impregnates the soul and hibernates, waiting for death so it can be triggered.

Ghouls, being undead, are extremely difficult to destroy. As part of their transformation their skin desiccates and hardens, granting them a bonus of 1 Armour Point to whatever natural protection they once had. In addition the dire potency of their animating curse allows them slowly to regenerate damage. Even a dismembered ghoul will eventually regrow new body parts at the rate of one Hit Point per location every week until it is complete once more. The only sure way to kill one is with fire, which inflicts normal damage.

Ghoul characteristics are based upon those of the originally infected creature. They gain +6 STR, +3 CON, +3 DEX, their INT is converted to INS and CHA is lost entirely. POW, no matter what it started with, is replaced with 1d6. The following ghoul is based on a human cadaver.

If a ghoul's bite penetrates armour the victim must make an unopposed Endurance roll to resist infection. Failing the roll means the victim is infected with the spirit curse that will create a new ghoul upon death. A standard ghoul tactic is to grip an opponent with its hands, and then target an area of exposed flesh. Once it has bitten it releases and flees, attempting to find somewhere to skulk until a threat has passed, and it can resume feeding.

Giant

Enormous humans, giants can range in size from several metres tall to potentially dozens, although at the upper range they are beyond the capability of most mortals to defeat. Their natural size, and whether or not they continue to grow in height, depends upon the setting. The most common giants are between four and ten metres tall. Whilst ostensibly a sapient race, a few giants are so dim-witted or ponderous of thought that they are in effect less intelligent than animals, and act accordingly.

Myth has it that giants are bad-tempered, sometimes desirous of human flesh, and bread made of bones and generally unpleasant to encounter. Some, like the fabled etten, have two heads. However, in truth, giants come in all dispositions, ranging from the nasty, through the surly to those who are genuinely friendly. Giants then, are as diverse as their smaller cousins, and need not be ground-stomping man-eaters. In Meerish legend the giants are the heralds of the gods. Myceras' herald is a gigantic minotaur who rides a chariot the size of a galley pulled by enormous bonacon. When the giants appear, legends say, the gods are preparing for war.

What is common to giant species though, is a relatively primitive culture. Most are solitary beings although some form complex, barbarian or perhaps civilised societies where giants as a race are common (although this tends to be a rarity). Their size makes the creation of artefacts, such as weapons and armour, quite difficult given the amount of raw materials and sheer logistics of production difficult. As such many giants rely on natural armour and improvised weapons, such as huge branches and tree-trunks. Given their size, such large weapons allow for sweeping effects and, of course, bigger giants can stomp their foes with massive feet using their Trample ability.

When battling any giant, melee combat Hit Locations are rolled on 1d10 or even 1d6 indicating the difficulty (or sheer impossibility) of reaching the upper areas of the body. Range weapon users roll 1d20 as normal.

The example given here is for a four metre giant. For each additional 2 metres of height add +3 STR, +6 SIZ and +1 Armour Point.

One Head or Two?

Some giants — commonly those found in British myths — have two heads. Each head has its own personality and it is common for the heads to argue with each other, agreeing only that whatever is standing before the giant is good enough to be stomped flat and ground-up for flour. Adding an additional head is unlikely to grant any serious combat advantage to the giant, but it does mean that severing only one head does not automatically kill it. Indeed, depending on the general disposition between the heads, the surviving bonce may even consider that its enemies have just done it a favour.

Giant		Attributes	
STR: 2d6+15 (22)	Action Points	2	
CON: 2d6+12 (19)	Damage Modifier	+1d10	
SIZ: 2d6+21 (28)	Magic Points	11	
DEX: 3d6 (11)	Movement	12m	
INT: 3d6 (11)	Initiative Bonus	11	
POW: 3d6 (11)	Armour	Thick skin	
CHA: 3d6 (11)	Abilities	Trample	
	Magic	Some may have Folk Magic	

1d20	Location	AP/HP
1–3	Right Leg	3/10
4–6	Left Leg	3/10
7–9	Abdomen	3/11
10-12	Chest	3/12
13–15	Right Arm	3/9
16–18	Left Arm	3/9
19–20	Head	3/10

Skills

Athletics 53%, Brawn 80%, Endurance 68%, Evade 42%, Perception 42%, Unarmed 63%, Willpower 42%

Passions

Greedy 75%, Like Beanstalks 60%, Hate Englishmen 90%

Combat Style & Weapons

Bash and Smash (Club, Maul, Great Club) 73%, Kick and Stomp 63%

Weapon	Size/Force	Reach	Damage	AP/HP
Tree Trunk	E	VL	2d8+1d10	4/30
Kick	L	M	1d6+1d10	As for Leg
Trample	L	M	1d6+1d10	As for Leg

Goblin/Orc

Stunted, twisted humanoids abound in myth and fantasy. They go by many names: goblin, hobgoblin, orc, and so on. They all have certain similarities; either grey or greenish skin, ugly to most eyes, vicious, peevish natures bent towards cruelty, and slow, dull-witted intellects. Goblins or orcs are the foot soldiers and minions of Evil Gods and their direct servants, perpetrators of terrible, murderous raids with sadistic, unpleasant fates for those unlucky enough to be captured. Larger, tougher goblin species are given an affix such as 'hob' (as in hobgoblin) or 'dai' (as in dai-bakemono, the Japanese name for such creatures) which means great, terrible or tough.

Goblins dislike the light, and make their homes beneath ground where they may well be natural enemies of dwarves. Their societies are crude – not much above the primitive– and they prefer to steal rather than create, making raids on communities where weapons, armour, food, and other commodities they want are found in abundance. Goblins are sly and pernicious; they cannot be trusted, and they even dislike and distrust their own kind.

Goblins are cowardly by nature: an outnumbered goblin will flee or surrender. They prefer to outnumber their foes, and so will not engage unless they have greater numbers (and usually hunt and raid in packs of 1d6+3).

The characteristics above are for a standard goblin or orc. Hobgoblins have 2d6+8 STR and SIZ, but otherwise the same characteristics. As leaders they can be expected to have better weapons and armour.

Goblin/Orc		Attributes	
STR: 2d6+4 (11)	Action Points	2	
CON: 3d6+3 (14)	Damage Modifier	None	
SIZ: 2d6+4 (11)	Magic Points	11	
DEX: 3d6 (11)	Movement	6m	
INT: 1d6+7 (11)	Initiative Bonus	11	
POW: 3d6 (11)	Armour	Thick skin. Some wear additional, scavenged, armour	
CHA: 2d6 (7)	Abilities	Night Sight	
	Magic	Some may have Folk Magic or specialised priests and shamans	

1d20	Location	AP/HP
1–3	Right Leg	1/5
4–6	Left Leg	1/5
7–9	Abdomen	1/6
10-12	Chest	1/7
13–15	Right Arm	1/4
16–18	Left Arm	1/4
19–20	Head	1/5

Skills
Athletics 52%, Brawn 42%, Deceit 57%, Endurance 48%, Evade 62%, Perception 61%, Unarmed 52%, Willpower 42%

Passions
Hate the Light 90%, Hate Non-Goblins 95%, Love Hurting Things 80%

Combat Style & Weapons
Goblin Warrior (Shortsword, Shield, Spear, Sling) 62%

Weapon	Size/Force	Reach	Damage	AP/HP
Shortsword	M	S	1d6	6/8
Shortspear	M	L	1d8+1	4/5
Target Shield	L	S	1d4	4/9

GORGON

In Greek myth the gorgons were sisters cursed to immortality, and a hideousness that turned mortals to stone instantly. Descriptions of these creatures vary, but MYTHRAS gorgons are mortal demons with the lower half of immense serpents, and the upper body of a woman. The face of a gorgon is truly hideous for mortals to gaze upon, and catching sight of an unreflected gorgon's visage petrifies living tissue as described below. In place of hair, living, writhing snakes frame the gorgon's deadly face, and their fingers terminate in claws of razor-sharp iron.

Such is the deadliness of a gorgon that these monsters must remain isolated from contact with the outside world. Temples, tombs and catacombs are their favoured retreats with those who worship them placing offerings of meat and drink at the very outer reaches of the lair before retreating swiftly. The unlucky souls who, out of curiosity, remained to see if the rumours were true stand as stone guardians, features twisted in cruel realization.

Despite their divine or infernal origin gorgons are vulnerable to mortal weapons. Their blood however is a deadly poison, so coming into contact with the ichor, whether being caught in a spray of blood (such as from a Bleed special effect) or when cleaning a blade used to wound the monster, forces the victim to resist its venomous touch.

Whilst having a monstrous nature and appearance, gorgons are not necessarily evil-doers. Victims of circumstance, their tempers have certainly been warped into murderous anger, but gorgons are intelligent, and from time to time use their beautiful voices to seduce servants who can walk abroad and do their bidding. Gorgons may give fair warning or hide their features so as to enter into discourse with those they need rather than killing them outright.

The primary means of offense is the Gaze attack, which the gorgon must activate on its turn at the cost of 1 Magic Point. Any mortal creature looking in the direction of the gorgon, who can potentially see its face, must make an opposed roll of its Willpower versus the gorgon's. If the gorgon wins the victim meets its gaze and is petrified completely, resulting in instant death. If gorgon loses, the victim manages to avert its eyes before the petrifaction can take effect.

In some Greek iconography the gorgons are depicted as winged women with broad round heads, serpentine hair, the tusks of boars, lolling tongues, flared nostrils, and sometimes short coarse beards. Clearly they were dreadful demons and Games Masters are encouraged to make their gorgons as grotesque and terrible as needed. They need not follow the serpentine form shown in this example and, indeed, may also possess wings.

FIGHTING A GORGON

Risking a gorgon's gaze directly is stupid and dangerous. However looking at the creature in reflection poses no risk of petrifaction. Those who are determined to slay a gorgon then, should use a mirror or the interior of a metal shield, polished to provide a mirror-like surface. Fighting using reflection reduces the hero's combat style by two difficulty grades. Another alternative is to fight blindfold or with the eyes obscured. In this case, the combat style is reduced by three grades…

Anyone surviving long enough to enter close combat with a gorgon must deal with the snake hair as well as the monster's tail and talons. The snakes attack as one entity, striking at Short reach. The individual fangs are too

small to inflict significant damage, but on a successful bite against an unprotected foe (or by use of the Inject Venom special effect) the gorgon will inject a venom with a potency equivalent to the gorgon's Endurance. The poison acts on the Combat Round after introduction paralysing the affected area. Paralysis of the abdomen means both legs stop working. Paralysis of the chest or head leads to death within a number of turns equal to the victim's CON as organs begin to fail.

The gaze attack of a gorgon head remains effective even after a gorgon's death, the Willpower of the monster being equivalent to its living form. Using a head in this manner however can be very dangerous since both friends and foes (and even the wielder if they fumble) can become ensnared by the indiscriminate gaze.

Gorgon	Attributes	
STR: 3d6+6 (17)	Action Points	3
CON: 2d6+9 (16)	Damage Modifier	+1d4
SIZ: 3d6+6 (17)	Magic Points	16
DEX: 3d6+6 (17)	Movement	6m
INT: 2d6+9 (16)	Initiative Bonus	14 (includes Armour Penalty)
POW: 2d6+9 (16)	Armour	Scales on serpentine locations; Hoplite armour on upper body.
CHA: 3d6 (11)	Abilities	Gaze Attack, Immunity (Poisons), Terrifying, Venomous
	Magic	Devotion 57%, Exhort 67% (Dismiss Magic, Enthrall, Fear, Illusion)

1d20	Location	AP/HP
1–3	Tail Tip	4/6
4–6	Mid Tail	4/7
7–9	Lower Body	4/8
10-12	Chest	5/9
13–15	Right Arm	5/6
16–18	Left Arm	5/6
19–20	Head	2/7

Skills
Athletics 64%, Brawn 74%, Deceit 57%, Endurance 72%, Evade 74%, Insight 62%, Perception 72%, Seduction 67%, Track 62%, Willpower 72%

Passions
Love Solitude 90%, Resent Mortals 70%, Hate Beauty 70%

Combat Style & Weapons
Gorgon Horror (Talons, Tail, Snake Hair, Gaze and Bow) 74%

Weapon	Size/Force	Reach	Damage	AP/HP
Talons	M	S	1d4+1d4	As for Arm
Tail	L	L	1d6+1d4	As for Tail
Recurve Bow	H	-	1d8+1d4	4/8
Snake Hair	S	S	Poison	As for head
Gaze	Special		-	-

Griffin/Hippogriff

Several spellings describe the same creature: griffon, gryphon, and the one used here. A combination of the head, forequarters and wings of a giant eagle, with the hindquarters of a lion. Griffins are tenacious airborne predators that make their eyries in high places and prey on livestock up to and including horses. Although not known for fixating on humans, attacks are not unknown especially if one wanders, mounted or on foot, into a griffin's hunting territory (which can span many kilometres from an eyrie.

Griffins are fast and clever, employing dive attacks to harry their prey, exhausting it before swooping down to snatch it up with their immense claws. Attacks from the air are favoured over those from ground, but on land a griffin is not the ungainly creature it might seem to be. It hunkers low, like a lion, to circle its prey, and strikes out with both beak and claws to grip and slash, immobilizing the foe before taking to the wing once more.

Griffins usually form mated pairs that share an eyrie, and carve out a wide hunting territory that is defended from other predators and other griffins. Mated pairs tend to hunt in concert save for when one remains to protect eggs or fledglings; yet if one gets into trouble it can unleash a powerful screech guaranteed to be heard by its mate, and bring them to aid. Thus, when dealing with one griffin, a second is never far away.

Griffins can be tamed and used as human mounts if captured as chicks and raised for the task. Full-grown griffins are too wild to be tamed although stories exist of bonds being formed between some individuals and humans. Griffin cavalry mounts are therefore a much sought-after thing in certain cultures leading to daring raids on griffin eyries for eggs and chicks; though the mortality rate for such adventures is high.

Hippogriffs are the result of a mating between a horse and a griffin. Hippogriffs combine the head, forequarters and wings of a giant eagle with the legs and hindquarters of a horse. These creatures inhabit similar territories to griffins but form quite separate communities – usually nesting in groups of up to twelve individuals.

Hippogriffs display a higher measure of tolerance to their griffin cousins and are somewhat easier to train and use as mounts. In all other respects they act as griffins.

Griffin	Attributes	
STR: 3d6+12 (23)	Action Points	3
CON: 3d6+6 (17)	Damage Modifier	+1d12
SIZ: 3d6+24 (35)	Magic Points	11
DEX: 3d6+12 (23)	Movement	8m, 18m (Flying)
INS: 2d6+6 (13)	Initiative Bonus	18
POW: 3d6 (11)	Armour	Feathers and Hide
CHA: 2d6+12 (19)	Abilities	Diving Strike, Flying
	Magic	None

1d20	Location	AP/HP
1-2	Right Hind Leg	1/11
3-4	Left Hind Leg	1/11
5-7	Hindquarters	1/12
8-10	Forequarters	2/13
11-12	Right Wing	2/10
13-14	Left Wing	2/10
15-16	Right Front Leg	2/11
17-18	Left Front Leg	2/11
19-20	Head	2/11

Skills
Athletics 76%, Brawn 78%, Endurance 64%, Evade 66%, Fly 76%, Perception 64%, Willpower 52%

Combat Style & Weapons
Combat Style: Death from Above (Beak, Claws) 86%

Weapon	Size/Force	Reach	Damage	AP/HP
Beak	H	M	1d10+1d12	As for Head
Claws	H	L	1d8+1d12	As for Leg

Halfling

Peaceful, civilised folk who live a largely agrarian existence, Halflings are diminutive humanoids who are shorter than dwarves by around a head, but lighter of frame. Their homes are farms and steads with villages forming close-knit communities. Halflings are not the most adventurous of races, and can go largely unnoticed as they pose no kind of threat to anyone.

Halflings might be mistaken for small dwarves but the differences are obvious to those in the know. Halflings have large, rugged feet that are oversized for the body. Shoes and boots are shunned; the feet are extremely thick-soled providing more than adequate protection against rocks and stones.

Whilst they are generally unadventurous, halflings are inquisitive. They like to know, and share, secrets. They adore stories, myths and fables, and have enquiring minds. This means that, when abroad, the world is a fascinating place to be questioned and taken in – and this can lead them into trouble. Otherwise they are a rather prosaic, content race that keeps to itself, and prefer neither to interfere with the wider world or have it interfere with them.

Halfling Characters

Despite being physically smaller and weaker than most other sapient species, halflings compensate with a certain nimbleness that serves

them well in sticky situations. Although unadventurous they are not cowardly: halflings might say they are, but when it comes to fighting for their homes and way of life they can summon enormous reserves of courage. In short, halflings make for good player characters – especially for those players who prefer sneaking around to stalking boldly across the moorland.

Culture

Halflings are Civilised, and use the Civilised skill choices found on pages 14 to 15. Their communities are closely-knit villages and small towns with several extended families forming the basis of the community. Their industries are basic: agriculture primarily, but also handicrafts such as pottery, weaving, leatherworking and textiles. They do work metals but very infrequently for weaponry, using the daggers of bigger folk as swords and child sized armour.

The common cultural unit for halflings is the Riding; an area bounded by three towns which makes the size of each riding vary considerably. A Borough is formed of three Ridings.

Cultural Passions

- Loyalty to Village, Town or Riding
- Love (Something emotional)
- Hate (Heavy Industry)

Professions

Beast Handler, Craftsman, Entertainer, Farmer, Fisherman, Herder, Merchant, Official, Physician, Scholar, Thief, Warrior

Starting Money

Halfling characters begin the game with commodities or currency worth 4d6 x30 silver pieces.

The Halfling Voice

'Our Riding – that is to say, the West Riding – was founded by the Hoarfoots who were joined by the Slintwistles, and then, later the Argreaves. Now, the Hoarfoots never liked the Slintwistles much on account of Old Man Slintwistle neglecting to invite Old Man Hoarfoot to his birthday party. Truth be told, he did, but forgot to post the invitation, so it just goes to show you what trouble forgetfulness can get you into.

Where was I? Ah, yes, the West Riding. So, there are three villages – because that's what Riding means: three – Hoarenderby, Slintenderby and Greavenderby named for each of the founding families you see. Hoarenderby is famed for its wool, because it has good, soft water coming down off those hills which are just perfect for grazing sheep. Slintenderby produces the finest vegetables out of any district you care to mention, and Greavenderby's beer is worth wearing shoes for.

Are you hungry? I am. In fact, why don't we walk to the Grey Lion at Greavenderby and have a jug of finest ale? I prefer Nadger's Tat myself, because it has that hoppiness, but I know you southerners prefer something a little lighter, so I'd say go for the Golden Honeydew. But, really, you can't go wrong with anything you drink at the Grey Lion because Duffer Widget – he's the landlord – knows his cellaring, and none of his beers are ever sour, off or watered. And they do a cracking plate of bread and cheese too…

C'mon… I know! Let's sing a walking song as we go…'

Halfling		Attributes
STR: 2d6+1 (8)	Action Points	3
CON: 3d6 (11)	Damage Modifier	-1d2
SIZ: 1d3+6 (8)	Magic Points	11
DEX: 3d6+3 (14)	Movement	4m
INT: 2d6+6 (13)	Initiative Bonus	14
POW: 3d6 (11)	Armour	None
CHA: 3d6 (11)	Abilities	None
	Magic	Usually none, but halfling specialists can follow any magical path.

1d20	Location	AP/HP
1–3	Right Leg	0/4
4–6	Left Leg	0/4
7–9	Abdomen	0/5
10-12	Chest	0/6
13–15	Right Arm	0/3
16–18	Left Arm	0/3
19–20	Head	0/4

Skills

Athletics 42%, Brawn 36%, Craft (any) 57%, Customs 66%, Deceit 46%, Endurance 62%, Evade 68%, Insight 54%, Locale 66%, Lore (Agriculture) 56%, Perception 64%, Sleight 55%, Stealth 67%, Unarmed 42%, Willpower 52%

Combat Style & Weapons

Halfling Constable (Sword, Sling, Shield) 52%

Weapon	Size/Force	Reach	Damage	AP/HP
Halfling Shortsword	S	S	1d4+1-1d2	6/8
Buckler	M	S	1d3-1d2	6/9
Sling	L	-	1d8	1/2

Harpy

Monsters from legend, harpies combine the head and breast of a woman – usually an ugly, peevish hag – with the lower body and wings of a vulture. Harpies are cruel, pernicious creatures that revel in tormenting and inflicting suffering. It is rare for them to kill a foe outright, preferring instead to snatch, scratch and bite before flying off to a safe distance and shrieking insults.

A favoured torment is the theft and despoiling of food. Harpies might target an outdoors feast or banquet, or deliberately steal from food stores, setting out to wreck a fine harvest or ruin what meagre supplies a community has managed to put down for the winter months. They rarely take food for their own sustenance: their delight is purely in denying others. Harpies typically dive and strike, aiming for the head and upper body, inflicting scratches with their sharp claws. Additionally they attempt to seize weapons and shields (using the Grip special effect) which they then carry away and drop, well out of reach.

Harpies are natural enemies of iqari. If iqari move into a region frequented by harpies they devote their efforts to driving off or killing the monsters as quickly as possible.

Harpy		Attributes
STR: 3d6 (11)	Action Points	3
CON: 3d6 (11)	Damage Modifier	None
SIZ: 1d6+9 (13)	Magic Points	11
DEX: 4d6+6 (20)	Movement	4m, 12m (Flying)
INT: 2d6+6 (13)	Initiative Bonus	17
POW: 3d6 (11)	Armour	Feathers
CHA: 1d6 (4)	Abilities	Diving Attack, Flying
	Magic	None

1d20	Location	AP/HP
1–3	Right Claw	1/5
4–6	Left Claw	1/5
7–9	Abdomen	1/6
10-12	Chest	0/7
13–15	Right Wing	1/4
16–18	Left Wing	1/4
19–20	Head	0/5

Skills

Athletics 51%, Brawn 44%, Deceit 57%, Endurance 42%, Evade 60%, Fly 71%, Perception 64%, Willpower 42%

Passions

Greed 99%, Spiteful 95%, Love Suffering 95%

Combat Style & Weapons

Snatch and Grab (Claws) 71%

Weapon	Size/Force	Reach	Damage	AP/HP
Claws	M	M	1d4	As for Claw

Horse

There are many varieties of horse, bred for different purposes. All have enormous stamina and capacity for hard work. Most cultures have domesticated the horse for use as a primary riding and beast of burden.

Wild horses sometimes fight to exert dominance within a herd, or to protect themselves against predators. Riding and chariot horses however rarely engage in combat, save for an occasional nip or kick to express displeasure. War horses are specially trained to fight against foot troops, but require a competent rider to initiate battle.

This example is for a standard riding mount that can be bought or hired by most adventurers. For a War Horse – one bred specifically for its size and reliability in battle – add a further 4 to both STR and SIZ. For a Heavy Horse – one used specifically for heavy agricultural work, add 8 to STR and SIZ instead.

Horse	Attributes	
STR: 2d6+15 (22)	Action Points	2
CON: 2d6+6 (13)	Damage Modifier	+1d12
SIZ: 2d6+24 (31)	Magic Points	7
DEX: 2d6+3 (10)	Movement	12m
INS: 2d6+4 (11)	Initiative Bonus	11
POW: 2d6 (7)	Armour	Hide
	Abilities	None
	Magic	None

1d20	Location	AP/HP
1–3	Right Hind Leg	1/9
4–6	Left Hind Leg	1/9
7–9	Hindquarters	1/10
10–12	Forequarters	1/11
13–14	Right Front Leg	1/8
15–16	Left Front Leg	1/8
17–20	Head	1/9

Skills
Athletics 52%, Brawn 83%, Endurance 66%, Evade 40%, Perception 48%, Willpower 34%

Combat Style & Weapons
Rear and Plunge (Hoofs) 62%

Weapon	Size/Force	Reach	Damage	AP/HP
Hoof	H	L	1d6+1d12	As for Leg

Insect Swarm

Insects on their own are a nuisance. As an angry swarm, they can be lethal. A swarm of bees or wasps can contain thousands of individuals, all acting in concert. Most swarms are not in response to a threat – although it is an effective tactic – but as part of the reproductive cycle. However, any disturbance of a hive can result in swarm activity, with individuals targeting exposed areas of flesh with stings, and bites to drive a foe away.

It is almost impossible to kill a swarm: there are simply too many individuals. The only hope is to either outrun it or find a way of taking cover (water is not always an effective way of evading a swarm of insects, since they often wait about for the victim to surface). A swarm may decide to cease an attack if it collectively feels a threat has been neutralized: after 1d3 rounds of combat, make a Willpower roll for the swarm. If the roll is successful then the swarm abates its attacks, and returns to its nest or previous activity.

A swarm *can* be harmed if an attack – magical or mundane – which inflicts area damage can be directed at the swarm, engulfing at least 75% of it. In such cases the swarm has a number of Hit Points equal to its SIZ, and any damage reduces the size of the swarm commensurately.

The normal characteristics for creatures are not applicable to swarms. Instead, only one characteristic is given: SIZ. This is used to gauge the volume of the swarm in comparison with an average human. A swarm of SIZ 6 is enough to engulf one half of the body. A swarm of 12 is enough to engulf the entire body. A swarm of SIZ 24 could engulf two opponents simultaneously. The lethality of the attack is based on SIZ, as follows:

Insect Swarm Damage

SIZ	*Sting/Bite Damage*	*Combat Actions*
1–5	1	1
6–11	1d2	2
12–18	1d3	3
19–25	1d4	4
26–33	1d6	5

The damage from stings and bites are applied simultaneously to every location covered by the swarm. Worn armour initially counts against this damage, but is reduced by 1 point for each successful attack, as the insects begin to crawl inside gaps in the clothing. For example, a victim wearing brigandine armour who stumbles into a swarm of SIZ 6, will be immune to the swarm's first three attacks but eventually the insects will find a way in. Normal clothing provides no protection, unless especially thick – for example winter wear.

Swarms do not generate Special Effects, and neither do they use Combat Actions to parry or evade unless attacked with an area affect assault. On the other hand a victim can use Evade to temporarily avoid a swarm. Otherwise they must flee, hide or seek cover. Swarms fly at a base Movement Rate of 4, but can augment this rate by using their Athletics skill.

Swarm Skills:

Athletics 60%, Fly 60%, Willpower 30%, Swarm Attack (Stings or Bites) 60%

Whenever a character is stung by a swarm of poisonous insects, he may succumb to the increasing levels of venom introduced into his body. Keep track of the accumulating value of the damage suffered from each attack, which represents the growing toxicity of the venom. Every time the character experiences another attack, they must make an opposed roll of their Endurance versus the new level of toxicity. Failure means that they suffer the effects of the insect's venom.

Iqari

A humanoid race with the head, wings and lower body of a giant raptor (eagle is the most common, but there are also hawk, owl, kestrel and osprey species), and the upper body of a human; the iqari dwell in the high places of the world: mountains and hills surrounded by open pastures and deep valleys. They shun contact with most other sapient races although it has been known for certain iqari, deemed mad by their kin, to seek out social contact with others.

Iqari are fierce and tenacious hunters, patrolling the skies above their territories in search of prey that can either be carried back to the eyries or killed, and butchered in-situ with meat then being returned. Iqari hunters always carry the tools requisite for the job: a hunting spear, flint knives (occasionally metal), and bone needles for sewing sacks from the skin of the prey to carry their spoils. Favoured quarry are mammals of most sizes, but iqari shy away from attacking anything too large because, even with superior numbers, butchering, and carrying away the remains would take too long and leave the hunting pack exposed.

Iqari are intelligent and social amongst their own kind. An eyrie consists of up to six or seven iqari (parents and young) with many eyries clustered together forming a settlement. They worship the spirits of the air and mountains, and iqari shaman can be powerful animists able to channel and harness both the great ancestor spirits and the spirits of the hunt and the winds. Their language is a complex amalgam of squawks, chitters, head movements, hand and wing gestures. They are incapable of speaking human tongues but can understand them and use sign language to communicate back. However, given their reclusive nature, opportunities for encountering an iqari capable of understand human language is rare.

They have few natural enemies, although there is competition between iqari, griffins and hippogriffs for hunting territories. This can result in spectacular and bloody aerial battles, ultimately ending in a certain degree of demarcation and co-operation. Iqari have very high standards of personal honour. A worthy sapient foe will be allowed to live to fight another day, and if the opponent was truly worthy of respect, the iqari warrior may gift it with a wing feather – the highest honour these creatures can bestow. The one creature iqari will aim to slaughter are harpies. These airborne hags are the complete antithesis of iqari, and the birdmen show little mercy when harpies stray into their regions.

The iqari's Paralysing Screech skill (base POW+CHA) forces those within 5 metres to make an opposed Willpower roll against the iqari's skill. Anyone who is unsuccessful is paralysed by the horrific noise for a single combat round and temporarily deafened. Those who make their roll are merely deafened for 1d6 melee rounds, unable to communicate verbally. Each successful use of this ability costs the iqari a single magic point.

Iqari	Attributes	
STR: 3d6+12 (23)	Action Points	3
CON: 2d6+6 (13)	Damage Modifier	+1d8
SIZ: 2d6+12 (19)	Magic Points	11
DEX: 2d6+12 (19)	Movement	6m, 18m (Flying)
INT: 2d6+6 (13)	Initiative Bonus	14 (includes armour)
POW: 3d6 (11)	Armour	Feathers, Leather Kilt and Vambraces
CHA: 3d6 (11)	Abilities	Diving Attack, Flying
	Magic	Iqari generally practice Mysticism (Meditation 56%, Mysticism 54%). Specialist shaman also gain Animism (Trance 64%, Binding 62%)

1d20	Location	AP/HP
1–3	Right Leg	2/7
4–6	Left Leg	2/7
7–9	Abdomen	3/8
10	Chest	0/9
11–12	Right Wing	0/7
13–14	Left Wing	0/7
15–16	Right Arm	1/6
17–18	Left Arm	1/6
19–20	Head	2/7

Skills

Athletics 62%, Brawn 62%, Endurance 56%, Evade 58%, Fly 82%, Paralyzing Screech 62%, Perception 64%, Sign Language 54%, Stealth 52%, Survival 54%, Unarmed 72%, Willpower 52%

Combat Style & Weapons

Iqari Warrior (Spear, Beak, Claw, Wing Strike) 72%

Weapon	Size/Force	Reach	Damage	AP/HP
Beak	M	T	1d4+1d8	As for Head
Claw	M	S	1d6+1d8	As for Leg
Wing Strike	L	VL	1d3+1d8	As for Wing
Longspear	L	VL	1d10+1+1d8	4/10

Iqari Characters

Playing an iqari can pose some challenges unless all the characters are also iqari. Those iqari who seek out the company of other races are considered insane by their own kind and, indeed, may be in the throes of some psychosis.

Iqari abhor confinement. Buildings and rooms hold a special fear for them as they have an innate need to see the open sky at all times. Venturing underground, even for brief periods, requires a successful Willpower roll which must be remade every hour. Failed rolls result in the iqari experiencing the equivalent of a panic attack, and this may result in extremely manic, and possibly even violent behaviour especially if an exit is not in evidence.

A further challenge is that of language. Iqari are not equipped with the vocal organs to even approximate human speech, and so sign language is essential if the creature is to make itself understood (although understanding sapient tongues is quite possible). And, as raptors, iqari are exclusively carnivorous preferring either live meat or raw, freshly killed food. This too may prove to be a challenge for non-iqari in a party.

Otherwise, iqari are an intelligent species with a sophisticated system of honour and its recognition. Iqari society has a rigorous set of laws to ensure that they do not return back to the beasts they were raised from. These are formalised into ritual songs which are repeatedly sung to the young. They are taught that the only thing preventing the iqari from devolving are their principles. Those who break

the laws have no honour, and are thus considered mindless animals. This sense of personal honour is so strong that if an Iqari breaks the codes, even by no fault of their own, the psychological backlash can drive them into insanity…and insanity generally equates to self destruction.

Culture

Iqari society is strange by human standards but most closely resembles the Primitive and Barbarian cultures, depending on the size and sophistication of the community. Smaller communities tend more towards the primitive whilst larger, older ones tend more to embody the barbarian. Skill choices should reflect one of these two cultures.

- Customs+40%, Native Tongue+40%
- Standard Skills: Brawn, Dance, Endurance, Locale, Perception, Sing, Unarmed
- Example Combat Styles: Iqari Hunter, Eyrie Sentinel, Fallen Psychotic
- Professional Skills: Courtesy, Craft (any primitive), Fly, Lore (any), Meditation, Mysticism, Navigation, Survival

Cultural Passions

- Loyalty to Eyrie
- Love (Freedom)
- Hate (Confinement)

Professions

Craftsman, Hunter, Shaman, Warrior

Starting Money

Iqari characters begin the game with commodities or currency worth 4d6 x10 silver pieces.

The Iqari Voice

'You shall not be an animal.
You shall not steal another's glory.
You shall not act against a brother without open challenge.
Let those with less glory act first.
Defend your eyrie or find another.
Give surplus to those less able.
Maiming during play is loss of self control.
Needless death threatens future eggs.
Fall not upon the prey at the first smell of blood,
lest someone be hunting yours;
Withhold the claw in times of insufferable insult,
lest it snatches away your reputation;
Eat not the flesh of thinking life,
lest your appetite consumes your soul.
A clear mind costs only patience.'

Typical Iqari mantra taught to fledglings.

Lion

Savannah and plains-dwelling big cats, lions form prides of between 10 and 20 (around five females and cubs, and two or three males). Males excluded from a pride can, and do, become rogue wanderers, and so lions can also be encountered singly. The females perform most of the hunting with the males guarding the pride's territory from other prides and interlopers.

Hunting is a co-ordinated business with three or more lionesses stalking and chasing-down prey over a protracted period. Such teamwork increases the success of the hunt. Each lioness in a hunting party has a preferred role, with a leader and stalkers who triangulate to reduce the chance of prey escaping.

It is rare for lions to prey on humans but not unheard of. Settlements with livestock populations that are established too close to a pride's territories increases the chance of attacks, and rogue males (particularly the sick or injured), driven by hunger, will look for whatever prey is available.

Lion	Attributes	
STR: 2d6+12 (19)	Action Points	3
CON: 3d6 (11)	Damage Modifier	+1d8
SIZ: 2d6+15 (22)	Magic Points	7
DEX: 3d6+6 (17)	Movement	8m
INS: 2d6+6 (13)	Initiative Bonus	15
POW: 2d6 (7)	Armour	Mane and Hide
	Abilities	Intimidate, Night Sight
	Magic	None

1d20	Location	AP/HP
1–2	Right Hind Leg	1/7
3–4	Left Hind Leg	1/7
5–7	Hindquarters	1/8
8–10	Forequarters	1/9
11–13	Right Front Leg	1/7
14–16	Left Front Leg	1/7
17–20	Head	3/7

Skills
Athletics 66%, Brawn 61%, Endurance 52%, Evade 54%, Perception 50%, Willpower 44%

Combat Style & Weapons
King Slayer (Bite, Claw) 76%

Weapon	Size/Force	Reach	Damage	AP/HP
Bite	L	S	1d8+1d8	As for Head
Claw	L	M	1d6+1d8	As for Leg

Lizard, Giant

Many species of giant lizard exist and, whilst appearances will differ, most giant lizards share very similar characteristics. They are all cold-blooded, all predators of some kind, and all need warm to hot conditions to thrive. Lizards are found throughout jungles, arid areas, hills and mountains as long as their environmental needs are being met.

Sight is highly important for most types of lizard, both for locating prey and for communication. Consequently many lizards have highly acute colour and heat vision, and therefore excellent perception.

Most lizards rely heavily on body language, using specific postures, gestures and movements to define territory, resolve disputes and entice mates, which leads to deliberate, almost ritualistic movements that some cultures reflect in religious dances and ceremonies.

Many lizards are brightly coloured to warn potential predators, but some keep their colouration hidden until needed (with crests, wattles, on the underside of the belly, and so forth). Lizards are territorial, and guard their territories against other predators but are, generally, ambivalent towards humans unless hungry or threatened. Some species, like the monitor lizards, are notorious for attacks, and will consider anything warm blooded and moving fair prey.

Lizards apply a number of different techniques when hunting, anything from launching ambushes from cover, dropping atop victims, or even running rapidly over concealed patches of quicksand or water to lure prey to a lingering death.

A defensive technique used by some lizard species is to shed the tail completely if it is grabbed and held by a predator. The tail will regenerate but is usually shorter and of a different hue to the original. Detaching the tail in this fashion causes the lizard no wound effects.

Lizard, Giant		Attributes
STR: 2d6+12 (19)	Action Points	3
CON: 2d6+6 (13)	Damage Modifier	+1d6
SIZ: 2d6+12 (19)	Magic Points	7
DEX: 1d6+12 (16)	Movement	10m
INS: 2d6+5 (12)	Initiative Bonus	14
POW: 2d6 (7)	Armour	Tough Scales
	Abilities	Adhering (some), Cold Blooded, Intimidate
	Magic	None

1d20	Location	AP/HP
1-3	Tail	3/7
4-5	Right Hind Leg	3/7
6-7	Left Hind Leg	3/7
8-10	Hindquarters	3/8
11-14	Forequarters	3/9
15-16	Right Front Leg	3/6
17-18	Left Front Leg	3/6
19-20	Head	3/7

Skills
Athletics 65%, Brawn 58%, Endurance 56%, Evade 72%, Perception 68%, Track 55%, Stealth 68%, Willpower 44%

Combat Style & Weapons
Scaly Hunter (Jaws, Claws) 75%

Weapon	Size/Force	Reach	Damage	AP/HP
Bite	M	T	1d6+1d6	As for Head
Claw	M	M	1d4+1d6	As for Leg

Lizardman/Ophidian

Classic creatures of fantasy literature Lizardmen and Ophidians are closely related species of bipedal sapient reptiles. Lizardmen are self explanatory, possessing muscular bodies, clawed hands and feet, elongated snouts filled with snaggle teeth, heavy tails and scaled, often beautifully coloured skin. Ophidians are similar but take their primary attributes from snakes rather than lizards; and thus have a leaner, more humanoid build, stubbier snouts, venomous fangs instead of peg teeth, and are more intelligent than their brethren.

Both species share a cold, reptilian outlook on life; but whereas lizardmen tend to form primitive or occasionally barbarian societies, the ophidians are naturally inclined to civilisation, and all the decadence and treachery which it brings. Like chalk and cheese, one is a race of illiterate savages, the other amoral and urbane. The lizardmen are more prone to direct physical confrontation whereas ophidians prefer subtle manipulation or assassination.

With their thick scales, and inured resilience towards both damp and desiccated environments, the reptilian races prefer to live in regions deemed living hells, such as burning deserts, arid wastelands, pestilent swamps, and steamy, tropical jungles. Within these fastnesses their civilisations rise and fall in cycles beyond the ken of other sapient species. Only when differing cultures are forced into each other's territory do folk begin to go missing, killed for trespassing or taken for sacrifice; or perhaps worse still captured to be eaten, for the lizardmen are prone to cannibalism, and have a taste for human flesh.

When not engaged in war, lizardmen often manufacture tools and weapons, usually for trade or as sacrifices to the local gods and spirits. Ophidians on the other hand have more refined tastes, and craft art or scholarly works, their focus more being towards the sorcerous or mystical talents.

Lizardman/Ophidian	Attributes	
STR: 2d6+9 (16)	Action Points	3
CON: 2d6+6 (13)	Damage Modifier	+1d4
SIZ: 2d6+9 (16)	Magic Points	11
DEX: 2d6+6 (13)	Movement	6m
INT: 2d6+6 (13)	Initiative Bonus	13
POW: 3d6 (11)	Armour	Tough Scales. Warriors can wear any.
CHA: 2d6 (7)	Abilities	Cold Blooded, Night Sight
	Magic	Specialists may practice Animism or Theism

1d20	*Location*	*AP/HP*
1-3	Tail	3/6
4-5	Right Leg	3/6
6-7	Left Leg	3/6
8-10	Abdomen	3/7
11-14	Chest	3/8
15-16	Right Arm	3/5
17-18	Left Arm	3/5
19-20	Head	3/6

Skills
Athletics 59%, Brawn 62%, Craft (Any primitive) 56%, Customs 56%, Endurance 66%, Evade 56%, Insight 44%, Locale 66%, Perception 54%, Swim 69%, Unarmed 59%, Willpower 52%

Passions
Loyalty to Tribe 90%, Hate Enemies 80%

Combat Style & Weapons
Lizardman Warrior (Stone Axe, Shortspear, Target Shield) 69%

Weapon	Size/Force	Reach	Damage	AP/HP
Bite	M	M	1d6+1d4	As for Head
Claw	M	T	1d4+1d4	As for Arm
Tail	M	L	1d4+1d4	As for Tail
Shortspear	M	L	1d8+1+1d4	4/5
Stone Axe	M	M	1d6+1+1d4	4/8
Target Shield	L	S	1d3+1+1d4	4/9

The characteristics above denote a lizardman. Ophidians have slightly different base characteristics, swapping the dice rolls for STR with POW and SIZ with INT. They have two less Armour Points than lizardmen, but in exchange have the Venomous trait, injecting the poison with their bite. Substitute Craft with a suitable Lore skill. Most ophidians know Folk Magic, and specialists study Sorcery or Mysticism.

Ophidian Venom

Ophidian venom has a Potency of 70%. A victim must win an opposed roll of his Endurance against the Potency of the venom else suffer the following symptoms. At the start of the round following being poisoned, the bitten location suffers the Agony condition, rendering it unusable for the next 2d6 minutes, and possibly disrupting any attempts at concentration or spell casting. One hour later the victim begins to suffer the combined effects of Hallucination and Mania, developing a rabid fear of snakes. This effect lasts 2d6 days, during which time the victim grows increasingly paranoid until they must eventually be tied up for their own safety. After the poison subsides the victim will have no recollection of what bit them or how.

Mammoth

Pachyderms that thrive in colder climates, mammoths are considerably larger and more dangerous than elephants. The Mythras mammoth stands some three and a half metres at the shoulder. With its woolly, shaggy covering of fur, this immense beast is truly a sight to behold.

The tusks of the mammoth are extremely long with a distinct outward bow and upward curve, making them both formidable weapons and highly prized sets of ivory. The skin and fur is extremely warm, and the layers of subcutaneous fat mean that, all in all, a mammoth is a much-hunted beast, especially amongst primitive cultures that share a similar climate to the mammoth's herd territories.

Mammoths, like elephants, live and move in herds of up to twenty creatures. All herd members will fight to protect themselves and their young. An enraged mammoth is not to be trifled with. Above and beyond their stampede and trampling ability, the vast tusks and strong, probing trunk mean that mammoths are daunting opponents.

Fur, on its own, is not enough to offer protection against the cold. Mammoths also have a layer of subcutaneous fat up to a hand width deep. This fat is an important commodity for many cultures, just as blubber is from whales. Where mammoths exist, one can therefore guarantee industries, even primitive ones, to exploit the mammoth's natural resources.

Mammoths attempt to trample first, taking advantage of their size and weight. If forced into close combat, the trunk is used to grip, and then hurl an opponent as far as possible (1d6+4 metres, with falling damage sustained by the victim). If the trunk cannot be engaged, then the tusks are used to smash small opponents (such as humans) or gore larger ones.

Mammoth		Attributes
STR: 2d6+40 (47)	Action Points	2
CON: 2d6+24 (31)	Damage Modifier	+2d10
SIZ: 2d6+56 (63)	Magic Points	11
DEX: 3d6 (11)	Movement	10m
INS: 2d6+4 (11)	Initiative Bonus	11
POW: 3d6 (11)	Armour	Woolly pelt and hide
	Abilities	Intimidate, Trample
	Magic	None

1d20	Location	AP/HP
1-2	Right Hind Leg	9/19
3-4	Left Hind Leg	9/19
5-8	Hindquarters	9/20
9-12	Forequarters	9/21
13-14	Right Front Leg	9/19
15-16	Left Front Leg	9/19
17	Trunk	9/18
18-20	Head	9/19

Skills
Athletics 58%, Brawn 130%, Endurance 92%, Evade 22%, Perception 52%, Willpower 52%

Combat Style & Weapons
Trampling Doom (Trunk, Trample, Gore) 78%

Weapon	Size/Force	Reach	Damage	AP/HP
Trunk	C	VL	1d10+2d10	As for Trunk
Tusks	C	VL	1d12+2d10	As for Head
Trample	C	T	4d10	As for Leg

ELEPHANTS

If an elephant is needed for a MYTHRAS game, the mammoth's statistics are the obvious starting point. Reduce STR and SIZ by 10 points to approximate the elephant's smaller stature (they typically weigh between 3 and 6 tons, compared with a mammoth's 5 to 10 tons). Elephants have shorter tusks, so reduce the Size to Huge and Reach to Long. An elephant's trunk is also longer than that of a mammoth, but there is no necessity to amend the trunk statistics from those given above.

The other obvious difference is that elephants are a tropical and sub-tropical species meaning that they lack both the fur and subcutaneous fat of the mammoth. Reduce the elephant's natural Armour Points to 7 across all locations.

The Intimidate and Trample abilities remain the same, as do skills and Combat Styles.

MANTICORE

A manticore is a wild beast, powerful, daring, as big as the largest lion, its thick fur of a red colour like cinnabar. Its face however is not that of a wild beast but of a man, and it has three rows of teeth set in its upper jaw, and three in the lower; these are exceedingly sharp and larger than the fangs of a hound. Its ears also resemble a man's except that they are larger and shaggy; its eyes are blue-grey and they too are like a man's, but its feet and claws are those of a lion.

To the end of its insectoid tail is attached the sting of a scorpion, which might be over half a metre in length; and the tail has barbs at intervals on either side. The tip of the tail gives a fatal sting to anyone who encounters it, and death is immediate.

The manticore can cast its barbs like arrows, by flicking its tail and shooting them a great distance. Most creatures that the missile hits are killed due to the beast's poison. These barbs replenish themselves constantly so that it rarely runs out of ammunition.

Manticora are all vicious predators feeding on whatever they can hunt, but for preference it will devour human beings; indeed it will slaughter a great number; utterly fearless, willingly ambushing two or even three men, and alone overcoming that number. As if this was not bad enough, a few are cursed with chaotic gifts which twist or deform them in some way, granting them wings for example.

Manticore venom has a Potency equal to the creature's Endurance. It takes effect 1 round after damage has been inflicted, and causes paralysis to 1d3 contiguous hit locations. If this affects the chest the victim begins to asphyxiate and will die unless treated.

Manticore	Attributes	
STR: 2d6+15 (22)	Action Points	3
CON: 2d6+9 (16)	Damage Modifier	+1d10
SIZ: 2d6+18 (25)	Magic Points	11
DEX: 3d6+6 (17)	Movement	10m
INS: 2d6+7 (14)	Initiative Bonus	16
POW: 3d6 (11)	Armour	Fur, Mane and Chitin
	Abilities	Chaos Feature, Frenzy, Leaper, Venomous
	Magic	None

1d20	Location	AP/HP
1-3	Tail	6/9
4-5	Right Hind Leg	3/9
6-7	Left Hind Leg	3/9
8-10	Hindquarters	3/10
11-14	Forequarters	3/11
15-16	Right Front Leg	3/9
17-18	Left Front Leg	3/9
19-20	Head	5/9

Skills
Athletics 69%, Brawn 61%, Endurance 72%, Evade 74%, Perception 65%, Stealth 71%, Track 60, Willpower 62%

Combat Style & Weapons
Man Hunter (Bite, Claws, Barbs and Sting) 79%

Weapon	Size/Force	Reach	Damage	AP/HP
Jaws	M	T	1d4+1d10	As for Head
Claws	L	M	1d6+1d10	As for Leg
Sting	H	L	1d8+1d10+Vencom	As for Leg
Flung Barbs	L	-	1d6+1d10+Venom	

MANTIS, GIANT

At three metres in length, the giant praying mantis is a quite formidable predator that feeds exclusively on creatures smaller than itself. It has two remarkable features: the elongated forelimbs that are used to catch and hold prey immobile, and its extremely long and flexible thorax which permits amazing limb dexterity whilst the body remains static. Also of note is the insect's field of vision. Its massive compound eyes and neck articulation grant the mantis a wide field of vision through 300 degrees, making it difficult to creep up on from behind.

Mantids are ambush hunters. The giant variety conceals itself in foliage and branches, remaining motionless for extremely long periods until suitable prey strays within range of its forelimbs. The insects can fly, doing so mainly at night to move between hunting locations, and some mantids have distinct territories that are heavily defended. During mating season females are known to kill and eat their mates once copulation is complete.

Mantis, Giant	Attributes	
STR: 2d6+6 (13)	Action Points	3
CON: 2d6+6 (13)	Damage Modifier	+1d4
SIZ: 2d6+12 (19)	Magic Points	4
DEX: 2d6+18 (25)	Movement	6m, 10m (Flying)
INS: 2d6+2 (9)	Initiative Bonus	17
POW: 1d6 (4)	Armour	Chitin
	Abilities	Camouflaged, Flying, Grappler
	Magic	None

1d20	Location	AP/HP
1	Right Rear Leg	3/6
2	Left Rear Leg	3/6
3-4	Metathorax	3/8
5	Mid Right Leg	3/6
6	Mid Left Leg	3/6
7-10	Prothorax	3/9
11–12	Right Wing	3/6
13–14	Left Wing	3/6
15–16	Right Forelimb	3/6
17–18	Left Forelimb	3/6
19–20	Head	3/7

Skills
Athletics 78%, Brawn 72%, Endurance 56%, Evade 80%, Fly 68%, Perception 53%, Stealth 74%, Willpower 48%

Combat Style & Weapons
Unseen Death (Scything Limbs, Bite) 78%

Weapon	Size/Force	Reach	Damage	AP/HP
Forelimb	L	VL	1d6+1d4	As for Limb
Mandibles	M	M	1d4+1d4	As for Head

Consummate ambushers, manti wait, motionless, for prey to wander close enough for an attack which happens with frightening speed. Match the mantis's Stealth against a victim's Perception (remembering the Camouflage penalty) in an opposed roll to determine the outcome of the ambush.

The mantis strikes with its forelimbs first, automatically gripping the prey if the attack is successful. If it wins a special effect it usually selects Pin Weapon (if the opponent has a drawn weapon or held shield) or Kill Silently. On its next turn the victim is yanked back to the mantis which delivers a bite with its powerful mandibles, aiming for the neck, chest or abdomen in a bid to quickly incapacitate. If a victim breaks free of the insect's grip or the initial attack fails, then the mantis will attempt to fly away and hunt something else. A mantis will not try to ambush a creature that is clearly larger than itself.

Minotaur

Bovine-headed and man-bodied, minotaurs are anthropomorphic hybrids of myth and legend. In the original Greek myth the minotaur was a single beast known also as Asterion, which dwelled in the labyrinth of Crete, beneath the palace of King Minos, where it received regular sacrifices.

Minotaurs are much larger than humans. Males average well over two metres tall. They are powerful and massively built, with a natural confidence and swagger amongst their own kind. Males are blessed with oversized horns, and proudly display battle scars as badges of honour. A few have the lower halves and the hoofed legs of bulls. Armour is rarely worn, more from the fact that none amongst their culture knows the art of smithing and salvaged war trophies rarely fit, rather than any philosophical attitudes towards it.

Their favoured weapons are great axes or two handed clubs, with which they delight in smashing opponents about. There is no doubting that minotaurs are tenacious fighters and have little trouble rising to aggression when the need calls for it. They are brave but merciless fighters, and believe in putting a foe down as quickly and brutally as possible.

When faced with chaos-tainted species, such as boar-kin and chaos hybrids, minotaurs show no mercy. They have an innate hatred of chaos and attempt to stamp it out whenever and wherever they can.

Socially most minotaurs tend to be bluff, gruff and taciturn with a reputation for being, at best, rude to other species and, at worst, outwardly aggressive. Some of this reputation comes with the struggle minotaurs have with human tongues. They can understand them well enough, but speaking them is difficult. No minotaur can speak a human tongue at higher than 50%, owing the sheer differences in minotaur physiology and vocal dynamics.

Minotaurs have a polygynous social structure. Males may take several wives and herd leaders always have a harem, which are won by demonstrating martial prowess and great deeds. Primarily vegetarians, minotaurs consume vast amounts of fruits and wild grains every day, supplementing their diet with milk and cheese from their herds. Minotaur warbands have been known to raid cattle herders who move into a minotaur grazing areas, sparing only the cattle (which they release) but massacring the herders.

Several minotaur tribes live in close proximity to Meeros although they maintain a respectful distance. Like the Meerish they revere Myceras, although they depict the War God as the primary deity of their cosmology - the father of all other gods.

They consider the Meerish pantheon to be a blasphemy against Myceras and do not recognise Meerish temples or rites.

They do, however, recognise the bravery that Myceras's warriors exhibit in battle and accord a level of respect to those who display courtesy and honour.

Minotaur Characters

More sociable minotaurs can make for excellent player characters as long as the limitations regarding language are remembered. Minotaurs are tough, proud and irascible, but they are also intelligent and can even be compassionate when the time calls for it. However if a party ever required a stoic, strong, silent, brute of a warrior, then nothing fits the bill quite like a minotaur.

Culture

Minotaurs form small societies well away from standard humans. They rarely tend to rise above the level of a Barbarian culture, and most are nomadic because their beliefs and behaviour are based on strength and survival rather than higher notions of art and social development. Since beasts of burden or wheeled vehicles are rarely used, minotaur possessions are limited to what they carry themselves. The Drive and Ride skills are redundant unless the minotaurs are from a culture where giant riding or pack animals are readily available.

- Customs+40%, Native Tongue+40%
- Standard Skills: Athletics, Brawn, Endurance, Influence, Locale, Perception, Unarmed
- Example Combat Styles: Minotaur Warrior, Horned Berserker, Hoofed Hunter
- Professional Skills: Commerce, Craft (any primitive), Healing, Language (any), Lore (any), Navigation, Survival, Track

Cultural Passions

- Loyalty to Herd
- Love (Freedom, Battle)
- Hate (Chaos)

Professions

Crafter, Farmer, Herder, Priest, Shaman, Warrior

Starting Money

Minotaur characters begin the game with commodities or currency worth 4d6 x20 silver pieces.

The Minotaur Voice

'These field and trails belong to the Buru-hrunz tribe and you trespass. Are you want make us angry? We will fight if have to, and my horns will drip your blood, but we want you go now, so we not have to kill you. If you come to trade, we happy to change goods but be quick about business. We have silver, bronze and want strong weapons and sharp tools.

So? You challenge me? Or what? You flee, you trade or you die. Simple.'

Minotaur	Attributes	
STR: 3d6+6 (17)	Action Points	2
CON: 2d6+6 (13)	Damage Modifier	+1d6
SIZ: 2d6+15 (22)	Magic Points	11
DEX: 2d6+3 (10)	Movement	8m
INT: 2d6+6 (13)	Initiative Bonus	12
POW: 3d6 (11)	Armour	Horns and Hide. Warriors may wear any armour
CHA: 3d6 (11)	Abilities	Intimidate, Trample
	Magic	Some herds may have specialist priests and shaman. Sorcery tends to be shunned.

1d20	Location	AP/HP
1–3	Right Leg	0/7
4–6	Left Leg	0/7
7–9	Abdomen	0/8
10-12	Chest	0/9
13–15	Right Arm	0/6
16–18	Left Arm	0/6
19-20	Head	3/7

Skills
Athletics 57%, Brawn 79%, Customs 66%, Endurance 66%, Evade 40%, Insight 44%, Locale 56%, Lore (Herding) 66%, Perception 54%, Unarmed 57%, Willpower 42%

Combat Style & Weapons
Minotaur Warrior (Great Axe, Shortspear, Hoplite Shield, Gore) 67%

Weapon	Size/Force	Reach	Damage	AP/HP
Minotaur Great Axe	E	VL	2d8+2+1d6	6/12
Minotaur Shortspear	H	VL	1d10+1+1d6	4/10
Hoplite Shield	H	S	1d4+1d6	6/15
Gore	L	M	1d8+1d6	As for Head

Mummy

Animated corpses, usually by sorcery or other magic, but sometimes through sheer force of will, which have been subjected to mummification processes to help preserve them in preparation for the afterlife. Mummies lack any functioning internal organs, and so are essentially bone, sinew and desiccated flesh. Like most undead this makes them naturally resilient to damage.

Mummies are, however, somewhat susceptible to fire. The bandages used in their preparation and the fluids used for embalming, are usually flammable. Any strike with a naked flame has a chance equal to the damage rolled of setting the creature alight. This means that the original damage continues to affect the hit location struck each round until extinguished, and also spreads to one adjacent hit location every round inflicting further damage.

There are three main types of Mummies:

- ***Marionette*** mummies animated through sorcery are mere automatons which need to be actively controlled by the caster, otherwise they have no purpose or direction. In effect the sorcerer 'wears' the body of the mummy as a proxy to perform some nefarious deed.
- ***Guardian*** mummies are those inhabited and controlled by a spirit, which has been bound into the corpse. Depending on the type of spirit this means that these mummies are usually instinct-driven and have no real intelligence, merely a subconscious command which they are compelled to perform.
- ***Vengeful*** mummies that self animate through sheer force of will are usually motivated to complete a specific act or task denied to them during life. This might be revenge (on a murderer, say) or protecting their burial chattels. These fearsome mummies display the same intelligence they held in life.

Mummy characteristics are based upon those of the original creature, maintained intact by the act of preservation, and further infused with an unnatural strength and vitality. They gain +2 Armour Points due to the bandaging, and bonuses to STR and CON particular to the power of the magic or spirit animating them. The INT, POW and CHA of the mummy are based upon what spirit or will currently animates it. The following statistics are for a human mummy of average physical characteristics, but which has been possessed by its ancient, former soul (treated as an Intensity 3 Undeath Spirit).

Unless buried or armed with a weapon, human mummies typically attempt to grapple their opponents in close quarters (see Grappling page 106). When possible they use the Choose Location (head) to grab their victim's throat and begin strangling, continuing to exert damage each turn whilst simultaneously asphyxiating them.

Mummy	Attributes	
STR: 3d6+9 (20)	Action Points	2
CON: 3d6+9 (20)	Damage Modifier	+1d6
SIZ: 2d6+6 (13)	Magic Points	22
DEX: 3d6 (11)	Movement	6m
INT: 2d6+6 (13)	Initiative	12
POW: 1d6+18 (22)	Armour	As per original creature with bandages and burial armour.
CHA: 3d6 (11)	Abilities	Imunity (Poison, Disease), Life Sense, Undead
	Magic	Some may retain the magical skills possessed in life.

1d20	Location	AP/HP
1–3	Right Leg	2/7
4–6	Left Leg	2/7
7–9	Abdomen	2/8
10-12	Chest	2/9
13–15	Right Arm	2/6
16–18	Left Arm	2/6
19-20	Head	2/7

Skills
Athletics 51%, Brawn 63%, Endurance 70%, Evade 42%, Perception 63%, Unarmed 71%, Willpower 84%

Combat Style & Weapons
Vengeful Strangler (Hands) 71%

Weapon	Size/Force	Reach	Damage	AP/HP
Hands	S	T	1d3+1d6	As for Arm

Octopus, Giant

These monstrous cephalopods may well be the source of sea-monster tales. The giant species can range in size from the average 10 metre arm span of the example provided below, to colossal monsters which can attack ships.

Octopuses have several offensive and defensive mechanisms. Their eight tentacles, lined with suction cups, allow them a huge range of movement and actions; also all octopuses are venomous, and in these gigantic varieties the venom is a threat to large species. Couple this with their ability to squirt ink, change the colour of their skin, regenerate tentacles, propel themselves at great speeds through the water, and to squeeze into and through very small spaces, and the giant octopus becomes a formidable predator.

An octopus is also an intelligent creature with excellent problem solving abilities. When attacking prey, such as creatures in boats or creatures in the water, they are selective, and capable of using as wide a range of combat Special Effects as any sapient species, despite having the INS characteristic.

Octopuses may use their tentacles to parry attacks, using the squidgy limbs to entangle weapons in their grip, forcing wielders to wrestle them free with opposed Brawn rolls. Any gripped opponent is either crushed in-situ or drawn towards the beak, whereupon the octopus bites into the creature and injects venom with a Potency equal to the octopus's Endurance. The venom paralyses the affected area within one Combat Round, and then spreads to the rest of the body 1d3+3 rounds later. It then feeds on the paralysed specimen at leisure, dragging it into the depths.

Octopus, Giant		Attributes
STR: 2d6+15 (22)	Action Points	6 (Multi-limbed)
CON: 2d6+12 (19)	Damage Modifier	+1d10
SIZ: 2d6+21(28)	Magic Points	7
DEX: 2d6+15 (22)	Movement	2m (land), 8m (water)
INS: 2d6+7 (14)	Initiative Bonus	18
POW: 2d6 (7)	Armour	Blubbery Skin
	Abilities	Camouflaged, Formidable Natural Weapons, Grappler, Multi-Limbed, Regeneration (can grow back lost tentacles at its Healing Rate in Hit Points per day), Swimmer, Venomous
	Magic	None, thankfully.

1d20	*Location*	*AP/HP*
01-02	Tentacle 1	1/10
03-04	Tentacle 2	1/10
05-06	Tentacle 3	1/10
07-08	Tentacle 4	1/10
09-10	Tentacle 5	1/10
11-12	Tentacle 6	1/10
13-14	Tentacle 7	1/10
15-16	Tentacle 8	1/10
17-18	Body	1/12
19-20	Head	1/11

Skills
Athletics 87%, Brawn 80%, Endurance 68%, Evade 74%, Perception 61%, Stealth 76%, Swim 71%, Willpower 54%

Combat Style & Weapons
Writhing Doom (Tentacles, Beak) 84%

Weapon	Size/Force	Reach	Damage	AP/HP
Tentacles	H	VL	1d8+1d10	As for Tentacle
Beak	M	T	1d6+1d10	As for Head

Ogre

The term *ogre* refers to any giant race of ugly, bad tempered humanoid. Smaller than true giants but every bit as mean – if not meaner – ogres tend to keep to themselves, living in hilly or forested regions where they make their primitive settlements. Ogres even dislike their own species: their sour temperaments making for solitary, bile-filled individuals. A few may be cursed by chaos, but such individuals are rare.

Whilst sapient, they have limited intellects and maintain a very primitive world-view. Many are so stupid they have reverted to bestiality and no longer understand speech. They make clothing for themselves but weapons and armour are either scavenged or relatively simple (leathers, stone, wood) or improvised (such as the proverbial ogre club – a heavy branch with a lump of stone fastened to it, more akin to a primeval mace).

Highly intelligent ogres may subjugate tribes of lesser humanoids in order to use them as slaves, or send them forth to gather food (although more bestial ones often face the opposite situation of being captured and used as savage pets). Ogres have a reputation for cannibalism and a taste for human flesh. This is true: they will eat whatever they can catch, and they seem to delight in catching other sapient species for torment and tastiness.

Ogre		Attributes
STR: 2d6+12 (19)	Action Points	2
CON: 2d6+9 (16)	Damage Modifier	+1d8
SIZ: 2d6+18 (25)	Magic Points	11
DEX: 3d6 (11)	Movement	8m
INT: 2d6+3 (10)	Initiative Bonus	8 (includes Initiative Penalty)
POW: 3d6 (11)	Armour	Scraps of Fur and Leather
CHA: 2d6 (7)	Abilities	None
	Magic	Sapient ogres may know some Folk Magic or Animism

1d20	*Location*	*AP/HP*
1–3	Right Leg	2/9
4–6	Left Leg	2/9
7–9	Abdomen	2/10
10-12	Chest	2/11
13–15	Right Arm	2/8
16–18	Left Arm	2/8
19-20	Head	2/9

Skills
Athletics 50%, Brawn 84%, Endurance 62%, Evade 42%, Locale 40%, Perception 38%, Survival 53%, Track 56%, Unarmed 60%, Willpower 42%

Combat Style & Weapons
Big, Hitty Things (Club) 70%

Weapon	Size/Force	Reach	Damage	AP/HP
Ogre Club	L	L	1d10+1d8	4/10

Female ogres seem to be smarter and more conniving than their male counterparts, being very much the brains of the relationship.

This assumes, of course, that ogres form meaningful and lasting relationships. Fables and legends often pair ogres together in marriage which indicates that, whilst solitary, finding a partner is advantageous.

Panthotaur

These creatures are a lean combination of a human with the furred head, abdomen, legs, tail and retractable claws of a large cat – either a lion, tiger, leopard, panther or jaguar. Panthotaurs retain their big cat ferocity and cunning and, in the case of lion panthotaurs, social behaviour by forming prides. Otherwise they exhibit near-human sapience. Visually they are beautiful to behold, parts of their body covered with a fine fur that matches the feline they are related to.

Their different psychologies and dietary requirements mean that panthotaurs do not mix easily with humans and so remain apart from them. Occasionally humans might find themselves as prey but, generally, panthotaurs opt for smaller game and give humans a wide-berth. Panthotaurs are territorial, occupying lands similar to their animal cousins (jungles, bush and savannah), and may even command prides or solitary individuals of their beast brethren.

Armed with effective natural weapons and incredible agility, these creatures rarely use armour or even weapons beyond a simple sling or spear. Rather they use speed and stealth to hunt and defend their territories. Hit and run techniques are preferred to toe to toe slugging matches.

The Panthotaurs of Anathaym's world inhabit the savannahs of the northern region, bordering the realm of the Badoshi. They revere the Sun Goddess Ar-Aya and, being master mathemeticians have built vast, stepped pyramids in her honour. Pictured below is one of the high priestesses of the Pantheris. Her collar is symbolic of her relationship with the sun, and marks her as a formidable theist magician.

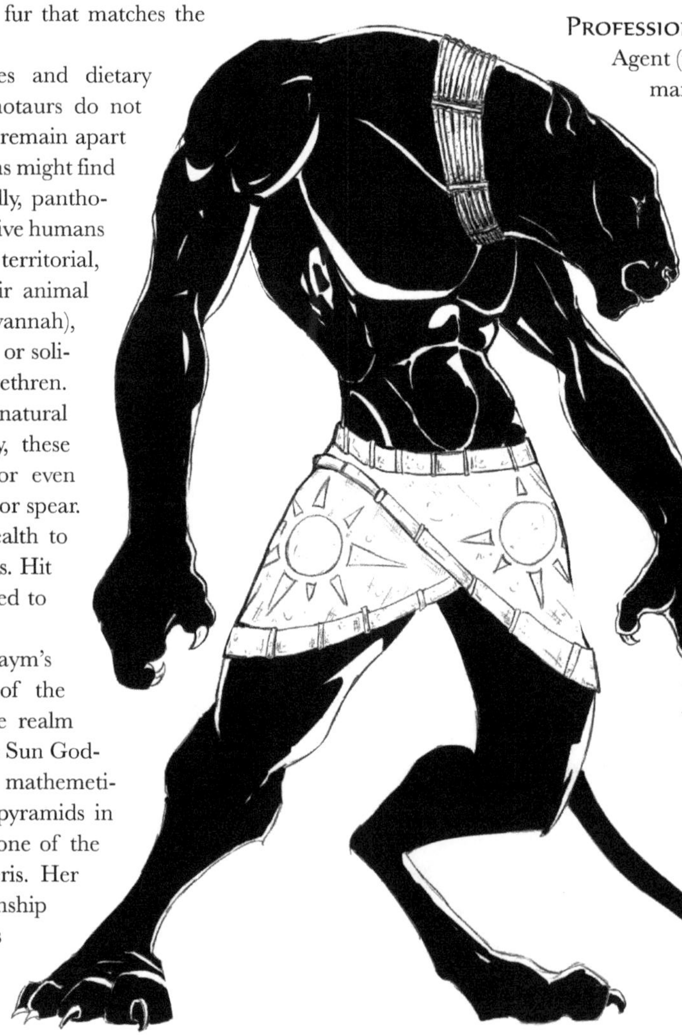

Panthotaur Characters

Panthotaurs can be used as player characters – although their solitary natures may make some aspects of integration with human characters difficult. The most social are the Leonitaurs (Lions) owing to their innate social organization. Tigrisotaurs (Tigers) tend to be the most solitary.

Culture

Panthotaurs live in pride-like, Barbarian-level societies often matriarchal in nature. The males are typically hunters and warriors, but dealings with other species are handled by the females.

- Customs+40%, Native Tongue+40%
- Standard Skills: Athletics, Brawn, Endurance, Influence, Locale, Perception, Unarmed
- Example Combat Styles: Panthotaur Warrior, Clawed Assassin, Silent Hunter
- Professional Skills: Commerce, Craft (any Barbarian), Healing, Language (any), Lore (any), Stealth, Survival, Track

Cultural Passions

- Loyalty to Pride
- Love (Freedom, Hunting)
- Hate (Chaos)

Professions

Agent (females), Crafter, Hunter, Priest, Shaman, Warrior

Starting Money

Panthotaur characters begin the game with commodities or currency worth 4d6 x40 silver pieces.

Panthotaur		Attributes
STR: 3d6+6 (17)	Action Points	3
CON: 2d6+6 (13)	Damage Modifier	+1d4
SIZ: 3d6+6 (17)	Magic Points	11
DEX: 2d6+12 (19)	Movement	8m
INT: 2d6+6 (13)	Initiative Bonus	15 (includes Initiative Penalty)
POW: 3d6 (11)	Armour	Fur and Leather Kilt
CHA: 2d6 (7)	Abilities	Intimidate, Night Sight
	Magic	Specialists can learn any magical discipline.

1d20	Location	AP/HP
1–3	Right Leg	1/6
4–6	Left Leg	1/6
7–9	Abdomen	2/7
10-12	Chest	1/8
13–15	Right Arm	1/5
16–18	Left Arm	1/5
19–20	Head	1/6

Skills

Athletics 66%, Brawn 54%, Endurance 56%, Evade 78%, Locale 56%, Perception 64%, Stealth 72%, Survival 54%, Track 56%, Unarmed 76%, Willpower 52%

Combat Style & Weapons

Panthotaur Warrior (Sling, Spear) 76%

Weapon	Size/Force	Reach	Damage	AP/HP
Bite	M	T	1d4+1d4	As for Head
Claw	M	M	1d6+1d4	As for Arm
Shortspear	M	L	1d8+1+1d4	4/5
Sling	L	-	1d8	1/2

Scorpion, Giant

Larger than a full grown human, giant scorpions are found mostly in hot, arid climates where they make their nests in caves and burrows, but they are natural survivors and can be found in almost any climate.

Scorpions have eight legs, two enlarged pincers, a long curved tail that finishes with a venom sac and stinger, and a segmented body with natural armour plating. They are generally nocturnal, opportunistic predators that wait for passing prey to stray into range of their pincers. Whilst voracious and capable of eating large amounts in one sitting, they can also go without food for long spans of time. The scorpion lacks a discernible head, with its eyes, mouth and other sensory organs located in the cephalothorax. The mouth consists of a pair of extremely sharp mandibles that can tear through tough skin or armour.

The giant species has few natural predators, placing it at the top of its local food chain. Its venom, tough exoskeleton, and ability to rapidly retreat to its burrow or cave makes capturing one of these scuttling arthropods difficult and risky.

Scorpion venom has a Potency equal to the creature's Endurance. It acts on the next round after injection and inflicts Agony on the location. After a further hour the venom slowly breaks down the tissue, causing the location to additionally lose 1 Hit Point per hour, which normally results in the loss of the limb (or death of the victim if head or torso) unless the poison is successfully treated. If desired the Games Master may substitute this venom with another, as the effects of giant scorpion venom can run a huge gamut of different effects depending on its species (see Poisons page 74 to create new ones).

Scorpions have incredibly resilient physiologies allowing them to survive the most extreme environmental conditions ranging from intense cold to extreme heat. Games Masters may therefore want to grant giant scorpions the Immunity (Cold) and Immunity (Heat) abilities - extending these even to resisting magical forms.

Scorpion, Giant		Attributes
STR: 2d6+12 (19)	Action Points	3
CON: 3d6+6 (17)	Damage Modifier	+1d8
SIZ: 2d6+15 (22)	Magic Points	4
DEX: 2d6+9 (16)	Movement	8m
INS: 2d6+2 (9)	Initiative Bonus	13
POW: 1d6 (4)	Armour	Chitin
	Abilities	Adhering, Burrowing, Formidable Natural Weapons, Venomous
	Magic	None

1d20	Location	AP/HP
01-02	Tail	6/8
03	Right Rear Leg	6/7
04	Left Rear Leg	6/7
05	Mid Right Leg	6/7
06	Mid Left Leg	6/7
07	Fore Right Leg	6/7
08	Fore Left Leg	6/7
09-12	Thorax	6/9
13-15	Right Pincer	6/8
16-18	Left Pincer	6/8
19-20	Cephalothorax	6/10

Skills

Athletics 65%, Brawn 71%, Endurance 64%, Evade 72%, Perception 53%, Stealth 65%, Willpower 48%

Combat Style & Weapons

Scuttling Horror (Sting, Pincers) 75%

Weapon	Size/Force	Reach	Damage	AP/HP
Pincer	H	L	1d8+1d8	As for Pincer
Sting	L	VL	1d6+1d8+Venom	As for Tail

Sea Serpent

Colossal denizens of deep water – both fresh and salt – sea serpents are vast, serpentine creatures equipped with fins, a head that is small in comparison with its body and an undulating motion through the water that results in a humped appearance when the body breaks the surface. For the most part they feed in the depths but may come to the surface to attack boats if disturbed.

Hungry sea serpents that encounter vessels generally pluck up a few sailors, swallowing them whole until their appetite is satisfied. Some clever captains will leave livestock (or perhaps unwitting passengers) on deck to feed a known monster in the hope it will depart peaceably. However, if harmed or driven to anger the creature will reduce a ship to driftwood, drowning most of its crew in the process. Killing such a monster is near impossible given its size and its ability to plunge back into the depths to flee an overwhelming attack against it.

Sea Serpent	Attributes	
STR: 2d6+30 (37)	Action Points	3
CON: 2d6+18 (25)	Damage Modifier	+2d10
SIZ: 2d6+60 (67)	Magic Points	11
DEX: 2d6+12 (19)	Movement	8m (Swim)
INS: 2d6+3 (10)	Initiative Bonus	15
POW: 3d6 (11)	Armour	Scales
	Abilities	Engulfing, Swimmer, Terrifying
	Magic	None

1d20	Location	AP/HP
1-3	Tail	6/19
4-5	Right Hind Fin	6/18
6-7	Left Hind Fin	6/18
8-10	Hindquarters	6/20
11-14	Forequarters	6/21
15-16	Right Front Fin	6/18
17-18	Left Front Fin	6/18
19-20	Head	6/19

Skills
Brawn 124%, Endurance 90%, Evade 58%, Perception 51%, Stealth 59%, Swim 82%, Willpower 52%

Combat Style & Weapons
Scourge of the Sea (Bite and Tail) 86%

Weapon	Size/Force	Reach	Damage	AP/HP
Bite	C	VL	1d12+2d10	As for Head
Tail Bash	C	VL	1d10+2d10	As for Tail

Shark

Sharks are consummate predators which roam the waters searching for prey and are merciless in its pursuit. They will attack anything that is helpless or panicking in the water, and are extremely sensitive to blood, allowing them to home in on prey from many kilometres away.

Once a shark tastes blood it does not stop in its attacks. Driving a shark away is exceedingly difficult and, by the time one shark has been deterred, another half dozen may have already arrived to join the feast.

Shark	Attributes	
STR: 2d6+18 (25)	Action Points	3
CON: 2d6+9 (16)	Damage Modifier	+2d6
SIZ: 2d6+35 (42)	Magic Points	7
DEX: 2d6+9 (16)	Movement	12m (Swim)
INS: 2d6+3 (10)	Initiative Bonus	13
POW: 2d6 (7)	Armour	Thick Hide
	Abilities	Blood Sense, Frenzy, Swimmer
	Magic	None

1d20	Location	AP/HP
1-3	Tail	2/12
4-6	Dorsal Fin	2/11
7-10	Hindquarters	2/13
11-14	Forequarters	2/14
15-16	Right Fin	2/11
17-18	Left Fin	2/11
19-20	Head	2/12

Skills
Brawn 87%, Endurance 62%, Evade 52%, Perception 57%, Swim 81%, Willpower 34%

Combat Style & Weapons
Jaws (Bite) 81%

Weapon	Size/Force	Reach	Damage	AP/HP
Bite	E	M	1d10+2d6	As for Head

Skeleton

Skeletons are the remains of dead creatures whose flesh has long rotted away, which are subsequently animated through magic. Any kind of skeleton can be animated, and need not specifically be bones, as even the empty husks of giant insects can be raised from their rest.

They are susceptible to weapons delivering blunt-trauma, which smashes the bone (or chitin), and disrupts the joints. Such weapons increase their damage dice by one step when used against skeletons (for example a club with 1d6 damage would become 1d8). On the other hand skeletons are resistant to slashing and thrusting weapons. Reduce the damage dice of slashing weapons by one step, and thrusting weapons by two steps.

Similar to mummies there are several types of skeletons depending on the type of magic used to animate them:

- Those animated through sorcery are automatons which must be actively controlled by the caster, otherwise they lapse into quiescence. Although powerful sorcerers can control several skeletons simultaneously their usefulness is limited by the concentration required to direct them.
- Skeletons raised by theism have the benefit that it is the supernatural entity being channelled by the priest who controls

them. This can often grant the undead a semblance of independent action, though their skills are dependent on the nature of the deity or demon called upon.

- Animists can send undeath spirits to possess the bones of dead creatures, granting the skeleton mental characteristics, and a degree of free will. This strength is also a weakness since the animating spirit can be blocked, exorcised or destroyed by magic which specifically targets such entities.

Skeleton characteristics are based upon those of the original creature, but modified to reflect the loss of flesh and muscle. Their STR and CON are halved (but receive bonuses according to the strength of the animating magic), and DEX is increased by half again – but never higher than the maximum for the species. The INT, POW and CHA of the skeleton are based upon the caster's own or the spirit that currently animates it.

The skill values of the skeleton are equal to those of its controller. For sorcerers and priests this is straight forward, but the skills of skeletons raised by animism are dependent on the spirit. Skeletons can wear armour, and wield any weapons they would naturally have in their previous life. The following statistics are for an average human skeleton which has been possessed by an Intensity 2 Spirit of Undeath (see page 153). All calculations have been factored in.

Skeleton	Attributes	
STR: 12	Action Points	3
CON: 12	Damage Modifier	None
SIZ: 13	Magic Points	16
DEX: 16	Movement	6m
INT: 11	Initiative Bonus	14
POW: 16	Armour	None
	Abilities	Undead
	Magic	None

1d20	Location	AP/HP
1–3	Right Leg	0/5
4–6	Left Leg	0/5
7–9	Abdomen	0/6
10-12	Chest	0/7
13–15	Right Arm	0/4
16–18	Left Arm	0/4
19–20	Head	0/5

Skills
Athletics 68%, Brawn 45%, Endurance 44%, Evade 72%, Perception 57%, Unarmed 68%, Willpower 72%

Combat Style & Weapons
Skeletal Warrior (Sword, Spear, Peltast Shield) 68%

Weapon	Size/Force	Reach	Damage	AP/HP
Shortspear	M	L	1d8+1	4/5
Peltast Shield	L	S	1d4	4/12
Shortsword	M	S	1d6	6/8

It is rumoured that the teeth of certain creatures, cursed with Chaos or undeath, can be buried and, with the right incantations, emerge from the ground as murderous skeletons of their host form. Of course this may simply be a myth used to terrify Meerish children into cleaning their own teeth properly. Or it may have something to do with a spell formula found in the infamous Death Scrolls of Bhast.

Slargr

A hulking, bad-tempered, bipedal lizard, slargr inhabit forests and swamps and establish extensive hunting grounds, targeting any creature smaller than themselves for food. Although omnivorous, slargr prefer fresh, raw meat; and despite their size are skilful yet silent ambush hunters. Their mottled grey-green skin offers excellent camouflage in the slargr's natural habitat making surprise attacks common. Rather strangely, the scales which cover them are thicker on the arms and head, but grow gradually thinner towards its tail, making it more vulnerable from the rear.

Although they appear slow and dull-witted, they are anything but. Slargr are intelligent. Their vast, clawed hands make all but the simplest brute tools difficult to use, but the beasts employ rocks, tree branches and other natural resources to aid in their hunting and even dig spike-lined death pits to aid in catching larger prey.

Slargr are, generally, solitary creatures. Intensely protective of their hunting territories, slargr cannot abide sharing with even their own kind. Companionship is sought for mating purposes only, and this happens once a year when the females become fertile and develop a pinkish-red sheen to their skin indicating a readiness to mate. At this time males compete in fights to the death for mating privileges, something the females encourage to ensure they will couple with the strongest male specimen they can.

Ostensibly bipedal, slargr will revert to all-fours when giving chase, thereby improving their speed. In combat they use their mass to overwhelm opponents, and a favoured tactic when dealing with weapon-using prey is to disarm the opponent first (especially shields) before bludgeoning and rending with claws and teeth. It has been known for humans to reason with slargr – persuading them to pursue better or larger prey – but such opportunities are rare. A hungry slargr has only one, driving desire, and it is not to enter into polite discourse.

The cover of this book depicts a typical adult slargr. The creature has been stalking Anathaym for some time before making a ferocious, unexpected attack.

Slargr	Attributes	
STR: 2d6+15 (22)	Action Points	2
CON: 2d6+12 (19)	Damage Modifier	+1d10
SIZ: 2d6+18 (25)	Magic Points	11
DEX: 2d6+6 (13)	Movement	6m
INT: 2d6+4 (11)	Initiative Bonus	12
POW: 3d6 (11)	Armour	Tough Scales
CHA: 2d6 (7)	Abilities	Blood Sense, Camouflaged, Formidable Natural Weapons, Grappler
	Magic	None

1d20	Location	AP/HP
1-3	Tail	2/9
4-5	Right Hind Leg	3/9
6-7	Left Hind Leg	3/9
8-10	Abdomen	3/10
11-14	Chest	3/11
15-16	Right Arm	4/8
17-18	Left Arm	4/8
19-20	Head	4/9
19-20	Head	4/9

Skills
Athletics 55%, Brawn 77%, Endurance 68%, Evade 46%, Perception 62%, Track 70%, Stealth 64%, Willpower 52%

Combat Style & Weapons
Slargr Hunter (Claws, Jaws and Tail) 75%

Weapon	Size/Force	Reach	Damage	AP/HP
Bite	L	S	1d8+1d10	As for Head
Claws	L	M	1d8+1d10	As for Arm
Tail	L	L	1d6+1d10	As for Tail

Smilodon

Often known as sabre-toothed tigers, although this is a misnomer, these big cats are noted for both their intimidating physical size and pronounced canine fangs which arch down well below the lower jaw and average around 30 centimetres in length. Smilodon are incredibly robust and strong when compared with other big cats – especially forequarters.

Built for power rather than speed, they are ambush hunters, using height to leap down on their prey, combining the delivery of a stabbing downward thrust with their incisors together with the impact of their sheer bulk to overwhelm their victims. Death is usually delivered by crushing the windpipe, a task made easier if the prey has been surprised, stabbed and then crushed under smilodon's weight.

Smilodon hunt in small family packs of between three and eight animals, although lone smilodon are also known. Their powerful forelimbs mean they are excellent climbers, and so they make use of any naturally high terrain to ambush their prey.

Smilodon	Attributes	
STR: 2d6+15 (22)	Action Points	3
CON: 2d6+6 (13)	Damage Modifier	+1d12
SIZ: 2d6+25 (32)	Magic Points	7
DEX: 2d6+9 (16)	Movement	8m
INS: 2d6+6 (13)	Initiative Bonus	15
POW: 2d6 (7)	Armour	Fur and Hide
	Abilities	Intimidate, Leaper, Night Sight
	Magic	None

1d20	Location	AP/HP
1–2	Right Hind Leg	2/9
3–4	Left Hind Leg	2/9
5–7	Hindquarters	2/10
8–10	Forequarters	2/11
11–13	Right Front Leg	2/9
14–16	Left Front Leg	2/9
17–20	Head	2/9

Skills
Athletics 78%, Brawn 84%, Endurance 66%, Evade 52%, Perception 50%, Track 66%, Stealth 69%, Willpower 44%

Combat Style & Weapons
Smilodon Ambush (Teeth, Claws) 78%

Weapon	Size/Force	Reach	Damage	AP/HP
Bite	H	M	1d10+1d12	As for Head
Claws	L	M	1d8+1d12	As for Leg

Snake, Giant

The largest naturally occurring large snakes (the constrictors, such as the python and anaconda) can reach huge lengths. This entry describes snakes of a more monstrous scale that are capable of swallowing prey whole and are truly terrifying in their appearance. The vast bulk of giant snakes are non-venomous: they rely on their size and strength to catch and then kill prey without the need to poison it for incapacitation. Of course, for added horror, giant snakes can be made venomous as well.

Snakes can adapt to most habitats although, being cold-blooded, they are sluggish in cooler climes. They can be found anywhere from deserts to jungles; forests to mountains. Wherever there is enough prey, giant snakes may not be far removed. All giant snakes are either camouflaged for their environment or possess the ability to mesmerise their prey. However, even the most brightly patterned serpents can be difficult to detect, and because snakes often remain motionless and silent for many hours, stumbling into a snake's path is not difficult to do.

All snakes have the inherent ability to unhinge their jaws in order to ingest subdued or slain prey. However since most serpents have a rather small head in proportion to their body length, and must spend hours swallowing victim, they do not receive the Engulfing ability in combat. Despite this minor restriction, a snake can swallow a creature of up to their own size. It takes one day per point of SIZ to fully digest the meal.

Whether they strike from ambush or hold mesmerised victims motionless whilst they approach, constrictors loop prey with their coils and wind themselves tight, cutting off circulation and air, suffocating and crushing the victim. Once the prey is dead or unconscious it is swallowed whole, and digested over a long period, meaning that snakes can take considerable periods between meals. Escaping from a giant constrictor's coils is a monumental feat requiring an opposed test of Brawn skills.

Snake, Giant	Attributes	
STR: 3d6+9 (20)	Action Points	3
CON: 3d6+12 (23)	Damage Modifier	+2d6
SIZ: 3d6+30 (41)	Magic Points	7
DEX: 2d6+12 (19)	Movement	8m
INS: 2d6+5 (12)	Initiative Bonus	16
POW: 2d6 (7)	Armour	Scales
	Abilities	Camouflaged or Gaze Attack (Mesmerism), Cold Blooded, Grappler
	Magic	None

1d20	*Location*	*AP/HP*
1–3	Tail Tip	4/13
4–5	Mid End-length	4/13
6–7	Fore End-length	4/13
8–9	Rear Mid-length	4/14
10–12	Mid Mid-length	4/14
13–14	Fore Mid-length	4/14
15–16	Rear Fore-length	4/13
17–18	Mid Fore-length	4/13
19–20	Head	4/13

Skills
Athletics 79%, Brawn 91%, Endurance 66%, Evade 68%, Perception 59%, Stealth 71%, Willpower 54%

Combat Style & Weapons
Crushing Death (Constrict, Bite and Writhe) 79%

Weapon	Size/Force	Reach	Damage	AP/HP
Bite	H	VL	1d8+2d6	As for Head
Constrict	E	T	2d6	As for Segment
Tail Slap	E	VL	1d6+2d6	As for Tail

Giant constrictors with the ability to mesmerise must engage the target in direct eye contact, which prompts an opposed roll of Willpower skills. If the victim loses, they remain motionless, unable to react or save themselves.

The first attack of the snake against a surprised or mesmerised target (if it generates a Special Effect) will target the chest or abdomen. No damage is inflicted but the attack automatically establishes a grapple. On the snake's next turn, it inflicts its Damage Modifier by tightening its coils applying the damage to the Chest or Abdomen area directly: armour does not protect against this constriction damage. Giant snakes usually keep their heads out of combat unless outnumbered by opponents.

Spider, Giant

Even hardened adventurers can harbour arachnophobia – the fear of spiders – which makes the giant variety even more terrifying. Giant spiders are excellent predators, using all manner of ingenious methods of luring and trapping prey. Whether they use concealed burrows (trap-door spiders), sticky webs, or are fast running hunter-killers; spiders are cunning, patient and deadly. When using a giant spider, decide how it hunts and use the appropriate combat techniques described here to run the encounter.

All giant spiders have the ability to adhere to vertical surfaces. This means they can squat on a cave ceiling and cling to or scurry up a wall at great speed. They have excellent vibratory, as well as visual perception, through the hairs on their legs, making them difficult to sneak up upon unless care is taken to move extremely slowly, and not disturb the silken trip lines which surround their lairs.

Spiders pinion prey with one or more of their legs before biting with their mandibles. Provided the bite penetrates any armour, it injects venom into the victim, which has a Potency equal to the spider's Endurance. Games Masters are free to develop their own poisons for particular species, but as a default use the following toxin.

Generic spider poison acts 1d6 rounds after injection (during which time the spider either retreats or maintains its grip), and paralyses the victim if not resisted. Once immobile the spider will wrap the victim in silk. Paralysis lasts for a number of hours equal to one quarter of the spider's CON. However, the venom has a more deadly secondary effect. Each hour after the initial poisoning, the victim loses 1 Hit Point from every location as his insides begin to liquefy. This continues until the victim is dead.

Spider silk is incredibly strong and sticky: treat a silk binding or a strand of web as having 6 Armour Points, and Hit Points equal to half the spider's SIZ. Touching an adhesive web glues the limb to the strand, unless the victim can win an opposed roll of their Brawn against the silk's Stickiness (equal to the spider's Endurance). If this fails they remain fastened, unable to break free by strength alone.

Attempting to cut free exposes the tool or weapon used to the same process. Despite popular belief, spider webs are not flammable, but a character might slowly burn their way through a web by using a flame to shrivel the strands (fire damage ignores the silk's Armour Points).

Some spiders are capable of leaping disturbingly long distances using their powerful musculature. If designing spiders that are hunter-killers, grant them the Leaping ability to reflect this method of chasing down prey.

Spider, Giant		Attributes
STR: 3d6+9 (20)	Action Points	3
CON: 3d6+6 (17)	Damage Modifier	+1d10
SIZ: 3d6+18 (29)	Magic Points	4
DEX: 3d6+9 (20)	Movement	10m
INS: 2d6+2 (9)	Initiative Bonus	15
POW: 1d6 (4)	Armour	Exoskeleton
	Abilities	Adhering, Earth Sense, Grappler, Venomous
	Magic	None

1d20	Location	AP/HP
01-02	Right Rear Leg	4/9
03-04	Left Rear Leg	4/9
05-06	Mid Right Leg	4/9
07-08	Mid Left Leg	4/9
09-10	Fore Right Leg	4/9
11-12	Fore Left Leg	4/9
13-14	Abdomen	4/12
15-16	Front Right Leg	4/9
17-18	Front Left Leg	4/9
19-20	Cephalothorax	4/11

Skills
Athletics 80%, Brawn 69%, Endurance 64%, Evade 80%, Perception 53%, Stealth 69%, Willpower 48%

Combat Style & Weapons
Eight Legged Horror (Legs, Mandibles) 80%

Weapon	Size/Force	Reach	Damage	AP/HP
Mandibles	L	T	1d6+1d10	As for Head
Legs	L	VL	Grapple	As for Leg

Tiger

With the exception of smilodon, tigers are the largest of the big cats. Highly territorial and generally solitary (save for females with cubs) they frequent many different climates including arctic environments. Their natural camouflage, usually with the characteristic black stripes, means they can move with high stealth, increasing their ambush capabilities. The pattern of stripes is unique to each tiger, and helps the animals to conceal themselves amongst the shadows, foliage and long grass as they stalk their prey.

The chief means of attack is the powerful bite, followed by claw rakes. A hungry tiger is tenacious and will stalk prey for a great distance if driven by an empty stomach. They are undeterred by prey larger themselves although these cats are still cautious given that - generally - they do not hunt in large numbers, and have little in the way of support.

Tiger		Attributes
STR: 2d6+15 (22)	Action Points	3
CON: 2d6+6 (13)	Damage Modifier	+1d10
SIZ: 2d6+18 (25)	Magic Points	7
DEX: 2d6+12 (19)	Movement	8m
INS: 2d6+6 (13)	Initiative Bonus	16
POW: 2d6 (7)	Armour	Fur and Hide
	Abilities	Camouflage, Intimidate, Night Sight
	Magic	None

1d20	Location	AP/HP
1–2	Right Hind Leg	2/8
3–4	Left Hind Leg	2/8
5–7	Hindquarters	2/9
8–10	Forequarters	2/10
11–13	Right Front Leg	2/8
14–16	Left Front Leg	2/8
17–20	Head	2/8

Skills
Athletics 71%, Brawn 68%, Endurance 66%, Evade 68%, Perception 60%, Track 56%, Stealth 72%, Willpower 54%

Combat Style & Weapons
Striped Death (Teeth, Claws) 81%

Weapon	Size/Force	Reach	Damage	AP/HP
Bite	L	S	1d8+1d10	As for Head
Claws	L	M	1d6+1d10	As for Leg

Troll

Having their roots in Scandinavian folklore, *troll* was originally a pejorative term for the *jotnar*, or giants. In time it has come to refer to a species of ugly, brutish, peevish humanoids who live in isolation from humans, often dwell in caves and cavern systems, and can be turned to stone if struck by the sun's rays. Trolls can be up to twice the size of a human, and are usually distinguished by their ugly, warty faces, oversized ears, straggling unkempt hair, a mouth full of tombstone-like teeth, and a tendency to eat human flesh when they can get it. Whilst this is true of most trolls, it is not true for all. Some trolls are far fairer in their appearance – although always large in size and stature– and their dispositions are as varied as for humans.

Many folk legends surround trolls, such as their ability to regenerate the damage of any wound. Such rumours are false but have their basis in the fact that the hide of a troll is naturally resistant to non-magical damage – an easy to make mistake when most battles against trolls are performed in the dark. Despite this, they can still drown, burn or suffer injuries from wrestling. Likewise the idea that trolls can be driven off by loud noises is also false; rather they are driven to rage by excessive noise which hurts their sensitive ears.

A peculiarity amongst trolls is possession and guardianship. Some trolls become absorbed with a particular fixture (such as a bridge), landmark (such as a tree or interestingly shaped outcrop of rocks) or possessions (club, hammer, stolen wealth), and become obsessive about its safety. Trolls caught in the grip of such an obsession always act aggressively when they think the subject of it is under threat, no matter how slight. Unprovoked attacks are common where a troll believes someone is after whatever it covets.

Direct sunlight can pose problems for trolls. Some are able to function in daylight, as long as the sky is overcast, whilst others – those who with the strongest links with to darkness – are, indeed, turned to stone when struck by the sun's rays.

This different reaction to sunlight differentiates troll species. To determine how a troll is affected, roll on the Troll Darkness Bond table.

Troll		Attributes	
STR: 3d6+9 (20)	Action Points	2	
CON: 3d6+6 (17)	Damage Modifier	+1d8	
SIZ: 3d6+12 (23)	Magic Points	11	
DEX: 3d6 (11)	Movement	8m	
INT: 2d6+3 (10)	Initiative Bonus	11	
POW: 3d6 (11)	Armour	Tough, Warty Hide	
CHA: 2d6 (7)	Abilities	Dark Sight, Immunity (Mundane Weapons)	
	Magic	Some trolls know Folk Magic 48% (Darkness or Extinguish, plus 1d3 others)	

1d20	*Location*	*AP/HP*
1-3	Right Leg	3/8
4-6	Left Leg	3/8
7-9	Abdomen	3/9
10-12	Chest	3/10
13-15	Right Arm	3/7
16-18	Left Arm	3/7
19-20	Head	3/8

Skills
Athletics 51%, Brawn 73%, Deceit 47%, Endurance 64%, Evade 42%, Perception 51%, Stealth 61%, Unarmed 71%, Willpower 42%

Passions
Obsession with Place/Thing 95%, Loathe Billy Goats 90%

Combat Style & Weapons
Troll Fury (Club, Maul, Thrown Rock) 61%

Weapon	Size/Force	Reach	Damage	AP/HP
Troll Club	L	M	1d8+1d8	4/10
Troll Maul	E	VL	1d12+3+1d8	4/10
Thrown Rock	L	-	1d6+1d8	-
Fists	L	M	1d4+1d8	As for Arm

Troll Darkness Bond Table

1d100	*Bond Srength*
01-20	Very weak bond. Troll can function without hindrance in slightly overcast conditions. Lesser cloud cover inflicts one level of Fatigue.
21-40	Weak bond. Troll can function without hindrance in completely overcast conditions. Lesser cloud cover inflicts three levels of Fatigue.
41-60	Average bond. Troll incurs five levels of Fatigue in any form of daylight, no matter the cloud cover.
61-80	Strong bond. As above, but the troll also suffers 1 Hit Point of damage to every location per hour.
81-00	Very strong bond. Any form of daylight petrifies the troll in 1d6+4 Rounds.

UNICORN

A pure-white horse with a long, graceful, spiralling horn emerging from the forehead, unicorns represent grace, dignity and purity. Killing a unicorn is said to curse the killer, and only those with pure hearts, minds and bodies can hope to approach, or tame, a unicorn. Those motivated by evil and chaos view unicorns as an enemy, and may try to seek-out the beasts for murder or torture, contributing to the animal's wariness. However certain circumstances might bring a unicorn into the vicinity of others – usually when someone of pure motive and heart needs help – or certain spells.

The unicorn's horn is magical, possessing the power of healing. If touched against an injured location, the horn restores a number of Hit Points equal to half the unicorn's Magic Points and any disease or poison currently suffered is neutralized. Each use of this power diminishes the unicorn's Magic Points by 1 so successive bouts of healing grow progressively weaker. Severed limbs cannot be reattached but crushed or maimed ones are restored. Such healing is performed at the will of the unicorn, which cannot be compelled or forced.

Any virginal character can attempt to gain a unicorn's help and trust through an Influence roll opposed by the creature's Willpower. If the character can also be considered to be pure of mind and spirit (and here the Games Master must decide if this is true) then the Influence roll becomes one grade easier. All other characters have no hope of gaining a unicorn's trust and any character openly following or tainted by chaos immediately causes the unicorn to flee.

A pure character who critically succeeds in gaining a unicorn's trust also gains its love. This forms a Passion between the two which can be used for securing aid or help in the future. Securing that unicorn's help becomes automatic, and gaining the help of other unicorns becomes one grade easier.

If killed a unicorn's horn retains some of its healing abilities. If ground into a powder (one horn creates 1d6+3 doses), and ingested it cures any disease or poison. However, killing a unicorn results in a curse for the killer. The exact nature is up the Games Master to decide but it can include Luck Points failing to regenerate, no natural healing, development of a disease or deformity, and so on.

The horn is considered a magical weapon with which the unicorn can parry attacks, but it only uses it this way if cornered or unable to canter. By preference a unicorn charges, if possible, trampling its victim on the way through.

Unicorn	Attributes	
STR: 2d6+21 (28)	Action Points	3
CON: 2d6+6 (13)	Damage Modifier	+2d6
SIZ: 2d6+30 (37)	Magic Points	19
DEX: 2d6+12 (19)	Movement	12m
INS: 2d6+7 (14)	Initiative Bonus	17
POW: 2d6+12 (19)	Armour	Hide
	Abilities	Formidable Natural Weapons, Life Sense, Trample
	Magic	None

1d20	Location	AP/HP
1–3	Right Hind Leg	1/10
4–6	Left Hind Leg	1/10
7–9	Hindquarters	1/11
10–12	Forequarters	1/12
13–14	Right Front Leg	1/9
15–16	Left Front Leg	1/9
17–20	Head	1/10

Skills
BAthletics 77%, Brawn 85%, Endurance 66%, Evade 78%, Perception 73%, Stealth 73%, Willpower 78%

Combat Style & Weapons
Indomitable Sentinel (Horn, Hoofs) 87%

Weapon	Size/Force	Reach	Damage	AP/HP
Gore	H	L	1d10+2d6	As for Head
Trample	E	T	4d6	As for Leg

VAMPIRE

Kings and queens of the undead, vampires sustain themselves through drinking of blood of sapient creatures. The following type of vampire is based upon European myth, but can be tweaked to fit the countless different versions of other cultures and fantasy worlds.

The manner of becoming a vampire depends on the campaign. In some settings vampirism may be the rare result of a curse, possession or deliberate self transformation. In others vampirism may be a contagious disease which affects anyone bitten by one of these monsters. Many superstitions surround the creation of vampires, and thus the real cause may remain obfuscated. About the only thing which is definitively known is that vampirism only affects sapient species.

When raised as a vampire, the creature receives the following benefits:

- The vampire gains the Undead ability, rendering it immune to the detrimental effects of most injuries and the affects of Fatigue, save for that lost by not feeding (see below).
- The vampire is infused by an unholy strength and speed. Multiply STR and DEX by two.
- The vampire's natural weapons are augmented by the growth of fangs and iron hard finger nails, if the species did not already possess something similar.
- The vampire becomes immune to most non-magical attacks, its flesh instantly re-knitting together or invulnerable unless specifically decapitated in a single blow – although it can still be destroyed by burning, drowning or exposure to sunlight.
- The vampire gains a gaze attack with the power to dominate sapient and animal victims. The vampire must spend a Magic Point on his turn and engage the target in an opposed Willpower roll. If the victim loses it falls under the control of the vampire's will (see below).
- The vampire might also develop an alternate form (roll on the Vampire Shape-Shift table). This form gains the same

immunities as its normal form, but provides it with alternate senses and means of locomotion. Shape-Shifting requires a successful Willpower roll to initiate, and takes 1d3 combat rounds to complete. It costs at least 1 Magic Point to shape-shift and 1 point per hour thereafter to maintain the form.

In return, vampires exhibit certain weaknesses, as follows:

- The need to consume blood weekly. For each week it does not feed, the vampire suffers a level of Fatigue which does not recover until it feeds again; each victim (who must be drained to death) reducing its Fatigue level by one. If the vampire drops to the level of Comatose they enter a state of suspended animation, but do not die.
- Susceptibility to sunlight, suffering 1d6 damage per round to each location it contacts.
- Catatonic sleepers, vampires find it difficult to awaken if disturbed during the hours of daylight. Consequently they try to find remote and easy to secure lairs.
- Vulnerability to impaling weapons of a particular type of wood (ash or hawthorne for example).

All other superstitions concerning vampires, such as its dislike of garlic or lack of reflection, are merely folklore, and need not have any basis in truth, although a fun concept would be a newly raised vampire who believes that they *are* true.

Vampires are fearsome opponents. In combat they are almost unstoppable without magical weapons or offensive spells, although for some reason their neck is vulnerable to decapitation if the blow does twice the Hit Points of the head in a single strike.

Impaling weapons made of certain types of wood can harm a vampire, bypassing their natural immunity to mundane weapons. These however do not actually kill the vampire, but instead prevent it from instantly regenerating the damage inflicted upon it. A headless spear, arrow or crossbow bolt which both Impales and inflicts a Major Wound, renders that particular location immobile. If this is the head or chest the vampire becomes quiescent. Removing the stake allows the creature to rise again.

Perhaps the most frightening power of vampires is their ability to dominate victims, turning folk into unwitting servants for the creature. Although this power requires direct eye contact and the investment of a Magic Point, which the vampire does not recover until he lets the domination drop, until that time the victim can be controlled anywhere within a range of the vampire's POW in kilometres. Whilst the victim may remain at the beck and call of its master, the vampire must actually concentrate to the exclusion of all else to actively control one of its servitors.

Vampire Shapeshift Table

1d100	Alternate Form
01-75	None. The vampire cannot shape-shift.
76-80	Wolf (use all physical characteristics for the wolf entry).
81-85	Bat (becomes a bat-like monstrosity but retains its original SIZ. It gains the Flying ability and Fly skill).
86-90	Swarm of Rats (becomes a pack of rats which can scatter in all directions to eventually coalesce at a later time).
91-95	Gaseous (becomes non-corporeal and can, in its mist-like form, pass through any gap permitting the flow of air).
96-100	Roll Twice – ignoring this result if rolled again.

Vampire		Attributes	
STR: 3d6x2 (22)	Action Points	3	
CON: 3d6 (11)	Damage Modifier	+1d4	
SIZ: 2d6+6 (13)	Magic Points	11	
DEX: 3d6x2 (22)	Movement	6m	
INT: 2d6+6 (13)	Initiative Bonus	18	
POW: 3d6 (11)	Armour	None	
CHA: 3d6 (11)	Abilities	Allergy (Sunlight), Darksight, Gaze Attack (Domination), Immunity (Mundane Weapons), Undead, Vampiric, Vulnerable (Special)	
	Magic	Some may retain the magical skills possessed in life.	

1d20	*Location*	*AP/HP*
1–3	Right Leg	0/5
4–6	Left Leg	0/5
7–9	Abdomen	0/6
10-12	Chest	0/7
13–15	Right Arm	0/4
16–18	Left Arm	0/4
19–20	Head	0/5

Skills

Athletics 74%, Brawn 65%, Deceit 54%, Endurance 62%, Evade 64%, Influence 62%, Perception 54%, Seduction 64%, Stealth 75%, Unarmed 84%, Willpower 62%

Passions

Covet Power 95%, Love to Seduce 90%, Abhor Life 80%

Combat Style & Weapons

Generally fights using Unarmed

Weapon	Size/Force	Reach	Damage	AP/HP
Bite	M	T	1d4+1d4	As for Head
Fists	M	S	1d3+1d4	As for Arm

Vampires do not normally feed during the midst of combat. However, if pressed, they can drain a victim of blood in a matter of moments, sucking one level of Fatigue per Round until interrupted or the victim is dead. Usually vampires prefer to take their time drinking rather than glutting themselves.

Japanese and Malaysian myths have similar vampiric forms (the rokuro-kubi and penannggi respectively). These vampiric creatures detach their heads from their bodies, somtimes dragging their entrails with them and take to the night skies to hunt fresh blood. At daybreak they return to their bodies and reform, with daily life continuing as normal.

Using these kinds of undead in MYTHRAS means adjusting the hit locations slightly: 01-15 strikes the entrails and 16-20 strikes the head. The creatures have the Flying ability and all other relevant abilities for traditional vampires. A rokuro-kubi or penannggi may not even be aware of what happens to them after sunset, living relatively normal lives during daylight hours.

Winged Ape

Winged apes resemble silverback gorillas save for the pair of huge, bat-like wings sprouting from the shoulders, giving them flight. Despite being flying creatures they are primarily ground-dwellers, using their flight simply to chase prey, move short distances quickly and intimidate others. They lack the strength to maintain sustained flight or even take off without a running start; often requiring a high place from which to launch themselves.

Winged apes frequent hilly, mountainous and jungle areas, often finding homes in ancient, overgrown ruins. They are omnivorous but follow a largely herbivorous diet, seeking meat only on rare occasions. That said, if an intruder is killed, winged apes will happily feed on the carcass.

The apes are highly territorial and extremely aggressive to those who their territory. They form groups of between 10 and 30 individuals with a strong and aggressive male as the pack leader, and supplemented by several strong beta males. The alpha male has the privilege of mating with all the females in the pack and other males must wait their turn or challenge the alpha male for breeding rights.

Winged Ape		Attributes
STR: 2d6+12 (19)	Action Points	3
CON: 2d6+9 (16)	Damage Modifier	+1d8
SIZ: 2d6+15 (22)	Magic Points	11
DEX: 2d6+6 (13)	Movement	4m (land), 8m (flying)
INS: 2d6+7 (14)	Initiative Bonus	14
POW: 3d6 (11)	Armour	Fur
	Abilities	Diving Strike, Flying, Formidable Natural Weapons
	Magic	None

1d20	Location	AP/HP
1–3	Right Leg	2/8
4–6	Left Leg	2/8
7–9	Abdomen	2/9
10	Chest	2/10
11–12	Right Wing	0/8
13–14	Left Wing	0/8
15–16	Right Arm	2/7
17-18	Left Arm	2/7
19-20	Head	2/8

Skills
Athletics 62%, Brawn 71%, Endurance 62%, Evade 46%, Fly 62%, Perception 55%, Willpower 52%

Combat Style & Weapons
Rip Apart (Fists, Teeth, Wing Strike) 72%

Weapon	Size/Force	Reach	Damage	AP/HP
Bite	M	T	1d3+1d8	As for Head
Fists	M	M	1d4+1d8	As for Arm
Wing	M	L	1d3+1d8	As for Wing

Wolf

Oldest of the canine species and feared pack-hunters, wolves are native to temperate and sub-arctic climates, preferring forests, hills and moorland. A pack consists of between 12 and 30 wolves led by an alpha male – usually the strongest of the pack but often the oldest. The pack hierarchy is incredibly strong; most individual wolves are subservient to the alpha male and challengers to the position are set-upon by the others. Any male that beats the leader generally assumes the alpha position, and may drive out the loser (if death does not result) or the loser may assume a life of subservience to the new leader, thereby retaining a place in the community.

Wolves are most active at night but can be roused to activity during the day. Hunting expeditions are highly co-ordinated affairs. A pack chooses and stalks its prey carefully and attacks, when they happen, consist of successive waves of between three and six animals aiming to incapacitate the prey before tearing out the throat or cutting off air at the windpipe. The alpha male feeds first, followed by the remainder of the pack in an established order. The youngest members of a pack may have to make do with scraps.

In combat wolves rely on their powerful bite rather than their claws. Once a bite takes hold the wolf locks its jaws, and continues to exert pressure through the canines and by vigorously shaking the head, deepening and lengthening the bites. Wolves therefore tend to choose the Grip and Choose Location Special Effects (always aiming for an exposed area). A Gripped victim sustains biting damage throughout the duration of the grip as the wolf worries at the wound.

If the alpha male is forced to flee then the pack follows suit, although braver individuals may attempt to gain status by remaining to fight.

Canines have been domesticated for as long as man has lived in settlements. Being relatively easy to train, tame and breed, it has led to a vast range of types, sizes and shapes. As well as being treated as pets or house-dogs, most dogs have been put to work in some capacity: hunting, guarding, herding and so on. If you need statistics for any dog, use those for the wolf (which is the progenitor of all canine breeds), and adjust the physical statistics (STR, SIZ and DEX) accordingly. All dogs are pack animals that choose a leader (even if this is considered to be a human owner) and, if kept in a pack, will exhibit wolf-like pack tendencies at some stage.

Prehistoric dire wolves are much larger specimens; double STR and SIZ. These can be used for stronger versions of lycanthropy, see below.

Lycanthropy

Lycanthropy is the condition that transforms a human into a wolf form through some appropriate environmental trigger (full moon, for example). Any character struck by lycanthropy transforms into a wolf of a SIZ similar to the human form, but replacing INT with INS. STR, CON, DEX and POW is the higher of the human or wolf form, as are the listed skills. Some lycanthropes also gain immunity to mundane damage, but retain a vulnerability, silver being their traditional weakness.

The wolf form lasts for a number of hours equal to the lycanthrope's CON. The transformation process takes 1d3 minutes and is excruciatingly painful.

Wolf	Attributes	
STR: 1d3+6 (8)	Action Points	2
CON: 3d6 (11)	Damage Modifier	-1d2
SIZ: 1d3+6 (8)	Magic Points	7
DEX: 3d6 (11)	Movement	8m
INS: 2d6+6 (13)	Initiative Bonus	12
POW: 2d6 (7)	Armour	Fur
	Abilities	Night Sight
	Magic	None

1d20	Location	AP/HP
1–2	Right Hind Leg	1/4
3–4	Left Hind Leg	1/4
5–7	Hindquarters	1/5
8–10	Forequarters	1/6
11–13	Right Front Leg	1/4
14–16	Left Front Leg	1/4
17–20	Head	1/4

Skills
Athletics 59%, Brawn 36%, Endurance 62%, Evade 52%, Perception 60%, Track 64%, Willpower 44%

Combat Style & Weapons
Pack Savage (Bite) 59%

Weapon	Size/Force	Reach	Damage	AP/HP
Bite	S	T	1d4-1d2	As for Head

Wyrm/Wyvern

Wyrms and wyverns are draconic entities that have serpentine bodies, a fierce, dragon-like head and wings. The only difference between the two is that wyrms lack any legs, whereas wyverns possess a set of hind legs. The wings in both species are too small to sustain flight over long distances which mean they normally traverse terrain by either wriggling or hop about with long, leaping bounds.

Neither creature has the intelligence of a dragon, being mere predatory beasts. They lack a breath weapon but make up for this with savage ferocity and imposing size. They are found in a diverse range of terrain, favouring hilly and moorland regions although both can be found in forests, jungles or swamps making their lairs in deep burrows. Wyrms are capable of hugging the ground and slithering, snake-like, to stalk prey. Wyverns are less discreet, relying on frontal assaults.

In the following table, Hit Location ranges have been included for both creatures.

An aquatic form of the wyvern exists, replacing the hindquarters and tail with the fins and tail of an enormous fish. The sea-wyvern gains the Aquatic ability and Swim at 74%.

Wyrm/Wyvern	Attributes	
STR: 2d6+18 (25)	Action Points	3
CON: 2d6+12 (19)	Damage Modifier	+2d6
SIZ: 4d6+30 (44)	Magic Points	11
DEX: 2d6+12 (19)	Movement	8m (land), 16m (flying)
INS: 2d6+5 (12)	Initiative Bonus	16
POW: 3d6 (11)	Armour	Scales
	Abilities	Cold Blooded, Dark Sight, Flying, Frenzy
	Magic	None

Wyrm	Wyvern	Location	AP/HP
1-4	1-3	Tail	6/12
-	4-5	Right Hind Leg	6/13
-	6-7	Left Hind Leg	6/13
5-8	8-10	Hindquarters	6/14
9-12	11-14	Forequarters	6/15
13-15	15-16	Right Wing	6/13
16-18	17-18	Left Wing	6/13
19-20	19-20	Head	6/14

Skills
Athletics 64%, Brawn 89%, Endurance 78%, Evade 68%, Fly 74%, Perception 63%, Willpower 62%

Combat Style & Weapons
Draconic Terror (Bite, Tail Sweep) 84%

Weapon	Size/Force	Reach	Damage	AP/HP
Bite	E	L	1d12+2d6	As for Head
Tail	E	VL	1d10+2d6	As for Tail

ZOMBIE

Any recently deceased corpse animated through magic or some exotic plague is a zombie. Mindless, decaying and driven by a desire to consume flesh and blood, zombies have no intellect to speak of. Magically created zombies are often under the control of a caster in a similar way to Skeletons (see pages 264-265).

The freshness of the original corpse at the time of its animation defines much of a zombie's toughness. Their characteristics start as equivalent to the creature in life, but (assuming no burial) are reduced by one point for each day which passes after death before it is raised. Once animated a zombie does not normally rot any further, but retains its foul stench.

Of course the rate of the initial degeneration depends on the environment. In cold or subterranean climates the rate may slow down to one point per week; whilst places like bogs or glaciers may preserve corpses indefinitely. However quickly it deteriorates, once a corpse has lost half of its STR or CON what remnants of flesh remain will simply slough off the underlying bones. From this point the body can only be raised as a skeleton.

Zombies are relentless in whatever task assigned to them and pursue it tirelessly. As per the Undead trait they are not subject to fatigue. Neither are they unduly affected by damage, and the only thing that will stop a zombie from moving is to destroy either the head or chest (whichever of the two the animating magic or disease is primarily located) by reducing it to a Major Wound. Thus fresh corpses can be quite difficult to put down, whereas badly rotted ones are rather vulnerable.

To create a zombie take a creature, decide the nature of its unlife, and zombify it.

- Magically raised zombies take on the mental characteristics and physical skills of the caster or spirit controlling the body. Note that some methods of animating zombies can grant the corpse bonuses to their deteriorated characteristics. In addition they can wear armour and wield any weapons they would naturally have in their previous life.
- A zombie created by some virulent plague is an autonomous creature, retaining the physical skills and degenerated mental characteristics of the original being, but any INT value is converted to INS. In addition it usually carries the disease which caused its own transformation. To make this type scarier, treat Zombie Plague as a mundanely incurable disease with a Potency of 80%. Anyone bitten by the zombie must make an opposed roll of their Endurance versus the potency. Failure to beat the plague means that they begin to rot before they die; losing characteristic points at a rate of one per hour. After 1d6 hours they expire from the disease and minutes later arise as a zombie.

The following statistics are for an average human zombie created by zombie plague, arising from death two hours after infection.

Average zombies are often little threat unless they mob opponents using superior numbers, are equipped with armour and weapons, or carry zombie plague.

Zombies created through magic need no sustenance. Those created by plague or contagion may need to consume blood, flesh, hearts or brains to remain functional. These zombies are driven by hunger and may possess the Life Sense ability to help them hunt.

Zombie	Attributes	
STR: 3d6-2 (9)	Action Points	2
CON: 3d6-2 (9)	Damage Modifier	-1d2
SIZ: 2d6+6-2 (11)	Magic Points	0
DEX: 3d6-2 (9)	Movement	6m
INS: 2d6+6-2 (11)	Initiative Bonus	10
POW: 3d6-2 (9)	Armour	None
CHA: 3d6-2 (9)	Abilities	Undead
	Magic	Some may retain the magical skills possessed in life.

1d20	Location	AP/HP
1–3	Right Leg	0/4
4–6	Left Leg	0/4
7–9	Abdomen	0/5
10-12	Chest	0/6
13–15	Right Arm	0/3
16–18	Left Arm	0/3
19–20	Head	0/4

Skills

Athletics 38%, Brawn 40%, Endurance 58%, Evade 38%, Perception 40%, Unarmed 58%, Willpower 48%

Passions

Brains... 99%

Combat Style & Weapons

Generally fights using Unarmed

Weapon	Size/Force	Reach	Damage	AP/HP
Bite	S	T	1+Disease	As for Head
Fists	S	S	1d3-1d2	As for Arm

Chaos Features

Certain creatures are tainted by Chaos, which warps and alters natural forms in subtle and not-so-subtle ways. Creatures so tainted may have one or more Chaos Features, chosen to fit the recipient or rolled randomly:

Chaos Features

1d100	Feature	Effect
01-02	Acidic	Possesses a flesh dissolving acidic ichor which sprays whenever the skin is damaged, causing damage to the attacker; roll 1d4 to determine the strength of the acid, 1=1d2, 2=1d4, 3=1d6 and 4=1d8 damage per wound.
03-04	Alluring	Produces pheromones which attract and seduce victims. The creature gains the Seduction skill at POW x5%. It can be resisted using Willpower as per any Seduction.
05-06	Asymmetric	One half of the creature is larger, longer or taller than the other, double the Hit Points for locations in the larger side and halve the Hit Points of locations for the smaller.
07-08	Boneless	The creature possesses resilient, malleable cartilage rather than bone. It can squeeze through any size of gap and takes no damage from any fall.
09-10	Brainless	Sensory organs are distributed over the entire body and sentience is located elsewhere – but not in the head. The brain is found in a random location.
11-12	Burning	The creature seethes with chaotic heat, injuring anyone within Short range; roll a d4, 1=1d2, 2=1d4, 3=1d6 and 4=1d8 damage per round.
13-14	Chameleon	Naturally blends with its surroundings and has an effective Stealth skill of 100%+POW.
15-16	Climbing	Gains the Adhering Ability.
17-18	Contagious	Inflicts a virulent disease with a delay of 1d8 hours and potency of CONx5%, which reduces a random characteristic by1d8 points: roll a d6, 1=STR, 2=CON, 3=DEX, 4=INT, 5=POW or 6=CHA.
19-20	Corroding	Weapons sustain 1d8 damage each time they strike the creature. Weapon Armour Points offer no protection.
21-22	Dampener	All magical effects within the creature's POW in metres are suppressed by 1d8 Magnitude. Spells reduced to zero Magnitude are dispelled unless part of a permanent enchantment.
23-24	Deathly	Drains the vitality of nearby plants and creatures. Those in Short range of the creature must succeed in an unopposed Endurance roll each round to avoid suffering 1 point of damage to every Hit Location, ignoring armour.
25-26	Disturbing	Creature is covered with unsettling forms, such as miniature arms, multiple eyes or mouths, writhing pseudopods, etc. Viewers must succeed in an unopposed Willpower test or be helpless with horror until they can make the roll successfully.
27-28	Domineering	Manipulates those around it with mental commands, which cannot be resisted unless the target is successful in an unopposed Willpower test.
29-30	Draining	Temporarily weakens the magical power of an opponent, draining 1d8 MP with each successful strike.
31-32	Droning	Produces a buzzing noise that sedates listeners. All within the creature's POW x5 in metres must succeed in an unopposed Willpower roll to avoid falling asleep for 1d8 minutes.
33-34	Entangle	Restricts the movements of those within melee range, who must succeed in an unopposed Brawn roll to avoid being rendered physically helpless each round.
35-36	Frightening	Creature appears terrifyingly dangerous; viewers must succeed in an unopposed Willpower roll or flee the creature immediately.
37-38	Icy	Radiates freezing waves of cold, injuring anyone within melee range; roll 1d4, 1=1d2, 2=1d4, 3=1d6 and 4=1d8 damage per round.
39-40	Intangible	Moves through solid objects as though non-corporeal. Whilst intangible it cannot be harmed, but neither can it attack.
41-42	Leaper	Has powerfully sprung limbs, multiplying its jump range by a factor of 1d4+1.
43-44	Levitating	Hovers above the ground giving it the ability to move over any surface without sinking or leaving tracks.
45-46	Mimic	Assumes the shape of a creature it successfully touches, maintaining its own Characteristics, but mimicking the locations and appearance of the being contacted.
47-48	Mournful	Appearance is sad or pathetic. Observers must succeed in an unopposed Willpower roll to be able to begin attacking it.
49-50	Mutated	Roll a random location and remove it from the creature. It no longer has this location, but it still functions perfectly well without it, even defying logic.
51-52	Nerveless	Does not feel any pain and ignores the effects of Serious Wounds.
53-54	Neutralising	Any spells cast at the creature are immediately neutralized.
55-56	Obfuscating	Produces a cloud of mist, spores or darkness that blinds observers. Those affected must succeed in an unopposed Perception roll every turn to see the creature.
57-58	Oversized	One location is swollen doubling its Hit Points.
59-60	Paralysing	Renders victims incapable of movement; those touched must succeed in an unopposed Endurance roll to avoid 1d8 minutes of paralysis.
61-62	Perceptive	Possesses an odd primary sense; roll a d6, 1=Echolocation (sonar), 2=Thermoception (heat), 3=Cerebralception (sapient consciousness), 4=Nociception (pain), 5=Ethoception (souls), 6=Thaumaception (magic). The creature does not rely on sight to perceive others and may lack eyes.

CHAOS FEATURES CONTINUED

1d100	Feature	Effect
63-64	Poisonous	One unarmed attack inflicts a venomous poison with a delay of 1d8 rounds and a potency of CONx5%, which inflicts a Poison Condition selected from page 75.
65-66	Polymorph	Changes shape every round, maintaining its Characteristics, but assuming the locations of the new form and carrying over any damage already suffered (Games Masters should prepare various forms in advance).
67-68	Projector	Any damage inflicted on the creature is felt by anyone within POW metres, who suffer the psychological, but not physical effects as if they had been wounded too.
69-70	Quick	Movement rate is multiplied by a factor of 1d4+1.
71-72	Reflecting	All magic cast on the creature is reflected back against the caster.
73-74	Regenerating	Recovers 1 Hit Point per round to every location, unless the creature has suffered a Major Wound in the injured location.
75-76	Roaring	Produces a thunderous roar, deafening listeners, who must succeed in an unopposed Endurance roll to avoid becoming temporally stunned for 1d3 Turns.
77-78	Scintillating	Possesses a shifting chromatic aura that confuses onlookers. All attacks against the creature are one grade harder.
79-80	Shadowy	The creature absorbs the ambient light in its immediate surroundings, creating a pool of total darkness with a radius equal to POW in metres.
81-82	Shocking	Charges itself with electricity, inflicting a shock on those that hit it (if using metal or uninsulated weapons, or are struck by it; roll 1d4, 1=1d2, 2=1d4, 3=1d6 and 4=1d8 damage per blow).
83-84	Silent	Completely inaudible – even its attacks.
85-86	Slimy	Cannot be grappled or gripped in close combat. The creature leaves a sticky mucus trail wherever it travels.
87-88	Stench	Releases nauseating odours that sicken inhalers, who must succeed in an unopposed Endurance roll to avoid uncontrollable vomiting for 1d3 Combat Rounds.
89-90	Sticky	Secretes a strong glue or mucus which causes items to stick to its skin, requiring a successful unopposed Brawn roll and a Combat Action to free.
91-92	Teleporter	Can freely teleport to a new location once per round. The location must be within a number of metres equal to POW x2.
93-94	Transmuter	Changes the substance of organic material it touches into another substance; living victims must succeed in an unopposed Endurance roll to avoid the struck location being changed into crystal, dust, stone, wine, bronze and so on.
95-96	Vampiric	Hit Point damage inflicted on an opponent is transferred to itself, healing any wounds currently suffered.
97-98	Warded	Invulnerable to one specific type of material; steel, wood, stone, flesh, etc.
99-100	Weakening	Temporarily reduces the STR of an opponent by 1d8 each successful (undefended) hit.

NON-HUMAN HIT LOCATIONS

The tables in this section are for Games Masters who enjoy creating their own creatures - or when a character might, through magic, be transmogrified into something else.

Arachnid	
1d20	*Location*
1-2	Right Rear Leg
3-4	Left Rear Leg
5-6	Mid Right Leg
7-8	Mid Left Leg
9-10	Fore Right Leg
11-12	Fore Left Leg
13-14	Abdomen
15-16	Front Right Leg
17-18	Front Left Leg
19-20	Cephalothorax

Centaurid	
1d20	*Location*
1-3	Right Leg
4-6	Left Leg
7-8	Hindquarters
9-10	Forequarters
11-12	Right Front Leg
13-14	Left Front Leg
15-16	Chest
17	Right Arm
18	Left Arm
19-20	Head

Draconic	
1d20	*Location*
1-2	Tail
3-4	Right Hind Leg
5-6	Left Hind Leg
7-8	Hindquarters
9-10	Right Wing
11-12	Left Wing
13-14	Forequarters
15-16	Right Front Leg
17-18	Left Front Leg
19-20	Head

Insect	
1d20	*Location*
1	Right Rear Leg
2	Left Rear Leg
3	Right Middle Leg
4	Left Middle Leg
5-9	Abdomen
10-13	Thorax
14	Right Front Leg
15	Left Front Leg
16-20	Head

Dorsal Finned Aquatic	
1d20	*Location*
1-3	Tail
4-6	Dorsal Fin
7-10	Hindquarters
11-14	Forequarters
15-16	Right Fin
17-18	Left Fin
19-20	Head

Tailed Biped	
1d20	*Location*
1-3	Tail
4-5	Right Leg
6-7	Left Leg
8-10	Abdomen
11-14	Chest
15-16	Right Arm
17-18	Left Arm
19-20	Head

Winged Quadruped	
1d20	*Location*
1-2	Right Hind Leg
3-4	Left Hind Leg
5-7	Hindquarters
8-10	Forequarters
11-12	Right Wing
13-14	Left Wing
15-16	Right Front Leg
17-18	Left Front Leg
19-20	Head

Pachyderm	
1d20	*Location*
1-2	Right Hind Leg
3-4	Left Hind Leg
5-8	Hindquarters
9-12	Forequarters
13-14	Right Front Leg
15-16	Left Front Leg
17	Trunk
18-20	Head

Tailed Quadruped,	
1d20	*Location*
1-3	Tail
4-5	Right Hind Leg
6-7	Left Hind Leg
8-10	Hindquarters
11-14	Forequarters
15-16	Right Front Leg
17-18	Left Front Leg
19-20	Head

Serpentine	
1d20	*Location*
1-3	Tail Tip
4-5	Mid End-length
6-7	Fore End-length
8-9	Rear Mid-length
10-12	Mid Mid-length
13-14	Fore Mid-length
15-16	Rear Fore-length
17-18	Mid Fore-length
19-20	Head

Winged Biped	
1d20	*Location*
1-3	Right Leg
4-6	Left Leg
7-9	Abdomen
10	Chest
11-12	Right Wing
13-14	Left Wing
15-16	Right Arm
17-18	Left Arm
19-20	Head

Tailed Arachnid	
1d20	*Location*
1-2	Tail
3	Right Rear Leg
4	Left Rear Leg
5	Mid Right Leg
6	Mid Left Leg
7	Fore Right Leg
8	Fore Left Leg
9-12	Thorax
13-15	Right Pincer
16-18	Left Pincer
19-20	Cephalothorax

Winged Insect	
1d20	*Location*
1	Right Rear Leg
2	Left Rear Leg
3-4	Metathorax
5	Mid Right Leg
6	Mid Left Leg
7-10	Prothorax
11-12	Right Wing
13-14	Left Wing
15-16	Right Forelimb
17-18	Left Forelimb
19-20	Head

Games Mastery

This chapter provides a range of notes for Games Masters – both those new to Mythras and old hands. It offers tips and techniques for running enjoyable games along with certain optional rules that Games Masters may wish to include in their campaigns. It is by no means exhaustive: Games Masters are continually developing new ideas and techniques and many of these will be unique to your own style of play.

This is Your Game

The Mythras rules are comprehensive and reasonably detailed. They work together through certain underlying concepts that are replicated throughout the different areas of game mechanics: character creation, combat, magic and so on. However there will always be occasions where…

- A particular rule does not fit a certain, unique situation or even an overall playing style
- Games Masters and players devise something that works better for them
- Rules found in a similar game system using similar mechanics are desired over those found in Mythras

Games Masters are encouraged to change, ignore and adopt rules to fit the style and needs of the campaign and players. Mythras has always been extremely flexible in this regard, and this edition of the game is no different. If something does not work how you think it should, change it. If you don't like a particular rule, and feel it's superfluous, drop it. If you find a rule in a sister d100 game that you really like, add it to your Mythras game. The chances are that you will not break anything found in Mythras – or can easily adapt imported or house-created rules to work with the core mechanics.

You should make Mythras your game. The rules are a pre-prepared guideline but nothing should be considered as written in stone. There is no right or wrong way to play any roleplaying game, and you should adapt what you find in these pages to make your own game sing the song you want sung.

Adapt, change, improvise, import. These are all useful and valid techniques for making your Mythras.

The Petersen Rules of Good Gaming

Sandy Petersen, celebrated game designer, has created five easy rules that are worthwhile for all Games Masters to bear in mind when running a gaming session.

1. *Make Bonuses Worthwhile.* If something is worth doing, it's worth doing on a grand scale. Bonuses (and penalties) to skills, whether offered through magic or in some other form, should mean something. This is why modifiers to skills (see the Skills chapter) are structured in the way they are. Modifiers range from influencing a skill's chance by increasing it by half again (Easy skills) or reducing by a third, through to being guaranteed success or making something simply impossible to accomplish. Higher magic, too, offers some quite substantial ways to influence skills and characteristics, whereas Folk Magic, simplest of all the magical systems, tends not to offer skill boosts or modifiers.
2. *The Right to Have Fun.* Mythras adventures should be fun from the minute the players gather at the table. Try not to spend too long in dull preamble or book-keeping and start the session with a bang. Take cues from movies and television shows: good ones involve the characters (and the viewer) immediately. Everyone should be involved and feel that they are involved. If things appear to be flagging, spice them up quickly using humour, excitement, tension or some other device that hooks everyone back into the game. It is worthwhile having a few such hooks pre-prepared for just such an occasion. You might not need to use them, but if you do, you'll be glad you made the effort.
3. *Show, Don't Tell.* Actions speak louder than words. If a non-player character is clearly a villain, have him act villainously. If a character is good, clean and wholesome, have them act

that way. If a situation is foreboding and sinister, pepper your description with signs (insects suddenly stop buzzing. A wolf howls. Thunder rumbles. The air grows suddenly cold. The characters break out in goose-bumps). You needn't worry about the players agreeing with your value perceptions, even you feel they are based in reality: the main idea is to convey an impression, an atmosphere, and a demonstration of what the characters experience. It all supports the Right to Have Fun.

4. *Three Strikes and You're Out.* If a player is making a decision that could make life very difficult for himself and others, try to give him at least three chances to make an informed decision and possibly escape his fate. Luck Points will help here, but there other techniques too. For example, a dragon might be threatening a small settlement; the first signal is the villagers warning of the dragon's lair. If this doesn't deter the characters, perhaps the dragon can be seen in the distance circling the mountain tops, casually incinerating the local undergrowth. If that still doesn't deter the characters, then a direct encounter with the dragon – which is the third and final chance – might be looming. However things turn out, the character has had ample opportunity to do something about the situation. If things end badly, at least the opportunities to avert disaster were presented.
5. *It's Always the Player's Fault.* By this we mean that, if things do go badly for a player, it should be a result of decisions made and actions taken, rather than being a fault in the game rules or their presentation by the Games Master. Players ought not to feel cheated by the game system or bad dice rolls. Players must feel that, if they had acted differently, they would have fared better and perhaps emerged victorious. Successful MYTHRAS sessions should not be Players versus the Game System, or Players versus the Games Master. Responsibility for actions must be taken by the players, and so part of the Games Master's job is to foster such opportunities using the game system to assist and inform, rather than oppose and penalise.

PREPARATION AND GAME AIDS

There are certain materials and game aids that you may find help manage each MYTHRAS session. They are not essential but experience has found that they can make life easier.

Scrap Paper – for making notes and especially during character creation. For the latter, have players create their characters in rough first, and when happy, transfer the information to a character sheet.

Pre-printed Character Sheets – you will find a sample MYTHRAS character sheet on pages 302 to 303. You are free to copy this for personal use (or download a copy from www.thedesignmechanism.com). It holds all the essential information needed by each player, and is structured to show the most useful play elements on the front page, with additional detail on the rear. In time players will find they outgrow their character sheets – or they become untidy, torn, spoiled, and so on. From time to time refresh the character sheets but keep the old ones for reference in case they are needed. It is also a good idea for the Games Master to take a personal copy of each player's sheet and hold it for both reference, and back-up. Every good Games Master knows the capabilities of his characters, and can use these to develop stories and scenarios that fit with what each character can do, and their backstory.

A supply of counters - coins, sweets, beads, buttons, bottle-tops, or poker chips – are a useful way of keeping track of variable attributes such as Action Points, Magic Points and Luck Points. Give each player a supply of different colours or types of counter according to their character's statistics and, when a point is spent on something (performing a Combat Action, casting a spell) have the player put the appropriate counter into a discard pile. In this way players can easily see what resources they have available, and do not need to constantly amend their character sheet. The Games Master will need a supply too, for tracking the actions of foes and monsters.

Combat Reference Sheets and Tracker – we strongly recommend printing a copy of the Special Effects for each player at the table. To begin with they will need to reference the different Special Effects so they can understand what each does and how it works. This will encourage variety of Special Effect use, and saves wear and tear on rulebooks. In time, as the players become more familiar with how Special Effects work, the sheets will be used less often, but making them available from the start, as part of a Character Pack, is a real help for getting to grips with the game. You will also find a Combat Tracker sheet, used for recording Initiative order, wounds, and so forth in the Reference section of MYTHRAS (or download from our website). This is designed to help with book-keeping during combat and is recommended for all Games Masters.

Miniatures, and Figures – Whilst MYTHRAS is not necessarily designed specifically for miniatures play, there is no doubt that having some form of character representation for combats and battles can help understand positioning, movement and engagement. There are hundreds of thousands of figures available, from those designed for roleplaying games (typically 25-28mm) to those designed for wargames (15-25mm). You can even find very cheap cardboard figures that you can print, cut out, and then use ad infinitum. Choose figures that approximate the look and feel of the setting, but otherwise you are spoilt for choice.

Battlemats and Movement Grids – used with figures, battlemats are usually pre-printed with either squares or hexagons, and used to regulate positioning and movement. The scale represented depends on the size of the figures used. Typically, with 25-28mm figures a square or hex will represent about one metre, but you can, of course, adjust the scale to fit the figures. Some battlemats are covered in wipe-clean finishes that let you use dry erase markers to sketch out rooms, walls, obstacles, and so on: a useful ad hoc mapping tool.

Wipeboard and Dry Erase Markers – a small wipeboard, about the dimensions of this book, can be easily bought from stationers along with dry erase markers. These tools are incredibly useful for recording combat details, Initiative order, notes on wounds, or to do a quick, temporary sketch-map rather than rely on reams of scrap paper. We recommend investing in a wipeboard and pens: its usefulness at the gaming table is unparalleled. Plus, some wipeboards are magnetic too, and you can easily buy magnetic counters and sheets that can then be customized to make Action Point trackers, initiative trackers and so on, that attach easily to the wipeboard, further extending its usefulness.

Games Master Screen – not an essential, but definitely useful. Screens should, on the Games Master's side, have all the most relevant tables and rules summaries used during play. The players' side can carry artwork or reference materials such as Special Effects so that all the players can easily see them. A simple screen can be made with a few sheets – 3 to 4 – of Letter or A4 card taped together. More expensive vinyl screens, with clear pockets for inserts, can be bought commercially, and these allow for infinite customisation of both Games Master and player information, simply by changing the insert. The reference sheets found in the Reference section of MYTHRAS are designed to work with such screens, or can be copied and glued onto a home-made cardboard screen.

Books, References and Electronic Aids – only the Games Master really needs the rulebook but a couple of additional copies are always useful in case players want to look something up. As an alternative, a PDF version of MYTHRAS can be easily chopped into appropriate pages or chunks (just print out what you need) that can then be used in place of the rulebooks, and obviously save on wear and tear. If you have PDF editing software you can compile your own Players' Book if needs be. And, of course, PDF displays very well on tablet devices that are becoming increasingly popular at the games table.

CREATING CHARACTERS

Character creation is best as a collaborative exercise – between the player and Games Master, but also amongst the players, which not only saves time but also offers other benefits.

Group character creation greatly helps in cementing the group together, giving each character a reason for adventuring with the others. Players can discuss and agree on differing and complementary character careers and backgrounds and, during the Culture and Community part of character creation, establish relationships between their characters that go merely beyond 'You all meet in a tavern…': For example:

- All the characters could come from the same cultural background, which makes logical sense.
- Characters can be family members, either close or extended, which creates bonds of blood and helps define beginning Passions, loyalties and family structures.
- Characters can belong to the same, or affiliated, cults or brotherhoods, again providing a reason for adventuring.

Tying the characters together during the character generation stage lends the group communal Luck Points, as discussed on page 81, representing their bonds and ties.

A group exercise can be invaluable in establishing a backstory for the characters that the Games Master can then use in future scenarios. When getting together to create characters as a group, look to answer several questions:

- How do we all know each other?
- How do we feel about each other?
- Does my character have a special relationship with any of the others (a brother, say)? If so, how?
- Why do we want, or need, to work together?
- Who else do we know?
- How do we serve our communities? What do our communities think of us?
- Where do we want to go and what do we want to do?

It is not necessary to address all of these questions immediately: answers often develop through time and play. But finding some answers at the character creation stage helps establish the group as a team and immediately starts to make things seem real. If all the characters have some form of common background element, be it culture, career, family, clan, cult or something else, they have a genuine reason for adventuring, and the Games Master does not need to rely on clichés such as meeting in a crowded drinking establishment.

WHAT SKILLS ARE NEEDED?

MYTHRAS's skill system is incredibly flexible, allowing you to play just about any character concept you can conceive. Every skill has a use in the game. Sometimes though, it is useful to know which skills are most likely to have a direct impact on play or be required in certain tense situations. This can help when assigning skill points at either cultural, career or free skill assignment stages.

Athletics: Used in a variety of combat opposed rolls (resisting a Bash, for example)

Brawn: Good Brawn helps in removing impaled weapons – either one you have impaled, or one that's been impaled in you.

Combat Style: The higher your combat style, the better you fight. Remember that a combat style covers several weapons, and has certain traits that come into play in certain circumstances. As well as being used to hit and defend against opponents, combat style is also used in opposed rolls for damage and certain Special Effects. It can also be used non-lethally. Why not use your Combat Style as a roll to intimidate opponents or as a way of identifying yourself to peers and contemporaries?

Endurance: A decent Endurance score helps in resisting the effects of Major and Serious Wounds. It is also used to resist certain targeted spells.

Evade: Essential for diving out of the way of missile weapons, charging monsters and certain targeted spells. It is also used for actively closing range or disengaging from a melee: it is a very useful skill.

Insight: Used for determining motivation, emotional state, plans and plots… Insight is an extremely useful skill for reading other people. In combat, use Insight to perhaps determine what an observed opponent is likely to do if he generates a Special Effect, or if a seemingly idle opponent is preparing a spell.

Passions: In combat, passions can be used to augment a combat style or other skill. If fighting for the clan's honour, Loyalty to Clan is a highly relevant augmentation to a Combat Style. The same is true for non-combat situations. Things a character feels strongly about constantly influence how certain other skills are used: Influence or

Deceit, for example. Know your Passions and consider how they can be used in different situations.

Willpower: Extremely useful for resisting certain spells, but also for resisting Influence and Deceit attempts. Willpower is always a good skill to develop.

Do not make the mistake of thinking that the above skills are the only ones that should be concentrated on for development: far from it. Mythras allows characters to develop both broad ranges of useful skills, and specialized skills for use in specific situations that reflect professional training and personal growth.

When it comes to investing skill points in skills during character creation, and in choosing skills to benefit from Experience rolls, think about your character's concept and career. Focusing on only a handful of potentially useful skills will penalize the character in other areas that may not be immediately evident.

In Mythras, characters are not necessarily intended to be archetypes, but fully rounded individuals that have a wider range of talents than merely fighting, sneaking or casting spells. Social skills are as every bit as useful as combat ones – especially if you need to talk your way out of trouble.

Developing a decent range of skills across a wide spectrum of areas improves your chances of succeeding in a multitude of situations. Within careers especially you have many options for developing a character that is unique, and goes against traditional archetypes and tropes. How about a warrior-poet? A duplicitous clan adviser? A scrupulous, honest diplomat fighting against the corrupt system? Even a lowly fisherman or farmer can, in time of need, become a hero of his people.

Mythras characters are what you make of them, and the rules provide you with the tools to create some truly memorable and unique characters that defy conventional moulds and stereotypes (although you can build such characters if you want to).

Equipment

The Economics and Equipment chapter offers a reasonable selection of items for characters to buy when beginning the game. However there are a number of caveats for Games Masters when players start to make equipment selections– and these apply also to defining Combat Styles too.

1. Consider the milieu: what is the general nature of the period in which the campaign will be set? If in something roughly analogous to the classical period (Ancient Greece, Rome, Mesopotamia, and so on) equipment, armour and weapon choices should reflect that milieu. Just because Mythras lists a piece of equipment does not mean it should be available. Use your judgement and the milieu of the setting to guide reasonable choices.
2. Consider the cultural background: would barbarians really have access to crossbows and heavy plate armour? Would a nomad, used to riding and fighting from horseback, encumber himself or his mount with a polearm? Would a city-dweller be trained in using a sling when the militia uses spears and bows? Weapon, armour and equipment choices should reflect cultural heritage as much as the milieu. Consider the environment too. Metal armour is generally impractical in very hot and humid climates and is also difficult to manufacture, or expensive to obtain, if a society lacks the raw materials needed. There is a reason why Masai warriors do not encumber themselves with heavy armour. Similarly, Greek hoplites, despite having very good access to bronze, left their limbs free or lightly armoured, to maximize manoeuvrability, and optimise weight. In some cultures, armour may even be viewed as a weakness.
3. Consider Game Impacts: heavy armour slows down the wearer in combat. Even though a character might be able to afford a suit of full, articulated plate, it is cumbersome to wear, hot, and restricts as much as it protects. The edge in combat is often won through speed rather than brute protection. And, traditionally, plate armour is reserved for wars; not for daily use. Anyone wandering around a city dressed as though for a battle will be incongruous and attract the wrong kinds of attention. Similarly, large, two-handed weapons certainly deal a great amount of damage, but they limit certain options for defence. And, again, walking through town with a great axe is a sure way to attract trouble. In Rome, all personal weapons were banned in the city: thus fantasy realms can, and should, have similar restrictions and taboos.
4. Consider What's Reasonable: Mythras does not go overboard on detailed rules for encumbrance but this does not mean that common sense should be ignored. It is simply impractical for a character to carry a kite shield, great axe, warhammer, longsword, crossbow, kit-pack and armour. Guide the players in these limits, and advise them what is logical and practical. There is no need for extremely detailed rules regarding what can and cannot be carried – merely a degree of common sense and practical consideration.

Social Class

Although the default position is to roll randomly for social class, this should not be considered as being the sole method. There are several reasons for choosing or assigning social class instead:

- Group integration is easier if all characters are from the same class.
- Financial disparities between characters are avoided.

This second point is worth some expansion. It is true that those born into a wealthy or privileged background have access to more and better equipment, supporting resources and ready cash: but such has it always been. That said, the income levels described in the Economics and Equipment chapter relate to the costs of maintaining an accustomed standard of living. Those born into a wealthy class will need to spend a far greater proportion of anything they earn to maintain that standard of living than, say, Freemen. And, having monetary wealth available does not always guarantee that its owner has any natural right to it. Wealthier social classes are not always debt-free – a bag of coins a nobleman has to hand may have been obtained from a moneylender with property used as collateral. What would happen if the debt was suddenly called in?

There is, though, always a certain perception of inequality associated with disparate levels of character wealth. For this reason, and especially if starting wealth is seen as necessary to a campaign, Games Masters should assign the same social class to all characters to maintain parity or limit wealthier classes from beginning the game with what might be perceived as an unfair advantage. In reality, society has always suffered such inequalities, and it should be remembered that simply being able to afford lots of equipment, arms and armour does not equate with being able to use any of it effectively.

On the other hand, one advantage of having someone move in advantageous social circles is access and influence in high places. There may be times when having a noble class in the party can assist in ways far more subtle than in simple monetary terms. The rich tend to move in circles of power and influence; this means that a character from a wealthy or noble social class can, when it is needed, draw on family and personal contacts that would otherwise be denied to characters of a more lowly station. This is important in all cultures, not just the civilised ones.

Sitting at the chieftain's table places one closer to her ear or the ear of his advisers. High ranking nomads ride closer to the khan's caravan; highly placed primitive peoples may have influence with the tribal elders or high shaman. Rank brings influence, and influence can be far more precious than money. Having disparate social strata within an adventuring group should be viewed pragmatically rather than with jealousy. Money isn't everything, and influence in the right places can assist when money's voice has fallen silent.

Investigations

Some scenarios rely more on research, mystery, intrigue, and detective work than on the use of the weapons. The gathering of clues to solve a puzzle or mystery is an essential element of such adventures but one problem frequently encountered is the missing of vital clues through failed skill rolls. Of course, Games Masters are quite at liberty to make clues obvious or even hand them out through roleplaying to ensure the smooth flow of the investigation, but this can take away some of the drama and excitement of uncovering a clue or piece of information through the skill rolls of an investigative process.

The most vital aspect of well designed scenarios is that they have alternate means of reaching their conclusion. A scenario, especially one centred upon investigation, should never come to a juddering halt if a crucial clue is not discovered. Even if a particular skill check is pivotal to the plot, a good Games Master should ensure that whatever the outcome, it pushes the storyline forwards. For example a failed investigative roll could result in:

- False information which leads characters to jump to the wrong conclusion
- Finding only part of the information which will lead them off on a roundabout side plot
- An intuitive itching that they are missing something, which resolves itself in a dream or flash of inspiration soon after
- The interruption of the investigation attempt, preventing the characters from locating the clue till they return at a later time
- Arrival of a scroll or informant soon after, to get the characters back on line, but at the expense of worsening the situation

The secret is to never stonewall the characters, but always keep the story flowing. In some situations, such as a sandbox style campaign, reaching an impasse on one plotline does not prevent characters from continuing others in the meantime; but the Games Master should make it clear that pursuing their investigation will, for the moment, be fruitless and quickly divert their attention with a pressing scenario elsewhere.

Of course the availability of personal Luck Points makes the risk of failing crucial investigation rolls less likely, providing the Games Master encourages the use of them in non-combat situations.

A way around this is through the use of those Luck Points provided through forming Personal Connections, as described in the Culture and Community chapter. This group pool of Luck Points could be used by characters when involved in an investigative situation where it is essential to gather clues and information to progress. Instead of making skill rolls, such as Perception, Insight, Lore or something else, the characters can opt to spend a group Luck Point to receive a vital piece of information in lieu of a skill roll.

Spending points in this way depletes the pool which will not refresh until the next game session, but it does guarantee that characters can, through judicious use and communal efforts, avoid the frustrations of bad dice rolls when searching for something they need. A Games Master could even restrict the use of the group's Luck Points to non-combat situations only, which would further encourage their use for investigation.

Using Luck Points to automatically discover clues is a purely optional feature and always at the Games Master's discretion – but they do provide a straightforward mechanism for conducting investigation and research without complete reliance on the vagaries of the dice; providing of course, that the investigation is not so complex that it burns through every available Luck Point.

Using Passions

Although Passions are offered as an optional rule in Mythras, Games Masters are recommended to consider using them as an active part of their games.

Throughout all kinds of fiction, and especially in fantasy, passion drives the plot. The desire to save the world from the evil dark lord; to pursue and gain power; to quest for glory and lost wisdom; to defend, find or avenge love. The variations are limitless and the Passions system is capable of handling them all.

Every individual is driven by some sort of passion. Passions both inform and cloud choices. The heart governs the head, and rational thinking is replaced by that overwhelming compulsion a true passion brings. There is nothing we will not do to save our loved ones. Our loyalty to leader or country drives us to selfless acts. Passions impel us, and in Mythras the Passions mechanics can help drive an entire campaign.

Games Masters can use passions in a variety of ways, designing entire scenarios around the feelings that a character holds for a particular subject or antagonist. These can be very fulfilling for players, especially when they begin to vicariously experience the emotions gripping their characters.

The course of a campaign can hinge on a single passion. Consider the Greek sagas and Shakespeare's tragedies. In The Iliad, Troy is besieged because the love between Paris and Helen causes them to act in a specific way, forcing Agamemnon to seek bloody revenge. In Macbeth, Lady Macbeth's ambition drives her weaker husband to commit regicide, plunging the kingdom into tyranny, paranoia, further bloodshed and, eventually, war.

Anathaym's Saga

Over the course of her adventuring career, Anathaym has developed the 'Hate Badoshi Warlords' passion. The Badoshi have continually threatened her homeland but now she has been chosen to lead a delegation sent to negotiate a crucial truce with these merciless barbarians.

At the Badoshi fortress she is continually insulted, belittled, and challenged – a typical Badoshi ruse that she ought to resist. The Games Master calls for Anathaym to roll against 'Hate Badoshi' to see if, finally, she can resist the constant snide attempts to demean her position. If her roll fails then she can control her overwhelming feelings to extract vengeance; if it succeeds, her hatred will overcome her, which is what the Badoshi want.

Her roll does, indeed, succeed, and she challenges the Badoshi champion to single combat, and kills him. The Badoshi Warlords expel the delegation after slaughtering half of them. Anathaym barely escapes with her own life. War, not peace, is assured. The delegation has failed as a result of Anathaym's hatred. The campaign will now follow a very different course due to the use of this Passion.

Anathaym's inability to allow her head to rule her heart results in a potentially disastrous outcome. It involved a straight roll against her Passion. However, consider the following alternative…

Instead of a straight roll versus 'Hate Badoshi Warlords' the Games Master rules that Anathaym should make an opposed roll of her hatred against her 'Loyalty to Meeros'. Her Loyalty roll wins the contest. Although Anathaym is filled with loathing for the treatment meted out to the delegation, her Loyalty prevails, and she weathers the insults. The Badoshi are secretly impressed by Anathaym's conduct, and the peace negotiations continue although so do the insults. However, war is averted, and Anathaym returns to her queen as a heroine: her head has ruled her heart, and many lives will be saved as a result.

Passions, then, can play a crucial part in a campaign at a personal level, or be at its heart and drive it, at a much higher level. Passions complicate choices, pose moral dilemmas and spur characters to acts of great heroism or flawed villainy. Naturally the Games Master must exercise a certain caution if using Passions to drive core behaviours, but, if used wisely and subtly, Passions can transform a campaign from a series of set pieces into a truly epic saga of heroism, treachery, victory and defeat.

Note that some players can find the use of passions in this manner an imposition, regarding it as a loss of personal control over their character; whilst others welcome the concept of using dice rolls to escape the responsibility of making a difficult choice, or simply enjoy the random vagaries of fate produced by rolling for such things. As such Games Masters should carefully consider whether passions suit their players, before introducing them in play.

Combat

Mythras combat can be deadly. A combination of good combat skills, Special Effects and weaponry can fell even the toughest opponent quickly. Here are some words of advice regarding combat generally and more specific situations.

Combat Styles

When preparing for character creation, Games Masters should give some consideration to Combat Styles. To summarise what a style is:

- The way a character has been trained to fight
- The weapons with which that character has been trained, usually dictated by culture and career.

Mythras does not prescribe any limits on the number of weapons a Combat Style can contain or cover. The primary reason for this is because such limits are always arbitrary, whereas a particular setting may have quite extensive training regimes. For instance, a Barbarian Hunter style may include weapons such as spear, sling, bow, net and bolas whereas a Barbarian Warrior style may only include sword and shield. Of course, Games Masters can ensure that all Combat Styles in their campaign are balanced in the number of weapons contained, but this is something that the Games Master should establish as part of campaign preparation.

There are, however, some recommendations we offer when developing Combat Styles:

- Always consider the culture developing the style. Different societies during different eras follow many diverse trends and fashions. For example, with the introduction of gunpowder weapons shields began to fall out of favour, leading to a range of very different fighting styles that eschewed the shield as a protective instrument. Whereas in feudal Japan shields were

always very uncommon, even in the periods when archery was considered the pre-eminent style of combat.

- Try to ensure that Combat Styles do not include overlapping weapons. If this is impossible, then a character should use the style most fitting to the current circumstances. For example a Barbarian Warrior trained in Sword, Spear and Bow may also be trained in the Shield Wall Combat Style which focuses on Sword, Spear and Shield. If the warrior finds himself in a shield wall situation then the Shield Wall Combat Style percentage would be used for measuring his Sword and Spear capability – because the shield wall imposes a very different fighting style. Similarly fighting from horseback requires very different weapon techniques to foot combat: a Cavalry combat style might contain Sword, overlapping with another style, and this would be used whenever a character engages in combat when mounted.
- Styles can include melee and ranged weapons. A thief, for instance, trained in the Shadow Walkers style (dagger, shortsword and garrotte, for instance), can reasonably be assumed to be able to throw his dagger as well as use it in hand to hand combat. Again though, culture and practice will determine if, and when, a weapon can also be used in ranged circumstances. Some styles will almost certainly focus only on ranged weaponry whilst others will focus completely on hand to hand combat.
- Discuss the different options with the players during character creation, and establish requirements according to each player's character concept, culture and profession. Allow for flexibility and creativity, and point out weapon specific Special Effects appropriate to their nature: this will help encourage creative use of Special Effects during combat scenes, leading to more interesting fights.

You Know, this isn't Necessary…

It should be obvious when superior numbers, displays of skill, good arms and armour will make a fight very one sided. Characters should always, before seeking to initiate combat, ask themselves if it is worthwhile; necessary; inevitable, or most important of all, if it is survivable!

Fighting should always be a last resort with alternative means – negotiation, trickery, or even retreating – being taken into consideration beforehand. Indeed, this can even form a phase of a potential combat, handled in Combat Rounds, but using social skills to adjudicate a potential outcome. For example, Insight can be used to judge whether an opponent has the stomach for a fight, despite obvious bravado. Influence and Passions could be used to negotiate a peaceful outcome before weapons are drawn.

Honourable and reasonable opponents will seek alternatives to fighting and not lose face in doing so. Creatures, if outnumbered or cornered, will flee rather than risk life and limb. Consider what can be done to reduce the risk of injury and death before rushing in to deal damage. An opponent may have unknown magical reserves or skills that make even what seems like the most obviously one-sided fight something different entirely.

Anathaym's Saga

Meeros finally falls to the army of monstrous beasts, let into the city by treachery. The populace flees to the fortified acropolis upon which the queen's palace, and most important temples stand, but the gates fail to shut due to some foul sorcery which has welded their hinges solid. Facing total slaughter, Anathaym stands in the gateway at the head of the remaining Scarlet Spears, and invokes every magic at her command, determined to cut down as many monsters as she can before her soul travels to Myceras.

Up the ramp approaches a mass of centaurs, satyrs, and Panthotaurs, led by their leader, a massive minotaur bedecked in armour, and wielding a great axe. To his side stands the traitor Xenos, who grins fiercely as he sees his hated foe preparing herself for her death. The minotaur king, and Anathaym recognise one another's status, and gesture to their fellows that this will be a single combat between heroes.

Both protagonists exchange many mighty blows back, and forth before the minotaur king suffers outrageous misfortune, his gold painted hoof slipping on a pebble, causing him to drop his axe, and fall prone beneath the ready, glowing tip of Anathaym's spear. Instead of plunging home her weapon into the near helpless minotaur, she honourably salutes her formidable opponent, and takes several steps backwards to allow him to rise. The bull king recognises this act of mercy, recovers his huge axe, and bellows that in exchange for his life he will allow Meeros to stand, then orders his army to depart.

The wrathful Xenos protests this act, demanding the minotaur hack down the presumptuous bitch, which the minotaur king blithely ignores. Finally, consumed by hatred, the pampered noble draws his own sword, and rushes ferociously at Anathaym, screaming angrily with each strike…

Death is not the Only Option

Victory need not, and should not, be dependent on killing every single opponent. An intelligent foe, beaten and helpless, is far more likely to surrender or call for mercy than fight to the absolute and bitter end. Captured opponents can be ransomed, questioned or even released in an honourable way, leading to perhaps a future alliance or a similar acts of mercy if the characters find themselves on the losing side. Injured opponents may simply try to flee. Just about every creature, sapient or not, seeks to *avoid* death and injury.

MYTHRAS provides many tools for bringing a fight to a victorious conclusion without wholesale slaughter. Characters should be encouraged to think about those options that can win a fight conclusively without necessarily drenching themselves in blood to do so. Special Effects such as Trip, Disarm, Press Advantage and Compel Surrender can all bring a fight to a satisfactory conclusion without death being a forgone conclusion.

Killing has Consequences

Whilst combat has always had pride of place in many roleplaying games, especially MYTHRAS, it should be remembered that mindless violence and death are frowned upon by most cultures, for the basic reason that it undermines society. Whilst killing is permitted in certain circumstances, in times of war or in self defence perhaps, there are usually conventions to observe. For instance not even on the battlefield is it always expected or even permitted to kill surrendered or helpless foes.

Characters should scale any violent reaction proportionately to the event which triggered it, suited to the culture they are in. For example, a thief who attempts to rob characters in a back alley at knifepoint rarely deserves to be slaughtered, since folks would consider frightening off the criminal, or at most giving him a beating, a more than sufficient retort. Of course, if that thief was also a murderer who killed his victims then a more violent response would be in order.

As a rule opponents in a fight are rarely willing to continue to the death unless driven by some overwhelming passion – be that religious fanaticism, protection of a loved one, or seeking to sate a need for vengeance. Generally, rather than death, foes will seek quarter, beg for mercy or attempt to flee. Killing at this point can bring serious repercussions.

Of course mishaps occur when weapons are being swung, but unnecessary butchery soon brings a double-edged reputation. On one hand the characters will become known as men not to be trifled with, but conversely they will alienate themselves from those they ostensibly protect.

Repetitive killing can draw unwelcome attention from local rulers whom rarely appreciate those who take matters of law or punishment into their own hands. Killing the wrong person can bring retribution from a powerful patron or perhaps start a vendetta with a slain victim's family, cult or brotherhood. A society usually has strict rules about death, even as part of an honourable duel or self defence. It may be something as simple as paying wergild to compensate the family of the slain or might result in exile to avoid ongoing disruption within the clan or settlement.

Games Masters are encouraged to consider what happens in our own world to those who practice gratuitous violence upon members of their own society. On the other hand it can be completely different to pursue the same degree of slaughter against an enemy culture, race or species.

Pacing Combat Encounters

Unlike some roleplaying games, healing magic is not ubiquitous, meaning that injured characters are not going to be able to fall back on a plethora of spells, potions and scrolls to regain lost hit points if they lurch from one combat to another. Natural healing can be slow and if the characters are in an isolated location, far away from places offering rest and sanctuary, healing will take longer, and characters be placed at greater risk.

It is therefore imperative for Games Masters to carefully pace violent encounters: too many and characters will soon die. Similarly, players will need to pace their activities according to any lingering wounds or injuries. If every character in a party is injured and there is no easy access to healing, magical or natural, a fight will be the last thing they need (unless they are all truly suicidal).

Of course not all scenarios need not involve combat at all, instead relying on social interaction, good roleplaying and use of wits to succeed. However, those adventurers that do involve physical conflict should limit themselves to several minor encounters, and one major.

Minor engagements are those where characters have significantly greater skills and perhaps armour than their opponents. Rabble and Underlings (see page 111) are often good fodder for these sorts of encounters, as are lone creatures whom the characters can gang up on.

Major engagements should be used as the climax of a scenario, being battles where the characters are evenly matched or slightly outclassed by their opponents. Such encounters should pose a considerable chance that they will be badly injured.

Games Masters need to be aware of these limitations in Mythras and structure their games accordingly. If combat becomes the focus of the campaign, occurring so frequently that there is little time to heal naturally or recover magical resources between encounters, the characters will either be unable to complete their quests or be slain from the accumulation of crippling injuries.

Players, in particular, need to understand that when bloodied and bruised from one violent encounter, another in quick succession is not the best way of making progress: hiding, fleeing or talking their way out of trouble may prove to be far more beneficial.

Action Points are Not the Be All and End All

Action Points certainly bestow advantage. Being able to do more in a combat round can make all the difference. However, characters that may feel penalized by only having 2 Action Points, rather than 3, (or 3 Action Point characters facing an creature with 4) still have many options available to help level the odds:

Speed Helps: Striking first, through a higher Initiative, offers a significant advantage. Lightly armoured characters can exploit this opportunity when facing slower, heavily armoured ones.

Numbers Matter: Outnumbering a foe can quickly resolve a fight because the foe cannot hope to use its own Action Points to effectively deal with two opponents who have 2 Action Points each. Conversely creatures that attack in packs use their weight of numbers to overwhelm their opponents, so numerical advantage should be exploited when possible.

Manoeuvring: A character who is outnumbered can make excellent use of the Outmanoeuvre Combat Action to keep multiple foes at bay, buying time for help to come or simply remaining unengaged (and possibly fleeing).

Use of Weapons: Long weapons, such as spears, can hold an opponent at a safe distance limiting what can be done even with a superior number of Action Points. And long weapons can be used to injure– and whittle down – an opponent without him getting close enough to attack. A long weapon impaled in a human-sized creature will severely hamper its skills and movement, leading to a massive disadvantage regardless of its Action Points. Remember: a weapon is a tool, and tools have multiple uses beyond the obvious.

Use of Special Effects: A common misconception is that special effects such as Choose Location and Maximise Damage are the most advantageous. They are definitely effective, but when faced with an opponent that has more Action Points those special effects that deny Action Points, or force them to be used for activities other than attack or defence, are often better choices. An overextended foe cannot attack on his next turn. A disarmed foe has to spend an Action Point to draw another weapon. Bash can force an opponent out of engagement, making him expend an Action Point simply to regain it.

Never Ignore Defence: Another misconception is that, if an attack against you fails, it makes little sense to spend an Action Point in defending – it could be more useful for an attack. However, a successful defence roll against an unsuccessful attack generates a Special Effect, and any opportunity to gain an advantage (especially if you have fewer Action Points) should not be ignored. All the defensive Special Effects have their uses, and some can easily dictate the outcome of a fight. A Blind opponent suffers a significant disadvantage for 1d3 turns; Opening Range can afford the defender valuable breathing space. Try not to overlook the use of defensive opportunities even when straight logic might dictate reserving Action Points for an attack.

Shields are Invaluable: Two handed weapons definitely do more damage and wielding a pair of swords looks impressive, but there is no substitute for a shield when it comes to pure defensive expedience. Shields block the damage of large weapons and creatures very effectively, and are the only way to defend against ranged attacks. But don't underestimate their usefulness in other areas: Passive Blocking keeps multiple locations defended, and a shield, when used to Bash, is more effective than other blunt-force weapons.

The best approach is a combination of all the above techniques in different circumstances. For one thing, combat becomes more interesting and can yield some interesting results. Good and clever use of techniques and tools can truly level the battlefield when it comes to Action Point disparity, and the Mythras combat system has been carefully designed to take into account the myriad combat options available and the fact that opponents are not always evenly matched.

Grading Opponents

"How should I grade opponents so that fights are balanced?" This is a frequently asked question, especially by Games Masters coming to Mythras from roleplaying games that have structures in place, such as experience and challenge levels, designed to maintain party/opponent parity.

The easiest way is to match opponent and character numbers, with the opponent's skills in roughly the same range (+/- 10%) as the characters' skills. However, this can lead to boring and repetitive combats – especially if neither the characters nor their opponents use Special Effects to their full advantage. Combats are usually at their best when opponents are challenging and not necessarily balanced. So, in addition to giving opponents a certain parity in terms of skills, here are some suggestions for also introducing challenges that are not so one-sided as to diminish players' enjoyment.

Anathaym's Saga

The battle between Xenos, and Anathaym is epic, fuelled by years of building hatred. At first the warrioress, despite her injuries, has the advantage; but Xenos uses his Hate Anathaym passion to boost his Combat Style, granting him the greater skill, forcing her on the defence. Several blows later, strengthened by his brutal, unrestrained rage he cuts through her spear shaft, and Anathaym is forced to draw her shortsword.

Gloatingly Xenos describes what he'll do to her sister once he has dealt with Anathaym, and the conceited queen who refused his marriage proposal. This incenses Anathaym so greatly that she uses her own Hate Xenos passion to augment her combat prowess. Then with consummate skill, she cuts off his sword hand at the wrist. Xenos screams in agony, and drops to his knees in front of the furious warrior.

This time there is no mercy in her heart. Heedless of the strident commands given her by the queen, and before anyone can interfere, she decapitates Xenos – claiming the vengeance she has long sought. She has little time to savour her victory. All too soon she is disarmed by her Scarlet Spear compatriots, and escorted to face judgement by the senate for killing the one man she was forbidden from harming.

Superior, but not overwhelming, numbers can help: take the party's size, and increase the number of opponents by two individuals.

Use packs of creatures, using pack tactics. Pack hunters, such as wolves, rarely stalk alone. Size a pack as above, but have the pack work differently to sapient opponents: surrounding, harrying, wearing down, and then sending multiple numbers against the most helpless seeming member. The party will be forced into measures that consolidate their numbers for safety and aim to drive the pack away.

Exotic arms and armour. Have that raiding group of goblins attack with nets and tridents rather than swords and shields, giving the opponents different Special Effect options that might be unfamiliar to the characters, such as Entangle.

Make use of ambushes and ranged attacks: ranged attacks can be difficult to counter, and doubly so if the enemy has taken advantage of excellent cover. The characters will be forced to find ways of closing whilst defending themselves, or be forced to use their own ranged attacks, to counter even a modestly-skilled opponent. If characters are surprised by an ambush, they will be forced to spend a round defending before they can counter attack, again making modestly skilled opponents a hazard and challenge in the earliest stages of a fight.

Consider use of magic. Sapient creatures are just as capable of using magic as the characters. Equipping a set of foes with spells such as Bladesharp and Demoralise can compensate for perceived lack of skill and force different tactics. A shaman, controlling several fetishes, can prove to be a match for any player-character spell caster or well-armed fighters. Remember that sapient creatures have access to similar resources as characters: use them wisely, and this will help grade the challenges characters face.

Have creatures fight according to their nature. The Creatures chapter gives more detail about how creatures tend to involve themselves in combat: read and use these guidelines which will help in making fights with non-sapient creatures far more interesting and challenging for the characters.

Use of local conditions and the environment. Adventurers are usually the strangers in a locale. This lends the incumbent species or opponents a distinct advantage in using terrain, staging surprise attacks, driving the characters into bottlenecks, and so forth. Many species are nocturnal or have excellent night-sight, making their attacks for more likely to occur during the hours of darkness, when characters should suffer from penalties due to the absence of light. Couple this with unfamiliar terrain, and even a simple fight may become very challenging.

Never forget fatigue. Sustained effort equals fatigue. If characters have been travelling through difficult country with heavy loads, then they may well be suffering from fatigue. Clever predators will keep watch for many hours to ensure a potential opponent is worn down whilst it is still fresh and able. Use the fatigue rules to simulate the toll on both characters and opponents. In this way, monsters that are seemingly very, very tough can be pitched against fresh-as-daisy characters if the monster is tired or tiring.

Ultimately 'balanced' encounters are less about relative combat skills, hit points, armour and weapons, and more about tactics and use of the environment. Games Masters should never forget two things when developing encounter challenges for characters:

- Characters have Luck Points – these can be life-savers.
- Characters are on the path to be being heroes– and should have the opportunity to act in this way. Stupidity and lack of planning should not be rewarded.

In Mythras even relatively low-skilled opponents can still fell a mighty warrior with a 120% Combat Style if they are cunning and selective in their tactics. Likewise a character with a mere 40% in bow and arrow can still attempt to bring down the fire-breathing dragon. Experience with the combat mechanics will help shape challenging encounters that include seemingly unbalanced opponents.

Non-Player Character Statistic Blocks

Although the Creatures chapter provides the same range of characteristics and attributes as for adventurers, Games Masters only rarely need this level of detail. And, in most circumstances, an average of a species is perfectly fine without the need to roll a completely bespoke example.

When running an encounter likely to result in combat, the following information is most crucial:

- Action Points, Initiative Bonus, Armour Point, Hit Points, Movement Rate, Magic Points
- Combat Style (with weapon values), Athletics, Brawn, Endurance, Evade, Perception, Stealth and Willpower.
- Important Traits. Unless a creature has a particular skill useful in combat or other encounter situations, then a more detailed skill list is superfluous. If a skill is unlisted and Games Masters need to assign a value in a hurry, give the opponent or creature either 30%, 60% or 90% depending on whether it can be expected to be poor, competent or good at the required skill. For example, a group of characters encounter a troupe of centaurs and end up negotiating with them rather than fighting; the Games Master has not listed Influence in the required statistics, but it can be assumed that at least one of the centaurs has Influence 60%, representing a reasonable level of negotiation skill.

Social Conflict

Social Conflict is the application of verbal and sociological techniques to force a change in thinking, behaviour or social standing. It can take many forms and need not be direct, but may ultimately result in injury to reputation, personal honour, codes of conduct, and so on. Various techniques are utilised which include trading insults, spreading rumours, uncovering scandals, personal argument, open debate, betrayal of secrets, and anything else one side or the other come up with.

The key recommendation for Games Masters is to roleplay, as far as possible, social conflict situations. However there are many players who feel uncomfortable of immersing themselves to this degree and prefer a mechanical method, more akin to combat, to help determine the outcome. Indeed, such mechanics can greatly speed up play and keep the action flowing.

The task system, described on page 65, used for crafting and manufacturing goods, can be tailored to help resolve social conflict situations. The system is straight-forward:

- Instead of a Craft or similar roll, characters use their social skills: Commerce, Customs, Deceit, Insight, Influence, Oratory, Passions and Willpower, as appropriate.
- The Games Master frames the social conflict setting: 'Persuade the senate to go to war' for instance; 'Defend your personal honour'; 'Cut a braggart down to size using cunning wit.' Next he decides how long achieving the objective is likely to take. This could be a few seconds of verbal sparring; a few minutes of impassioned rhetoric; or many hours of detailed and tense negotiations.
- The aim of the characters (or the opponent) is to score 100% or more over the course of the conflict. Each participant may

Anathaym's Saga

Anathaym faces her queen's wrath for killing Xenos. The ruler had expressly wanted the traitor alive, not only to gather information concerning how the city fell so quickly, but also to weaken the political power of certain members of the Senate. Worse still, Misogynistes, the father of Xenos, has charged Anathaym with breaking the ancient law forbidding the slaying of a member of the sacrosanct founding families. With her grip on the throne weakened by the devastating sack on Meeros, the queen has little option but to let the trial continue.

The Games Master decides the trial takes place over the course of several days, with each roll representing one day of game-time. As a guilty member of the conspiracy Misogynistes uses his Deceit skill to misrepresent evidence against the warrioress, twisting well known tales of her years actively persecuting his son. To counter his honey-tongued fabrications, Anathaym uses her Influence skill in an attempt to show that she has always faithfully served the city.

Day One: Anathaym's Influence roll is a success, whilst Misogynistes' (still overwhelmed by his son's loss) fails. She scores 25% towards her goal of 100.

Day Two: This time Misogynistes scores a critical success whilst Anathaym only succeeds. Both parties now have a score of 50%, and the trial is neck, and neck, fuelling much impassioned debate in the taverns that evening.

Day Three: Only Anathaym succeeds, as Misogynistes fails to arrive at the senate house that day (automatic failure). Her stoic defence against the senate's questions allows her to draw ahead with 75%.

Day Four: Anathaym is stunned to silence when Misogynistes turns up, claiming that it was Anathaym herself who opened the city gates, and staged the battle with the minotaur king. The forged scroll he presents as conclusive proof of his son's innocence, which details the looting of the city, bears the wax impression of Anathaym's own familial seal ring. Misogynistes wins a critical whilst Anathaym fails entirely.

With his 100%, the senate finds the Champion of Meeros guilty of Treason, the murder of Xenos, and attempted Regicide. She is sentenced to be stoned to death immediately, before the senate house.

However, as the senators rise the sacred statue of Myceras groans with cyclopean displeasure, and topples as an earthquake strikes the city...

And so Anathaym's Saga concludes. For now...

roll against the relevant social skill, and accumulate the result for that particular period of sparring:
Critical: 50%
Success: 25%
Failure : 0%
Fumble: –25%

- The first side to reach 100% or more wins the conflict, with any excess above 100 reflecting a greater degree of outcome. If the contest ends in stalemate, with two or more participants ending with the same 100%+ score, then the Games Master has the option of permitting the contest to end in an unresolved standoff; or the leading contestants can make a straight opposed roll between them, the victor of the roll winning the contest.
- The outcome may not be clear-cut, depending on the intended result, and will depend on whether the method of invoking social conflict is direct or indirect.

This system can be applied to just about any form of social interaction – not just conflict; attempting to seduce someone, for instance. The abstracted timeframe allows for actions that might take weeks to be condensed into a few minutes of dice rolls, hopefully supported by some roleplaying to help add flavour, and not reduce something of fundamental importance to a purely mechanistic exercise.

Characters can change the skill used from one round to the next, as long as the skill is appropriate to the direction of the interaction. For instance, a character could start a debate with Influence in the first round, change to Oratory in the next, and then back to Influence in the third. Games Masters can force such a change depending on how the social conflict needs to play out, and how the outcome has been framed. In this example, the first round might simulate persuading a senator to table a motion before the senate. In the second round the character is called upon to give a speech laying out his reasons; and in the third, the character must return to persuasion to swing the crucial vote in his favour.

Using Traps

Traps are a traditional element of tomb raiding or the protection of famous treasures. Although their prevalence in Sword & Sorcery belies their actual rarity in historical record, this should not prevent the Games Master from using them as an important element of their scenarios. Some degree of thought should be given to the occurrence, purpose and deadliness of traps however.

The most commonplace traps are merely warning devices, used to alert guardians of whatever has been trapped. Scattering dried leaves around a campsite or balancing a chair against the door of a rented room in a tavern, are traps designed to reveal the presence of stalkers or thieves. These are good challenges to place against characters since the only outcome is the revelation of their presence, leaving them free to negotiate or flee as the circumstances denote.

Ensnaring traps are more often used by hunters to capture prey, usually for the purpose of gathering food. Yet pits, snares and dropping portcullises can just as easily be used against characters. They are also good to use against characters, especially when the noise of their triggering attracts those that set them, preventing sapient victims from freeing themselves or being freed by others. This will of course place captured characters at some disadvantage, but will not unduly injure them.

The point at which Games Masters need to be careful is when placing traps intended to maim or kill in his scenario. Such devices are not always intended to be easily bypassed or avoided. After all, it would be crass stupidity for the tomb of a powerful king to have traps which can be circumvented, since there is no reason for anyone to enter the sepulchre once the dead ruler is interred. A palace treasury on the other hand, may need to be opened on a regular basis and thus requires some secretive method of safe entry.

A properly designed death-trap should be – once triggered – utterly lethal otherwise it is not performing its function correctly. This however may be of little consolation to players whose characters have just been crushed to bloody pulp or lie at the bottom of a pit transfixed by stakes. When using such traps to guard important locations and treasures, the Games Master should provide plenty of warning that 'no man has ever returned from entering' the infamous place. Clues can be placed in ancient scrolls describing its legend, carved across the entry as dire curses or even passed down by word of mouth by storytellers and burglars.

No matter how deadly the trap, there should always be some method of escaping its effect, even if this is merely diving back the way they came. This is not the same as circumventing the trap, merely avoiding the worst of what occurs when it is set off. Yet because of the binary nature of resistance rolls in Mythras, injury-inflicting traps should be used sparingly as characters will eventually fail their roll; although Luck Points can add considerably to survivability.

Since most traps are but a single use, characters should sometimes encounter traps which have already been sprung – often with the remains of a previous victim still caught upon them. This is more relevant to traps built in long forgotten or abandoned places, rather that those still frequented by living folks. In fact nothing prevents a scenario being designed around a necropolis of previously sprung traps with no active ones left, simply to unnerve the characters. Conversely tomb maintenance could be the duty of a nearby cult or brotherhood, to ensure that the secrets of such places remain unsullied by acts of desecration.

Due to the considerable investment of time (and sometimes money) required to construct traps, especially larger scaled devices, it should be reasonably rare to encounter multiple incidences of them. Building a sprawling death-trap dungeon for example would require years of effort and a modest fortune to pay the workers, but to what purpose? There would be little chance of suppressing the fact that the dungeon existed and rumours concerning its precise secrets might escape, unless of course all of its labourers were slain.

Depending on its ultimate intention, this might not be an issue. The constructor of a death-trap dungeon might wish for people to hear of its infamy, drawing them to an annual festival where adventurers compete to survive the dungeon for the promise of a priceless reward. Equally the dungeon may guard the entrance to a royal necropolis, and its fame spread far and wide by display of dead thieves outside its entry – freely advertised and unguarded – to ensure few ever try once the reputation of its deadliness is established.

Creatures as Player Characters

A great deal of fun can be had with non-human characters, and one of the beauties of Mythras is that just about any race can be used in this way. Players will, no doubt, flip through the Creatures chapter and petition the Games Master to play an Ogre, Minotaur, or even a Gorgon or Dragon. What is a beleaguered Games Master to do?

Just because a creature *can* be played as a character does not mean that it *should*. The Games Master is always the final arbiter and even uncontroversial choices, such as dwarves and elves, may not be in keeping with the flavour of a campaign. The Games Master must base his decision on the following considerations:

- How well does a particular race fit with the nature and themes of the campaign? Any creature but humans would be out of place in an historical setting for instance. Whereas a high fantasy campaign could be assumed to have one or more elder races (a common high fantasy theme).
- Is the creature sapient? Sapience denotes free will, informed decision-making and the capacity to act in a rational, judgmental way rather than one based on instinct. Sapient characters are far easier to relate to and therefore play, than those which are merely sentient. Of course, some sentient creatures may have been raised to sapience through magic or other means, and therefore be applicable for play, but generally true sapience is the key.
- What is the creature's level of power when compared with the rest of the characters? As a rule of thumb, Games Masters should deter players from choosing creatures that are clearly much more powerful than the other characters. The easiest way to measure power levels are to compare attributes. Creatures with substantially more Action Points, significantly higher Damage Modifiers, high Hit Points and natural armour, will have a large advantage over more modest character types. This can prove to be difficult when it comes to balancing encounters for the whole party and it may also cause resentment amongst other players – especially if, in combat situations, the creature character clearly hogs the limelight.
- How will the creature fit in with other races? Both Games Masters and players need to consider questions of prejudice, social acceptance, and general logistics of mixing races in the same group. A group may find it is barred or banished from many areas if it contains a troll or chaos hybrid in its number; worse, it may attract attacks from those who seek to stigmatise and punish difference. A group with a giant as a member will likely strike terror from many kilometres away and, even if they do not, find that the giant character simply cannot enter a city's walls due to its size, thereby causing the player to sit-out much of the fun. Another consideration is that of tolerance within the group. Different races have radically different views regarding morality, and these might be so disparate as to lead to intra-party conflict and strife. A further consideration is language. If different races have trouble communicating, this can also lead to tensions and difficulties.
- Is the creature suitable? Some of the creatures in Mythras are intended to be non-player characters: contacts, arch-villains, boss-monsters, and so on. A Gorgon, for example, would never make a suitable player character simply due to its nature and powers. This, again, comes back to the adage that just because a creature can be played as a character, it does not mean that it should – or was even intended to be.

Culture, Careers and Development

Where a non-human race is acceptable, the Creatures chapter offers some guidance on developing a species with an appropriate culture, career, and so forth. Where such guidance does not exist, the character creation rules are flexible enough to be applied to just about any race without special rules or requirements. Choose a cultural background that reflects the creature's type, a profession that fits with its description and culture, and then continue the character creation process as for humans. Where a species has character development notes included, use these in preference to the human character creation system; you may also find that these notes fit several other species and they need not be considered unique or restricted.

Magic

What types of magic are used and how common they are, are specific to the campaign. A magically rich campaign could have all five of the magical disciplines whereas a low-magic campaign might have only one, reflecting a single, dominant power in the universe. Games Masters must carefully consider how prevalent magic will be in the world before allowing players to develop magic-using characters. Not all of the magical disciplines need to be used, and indeed, some uniquely interesting combinations can be created by mixing and matching them.

With five separate magic systems Games Masters have a great deal of choice when it comes to deciding what types and levels of magic should be present in the campaign. Some points for all Games Masters to consider:

- What is magic's presence? Is it extremely rare and in the hands of only a few, fabled practitioners, or is it more common-place?
- Is magic a specialised art, relegated to members of only a few careers that dedicate their lives to its pursuit? Or is it possible for all careers to learn magic in some form, irrespective of how rare it is?
- How is magic viewed by most societies? If magic is relatively rare then the chances are that most people will view it with awe, respect and, perhaps, suspicion and fear. If it is more common then magic may be something that, whilst remarkable in its own way, is an accepted part of daily life.

Which of the magic systems will be represented in your campaign?

Folk Magic – magic may be restricted to very simple, local effects that are understood primarily by hedge wizards, witches, wise men and women, and so on. Much is based on folk-lore and a deep understanding of the natural world, coupled with certain powers that may be inherited through a bloodline or awoken through exposure to such knowledge.

Animism – the spirits are vital entities to the world and communion with them a natural part of life. Whilst animists are often viewed as primitive, there are many civilised and sophisticated societies practicing animism, such as the Shinto religion of Japan.

Mysticism – ascetics seek to enlighten themselves through a personal understanding of reality and control over their bodies' unrealised potential. Mysticism is prevalent in many cultured societies that have their basis in reason, rationality and deep philosophical understanding. Mysticism is not necessarily a religious path though, and may be found in many secular societies.

Sorcery – sorcery implies that mortals have mastered the arcane laws of the universe and bend them to their will. The gods may not exist, may be absentee landlords, or their worship has diminished to the point that they cease to be relevant. Sorcerers, especially the very powerful ones, may be looking to fill this gap, and assume a godhead role themselves. This is a typical trope of most Sword and Sorcery.

Theism – this implies that the gods exist, and are prepared to allow their powers to be channelled and used by mortals in return for worship. This is typical of many ancient myths and religions, particularly those of the ancient world such as India and Mesoamerica.

Whatever combination of styles you choose for your campaign– and there is no need to have all five present, unless you desire a truly magic-rich campaign – study the magic systems carefully:

- Understand how they work and what powers they grant to their practitioners. Reading a spell on its own is not enough: the mechanics for each magic system can enhance an individual spell's effect considerably.
- Do different cultures practice different magical traditions? Experiment with different themes. Perhaps the barbarians of the steppes are masters of sorcery whilst the civilised cultures cleave to spirit worship. Maybe only the superstitious primitive tribes believe in the gods whilst the nomads - arch-survivalists – have developed many mystical traditions to aid in their daily life.
- Choose what spells will be made available. Games Masters should not feel compelled to make every spell listed for a magic type available. Some will be unknown, rare, or extremely difficult to learn. Some will not be appropriate to the flavour of the campaign. Build your own spell lists. Doing so will help manage players' expectations when choosing magic, and give the Games Master control over magic that could be overly powerful in a campaign's early stages. You can always expand your list later. Indeed, magical research can be a very good driver for certain scenarios.
- Decide what magic will be available to characters at character creation. Do characters need to join a cult to learn higher magic? Can they choose magic-using careers from the very start, and develop cult membership (or some other form of magical education) as a part of character creation? Should they have any magic at all? Might gaining access to it, through adventuring and experience, be the route to magical power? Many fantasy stories use this premise very successfully as a way of showing individual journeys of discovery and realisation.
- Consider what consequences a magical type will have on the world. Magic is a path to power, and all paths to power lead to some form of ruling class, which will, eventually, seek to consolidate and protect its position. How does this influence the lower social strata? Is magic used to control the populace or oppress them? Do certain forms of magic corrupt spiritually and morally? Have other magical paths been forgotten but could be awoken in some way?

Cults and Brotherhoods in the Campaign

The Cults chapter provides an extensive range of bare-bones cults for Games Masters to develop, depending, of course, on whether or not cults form an important part of the campaign. Although cults have always been an integral part of Mythras, there is no need to make them the focus of attention or indeed, even include them at all. There are some excellent reasons for their inclusion: history and fantasy include many cult examples, and some ancient societies were defined by them. But some settings may use cults very differently:

- Cults may be rare or difficult to join, being restricted to certain cultures, social classes, or careers. Only a small elite might be entitled to progress through the cult ranks.
- Some fantasy genres – Swords and Sorcery in particular – depict the universe as a cold, uncaring place where the gods are largely absent, and cults are reserved for a tiny minority who are bent on achieving power at all costs. In such cases cults are the province of powerful non-player characters (typically malevolent sorcerers), and form the focus of characters' opposition.
- Worship of gods simply has little or no overt organization. Worship is personal and although temples and clerical classes exist, there is no established hierarchy of progression outside of a purely clerical career – which may be highly restrictive in terms of adventuring.
- In worlds or settings where magic is rare or absent, cults are purely a social mechanism rather than one that offers benefits for its initiates: cults therefore provide background colour rather than an integral game mechanic for magical development.

So, give some thought to the place and role of cults in the campaign. Many settings– and some published specifically for Mythras – will use them extensively, whilst others may include them to a much lesser degree. Brotherhoods, on the other hand, are likely to be far more common: people, being social animals, naturally form brotherhoods and societies for mutual support, advancement and protection. Brotherhoods can effectively replace cults in some settings, or happily co-exist with them.

If cults are to be used, they require a little work. Cults can be as detailed or as nebulous as one desires; but to get the very most from a cult, the following framework elements can be used as the basis for developing a fully-realised cult.

- Concept
- Object of Veneration
- History and Context
- Myths
- Magic and Powers
- Obligations and Deficits
- Membership and Ranks
- Training

When developing a cult, approach each element in order, allowing ideas to build, based on the decisions made for the preceding element. Although the following steps are phased specifically for cult organisations, the same elements can be applied for the creation of Brotherhoods too.

Concept

What is the basis of the cult? Is it a formal religion covering an empire, a nation, a community or a small body of people? Is it, perhaps, outside of an over-arching religion due to a difference of belief, although agreeing with it on most aspects of orthodoxy? Is the god living or dead? Is the god represented by a prophet or ideal that forms the basis of the belief? Is the cult focused on worshipping a particular aspect of a god's nature? Is the focus of the cult a charismatic individual who might become a god? Or is it a personality of such heroic, charismatic stature that veneration is the only way to show the appropriate love and respect?

The concept need not be detailed, but it needs to have a substantive hook for the rest of the framework. It might be as simple as a sentence, or a more detailed paragraph or so that clearly outlines the concept. Do not feel compelled to go into too much conceptual detail. Concepts change over time, so if the concept is relatively simple and straightforward, it is easier for characters to understand and depth will come through active gameplay.

Object of Veneration

Cults are usually formed to venerate someone or something. The object of veneration for the cult – its heart and focus – should be defined. There are many different kinds of objects for veneration but the most common are:

- A single god or goddess – such as Zeus, Odin or Gurghul the Avenging God of Foetid Mists. Or a group of gods and goddesses – a pantheon.
- An aspect of a god or goddess's nature – one particular form of behaviour that adherents find sacred.
- Someone who embodies both the nature of mortals and gods – a demigod.
- A holy prophet or messenger.
- A creature or monster of singular power A charismatic individual, either living or dead, who inspires love and devotion – a Personality or Hero cult
- A philosophy of existence leading to some form of unearthly reward – Buddhism, for instance.
- An object or relic of power or significance.

History and Context

What is the history behind the cult? What role does it play in society? Much depends on the cult's size, but small cults can be very powerful in a local area, and large ones weak when their influence is spread across distances.

- Who founded the cult, or how did it come into being?
- When was it founded – recently or long ago?
- How has it maintained its position – has it changed over time?
- Does the cult have enemies? What other cults is it affiliated with?
- Is the cult part of a pantheon? How does it contribute to the overall myths of that pantheon?
- Does the cult worship differently, or believe different things to similar cults? If so, is it considered heretical?
- What social services does the cult offer to its lay members? Is it a beneficent cult or inherently selfish? Does it care a jot for the welfare of others?
- What is the cult's future? Are new members being attracted or is its influence on the wane? Are new beliefs eroding old ones from within?

The history and context should be a narrative that addresses some, or all, of the above questions. Again, it need not be too complex or detailed, growing instead through game play and continued Games Master development.

Myths

Many cults have myths. A myth is a story or set of stories that describe and exemplify what the cult stands for and how it behaves. Myths are, typically, timeless and concern the deeds of gods or the object of veneration. They may be considered unassailable truths, or stories that provide a meaning or parable, but are known to be a work of fiction. The important fact is that a myth explains, teaches and promotes the ethics, values and behaviours of the cult.

Myths can be as simple or elaborate as the Games Master wishes them to be. Many myths concern the eternal questions of:

- How was the world made?
- How did people come into being?
- How does the venerated being handle certain challenges and problems?
- How were enemies defeated?
- How will the world follow its course and how might it end?
- What does the object of veneration do for me?

It is usually the case that no one knows who created the myth and how it came into being; a myth simply is – whether written down or communicated through word of mouth. Myths are typically unquestioned (although the myths of other cults, especially where they conflict with a cult's own myths, may certainly be challenged, even violently), even when it is known that much is fabrication, because the power of the lesson is inherent in the myth's structure. It is easier to reinforce behaviour if one tells a story to show that behaviour in action, rather than simply listing a set of rules and restrictions. Children are particularly receptive to the power of myth, and cults ensure that myths form a part of a child's education so that patterns of behaviour and belief can be established early-on.

Myths become ingrained into the psyche and enforce certain patterns of behaviour. Stronger myths are more successful at this. For every myth created, decide what forms of behaviour it seeks to exemplify. These should be simple, clear statements such as...

- Lying is wrong
- Bravery is necessary
- Tricksters cannot be trusted
- Hospitality to enemies and friends is essential
- Hard work provides the best rewards

Magic

What magic can a cult offer to its members? This is dependent on a number of things:

- Whether or not the cult reveres a god, personality or ideal – the latter two cannot offer Theist Magic, but may be able to offer Animism, Mysticism, Sorcery or Folk Magic.
- If the cult offers Magic to its membership. Some cults don't provide any magic at all, or limit it to those of higher cult rank than the common members.

The sample cults in the Cults and Brotherhoods chapter give ample examples of the ranges of spells and types of magic available, but Games Masters can be creative. Theist cults might also offer sorcery as part of their nature; or sorcery orders might also worship a particular god who offered sorcerous knowledge as a gift.

Obligations and Deficits

Obligations and Deficits are another framework method for enforcing certain kinds of behaviour. Essentially, cult members are rewarded for acting in the right ways and penalised for acting against the behavioural norms of the cult. These things can take different forms and it is up to the Games Master to decide which (and they can be mixed and matched) are most appropriate to the campaign and thus available as part of the Cult Framework. The Cults chapter offers several different ways of creating obligations and deficits through the use of taboos, geases and superstitions. These are regular tropes in myth and fantasy, and often used as the basis for adventure and stories.

Membership and Ranks

This cult framework element is of substantial importance to both cults and characters. It defines how people join the cult and what stages are open to them through cult progression. Becoming a member of a cult can be as simple as proclaiming worship of a god, following of personality or ideal, or undergoing some form of initiation rite. For most, this is enough for their personal requirements, and they will progress no further in the cult and have no desire to do so.

However, the more steadfast and devout – those who want to make a real commitment to the focus of their veneration – must go somewhat beyond the Common Membership requirements and become Dedicated Members. These dedicate themselves to the inner workings of the cult and place themselves on a track for progression, allowing the cult to become the focus for their activities.

Initiation involves a ritual of some form. The precise nature can be defined as part of the cult framework, and can take any of a number of forms: some examples are:

- Initiation ritual involving much pomp or ceremony, such as a communion rite, baptism or other, symbolic acceptance into the cult's ways
- Trial or ordeal
- Vigil, fasting or abstinence
- Swearing of a binding oath
- Making a sacrifice

Performing the initiation ritual can either be a focus of a roleplaying session, or, for simplicity, abstracted to a roll against a particular skill (such as Endurance, Willpower, or a Passion). Once the initiation rite is complete, and if the initiate meets any prerequisites for membership, then he is considered a Dedicated Member.

Training

Cults may teach skills as part of the rewards offered to their active members, and look for certain skills when recruiting members. The kinds of skills offered reflect two things: the cult's nature and purpose (pious, peaceful cults will focus on lore and communication skills; martial cults will offer weapon skills); and the kinds of qualities the focus of veneration exemplifies. Therefore, as part of the cult framework process, give some thought to the following questions when choosing cult skills:

- What skills does the object of veneration display and promote?
- What skills are used in the myths fundamental to the cult?
- What skills are important to the cult in achieving its aims?
- What skills might members naturally bring to the cult, given the culture and campaign background?

Cults tend to offer training in order to enforce certain kinds of behaviour, but also to make sure that the cult is equipped with what it needs to achieve its goals and ensure its survival. Training happens in several ways:

- Through dedicated training academies, supported by the cult
- Through the indenturing of lower ranks to higher ones
- Through mentoring and required study
- Natural transfers of knowledge through religious ceremonies, festivals and services
- Through the teaching of myths and beliefs.

Consider which ways are available through the cult. There is no need to formalise each and every academy, rite, mentor, and so on; simply a consideration of which methods of teaching suit the cult the best.

Rounding Out the Cult

Having worked through this framework, you should have a good idea of a cult's focus, function, history, myths, magic and structure. It is now time to apply some finishing touches that can be used during gameplay. None of these finishing elements are crucial, but they offer completeness.

- Roll 1d4+1 – this is the number of Holy Days the cult observes during the year. At least one day will mark the founding of the cult, and one will mark another major point of importance, reflecting a key myth or deed (such as the martyrdom of a prophet or hero). Decide where in your game calendar these Holy Days will appear and their importance to members of different ranks. The founding day and additional day of importance will be marked by all cult members; other days may be marked by only one rank and hold lesser significance.

- What are the ceremonies for the cult? How is worship conducted? Are ceremonies formal and highly ritualised, or are they loosely structured and simple in approach? Do different Holy Days require different ceremonies? Be as vague or as detailed as you wish, but assemble some notes on what ceremonies usually require, using myths, history and other elements of the cult framework to determine what they consist of.
- Where is the cult's home? This might be obvious, if the cult is local to a small community, but large cults generally have a base of focus, where the major temple, church or shrine is located. Agree this with the Games Master.
- What happens to those who stray from the cult's path, betray its ideals or attempt to leave the cult? Are magical punishments enforced? Are apostates condemned to death? Is there no sanction at all? Consider the cult's nature, and outline the punishments, if any, for going against the cult's ideals. Some cults use the threat of punishment as a propaganda tool to enforce behaviour but may never carry out the threat; others will do so rigorously and publicly.

Index

A

Abjure 166
Absorption 182
Accidental Injury 96
Accommodation 58
Acephali 225
Acid 68
Acrobatics 44
Acting 44
Action Points 8
  Managing 285
Action, Time, and Movement 68, 69
Adhesion 157
Aegis 182
Aerial Tactics 103
Age 31
Ageing 32, 68, 70, 71, 166
Agent 27
Age Table 32
Aiming 107
Alarm 123
Alchemist 27
Allergy 215
Allies 22, 25, 207, 208, 209, 210
Ammunition, Ranged Weapon 62
Anathaym's Saga 7, 11, 17, 21, 27, 32, 41, 50, 54, 56, 58, 70, 74, 77, 80, 87, 89, 90, 92, 101, 102, 109, 111, 123, 193, 197, 198, 203, 205, 206, 283, 284, 286, 287
Ancestor Spirits 145
Animate 166
Animism 130
  Binding 130, 131
  Spirit Damage 131
  States of Being 130
  Trance 130
  Trance Preparation Time 131
  What Are Spirits? 130
Animism Tricks 140
Ant, Giant 225
Appraise 123
Aquatic 215
Arise 96
Armour 57
Armour Material Types 58
Armour Penalty to Initiative 58
Arrowcut 157
Art 44
Asipatra 226
Asphyxiated 41
Asphyxiation 43, 68, 71, 75, 76, 78, 143, 174
Assess Situation 93
Astral Projection 157
Athletics 38
Attack 91
Attacks and Parries 94
Attract 167
Attributes 5, 8
Augmenting Skills 50
Aura 157
Aurochs 226
Avert 123
Awaken 182
Awareness 157

B

Babble 123
Baboon 227
Background Events 18
Backlash 183
Bagini 227
Bakru 228
Bane Spirits 147
Banish 167
Barbarian 14
Bartering and Haggling 55
Bash 96
Basilisk 229
Bear 230
Beastcall 124
Beast Form 183
Beast Handler 27
Beetle, Giant 230
Befuddle 124
Behold 183
Bezainted 57
Bind Ghost 183
Binding 44, 131
  Creating a 136
Bleed 96
Bleeding 41
Bless Crops 183
Blind Opponent 96
Blood Loss 68, 71, 75, 78, 96
Blood Sense 215
Bludgeon 124
Boar 231
Boar-Kin 232
Boating 39
Body Snatching 141
Bonacon 232
Bonus Skill Points 32
Brace 91
Brawn 39
Breaking 39
Breath 124
Breathe Flame 215
Breathe Water 183
Brotherhoods 193
Bureaucracy 45
Burrower 215
Bypass 124
Bypass Armour 96

C

Calculate 124
Calling on the Gods 178
Call Winds 183
Calm 124
Camouflaged 215
Capping 50
Careers 26
Careers by Cultural Background, examples 26
Cast Magic 91
Centaur 233
Chameleon 184
Change Range 91
Chaos Aura 215
Chaos Feature 215
Chaos Features 275
Chaos Hybrid 234
Character Concept 6
Character Improvement 68, 71
Characteristic 5
Characteristic Drain 215

Characteristics 6
Increasing 72
Characteristics, Calculating 8
Charging 102
Charisma 8
Chill 124
Chimera 236
Choose Location 96
Circumvent Cover 96
Circumvent Parry 97
Civilised 14
Cleanse 125
Clear Skies 184
Climbing 38
Close Combat
Engagement 101
Situational Modifiers 101
Close Range 97
Closing Range 107
Clothing 59
Cloud Call 184
Cockatrice 229
Cold-Blooded 215
Colleges 194
Combat
Components of 86
Games Mastery 283
Pacing 285
Combat Actions 91
Free Actions 93
Proactive 91
Reactive 92
Combat Round 5
Combat Styles 12, 86
Combat Styles, Sample 87
Combat Style Traits 89
Combat, Unusual Conditions 106
Commerce 45
Communal Mind 215
Community 21
Comnbat Styles, Weapon Choices 88
Companies 194
Compel Surrender 97
Conceal 39
Connections, Personal 22
Connections Table 25
Consecrate 184
Constitution 7
Contacts 22, 25
Contested Rolls 50
Contests of Strength 39
Cool 125
Coordination 125
Copper Piece 54
Counter Spell 92
Courtesan 27
Courtesy 45
Courtier 27
Cover 102
Crab, Giant 236
Craft 45
Crafter 28
Creating Characters 280
Creature Competence 219
Creatures 214
Abilities 214
Armed Combat Considerations 222
As Player Characters 289
Designing Your Own 223
How Creatures Fight 220
Intelligence and Instinct 214
Unarmed Combat Considerations 221
Creatures as Characters 218
Critical Success 37
Crocodile/Alligator 237
Cult Membership 34
Cults 113
Availability by Culture 196
Benefits 199
Comparative Rank Titles 197
Cult and Brotherhood Centres 205
Demonstrations of Worthiness 195
Divine Intervention 201
Geasa 204
Gifts 201
Magic 200
Material Aid 200
Membership 195
Monasteries 206
Oaths 201
Progression 196
Protection 199
Ranks 197
Restrictions 201
Sample 206
Shrines 206
Social Status 200
Superstitions 204
Taboos 204
Temples 206
Training 199
Why Join? 194
Cults and Brotherhoods in the Campaign 290
Cults and Miracles 179
Cults & Brotherhoods 192
Cultural Skill Points 13
Culture 45
Culture & Community 13
Cure Malady 185
Curse 125
Curse Spirits 147
Custom Career, Creating a 31
Customs 40
Cycle 5
Cycles 90
Cyclops 237

D

Damage and Wound Levels 109
Damage Modifier 8, 107
Damage Reduction 94
Damage Weapon 97
Dance 40
Dark Sight 158, 215
Death Sense 215
Death Spirits 148
Deceit 40
Delay 91
Denial 158
Designing A Character 6
Devotion 45
Devotional Pools 180
Dexterity 7
Dice Roll, Assign 8
Dice Roll, In Order 8
Dice Step 5
Dice Used in the Game 5
Differential Roll 5
Differential Rolls 51
Difficulty Grades 38
Diminish 167
Disarm Opponent 97
Disease 68, 74
Traits 74
Disease and Poison Conditions 75
Disease Immunity 215
Diseases and Poisons, Treating 46
Diseases, Sample 75
Disguise 45
Dishevel 125
Dismiss Elemental 185
Dismiss Magic 185
Disruption 125
Distance Penalties 108
Dither 91
Divine Intervention 201
Diving Strike 215
Dominate 167
Dragon 238
Drive 40
Drop Foe 97
Drop Weapon 93
Drowning 68, 71, 237
Dry 125
Duck Back 97
Dullblade 125
Dwarf 239

E

Earthquake 185
Earth Sense 158, 215
Echolocation 158, 215
Economics & Equipment 54
Elementals 241
Elemental Spirits 148
Elemental Summoning 186
Elephant 256
Elf 243
Enchant 168
Encumbrance 56, 57, 68, 77
Alternative Rules 77
Capacity 77
Non-Human Armour ENC 77
Endurance 41
Endurance and Willpower, Limits to 44
Engineering 46
Engulfing 215
Enhance (Characteristic) 169
Enhancements, Equipment 66
Enhance Parry 97
Enlarge 169
Entangle 97, 186
Entertainer 28
Enthrall 186
Equipment Culture/Milieu 57
Equipment Manufacturing and Quality 65
Equipment Price 56
Equipment, Starting 32
Evade 41, 92
Evading 103
Excommunicate 186
Exhort 46
Exorcism 140, 186
Experience Modifier 9
Experience Rolls 71
Extended Family Table 25
Extension 186

F

Falling 44, 68, 78, 158
Falling Objects 78
From a Moving Vehicle 78
Families 21
Family & Connections 25
Fanaticism 126
Farmer 28
Fatigue 43, 48, 68, 69, 70, 71, 75, 76, 77, 78, 79, 82, 84, 96, 117, 125, 129, 155, 156, 158, 159, 183, 188, 209, 211, 212, 215, 216, 218, 228, 233, 235, 269, 271
Physical Effort 78
Effects of 78
Recovering from 79
Managing 79
Fear 186
Featherlight 158
Fecundity 186
Fetches 149
Fetishes 135
Fighting at the Longer Reach 106
Fighting at the Shorter Reach 106
Find 126
Firearrow 126
Fireblade 126
Fires 68, 79
Firing into a Crowd 108
Firing on the Move 108
First Aid
First Aid Actions 41
Fisher 28
Flurry 97
Fly 170
Flying 216
Flying Combat 103
Folk Magic 46, 121
Access to 121
Alarm 123
Appraise 123
Avert 123
Babble 123
Beastcall 124
Befuddle 124
Bladesharp 124
Bludgeon 124
Breath 124
Bypass 124
Calculate 124
Calm 124
Chill 124
Cleanse 125
Cool 125
Coordination 125
Creating New Spells 129
Curse 125
Darkness 125
Deflect 125
Demoralise 125
Dishevel 125
Disruption 125
Dry 125
Dullblade 125
Duration of Spells 123
Extinguish 125
Fanaticism 126
Find 126
Firearrow 126
Fireblade 126
Frostbite 126
Glamour 126
Glue 126
Heal 126
Heat 127
Ignite 127
Incognito 127
Ironhand 127
Knock 127
Learning 121
Light 127
Limits to Capacity 122
Lock 127
Magnify 127
Might 127
Mimic 127
Mindspeech 127
Mobility 127
Nature of 121
Pathway 127
Perfume 128
Pet 128
Phantasm 128
Pierce 128
Polish 128
Preserve 128
Protection 128
Repair 128
Repugnance 128
Shock 128
Shove 128
Sleep 128
Slow 128
Speedart 128
Spiritshield 129
Starting 121
Tidy 129
Tire 129
Traits 123
Translate 129
Tune 129
Ubiquitous 122
Using 122
Ventriloquism 129
Vigour 129
Voice 129
Warmth 129
Witchsight 129
Follower 131
Food 59
Force 107
Force Failure 97
Formidable Natural Weapons 158, 216
Fortify 186
Freely Improving Skills 72
Frenzy 216
Fumble 37

G

Gambling 46
Games Mastery 278, 301
Game System 68
Gangs 194
Gaze Attack 216
Geasa 204
Ghoul 244
Giant 245
Gifts 201
Sample Gifts 202
Glamour 126
Glossary of Terms 5
Glue 126
Goblin 246
Gold Piece 54
Gorgon 247
Grading Opponents 286
Grappler 216
Grappling 106
Griffin 248
Grip 97
Group Rolls 51
Growth 186
Guardian Spirits 149
Guilds 113, 194

H

Haggling 45, 51, 55, 56
Halfling 249
Harmonise 186
Harpy 250
Haunts 150
Heal 126
Heal Body 186
Healing 46
Magical 80
Permanent 80
Healing from Injury 68, 80, 110
Healing Rate 9
Heal Mind 186
Heal Wound 187
Heart Seizure 187
Heart Slow 158
Heat 127
Height, and Weight 9
Herder 29
Heroic Last Actions 110
Hide Life 170
High Shaman 131
Hinder 170
Hippogriff 248
Hit Locations 109
Hit Locations, Non-Human 276
Hit Points 10
Hold Breath 216
Holdfast 170
Hold Magic 91
Hoplite 57
Horse 251
Hunter 29

I

Ignite 127
Illusion 187
Immunity 158, 216
Impale 97
Impaled 41
Impaling Ranged Attacks 108
Inanimate Objects 68, 81
Using Weapons Against 81
Incognito 127
Income 54
Income between Adventuring 55
Indomitable 158
Influence 42
Initiative 5, 90
Calculating 90
Penalty 90

Initiative Bonus 10
Inject Venom 218
Insect Swarm 251
Insight 42
Intelligence 7
Intelligence and Instinct 214
Intensity 5
Interrupt 92
Intimidate 216
Intuition 170
Investigations 282
Invocation 47
Invoking a Spell 164
Iqari 252
Ironhand 127

J

Jumping 39

K

Kara 7, 21, 22, 49, 120, 123, 179, 181, 184, 193, 197
Kill Silently 98
Knock 127
Knockback 104

L

Language 47
Lay to Rest 187
Leader 199
Leaper 216
Leaping Attacks 104
Leeching 187
Life Sense 158, 216
Lifting 39
Light 127
Linguistic Fluency 47
Linothorax 57
Lion 253
Literacy 47
Livestock 59
Lizard, Giant 254
Lizardman 254
Loading Ranged Weapons 109
Locale 42
Lock 127
Lockpicking 47
Lore 47
Luck Points 8, 10, 11, 22, 68, 81, 111, 143, 159, 204, 270, 279, 280, 282, 287, 288
  Using 81
  Group 81
Lycanthropy 273

M

Madness 187
Magic
  and Characters 118
  Animism 112
  Casting Requirements 119
  Destruction and Consumption 117
  Dismissing One's Own 120
  Enduring Costs 120
  Folk 112
  How Many Abilities? 114
  Interrupting Casting 119
  Learning New Abilities 118
  Learning New Traditions 119
  Magical Locations 116
  Magnitude and Intensity 120
  Mysticism 113
  Restricted Actions 120
  Ritualistic Casting Times 115
  Royalty and Noble Houses 114
  Sacrifice 116
  Self 116
  Social Castes 114
  Sorcery 113
  Stacking 120
  Starting Magic 118
  Tailoring 112
  Teachers 114
  Theism 113
  Totems 114
  Traditions 113
  Using 119
  Veneration 117
  Where Do Magic Points Come From? 115
Magical Discipline 5
Magical Energy 115
Magical Tradition 5
Magic Points
  Recovering 117
  Rule of Recovery 117
  Running Out Of 117
  Sacrificing 116
Magic Sense 158, 216
Magnitude 5
Mail Armour 57
Major Injury 41
Major Wound 110
Mammoth 255
Manticore 256
Mantis, Giant 257
Mark 170
Marksman 98
Marriage 23
Maximise Damage 98
Mechanisms 47
Medicine Spirits 151
Meditation 48, 154
Meeros 1, 7, 14, 17, 22, 27, 34, 50, 54, 56, 80, 92, 111, 115, 123, 158, 159, 164, 168, 179, 193, 197, 199, 203, 205, 210, 259, 283, 284, 287
Melee Weapons 61
Merchant 29
Mimic 127
Mindblast 188
Mindlink 188
Miner 29
Minor Injury 41
Minor Wound 110
Minotaur 258
Miracle
  Exhortation Time 181
Miracles
  Absorption 182
  Aegis 182
  Awaken 182
  Backlash 183
  Beast Form 183
  Behold 183
  Berserk 183
  Bind Ghost 183
  Bless Crops 183
  Breathe Water 183
  Call Winds 183
  Chameleon 184
  Clear Skies 184
  Cloud Call 184
  Consecrate 184
  Corruption 184
  Cost of Requesting 181
  Cure Malady 185
  Cure Sense 185
  Descriptions 182
  Dismiss Elemental 185
  Dismiss Magic 185
  Dispelling 182
  Earthquake 185
  Elemental Summoning 186
  Entangle 186
  Enthrall 186
  Excommunicate 186
  Exorcism 186
  Extension 186
  Fear 186
  Fecundity 186
  Fortify 186
  Growth 186
  Harmonise 186
  Heal Body 186
  Heal Mind 186
  Heal Wound 187
  Heart Seizure 187
  Illusion 187
  Lay to Rest 187
  Leeching 187
  Limitations 182
  Madness 187
  Magnitude and Intensity 182
  Mindblast 188
  Mindlink 188
  Mirage 188
  Obliterate 188
  Pacify 188
  Perseverance 188
  Propitiate 188
  Rain of (Substance) 188
  Raise Undead 188
  Reflection 189
  Rejuvenate 189
  Resurrect 189
  Ripen 189
  Sacred Band 189
  Sever Spirit 189
  Shield 189
  Soul Sight 190
  Spirit Block 190
  Steadfast 190
  Sunspear 190
  Sureshot 190
  Thunderclap 191
  True (Weapon) 191
Miracles by Cult Rank 190
Miracles, Requesting 181
Mirage 188
Mju 7, 120, 155, 156, 158, 159
Monasteries 206
Money, Starting 21
Mount 91
Mounted Combat 104
Move 91
Movement Rate 10
Multi-Headed 216

Multi-Limbed 216
Multiple Opponents 104
Mummy 260
Musicianship 48
Mystic 29
Mystical Orders 193
Mysticism 154
  Augmenting Skills 156
  Enhancing Attributes 159
  Implementing a Talent 156
  Invoking Traits 156
  Magnitude and Intensity 156
  Paths and Talents 155
  Spirit Sense 158
  Starting Mystics 155
  Talent Descriptions 156
  Using 156
Mystic (Sense) 171

N

Native Tongue 42
Nature Spirits 151
Navigation 48
Neutralise Magic 171
Night Sight 158, 217
Nomadic 15
Non-Human Species 6

O

Oaths 201
Obliterate 188
Octopus, Giant 261
Official 29
Ogre 261
Opening Range 107
Open Range 98
Ophidian 254
Opposed Roll 5
Opposed Rolls 50
Opposed Skills Over 100% 51
Oratory 48
Orc 246
Organisation 4
Outmanoeuvre 92
Outmanoeuvring 104
Overextend Opponent 98
Overpenetration 98
Overseer 198

P

Pacify 188
Pain Control 158
Palsy 171
Panthotaur 262
Parents Table 25
Parry 93
  Unable to 95
  Failed to 95
Parrying a Missed Attack 95
Passions 22
  Increasing 72
  Using 282
Passive Blocking 105
Pathway 127
Perceive (Sense) 171
Perception 42
Perseverance 188
Petersen Rules of Good Gaming 278
Phantom (Sense) 171
Physician 30
Pin Down 98
Pin Weapon 98
Pitfall 84
Points Build 8
Points Build, Non-Human 219
Poison 74
Poison Immunity 217
Poisons, Sample 76
Possession 140
Possession, Covert 217
Possession, Dominant 217
Power 7
Predator Spirits 151
Preparation and Game Aids 279
Prepare Counter 98
Press Advantage 98
Priest 30
Primitive 16
Professional Skills 13, 44
Propitiate 188
Proportional Skill Success 52
Protective Ward 173
Proven 198
Pulled Blows 105

R

Rabble 111
Rain of (Substance) 188
Raise Undead 188
Range 107
Ranged Combat, Situational Modifiers 107
Ranged Weapons 61
Range Penalties, Realistic 109
Rapid Reload 99
Ready Weapon 92
Reflection 189
Regain Footing 92
Regenerate 173
Regeneration 217
Regiments 194
Rejuvenate 189
Ranged Combat
  Force 107
  Damage Modifier 107
  Range 107
Reload 107
Remise 99
Repair 128
Repugnance 128
Repulse (Creatures) 173
Reputation Table 25
Resources 65
Resurrect 189
Revivify 173
Ride 43
Ripen 189
Rivals 22, 25
Running 39

S

Sacred Band 189
Sacrosanct Locations 180
Sailor 30
Scar Foe 99
Scholar 30
Scorpion, Giant 263
Scout 30
Seamanship 48
Sea Serpent 264
Seduction 48
Select Target 99
Sense (Object, State or Substance) 174
Serious Injury 41
Serious Wound 110
Serious Wounds, Treating 46
Sever Spirit 189
Shaman 30, 131
  Surviving after Death 141
Shapechange 174
Shape-Shifting Spirits 152
Shaping 49
Shark 264
Shield 189
Shields 63
Shock 128
Shove 128
Shrines 206
Shrink 174
Siblings Table 25
Sickness Spirits 152
Siege Weapons 62
Signal 93
Silver Piece 54
Sing 43
Size 7
Skill 5
Skills 37
  Capping 50
  Contested 50
  Increasing 72
  Learning New 73
  Reattempting 50
  Different Situations 50
Skills, Modifying 38
Skills Summaries 53
Slargr 265
Sleep 128
Sleight 49
Slip Free 99
Slow 128
Smilodon 266
Smother 174
Snake, Giant 266
Social Class 21, 23, 24, 28, 54, 59, 281
Social Conflict 287
Sorcerer 31
Sorcery 161
  Abjure 166
  Animate 166
  Attract 167
  Banish 167
  Bypass Armour 167
  Castback 167
  Combine 162
  Damage Enhancement 167
  Damage Resistance 167
  Diminish 167
  Dispelling a Sorcery Spell 165
  Dominate 167
  Draw 168
  Duration 162
  Enchant 168
  Enhance (Characteristic) 169
  Enlarge 169
  Enslave (Creatures) 169

Evoke 169
Fly 170
Further Extending Duration 162
Hide Life 170
Hinder 170
Holdfast 170
Imprison 170
Intuition 170
Invocation 161
Invocation Costs 165
Invocation Time 165
Invoking a Spell 164
Learning Spells 164
Limitations 165
Magnitude 163
Magnitude and Intensity 165
Mark 170
Mystic (Sense) 171
Neutralise Magic 171
Palsy 171
Perceive (Sense) 171
Phantom (Sense) 171
Portal 172
Project (Sense) 172
Protective Ward 173
Range 163
Regenerate 173
Repulse (Creatures) 173
Restricting Components 165
Revivify 173
Schools and Spells 163
Sculpt (Substance) 173
Sense 174
Shapechange 174
Shaping 161
Shrink 174
Smother 174
Spell Resistance 174
Spirit Resistance 175
Starting Sorcerers 163
Store Manna 175
Summon 175
Summoning Otherworld Entities 169
Switch Body 175
Tap (Characteristic) 175
Targets 163
Telepathy 175
Teleport 176
Transfer Wound 176
Transmogrify 176
Trap Soul 176
Undeath 177
Using 164
Wrack 177
Sorcery Orders 193
Sorting Roll 52
Speak 93
Spear Trap 84
Special Effect 5
Special Effects 95
Special Effects Summary 100
Speedart 128
Spell Resistance 174
Spider, Giant 267
Spirit Block 190
Spirit Combat 137
Consequences of Defeat 138
Engaging 137
Options 139
Physical Damage 139
Special Effects 138
Tenacity 139
Spirit Cults 193
Spirit Damage 131
Spirit Resistance 175
Spirits
Abilities 142
Ancestor 147
Animate 142
Applying Spirit Powers 142
Attitude 134, 137
Attributes 133
Autonomy 142
Bane 147
Binding 135
Binding a Soul into a Living Creature 141
Binding Huge Spirits 141
Bless 142
Body Snatching 141
Cannibalistic 142
Characteristics 133
Comprehension 143
Conjugate 143
Covert 143
Curse 143, 147
Deadly 143
Death 148
Defining 132
Demesne 143
Designing 142
Diabolic 140
Different Settings 141
Discorporate 143
Disease 143
Domination 144
Elemental 148
Endowment 144
Eternal 144
Examples 145
Fetches 149
Fetishes 135
Glamour 144
Guardian 149
Haunts 150
Healing 144
Intensity 133
Limits to Bound 136
Locating 134
Mana 144
Manifestation 144
Medicine 151
Miasma 144
Nature 151
Negotiation 134
Observing 137
Passion 144
Perceptive 145
Persistent 145
Possession and Exorcism 140
Predator 151
Puppeteer 145
Recurring Trait 138
Rejuvenating 140
Sagacity 145
Shapechange 145
Shape-Shifting 152
Sickness 152
Spellcasting 145
Subjugate 145
Summoning a 136
Telekinesis 145
Traps 141
Types 142
Undeath 153
Warding 145
Wither 145
Wraiths 153
Spiritshield 129
Spirit Societies, Cults & Traditions 131
Spirit Worshipper 131
Spoil Spell 99
Squeeze 159
Standard Skills 11
Stand Fast 99
Steadfast 190
Stealth 43
Store Manna 175
Streetwise 49
Strength 7
Striking 106
Struggle 92
Stun Location 99
Success, Automatic 37
Suffocation 68, 71
Summon 175
Sunder 101
Sunspear 190
Superstitions 204
Sureshot 190
Surgery 47
Surprise 105
Survival 14, 16, 27, 28, 29, 30, 31, 42, 49, 53, 59, 68, 82, 84, 155, 209, 211, 212, 219, 225, 227, 230, 232, 235, 240, 241, 252, 253, 259, 262, 263
Sweep Attacks 105
Swim 43
Swimmer 217
Switch Body 175

T

Taboos 204
Take Weapon 101
Tap (Characteristic) 175
Task Rounds 65
Task Rules in Other Circumstances 67
Teach 49
Teachers 73, 114
Teaching, General vs Specific 49
Team Roll 52
Temples 206
Tenacity 139
Terrifying 217
Theism 178
Cults and Miracles 179
Devotion 178
Devotional Pools 180
Donating Magic Points 180
Exhort 178
Joining More Than One Cult 180
Learning Miracles 179
Sacrosanct Locations 180
Starting Theists 179
Using Theism 180
Theist Cults 193
Thief 31
Throwing 39
Thunderclap 191
Tidy 129

Tiger 268
Tire 129
Tools 60
Track 49
Training 49, 73, 74, 199, 207, 291, 292
Trample 218
Trance 49
Trance Preparation Time 131
Transfer Wound 176
Translate 129
Transmogrify 176
Traps 60, 68, 82, 83, 141, 288
  Using 288
Trap Soul 176
Traps, Sample 83
Trip Opponent 101
Troll 269
True (Weapon) 191
Tune 129
Turn 5
Turns 90

U

Unarmed 43
Unarmed Combat 105
Unconsciousness 41
Undead 218
Undeath 177
Undeath Spirits 153
Underlings 111
Unicorn 270
Use Luck Point 93

V

Vampire 270
Vampiric 218
Vehicles 62
Venomous 218
Ventriloquism 129
Vigour 129
Visibility 68, 84
Vulnerable 218

W

Ward Location 93
Warrior 31
Weapon Malfunction 101
Weapon Reach Categories 94
Weapon Reach – Closing and Opening Range 106
Weapon Size and Reach 94
Weapon Size Categories 94
Weapons, One Handed 63
Weapons, Ranged 65
Weapons, Two Handed 64
Weather 68, 84, 184
  Precipitation 84
  Temperature 84
  Wind 85
Willpower 44
Winged Ape 272
Witchsight 129
Withdraw 101
Withdrawing 107
Wolf 272
Wounding Opponents with an Endurance over 100% 110
Wrack 177
Wraiths 153
Wyrm/Wyvern 273

X

Xenos 7, 21, 74, 80, 180, 205, 284, 286, 287

Z

Zamothis 7, 27, 74, 90, 92, 95, 101, 109, 111
Zombie 274

Appendix: Play Aids

Mythras has plenty of play aids and resources, many of which are free to use or download, and we have listed our favourites in this section. Over the next three pages we also provide a character sheet and a combat tracking sheet; both are valuable resources for both players and Games Masters. Feel free to make copious copies of these for personal use.

Other resources that you may find useful are as follows:

Mythras Games Master's Guide

This free PDF collects together all the essential tables and charts from the game into a handy PDF that can be printed and chopped up to create a custom GM screen. The guide also includes two starting scenarios, one of which following Anathaym's fate after the earthquake that shakes Meeros.

Mythras Imperative

This free booklet is a beginners' introduction to Mythras. Condensing the rules into less than 50 pages, this is the ideal way for players and GMs new to Mythras - and d100 gaming in general - to get to grips with the system. Imperative is free to download from the Design Mechanism website, DrivethruRPG, and other online game sites. You can also buy a printed copy from Lulu - see the list of links, opposite.

Mythras Combat App

Designed for Android, this app presents all the Special Effects in an electronic format, showing at a glance what effects are available, what they do, and additional information relating to combat results. It can be downloaded from Google Play.

Mythras Combat Cards

All the Special Effects presented in a deck of 60 playing cards. Each card deals with a single effect, one side illustrating the effect with an evocative woodcut, and the other side noting the specifics of the effect. Presented as cards, this deck is ideal for those new to Mythras as a handful of effects can be agreed on and held in-hand, thereby focusing choices and making it easier to envisage the effect and when best to use it. It also makes Special Effects even more fun than simply consulting a list. Available from DrivethruRPG.

Mythras Enemy Generator

This online tool rapidly creates statistics for hundreds of Mythras creatures and NPCs. Individual enemies or entire gangs of them can be created at the press of a button and then exported to PDF if one wishes.

Links to Play Aids

Design Mechanism Website
www.thedesignmechanism.com/products

DriveThruRPG
www.drivethrurpg.com/browse/pub/4057/Design-Mechanism

Enemy Generator
http://skoll.xyz/mythras_eg/

Lulu Webstore
http://www.lulu.com/spotlight/Mythras

Mythras

Character Name: ____________________

Player Name: ____________ Race/Culture: ____________

Gender: ______ Frame: ______ Homeland: ____________

Age: ______ Height: ______ Career: ____________

Handedness: ______ Weight: ______ Social Class: ____________

Description: ____________________

Experience Rolls

Notes (Background, Culture, Family, ...)

Money & Wealth

Income	day	week	season	year
Silver Pieces	____	____	____	____

Characteristics & Attributes

Characteristic		Attribute	
Strength		Action Points	
Constitution		Damage Modifier	
Size		Experience Modifier	
Dexterity		Healing Rate	
Intelligence		Initiative	
Power		Luck Points	
Charisma		Movement Rate	

Cult Information

Ranks, Benefits, Restrictions, Gifts, ...

Devotional Pool: ____ / ____

Standard Skills

Skill	Base %		%
Athletics	STR + DEX	☐	____
Boating	STR + CON	☐	____
Conceal	DEX + POW	☐	____
Customs	INT x2	☐	____
Dance	DEX + CHA	☐	____
Deceit	INT + CHA	☐	____
Drive	DEX + POW	☐	____
First Aid	INT + DEX	☐	____
Influence	CHA x2	☐	____
Insight	INT + POW	☐	____
Locale	INT x2	☐	____
Perception	INT + POW	☐	____
Ride	DEX + POW	☐	____
Sing	CHA + POW	☐	____
Stealth	DEX + INT	☐	____
Swim	STR + CON	☐	____
Unarmed	STR + DEX	☐	____

Resistances

Skill	Base %		%
Brawn	STR + SIZ	☐	____
Endurance	CON x2	☐	____
Evade	DEX x2	☐	____
Willpower	POW x2	☐	____

Professional Skills

Skill	Base %		%
____	____	☐	____
____	____	☐	____
____	____	☐	____
____	____	☐	____
____	____	☐	____
____	____	☐	____
____	____	☐	____
____	____	☐	____
____	____	☐	____
____	____	☐	____
____	____	☐	____
____	____	☐	____
____	____	☐	____
____	____	☐	____
____	____	☐	____

Languages (INT+CHA)

Skill		%
Native (____)	☐	____
____	☐	____
____	☐	____
____	☐	____
____	☐	____
____	☐	____

Magic Points

0	1	2	3	4	5	6	7	8	9	10
11	12	13	14	15	16	17	18	19	20	
21	22	23	24	25	26	27	28	29	30	

Used MP (active effects): ____

Magical Skills

Skill	Base %		%
____	____	☐	____
____	____	☐	____
____	____	☐	____
____	____	☐	____
____	____	☐	____
____	____	☐	____
____	____	☐	____
____	____	☐	____
____	____	☐	____

Passions

Passion	%
____	____
____	____
____	____
____	____
____	____
____	____

Design and Layout by Evelyn H.

Magic & Abilities

Spells, Spirits, Talents, Miracles, ...

Fatigue

	State	Skills	Move	SR	AP	Time
☐	Fresh	-	-	-	-	-
☐	Winded	Hard	-	-	-	15 min.
☐	Tired	Hard	-1m	-	-	3 hours
☐	Wearied	Form.	-2m	-2	-	6 hours
☐	Exhausted	Form.	Half	-4	-1	12 hours
☐	Debilitated	Herc.	Half	-6	-2	18 hours
☐	Incapacitated	Herc.	None	-8	-3	24 hours
☐	Semi-Conscious	Hope.	No Activity Possible			36 hours
☐	Comatose		No Activity Possible			48 hours
☐	Dead		No Activity Possible			Never

Hit Locations

1d20	Location	Max HP	HP
19 - 20	Head		
16 - 18	Left Arm		
13 - 15	Right Arm		
10 - 12	Chest		
- 9	Abdomen		
- 6	Left Leg		
- 3	Right Leg		

Wounds: ______

Armour

Armour Worn	AP	ENC

Total Armour ENC: ______

Armour Penalty (Armour ENC/5): ______

Equipment

Item	ENC

Total ENC (worn armour counts half): ______

Burdened (STRx2): ______

Overloaded (STRx3): ______

Combat Styles (STR+DEX)

Style	Weapons	Trait		%
			☐	
			☐	
			☐	
			☐	
Unarmed			☐	

Weapons & Shields

Melee Weapons & Shields	Damage	Size	Reach	Traits	Combat Effects	AP	HP	ENC
							/	
							/	
							/	
							/	
							/	
							/	
							/	

Ranged Weapons	Damage	Force	DM	Range	Load	Combat Effects	AP	HP	ENC
				/ /				/	
				/ /				/	
				/ /				/	

Design and Layout by Evelyn H.

www.ingramcontent.com/pod-product-compliance
Ingram Content Group UK Ltd.
Pitfield, Milton Keynes, MK11 3LW, UK
UKHW051043120926
8556IPUK00031B/875

9 781911 471066